D1397896

HANDBOOK OF HYPERACTIVITY IN CHILDREN

Johnny L. Matson

EDITOR

Louisiana State University

Allyn and Bacon

Boston   London   Toronto   Sydney   Tokyo   Singapore

Copyright © 1993 by Allyn and Bacon
A Division of Simon & Schuster, Inc.
160 Gould Street
Needham Heights, Massachusetts 02194

All rights reserved. No part of the material protected by this copyright notice may be reproduced or utilized in any form or by any means, electronic or mechanical, including photocopying, recording, or by any information storage and retrieval system, without written permission from the copyright owner.

Library of Congress Cataloging-in-Publication Data

Handbook of hyperactivity in children / Johnny L. Matson, editor.
    p.   cm.
    Includes bibliographical references and index.
    ISBN 0-205-14591-4
    1. Attention-deficit hyperactivity disorder. I. Matson, Johnny L.
    [DNLM: 1. Attention Deficit Disorder with Hyperactivity—
diagnosis. 2. Attention Deficit Disorder with Hyperactivity—
etiology. 3. Attention Deficit Disorder with Hyperactivity—
therapy. WS 350.6 H237]
RJ506.H9H36 1993
618.92'589—dc20
DNLM/DLC
for Library of Congress   91-2459
                                  CIP

ISBN 0-205-14591-4

H45917

Printed in the United States of America
10 9 8 7 6 5 4 3 2 1   97 96 95 94 93

618.92589
H23

93-1616
233217930

CONTENTS

PREFACE

Hyperactivity, attention deficit disorder, or whatever term you choose to use is a frequent problem among children. The topic has received perhaps more attention than any other from researchers in the child psychopathology field. Further, in clinical settings it is the most common reason for referrals to mental health clinics and is an issue of frequent concern for teachers and school psychologists. The magnitude of the problem among children also accounts for the rapid evolution of the field. As a result, a volume updating what we know and what we need to know about hyperactivity is needed.

The present volume is one such effort. The book is broken into three sections: general issues, assessment, and treatment. The first of these, general issues, covers the history of the field, diagnostic and definitional parameters, theories, etiology, and methodology. Much has been learned about hyperactivity. The chapters by eminent researchers in the field should, we hope, adequately reflect the latest developments.

Assessment and diagnosis of hyperactivity have proven to be more complex than many researchers and clinicians would have hypothesized just a few years ago. It has become apparent that a variety of instruments are needed and that the measures need to be specific to particular behaviors and environments. Further, and paralleling research in other areas of child psychopathology, assessment measures are needed for diagnosis, to delineate targets for intervention, and to evaluate treatment outcome. Researchers have been able to demonstrate that hyperactivity affects particular skills and skill areas, thus, entire methodologies have emerged to assess the effects of hyperactivity on specific skill areas such as academic skills.

The section on treatment covers drug therapies, which have constituted the primary intervention strategy for this disorder. However, other interventions are also available, particularly those that emphasize behavioral training strategies. Given the need for specificity in these interventions, we have divided them into school and home or clinic-based treatments. Nutrition is also covered in this section. Given the popularity of nutrition in clinical practice, a book of this sort would be incomplete without coverage of this area.

The collaboration of various mental health disciplines is viewed as quite important, given the complexity of the problem and the emergence of multiple assessments and interventions. Further, the need to assess and treat the problem in a variety of settings (e.g., school and home) has by necessity drawn in a variety of professionals. We conclude with some predictions of future developments and an overview of the field and its present status.

We hope this volume will serve as an update on a fascinating and rapidly expanding topic in the field of child psychopathology. The authors of the chapters have all made significant contributions to the field of hyperactivity. Our intent is to provide readers with a state-of-the-art description of where we are and where we are likely to be in the future.

ACKNOWLEDGMENTS

This book is dedicated to my wife Deann, my children Michael and Meggan, and my parents Mary and Walter. My gratitude to Jerry Frank and Phyllis Hall from Pergamon, whose support and encouragement made this volume possible. Thanks also to Kelley Francis, Linda Le Blanc, and Karen Linton, who helped with the production of the book.

ABOUT THE EDITOR AND CONTRIBUTORS

EDITOR

Johnny L. Matson received his Ph.D. in psychology from Indiana State University in 1976. He is currently Professor and Director of Clinical Training in the Department of Psychology at Louisiana State University. Previous positions include Assistant Professor of Psychology and Psychiatry at the University of Pittsburgh and Professor of Special Education at Northern Illinois University. He is the author of over 280 publications, including 30 books. Dr. Matson is the past President of the Psychology Division of the American Association on Mental Retardation and the Developmental Disabilities division of the American Psychological Association. He has served on the editorial boards of 12 journals, including *Behavior Therapy* and the *Journal of Applied Behavior Analysis,* and has been the editor-in-chief of *Research in Developmental Disabilities* for 14 years.

CONTRIBUTORS

Peggy T. Ackerman received her B.A. degree from Hendrix College in Conway, Arkansas, in 1952. She was awarded a Carnegie fellowship to George Peabody College, Nashville, Tennessee, and received her M.A. (Psychology) there in 1953. In 1954–1955, she did additional work at the University of Wisconsin, where she served as a research assistant to Dr. Julian C. Stanley. In 1957, she became a research assistant in the Department of Psychiatry, University of Arkansas for Medical Sciences (UAMS) in Little Rock. There, she began her collaboration with Dr. Roscoe A. Dykman, which has resulted in over 50 publications in the areas of learning disability and attention disorders. At present, she has a joint appointment in the Departments of Psychiatry and Pediatrics at UAMS.

Russell A. Barkley, Ph.D., is Professor of Psychiatry and Neurology and Director of Psychology at the University of Massachusetts Medical Center. He has served as President of the Section on Clinical Child Psychology, Division 12, American Psychological Association and is now President-Elect of the Society for Research in Child and Adolescent Psychopathology. He received his Ph.D. in clinical psychology from Bowling Green State University and internship training at the Oregon Health Sciences University. He is a Diplomate in both Clinical Psychology and Clinical Neuropsychology from the American Board of Professional Psychology, Inc. He has authored or coedited 4 books and has published 35 book chapters and more than 55 scientific papers on attention deficit hyperactivity disorder, parent training, and child neuropsychology. He currently serves on the editorial boards of six psychology journals and is a consulting reviewer for many others.

Rowland P. Barrett, Ph.D., is Associate Professor of Psychiatry at the Brown University Program in Medicine and Chief of Service for Autism and Developmental Disabilities at the Emma Pendleton Bradley Hospital where he also serves as the

Director of Psychology. He received his Ph.D. from the University of Pittsburgh in 1978. Dr. Barrett has published extensively in the areas of behavioral assessment, behavior therapy, and operant behavioral pharmacology.

Ralph Mason Dreger is Professor Emeritus of Psychology at Louisiana State University in Baton Rouge. After receiving his Ph.D. from the University of Southern California, he taught at Florida State University and Jacksonville University before settling at LSU, where he taught in the clinical psychology program until retirement. Author of 100 articles and scholarly reviews in scientific journals, Dr. Dreger has authored and/or edited 4 books and serves as Associate Editor of one journal and Consulting Editor of another, as well as being a regular reviewer for other journals. His major research interests include behavioral classification of behavior disorders and clustering of individuals on the basis of their profiles on such disorders.

George J. DuPaul received his Ph.D. in School Psychology from the University of Rhode Island in 1985 and is currently an Assistant Professor of Psychiatry at the University of Massachusetts Medical Center. His research interests are in the assessment and treatment of attention deficit hyperactivity disorder and related behavioral difficulties.

Roscoe A. Dykman, Ph.D., is Professor Emeritus and Director of the Psychophysiology Laboratory, CARE Unit, Arkansas Children's Hospital. He received his Ph.D. in Human Development, University of Chicago, in 1949. His specialty is physiological psychology, but he has also had considerable training and experience in group psychotherapy. He is author or coauthor of some 200 scientific articles in the fields of psychophysiology, behavioral genetics, attentional deficit disorders, and learning disabilities. He has been a panel member on four different NIMH/NICHD committees and is currently a member of the NICHD Mental Retardation Committee. He is also on the editorial board of two journals.

Josephine Elia, M.D.: Vita unavailable.

Virginia E. Fee, Ph.D., Assistant Professor of Psychology at Mississippi State University, is currently pursuing research in the areas of ADHD, social acceptance and rejection, and developmental disabilities.

Christina M. Fremer received her M.S. from Eastern Michigan University, Ypsilanti, Michigan, in 1986. She is presently a Behavioral Consultant with the John Merck Multiple Disabilities Clinic in Pittsburgh, Pennsylvania. Her clinical and research interests include assessment and behavioral intervention of learning disabled and behaviorally disordered children.

Kenneth D. Gadow received his Ph.D. in special education from the University of Illinois in 1978. He is currently Professor of Child Psychiatry, State University of New York at Stony Brook. He is the author of *Children On Medication* (Vols. 1 & 2), numerous journal articles, and is the editor of the research annual, *Advances in Learning and Behavioral Disabilities*. His research interests are in pediatric psychopharmacology, hyperactivity, childhood aggression, and television violence.

Liam K. Grimley, Ph.D., is Professor of Educational and School Psychology and Director of Training Programs in School Psychology at Indiana State University. He holds five graduate degrees from European and American universities, including a Ph.D. degree in school psychology from Kent State University. He is currently chairman of the State of Indiana Advisory Council for the Education of Handicapped Children and Youth. He is a former editor of *School Psychology Digest* (now *School Psychology Review*), the quarterly professional journal of the National Association of School Psychologists. He is author of numerous journal articles, editor of *Historical Perspectives on School Psychology,* and coauthor of a book on attention deficit disorder.

David C. Guevremont received his Ph.D. in clinical psychology from West Virginia University in 1987. His general theoretical orientation is in the area of applied behavior analysis and behavior therapy with children and families. Dr. Guevremont is currently an Assistant Professor of Psychiatry at the University of Massachusetts Medical Center and a full-time faculty member in the Department of Psychiatry's Attention Deficit Hyperactivity Disorders Clinic. He is actively involved in both clinical work and research on the assessment and treatment of ADHD in children and in adolescents. Current research interests have focused on family-based treatments of ADHD adolescents and social competence and peer relationships of children with ADHD. His book, co-authored with Dr. Michael Spiegler, will be published next year.

William J. Helsel, Ed.D., is Director of the Intensive Treatment System at Western Carolina Center in Morganton, North Carolina. He received his Ed.D. in education psychology from Northern Illinois University in 1985. His clinical research interests are in working with people evincing mental retardation, psychopathology, and severe behavior disorders.

Kelly Hern is a 1990 graduate of the University of Georgia where he received his doctorate in School Psychology with minors in Neuropsychology and Personality Assessment. His research interests and publications have focused on neuropsychological and neurophysiological differentiation of ADD subtypes, as well as effective intervention methodology. Dr. Hern is a Nationally Certified School Psychologist and serves as a Fellow in Pediatric Psychology at the University of North Carolina School of Medicine.

George W. Hynd, Ed.D., is Chair of the Division for Exceptional Children and Research Professor of Special Education and Psychology. He also is the Director of the Center for Clinical and Developmental Neuropsychology at the University of Georgia. His research interests focus on the neurobiological basis of childhood learning disabilities and attention deficit disorders. He has authored or edited 10 books and authored over 120 chapters and scientific articles.

Roger C. Katz, Ph.D., is a Professor of Psychology at the University of the Pacific in Stockton,

California, where he also has a part-time private practice in clinical psychology. Dr. Katz received his B.A. degree from the University of California, Berkeley, and M.A. and Ph.D. degrees in clinical psychology from the University of Utah. His research and scholarly writings are principally in the areas of child behavior disorders and behavioral medicine.

Kevin L. Kelly, M.A., is the senior research specialist and program coordinator for the inpatient child psychiatry unit of the University Hospital, State University of New York at Stony Brook. He received his M.A. in experimental psychology from the University of Rhode Island and is currently a doctoral candidate in the biopsychology program at SUNY Stony Brook. His research interests include neuropsychological assessment in pediatric psychopathology and psychopharmacology.

James Kirby, M.D.: Vita unavailable.

Linda Krein, R.Ph., M.S., is currently a predoctoral intern at the Veteran's Administration Medical Center in Denver, Colorado. She received a B.S. in pharmacy from North Dakota State University in 1970, and a M.S. in psychology from Colorado State University in 1988. Her research and clinical interests are in the areas of child development and neuropsychology.

Alison R. Lorys-Vernon received her Ph.D. in school psychology from the University of Georgia in 1990. She is currently a neuropsychologist at North Shore University Hospital in Manhasset, New York. Her research interests include pediatric neuropsychology, attention deficit disorders, and developmental language disorders.

Heikki Lyytinen, Ph.D., is Associate Professor of Psychology at the Department of Psychology, University of Jyvaskyla, Finland. He is also the Director of the Niilo Maki Institute. His main research interests are in psychophysiology and developmental neuropsychology.

Jennifer Mauro is currently completing her internship at the Newington Children's Hospital and will receive her Ph.D. from the University of Oregon this year. Her clinical interests include the use of art and play therapy, post-traumatic stress disorder in children, and the treatment of eating disorders. Her past research has focused on parent-child attachment, temperament, and development of imaginary companions.

Susan G. O'Leary, is Associate Professor of Psychology and Director of the Doctoral Program in Clinical Psychology at the University at Stony Brook, where she received her Ph.D. in 1972. She conducts research on the prevention and treatment of oppositional, conduct, and hyperactivity attention deficit disorders, with an emphasis on the effects and parameters of discipline. She is presently an Associate Editor for *Behavior Therapy*.

Dean X. Parmelee, M.D., is a graduate of the original Antioch College, received his M.D. from the University of Rochester School of Medicine and Dentistry, and completed his residency programs at the Harvard Medical School. He is Chairman of Child and Adolescent Psychiatry at the Medical College of Virginia and his main research interest is in the area of models and systems of mental health care for children and youth.

Linda J. Pfiffner completed her doctoral training in clinical psychology at the State University of New York at Stony Brook in 1987. She is currently a licensed clinical psychologist at the Child Development Center at the University of California, Irvine, where she is active in coordinating the clinical services and leading a number of research projects. Her research and clinical work has focused on childhood psychopathology and includes diagnostic/ assessment issues (including the field trials for DSM-IV), classroom management, and family-based interventions. She has published a series of articles examining classroom interventions for ADHD children and has also published in the areas of parenting and family factors related to childhood behavior problems.

Judith L. Rapoport, M.D., received her medical degree from Harvard University in 1959. Currently, she is the Chief of the Child Psychiatry Branch, National Institute of Mental Health. She has published over 100 articles and 3 books in her major fields of research interest: psychiatric diagnosis, hyperactive children, biological aspects of child psychiatry, pediatric psychopharmacology, and obsessive compulsive disorder.

Mark D. Rapport, Ph.D., is an Associate Professor of Psychology and Psychiatry at the University of Hawaii and received his Ph.D. in both Clinical Psychology and School/Community Psychology from Florida State University. Dr. Rapport presently serves on the editorial boards of *Behavior Modification* and the *Journal of Psychopathology and Behavioral Assessment*. He has authored 10 book chapters and over 30 scientific papers on attention deficit hyperactivity disorder and is the inventor of the *Attentional Training System* for treatment of children with ADHD. His research interests are in pediatric psychopharmacology, childhood psychopathology, the design of computerized instruments to assess children's neurocognitive function, and behavioral-classroom interventions for children with ADHD.

Lee A. Rosén, Ph.D., is an Associate Professor of Psychology at Colorado State University. He received his Ph.D. in clinical psychology from the State University of New York at Stony Brook in 1984. His clinical and research interests include hyperactivity, developmental disabilities, and behavioral treatment of disruptive behavior disorders in children.

Elizabeth A. Schaughency received her Ph.D. from the University of Georgia and is currently Assistant Professor of Psychology in the Clinical Training Program at the University of Oregon. Her research interests include classification of childhood psychopathology, particularly ADHD, and the interaction of differing childhood behavior disorders with outcomes in important areas functioning.

Dionne Schissel received her Ph.D. in counseling psychology from Colorado State University in 1990. She is currently the education administrator and a therapist at a residential treatment facility for severely emotionally disturbed children in San Francisco. Her clinical interests are in the treatment of sexually and physically abused children and children with attentional and conduct problems.

Nirbhay N. Singh received his Ph.D. from the University of Auckland, New Zealand, in 1979. He is a Professor of Psychiatry at the Medical College of Virginia, and Director of Research at the Commonwealth Institute for Child and Family Studies in Richmond, Virginia. He is the editor-in-chief of the *Journal of Behavioral Education* and the *Journal of Child and Family Studies*. His research interests include pediatric psychopharmacology and psychiatric disorders in children and adolescents.

Aradhana A. Sood, M.D., is a graduate of the Jiwaji University, Gwalior, India. She completed her residency program at the University of Missouri in Kansas City, Missouri, and her fellowship in child psychiatry at the Ohio State University in Columbus, Ohio. Currently, she is an Assistant Professor of Psychiatry at the Medical College of Virginia in Richmond, Virginia. Her main research interests are in adolescent mood disorders, bereavement in children and adults, and child and adolescent psychopharmacology.

Susan Taylor received her Ph.D. from Colorado State University in 1990. She is in private practice part time and also works as an evaluator for Adams Community Mental Health Center in Denver, Colorado.

Kathryn Vannatta is currently completing her internship at the Duke University Medical Center and will receive her Ph.D. from the University of Oregon this year. Upon completion of her internship, she will begin a postdoctoral fellowship in pediatric psychology at the University of Cincinnati School of Medicine. Ms. Vannatta's research interests include correlates and antecedents of childhood sociometric status.

Anne S. Walters is a Clinical Assistant Professor in the Department of Psychiatry and Human Behavior, Brown University Program in Medicine, and Staff Clinical Psychologist at the Emma Pendleton Bradley Hospital, East Providence, Rhode Island. She received a Ph.D. in 1988 from Georgia State University, Atlanta, Georgia, with a specialty in Child/Family, and completed a two-year postdoctoral fellowship in Clinical Psychology from Brown University Program in Medicine in 1989 with a specialty in Developmental Disabilities. Clinical interests include dual diagnosis in children and treatment of ADHD. Research interests include suicidal behavior in mentally retarded children and adolescents and the observational assessment of social behavior in pervasive developmental disorders. She has published in the areas of mother-infant interaction, social behavior in autism, and psychopathology in developmentally disabled children and adolescents.

John S. Werry is Professor and Head of the Department of Psychiatry and Behavioural Science, School of Medicine, University of Auckland. He received his medical degree in New Zealand and his psychiatric training at McGill University. He was at the University of Illinois before returning to New Zealand. His interests include psychopharmacology, ADHD, child and adolescent schizophrenia and bipolar disorder, and clinical information systems.

CHAPTER 1

THE HISTORY OF HYPERACTIVITY

Anne S. Walters
Rowland P. Barrett

Hyperactivity, or attention deficit hyperactivity disorder (ADHD) (American Psychiatric Association, 1987), is one of the most widely debated disorders of childhood development as well as one of the most common. Estimates of prevalence range from 2% to 20% of the U.S. school-age population, with the clustering of estimates at 2% to 5% translating to roughly one child in every classroom (Barkley, 1981, 1982; Ross & Ross, 1982). Though efforts to reach consensus about symptomatology have yielded a remarkably stable cluster of symptoms over time, syndrome definition has been marked by shifting focus and dissent among researchers in the field. These shifts have been most notable in the areas of diagnosis and etiology. In fact, a listing of former terms for ADHD provides a brief tour of the history of hyperactivity: "Fidgety Phil," per Hoffman in 1854 (cf. Conners & Wells, 1986), brain damage syndrome (Still, 1902), "organic drivenness" (Kahn & Cohen, 1934), organic behavior syndrome (Bradley & Bowen, 1941), minimal brain damage syndrome (Strauss & Kephart, 1955), hyperkinetic impulse disorder (Laufer & Denhoff, 1957), minimal brain dysfunction (Clements & Peters, 1962), hyperactivity (Werry, 1968), hyperkinetic syndrome (Rutter, Graham, & Yule, 1970), hyperactive child syndrome (Cantwell, 1975a), attention deficit disorder (American Psychiatric Association [APA],

1980), and attention deficit hyperactivity disorder (APA, 1987).

Further elucidation of the history of ADHD yields a bird's-eye view of the history of thinking about childhood psychopathology in general. Efforts to define a syndrome of ADHD have followed the progression outlined by Achenbach (1988) with reference to the typical evolution of taxonomic paradigms in childhood psychopathology—from mental disorders viewed as brain diseases, to nosologies based on clinical descriptions of symptoms or signs, to multivariate methods of clustering symptoms and syndromes. Thus, an outline of the history of the diagnosis of hyperactivity provides an interesting perspective on the manner in which taxonomy has both informed and clouded struggles to delineate etiology and treatment of this disorder.

BEHAVIORAL SEQUELAE OF KNOWN BRAIN INJURY

Although Hoffman, a German physician, first described a patient nicknamed "Fidgety Phil" in 1854, the initial behavioral description corresponding most closely to ADHD is generally attributed to George F. Still in 1902. Popularly known as "Still's Disease," the behavioral condition was termed *brain damage syndrome* by Still (1902), who postulated that the syndrome stemmed from a "defect in moral control." By this rather puzzling description, Still referred to "the control of action in conformity with the idea of the good of all" (p. 1008), thus also providing a preview of diagnostic groupings that have included ADHD under the more general heading of behavior disorders. Still associated some "defects of moral control" with a broad impairment of intellect and speculated that the general aim of behavioral excess in these children was self-gratification. More specific characteristics in "imbecile children," as well as in children of normal cognitive functioning, involved "passionateness, spitefulness/cruelty, jealousy, lawlessness, dishonesty, wanton mischievousness/destructiveness, shamelessness/immodesty, sexual immorality and viciousness" (p. 1009).

Still (1902) viewed these symptoms in mentally retarded children as an associated feature of their cognitive limitations but also noted that there was no direct correlation between level of symptomatology and cognitive limitations; nor was there a tie to injury to a particular area of the brain. He further described two additional groups of children: one with symptoms tied to an observable disease process (such as encephalitis, epilepsy, head injury, and/or brain lesion), and a second with no signs of disorder other than behavioral symptoms. "There are certain children," Still (1902) remarked in addressing this second group, "who show so marked a deficiency of mental control that even in large institutions containing some hundreds of children they can be picked out at once as different in this respect from all the others" (p. 1079). In this latter group, Still (1902) noted unusual physical characteristics as well as a possible relationship to parental disorder. Though Still's symptom clusters appeared not to distinguish between conduct disorder, oppositional disorder, and ADHD (a distinction currently debated), he provided a method of grouping varied associated conditions and etiologies that forms the basis of the symptom clustering and exclusionary criteria currently in use.

The early link between brain damage or central nervous system dysfunction and hyperactivity was further strengthened by observations of the survivors of the U.S. encephalitis epidemic from 1917 to 1918. These children frequently developed behavioral disorders that closely resembled those previously de-

scribed by Still (1902) and, subsequently, postulated by Kahn and Cohen (1934) to be "organically driven." Kahn and Cohen (1934) noted the primary characteristics of this disorder as general hyperkinesis, clumsiness of motor movements, and behavioral disinhibition, and tied these characteristics to damage to the brain stem. As an aside, the authors also contended that *organic drivenness* may be related to prenatal injury or birth injury, or may be the result of a genetic predisposition which they termed a "constitutional variant" (p. 752).

Kahn and Cohen (1934) were perhaps the first to infer common causality based on observations of similar symptomatology across groups of affected individuals. They speculated that the "surplus of inner impulsion," or organic drivenness, was a consequence of damage to the brain stem. Citing case studies as support, they described individuals whose hyperkinesis was secondary to known signs of brain stem dysfunction. Bender (1942) echoed these observations of the postencephalitic syndrome, with hyperkinesis noted as the primary symptom; she also agreed with the attribution of damage to the brain stem.

Strauss and Lehtinen (1947) published extensive descriptions of the symptoms and disabilities of the brain-injured child and are generally thought to have originated the concept of *minimal brain dysfunction*. They noted that brain damage in children resulted in a specific behavioral syndrome that was demonstrably different from behaviors of non–brain-injured, mentally retarded children. They, too, identified symptoms of the syndrome that constituted behavioral sequelae of encephalitis as well as other forms of parent-identified damage, including "instability, lack of inhibition, impulsivity, (and) hyperactivity" (p. 90).

Strauss and Lehtinen (1947) focused on defining the nature of the handicaps present in these children with diffuse brain damage, with little attention paid to the definition of a specific syndrome of hyperkinesis. However, the association of the symptoms of excessive motor activity and distractibility with brain damage became firmly entrenched as a result of these early descriptions of the behavioral sequelae of known and inferred brain injury. In a later volume, Strauss and Kephart (1955) discussed similar behavioral symptoms in children of normal intellectual functioning with known and inferred brain damage. These authors were the first to suggest that reductions in external stimulation (environmental management) would be of benefit in reducing hyperkinetic behavior, a recommendation that endures within the modern classroom despite little supportive evidence (Routh, 1978).

BEHAVIORAL SEQUELAE OF INFERRED BRAIN DAMAGE

In the United States throughout the 1930s and 1940s, behavioral disorders with excessive motor activity as a primary symptom continued to be strongly associated with terms indicative of brain damage or dysfunction, although diagnostic efforts were extended to cases without known history of damage. In the late 1930s, Charles Bradley, a physician and director of the Emma Pendleton Bradley Home in Providence, Rhode Island, initiated the first of a series of studies that would eventually span more than 40 years at that facility and greatly influence the field of hyperactivity research. He used dextroamphetamine (Benzedrine) to treat children with "syndromes of cerebral dysfunction" or *organic brain syndrome* (Bradley, 1937). The children in Bradley's studies were diagnosed with behavioral syndromes attributed both to encephalopathy or, more generally, to "difficulties at birth." Bradley documented improvement on school-related tasks in 60% to 75% of patients treated with stimulant medication (Bradley, 1937, 1950; Bradley & Bowen, 1940, 1941; Bradley & Green, 1940), though he was conscientious about noting the lack of relationship between specific diagnosis (e.g., behavioral problems associated with convulsive disorders, psychopathic personality, schizoid personality, etc.), level of intellectual functioning, and improvement in general functioning in the classroom. In fact, Bradley (1937) attributed improvement to the changed "emotional attitude" of patients toward their academic tasks and noted that this change might well be a nonspecific one.

Maurice Laufer and Eric Denhoff, a child psychiatrist and pediatrician working out of the same residential school at the Emma Pendleton Bradley Home, are generally credited with providing the first behavioral description of a hyperactivity syndrome (Laufer & Denhoff, 1957; Laufer, Denhoff, & Solomons, 1957). However, it was Charles Bradley, once again, who first described a behavioral syndrome with an identified cause nine years before Laufer and Denhoff published their initial papers (Rosenfeld & Bradley, 1948). Bradley defined the primary characteristics of the hyperactivity syndrome as involving short attention span, dyscalculia, mood lability, hyperactivity, impulsiveness, and poor memory. Rosenfeld and Bradley (1948) attributed these symptoms to the effects of "asphyxiant illness" in infancy or the sequelae of anoxia or hypoxia at birth and later illnesses such as pneumonia. It is interesting that none of the children studied were formally diagnosed as mentally retarded; rather, their symptoms were interpreted as reflecting nonspecific dysfunction of the central nervous system.

Laufer (1979) later reported that Bradley's early papers served as an inspiration for his continuing work at the Emma Pendleton Bradley Home in further defining hyperkinetic impulse disorder, (HID). Laufer and Denhoff (1957) delineated the following symptoms as characteristic of this disorder: hyperactivity, or higher than normal levels of motor activity, motor development that was often advanced, short attention span and poor concentration, variability in behavior, impulsiveness and inability to delay gratification, irritability, low frustration tolerance, fits of anger, explosiveness, and poor school performance. They further noted that the disorder could be observed in infancy or early childhood, that it was observed more frequently in males and first-borns, and that the syndrome often dissipated between the ages of 8 and 18. Laufer and Denhoff (1957) discussed a specific site of damage in the diencephalon as a result of pre- or perinatal complications, such that affected children were unusually sensitive to stimuli in the peripheral receptors and viscera. Finally, they outlined the reciprocal interaction between infants and their caretakers, secondary to HID, which they postulated as the origin of secondary emotional disturbance.

Laufer and Denhoff continued the tradition of the leading edge hyperactivity research begun by Charles Bradley and the Emma Pendleton Bradley Home staff in 1937 by publishing manuscripts on the topic throughout the early 1970s (Denhoff, 1971, 1973, 1979; Laufer, 1973), further developing their notions about the loci of brain dysfunction and the development of diagnostic procedures. Further, they emphasized the developmental changes in hyperactivity observed across ages. Although they initially noted that many aspects of the syndrome dissipated in adolescence, they later reported that symptoms may persist into adulthood (Laufer, 1979). Their research marked the movement of notions of hyperactivity away from symptoms associated with known cerebral damage or trauma (seizure disorders, cerebral palsy, postencephalitic syndromes) and toward a transactional view of hyperactivity as related to brain dysfunction influenced developmentally by a variety of external circumstances.

MINIMAL BRAIN DYSFUNCTION

During the 1960s, researchers continued to emphasize the distinction between brain dysfunction and known brain damage in their efforts to delineate a syndrome of hyperactivity. Pasamanick and Knobloch (1966) proposed a "continuum of reproductive casualty" based on their studies of normal and preterm infants. They postulated that when damage to brain areas was severe, death resulted; whereas milder forms of damage resulted in syndromes such as cerebral palsy and seizure disorders. They proposed a category of *minimal brain damage* characterized by abnormal neurological signs that dissipated by 18 to 24 months. In a later publication, they reported a higher incidence of pre- and perinatal complications in a group of hyperactive, clinic-referred children (Pasamanick & Knobloch, 1966).

At the time of Pasamanick and Knobloch's research, other researchers were urging caution with respect to the use of the term *brain damage* given the lack of demonstrable evidence (cf. Birch, 1964). The Oxford Conference in 1962 concluded that the inference of brain damage in behaviorally disordered children was not a sound one and further suggested that the term *minimal brain damage* be discarded (Bax & MacKeith, 1963). Clements and Peters (1962) agreed, terming the disorder *minimal brain dysfunction*. Further, they stressed the notion of

central nervous system deviation, and outlined possible symptoms, which included specific learning deficits, perceptual-motor deficits, general coordination deficits, hyperkinesis, impulsivity, emotional lability, short attention span and/or distractibility, "equivocal" neurological signs, and borderline abnormal or abnormal electroencephalographic (EEG) studies.

Though Clements and Peters (1962) commented on the interaction between the postulated organic basis of hyperactivity and psychosocial stressors, clearly their emphasis was on neurological dysfunction. Their rationale for continuing the notion of brain dysfunction as contributory was based on their observations of the similarities between symptoms of children with known brain injury and those without, correlations between complications in pregnancy and delivery and the emergence of behavioral or learning disorders, response to medication, and clustering of symptoms. Results of a later task force proposed that a definition of minimal brain dysfunction be established, such that the term *minimal brain dysfunction syndrome* referred to children of near-average, average, or above-average general intelligence with certain learning or behavioral disabilities ranging from mild to severe, associated with deviations of central nervous system functions. These deviations were manifested by various combinations of impairment in perception, conceptualization, language, memory, and control of attention, impulse, or motor functions (cf. Rie, 1980).

HYPERACTIVITY

Other researchers, such as Werry (1968), in his description of developmental hyperactivity, attempted to separate a syndrome of hyperactivity from the umbrella term of *minimal brain dysfunction*. Werry (1968) argued for the establishment of norms against which to evaluate excess motor activity (defined as 2 standard deviations above the mean), as well as pointing out the need for assessing the "situational appropriateness of a (motor) movement." Accordingly, Werry (1968) developed norms for and published one of the first widely used scales for assessing symptoms of hyperactivity and monitoring treatment effects over time. Werry (1968), like earlier authors, noted a similar constellation of symptoms, although he made two additional distinctions: (a) the varying picture of symptoms over development, and (b) the need to recognize that "soft signs" and hyperactivity were not necessarily causally related. His research was notable for the explicit separation of developmental hyperactivity and hyperactivity associated with major central nervous system damage (organic hyperactivity). In a later article reviewing published studies of brain injury in children, Werry (1972) noted that psychopathology was not more common in brain-injured children than in control children without brain injury and, further, that when behavioral symptoms were present, the least common was hyperkinesis.

Other researchers publishing in the late 1960s and early 1970s criticized the circular reasoning inherent in concepts of inferred brain damage. Ultimately, the notion of demonstrable or inferred diffuse brain damage was abandoned. Birch (1964) noted that brain damage had come to refer to a concept or to a pattern of behavioral disorders, a pattern that children with demonstrable brain injury did not always share. Further, research had failed to support the notion that the incidence of brain damage in ADHD populations was higher than expected, and continued research failed to support a relationship between pre- or perinatal distress and later ADHD symptoms. Thus, even the term *minimal brain dysfunction* began to be viewed as both misleading and overly inclusive, referring to some ill-defined group that included learning disabled, brain-injured, and hyperactive children.

The *Diagnostic and Statistical Manual of Mental Disorders,* second edition (DSM-II, APA, 1968), provided a definition of the hyperkinetic reactions of childhood that included several of the areas that both Clements and Peters (1962) and Laufer and Denhoff (1957) had focused on, most notably excessive motor activity and inattention. However, the *DSM-II* approach was to describe symptoms in behavioral terms rather than including organic findings or speculating about etiology, moving toward a definition of hyperactivity closer to Werry's (1968, 1972) than to earlier concepts of *minimal brain dysfunction.*

Other developments included Cantwell's (1972) contributions with regard to examining possible genetic components of hyperactivity. In a study comparing parents of 50 hyperactive children and 50 control children without hyperactivity, Cantwell (1972) reported increased rates of alcoholism, sociopathy, and hysteria in the parents of hyperactives. Further, 10% of the parents were also reported to be hyperactive as children. Cantwell (1972) noted the absence of direct evidence of brain injury in these children and concluded that the presence of these adult disorders in the families of hyperactive children suggested familial transmission. In a later study of 39 hyperactive children, Cantwell (1975b) noted a higher incidence of psychiatric disturbance in biological parents compared to adoptive parents, further suggesting a process of genetic transmission. Kinsbourne (1977) expanded on this notion of genetic transmission to propose the idea of a continuum of temperamental characteristics with respect to impulsivity, with hyperactive individuals representing the population at one extreme of the distribution.

ATTENTION DEFICIT DISORDERS

The decade of the 1970s marked a shift in defining characteristics of the syndrome to include inattention, with observations of excessive motor activity. Inattention appeared to be better suited to standardized measurement than level of activity, making development of norms and comparison groups feasible. Douglas (1972), using the catch words "stop, look and listen," identified impulsivity, inability to sustain attention, and difficulty modulating arousal as the characteristics that best distinguished hyperactive children from normal children. In contrast with other perspectives at the time, Douglas did not find evidence to support a high degree of distractibility in hyperactive children. She did, on the other hand, support the notion of a deficit in sustained attention, a deficit that was found to be present regardless of whether children were subjected to stimulus reduced conditions.

Douglas's work during the late 1960s and through the 1970s (e.g., Douglas, Parry, Martin, & Garson, 1976; Douglas & Peters, 1979), was instrumental in encouraging other researchers (e.g., Werry) to compare hyperactive children with otherwise normal children on several dimensions of behavior (in addition to activity level) typically identified as affected. Further, she used her findings on differences in sustained attention and ability to modulate levels of arousal, and her theories about the effects of these deficits on higher order perceptual thinking and problem-solving abilities to develop a cognitive approach to treatment (Douglas, 1980a, 1980b).

An additional development during the 1970s was the increasing support for the notion of hyperactivity as the result of delayed maturation. From this perspective, the hyperactive child was viewed as abnormal only in the rate of acquisition of attentional competencies and capacities to inhibit activity level and impulsive responding. The notion of developmental delay has been supported by comparisons of hyperactive children with control children in neurological examinations and in electroencephalographic (EEG) studies (Barkley, 1981). However, diagnostic use of these diverse findings continued to be problematic.

By the end of the 1970s, the shift in focus to attentional deficits was evident in the *Diagnostic and Statistical Manual of Mental Disorders,* third edition (DSM-III, APA, 1980), with hyperactivity identified as a symptom that may or may not be associated with *attention deficit disorder,* as the syndrome was newly titled. In addition, onset prior to age seven was identified as one of the defining criteria of the syndrome. Finally, several exclusionary criteria were identified, including such handicapping conditions as psychosis, sensory defects, neurological disease, and mental retardation. These criteria were in marked contrast to symptoms of the syndrome as it was initially considered by researchers at the Emma Pendleton Bradley Home (i.e., Bradley, 1937; Laufer & Denhoff, 1957). These authors explicitly included these diagnostic groups as among those that exhibited characteristics of hyperkinetic impulse disorder.

Efforts to exclude children with associated but theoretically unrelated (at least in terms of etiology) symptomatology were accompanied by a growing number of voices arguing against the notion of attention deficit disorder as a syndrome (Shaffer & Greenhill, 1979). Shaffer and Greenhill (1979) noted that while some researchers argued for the utilization of hyperactivity as a "phenotypic description," widespread clinical practice continued

to correlate hyperactivity with minimal brain damage and its concomitant associations about etiology. Further, they stressed that available instruments designed to assess hyperactivity did not reliably discriminate between normal and hyperactive children on the basis of activity level alone. Nor did hyperactivity as a variable facilitate discrimination between other forms of psychiatric symptomatology. Finally, Shaffer and Greenhill (1979) reiterated Charles Bradley's (1937) early speculation that response to stimulant medication is nonspecific, also noting that the diagnosis does not allow consistent predictions about outcome later in life.

Sandberg, Rutter, and Taylor (1978) also spoke out against the notion of hyperactivity as a syndrome. They noted the inconsistency of factor analytic studies, and pointed out that even when factors could be identified on a specific measure, validity coefficients between instruments were low, suggesting the possibility that such measures were actually measuring factors other than hyperactivity. Results of their studies indicated that most children with diagnosable psychiatric disorders were rated as "inattentive" and "overactive," but these symptoms appeared usually to be situation-specific rather than specific to the disorder. The authors concluded by recommending that the notion of a definable and measurable syndrome be abandoned but that the possibility of a subgroup demonstrating pervasiveness of symptoms be further investigated.

DeFilippis (1979) summarized the results of factor analytic studies, noting that although these studies had not identified a single factor that included the primary symptoms, several of the behavioral characteristics did tend to cluster. Based on these studies, DeFilippis outlined inclusion and exclusion criteria for the disorder, with the presence of "unequivocal signs" of brain damage viewed as criteria for exclusion (soft neurological signs and abnormal EEGs were not seen as constituting unequivocal signs).

Researchers in the early 1980s have echoed these observations. Recently, Rutter (1989) has reemphasized the finding that brain dysfunction is linked nonspecifically to a variety of psychiatric disturbances, and further, that the link between birth complications and ADHD has proved to be insubstantial. Ross and Ross (1982) reiterated that factor analytic studies of ADHD do not yield the clustering of symptoms that is characteristic of true syndromes, and noted that there is neither an identified and common etiology nor a predictable course. Echoing Sandberg et al.'s (1978) observation that distinguishing ADHD symptoms from those of other psychiatric disorders is notoriously difficult, Ross and Ross (1982) observed that the overlap between learning disabilities, conduct disorder, and ADHD has been particularly troublesome and commented on the increasing number of researchers who advocate collapsing these categories to form a broad-based externalizing disorder.

In contrast, researchers such as Rutter (1989) have taken the position that a more narrowly defined syndrome would be useful. From such a perspective, the pervasive nature of both overactivity and inattention is critical as is the onset of symptoms from preschool. Taylor (1988) noted that factor analytic studies have demonstrated the existence of a hyperactivity-inattention factor as distinct from conduct disorder or aggressiveness factors. Further, he agreed that attempts to distinguish "true" hyperactive children, that is, those demonstrating pervasiveness of symptomatology, will yield clearer diagnostic categories. Support for this relatively small group of pure hyperactive children is widespread (Barkley, 1981; Rutter, 1989; Taylor, 1988; Weiss & Hechtmann, 1986). Thus, current efforts to identify subtypes appear to be divided into the following categories: aggressive or oppositional versus nonaggressive ADHD, and pervasive versus situational ADHD (Barkley, 1988).

SUMMARY AND CONCLUSIONS

This history of the diagnostic concept of hyperactivity was traced to its roots in Hoffman's 1854 behavioral description of "Fidgety Phil" and, somewhat later, to the original work of George F. Still in 1902.

Since its introduction to the literature nearly 90 years ago, the concept of hyperactivity has been among the most widely debated disorders of child development. Although the cluster of symptomatic behaviors agreed on as making up hyperactivity has

been remarkably stable over this long period of time, shifting focus and dissent among clinicians and researchers has led to a variety of diagnostic labels for the disorder. No fewer than 13 diagnoses have either alluded to the etiologic mechanism thought to be responsible for the disorder or sought to describe those behaviors most characteristic of it and comprising its core symptoms. As a result, depending largely on their age cohort, similarly inattentive, impulsive, and overactive children have been variously diagnosed (see Table 1.1.).

Although it would appear that hyperactive children have been less than uniformly diagnosed across time, the relative stability of a cluster of behaviors consensually acknowledged as characteristic of the disorder has allowed some semblance of diagnostic continuity to exist despite often marked disagreement among clinicians and researchers as to the magnitude and relevance of a particular symptom to the overall disorder.

Currently, the controversy persists as to whether hyperactivity is a separate and unique disorder, the relative contributions of its core symptoms, and its relationship with conduct disorders as well as other diagnostic groups such as Tourette's syndrome and tic disorders (cf. Cohen, Bruun, & Leckman, 1988). The symptom cluster has persevered, however, and continues to drive basic and applied research as well as the treatment of the disorder.

What may be concluded on the basis of nearly 90 years of examining the concept of hyperactivity is hardly definitive, as may be seen in the following statement by Barkley (1989):

ADHD appears to be a developmental disability in the domains of sustained attention, impulse control, and the regulation of activity level. . . . It arises during early childhood . . . and is . . . chronic in nature. Future research may reveal an as-yet-unspecified deficit in the manner in which consequences regulate behavior, suggesting that the disorder may be . . . motivation(al) rather than attention(al). Present knowledge strongly points to a biological predisposition to the disorder, with multiple etiologies being implicated. Environmental influences appear to play a role in determining the severity of ADHD symptoms, the development of oppositional and defiant behavior as well as conduct disorders, and the long-term prognosis for the disorder. (p. 65)

Table 1.1. Chronological Listing of Historically Used Diagnoses for Attention Deficit Hyperactivity Disorder

TAXONOMIC GROUPINGS AND DIAGNOSIS	REFERENCE
Sequelae of Known Brain Damage	
Brain damage syndrome	Still, 1902
Organic drivenness	Kahn & Cohen, 1934
Sequelae of Inferred Brain Damage	
Organic brain syndrome	Bradley, 1937
Organic behavior syndrome	Bradley & Bowen, 1941; Rosenfeld & Bradley, 1948
Minimal brain damage	Strauss & Kephart, 1955
Hyperkinetic impulse disorder	Laufer & Denhoff, 1957
Minimal brain dysfunction	Clements & Peters, 1962
Developmental Psychopathology	
Hyperactivity	Werry, 1968
Hyperkinetic syndrome	Rutter, et al., 1970
Hyperactive child syndrome	Cantwell, 1975a
Minimal brain dysfunction syndrome	Laufer, 1979
Attention Deficit Disorder	American Psychiatric Association, 1980
Attention Deficit-Hyperactivity Disorder	American Psychiatric Association, 1987

It is interesting that Barkley's conclusion is similar to the observations of Still (1902), who originally speculated that the disorder represented a "defect in moral control" attributable to brain damage. They are also similar to those of Rosenfeld and Bradley (1948), who first listed the cardinal characteristics of the disorder as consisting of a short attention span, impulsiveness, and restlessness while alluding to an overlap with conduct disorders and learning disabilities by noting that such children also may present with "an unpredictable variation in mood, fluctuant ability to recall material previously learned, [and] . . . a conspicuous difficulty in arithmetic."

Despite a variably articulated but generally unchanged conceptualization of the disorder across the years, the field of hyperactivity research and treatment has not been without advances. Perhaps the most influential of these has stemmed from the unique contributions of Charles Bradley, Maurice Laufer, Eric Denhoff, George Rosenfeld, Margaret Bowen, Emily Green, and Gerald Solomons of the Emma Pendleton Bradley Home, with respect to their pioneering research in the use of stimulant drugs across the 20-year period of 1937 to 1957.

Since Bradley's (1937) original observation of the effects of dextroamphetamine (Benzedine) on 30 child patients, the study of stimulant drug use in behaviorally disordered children has become commonplace. Recent estimates have indicated that over 600,000 children are treated each year for ADHD with stimulant drugs (Barkley, 1981). Moreover, it remains that the effect of stimulant drugs on the symptom cluster first described by Rosenfeld and Bradley (1948) and further developed by Laufer and Denhoff (1957) continues to drive contemporary research in the neurobiology of ADHD, where the goals of understanding the mechanism of action of stimulant drugs and pathophysiology of the disorder are yet to be achieved (cf. Zametkin & Rapoport, 1987).

REFERENCES

Achenbach, T. M. (1988). Integrating assessment and taxonomy. In M. Rutter, A. H. Tuma, & I. S. Lann (Eds.), *Assessment and diagnosis in child psychopathology* (pp. 300–343). New York: Guilford Press.

American Psychiatric Association. (1968). *Diagnostic and statistical manual of mental disorders* (2nd ed.). Washington, DC: Author.

American Psychiatric Association. (1980). *Diagnostic and statistical manual of mental disorders* (3rd ed.). Washington, DC: Author.

American Psychiatric Association. (1987). *Diagnostic and statistical manual of mental disorders* (3rd ed. rev.). Washington, DC: Author.

Barkley, R. A. (1981). *Hyperactive children: A handbook for diagnosis and treatment*. New York: Guilford Press.

Barkley, R. A. (1982). Hyperactivity. In E. J. Mash & L. G. Terdal (Eds.), *Behavioral assessment of childhood disorders* (pp. 127–184). New York: Guilford Press.

Barkley, R. A. (1988). Attention deficit disorder with hyperactivity. In E. J. Mash & L. G. Terdal (Eds.), *Behavioral assessment of childhood disorders* (2nd ed.) (pp. 69–104). New York: Guilford Press.

Barkley, R. A. (1989). Attention deficit-hyperactivity disorder. In E. J. Mash & R. A. Barkley (Eds.), *Treatment of childhood disorders* (pp. 39–72). New York: Guilford Press.

Bax, M. C. O., & Mackeith, R. C. (1963). Minimal brain damage: A concept discarded. In R. C. MacKeith & M. C. O. Bax (Eds.), *Minimal cerebral dysfunction*. Clinics in Developmental Medicine, No. 10. London: Spastics International Medical Publications, in association with William Heinemann Medical Books.

Bender, L. (1942). Post-encephalitic behavior disorders in childhood. In J. B. Neal (Ed.), *Encephalitis: A clinical study* (pp. 361–384). New York: Grune & Stratton.

Birch, H. G. (1964). The problem of "brain damage" in children. In H. G. Birch (Ed.), *Brain damage in children: The biological and social aspects* (pp. 3–12). Baltimore: Williams and Wilkins.

Bradley, C. (1937). The behavior of children receiving benzedrine. *American Journal of Psychiatry, 94*, 577–585.

Bradley, C. (1950). Benzedrine and dexedrine in the treatment of children's behavior disorders. *Pediatrics, 5*, 24–36.

Bradley, C., & Bowen, M. (1940). School performance of children receiving amphetamine (benzedrine) sulfate. *American Journal of Orthopsychiatry, 10*, 787–788.

Bradley, C., & Bowen, M. (1941). Amphetamine (benzedrine) therapy of children's behavior disorders. *American Journal of Orthopsychiatry, 11*, 92–103.

Bradley, C., & Green, E. (1940). Psychometric performance of children receiving amphetamine (benzedrine) sulfate. *American Journal of Psychiatry, 97*, 388–394.

Cantwell, D. P. (1972). Psychiatric illness in the families of hyperactive children. *Archives of General Clinical Neuropsychology, 1*, 15–19.

Cantwell, D. P. (1975a). Clinical picture, epidemiology, and classifications of the hyperactive child syndrome. In D. P. Cantwell (Ed.), *The hyperactive child: Diagnosis, management, current research* (pp. 3–16). New York: Spectrum Publications.

Cantwell, D. P. (1975b). Familial-genetic research with hyperactive children. In D. P. Cantwell (Ed.), *The hyperactive child: Diagnosis, management, current research* (pp. 93–108). New York: Spectrum Publications.

Clements, S. D., & Peters, J. D. (1962). Minimal brain dysfunction in the school-age child. *Archives of General Psychiatry, 6*, 185–197.

Cohen, D. J., Bruun, R. D., & Leckman, J. F. (Eds.). (1988). *Tourette's syndrome and tic disorders*. New York: John Wiley & Sons.

Conners, C. K., & Wells, K. C. (1986). *Hyperkinetic children: A neuropsychological approach*. Beverly Hills, CA: Sage Publications.

DeFilippis, N. (1979). The historical development of the diagnostic concept of hyperkinesis. *Clinical Neuropsychology, 1*, 15–19.

Denhoff, E. (1971). To medicate, to debate, or to validate. *Journal of Learning Disabilities, 4*(9), 467–469.

Denhoff, E. (1973). Hyperkinetic behavior syndrome: Clinical reflections. *Pediatric Annals*, 15–28.

Denhoff, E. (1979). Clinical aspects of minimal brain dysfunction: Diagnosis and management. In E. Denhoff & L. Stern (Eds.), *Minimal brain dysfunction: A developmental approach* (pp. 57–67). New York: Masson Publishing.

Douglas, V. I. (1972). Stop, look, and listen: The problems of sustained attention and impulse control in hyperactive and normal children. *Canadian Journal of Behavioral Science, 4*, 259–282.

Douglas, V. I. (1980a). Higher mental processes in hyperactive children: Implications for training. In R. Knights & D. Bakker (Eds.), *Treatment of hyperactive and learning disordered children* (pp. 65–92). Baltimore MD: University Park Press.

Douglas, V. I. (1980b). Treatment and training approaches to hyperactivity: Establishing internal and external control. In C. K. Whalen & B. Henker (Eds.), *Hyperactive children: The social ecology of identification and treatment* (pp. 283–318). New York: Academic Press.

Douglas, V. I., Parry, P., Martin, P., & Garson, C. (1976). Assessment of a cognitive training program for hyperactive children. *Journal of Abnormal Child Psychology, 4*, 389–410.

Douglas, V. I., & Peters, K. G. (1979). Toward a clearer definition of the attentional deficit of hyperactive children. In G. A. Hale & M. Lewis (Eds.), *Attention and the development of cognitive skills* (pp. 173–248). New York: Plenum Publishing.

Kahn, E., & Cohen, L. H. (1934). Organic drivenness: A

brain stem syndrome and an experience with case reports. *New England Journal of Medicine, 210,* 748–756.

Kinsbourne, M. (1977). The mechanism of hyperactivity. In M. Blaw, I. Rapin, & M. Kinsbourne (Eds.), *Topics in child neurology* (pp. 289–306). New York: Spectrum Books.

Laufer, M. W. (1973). Psychiatric diagnosis and the treatment of children with minimal brain dysfunction. *Annals of the New York Academy of Sciences, 205,* 303–309.

Laufer, M. W. (1979). Defining the minimal brain dysfunction syndrome. In E. Denhoff & L. Stern (Eds.), *Minimal brain dysfunction: A developmental approach* (pp. 5–16). New York: Masson Publishing.

Laufer, M. W., & Denhoff, E. (1957). Hyperkinetic behavior syndrome in children. *Journal of Pediatrics, 50,* 463–474.

Laufer, M. W., Denhoff, E., & Solomons, G. (1957). Hyperkinetic impulse disorder in children's behavior problems. *Psychosomatic Medicine, 19,* 38–49.

Pasamanick, B., & Knoblock, H. (1966). Retrospective studies on the epidemiology of reproductive causality: Old and new. *Merrill Palmer Quarterly, 12,* 7–26.

Rie, H. E. (1980). Defunctional problems. In H. E. Rie & E. D. Rie (Eds.), *Handbook of minimal brain dysfunctions: A critical view* (pp. 3–17). New York: John Wiley & Sons.

Rosenfeld, G. B., & Bradley, C. (1948). Childhood behavior sequelae of asphyxia in infancy. *Pediatrics, 2,* 74–84.

Ross, D. M., & Ross, S. A. (1982). *Hyperactivity: Current issues, research, and theory.* New York: John Wiley & Sons.

Routh, D. K. (1978). Hyperactivity. In P. Magrab (Ed.), *Psychological management of pediatric problems* (pp. 3–48). Baltimore: University Park Press.

Rutter, M. (1989). Attention Deficit Disorder/Hyperkinetic Syndrome: Conceptual and research issues regarding diagnosis and classification. In T. Sagvolden & T. Archer (Eds.), *Attention deficit disorder: Clinical and basic research* (pp. 1–29). Hillsdale, NJ: Lawrence Erlbaum Associates.

Rutter, M., Graham, P., & Yule, W. (1970). *A neuropsychiatric study in childhood.* London: Spastics International Medical Publications in Association with William Heinemann Medical Books.

Sandberg, S. T., Rutter, M., & Taylor, E. (1978). Hyperkinetic disorder in psychiatric clinic attenders. *Developmental Medicine and Child Neurology, 20,* 279–299.

Shaffer, D., & Greenhill, L. (1979). A critical note on the predictive validity of the hyperkinetic syndrome. *Journal of Child Psychology and Psychiatry, 20,* 61–72.

Still, G. F. (1902). The Coulstonian lectures on some abnormal psychical conditions in children. *Lancet, 1,* 1008–1168.

Strauss, A. A., & Kephart, N. C. (1947). *Psychopathology and education of the brain-injured child* (Vol. 2). New York: Grune & Stratton.

Strauss, A. A., & Kephart, N. C. (1955). *Psychopathology and education of the brain-injured child* (Vol. 2). New York: Grune & Stratton.

Taylor, E. (1988). Attention deficit and conduct disorder syndromes. In M. Rutter, A. H. Tuma, & I. S. Lann (Eds.), *Assessment and diagnosis in child psychopathology* (pp. 377–407). New York: Guilford Press.

Weiss, G., & Hechtmann, L. T. (1986). *Hyperactive children grown up: Empirical findings and theoretical considerations.* New York: Guilford Press.

Werry, J. D. (1968). Developmental hyperactivity. *Pediatric Clinics of North America, 15,* 581–599.

Werry, J. D. (1972). Organic factors in childhood psychopathology. In H. C. Quay & J. D. Werry (Eds.), *Psychopathological disorders of childhood* (pp. 83–123). New York: John Wiley & Sons.

Zametkin, A. J., & Rapoport, J. L. (1987). Neurobiology of Attention Deficit Disorder with Hyperactivity: Where have we come in 50 years? *Journal of the American Academy of Child and Adolescent Psychiatry, 26,* 676–686.

CHAPTER 2

CLUSTER VERSUS DIMENSIONAL ANALYSIS OF ATTENTION DEFICIT DISORDERS

Roscoe A. Dykman
Peggy T. Ackerman

A dimensional analysis requires that we first select tests and/or measures that we hope will emerge in a statistical analysis as reliable measures of relatively independent dimensions. The dimensions must be descriptive of and relevant to the given area of concern, which in this chapter is attention deficit disorder (ADD). Children with ADD will occupy different and overlapping areas in multidimensional space. There need not be any attempt to assign subjects to discrete groups as is done in cluster analysis. Dimensional analysis insists ADD or any subcategory of ADD is at best a figment of imagination, an ideal-type construct, and a heuristic for differentiating an entity that, in fact, is not homogeneous.

Nonetheless, we believe that both clumping (cluster) and dimensional analyses are useful and valid, and the choice is a matter of the investigation's purpose; that is, whether to find types composed of individuals more or less alike or tests more or less alike. Ellis (1985) has said much the same thing in discussing dyslexia:

What the dimensional model predicts, however, is that there will be a complete and unbroken gradient of intermediate dyslexics linking such extreme cases. A dimensional model does not deny heterogeneity, only homogeneity of subtypes. . . . It does not preclude the study of selected individuals to highlight dimensions of difference, nor does it prevent one from drawing conclusions about the reading process in general from the obtained individual differences. (p. 192)

Cantwell and Baker (1988) in discussing dimensional analysis say:

As with most classification systems for childhood psychiatric disorders, the DSM system consists of categories that were derived from initial clinical impressions. Another approach to the classification of children's psychiatric disorders, generally known as the dimensional method, begins with mathematical and statistical procedures to measure the tendency of specific items of behavior to occur together. Once these "dimensions of behavior" are identified (for example by factor analysis), individuals or patients can be classified into mutually exclusive groups (e.g., using cluster analysis). The use of mathematical procedures eliminates unreliability of an interobserver type that can occur when two clinicians combine the same data differently. Different results, however, can be obtained in dimensional classification, depending upon the mathematical criteria selected. For example, some techniques will allow the investigator to say how similar patients must be in order to be grouped together. Other techniques require that the investigator begin by specifying the number of categories to be used. Some techniques allow for unclassified patients, whereas others do not. Studies of adult patients have shown that, depending on the methods of analysis used, the same patients can be classified in different groupings. . . .

Proponents of the dimensional approach to categorization consider a major argument for their system to be the fact that *all* its classifications are empirically derived. Thus, because of its empirical foundation, the dimensional approach produces groupings that are more reliable, more homogeneous, and more closely tied to their assessment tools. Also, because the classification is based on numerical scores obtained on specific assessment tools, a patient's responses to treatment can be more easily determined under the dimensional system. In addition, the dimensional approach provides maximal coverage, because arbitrary cut-off scores are established in order to categorize all individuals. However, the requirement that each individual be categorized into one and only one class presents problems when patients have more than one psychiatric illness. Such patients are more naturally handled by the categorical system, under which it is simple to specify membership in more than one class. . . .

> Another problem with the dimensional approach is that, although factor analysis and principal component analysis produce statistically meaningful correlates between items, the statistically significant dimension of behavior created may not be *clinically or theoretically* meaningful. . . .
> Another difficulty with the dimensional approach is that its categories, being based on mathematical scores, require cumbersome definitions. Not being tied to clinical intuition, the dimensional categories are more difficult to remember and are less likely to facilitate professional communication. (pp. 522–523)*

* D. P. Cantwell & L. Baker, Issues in the classification of child and adolescent psychopathology, *Journal of the American Academy of Child and Adolescent Psychiatry, 27,* 521–533, 1988, © by American Academy of Child & Adolescent Psychiatry. Reprinted by permission.

Cantwell and Baker (1988) are perhaps wrong in saying that the categorical approaches (like those in the *Diagnostic and Statistical Manual of Mental Disorders,* third edition, revised [DSM-III-R; APA, 1987]) are better able than dimensional approaches to handle the problems of multidimensionality and meaningfulness. Again, these authors seem to be thinking about cluster analysis as a dimensional approach, which it can be if we look at the distribution of individuals in cluster space rather than the categories that emerge. Some writers, including us, see cluster analysis as a categorization or clumping procedure and not as a dimensional analysis (Stanovich, 1988). Factor scores provide dimensional information. Cantwell and Baker say that individuals get assigned to only one category, which is the general aim of cluster analysis. However, even in cluster analysis, some individuals cannot be classified (they fall in the cracks). Also, persons assigned to clusters do, in fact, vary in distance measures; that is, individuals in a cluster are only more or less alike. And true dimensional approaches do not attempt to put individuals into categories. Cluster analysis can handle multiple categories at least as well as the DSM-III approach; and the categories that emerge can be logical, meaningful, and tied to clinical intuition. Also, dimensional approaches (factor analysis) are generally more concerned with the structure of items or variables than with the structure of groups.

When dimensional analysis is based on items that are used to assign children to categories in the first place, there is a good but by no means certain chance of coming up with a priori categories or closely related categories. In this case, cluster analysis of raw scores or factor scores, or Q factor (person analysis) techniques would be useful. The factors emerging from an R analysis (correlations of tests) can be left in dimensional form or the resulting factor scores subjected to a cluster analysis (see below). Moreover, if the factors are correlated, the factor scores themselves can be factored to obtain higher order factors.

Cantwell and Baker (1988) recognize that multivariate techniques can be combined with clinically based approaches to construct classification systems that match a priori hypotheses. They cite a paper by Pfol and Andreason (1978) that outlines a four-step approach: (a) selection of patients and variables, (b) division of patients into groups, (c) development of diagnostic criteria, and (d) evolution of the diagnostic system.

Skinner (1981) has proposed comparable safeguards in an elegant theoretical article on cluster methodology in which he argues first that cluster analyses must be theory driven. That means that we must choose subjects and variables that test specific hypotheses: for example, if inattentiveness is the basic defect of hyperactive children, then we should employ measures of both activity and attention. Also, we must specify in advance the classifications that are expected to emerge.

Skinner argues for a continuous interplay of theory development and empirical analyses. Beyond the construction of a priori hypotheses, he specifies two other necessary processes: internal validation involving convergent methods, and external validation involving predictive validity, clinical meaningfulness, descriptive validity, and generalizability to other populations. Cluster methods following the recommendations of Skinner may be found in several papers in the general area of learning disorders (LD) (Fletcher, 1985; Fletcher, & Taylor, 1984; Morris, Blashfield, & Satz, 1981; Satz & Morris, 1981; Satz, & Sparrow, 1970).

There are still questions about what elements should be included as measures of dimensions or clusters (see below the problems that arise with the ADD diagnosis). For example, persons with diabetes differ widely in behaviors, medical symptoms, and signs. However, the inclusion of categories mapping their differences would miss the essence of the disorder if the role of insulin in this disease were not known. Neither cluster nor dimensional analysis would be helpful in pinpointing the basic underlying defect without knowledge of the physiology of insulin. However, with no knowledge of the cause of the disease, these analyses could be useful in placing patients with diabetes into meaningful subcategories, and these categories could be important in prognosis.

Some researchers have argued that the traditional disease model is not relevant for ADD; they contend that ADD is more like obesity (Ellis, 1985) or IQ in that individuals differ not in having or not having the traits but rather in degree of manifestation. But much the same argument can be made for any disease; consider the example of diabetes above. Presently, whether or not we choose to call a child hyperactive depends on where we set our cutting lines on teacher, parent, and child rating scales or some composite of them. DSM-III diagnoses are based on clinical ratings derived in part from reports from sources other than the patient. In any case, it is useful to conceive of activity level, aggression, and attentiveness as normally distributed traits in the population. Each is inherited, we believe, in a quantitative manner conforming to a diathesis-stress model with the ultimate manifestation shaped by both heredity and environment. Hyperactivity, for example, is not inherited. What is inherited is the potential to become hypoactive or hyperactive. With a high genetic loading, hyperactivity is likely to surface, whatever the environment; similarly, it is unlikely to appear when there is low genetic loading. But in the middle range, life circumstance and learning greatly influence the outcome.

Presently, essentially nothing is known for sure about the neural or biochemical bases of ADD or LD. The research that has been done, however, is supportive of the idea that the disorders are biologically based, and that manifestations of them vary appreciably depending upon an individual's mix of genetic and environmental inputs. Anyone who believes that hyperactivity and its associated attention deficits are purely environmental should take a close look at mental health research, in general. Psychiatric disorders are moving from mental health to medicine. There are several neural systems whose overactivity or underactivity could explain ADD. Two that have been hypothesized as possibly important (Dykman Ackerman, Clements, & Peters, 1971) are the brain stem reticular formation and the inhibitory forebrain system as described by Clemente (1968). The former plays a critical role in emotion, alertness, sleep, and motor restlessness as well as in the inhibition of nondominant stimuli on their way to the cortex (Lindsley, 1951; Samuels, 1959). The inhibitory forebrain system is important in the inhibition of both somatic and visceral systems. Electrical stimulation of this system suppresses movement, synchronizes electrical cortical activity (brain waves), and produces sleep. This system can be conditioned, and it is easy to imagine cues in the classroom being conditioned to the activation of this system, explaining the passivity we and others have noted in many nonhyperactive LD children (Dykman et al., 1971). Moreover, it is clear that the frontal lobes play a critical role in distractibility, attention, and stimulus selectivity.

We have summarized much of the psychophysiological literature pertaining to ADD elsewhere (Dykman, Ackerman, Holcomb, & Boudreau, 1983). Our general conclusion in 1983, which still holds, is that the studies in this area have fared well in showing that LD and hyperactive children differ from controls, but not so well in revealing consistent differences between solely LD, solely hyperactive, and hyperactive children who are also LD (Delamater, Lahey, & Drake, 1981; Dykman & Ackerman, 1985; Ferguson, Simpson, & Trites, 1976). While differences have been reported by us and others (Dykman, Ackerman, Oglesby, & Holcomb, 1982; Dykman, Holcomb, Oglesby, & Ackerman, 1982; Holcomb, Ackerman, & Dykman, 1985, 1986; Werry & Quay, 1972), it appears that psychophysiological similarities outweigh psychophysiological differences. At present, we have no laboratory measures of attentiveness, hyperactivity, or aggressivity that can be used to make a diagnosis. We have evidence only that groups formed on the basis of rating scales differ in such measures as reaction time, heart rate, and event-related potentials in certain paradigms and not the reverse. We cannot at present make diagnoses on the basis of objective laboratory measures and may never be able to do this. One wonders if groups formed on the basis of laboratory measures would even be acceptable if they failed to validate categorizations now made by ratings. Whatever the circumstances, this report focuses on rating scales, which represent the present state of the art.

A BRIEF HISTORY

When we came into this field in 1965, the term *minimal brain dysfunction* (MBD) was commonly used to describe children of near-average, average, or above-average intelligence who were hyperactive (Hyper) or LD or both. The MBD label was first used in an early paper from our institution written by Clements and Peters (1962) and by a subsequent task force headed by Clements in 1966. Subsequently,

Wender (1971) did much to popularize the appellation MBD in a book entitled *Minimal Brain Dysfunction in Children*. In 1971 Dykman et al. asked what makes LD children alike whether or not they are hyperactive. The conclusion was contained in the title of the paper: "Specific Learning Disabilities: An Attentional Deficit Syndrome." The term *attentional deficit,* intended to cover all children then labeled as MBD, was considered by many child specialists a "weighty" label. In the paper, we reviewed evidence supporting the hypothesis that there is a specific learning disability syndrome with a cardinal symptom of defective attention. Attention was treated as a composite trait consisting of several components: alertness, stimulus selection, focusing, and vigilance. We stated that future research could show these components to be independent, but felt then as now that much could be gained by treating attention globally.

This was the first paper to suggest specifically that MBD be replaced by the label attention deficit syndrome. Many people reading the 1971 paper believed that we were talking only about LD children, but in fact most of our studies at that time included children who were hyperactive alone (but typically underachieving in one area or another), LD alone, or both. Our belief was that the majority of children referred to our clinic for academic problems were both hyperactive and LD. For one study, summarized in the 1971 paper, we divided LD children into three activity levels (hyper, hypo, and normal); these subjects were also divided into three neurological groups on the basis of the number of classical neurological signs they exhibited (Peters, Romine, & Dykman, 1975). Subsequently we wrote several papers in which we contrasted solely hyperactive and solely LD children with children who were both LD and hyperactive (see Dykman, Ackerman, & Holcomb, 1985, for a summary).

When DSM-III (APA, 1980) came along much later, it proposed three types of ADD: children who were and were not hyperactive and a residual type. DSM-III-R (the revised version; APA, 1987) did away with the subcategory ADD without hyperactivity saying it is a diagnosis that is rarely made and that ADD with and ADD without hyperactivity are probably subtypes of a single disorder.

Our research is very consistent in supporting the idea that attention problems are common to the majority of LD as well as ADD children. Whether attention problems in these children should be considered a global entity is moot. At a minimum we should attempt to develop rating scales and laboratory paradigms assessing selective and sustained attention as well as distractibility. Is distractibility (the inability to focus) the opposite of attention, or is it a separate dimension of attention? Moreover, we should look at attention in relation to working memory, that is, what a person has to retain in memory at the moment to be able to solve problems or to comprehend what is just heard or read. But for now, we have little choice. Rating scales are very poor in assessing selective attention. This assessment can be done in laboratory experiments, but the paradigms used so far have not been very successful in delineating solely ADD children from solely LD children (Holcomb, Ackerman, & Dykman, 1987). Sustained attention and distractibility are far easier to rate and far easier to study than selective attention even in the laboratory. Still, every sustained attention task involves certain elements of selective attention, but these can be rather minimal as, for example, in simple versions of the standard vigilance task. Paradigms separating selective and sustained attention are difficult to design for the simple reason that the load on sustained attention increases with increased demands on stimulus selection.

Even though the majority of reading disabled (RD) children exhibit ADD symptoms, ADD cannot be said to be the sole or major cause of reading disability. Many ADD children, even hyperactive ones, learn to read and spell at an age-appropriate rate. We came to believe that the major problem for RD children might be more in the area of selective attention and for hyperactive children more in the domain of sustained attention. Moreover, we theorized that the failure of hyperactive children to sustain attention was due to their lack of will to do so (Dykman & Ackerman, 1976a,b), moving into an area that William James referred to as *intention*. We further speculated that intention (sustained effort) reflects frontal lobe action whereas selective attention, especially as used in reading, reflects temporal lobe involvement. The role of temporal lobes and hippocampus in recall and consolidation of memory were well known at this time.

To study intention, we modified a paradigm that

Karl Pribram (1967) had used to study frontal and temporal lobe functioning in monkeys (Dykman, Ackerman, & McCray, 1980; Dykman, Ackerman, & Oglesby, 1979). Our children-subjects were asked to scan a visual field, discover the target symbol, learn to stay with the target for five trials, search for a new target, and so on. Each child began with a visual field size of only 2 symbols, but the field size was increased in steps up to 12 symbols. At this final level of difficulty, the child had to find which of 12 visual stimuli was "it," stay with it for 5 trials, and then find another. Symbol presentation was under computer control, and any given symbol could occur in any of 12 windows.

Unfortunately for the specifics of the theory, the RD group did not differ from the adequate reading hyperactive children in the number of search trials, after-search lapses, or reaction time (RT). Both clinical groups, however, were inferior to controls. When we later studied mixed RD plus hyperactive subjects, they, too, were inferior to controls but not distinguishable from the "pure" clinical groups on Pribram performance measures. If we were to regard Pribram's paradigm as a valid test of selective attention and inattention, we could conclude that both hyperactive and RD children are defective in both temporal and frontal lobe functioning.

The kinds of behavioral deficiencies produced by injuries of the frontolimbic areas and associated cortex (Milner, 1963) are very similar to those seen in ADD children, that is, hyperactivity, attraction to novelty, task impersistence, impulsivity, perseveration or inability to switch from one motion to another, dissociation of action and verbalization, and disregard for rules and consequences. Half the hyperactive children told us they had become tired and wanted to quit the Pribram task. The RD children, though tired, did not want to quit, yet they became inattentive as the difficulty of the task increased. The hyperactive boys were more attracted to novelty than the RD children. In the early trials of one procedural condition, where the new symbol added to the visual field was always the one to be chosen for reward, hyperactive children tended to choose the novel stimulus immediately whereas RD children did not (Dykman et al., 1979). Hence, the experiment as a whole validated the concept of frontal lobe impairment in hyperactive children.

In another sample of ADD, hyperactive and RD boys, the majority, when unmedicated, exhibited lapses of attention and extraneous responding (key-play) in the intertrial intervals of the Pribram task (Dykman, Ackerman, & McCray, 1980). As with the first sample, the hyperactive boys were far more deviant in extraneous responding than were the RD subjects. Methylphenidate dramatically decreased extraneous responding, particularly in hyperactive subjects, and improved the performance of all clinical groups about equally (Dykman, Ackerman, & McCray, 1980). It is interesting that the drug had a greater effect in decreasing after-search errors than in decreasing search trials; that is, it improved sustained, more than selective, attention (or memory).

The onslaught of modern research on children with RD indicates that the major problem for most is in phonics or phonetic awareness and not attention (Bradley & Bryant, 1983; Gough & Tumner, 1986; Liberman & Shankweiler, 1985; Morrison, 1987; Stanovich 1986, 1988; Vellutino, 1979; Wagner & Torgeson, 1987). The work by Bradley and Bryant suggests a causal link between phonological awareness measured prior to reading instruction and later skills in reading. The whole issue of whether there are subtypes of dyslexia is under study in well-funded National Institute of Child Health and Development (NICHD) projects at major universities. This is not to say that attentional problems are not also important in dyslexia or LD, in general. Our studies are clear in showing that RD children have attentional problems (Dykman, Walls, Suzuki, Ackerman, & Peters, 1970; Dykman, Holcomb, Ackerman, & McCray, 1983), but we need to consider more general information processing models to explain both ADD and LD (Ackerman, Anhalt, Dykman, & Holcomb, 1986).

CRITIQUES OF ADD/HYPERACTIVITY

The terms *hyperactivity* and/or *ADD* are exceedingly controversial. McNellis (1987), who gives us credit for the ADD term, promptly rejects it, saying, "There is no support for the notion of an attentional deficit as a syndrome affecting LD children." She

believes that differences in reaction time between LD children and age-matched controls are due to differences in motivation. "One cannot help but wonder," she writes, "whether a very interesting reward (say, brief glimpses of nudes) would eliminate possible group differences" (pp. 65–66). We have not tried nudes, but money does not eliminate the differences (Dykman, et al., 1985). Also, McNellis assumes that we were talking only about LD children in our 1971 paper, but we were, as noted above, talking about children then labeled as MBD.

Others have also complained about the ADD and hyperactivity constructs (Barkley, 1981, 1982; Loney & Milich, 1982; Rutter, 1983). Prior and Sanson (1989) argue that ADD is too heterogeneous and poorly defined to be a reasonable diagnosis. From a review of the literature, they conclude that there is an absence of definition because there is no unequivocal evidence for poor attention in hyperactive children. That attentional problems occur not only in ADD but in a large number of childhood disorders is taken as evidence by Prior and Sanson to support the idea that ADD is not a reasonable diagnosis. However, the fact that attention problems are common to many psychiatric and neurological disorders does not invalidate the concept of ADD, inasmuch as ADD with and without hyperactivity occurs in children with no other disorder. Hinshaw (1987) in an otherwise excellent review writes:

> The term hyperactivity is among the most confusing in all of psychopathology. It may connote, in various contexts, a set of symptoms or behaviors related to motor restlessness and over activity, a putative syndrome involving implicit brain dysfunction, or in the case of DSM-III definition—a second aspect of a disorder thought to involve core deficits in sustained attention. Such confusion in terminology has clearly contributed to the dispute over the boundaries of this category. (p. 444)

Why this is so confusing is difficult to understand. There is nothing to say that hyperactivity cannot be all of the above and more. There is a significant gap in reasoning that leads from the use of the term in different contexts to the conclusion that chaos rules. Nonetheless, Hinshaw, after discounting medical criteria as not revealing a differential pattern of biological/etiological precursors, concludes in discussing conduct disorders and hyperactivity that

> separate (but correlated) behavioral dimensions in the two areas are usually revealed in factor analytic studies. . . . Although the overlap in these two domains is often rather substantial, subgroups of children within these two domains differ in several important respects. Specifically, antisocial parents, family hostility, and low SES [socioeconomic status] typically plague conduct-disordered children but not the hyperactive/attention disordered children, whereas the latter group more often displays cognitive and achievement deficits. In addition, children with hyperactivity/attention deficits are more frequently off task in classroom and playroom situations, but they are not at greatly increased risk for behavioral deviance in adolescence. In contrast, conduct-disordered/aggressive youngsters are more frequently on task in structural settings and tend to be popular as well as rejected, suggesting greater volitional control of behavior and better social skills. . . . Yet their behavioral and social outcomes are far worse. (p. 458)

Here we have one of the major problems in the field: reasonable behavioral definition from rating scales but poor definition from biological or medical measures. This state of affairs could result because the paradigms used in biological research may not be those best suited to bringing out differences. We question the validity of Hinshaw's comment on differential response to known treatments. We doubt, for example, that methylphenidate would be as effective in treating severe conduct disorders as it is in treating children who are only inattentive and/or hyperactive and moderately aggressive. Moreover, there are numerous drugs that are effective in treating unrelated psychological and neurological disorders, but this does not mean that the disorders are the same; for example, treatment of enuresis by the antidepressant imipramine.

SUBTYPING STUDIES

The subtyping of ADD and dyslexic children has been a topic of considerable interest in the last three years. Dyslexic and/or ADD subtyping studies financed by NICHD are underway at several major universities including Yale, Harvard, Bowman Gray, and the University of Miami. We know

of four papers other than the one by Hinshaw that have been concerned with the interface of ADD with conduct, oppositional, anxiety, and/or affective disorders (Reeves, Werry, Elkind, & Zametkin, 1987; Taylor, Shachar, Thorley, & Wieselberg, 1986; Taylor, Everitt, Thorley, Schacharr, Rutter, & Wieselberg, 1986; Werry, Reeves, & Elkind, 1987).

In the first paper of two, Taylor, Schachar et al., (1986) ask whether a division of hyperactivity, separate from one of antisocial conduct, is valuable for describing children attending psychiatric clinics. The analysis is based on 64 boys referred to psychiatric clinics for the treatment of antisocial or disruptive behavior. The sample included aggressive and/or hyperactive children. Subjects were admitted to the study with IQs as low as 65. Measures of hyperactivity, defiance, and emotional disorder were taken from a standardized, semistructured interview of parents (PACS). The PACS was shown to have adequate interrater reliability, internal consistency, and factorial validity. Factor analysis of the PACS indicated a hyperactivity factor comprising overactivity, attention span, distractibility, fidgetiness, and social disinhibition. Taylor et al. had, in addition, teacher ratings (Conners' TQ) and a psychiatric interview carried out in the format of Rutter and Graham (1968). Also available were data from a continuous performance test (CPT), a paired associate learning task (PAL), a test of selective listening for digits (SLD), and Porteus mazes. A composite scale of attention test performance was derived by summing the log and z-transformed scores on the CPT, the percentage success rate on the PAL, the age score from the Porteus mazes, the selectiveness score from the SLD, and the digit span from the same test.

Taylor, Schachar et al. (1986) found the activity scales, but not the defiance scales, to be associated with greater activity, younger age, poorer cognitive performance, and abnormality on neurological examination. On the other hand, the defiance scales, but not the hyperactivity scales, were associated with impaired family relationships and adverse social factors. It was concluded that a dimension of inattentive, restless activity exists independently of one of antisocial, defiant conduct.

In the second paper Taylor, Everitt et al. (1986)

report a cluster analysis using the same subjects described in their first report. Two methods of cluster analysis (Wards method and the method of complete linkage) were used on reliable measures of hyperactivity, defiant behavior, emotional disorder, and attention deficit. The investigators opted for a four-group cluster solution on the grounds of clinical relevance and because of consistency of the two methods. Only six cases were classified into different groups by the two procedures. One cluster (Hyper) was composed of children (N = 15) with high scores on the activity scales in three situations (home, school, and clinic) and poor scores on attention, but little evidence of overt emotional disorder. Cluster C (21 cases), characterized by an absence of high scores on most variables, was high on teachers' ratings of defiance (and to a lesser extent hyperactivity). These children appeared to have a "situation-specific" problem of conduct. Cluster A (N = 13) was high on teacher and parent ratings of emotional distress, but not on depression. These children were neither hyperactive nor defiant. Cluster D (N = 11) had high scores on depression from the psychiatric examination. Cluster groupings were a significant predictor of methylphenidate response. Of the 38 children treated, 11 showed a positive response and of these 8 were in the cluster Hyper. Only 3 of the 27 who showed a lesser response were in the Hyper cluster. Methylphenidate response was assessed in terms of clinical judgment and a reduction in ratings of hyperactivity.

Rutter (1978) said that for a syndrome to be useful it must predict something other than what was used to define the group in the first place. Taylor, Everitt et al. (1986) contend that their results support the concept of a hyperactive syndrome, because relative to other groups studied, hyperactive children had lower IQs, higher frequencies of sensorimotor incoordination, a greater number of developmental disorders, and a better response to methylphenidate.

Werry, Reeves, and Elkind (1987) reviewed studies comparing ADD, anxiety, and conduct disorders, emphasizing the fallacy that the Chapmans (1973) made famous; namely, that of comparing controls and clinical groups without a clinical control group (see chapter 7 by Werry). Werry et al. (1987) say that the few studies that *have* compared ADD with conduct disorder, with or without anxiety disorder,

"suggest that ADDH may be a cognitive disorder, possibly of neurodevelopmental origin; conduct disorder one of social relationships of psychosocial origin; and anxiety disorder less predominantly male, associated with perinatal anxiety, and less severe in every way than the other two" (pp. 133). The writers conclude that coexistence of these disorders is probably common, and that it is senseless to attempt to revise the DSM-III "until we know what is right and wrong with it." This opinion also concurs with our opinion and that of Cantwell and Baker (1988).

A second paper from the Werry group (Reeves, Werry, Elkind, & Zametkin, 1987) is based on 105 children (ages 5–12) with diagnoses of anxiety, ADDH, and conduct or oppositional disorders. Reeves et al. report (no cluster analysis) that conduct and oppositional disorders resemble each other and seldom occur in the absence of ADDH. These cases then were grouped together and called an ADDH and conduct disorder group (N = 35). Werry, Methven, Fitzpatrick, and Dixon (1983) had earlier suggested that the combination of conduct and oppositional disorders improved the reliability of the diagnosis of conduct disorders. But Reeves et al. also found a pure ADDH group (N = 39) and an anxiety disorder group (N = 21). Diagnosis was made via the Diagnostic Interview Schedule for Children-Parent Version (DISC-P) of the National Institute of Mental Health (NIMH) (Costello, Edelbrock, & Costello, 1985). A total of 180 diagnoses were given to the 105 children.

The above studies, in addition to the extensive review of Hirshaw, indicate that there are subtypes of ADD children: some with hyperkinesis only, and some with conduct and/or oppositional disorders. This finding leaves open the question of whether subjects in these subtypes are sufficiently homogeneous to be grouped together or, in fact, shade into many other categories. We recently explored this question with a large ADD sample in our laboratory. The results are discussed below.

CATEGORIZATION RESULTS IN A LARGE ADD SAMPLE

Two recently published papers (Dykman & Ackerman, 1991; Livingston, Dykman, & Ackerman,

1990) report basic findings from this study, but here we will add some theoretically based analyses not previously described. The clinical subjects (N = 182) were children evaluated in our Child Study Center for school-related problems. All clinic referrals to the project were administered the Diagnostic Interview for Children and Adolescents (DICA), developed by Herjanic and Reich (1982) and Herjanic, Herjanic, Brown & Wheatt (1975). Those admitted met the criteria for Attention Deficit Disorder (ADD) based on the DICA attention items endorsed by each child's primary caretaker. As the child rated himself, parents were asked to agree or disagree with each answer. Each ADD subject admitted also met other criteria: (a) age between 7 and 11 years, (b) Full Scale IQ of at least 85, (c) good physical health with no uncorrected sensory impairments, and (d) normal educational experience. Children with known or suspected brain damage were excluded as were those having movement disorders, autism, or schizoid disorders. But children also meeting the DICA criteria for developmental reading, language, or arithmetic disorders, conduct disorder, oppositional disorder, anxiety disorder, phobic disorder, adjustment disorder, or depressive disorder, were admitted provided ADD was a primary diagnosis. The aim was to enroll a broad spectrum of clinic-referred children with ADD. The ADD sample included 153 boys and 29 girls; 164 children were Caucasian (138 boys, 26 girls) and 18 were black (15 boys and 3 girls).

Control children (33 males, 19 females, all Caucasian except 1 black male) were recruited during summer months mainly from local Boy and Girl Scout troops and vacation church schools. Some children of medical center employees also participated. None had been referred to school personnel or child guidance clinics for behavioral or academic problems. These children had to meet the four criteria listed above for ADD subjects.

The primary reason for recruiting a normal control group was to establish mean and variability figures for the laboratory tasks. For the cognitive, achievement, and behavioral ratings (except for the Yale teacher questionnaire), adequate normative data exist. The invitation to parents of controls specified that the child must not have experienced either behavioral or academic difficulties; therefore, as expected, this group had higher Wide Range Achievement Test (WRAT) scores and higher IQs than the total ADD sample, and means on behavioral ratings were in the normal range.

Additional Preliminary Workup

In addition to the WISC-R, the children were administered the revised Wide Range Achievement Test (WRAT-R), and their teachers and parents completed several questionnaires. Teachers were paid $10.00 to fill out three forms: our expanded Conners questionnaire (which includes 10 items assessing the ADD behaviors listed in DSM-III); the Matthews Youth Test for Health or MYTH (Matthews & Angulo, 1980), which assesses two components of Type A behavior (competitiveness and aggressivity-irritability); and the Yale Psychoeducational Questionnaire (Shaywitz, 1979), which we factor analyzed for research purposes. This analysis produced five factors: sustained attention, academic aptitude, hyperactivity, impulsivity, and socialization. Parents or guardians filled out the Conners parent questionnaire as well as Achenbach and Edelbroch's (1983) Child Behavior Checklist, which yields nine factors and two broad band or composite scores (Internalizing and Externalizing).

Laboratory Visit

On the day of the laboratory visit, the child was administered two self-rating scales, the Junior Personality Inventory (Eysenck, Eastings, & Eysenck, 1970), and the Arkansas Thrill Seeking Scale, modeled after the Sensation Seeking Scale developed by Zuckerman (1979). The subject was also given Gordon's (1979) differential reinforcement of low response rates (DRL), a task which purports to measure impulsivity; the Trail-making test (parts A and B), a part of the Halstead-Reitan battery (Golden, 1981) sensitive to brain dysfunction; a 10-minute coding task, an expanded symbol inverted version of the WISC-R subtest, thought to be a good measure of sustained attention; and a timed arithmetic test (20 simple addition and subtraction problems). The latter three tasks were administered in the hospital cafeteria during the noon hour; we wished to see how well the children could concentrate in a distracting environment, with and without methylphenidate.

DICA Diagnostic Procedure

The DICA was administered by a licensed and clinically experienced psychological examiner who was trained for the procedure by the project child psychiatrist. The psychiatrist then scored each protocol using DSM-III criteria. He decided whether a given diagnosis was *possible* (one symptom short of criteria), *probable* (enough symptoms but uncertain or lacking in criteria of duration or severity), or *definite,* and whether the diagnosis was current or not; for purposes of this report, these divisions are collapsed. Thus, the figures given are lifetime rates at any of the three degrees of diagnostic certainty. Also, anxiety and mood disorders were lumped, except for special treatment of separation anxiety in some analyses. Seven children endorsed enough items to warrant consideration of a diagnosis of psychosis, but on subsequent interview the psychiatrist discounted this diagnosis. All these children had other diagnoses, which were tabulated and used.

Behavioral Group Classification Procedure

Following Skinner (1981), we hypothesized that there would be three major behavioral subgroups in our large heterogeneous clinic sample: ADD only, ADD plus hyperactive (ADDH), and ADD plus hyperactive-aggressive (ADDHA). We did not expect to find many ADD-aggressive subjects who were not also rated as hyperactive. To confirm this hypothesis, we performed a K-means cluster analysis (BMDP KM program) of ADD subjects using three teacher rated behaviors: Loney and Milich's (1982) Iowa hyperactivity (IHY) and aggression (IAGG) factors (derived from the Conners questionnaire) and the Arkansas ADD index, which incorporates the DSM-III criteria for ADD. A three-cluster solution mirrored our hypothesis. Mean scores on the clustering variables suggested cut-scores on the pretreatment aggression and hyperkinesis factors (hereafter called the Iowa factors) that permitted division of the ADD sample into three groups that replicated

with a few exceptions, the results of the cluster analysis. The cut scores were as follows:

$$ADD = IHY \leq 8 \text{ and } IAGG \leq 6$$
$$ADDH = IHY > 8 \text{ and } IAGG \leq 6$$
$$ADDHA = IHY > 8 \text{ and } IAGG \leq 6$$

Reading Group Classification Procedure

In addition to behavioral groups, we wished to compare ADD children with and without developmental reading disorders (RD), or dyslexia, which was operationally defined by a discrepancy formula. More specifically, each child termed dyslexic had a mean WRAT reading plus spelling standard score less than 90 (lowest quartile) and this score was at least 10 points lower than his or her Full Scale WISC-IQ. This maneuver ensures that each dyslexic child will be a poor-for-age reader as well as an underachiever. Other formulas (e.g., quotients) can result in including underachievers for IQ who are nonetheless adequate for age as well as including slow learners as adequate readers simply because their reading and spelling scores are matched by IQ. The usual linear regression formulas for subtyping children as dyslexic fail to consider adequately over- and underachievement.

Our inclusion of spelling in the definition of dyslexia has been criticized by some reviewers in articles submitted for publication. We believe that this inclusion is justified for two reasons: first, the literature reviewed above indicates that phonic sensitivity is a precursor of both reading and spelling skill, and second, there are close and highly statistically significant correlations between reading and spelling. Reading and spelling on the WRAT were correlated 0.88 ($p < .01$) in our clinical children.

In the ADD sample, 82 children (74 boys, 8 girls) met criteria for dyslexia. Twelve others (9 boys, 3 girls) were poor-for-age readers but their mean WRAT reading-spelling score was not 10 points lower than their IQ. These children are better considered as slow learners. The normal reading ADD subjects included 65 boys and 18 girls. (Five children had missing WRAT data). Among the normal readers were 13 children with reading-spelling scores over

100 whose Full Scale IQ (FSIQ) was at least 15 points higher and another six with IQs 10 to 14 points higher. In summary, over half the sample were dyslexic or slow learners and proportionately more boys than girls were affected. The ratio of boys to girls for the entire sample was about 5:1 and the ratio of dyslexic boys to girls about 9:1.

Of the black children, 7 boys and 1 girl were dyslexic, 3 boys and 1 girl slow learners, and 4 boys adequate readers. Thus, a higher proportion of black children were poor readers, but the sex ratios were similar to those for the Caucasian children.

Because we had hoped to be able to include more ADD girls, we recruited a disproportionate number of normal girls. Overall, the girls had marginally higher reading scores and less adverse behavioral scores than boys ($p < .10$). We had also hoped that more black children could be recruited, especially black girls. The ratio of white to black ADD males is 9:1, which is markedly out of line with the ratio within the area served by our Child Study Center. For this reason, and because proportionately more of the black ADD males were from lower income families, comparisons with the white ADD sample must be viewed with caution. The black ADD males had significantly lower verbal and performance IQs and WRAT subtest scores than the white ADD males, and classroom teachers rated the black males significantly higher on hyperactive and aggressive behaviors but not on ADD behaviors.

ADD VERSUS DYSLEXIA

Using white males only, we did a number of comparisons of ADD subjects not RD with ADD subjects who were RD. The ADD not RD children did not differ from controls in IQ measures or achievement measures with the exception of lower WRAT spelling scores. Both the control and ADD not RD groups scored higher on cognitive measures (WISC-R and WRAT) than did the RD groups.

SUBGROUP ANALYSES

For each variable of interest, we did a two-way analysis of variance (ANOVA) (white males only)

with the RD group (dyslexic or not) as one factor and the behavior group (ADD, ADDH, and ADDHA) as another. A significant main effect in reading means that the RD boys differed from the not RD boys (behavioral groups ignored). Likewise, a significant main effect for behavior ignores the RD dichotomy. When both main effects are statistically significant it generally means doubly affected subgroups that differed from all other ADD-RD groups. Bonferroni tests on each separate ANOVA were used to contrast pairwise subgroup means in the event of a significant interaction. We recognize that when one makes many statistical tests there is an increased probability of type I errors. Yet, if we were to apply the Bonferroni method across all ANOVAs, there would be an appreciable chance of type II errors. It seems best in view of our knowledge at present to err on the side of type I rather than type II errors. But, we will emphasize only those findings significant at $p < .01$.

There were no significant interactions in these analyses, which means that RD did not add or subtract differentially from behavior groups and vice versa. As shown in Table 2.1, the RD children were lower than non-RD children in most cognition measures.

The corresponding data for behavioral groups appears in Table 2.2. Not shown, ADDHA children had higher mean scores in WRAT Reading than the other two behavioral groups ($p < .05$) and the means for sustained attention problems as rated on the Yale questionnaire were 1.8, 2.9, and 3.3 for ADD, ADDH, and ADDHA, respectively ($p < .02$).

COMORBIDITY OTHER THAN RD

As for additional DICA diagnoses, the ADDHA groups had the highest overall rate of diagnoses per child (0.94), with ADD next (0.90), and ADDH lowest (0.75). There was a tendency for more ADDHA boys to have diagnosis of conduct disorder (chi-square = 4.66, $p < .10$, 2 df), but no other differences in rates of disorders were found. Within and across the three ADD groups, those with and without RD did not differ in rates except in one

Table 2.1. Significant Reading Disability Results ($p < .01$)

TEST	NOT DYSLEXIC (N = 58)	DYSLEXIC (N = 64)
WISC-R		
Verbal IQ	113.8	99.7
Performance IQ	112.0	104.6
WRAT		
Reading	104.8	79.2
Spelling	98.7	78.5
Arithmetic	101.3	88.4
Yale		
Sustained Attention*	3.0	3.2
Academic Aptitude*	2.1	2.6
Performance		
Coding	126.7	97.5
Math (correct)	17.0	14.5
Math (seconds)	222.4	302.8

*Problems increase with score.

Table 2.2. Significant Differences for Behavioral Groups ($p < .01$)

TEST*	ADD	ADDH	ADDHA
Conners Hyperactivity	11.0	18.3	23.2
ADD	16.5	21.1	23.4
IAGG	0.8	2.1	10.9
Yale			
Hyperactivity	1.8	2.9	3.3
Socialization	1.7	1.6	2.3
Impulsivity	1.5	2.0	2.7
Myth			
Aggression	23.0	27.9	34.7
Child Behavior Checklist (CBCL)			
Externalization	19.7	27.0	31.1

*Problems increase with score.

category; overall, significantly more RD than normal reading children met the criterion for separation anxiety (chi-square = 4.86, $p < .05$).

We next divided the white males into four DICA groups, those with separation anxiety and/or other emotional disorders (EMOSA), those with conduct or oppositional disorders (OPPCON), those with diagnoses in both the preceding bins (BOTH), and those with no diagnosis (Neither). Figure 2.1 shows the number of boys in the ADD subgroups who fell into each of the four DICA groups. Dyslexic subjects were not over- or underrepresented in any DICA groups.

Parent ratings of their children on the Child Behavior Check List (CBCL) were reasonably concordant with DICA diagnoses (self-ratings of child). The ADD boys who satisfied DICA criteria for internalizing behaviors (EMOSA) were rated by parents on the checklist as more internalizing. Teacher ratings did not mirror DICA diagnoses as well as was expected. Even the boys who endorsed enough items to be placed in the conduct disorder category were not rated by teachers as significantly more aggressive (IAGG) or impulsive or less socially adaptive (Yale factors).

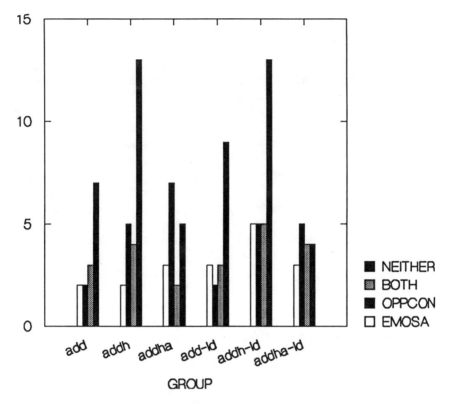

Figure 2.1. The percentage of Caucasian children in each ADD/dyslexic category in each of four DICA diagnostic bin. *Note:* OPPCON = oppositional or conduct disorder; EMOSA = emotional disorder and/or separation anxiety.

CLUSTER ANALYSIS OF FACTOR SCORES

In our initial subtyping analyses, we took the most straightforward tack, using raw scores on key variables. Below is a discussion of whether the subtyping could be improved with other techniques.

Here we use the same measures as before (IHY, IAGG, and the Arkansas ADD Index), but report a cluster analysis of factor scores. We factored IHY, IAGG, and the ADD scale (Principal Components Analyses [PCA] followed by Varimax rotation). As before, we hypothesized three behavioral groups: ADD, ADDH, and ADDHA. However, to obtain three factors we had to set the eigenvalue level to 0.30; otherwise, IHY and ADD show up on the same factor. This could be taken to mean that hyperactivity and attention are a single factor and not two separate factors. However, we prefer to regard them as

separate for the following reason: we do see children with attentional problems who are not hyperactive although the reverse is rarely the case. This latter group might be found in greater numbers in a school population. The intercorrelations suggested three factors: AGG correlated 0.56 with IHY and 0.37 with ADD (182 clinical cases). The remaining correlation IHY and ADD was 0.64 ($p < .01$ for all correlations).

The factor scores from this analysis were entered into a K means clustering program (BMDPKM) requesting three a priori groups: ADDHA, ADDH, and ADD. This analysis resulted in three clusters consisting of 45 ADDHA subjects, 65 ADDH subjects, and 77 ADD subjects. Note that a higher number of subjects was assigned to the ADD category than was obtained in the paper described above, that is, analysis of raw data and factor scores result in similar but not identical clusters.

INTERNAL CONSISTENCY OF FACTOR SCORE CLUSTERS

We next entered the three key variables (ADD, IHY, and IAGG) into a discriminant analysis where the groups were the three clusters formed with factor scores. Only two cases were incorrectly classified. The number of errors increased to four when we used the jackknife method in which each case was classified into a group according to classification functions computed from all cases except the case being classified.

Internal consistency was further checked by drawing a random sample of 16% of the cases. Discriminant (classification) functions were then computed for the remaining cases and these were used to classify the 30 subjects in the subsample. The variables entering the discriminant function were the same ones that had previously been used to derive factor scores, that is, ADD, IHY, and IAGG. Here we wished to see if the variables in raw score form (not factor scores) were consistent in identifying the groups derived by cluster analysis using factor scores. Of the 16%, there was only one misclassification error in 30 cases. Nonetheless, it was clear as we inspected the scatterplots of cluster scores, that the three groups overlapped to a rather appreciable extent (see dimensional graphs below).

We used factor scores instead of raw scores for the following reasons: First, the results for the two methods are not identical and the factor scores appear to be a somewhat better measure of the underlying variables than the scores themselves. Second, there is an advantage in using factor scores when there are more variables than the number of components one desires to retain: The larger set can be reduced to the smaller set of hypothesized principal variables. We could have used all the teacher ratings to derive our three behavioral groups but did not do so because we wished to use those most like the Iowa variables that have been used in previous studies (Loney & Milich, 1982).

EXTERNAL VALIDATION: TEACHER DATA

To check the external validation by teacher data, we first used the cluster program to assign subjects to the three behavioral groups (ADD, ADDH, and ADDHA). Then the other teacher variables were used to see how well they discriminated the three behavioral groups. The other variables were the two MYTH factors and the five Yale factors. By univariate analysis, we found the following variables to be statistically significant in differentiating the three behavioral groups: Myth aggression ($F = 10.72, p < .01$); Yale sustained attention ($F = 2.74, p < .02$), and Yale sociability ($F = 9.53, p < .01$). This analysis was done only on those cases for which we had data on all the variables entering the discriminant analysis (df = 2,143). The discriminant analysis (stepwise) yielded three Yale variables in the following order of importance: Yale hyperactivity, Yale sociability, and Yale impulsivity. Myth aggression dropped out because it was correlated substantially with the three Yale factors: 0.73 with Yale hyperactivity, 0.35 with Yale sociability, and 0.67 with Yale impulsivity. Hence, MYTH aggressiveness contributed nothing new to the classification function after the Yale factors were extracted. The classification matrix while statistically significant was not outstanding. The discriminant function correctly classified 74% of the ADDHA cases, 73% of the ADDH cases, and 71% of the ADD cases ($F = 32.08$, df = 6,284, $p < .01$). The jackknifed classification, which excludes the case being classified when the classification function is computed, yielded slightly lower estimates of overall accuracy as is generally the case in jackknifed classifications: 69% for ADDHA, 73% for ADDH, and 71% for ADD. The overall accuracy for the classification function was 72.8% and for the jackknifed classification 71.4%. Note that we are talking about an error rate of roughly 30% in assigning subjects to clusters formed on the basis of IHY, IAGG, and ADD (three other teacher measures). Yet, the overall thrust of this analysis, considering the vagaries of rating scales, lends credence to the hypothesis of three behavior groups. The correlations of teacher variables may be found in Table 2.3.

EXTERNAL VALIDATION: PARENT DATA

Like others, we found that behavior ratings from different sources do not agree well (Loney & Milich, 1982). This is not just a consequence, in our view,

Table 2.3. Teacher Correlations

	ADD	IHY	IAGG	MYC	MYA	SATT	HYP	ACAP	SOC
ADD	—								
IHY	0.66	—							
IAGG	0.40	0.56	—						
MYC	−0.27	0.08	0.14	—					
MYA	0.25	0.57	0.68	0.41	—				
SATT	0.66	0.42	0.24	−0.36	0.01	—			
HYP	0.31	0.70	0.54	0.32	0.73	0.15	—		
ACAP	0.50	0.20	0.06	−0.34	0.02	0.38	0.13	—	
SOC	0.40	0.37	0.52	−0.29	0.35	0.28	0.25	0.30	—
IMP	0.27	0.45	0.69	0.22	0.67	0.05	0.50	0.12	0.34

of different perspectives and situations in which children are observed, but is at least in part, a function of differing interpretations of items, even for items in which the content is the same.

For the parent discriminant function we entered the internalizing and externalizing T scores from the CBCL, the Conners parent hyperactivity factor, and the Conners parent ADD factor. All these variables were significantly correlated in the statistical sense ($p < .01$): parent ADD correlated 0.67 with parent hyperactivity, 0.42 with internalization, and 0.49 with externalization; and parent hyperactivity correlated 0.54 with internalization and 0.73 with externalization. The surprise was that internalization and externalization correlated so highly (0.70). These correlations, as expected, yielded only one clear factor.

In univariate tests, two variables were significant in differentiating the three behavioral groups: parent hyperactivity ($F = 9.58$, df = 2,165, $p < .01$) and the externalization score on the CBCL ($ = 9.21$, df $= 2,165$, $<.01$). Again, tests included only clinical cases for which we had a complete set of parent data. While the parent ADD score was not significant at the univariate level, it did enter the classification function. Stepwise discriminant analysis (variables entered in order of importance) used only the two Conners measures of ADD and hyperactivity ($F = 8.61$, df = 4,328, $p < .01$). The analysis correctly placed 63% of the ADD subjects, 49% of the ADDHA subjects, but only 31% of the ADDH subjects. It is apparent that the parent ratings are less accurate as external validation measures than the teacher measures. This result is most likely because the teacher external validation rating measures were made by the same teachers who made the ratings

entering the cluster analysis ("halo effect"). However, the overall significance in the parent data, despite the lack of precision in classification, supports the notion that parents and teachers are identifying similar categories.

EXTERNAL VALIDATION: CHILD SELF-REPORT DATA

The measures entering the discriminant function here were the four Eysenck factors (introversion, extraversion, psychoticism, and the lie scale) and the thrill-seeking index, and DICA diagnoses. There were only modest correlations: Eysenck psychoticism with Eysenck lie (−0.46) and thrill seeking (0.43), and Eysenck neuroticism with Eysenck lie (−0.36). Not one of the child variables attained statistical significance at the .05 level in separating the behavioral groups. However, one variable, hyperactivity as measured by the DICA, did enter the discriminant function and it reliably separated the ADDHA and ADDH children from the ADD group ($p < .05$).

EXTERNAL VALIDATION: PERFORMANCE TEST DATA

A factor analysis of the performance scores including IQ and WRAT scores (direct quartimin rotation) yielded three factors (the first two correlated at 0.40). The first consisted of the three tests given in the cafeteria: coding, arithmetic, and trail making. Coding and correct arithmetic responses loaded negatively (−0.77 and −0.62) whereas time to complete arithmetic problems and time to complete the two trail-making tests loaded positively (0.67, 0.56,

0.86, respectively). The second factor consisted of the three achievement tests and Verbal IQ. The loading for WRAT reading was 0.94; for WRAT spelling, 0.99; for WRAT arithmetic, 0.76; and for verbal IQ, 0.50. Only one measure, the Gordon DRL efficiency score, showed up on the second factor (0.85). The discriminant analysis on this set of factors was negative; that is, the three behavior groups did not differ from each other collectively on these measures. Moreover, only arithmetic time was significant in the univariate test ($F = 3.26$, df = 2,163, $p < .05$).

DIMENSIONAL ANALYSES

It is clear from Figure 2.2 that the factor scores representing the three subtypes of ADD are continuously distributed and that any carving up of regions

into distinct homogeneous subtypes is not possible. The same degree of scatter was manifest in the plots of the actual scores on ADD, IHY, and IAGG (figure not shown). We looked at the data from each source separately because we found that data could not be rationally combined across sources; that is, the factors that emerge are source dependent and not content dependent.

TEACHER VARIABLES

In the original cluster analysis based on raw scores, the teacher ratings produced the greatest number of statistically significant behavioral differences, with the Yale factors and MYTH showing highly significant group differences. But this finding leaves open the question of pattern differences among the whole set of teacher ratings, which we now describe using

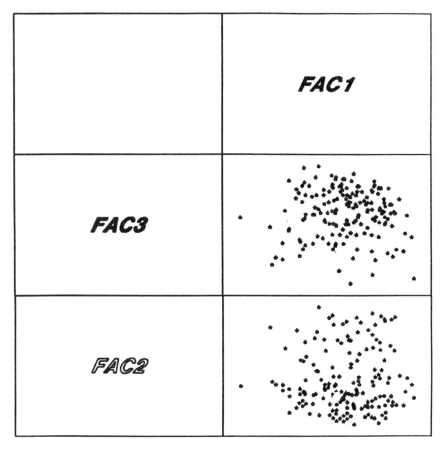

Figure 2.2. Factor 1, Factor 2, and Factor 3 represent factor scores for ADD, IHY, and IAGG, respectively. The plots for Factors 2 and 3 are not shown (much the same as these).Yh

two different dimensional approaches: canonical correlations (BMDP program) and LISREL (Joreskog & Sorbom, 1984).

The canonical analyses of teacher variables yielded three significant canonical variates ($p < .001$ by Bartlett's test for remaining eigenvalues as described in the BMDP manual). The canonical correlations were 0.87, 0.70, and 0.50. Table 2.4 gives the results of the teacher analysis. Set one consisted of the three variables used to define the clusters (ADD, IHY, and IAGG), and these were interdependent with 54% of IHY explained by ADD and IAGG, 44% of ADD explained by IHY and IAGG, and 32% of IAGG explained by ADD and IHY. The second set of variables consisted of the remaining teacher variables. MYTH aggression (MYA) had the highest squared multiple correlation of all the variables in this set: 71% of its variance was explained by the other variables in the set which included MYTH Competitiveness (MYC), Yale Sustained Attention (SATT), Yale Hyperactivity (HYP), Yale Academic Aptitude (ACAP), Yale Sociability (SOC) and Yale Impulsivity (IMP). The squared multiple correlations for HYP, IMP, MYC, SOC, and SATT were 0.57, 0.47, 0.47, 0.38, 0.25, and 0.24, respectively (squared multiple correlation equals the percentage of variance explained).

The canonical correlation is a double-barreled principal component analysis with the first canonical variate maximizing the variance removed by each successive factor with the restriction that factors are orthogonal. For the first canonical variate, a positive score on IHY and IAGG (presumably the ADDHA variable) went with positive scores on MYA, SATT,

HYP, SOC, and IMP. Positive scores on ADD were associated mainly with positive scores on ACAP and SATT and negative scores on HYP in the second canonical variate. The third component, IAGG (aggressiveness) was positively associated with HYP and negatively related to MYA, SOC, and IMP.

The LISREL model appears in Figure 2.3 which shows only the statistically significant paths ($p < .01$ for each path shown). The chi-square for the fit of this model was excellent ($p = .90$ with 6 degrees of freedom). The proportion of variance in ADD explained by all the variables in the teacher subset, which includes very minimal contribution from nonsignificant paths not drawn, was 0.64. The corresponding explained variance for IHY and IAGG was 0.67 and 0.60, respectively. We know that the variables within two sets (predictors and criterion) are substantially interdependent. Hence, a variety of LISREL models could be produced, all of which would fit the data reasonably well with nonsignificant chi-square differences between models. It will be noted that in the LISREL model IHY (hyperactivity) is related to only two variables (sustained attention on the Yale, and hyperactivity on the Yale). ADD is also related significantly to only two variables. Aggressivity is related significantly to four variables. Most interesting, if valid, are the two-way relationships between the criterion variables. The paths (one-way or two-way from ADD to IAGG or ADD to IHY were not significant; that is, the ADD variables, as Loney et al. say, are independent of IAGG. The path from IHY to ADD is much stronger ($p < .01$) than the reverse path (not

Table 2.4. Standardized Canonical Coefficients for Teacher Data

	CAN 1		CAN 2		CAN 3	
	Y_1	X_1	Y_2	X_2	Y_3	X_3
ADD	.036		1.297		−0.321	
IHY	.489		−0.579		1.272	
IAGG	.616		−0.320		−0.992	
Myth Competitiveness		−0.008		−0.147		−0.066
Myth Aggression		0.268		0.067		−0.318
Sustained Attention		0.336		0.595		0.103
Hyperactivity		0.336		−0.351		1.159
Academic Achievement		−0.112		0.530		0.041
Sociability		0.248		−0.085		−0.379
Impulsivity		0.323		−0.081		−0.624

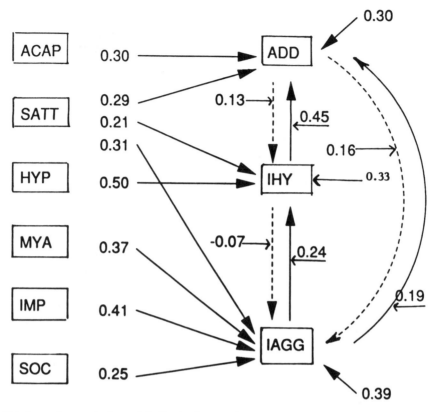

Figure 2.3. This figure shows only the statistically significant pathways (p < .05), except for 2-way connection. The nonsignificant 2-way pathways are shown by a dotted line.

significant), meaning that hyperactivity is more likely to "cause" attention problems than the reverse. Also, there is a tendency for aggression to have a greater effect on hyperactivity ($p < .01$) than the reverse (not significant), and a tendency for IAGG to have a greater effect on ADD ($p < .01$) than the reverse (not significant).

The LISREL and canonical analyses were concordant overall. This could more easily be seen if all the Lisrel paths were drawn and not just the statistically significant ones. The Lisrel model based on maximum likelihood methods seems to be more precise in showing the interdependencies of variables, and it shows both the direct effect of a variable as well as its indirect effects through other members of the same set; for example, the indirect path from HYP to IHY to ADD ($0.50 \times 0.43 \times 0.45 = .096$). This implies that some 10% of the variance in ADD can be attributed to this indirect path.

PARENT DATA

The analyses of parent ratings on the clusters (see cluster analysis section above) indicated that the three behavior groups differed on the CBCL externalization broad-band factor with ADD < ADDH < ADDHA. The canonical analysis yielded one significant eigenvalue ($p < .01$). Some 44% of the variance in parent ADD scores was explained by the parent hyperkinesis scale, internalization, and externalization. Corresponding percentages for the other three were 65% for parent rated hyperkinesis, 49% for internalization, and 65% for externalization. Hence, it appears that not only is there a significant overlap, but if we enter one factor, for example externalization, we simultaneously remove other factors. This analysis (see Table 2.5) indicated that high scores in IHY were associated with low scores on parent ADD, high scores on parent hyperkinesis, low scores on internalization, and high scores on externalization. The canonical correlation for this factor was 0.52. The second factor had a canonical correlation of only 0.26. See Figure 2.4 for LISREL model of parent data.

It will be noted that parents and teachers tend to see the interrelation of ADD, IHY, and IAGG differently. Here, high scores on ADD increase IHY and IAGG more than do the reverse pathways, a conception opposite to what the teacher model indicated and opposite to common sense conjectures.

Table 2.5. Standardized Canonical Coefficients for Parent Data

	Y_1	X_1
ADD	−0.136	
IHY	0.890	
IAGG	0.280	
Parent ADD		−0.518
Parent Hyperactivity		0.766
Internalization		−0.624
Externalization		0.864

The dominant pathway from IAGG to IHY (0.42) is logical. We can only assume from the pathways shown (direct and indirect) that parents do not discriminate the behavioral groups as well as teachers do.

CHILD DATA

As noted earlier, there was nothing significant in the ANOVAs of the child self-report data. Here the issue was whether the groups formed by clusters differed on Eysenck factors and/or thrill seeking. The two additional dimensional analyses added some useful information, suggesting that the child data were not quite as negative as originally thought.

The canonical correlation of ADD, IHY, and IAGG (set 2) with the four Eysenck factors and thrill seeking produced no significant variates by Bartlett's test for remaining eigenvectors; that is, this analysis indicated that the scores that entered the original cluster analysis were not significantly related to any

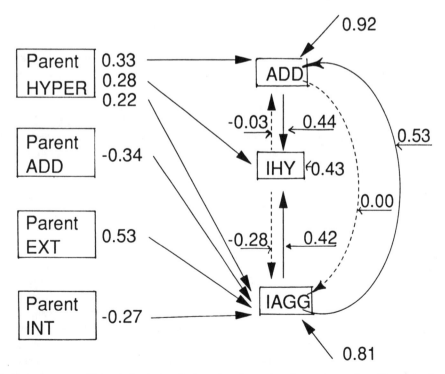

Figure 2.4 Path diagram (standardized) for the prediction of teacher ratings from parent ratings. The paths shown are staticsically significant ($p < .05$) except for dotted lines.

of the child self-ratings. Note that here we are talking about a disparity between teacher and self-ratings.

The LISREL model indicated that the variance explained by ADD, IHY, and IAGG in the four Eysenck variables and thrill seeking were 21%, 69%, and 53%, respectively, indicating that the child self-ratings are more closely tied to teacher ratings of hyperactivity and aggression than to teacher ratings of ADD.

No single variable, although one was statistically significant, had an appreciable effect on IHY or IAGG. The paths from thrill seeking to ADD and IHY were statistically significant ($p < .05$). IHY had the clearest structure as might be expected from its shared variance: Eysenck neuroticism scores and thrill-seeking scores were positively related to IHY and Eysenck psychoticism scores were negatively related to IHY.

CONCLUSIONS

It is unfortunate that we have to rely so heavily on rating scales in making diagnoses. There is no glucose tolerance test for ADD. Note also that DSM-III and DSM-III-R are rating scales: a certain arbitrary number of check marks produces a diagnostic label. While we and others have found objective laboratory measures to be statistically associated with diagnoses made by ratings (either DSM-III or the scales used in this report), they do not yield as clear a separation of subgroups as do other rating scales. No one thus far has developed an objective battery of laboratory measures sufficiently diverse to subtype ADD children reliably. We should attempt to construct batteries of laboratory measures broad enough in scope to assess all major dimensions of ratings scales so that we could type on the basis of physiological and performance measures in the laboratory and then determine how well these results relate to ratings and clinical impressions. In any event, our writing here has to do with rating scales and their inherent limitations.

The results of our analyses are clear in showing that we can derive subgroupings or clusters that mirror clinical reality. The teacher results suggest at least three basic and related types of ADD children: ADD only, ADDH, and ADDHA. We know from other analyses of these data that about one-half of

each group is dyslexic (poor in reading and spelling). Unfortunately, external validation in ratings other than those made by the teacher is only fair. While parent ratings are more closely associated with the teacher ratings than are the self-ratings of children, parents tend to see these children as belonging to one group rather than three groups. It would appear from our results that the teacher is the best source of diagnostic information, probably because he or she sees the child in a performance-demanding situation and in relation to other children the same age.

The dimensional analyses done in the last section above appear to reflect clinical reality better than the cluster analyses, but this is a matter of degree. It is absolutely clear that the clusters derived from teacher ratings are not homogeneous. Any one of the three groups have individuals located in the space of the other groups. While dimensional analysis is far more revealing in showing the structure of variables, it does not provide information about the structure of groups.

One might question whether anything worthwhile is gained by the subtyping of ADD children. In terms of presently available treatments, we probably do not need to subgroup them. Whatever the diagnostic category, treatment plans should take into account all variables related to problems at school and home. These include IQ, achievement, and ratings from various sources including the self-ratings of the child. Hence, every child must be treated somewhat differently. At the same time, most ADD children, whatever their subcategory, can be helped by low to moderate doses of stimulant medication. Still, we do not think subgrouping is a waste of time. Specific treatments will likely evolve once practitioners recognize that these children fall into reliable subgroups. We have some evidence to support this now. In results reported elsewhere (Dykman & Ackerman, 1991), we found that the three behavioral groups did not differ in response to methylphenidate. However, when we looked at other DSM-III diagnoses in these children (Livingston et al., 1992), we found that those who had both an externalizing and internalizing diagnosis (e.g., oppositional or conduct disorder and an anxiety disorder) did better on a higher dose of methylphenidate (0.6 mg/kg) than a low dose (0.3 mg/kg). It is also clear that since aggressive-type

ADD children have more serious problems later in life than other types (see review by Hinshaw, 1987), additional intervention is needed for them.

To turn now to the question of etiology, are we dealing with a single pleiotropic trait like PKU whose manifestations may vary in several directions—learning, inattentiveness, activity level, aggressiveness, and so on? Or are we dealing with subcategories that represent different combinations of different major genes? We doubt that any of the major dimensions are programmed by a single gene. It seems best to assume independent modes of inheritance for ADD, ADDH, and ADDHA youngsters. If we add to this the notion of continuous variation in multiple dimensions, which our data clearly support, we are talking about the additive and nonadditive effects of multiple genes, no one of which has a visible effect. We hasten to emphasize that this theorizing does not deny environmental influence. The object for research is the specific contribution of environment and genotype to each trait that enters the diagnosis. From this standpoint, we should probably discard all present-day childhood diagnostic categories and turn to variations in underlying variables such as anxiety, activity, attention, and intelligence, realizing that the equations may be different for the sexes.

In sum, we come back to the conclusion stated in the introduction, but with one additional caveat. Whether we cluster or factor analyze depends on our purposes, and both approaches can readily be combined. One is best for discovering individuals who are alike and the other best for discovering tests and measures that are alike. Once the major components are identified, they can be used to construct subgroups. Here we did not go beyond three variables (ADD, IHY, and IAGG) in constructing subgroups (clustering), but we could have utilized the whole battery of teacher measures. The three we chose matched, as said above, our a priori theoretical structure.

We had hoped that we would be able to combine data across sources. Much confusion would be eliminated if parents and teachers could agree. However, one encounters great difficulty when variables are combined in this way; LISREL, for example, rejected every across-source model we tried, and many were tried. The same was true for exploratory factor analysis; the tests segregated into factors by source rather than by content. With sufficient attention to design and numerous tryouts, it might be possible to bring at least the teacher and parent ratings into better concordance. If we were to do this, we would design items for each source that assess the three factors found in our research—attention, hyperactivity, and aggressiveness. But items that assess aggressiveness, for example, might be completely different for parents and teachers, even though they are measuring the same trait. The task would be to write items, even though different in content, that would measure the same thing. Perhaps a checklist of behaviors that are present or absent would work best for parents since they do not see the child in relation to other children in the same way teachers do; they would need an instrument such as the CBCL that does not make comparisons. The correlation of CBCL aggressiveness and IAGG was 0.39 ($p < .01$). While this is not very impressive it indicates a degree of overlap that might be improved with revised items. The caveat is that it is dangerous to combine sources from present-day rating scales. Parents seem to recognize one major dichotomy, pathology or not pathology. Teachers on the other hand do seem to be able to sort out the three separate major aspects of behavior we see in the clinic (attention, aggression, and hyperactivity). And physicians rarely spend enough time with a child to make a reliable diagnosis; they rely mainly on parent reports.

A final point has to do with the relevance of our research for psychiatric diagnosis. We admit to bias regarding the axis placement of attentional deficit disorder (ADD) in the DSM-III-R of the American Psychiatric Association (APA, 1987). In DSM-III-R, ADD is placed on Axis I, which includes mental conditions such as anxiety disorders and schizophrenia. We see no reason to consider ADD a mental disorder. The learning disabilities (LDs) are correctly placed on Axis II, presumed developmental disorders, which also includes disorders such as mental retardation, autism, and the personality disorders. We believe it best in view of current knowledge to consider all childhood psychopathologies as developmental disorders. There is certainly no good reason to place ADD and LD or ADD and conduct disorders on separate axes.

REFERENCES

Achenbach, T. M., & Edelbrock, C. S. (1983). *Manual for the child behavior checklist and revised child behavior profile*. New York: Queen City Printers.

Ackerman, P. T., Anhalt, J. M., Dykman, R. A., & Holcomb, P. J. (1986). Presumably innate and acquired automatic processes in children with attention and/or reading disorders. *Journal of Child Psychology and Psychiatry, 27*, 513–529.

Ackerman, P. T., Peters, J. E., & Dykman, R. A. (1971). Children with learning disabilities: WISC profiles. *Journal of Learning Disabilities, 4*, 150–166.

American Psychiatric Association. (1980). Diagnostic and statistical manual of mental disorders (3rd. ed.). Washington, DC: Author.

American Psychiatric Association. (1987). Diagnostic and statistical manual of mental disorders (3rd. ed., rev.). Washington, DC: Author.

Barkley, R. (1982). Guidelines for defining hyperactivity in children: Attention deficit disorder with hyperactivity. In B. E. Lahey & A. B. Kasdin (Eds.), *Advances in clinical psychology* New York: Plenum Publishing.

Barkley, R. A. (1981). *Hyperactive children: A handbook for diagnosis and treatment*. New York: Guilford Press.

Bradley, L., & Bryant, P. (1983). Categorizing sounds and learning to read: A causal connection. *Nature* (London), *271*, 746–747.

Cantwell, D. P., & Baker, L. (1988). Issues in the classification of child and adolescent psychopathology. *Journal of the American Academy of Child and Adolescent Psychiatry, 27*, 521–533.

Chapman, L. J., & Chapman, P. V. (1973). *Disordered thought in schizophrenia*. New York: Appleton-Century-Crofts.

Clemente, C. (1968). Forebrain mechanisms related to internal inhibition and sleep. *Conditional Reflex, 3*, 145–174.

Clements, S. (1966). *Minimal brain dysfunction: Terminology and identification*. Washington, D.C.: Department of Health, Education and Welfare.

Clements, S. D., & Peters, J. E. (1962). Minimal brain dysfunctions in the schoolage child—diagnosis and treatment. *Archives of General Psychiatry, 6*, 185–197.

Costello, E. J., Edelbrock, C. S., & Costello, A. J. (1985). Validity of NIMH diagnostic interview scale for children. *Journal of Abnormal Child Psychology, 13*, 574–596.

Delamater, A. M., Lahey, B. B., & Drake, L. (1981). Toward an empirical subclassification of "learning disabilities": A psychophysiological comparison of "hyperactive" and "nonhyperactive" subgroups. *Journal of Abnormal Child Psychology, 9*, 65–77.

Dykman, R. A., & Ackerman, P. T. (1976a). An information processing model of minimal brain dysfunction. In D. V. Sankar (Ed.), *Mental health in children* (pp. 375–409). Westbury, N.Y.: PJD Publications.

Dykman, R. A., & Ackerman, P. T. (1976b). The MBD problem: Attention, intention and information processing. In: R. P. Anderson & C. G. Holcomb (Eds.), *Learning disability/minimal brain dysfunction syndrome*. Springfield, IL: Charles C Thomas.

Dykman, R. A., & Ackerman, P. T. (1991). Attention deficit disorder and specific reading disability: Separate but often overlapping disorders. *Journal of Learning Disabilities, 24*, 96–103.

Dykman, R. A., Ackerman, P. T., Clements, S. D., & Peters, J. E. (1971). Specific learning disabilities: An attentional deficit syndrome. In H. R. Myklehurst, (Ed.), *Progress in learning disorders* (pp. 56–98). New York: Grune & Stratton.

Dykman, R. A., Ackerman, P. T., & Holcomb, P. J. (1985). Reading disabled and ADD children: Similarities and differences. In D. Gray (Ed.), *Biobehavioral measures of dyslexia* (pp. 47–62). Parkton, MD: York Press.

Dykman, R. A., Ackerman, P. T., Holcomb, P. J., & Boudreau, A. Y. (1983). Physiological manifestations of learning disability. *Journal of Learning Disabilities, 16*, 46–53.

Dykman, R. A., Ackerman, P. T., & McCray, D. S. (1980). Effects of methylphenidate on selective and sustained attention in hyperactive, reading-disabled, and presumably attention-disordered boys. *Journal of Nervous and Mental Disease, 168*, 745–752.

Dykman, R. A., Ackerman, P. T., & Oglesby, D. M. (1979). Selective and sustained attention in hyperactive, learning-disabled, and normal boys. *Journal of Nervous and Mental Disease, 167*, 288–297.

Dykman, R. A., Ackerman, P. T., & Oglesby, D. M. (1980). Correlates of problem solving in hyperactive, learning disabled, and control boys. *Journal of Learning Disabilities, 13*, 309–318.

Dykman, R. A., Ackerman, P. T., Oglesby, D. M., & Holcomb, P. J. (1982). Autonomic responsivity during visual search of hyperactive and reading disabled children. *Pavlovian Journal of Biological Science, 17*, 150–157.

Dykman, R. A., Holcomb, P. J., Ackerman, P. T., & McCray, D. S. (1983). Auditory ERP augmentation-reduction and methylphenidate dosage needs in attention and reading disabled children. *Psychiatry Research, 9*, 255–269.

Dykman, R. A., Holcomb, P. J., Oglesby, D. M., & Ackerman, P. T. (1982). Electrocortical frequencies in hyperactive, learning disabled, mixed, and normal children. *Biological Psychiatry, 17*, 675–685.

Dykman, R. A., Walls, R. C., Suzuki, T., Ackerman, P. T., & Peters, J. E. (1970). Children with learning disabilities: Conditioning, differentiation, and the effect of distraction. *American Journal of Orthopsychiatry, 40*, 766–782.

Ellis, A. W. (1985). The cognitive neuropsychology of developmental (and acquired) dyslexia: A critical survey. *Cognitive Neuropsychology, 2*, 169–205.

Eysenck, H. J., Eastings, M. S., & Eysenck, S. B. G. (1970). Personality measurement in children: A dimensional approach. *Journal of Special Education, 4*, 261–277.

Ferguson, H. G., Simpson, S., & Trites, R. L. (1976). Psychophysiological study of methylphenidate responders and non-responders. In R. M. Knights & D. J. Bakker (Eds.), *The neuropsychology of learning disorders*. Baltimore MD: University Park Press.

Fletcher, J. M. (1985). External validation of learning disability typologies. In B. P. Rourke (Ed.), *Neuropsychology of learning disabilities: Essentials of subtypal analysis*. New York: Guilford.

Fletcher, J. M., & Taylor, H. G. (1984). Neuropsychological approaches to children: Towards a developmental neuropsychology. *Journal of Clinical Neuropsychology, 6*, 39–56.

Gordon, M. (1979). The assessment of impulsivity and mediating behaviors in hyperactive and non-hyperactive boys. *Journal of Abnormal Child Psychology, 6*, 221–236.

Gough, P. B., & Tunmer, W. E. (1986). Decoding, reading, and reading disability. *Remedial and Special Education, 7*, 6–10.

Herjanic, B., Herjanic, M., Brown, F., & Wheatt, R. (1975). Are children reliable reporters? *Journal of Abnormal Child Psychology, 3*, 41–48.

Herjanic, B., & Reich, W. (1982). Development of a structured psychiatric interview for children: Agreement between child and parent on individual symptoms. *Journal of Abnormal Child Psychology, 10*, 307–324.

Hinshaw, S. P. (1987). On the distinction between attentional deficits/hyperactivity and conduct problems/aggression in child psychopathology. *Psychological Bulletin, 101*, 443–463.

Holcomb, P. J., Ackerman, P. T., & Dykman, R. A. (1985). Cognitive event-related brain potentials in children with attention and reading deficits. *Psychophysiology, 22*, 656–666.

Holcomb, P. J., Ackerman, P. T., & Dykman, R. A.

(1986). Auditory event-related potentials in attention and reading disabled boys. *International Journal of Psychophysiology, 3*, 263–273.

Holcomb, P. J., Ackerman, P. T., & Dykman, R. A. (1987). Event-related potentials of RDs during memory scanning. In S. Ceci (Ed.), *Handbook of cognitive social, and neuropsychological aspects of learning disabilities* (pp. 343–368). Hillsdale, NJ: Lawrence Erlbaum Associates.

Joreskog, K. G., & Sorbom, D. (1984). *LISREL VI. Analysis of linear structural relationships by maximum likelihood, instrumental variables, and least squares methods*. Mooresville, IN: Scientific Software.

Liberman, I. Y., & Shankweiler, D. (1985). Phonology and the problems of learning to read and write. *Remedial and Special Education, 6*, 8–17.

Lindsey, D. (1951). Emotion. In S. Steven (Ed.), *Handbook of experimental psychology* (pp. 473–516). New York: John Wiley & Sons.

Livingston, R. L., Dykman, R. A., & Ackerman, P. T. (1990). Prevalence and significance of additional DSM-III diagnoses in ADD children. *Journal of the American Academy of Child and Adolescent Psychiatry, 18*, 465–478.

Livingston, R. L., Dykman, R. A., & Ackerman, P. T. (1992). Psychiatric comorbidity and response to two doses of methylphenidate in children with ADD. *Journal of Child and Adolescent Psychopharmacology, 2*, 115–122.

Loney, J., & Milich, R. (1982). Hyperactivity, inattention and aggression in clinical practice. In M. Wolraich *Advances in behavioral pediatrics* (pp. 113–145). Greenwich, CN: JAI Press.

Matthews, K. A., & Angulo, J. (1980). Measurement of the Type A behavior pattern in children: Assessment of children's competitiveness, impatience-anger, and aggression. *Child Development, 51*, 466–475.

McNellis, K. L. (1987). In search of the attentional deficit. In S. J. Ceci (Ed.), *Handbook of cognitive, social, and neuropsychological aspects of learning disabilities* (pp. 63–81). Hillsdale, NJ: Lawrence Erlbaum Associates.

Milner, B. (1963). Effects of different brain lesions on card sorting. *Archives of Neurology, 9*, 90–100.

Morris, R., Blashfield, R., & Satz, P. (1981). Neuropsychology and cluster analysis: Problems and pitfalls. *Journal of Clinical Neuropsychology, 3*, 79–99.

Morrison, F. J. (1987). The nature of reading disability: Toward an integrative framework. In S. J. Ceci (Ed.), *Handbook of cognitive, social and neuropsychological aspects of learning disabilities, Vol II* (pp. 33–62). Hillsdale, NJ: Lawrence Erlbaum Associates.

Peters, J. E., Romine, J. S., & Dykman, R. A. (1975). A

special neurological examination of children with learning disabilities. *Developmental Medicine and Child Neurology, 17,* 63–78.

Pfol, B., & Andreasen, N. C. (1978). Development of classification systems in psychiatry. *Comprehensive Psychiatry, 19,* 197–207.

Pribram, K. H. (1967). Memory and the organization of attention. In D. B. Lindsley & A. A. Lumsdaine (Eds.), *Brain function and learning.* Berkeley: University of California Press.

Prior, M., & Sanson, A. (1989). Attention deficit disorder with hyperactivity: A reply. *Journal of Child Psychology and Psychiatry, 29,* 223–225.

Reeves, J. C., Werry, J. S., Elkind, G. S., & Zametkin, A. (1987). Attention deficit, conduct, oppositional, and anxiety disorders in children: II. Clinical characteristics. *Journal of the American Academy of Child and Adolescent Psychiatry, 26* 144–155.

Rutter, M. (1978). Diagnostic validity in child psychiatry. *Advances in Biological Psychiatry, 2,* 2–22.

Rutter, M. (1983). *Development neuropsychiatry.* New York: Guilford Press.

Rutter, M., & Graham, P. (1968). The reliability and validity of the psychiatric assessment of the child: I. Interview with the child. *British Journal of Psychiatry, 114,* 563–579.

Samuels, I. (1959). Reticular mechanisms and behavior. *Psychological Bulletin, 56,* 1–25.

Satz, P., & Morris, R. (1981). Learning disability subtypes: A review. In F. J. Priozzolo & M. C. Wittrock (Eds.), *Neuropsychological and cognitive processes in reading.* New York: Academic Press.

Satz, P., & Sparrow, S. S. (1970). *Specific developmental dyslexia: A theoretical formulation.* Rotterdam: Rotterdam University Press.

Shaywitz, S. (1979). *Yale neuropsychoeducational assessment scales.* New Haven, CT: Yale University Press.

Skinner, H. A. (1981). Towards the integration of classification theory and methods. *Journal of Abnormal Psychology, 90,* 68–97.

Stanovich, K. E. (1986). Cognitive processes and the reading problems of learning disabled children: Evaluating the assumption of specificity. In J. Torgesen & B. Wong (Eds.), *Psychological and educational perspectives on learning disabilities* (pp. 87–131). Orlando, FL: Academic Press.

Stanovich, K. E. (1988). Explaining the differences between the dyslexic and the garden-variety poor reader: The phonological-core variable-difference model. *Journal of Learning Disabilities, 21,* 590–604.

Taylor, E., Everitt, B., Thorley, G., Schacharr, R., Rutter, M., & Wieselberg, M. (1986). Conduct disorder and hyperactivity. II. A cluster analytic approach to the identification of a behavioral syndrome. *British Journal of Psychology, 149,* 768–777.

Taylor, E., Schachar, R., Thorley, G., & Wieselberg, M. (1986). Conduct disorder and hyperactivity: I. Separation of hyperactivity and antisocial conduct in British child psychiatric patients. *British Journal of Psychiatry, 149,* 760–767.

Vellutino, F. R. (1979). *Dyslexia: Theory and research.* Cambridge, MA: MIT Press.

Wagner, R. K., & Torgesen, J. K. (1987). The nature of phonological processing and its causal role in the acquisition of reading skills. *Psychological Bulletin, 101,* 192–212.

Wender, P. H. (1971). *The minimal brain dysfunction syndrome in children.* New York: Wiley-Interscience.

Werry, J. S., Methven, R. J., Fitzpatrick, J., & Dixon, H. (1983), The interrater reliability of DSM-III in children. *Journal of Abnormal Child Psychology, 11,* 341–354.

Werry, J. S., Reeves, J. C., & Elkind, G. S. (1987). Attention deficit, conduct, oppositional, and anxiety disorders in children: 1. A review of research on differentiating characteristics. *Journal of the American Academy of Child and Adolescent Psychiatry, 26,* 144–155.

Zuckerman, M. (1979). *Sensation seeking: Beyond the optimal level of arousal.* Hillsdale, NJ: Lawrence Erlbaum Associates.

CHAPTER 3

THEORY AND HYPERACTIVITY

William J. Helsel
Christina M. Fremer

Thousands of scientific writings on hyperactivity have been published (Whalen, 1990) including 7,000 articles that appeared in the 3-year period between 1977 and 1980 (Weiss, 1985). There is little reason to believe this proliferation has abated (Whalen, 1990). Given this vast literature from a variety of disciplines, it would be reasonable to assume that much is known about hyperactivity, and indeed, this is the case. For instance, the literature describes the various biological aspects of hyperactivity, such as contributions from genetics (Lahey, Piacentini, McBurnett, Stone, Hartdagen, & Hynd, 1988; Stewart, DeBlois, & Cummings, 1980), neuroanatomy (Lou, Henriksen, Bruhn, Borner, & Nielsen, 1989), neurochemistry (Levy & Hobbes, 1988; Zametkin, Linnoila, Karoum, & Sallee, 1986), pharmacology in both animals (Bedford, Marquis, & Wilson, 1984; Nielsen, Duda, Mokler, & Moore, 1984) and human beings (Barkley, 1977; Triantafillou, 1972; Weizman, Bernhout, Weitz, Tyano, & Rehavi, 1988; Zametkin, Rapoport, Murphy, Linnoila, & Ismond, 1985), and psychophysiology (see Hastings & Barkley, 1978). A great deal of work has also been published on psychosocial aspects of hyperactivity, including studies of mother-child interactions (Mash & Johnston, 1982), cognitive processes (Abikoff & Gittelman, 1985; Hamlett, Pellegrini, & Conners, 1987; Satterfield, Schell, Nicholas, & Backs, 1988),

behavior therapies (see Wells, 1987), and psychometrics of rating scales (Ullmann, Sleator, & Sprague, 1985). Some studies have looked at the interaction of biological and psychosocial aspects of hyperactivity (Hicks, Gualtieri, Mayo, Schroeder, & Lipton, 1985; Speltz, Varley, Peterson, Beilke, 1988; Vyse & Rapport, 1989).

In spite of the thousands of articles that have been published, however, much remains to be learned about hyperactivity. This is true of a number of additional psychiatric disorders, but few (e.g., schizophrenia and depression) rival hyperactivity in proliferation of literature. The rate of publishing on this topic is unrivaled among childhood psychiatric disorders. Given this remarkable level of interest, it is surprising that recently published articles question something as fundamental as the existence of hyperactivity (Bloomingdale, 1984). As noted in the first chapter of this handbook, much confusion has evolved out of the ongoing debate of appropriate labeling (e.g. MBD vs. ADD vs. ADHD). Some practitioners question whether hyperactivity is its own entity or a sequelae of a variety of other childhood disorders (Rutter et al., 1969). At the very least this apparent confusion is a curiosity, given the millions of dollars and thousands of workforce hours already expended in the investigation of something that may not even exist. One possible explanation for this inefficient approach to the examination of hyperactivity is the conspicuous absence of a general theory.

Consequently, the purpose of this chapter is to demonstrate the importance of theory in moving toward a better understanding of hyperactivity and its treatment. To accomplish this goal the chapter is presented in three major sections. The first is a discussion of theoretical underpinnings and theory characteristics. It should be noted that the word *theory* is used here, but *hypothesis* or *paradigm* can be substituted with little change in meaning (Eaglen, 1978). The second section examines a theoretical framework of general psychopathology suggested by Matson (1985). The third and final section calls for a change in the way theory building is currently structured, and a move to an integrated interaction theory, with the implications of such a change. This chapter is not, however, a comprehensive review of currently espoused theories of hyperactivity. Instead, it is a demonstration of the current role theory plays in the investigation of hyperactivity.

SCIENCE AND THEORY

Prior to a discussion of science and the role theory plays, it is necessary to examine the scientific method among alternative methods of inquiry, which are fundamental to the actions of professionals interested in hyperactivity—so fundamental, in fact, that little thought is given to their importance in the day-to-day activities of these professionals interested in the study of hyperactivity. As noted in the introduction of this chapter as well as the contents of this handbook as a whole, many articles have been written on hyperactivity. Further, the majority of these articles are attempts to understand the structure and workings of this disorder. In other words, empirical science is the method of inquiry that predominates the study of hyperactivity. What are the alternatives to empirical science? Why has empirical science become so dominant in the pursuit of information? What are the implications of selecting empirical science as the preferred method of inquiry? (An epistemological examination of pragmatism or logical positivism is not conducted here. See Krasner and Houts [1984] for a review of the issues of logical positivism in the behavioral sciences.)

Alternative Methods of Inquiry

To begin to understand the role of theory, an examination of that which underlies professional activity is necessary. This underlying motivation goes beyond the obvious reinforcers of the individual professional (e.g., academic position, tenure, financial reward, intrinsic reward) and permeates the collective group interested in questions of psychopathology and hyperactivity in particular. In fact, engaging in a method of inquiry, adapting beliefs, or gaining knowledge are apparently fundamental processes of man (Randall & Buchler, 1971). Human beings have a source of belief and a definite attitude in connection with this source. For professionals interested in hyperactivity and its investigation, the source is the scientific method. To understand the implications of this selection, alternative methods of inquiry should be reviewed.

Randall and Buchler (1971) discuss three methods of inquiry in addition to the scientific method. The first evolves from man's natural tendency to view his beliefs as correct and preferable. This steadfastness of belief is called faith, which has at least three forms. Faith as tenacity is the first and perhaps most dangerous. It is belief in spite of evidence to the contrary. The study of hyperactivity is fraught with examples of people adhering to a belief that has been repeatedly called into question. For instance, research findings on the role food additives play in hyperactivity are inconsistent at best (see Conners, 1980), yet diet adjustments have become common clinical practice. Research with consistent findings is not immune from faith in tenacity as in the case of those opposing methylphenidate usage (Citizens Commission on Human Rights, 1987). Only compatible beliefs are adopted, and new evidence is viewed suspiciously and with hostility.

The second form of faith is belief in the absence of evidence. Because of man's aversion to doubt or uncertainty he seeks out something to believe in and "latches on" to this belief. Formal religion is the most common example of this form of faith and is believed by many to be essential to man's existence (see Burton, 1974). The aversion to doubt being avoided by faith in the absence of evidence is revisited in a later section of this chapter and should be considered a major source of motivation for professionals interested in the study of hyper-activity.

The third and final form of faith to be considered is based on experience. It is a faith that better understanding of hyperactivity is inevitable because of previously disclosed positive evidence related to the study of other disorders as well as features of hyperactivity itself. This form of faith, also, has inherent in it a source of motivation. It is the belief that instances of failure will be dispelled by further investigation. This notion is paramount to the discussion of scientific method.

The second method of inquiry is authority. In this method man relinquishes his "independent efforts to determine what is true and false" (Randall & Buchler, 1971, p. 51). By definition this method of inquiry cannot tolerate alternative opinion; to question authority is the employment of an alternative method. The justification of authority as a method of inquiry is that individuals make errors. This justification is not adequate: if an individual can be in error, so can a group. Because authoritarianism is intolerant of alternative inquiry, high-rate error is likely, and in fact, will be perpetuated. Historical authority or tradition can preserve both wisdom and error; both good and bad survive.

At this juncture it is necessary to make a distinction between two types of authority. Dogmatic authority is quite different from expert authority. The former type relies on the opinion of an organized group that does not avail itself of an examination of how it was reached. In the latter type of authority, reliance is on a conclusion drawn from the scientific method that not only enables, but requires examination of how it was reached.

The third method of inquiry to be discussed is intuition, which gives man an opportunity to exercise his intellect. This method rests on the assumption that man has a natural capacity for acquiring knowledge; he has direct insight or an immediate awareness. The notion is that there are certain principles that are self-evident or need no evidence; "they are their own evidence, they guarantee their own truth" (Randall & Buchler, 1971, p. 54). The primary disadvantage of this method of inquiry is the determination of what is self-evident. With this method the offering of proof in favor of one view of a principle implies that the principle is not self-evident.

The method of inquiry is by definition the source of belief in what professionals interested in understanding hyperactivity do in their day-to-day lives. Yet little time is spent examining the "why" or philosophy of such a choice. Of primary interest is the choice evinced by this handbook and its contents. The three methods of inquiry just reviewed are actively rejected in favor of a fourth source of belief, the scientific method. At the base of this choice is the historic demonstration that "knowledge acquired by this method has increased, has grown and progresses steadily" (Randall & Buchler, 1971, p. 57). This documented success is an outcome of the basis of the scientific method; that is, the evidence accumulated is public. In examining a hypothesis to test a theory, if the results lead to rejection of the null hypothesis, it is not because the researcher says so (i.e., authority), not because of ethical or emotional reasons (i.e., faith), not because of feelings of certainty (i.e., intuition), but because the evidence is compelling. In this method the emotional or subjective element of man is reduced to a minimum. All of us have our idiosyncrasies, but they are our shortcomings, not an attribute of the method itself. In other words, the scientific method is not free of abuse, but its dependence on abuses is minimized. The scientific method's greatest strength and difference from the other three methods of inquiry is that it admits fallibility. Because of this a priori admission, science is self-perpetuating. There is no end to the "process of testing theories, improving their expression, and interrelating them with one another" (Randall & Buchler, 1971, p. 60). In fact, a distinguishing factor of the scientific method is the manner in which theories become transformed into knowledge.

At the risk of offending some readers, this review of methods of inquiry was conducted to raise awareness of the unavoidable role of philosophy in the study of hyperactivity, which is essential to the remainder of this chapter. Professionals interested in the study of hyperactivity must be conscious of the choice made in selecting the scientific method as the source of their beliefs. Once this notion is realized, it becomes apparent that it is the individual who plays a major role in science. Returning to the historical record, it is great theories that have advanced science, theories put forth by individual imagination. As stated by Dewey, "The end that we achieve is intimately tied up with and its character is influenced by the means we employ in achieving it. In other words, the kind of knowledge we attain is partly determined by the way we attain it" (Randall & Buchler, 1971, p. 138).

Scientific Theory

Once facts have been gathered, they must be integrated, organized, and classified.

> Facts do not have intellectual significance unless interpreted by a hypothesis or general principle; they do not, as is popularly supposed, speak for themselves. Theories unsupported by facts are baseless, facts uninterpreted by theories are unilluminating and blind. Each is essential to the other, and each derives a greater value from the other. (Randall & Buchler, 1971, p. 71)

The relationship between theory, whether implicit or explicit, and fact is interdependent whereby theories interpret facts and facts confirm theories. Because of this inevitable relationship, consideration must be given to the purpose of theory and its features.

Explanation and Prediction

"Prediction and explanation are central concepts in scientific research, and indeed they are in human action and thought" (Pedhazur, 1982, p. 135). Much has been written about these two concepts, which, like the methods of inquiry, underlie our professional behavior. Some have argued that these two terms are essentially identical, while others maintain that they are quite distinct. The latter orientation is compelling and is the chosen perspective of this chapter. Research designed for prediction is different from that designed for explanation. Rachlin (1988) traces the distinction back to the philosophers who have come to represent explanation and prediction. Aristotle sought intelligibility or the ability to understand why things are as they are. He sought explanation. In contrast, Plato sought to help us live a better life. Our ability to live a better life is dependent on our ability to predict and control our own behavior.

In explanatory research we seek to understand, whereas in predictive research we emphasize practi-

cal applications. This distinction is not merely a semantic frivolity; instead, it is imperative for professionals with scientific method as their source of belief to be aware of it in their day-to-day activities. It is commonplace to offer explanations that go beyond the results of studies, either in the discussion section of published papers or in formal and informal meetings with colleagues. As noted in the methods of inquiry section, the aversion to doubt and uncertainty that motivates a belief in the absence of evidence also motivates explanation in the absence of evidence. Consequently, when findings do not support individual opinion or some minor theory, researchers begin to postulate about the roles of unknowns in the etiology of hyperactivity. This natural tendency toward explanation in the absence of evidence is at the same time a strength and a weakness. The desire to explain hyperactivity motivates researchers to continue their efforts, but this unbridled motivation has resulted in a proliferation of information without a corresponding ability to predict and control hyperactivity. Unfortunately, explanation in the form of individual opinion or minor theory can lead to a great deal of discussion and speculation, but little else. The primary risk in seeking explanation is sacrificing prediction and control (Rachlin, 1988). An experiment that results in the ability to predict and control human behavior is far more useful, particularly in dealing with questions of psychopathology, than studies that explain a phenomenon. The ultimate goal of professionals interested in hyperactivity must be the ability to predict the disorder and control the behaviors.

Theory Characteristics

In theory development, explanation, prediction, and control must be treated as if they were mutually exclusive. In this way a theory can serve to summarize existing knowledge, to explain observed events and relationships, and to predict the occurrence of unobserved events and relationships (Ary, Jacobs, & Razavieh, 1985). According to Ary et al. (1985) there are four primary characteristics of a sound theory. The first is an outgrowth of the principle of parsimony. A theory should explain observed facts relative to a particular problem in the simplest form possible. This characteristic assumes an inductive-deductive method of scientific approach or a move inductively from observations to hypothesis and then deductively from hypothesis to logical implications of the hypothesis. Consistency with observed facts and with the already established body of knowledge is a second characteristic of theory development. The third characteristic leads to the "golden rule" of theory development. Theory should not be thought of as true or false or right or wrong; instead, it should be thought of as useful or not useful in predicting observable consequences. The consequences are those subjected to the third characteristic of theory, verification. A fourth and final characteristic is that a theory must stimulate new discoveries as well as those in need of further investigation.

Before examining theory specific to psychopathology, a further explication of the golden rule seems prudent. Eysenck (1988) has stated that "to reject a theory because it is imperfect is to reject all scientific theories" (p. 48). The notion of verifiability can be traced back in American thought to Pierce's pragmatism. The pragmatist argued, "It is not essential for us actually to know that a statement is true or false, but essential only that it be possible to take steps to such knowledge" (Randall & Buchler, 1971, p. 130). Further, an idea is not called true because it is satisfactory; it is called satisfactory because it is true. Truth for the pragmatist signifies scientific success and success occurs through the process of verification.

The hyperactivity literature is voluminous as a result of investigators' scientific success, but little time has been allocated to finding out "why." Increased attention must be focused on summarizing, not simply reviewing, existing knowledge. In particular, efforts must be made to explain and predict various forms of psychopathology (e.g., hyperactivity).

THEORY AND PSYCHOPATHOLOGY

In 1985, Matson published a paper entitled "Biosocial Theory of Psychopathology: A Three by Three Factor Model." The primary focus of this paper was on psychopathology and mental retardation, but what was written is applicable to psychopathology in the general population. Matson's 11 points of theory development are the focus of this section. The first of the 11 points discussed by Matson can be summarized in one word: flexibility. Any theoretical framework of human behavior will need to provide for open-ended conclusions, which promote further study of likely multifaceted etiologies of psychopathology.

Matson's second point is a call for more complex multidimensional theories. Professionals must move from "one dimensional figures, knowledgeable in one area but ignorant in all others" (Eysenck, 1988, p. 67). The study of psychopathology can be viewed like the growth of a tree. At its roots were eminent professionals like Kraeplin (1889) and Freud (1894–1953). As these founding fathers' works were disseminated, people from a variety of disciplines became interested in psychopathology and brought with them their specific "tools" of the trade as well as theoretical underpinnings. From this early growth, the tree has grown many branches that continue to reach out further and further even though a review of the literature reveals little realization that these many branches coexist and are all part of one tree—the examination of psychopathology. Some branches are stronger than others, some reach further, but each is part of a tree with a trunk and a root system that gives the tree its strength and vitality. If we do not return to the trunk and root system and begin to integrate the various branches of knowledge, the tree will outgrow its root system, the branches will break off and die, and eventually the tree will die, too, curtailing further understanding.

The third point noted by Matson was the issue of verifiability, which was expanded on in the closing paragraphs of the previous section. Points four and five have been grouped together and viewed, not so much as characteristics of theory, but as a means of developing more complex and multifaceted theories (i.e., point number two). In raising these points for discussion, Matson calls for a reconciliation of etiology, assessment, diagnosis, and treatment. Similar to Eysenck (1988) and Ary et al. (1985), he argues for a common ground "so that theories have both academic and clinical utility" (Matson, 1985, p. 205). As part of this reconciliation, a call is made for recognition of existing data and theories. This idea was addressed earlier by Ary et al. (1985) in their second characteristic of theory development—in particular, with their contention that a theory must be consistent with both currently observed facts and with the established body of knowledge. Implications are addressed in Matson's sixth point, which is also related to the concept of flexibility expressed in point one. A theory should encompass a broad spectrum of demographics including gender, race, age, and level of intellectual functioning. Predictability is the seventh point raised, which has been discussed in some detail as it compares to explanation.

The eighth point raised by Matson is a call for inclusion of a time dimension that is crucial to any theory of psychopathology. Questions of chronicity and effect of a disorder over time are essential to any theory. In the case of hyperactivity, there has been a recent proliferation of studies examining the course of this disorder from chilhood through adolescence and into adulthood (Brown & Borden, 1986; Gittelman, Manuzza, Shenker, & Bonagura, 1985). There remains, however, a need for continued efforts in the examination of time-related issues.

Ecological validation is the mainstay of Matson's ninth point. Implicit here is the a priori assumption that to be valid a theory must have its basis in "natural settings." This assumption can be viewed as one of utility, which is a fundamental characteristic of theory development. A theory of psychopathology must have utility if the marriage proposed by Matson of researchers and clinicians is to occur. A theory that evolves interdependently with laboratory research must be "transferable" to the natural setting. An example of the importance of point nine can be found in a recent publication, which examines the role of theory in behavior therapy (see Fishman, Rotgers, & Franks, 1988). One way to avoid the difficult question of transferability would be to develop theory based on empirical data collected in the natural setting and to collect empirical data based on a theory founded in the natural setting. In addition, these data should be gathered with research methodology conducive to prediction as well as explanation.

Matson's tenth point is a call for adherence to the scientific method as the preeminent method of inquiry. Theory that is not empirically based is likely to be baseless. The eleventh and final point is a call for a move to a pyramid model of psychopathology with a series of subset theories that clarify and hold together the superordinate theory. A move to a pyramid model of psychopathology has a number of implications for the remaining sections of this chapter. Tacit in the call for a pyramid model is the movement away from a parallel model, which has been traditional in the social and biological sciences. In this traditional model, researchers and clinicians are in competition with and between each other; consequently, the approach is to refute or ignore the existing empirical evidence gathered by people in different theoretical camps (i.e., different branches of the tree). Eysenck (1988) points out that proponents of different theories lack a common base of knowledge, which precludes any meaningful discourse. The parallel model encourages the rapid proliferation of specific pieces of knowledge (i.e., the branching-out of the tree) in an effort to "get the facts," but precludes discourse that is necessary to form complex theories. In the pyramid model, professionals from a variety of disciplines continue their individual work for the purpose of contributing to a superordinate theory. Returning to the metaphor of the tree, a call to pyramid model theory building is a call for the realization that there are many branches, a trunk, and a root system. Further it is a call for the move away from "territoriality" toward mutual respect for equally valuable contributions to our collective understanding of psychopathology. Such an understanding will facilitate both explanation and, more important, prediction of mental disorders.

SUMMARY

In this section the methods of inquiry, a precursor to any discussion of theoretical thought, were reviewed. From this review of the four sources of our beliefs it should be apparent that the scientific method, although not infallible, is the preferred method of inquiry. In fact, the strength of the scientific method over the other three is derived from its built-in admission of fallibility. Once this method of inquiry is selected a discussion of theory is necessarily engaged.

A quick review of the table of contents of this handbook, the list of contributing authors, and the pages of referenced works reveals that the scientific method is the preferred modality of inquiry. As we have selected empirical science to understand the "structure and workings of nature," we necessarily select theory as integral to this understanding. The gathering of facts and development of theory are each "essential to the other and each derives a greater value from the other" (Randall & Buchler, 1971, p. 71). Because of the apparent selection of scientific method and the interdependence of fact and theory, we reviewed characteristics of theories in general (Ary et al., 1985) and specific to psychopathology (Matson, 1985). Two themes common to each review were the flexibility necessary to stimulate further investigation and the verifiability of these investigations. Particularly important for this chapter is Matson's call for a move away from a parallel to a pyramid model of theory development. Such a move is a call for change in the daily behavior of professionals. A move to a pyramid model will result in a decrease of professional "territoriality" and a positive rather than negative approach to investigation. Instead of attempting to disprove a parallel theory, the focus will be on proving an overall theory that encompasses a number of subtheories, which in turn clarify the overall theory. At this point it should be noted that the debunking of parallel theories has been a powerful impetus for the biological and social sciences. It will be interesting to see whether support of a general theory will be as motivating. Nonetheless, the Matson recommendation for a move to a pyramid model of theory development is the basis for the remainder of this chapter.

THEORY DEVELOPMENT

Akiskal and Mckinney (1975), in an effort to move toward a "unified hypothesis," reviewed five major theories (i.e., branches) believed to be integral to the study of psychopathology: psychoanalytic, behavioral, sociological, existential, and biological. Matson (1985) argued "that theories in psychology and psychiatry should follow a simple blueprint based on points inherent in some previous theories and general points which are likely to enhance further model development" (p. 203). The notion raised in these two papers is an old point of view that moves in and out of favor as attitudes in philosophy change (Lunde, 1974). It is a call for eclecticism, which is a derivative of the Greek word meaning *select* and means to select parts from a variety of theories or

set of facts. Eysenck (1988) recently argued against such an approach. He views eclecticism as "eager to detect virtue in every passing fancy, but unwilling to submit itself to strict scientific discipline" (p. 62). He sees eclecticism as nebulous. It is interesting that Eysenck (1988) and Lunde (1974) put forth a common argument using Newtonian physics. Both authors, one opposed to and one in favor of eclecticism, discuss how Newtonian mechanics is wrong given Einstein's principle of relativity and yet, Newtonian physics has been quite functional for 300 years. The difference comes not in the meaning of eclecticism but in its application.

The notion of eclecticism applied to the integration of parallel theories in support of a superordinate theory (i.e., the pyramid model) must be examined. This call for eclecticism can be viewed from two perspectives. The first point of view evolves from the long tradition of parallel theory development and sees the selection of parts from the major theories as a means of forming another parallel theory which, as alluded to earlier, engenders an adversarial approach to science and may possibly be fanciful, as suggested by Eysenck. A second perspective, which is essential to a pyramid model, holds that each parallel theory is and has always been only part of a superordinate theory. Consequently, the selection of parts is not merely a "detection of virtue," but is a necessary ferreting out of essential components of a complex theory of psychopathology. In other words, parallel theories are composed of the necessary explicit and implicit assumptions to which a discipline adheres (Kuhn, 1962), but are not and have never been, in and of themselves, sufficient to a theory of psychopathology. For instance, the search for a neurochemical link to hyperactivity is necessary, but it is unlikely that any one substance or combination of substances is sufficient to explain and predict the myriad of variables related to the disorder (see Sokol, Campbell, Goldstein, & Kriechman, 1987). Neurochemistry was selected arbitrarily for this example and could have been replaced with any other biological or psychosocial variable, but the outcome would have been the same—necessary, but not sufficient.

At this point it is helpful to return to Matson's (1985) points four and five of psychopathology theory development. Here he called for the reconciliation of etiology, assessment, diagnosis, and treatment. This harmonization of four distinct branches can only be considered in a pyramid model. Numerous reviews exist that break the investigation of hyperactivity into categories either by discipline (e.g., neurology, psychology) or area (e.g., etiology, diagnosis) of interest (Sagvolden & Archer, 1989; Whalen, 1990). Such organization is necessary for the management of information available, but whatever the breakdown, it is artificial. Etiology, assessment, diagnosis, and treatment are inextricably bound and can be separated only for review purposes; they must be viewed collectively for any meaningful understanding. For instance, is it possible to conduct research on the etiology of a disorder without first engaging in assessment and diagnosis? The focus of a pyramid model is on this inseparable commonality. An example may prove easier to follow than the theoretical discussion to this point. A common criticism of all research on hyperactivity is sample heterogeneity (Whalen, 1990). The implications of this pervasive problem are threefold:

> First, it is likely to be a primary cause of many of the inconsistencies that are found in the literature. . . . Second, research findings should not be translated into clinical applications without replication and a careful consideration of sample characteristics. Third, substantial weight should be attached to those findings that are robust enough to emerge time after time, study after study, despite the noise created by sample heterogeneity. (Whalen, 1990, p. 134)

Sample heterogeneity is inherent in a parallel theories model because an adversarial relationship precludes the necessary interaction required for amelioration. Practically speaking, how does the neuroanatomist know he is examining a "hyperactive brain" without first engaging in assessment and diagnosis? How does the diagnostician know what behaviors are present without first engaging in assessment? How does the clinician know what treatments to apply without first engaging in assessment and diagnosis as well as having a knowledge of etiology?

This reconciliation of the integral components of psychopathology investigation (i.e., eclecticism) suggested by Matson (1985) is a first step in moving toward a common knowledge base. Also, it is a tacit endorsement of Matson's step eleven and the call for a pyramid model of theory development. The realization that each area of investigation or discipline are branches of a tree will strengthen the study of psychopathology. If the parallel theories approach is continued, the strength of a subtheory will be diminished by the weakness of other subtheories. Subtheories must be viewed as necessary to continued growth of the tree by their continued investigation of specific assumptions, but not sufficient to the growth of understanding psychopathology.

An Integrated Interaction Theory

The move to a pyramid model requires either the discovery of an existing theory general enough to sustain growth in understanding or the creation of a new theory. An investigation of the former prior to the latter seems prudent. Philip Hineline (1990) authored a review paper on the origins of environment-based theory that conveys a general theory that accommodates both organism-based (i.e., biologic) and environment-based (i.e., psychosocial) interpretations. For the purposes of this chapter, features of the Hineline article have been selected while others are ignored. I assume full responsibility for points emphasized and ideas expressed. The reader is referred to the Hineline paper for a far more in-depth analysis of psychological theory. Hineline discusses a tripartite model that includes the organism (i.e., present situation, expectations, representations, motivational states, genetic code); environment (present situations, past behavior-environment interactions, and evolutionary history); and present behavior. The content of each piece of the tripartite model is important, but for our purposes the focus is on the functioning of the model. Not unlike Bandura's reciprocal determinism applied to the self (Bandura, 1978), Hineline's model is based on the interaction between the organism, environment, and present behavior. Consequently, behavior is viewed as both biologic and environmental and any notion of its being one or the other is an artificial dichotomy. Hineline refers to this as bipolar explanatory prose.

Such a dichotomy has existed throughout the tradition of parallel theory development and has furthered the adversarial relationship. The most common example is the "nature versus nurture" controversy that, as Hineline suggests, can be more productively addressed by considering the interactions between phylogenic and ontogenic contributions of behavior. Behavior (e.g., psychopathology) cannot be understood unless it is part of an interactional model that simultaneously considers the organism, environment, and present behavior.

The basis of Hineline's review emanates from B. F. Skinner's oftentimes misunderstood text, *The Behavior of Organisms*. It may be that Skinner and operant conditioning were prematurely relegated to a learning theory, which was just another parallel theory. Skinner's features of theory may be quite conducive to a pyramid model, especially as viewed through Hineline's eyes. The dispelling of a myth and common misunderstanding of Skinner's work may serve as an example of this potential. For instance, Skinner never denied the existence nor the importance of physiology (e.g., neurology). Instead, he argued that those interested in establishing neurological bases must first describe behavior (i.e., an implicit call for Matson's reconciliation). Further, examination of structured and functional changes in tissue might avoid behavioral assessment, but the meaning of such change is baseless without an ability to "account for a fact of behavior."

If the notion of either biologic or psychosocial effects that have evolved out of the parallel theory tradition can be proven insufficient, then the integrated interaction model suggested by Hineline for behavior analysis can be considered as a general theory of psychopathology. The areas of disagreement with such a proposal have been twofold (Hineline, 1990). First, the status of behavior has been a source of disagreement. Organism-based theorists view behavior as an index of processes within the organism whereas the environment-based theorists view behavior as the main focus. Consequently, the second source of disagreement is process. Organism-based theorists view process as underlying behavior and located within the organism whereas environment-based theorists view process as consisting "in and of" the interaction between behavior and environmental events. To resolve this disagreement it is

necessary to determine its source. Hineline (1990) traces the history back to the evolution of the mechanistic-organismic versus the mechanistic-contextualistic (environment) metaphors, which are referred to as the root metaphors. He argues that these metaphors are "fundamentally conflicting" and that integration is not possible as a result of this incompatibility. Unfortunately, a resolution of this "conflict" is necessary before a sufficient theory of psychopathology can be developed.

Whalen (1990), in her review of the hyperactivity literature, highlighted the inadequacies of the parallel theories model with the "repeated failure to demonstrate organism deficiencies"; the absence of "compelling evidence to support psychosocial etiology"; and "recent findings [that] have provocative implications regarding physiological interpretations." As a result she concludes her review by calling for a move towards "interaction perspectives." But, is such a perspective possible with conflicting root metaphors. To move to an integrated interaction perspective (i.e., pyramid model) necessitates a return, once again, to the discussion of eclecticism. In the view of Eysenck, or as alluded to by Hineline, eclecticism is nebulous. If this confusion is inherent in eclecticism, but eclecticism is necessary for a move to a pyramid model, then a determination of the source of confusion must be sought. One possible source is the conflicting metaphors. Further, if these incompatible figures of speech result in an inability to integrate theories, a resolution of the conflict must be found. This analysis, in turn, requires a return to the methods of inquiry discussion presented at the outset of this chapter.

The scientific method has been demonstrated to be the preferred method of inquiry in the investigation of hyperactivity. Given this selection, faith in the absence of evidence is ruled out as a source of belief as are the other forms of faith and methods of inquiry. Yet, the view of behavior as an index of processes within the organism despite the absence of evidence, which emanates from the mechanistic-organismic root metaphor, is the source of conflict preventing integration of theories. How can this situation arise? First remember that man's aversion to doubt or uncertainty motivates him to latch on to this belief. Those who engage in the scientific method are not immune to this form of faith. In fact, as discussed at the outset of this chapter, faith in the absence of evidence is thought by many as necessary for the existence of man. As noted in the discussion of explanation versus prediction, professionals have a natural tendency toward explanation in the absence of evidence. It is quite common to postulate about roles of unknowns in the etiology of hyperactivity. Consequently, is it reasonable or even possible to suggest this form of faith be precluded from the study of human behavior? The answer to such a question is a resounding "no." Faith in the absence of evidence, or possibly faith based on experience is a fundamental source of belief and, consequently, motivation. Nevertheless, a theory based on either form of faith is in sharp contrast to theory as part of empirical science.

Therefore, the confusion that arises out of an attempt to integrate organism-based and environment-based theories is a result of the conflicting root metaphors. This conflict is not one of scientific theory, but is instead, a more fundamental one of methods of inquiry. Parsimoniously, organism-based theories are founded in faith whereas environment-based theories are founded in scientific method. Consequently, the disagreement of the root metaphors is not amenable to scientific investigation but lies instead in philosophical debate, which is beyond the realm of this chapter. If scientific method is to be the source of belief (i.e., Matson's tenth point of theory development), then Hineline's interaction model with an environment-based orientation can be considered a general theory of psychopathology. The evidence for behavior viewed as the main focus and "in and of" the interaction of organism, environment, and present behavior can be gathered through the scientific approach (i.e., the inductive-deductive method). Subtheories can continue to investigate explicit and implicit assumptions with faith in the existence of underlying processes and provide the necessary information to a superordinate theory of psychopathology. However, the superordinate theory must be consistent with observed facts and with the already established body of knowledge. This outcome of a pyramid model will focus on explanation of observed events and relationships and, more important, predict the occurrence of unobserved events and relationships.

CONCLUDING REMARKS

The role of theory in science was presented as essential to the advancement of usable knowledge. Little has been done to illuminate an apparently unabated proliferation of literature reporting empirical findings. Without a theory to pull together these facts there is little hope that they will have any practical utility. Studying psychopathology with little concern for utility serves only to further explanation and does little for the person exhibiting behaviors characteristic of some syndrome/disorder.

Scientific method was assumed throughout the chapter. Given interdependence of theory and science, parallel theory development and pyramid theory development were reviewed. Although parallel theory development will continue to result in a proliferation of literature, it is not at all clear that such growth will result in improved prediction and control of hyperactivity. The pyramid model was introduced as an alternative in hope that it will result in a more expedient move to usable findings.

An integrated theory without focus on whether it is biologically or psychosocially based was presented as a possible superordinate theory. The advantages of such a theory are that it marks a return to complex theory (induction vs. deduction) about a complex problem, it lessens the emphasis on importance of specific disciplines or areas of research, it continues to promote the specific research of subtheories, and is more likely to result in a theory of utility. This last benefit is of particular importance. A theory with utility is one that provides prediction and control. There currently exists research methodology designed to examine complex interactions with prediction (Pedhazur, 1982). A theme that permeated this entire chapter was that a theory that predicts through understanding complex interactions is essential to efficacious treatment of psychopathology, which is the only meaningful result of our efforts.

REFERENCES

Abikoff, H., & Gittelman, R. (1985). Hyperactive children treated with stimulants: Is cognitive training a useful adjunct? *Archives of General Psychiatry, 42,* 953–961.

Akiskal, H. S., & McKinney, W. T. (1975). Depressive

disorders: Toward a unified hypothesis. *Science, 182,* 20–29.

Ary, D., Jacobs, L. C., & Razavieh, A. (1985). *Introduction to research in education* (3rd ed.). New York: Holt, Rinehart, and Winston.

Bandura, A. (1978). The self system in reciprocal determinism. *American Psychologist, 33,* 344–358.

Barkley, R. A. (1977). A review of stimulant drug research with hyperactive children. *Journal of Child Psychology and Psychiatry, 18,* 137–165.

Barkley, R. A. (1990). [Review of *Attention Deficit Disorder: [Clinical and basic research]*. *American Journal of Mental Retardation, 95,* 358–362.

Bedford, J. A., Marquis, D. K. L., & Wilson, M. C. (1984). The effects of several anorexigenics on monkey social behavior *Pharmacology, Biochemistry & Behavior, 20,* 317–321.

Bloomingdale, L. M. (1984). Whither ADD (Attention Deficit Disorder)? *The Psychiatric Journal of the University of Ottawa, 9,* 175–186.

Brown, R. T., & Borden, K. A. (1986). Hyperactivity at adolescence: Some misconceptions and new directions. *Journal of Clinical Child Psychology, 15*(3), 194–209.

Burton, A. (Ed.). (1974). *Operational theories of personality.* New York: Brunner/Mazel.

Citizens Commission on Human Rights. (1987). *Ritalin: A warning for parents.* Los Angeles, CA: Church of Scientology.

Conners, C. K. (1980). *Food additives and hyperactive children.* New York: Plenum Publishing.

Eaglen, A. (1978). Learning theory versus paradigms as the basis for behavior therapy. *Journal of Behavior Therapy and Experimental Psychiatry, 9,* 215–218.

Eysenck, H. J. (1988). Psychotherapy to behavior therapy: A paradigm shift. In D. B. Fishman, F. Rotgers, & C. M. Franks (Eds.), *Paradigms in behavior therapy: Present and promise* (pp. 45–76). New York: Springer.

Fishman, D. B., Rotgers, R., & Franks, C. M. (Eds.). (1988). *Paradigms in behavior therapy: Present and promise.* New York: Springer.

Freud, S. (1953). The defense neuropsychoses. In J. Strachey (Ed.), *The standard edition of the complete psychological works of Sigmund Freud* (Vol. I). London: Hogarth Press. (Original work published 1894)

Gittelman, R., Manuzza, S., Shenker, R., & Bonagura, N. (1985). Hyperactive boys almost grown-up: I. Psychiatric status. *Archives of General Psychiatry, 42,* 937–947.

Hamlett, K. W., Pellegrini, D. S., & Conners, C. K. (1987). An investigation of executive processes in the problem-solving of attention deficit disorder—hyperactive children. *Journal of Pediatric Psychology, 12,* 227–240.

Hastings, J. E., & Barkley, R. A. (1978). A review of psychophysiological research with hyperkinetic children. *Journal of Abnormal Child Psychology, 6,* 413–447.

Hicks, R., Gualtieri, C. T., Mayo, J. P., Schroeder, S. R., & Lipton, M. A. (1985). Methylphenidate and homeostasis: Drug effects on the cognitive performance of hyperactive children. In L. M. Bloomingdale (Ed.), *Attention deficit disorder: Identification, course and treatment rationale* (pp. 131–141). New York: Spectrum.

Hineline, P. N. (1990). The origins of environment-based psychological theory. *Journal of the Experimental Analysis of Behavior, 53,* 305–320.

Kraeplin, E. (1889). *Psychiatrie: Ein lehrbuch fur studierende und aertze* (6th ed.). Leipzig, Germany: Barth.

Krasner, L., & Houts, A. C. (1984). A study of the "value" systems of behavioral scientists. *American Psychologist, 39,* 840–850.

Kuhn, T. S. (1962). *The structure of scientific revolutions.* Chicago: University of Chicago Press.

Lahey, B. B., Piacentini, J. C., McBurnett, K., Stone, P., Hartdagen, S., & Hynd, G. (1988). Psychopathology in parents of children with conduct disorder and hyperactivity. *Journal of the American Academy of Child and Adolescent Psychiatry, 27,* 163–170.

Levy, F., & Hobbes, G. (1988). The action of stimulant medication on attention deficit disorder with hyperactivity: Dopaminergic, noradrenergic, or both? *Journal of the American Academy of Child and Adolescent Psychiatry, 27,* 802–805.

Lou, H. C., Henriksen, L., Bruhn, P., Borner, H., & Nielsen, J. B. (1989). Striatal dysfunction in attention deficit and hyperkinetic disorder. *Archives of Neurology, 46,* 48–52.

Lunde, D. T. (1974). Eclectic and integrated theory: Gordon Allport and others. In D. Burton (Ed.), *Operational theories of personality* (pp. 381–404). New York: Brunner/Mazel.

Mash, E. J., & Johnston, C. (1982). A comparison of the mother-child interactions of younger and older hyperactive and normal children. *Child Development, 53,* 1371–1381.

Matson, J. L. (1985). Biosocial theory of psychopathology: A three by three factor model. *Applied Research in Mental Retardation, 6,* 199–227.

Nielsen, J. A., Duda, N. J., Mokler, D. J., & Moore, K. E. (1984). Self-administration of central stimulants by rats: A comparison of the effects of d-amphetamine, methylphenidate, and McNeil 4612. *Pharmacology, Biochemistry, & Behavior, 20,* 227–232.

Pedhazur, E. J. (1982). *Multiple regression in behavioral*

research: *Explanation and prediction* (2nd ed.). New York: Holt, Rinehart, and Winston.

Rachlin, H. (1988). Molar behaviorism. In D. B. Fishman, F. Rotgers, & C. M. Franks (Eds.), *Paradigms in behavior therapy: Present and promise*. New York: Springer.

Randall, J. H., & Buchler, J. (1971). *Philosophy: An introduction* (2nd ed.). New York: Barnes & Noble.

Rutter, M., Lebovici, S., Eisenberg, L., Sneznenvskij, A. V., Sadoun, R., Brooke, E., & Lin, T-Y. (1969). A tri-axial classification of mental disorders in childhood. *Journal of Child Psychology and Psychiatry, 10,* 41–61.

Sagvolden, T., & Archer, T. (Eds.). (1989). *Attention deficit disorder: Clinical and basic research*. Hillsdale, NJ: Lawrence Erlbaum Associates.

Satterfield, J. H., Schell, A. M., Nicholas, T., & Backs, R. W. (1988). Topographic study of auditory event-related potentials in normal boys and boys with attention deficit disorder with hyperactivity. *Psychophysiology, 25,* 591–606.

Sokol, M. S., Campbell, M., Goldstein, M., & Kriechman, A. M. (1987). Attention deficit disorder with hyperactivity and the dopamine hypothesis: Case presentations with theoretical background. *Journal of the American Academy of Child and Adolescent Psychiatry, 26,* 428–433.

Speltz, M. L., Varley, C. K., Peterson, K., & Beilke, R. L. (1988). Effects of dextroamphetamine and contingency management on a preschooler with ADHD and oppositional defiant disorder. *Journal of the American Academy of Child and Adolescent Psychiatry, 27,* 175–178.

Stewart, M. A., DeBlois, C. S., & Cummings, C. (1980). Psychiatric disorder in the parents of hyperactive boys and those with conduct disorder. *Journal of Child Psychology and Psychiatry, 21,* 283–292.

Triantafillou, M. (1972). Pemoline in overactive mentally handicapped children [Letter to the editor]. *British Journal of Psychiatry, 121,* 577.

Ullmann, R. K., Sleator, E. K., & Sprague, R. L. (1985). A change of mind: The Conners Abbreviated Rating Scales reconsidered. *Journal of Abnormal Psychology, 13,* 553–565.

Vyse, S. A., & Rapport, M. D. (1989). The effects of methylphenidate on learning in children with ADDH: The stimulus equivalence paradigm. *Journal of Consulting and Clinical Psychology, 57,* 425–435.

Weiss, G. (1985). Hyperactivity: Overview and new directions. *Psychiatric Clinics of North America, 8,* 737–753.

Weizman, A., Bernhout, E., Weitz, R., Tyano, S., & Rehavi, M. (1988). Imipramine binding to platelets of children with attention deficit disorder with hyperactivity. *Biological Psychiatry, 23,* 491–496.

Wells, K. C. (1987). What do we know about the use and effects of behavior therapies in the treatment of ADD? In J. Loney (Ed.), *The young hyperactive child: Answers to questions about diagnosis, prognosis and treatment*. (pp. 111–122). New York: Haworth Press.

Whalen, C. K. (1990). Attention deficit and hyperactivity disorders. In T. H. Ollendick & M. Hersen (Eds.), *Handbook of child and adolescent assessment* (pp. 131–169). New York: Plenum Publishing.

Zametkin, A. J., Linnoila, M., Karoum, F., & Sallee, R. (1986). Pemoline and urinary excretion of catecholamines and indoleamines in children with attention deficit disorder. *American Journal of Psychiatry,*

Zametkin, A., Rapoport, J. L., Murphy, D. L., Linnoila, M., & Ismond, D. (1985). Treatment of hyperactive children with monoamine oxidase inhibitors: I. Clinical efficacy. *Archives of General Psychiatry, 42,* 962–966.

CHAPTER 4

ETIOLOGY OF ATTENTION DEFICIT HYPERACTIVITY DISORDER

Alison R. Lorys-Vernon
George W. Hynd
Heikki Lyytinen
Kelly Hern

During the past two decades, perhaps the most frequently diagnosed childhood psychiatric disorder has been characterized by deficits in attention, impulsivity, and in most cases, excess motor activity. An estimate of the incidence rate suggests that 3% to 5% of school-age children may be affected, with 30% to 40% of the total referrals to child guidance clinics resulting from concerns regarding deficits in these areas (Barkley, 1982). Consistent gender differences appear to exist, with 5 to 10 times as many boys as girls affected by what is typically referred to as hyperactivity.

NOSOLOGICAL CONSIDERATIONS

Historically, controversy has surrounded the identification and classification of this disorder. Wender (1971) applied the terms *Minimal brain damage* or *Minimal brain dysfunction* (MBD), implying an etiologically based nosology. However, as clinical studies yielded inconsistent results re-

garding factors thought to be involved in hyperactivity, the more behaviorally oriented terms of *hyperactivity* or *hyperkinetic syndrome* became prevalent in the literature (Ross & Ross, 1982). The last three nosological systems published by the American Psychiatric Association (*Diagnostic and Statistical Manual of Mental Disorders,* 2nd ed. [DSM-II, APA, 1968], 3rd ed., [DSM-III; APA, 1980], & 3rd ed., rev. [DSM-III-R; APA, 1987) proposed diagnostic categories for this disorder that reflected a shift away from the etiologically (e.g., neurologic) based classification systems toward a behavioral-descriptive nosology.

For example, DSM-II (American Psychiatric Association [APA], 1968) classified the disorder as hyperkinetic reaction of childhood. Diagnostic emphasis was placed on a high motor activity level with a lesser emphasis on inattention problems. With the publication of DSM-III (APA, 1980), *Hyperkinetic reaction* was replaced with the term *attention deficit disorder* (ADD). Within this nosology, children could be diagnosed as exhibiting ADD with hyperactivity (ADD/H) or ADD without hyperactivity

(ADD/WO) depending on whether they exhibited excess motor activity concurrently with deficits in attention and impulsivity.

This nosological change reflected the influence of the contrasting behaviorally descriptive diagnostic approach that no longer stressed the importance of excess motor activity but rather emphasized the relevance of deficits in attention and impulse control (Lahey, Schaughency, Hynd, Carlson, & Nieves, 1987). The shift from an emphasis on overactivity may have been due to the paucity of consistent experimental findings demonstrating reliable differences in motor activity levels between hyperactive and nonhyperactive children.

Subsequent to the introduction of ADD/H and ADD/WO, the differentiation of subtypes was criticized as being empirically unfounded. It was believed that children with ADD constituted a homogeneous rather than a heterogeneous group. In reaction to this view and contrasting with DSM-III, the current DSM-III-R nosology (APA, 1987) adopted the categories of attention deficit hyperactivity disorder (ADHD) and undifferentiated attention deficit disorder (UADD) to diagnose children with these deficits. These diagnostic categories further complicated the inattention versus motor activity controversy and returned the emphasis in diagnosis to excess motor activity. However, the inclusion of UADD maintained the concept that "disturbances in which the predominant feature is the persistence of developmentally inappropriate and marked inattention that is not a symptom of another disorder" (APA 1987, p. 95) may occur. In this way, the idea that attention deficits could occur without hyperactivity was retained. This differentiation was important, as an experimental literature comparing these two behaviorally differentiated subtypes indicates that they do differ in very significant ways (Hynd, Lorys, Semrud-Clikeman, Nieves, Huettner, & Lahey, 1989; Lahey et al., 1987).

For example, children with ADD/H are more impulsive and distractible (Lahey, Schaughency, Frame, & Strass, 1985; Lahey et al., 1987), appear to be more socially rejected (King & Young, 1982; Lahey, Schaughency, Strauss, & Frame, 1984), and exhibit more aggression and conduct problems (King & Young, 1982; Lahey et al., 1984; Lahey et al.,

1987). In comparison, ADD/WO children are rated as more shy and anxious (Lahey et al., 1984; Lahey et al., 1987), exhibit a more sluggish cognitive tempo (Lahey et al., 1985), and experience more academic difficulties than children with ADD/H, although ADD/H children also exhibit academic difficulties (Edelbrock, Costello, & Kessler, 1984; Lahey et al., 1984).

RELEVANCE OF NOSOLOGY TO AN EXAMINATION OF NEUROLOGIC ETIOLOGY

Why are these nosological considerations so vital in addressing the neurological etiology of ADHD? If one examines the listing of symptoms for ADHD found in DSM-III-R, it can be seen that any child with a previous diagnosis of ADD/H will most likely be diagnosed as ADHD. However, it is entirely possible for previously diagnosed ADD/WO children to receive also a diagnosis of ADHD under DSM-III-R criteria. Consequently, in the face of evidence to the contrary, DSM-III-R criteria treat ADHD as a homogeneous classification (Cantwell & Baker, 1988).

The importance of this uniformity cannot be overemphasized. When examining for subtle differences in brain morphology or other potential etiologies, the most discretely and reliably diagnosed children should be used in forming as nearly perfect as possible a representation of ADHD considering what is known about the behavioral phenotype. Without this effort, if one were to employ children diagnosed as ADHD, it could not be assumed that there may not also be ADD/WO children in the clinic group. This factor may not seem initially important but it is relevant because of the significantly higher incidence of developmental learning disabilities found in ADD/WO groups. Hynd et al. (1989) found in a carefully diagnosed sample that 60% of the ADD/WO children also had a codiagnosis of a developmental learning disorder whereas none of the ADD/H children had such a diagnosis. Further, the performance of ADD/WO children was significantly poorer on rapid naming tasks, similar to the performance of learning disabled children (Wolf,

Bally, & Morris, 1986). Consequently, if ADD/WO children were present in an ADHD sample, one might be examining two clinical populations: one with relatively pure ADD/H and another who more closely resemble learning disabled children. Since there is good evidence to suggest that the brains of learning children, particularly reading disabled children, are morphologically different from those of normals (Hynd & Semrud-Clikeman, 1989), the inclusion of ADD/WO children in neuroimaging or other studies investigating etiologies of ADD/H seems inappropriate if one is initially trying to document whether differences exist, for example, in the brains of ADHD children.

With these thoughts in mind and with the knowledge that these issues are more fully examined elsewhere in the volume, it is appropriate to turn attention to those studies that have addressed differences in children and adolescents who suffer deficits in attention, impulse control, and motor regulation. The etiologies proposed for ADHD are numerous, as are the names under which it has appeared in the literature. Most of the theories of etiology (as well as the theories regarding the best methods of treatment) were developed post hoc to trials of various drug therapies or after clinical observations of patients with head injury or known neurological damage who exhibited such behaviors. The majority of recent studies on the etiology of ADHD have focused on the hyperactive behavior symptoms in addition to the deficits in attentional abilities. Commonly suspected etiologies include biologic causes, environmental influences, psychological or psychosocial factors, and neurologic factors. This chapter reviews these suspected causes and attempts to provide a framework for understanding this disorder.

It will be noted that several different terms are utilized in reference to the population known in the current nosology as ADHD. These terms are reflective of the diagnostic nosologies in use at the time the studies were conducted. The reader should interpret these terms to delineate those children who have deficits in attention as well as excess motor activity but also recognize that there is a lack of diagnostic rigor in regard to ADHD and that subject groups may not have been as "pure" as originally hoped.

THEORIES OF ADHD ETIOLOGY

Although numerous influences and factors have been hypothesized in the etiology of ADHD, these causes all have the potential to affect brain functioning. Therefore, on a more molar level, ADHD can be considered a disorder of brain function no matter what the etiology.

The factors and influences discussed in the following sections should not be thought of as all encompassing. There are numerous medical as well as nonmedical conditions and disorders that also manifest in symptoms of ADHD. However, the factors and possible bases for ADHD that are considered below are felt by the current authors to represent the more commonly researched and more widely accepted possibilities for the etiology of ADHD.

Biologic Factors

Biologic factors such as known genetic disorders as well as suspected genetic links have been associated with the etiology of ADHD. Hier (1980) demonstrated that boys with an extra Y chromosome (XYY) showed an increased incidence of hyperactivity in addition to depression of both verbal and performance abilities. Fragile X syndrome, named for a fragile site of Q27 of the X chromosome, has also been associated with ADHD. Hagerman, Kemper, and Hudson (1985) indicated that attentional problems as well as learning difficulties may result from this definable genetic defect. Although most children with Fragile X Syndrome are mentally retarded, the boys in the Hagerman et al. (1985) study were not retarded but did demonstrate attentional problems and learning disabilities. The results of Hagerman et al. (1985) should be read with caution as the small number of subjects (four) precludes the drawing of more definitive conclusions until additional reports are gathered.

Genetic disorders and ADHD are not limited exclusively to males although there is a higher incidence of ADHD in males, as noted above. Pennington and Smith (1983) found that girls with 45, XO manifested attentional deficits as well as handwriting and copying task problems. Not surprisingly, these girls also obtained depressed performance IQ scores. Eliason (1986) indicated that children with neurofibromatosis, a genetic disorder, also demonstrated a high incidence of visual-perceptual problems and language impairments in addition to a high incidence of learning and attentional problems.

In a related vein, Aman, Mitchell, and Turbott (1987) noted a deficiency of essential fatty acid (EFA) metabolites in hyperactive children. However, they found minimal or no improvements in children treated with efamol, an EFA supplement.

As a final note relative to genetic factors, heredity is believed to play a role in the etiology of ADHD. Positive family history of ADHD symptoms in close family members is commonly found in children with ADHD. Cantwell (1972) found hyperactivity to be four times as common in parents of hyperactive children as in parents of control children. Furthermore, results of Lahey et al. (1988) indicated that these is more marked aggression and illegal activity in fathers of children with conduct disorder and ADHD co-occurring. The authors concluded that there is a probable familial pattern of transmission for ADHD.

Environmental Factors

Numerous endogenous toxins have been associated with the etiology of ADHD. Lead poisoning has been shown to produce hyperactivity, short attention span, and impulsivity (Rummo, Routh, Rummo, & Brown, 1979). David and his colleagues (David, 1974; David, Clark, & Hoffman, 1979; David, Clark, & Voeller, 1972) provided well-documented evidence that body-lead burden, even below levels required to produce overt symptoms of toxicity, could induce hyperactive behavior in children. However, it may be that factors common to both lead ingestion and behavioral problems, such as social adversity and social class, may also be partial contributors to findings regarding lead and ADHD (Taylor, 1986).

Feingold, in his famous series of studies (Feingold, 1973a; 1973b; 1975a; 1975b; 1975c; 1976; Feingold, German, Brahm, & Simmers, 1973), implicated food additives in hyperactivity. This research spurred media attention and a nationwide

reaction. However, little empirical evidence has been found for the food additive-hyperactivity link (Bierman & Furukawa, 1978). Wender (1986), in his review of the available studies on the Feingold diet, concluded that food colorings and other additives had little effect on the behavior of hyperactive children. Zametkin and Rapoport (1986) noted that the popularity of dietary treatment of ADD persists because of the power of food as a conditioned stimulus. The saliency and availability of dietary treatment also adds to the popularity and continued use of this treatment. However, no consistent evidence for such "allergic reactions" have been found that characterize all hyperactive children (Hazel & Schumaker, 1988) and studies criticizing Feingold's hypothesis have themselves been criticized because of their methodological flaws.

Refined sugar has been suggested as a cause of ADHD but these accounts are difficult to interpret. Behar, Rapoport, Adams, Berg, and Cornblath (1984) compared sucrose ingestion and behavior in ADHD boys. Results indicated no difference in performance on the research task between groups. In addition, Kaplan, Wamboldt, and Barnhardt (1986) conducted a study in which they allowed children to regulate their own amount of sweetened breakfast. An additional variable (administration of methylphenidate) was included in the study. Results indicated that although the medication condition could be distinguished from the nonmedication condition, aspartame and sucrose conditions could not be differentiated. While it is impossible to say that ingestion of sugar does not worsen behavior in any child in any way, the research literature fails to demonstrate that sugar ingestion significantly contributes to ADHD.

Cultural and Psychosocial Factors

Adverse social conditions such as disruptive family relationships have also been linked to ADHD. As Shaywitz and Shaywitz (1988) note, findings from the National Collaborative Perinatal Project (NCPP) (Broman, Brien, & Shaughnessy, 1985; Nichols & Chen, 1981) provide good evidence for environmental and cultural influences in the etiology of ADHD. For example, children in the study who were termed *hyperactive-impulsive* were more likely to come from homes where the father was absent. Werner and Smith's (1977) findings from Kauai indicated similar results.

Cultural influences are also considered a probable basis for ADHD. For example, Mintz and Collins (1985) demonstrated that loudness and contextual inappropriateness led to parental perception of hyperactivity and a more negative parental evaluation of children's behaviors. It follows that in cultures and environments where ADHD behaviors are more accepted and less obvious, children displaying these behaviors are not seen as problematic or pathological. This variable is a consideration to be taken into account in interpreting cross-cultural studies of ADHD etiology. Other behavioral problems of childhood, such as depression and oppositional disorders, in addition to memory, achievement, language, auditory processing problems and general intelligence, may also manifest in symptoms of ADHD (Goldstein & Goldstein, 1989). Many practitioners believe that if interventions were aimed at remediation of these influences, remediation of ADHD would also occur. However, the following discussion of neurologic factors may color this notion.

Neurologic Factors

As described above, ADHD can be considered a disorder of brain function. Potential neurologic etiologies discussed here include hypotheses and theories regarding localization, neurotransmitters, and brain morphology.

The disorder investigated by the early theorists may not be identical to that known as ADHD today. Many of the children identified in early studies might not have met current criteria for ADHD. Indeed, they might not have received any diagnosis as the behavioral symptomatology of hyperactivity was extremely subjective, was dependent on clinical judgment, and was not a codified diagnosis. Other children used in these early studies could have received a diagnosis of minimal brain dysfunction (MBD) which included even less specific criteria than ADHD. However, though probably different, the description of the behaviors displayed by these children is very similar to those displayed by children

diagnosed as ADHD and thus earlier research should not be discounted prematurely.

Early in this century, excess motor activity in children was attributed to some form of brain damage that had resulted from severe illness, injury, or prenatal and perinatal difficulty (Still, 1902; Strecker & Ebaugh, 1924). Kahn and Cohen (1934) described a syndrome of "organic drivenness" in which behaviors were similar to the hyperactivity and distractibility noted in children who had recovered from Von Economo's disease, although the disease was not present. They postulated that this disorder was therefore due to some brainstem neuropathology. Bradley (1937) noted that benzedrine had a dramatic calming effect on the behaviors of hyperactive children, adding support to the notion of a neurological etiology. Strauss and Lehtinen (1947) stated that the syndrome of hyperactivity was a neural disorder that developed prenatally or early in postnatal life and that did not manifest itself in some common form of neuropathology but rather in abnormalities of behavior, emotion, and cognition.

Localization Theories

One of the first widely accepted neurological theories was advanced by Laufer, Denhoff, and Solomons (1957) who found that hyperkinetic subjects exhibited photically induced spike-wave EEG discharges similar to those seen in minor seizures after the administration of metrazol. This finding was attributed to a state of "over-arousal" due to a dysfunction of the diencephalon. Hyperkinetic children were viewed as having difficulty in the selective filtering of information and as being particularly sensitive to peripheral stimulation. Knobel, Wolman, and Mason, (1959) suggested that the cortex overcompensates for this subcortical dysfunction. This hyperarousal of the cortex was considered to be the source of hyperactivity and inappropriate behaviors exhibited by children with this syndrome.

The theory of overarousal was refuted by Douglas and her colleagues (Douglas, 1972; Douglas & Peters, 1979). She found that hyperactive and normal children performed equally well on tasks of selective attention but that the performance of the hyperactive children was significantly worse on tasks that required sustained attention. Kinsbourne (1984) also promoted the idea that a deficit in sustained attention was central to the diagnosis of ADD. He stated that "the machinery for efficient behavior control exists in the ADD child. Extra activation is needed, however, to enable it to participate consistently in controlling the way these children live" (p. 145).

Also in contrast to the hyperarousal hypothesis, Satterfield and his colleagues (Satterfield, Cantwell, Lesser, & Podosin, 1972; Satterfield, Cantwell, & Satterfield, 1974; Satterfield & Dawson, 1971) postulated a theory of underarousal as the basis for hyperactivity. They proposed that "the increased amount of motor activity seen clinically is secondary to lowered levels of Recticular Activating System (RAS) excitation, and represents an attempt on the part of the patient to increase his proprioceptive and exteroreceptive sensory input" (p. 196). However, it should be noted that Satterfield's early data dealt with electrodermal responses. He later reversed his decision based on the results gathered from evoked potential (EP) research. Satterfield and Braley (1977) recorded EPs from younger and older hyperactive children and found that younger children with hyperactivity could not be distinguished from normals on the basis of arousal levels as indicated by EPs.

Another theorist, Wender (1972), in one of his earlier publications, argued that lesions in the medial forebrain bundle, or hypothalamus, areas in the limbic system that are implicated in feedback reinforcement could cause hyperactivity in children. He proposed that there was a deficit in feedback reinforcement that was due to an arousal deficit produced by such lesions. Motor hyperactivity was proposed as a consequence of a paucity of feedback.

To further complicate matters, Le Moal and his colleagues (Le Moal, Cardo, & Stinus, 1969; Le Moal, Galey, & Cardo, 1975; Le Moal, Stinus, & Galey, 1976; Le Moal et al., 1977) reported that lesions in the ventral tegmental area (VTA) of adult rats produced a permanent syndrome with symptoms analogous to hyperactivity. Oades (1982) found that rats with electrolytically induced VTA lesions did poorly on a task analogous to the Pribam visual search task (Pribam, 1971) and noted patterns of responses similar to those observed in hyperactive children performing the Pribam task. Based on these studies, Solanto (1984) implicated the mesolimbic, meso-

corticolimbic, and nigrostriatal pathways in the etiology of ADD.

Dykman and his colleagues (Dykman, Ackerman, Clements, & Peters, 1971) developed a theory in which the deficit in attention was considered the central diagnostic factor for hyperactivity. They postulated the existence of an attentional inhibitory system in the forebrain that has major control over both the brainstem reticular formation and the "switching mechanism" of the thalamus. These researchers stated that a deficiency in this system leads to inefficient transfer of attention. They further stated that due to this lack of inhibitory control, there are diffuse patterns of electrical discharge from the thalamus and brainstem that may account for the hyperactive behaviors. This theory is comparable to the theory of overarousal proposed by Laufer et al. (1957). The child with ADHD is considered to be so overattentive to the environment that he becomes easily distracted and prone to engage in high levels of motor activity.

Rosenthal and Allen (1978) proposed a dysfunction in the forebrain "Arousal System II" (Routtenberg, 1968), a group of structures in the limbic system and frontal cortex, was the causal factor in hyperactivity. According to Routtenberg (1968), the forebrain and reticular systems maintain a reciprocal, functional relationship. Rosenthal and Allen (1978) stated that a dysfunction in this system would lead to poorly modulated RAS activity. This view is consistent with the theory of deficient forebrain inhibition proposed by Dykman et al. (1971). The authors noted that a similar syndrome that includes hyperactivity, impulsivity, poor attention, and a form of learning disability had been produced in animals. Lesions of the medial septum, orbitofrontal cortex, and posterior hippocampus each invoked these behaviors. They discussed previous research in which septal and frontal lesions in animals produced enhanced evoked potentials similar to those found in children with MBD (Buchsbaum & Wender, 1973). Furthermore, Davis (1957) demonstrated that amphetamines and methylphenidate reduced the hyperactivity and attention deficits seen in monkeys with orbitofrontal lesions. Therefore, Rosenthal and Allen (1978) theorized that some dysfunction, or possibly a maturational delay, in the septo-hippocampal region may be the central etiological factor in this syndrome.

Gorenstein and Newman (1980) discussed the disinhibitory effects of medial-septal lesions in animals and likened the behaviors of these animals to the impulsivity and hyperactivity seen in ADHD children. They stated, "We refer to septal dysfunction but might well have spoken of dysfunction within an entire system composed of the medial septum, the hippocampus, and orbitofrontal cortex" (p. 308).

The Dorsal Bundle Extinction Effect (DBEE) was discussed by Mason (1979, 1980) as possibly accounting for attention deficits. He stated that this noradrenergic projection may be involved in relaying instructions to the hippocampus that "memories are not to be laid down about the irrelevant stimulus" and to the cortex "not to continue processing the information contained in that stimulus [and] inhibit the cerebellum from using that stimulus to lay down motor learning" (Mason, 1979, p. 83). Therefore, no incoming stimulus is considered irrelevant when there is a disruption of the frontal lobe dorsal bundle fibers. This disruption results in impairment of attention and possibly perseveration of inappropriate behavior such as excess motor activity due to a resistance to the extinction of these behaviors.

In more recent studies, Huessy (1984) implicated the frontal-mesolimbic system as the site of dysfunction in children with ADD. He reported rat studies in which minute doses of amphetamines placed in the nucleus acumbens produced an immediate behavioral control. Voeller (1986) found behavioral disturbances and neurological findings consistent with right hemisphere damage or dysfunction in 15 children, all of whom had a diagnosis of ADD. Lateralizing neurological signs such as motor impersistence, spatial neglect, and social inadequacies implicated neurologic systems in the right hemisphere (Voeller & Heilman, 1988a, 1988b).

The localization theories of ADHD are plagued by the same maladies as all concepts of localization of disorders. The brain-behavior relationship is hypothetical for the most part and based on educated guessing. Causal relationships cannot be definitively stated because no direct examination of the neural areas in question in these children are available. However, indirect measures used in studies have proven to be successful in prediction of areas of neural abnormalities such as left hemisphere speech

centers. Therefore, proposed neurologic etiologies are felt to be more than simple conjecture.

Neurotransmitter Theories

One of the first theories on the etiology of ADHD based on an imbalance of neurotransmitters was published by Kornetsky (1970). He argued that drugs used in the treatment of hyperactivity have a marked effect on catecholamine levels; therefore, chemical imbalances in the brain systems that utilize the neurotransmitters appear likely to be involved in ADHD.

In support of this notion, Wender, Epstein, Kopin, and Gordon (1970) speculated that a biochemical imbalance involving one or more of the neurotransmitters (dopamine, norepinephrine, and serotonin) were related to hyperactivity. In 1972, Wender noted low levels of platelet serotonin in MBD children. In addition, Fuxe and Ungerstedt (1970) found that serotonin inhibited locomotor activity and aggression as well as resulting in more widespread inhibitory effects.

However, subsequent investigations of the serotonergic hypotheses have been inconsistent and not supportive of this theory. Wender later abandoned serotonin as a central factor in favor of catecholamines (Wender, 1974, 1976). In a 1984 review, he stated that he favored a dopamine hypothesis, noting evidence that tricyclic antidepressants that increased activity in noradrenergic and serotonergic systems did not provide adequate results in the treatment of children with ADD. Wender argued that the symptoms associated with ADD were often caused by decreases in dopaminergic or phenethylamingergic activity. Relative to this notion, Shaywitz, Yager, and Klopper (1976) proposed an animal dopaminergic model for ADHD. By injecting hydroxydopamine directly into rats' brains, they produced "hyperactive" rats by depleting brain dopamine levels. They concluded that their results supported a dopamine hypothesis.

Norepinephrine has also been implicated by many authors as the catecholamine most involved in the etiology of ADD. Similar to Shaywitz et al.'s (1976) study with dopamine, animal models of attention deficit and hyperactivity have been produced by the depletion of norepinephrine

(Lordon, Rickert, Dawson, & Pellymounter, 1980; Mason & Fibiger, 1978, 1979). Zametkin and Rapoport (1986) offer three types of evidence to support this hypothesis. First, MHPG, the major metabolite of norepinephrine, appears in decreased levels in urine studies of ADD/H children in comparison to normals. Second, drugs that ameliorate ADD/H also work to alter MHPG. Last, the effects of methylphenidate on urinary catecholamine are primarily noradrenergic.

Mikkelson and his colleagues (Mikkelson, Lake, Brown, Ziegler, & Ebert, 1981) speculated that alpha receptors for norepinephrine might be supersensitive in children with ADD/H. They found no difference between normals and ADD/H children in blood plasma levels of norepinephrine, but noted that the ADD/H group had higher blood pressure when standing. They reasoned that this was a tenable hypothesis considering that the alpha receptors that are involved in the regulation of blood pressure are affected by the drugs found most effective in the treatment of ADD.

A dual catecholamine hypothesis has also been suggested (Wender, 1975). Pharmacological data have suggested that the action of d-amphetamine, a drug often used in the treatment of ADD, is mediated by brain catacholernergic mechanism (Heikkila, Orlansky, Mytilineous, & Cohen, 1975). Kostowski (1980) noted that norepinephrine and dopamine both play an important role in the regulation of motor activity. Also, previous data suggested that increased activity in neurons utilizing norepinephrine may enhance the responses of dopamine receptors in the brain (Kostowski, 1980). Some researchers have argued that these neurotransmitters may have effects on other receptor sites.

All three neurotransmitters actually may be involved in some form in the etiology of ADD. Wender (1984) wrote that amphetamines generated the best behavioral results in children with ADD. Amphetamine is an monoamine oxidase inhibitor (MAOI) and thus a direct agonist causing release from storage of dopamine, norepinephrine, and serotonin. Its usage in treatment for ADD therefore has a threefold effect biochemically. Paul (1983) discussed the interdependency of these three neurotransmitters through the neuronal interconnections between the substantia nigra and locus coeruleus. These brain areas are involved in motor functions and thus may be related to hyperactivity.

Lastly, acetylcholine (ACH) has also been implicated in ADD. Anisman (1975) suggested that excessive activation of adrenergic systems may lead to rebound excitation of ACH neurons. Rosenthal and Allen (1978) proposed that this rebound excitation might lead to more successful forebrain modulation of the norepinephrinergic reticular system. They stated that "those hyperkinetic children who respond positively to a stimulant do so because of a cholinergic rebound and that those who do not respond positively exhibit this effect to a smaller degree" (p. 710). In support of this hypothesis, Zametkin and his colleagues (Zametkin, Karoum, Rapoport, Brown, & Wyatt, 1984) viewed the cholinergic system as participatory in the etiology of ADHD. They noted that the development of the fine motor coordination is often delayed in ADHD children and that dysfunctions in the nigrostriatal and tuberoinfidibular tracts fit the symptomology. Shader and Jackson (1975) stated that cholinergic-dopaminergic interactions are critical in these structures for the control of smooth motor functions.

The methodology utilized in all neurotransmitter studies can be questioned. Body chemical samples are generally taken from urinalyses that have failed to show consistent one-to-one relationships with brain neurotransmitter levels. Furthermore, drug studies are "unclean" and fraught with confounding factors. Psychopharmacology is a young field, and a unique mode of action for many medications is not clear. Most drugs affect more than one system; thus, analysis in isolation of a single neurotransmitter or other body chemical is somewhat implausible. Animal models often used in these analyses are also questionable because of the difficulty in generalizing paradigms. Nonetheless, these studies should not be disregarded. As knowledge increases, more will be learned about such relationships, and early hypotheses have been partially supported in some respects.

Brain Morphology

While there has traditionally been a presumption that the behavioral manifestations of this disorder reflect dysfunctional neurological systems, little evidence exists that directly ties the symptoms of hyperactivity to abnormal brain systems or structures in children without a history of documented head injury (Hynd & Willis, 1988). There are no post-mortem or cytoarchitectonic studies of the brains of children who experience hyperactivity as there are with other developmental disorders such as dyslexia (Hynd & Semrud-Clikeman, 1989). Consequently, one must rely on psychopharmacological or neuroimaging studies when attempting to articulate the neurological basis of hyperactivity. An initial study by Shaywitz, Shaywitz, Byrne, Cohen, and Rothman (1983) examined CT scans obtained on 35 children diagnosed as ADD according to DSM-III criteria. No note was made in the study as to whether only ADD/H children were included in the sample or whether it also included ADD/WO children. Using a midaxial slice, measurements were obtained for the anterior horns of the lateral ventricles, bifrontal width, and right and left hemispheres. Standard indices obtained from these data revealed no significant differences between the brains of the ADD and clinic contrast groups. The authors concluded that CT was not diagnostically useful with ADD and that if differences did exist in the brains of ADD children, CT technology could not discern brain anomalies in this population. They did suggest, however, that other neuroimaging procedures might hold more promise.

As a preliminary study, the Shaywitz et al. (1983) study was well controlled and relevant in that standard indices of brain morphology were employed to examine brain structures that may be revealing. Prior to this study, standardized indices were not evident. One may hypothesize that the lateral ventricles were examined in the study for evidence of dilation that could be a possible indication of early trauma. The bifrontal width may have been examined because the behavioral manifestations of ADHD are often characterized as possibly correlated to anterior dysfunction (Hynd & Willis, 1988). While these analyses do make conceptual sense, the failure to find significant differences in the Shaywitz et al. (1983) study perhaps could have reflected the inclusion of ADD/WO children or the employment of a clinic control group (referred for neurological problems but found to be free of overt neurological involvement). Further, other structures that similarly may be implicated in ADHD were not examined.

Consequently, this first study, while not providing significant findings, may have indicated the direction for neuroimaging studies that followed.

While CT may be useful in visualizing neuroanatomic structures, it can also be employed to chart regional metabolic activity correlated with blood flow to the brain. While this is clearly an invasive procedure, it has been used successfully in two studies focusing on ADHD children. In a preliminary study, Lou, Henriksen, and Bruhn (1984) examined regional cerebral blood flow/computed axial tomography (rCBF/CT) in children diagnosed as ADD. Results indicated that these children, when compared to normals, evidenced hypoperfusion in the frontal and central regions of the brain. This low metabolic activity presumably correlated with the behavioral symptoms of ADD: These children were administered methylphenidate, and metabolic activity increased to normal levels as serum blood levels rose in relation to the administration of the drug.

In an expanded study that included additional subjects, Lou, Henriksen, Bruhn, Borner, and Nielsen (1989) found that the low metabolic activity was especially significant in the right striatum for ADHD children. For those children who were diagnosed as ADHD+ (plus additional neurological signs such as dysphasia, mild MR), there was bilateral hypoperfusion in the striatum. Again, the administration of methylphenidate increased metabolic activity in the striatal region in the ADHD children.

While these two studies provide provocative data regarding the neurological etiology of ADHD, they included a small number of subjects, some of whom participated in both studies. Further, the inclusion of children with other neurological disorders (in the ADHD+ group) raises the question of how discretely representative of the ADHD phenotype these subjects were.

What can be concluded from these studies? The CT study by Shaywitz et al. (1983) failed to reveal any morphometric differences, perhaps because the subjects were not carefully differentiated according to ADD subtype or perhaps because of the limitations of the CT technology itself. The studies by Lou et al. (1984; 1989) do provide evidence that neurometabolic systems may be compromised in ADHD. However, differences in morphology were not examined so it is not known whether the metabolic differences reflected anomalies in structural or only metabolic integrity. Nonetheless, these studies do support further examination of possible differences in brain structures of systems that may be correlated to the behavioral manifestations of the ADHD syndrome.

Therefore, the remainder of this chapter presents an analysis of magnetic resonance imaging (MRI) data on children diagnosed as ADHD. The MRI data presented in the following discussion is derived in part from a study reported by Hynd, Semrud-Clikeman, Lorys, Novey, and Eliopolus (1989). The analyses reported here, however, are unique to this chapter.

MORPHOMETRIC ANALYSIS OF MRI IN CHILDREN WITH ADHD

The prior discussion stressed the relevance of accurately subtyping ADD subjects and noted that DSM-III-R (APA, 1987) presently denotes the diagnostic category of ADHDH. Therefore, the children in the study are referred to as ADHD. However, in each case, careful consideration was given to diagnostic criteria for ADD/H so that only subjects who met both criteria for ADHD and ADD/H were included in these analyses. It was felt this procedure would ensure that the children who participated in this MRI study represented a discrete and carefully diagnosed group of children who all suffered significant difficulties in attention, impulse control, and regulation of motor activity. Furthermore, the use of this selection criteria alleviated the possibility that any children who would meet diagnostic criteria for ADD/WO and ADHD would be included. As previously noted, ADD/WO children's brains may be morphologically similar to those of learning disabled children, therefore contaminating the sample and confounding the results. Last, the ADHD children were all judged by their parents and physicians to be favorable responders to stimulant medication.

Diagnostic decisions about each child were based on a review of all referral, psychometric, and behavioral information gathered in an evaluation. Two staff psychologists made independent diagnoses

and only those children about whom there was complete agreement were included in this study. The normals received no DSM-III or DSM-III-R diagnoses and had never been referred in the schools for behavioral or academic problems.

The MRI protocol employed sequential T1 weighted sagittal and axial MRI planes using a .6 tesla Technicare Scanner. The protocol involved 15, 7.5 mm sagittal planes (TR = 690; TE = 32) and 11, 5 mm axial planes (TR = 500; TE = 32). As in previous studies, reliable region of interest measurements (ROI) were obtained using the Technicare ROI measurement software system (Hynd et al., 1989). The use of the ROI program represented a significant improvement over previous studies with other populations as the measurements were made on the MRI scan itself and the high reliabilities obtained ($X = .95$) were much greater than reported for other neuroimaging studies (Hynd & Semrud-Clikeman, 1989).

The following analyses used a midaxial MRI scan that transversed the brain at a level bisecting the anterior horns of the lateral ventricles, superior temporal region, and posterior regions at the splenium. This slice corresponded to Pieniadz and Naeser's (1984) slice SM, which was the only one that provided morphometric data that correlated with postmortem measurements. All measurements were either in centimeters (for length or width) or square centimeters (for area). Figure 4.1 illustrates how these measurements were obtained on the MRI scan using the manually operated cursor. ROI measurements were obtained for the areas of the right and left cerebral hemispheres, area of the anterior horns of the lateral ventricles, areas of the right and left anterior and posterior regions, widths of the right and left anterior and posterior regions, lengths of the left and right plana, and lengths of the right and left insular region.

Prior to presenting the results of the analyses, two points need to be made. First, the ROI measurements represent, at best, crude indices of regional brain variation. As an initial methodology they may, however, reveal differences in brain morphology that perhaps correlate with behavioral observations. Further, they may highlight regions that deserve more focused analysis in future studies. Second, since the size of the brain does not vary

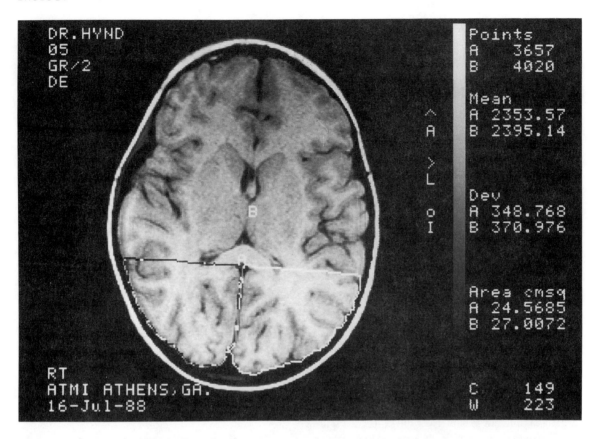

Figure 4.1. A midaxial MRI scan of a child with ADHD. Keeping in mind that these scans are reversed in orientation (e.g., left = right, right = left side), it can be seen that the area measurements for the left and right posterior regions are 27.0072 sq cm and 24.5685 sq cm, respectively.

significantly in overall morphology after the pre-school year (Fukuyama, Miyao, Ishizu, & Maruyama, 1979), the age range of these subjects should not be a factor. In fact, an analysis of correlations between these ROI measurements and age and IQ revealed no significant ($p > .05$) relationships as expected. All scans were read as within normal limits by a neurologist.

Areas of the Right and Left Cerebral Hemispheres

An analysis of the gross areas of the right and left cerebral hemispheres revealed no significant group, hemisphere, or group x hemisphere interactions. Consequently, it seems that at a macular level, there

were no obvious deviations in the morphology of the brain.

Areas of the Right and Left Anterior Horns of the Lateral Ventricles

Consistent with Shaywitz et al. (1983), no significant group, hemisphere, or group x hemisphere interactions were found for the right and left anterior horns of the lateral ventricles. These results support the notion that ADHD is not related in an obvious fashion to early damage that might result in dilation of the lateral ventricles. It might be of interest to note, however, that the ADHD children had smaller ROI measurements bilaterally than the normals, although this difference did not reach statistical significance.

Areas of the Right and Left Anterior and Posterior Regions

Table 4.1 presents the data for the ROI measurements of the right and left anterior and posterior regions. These measurements were obtained by measuring the area anterior to a line drawn horizontally across the tip of the genu for each hemisphere and for the right and left regions posterior to the end of the splenium.

Table 4.1 shows that there were no significant area effects for group, hemisphere, or group x hemisphere interactions for the anterior region. However, for the posterior region, a significant hemisphere effect emerged. Consistent with the literature, both ADHD and normal children showed left > right asymmetry in this region (Hynd & Semrud-Clikeman, 1989). However, in a further analysis incorporating only those ADHD children who obtained a T score of >70 on the Personality Inventory for Children (PIC) Hyperactivity scale (N = 7), a significant group effect did emerge. Figure 4.2 shows that the significant group effect reflects a smaller posterior region bilaterally but it also appears that the right posterior region is much smaller in area than in the normals. Future studies

with larger groups of children will need to explore correlated behavioral indices that may reflect deviations in ontogeny in these posterior regions among ADHD children.

Widths of the Right and Left Anterior and Posterior Regions

Again, consistent with the study reported by Shaywitz et al. (1983), no significant group, hemisphere, or group x hemisphere effects emerged in an analysis of variance for the anterior and posterior regions. There was a trend ($F = 3.02$, $p < .08$) toward a significant group effect for the anterior width, however. The small number of subjects may have obscured possible significant differences in the widths of the anterior regions for these subjects, and future studies will need to determine more fully whether ADHD children have bilaterally smaller anterior widths.

Lengths of the Right and Left Plana

The literature highlighting the importance of the right and left plana is derived from studies of the brains of dyslexics (Hynd & Semrud-Clikeman, 1989). Because ADHD (particularly ADD/H) children are not necessarily characterized by co-occurring learning disabilities (Hynd et al., 1989), it would be expected that these children would not show significant variation in the normal (L > R) patterns of plana asymmetry. Consistent with this notion, there were not significant differences in the normal pattern of plana asymmetry (70% had L > R) and no significant group, hemisphere, or group x hemisphere interactions were found (see Table 4.2 and Figure 4.3).

Table 4.1. MRI DATA: Area of Right and Left Anterior and Posterior Regions (sq cm)

| | Insular Cortex* | |
	Left	Right
ADD/H	4.80 (.54)	4.64 (.66)
Normals	5.17 (.53)	5.22 (.53)

*No significant group, hemisphere, or group x hemisphere interaction effects.

**Trend toward a significant group effect ($F = 3.16, p < .08$). Significant hemisphere effect ($F = 4.11, p < .05$). No significant group x hemisphere interaction effect.

[1] When only subjects with > 70 t-score on PIC Hyperactivity Scale included (N = 7), significant group effect emerged ($F = 4.54, p < .03$).

Lengths of the Right and Left Insular Regions

The insular region of the brain includes cortical matter; interior to the cortex are interhemispheric fibers that serve to interconnect the posterior and

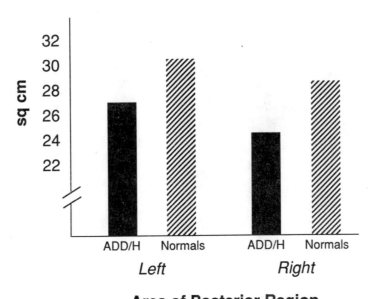

Area of Posterior Region

Figure 4.2. Areas of the left and right posterior regions in normal control and ADHD children.

anterior cortical zones. Lesions of the left insular region may disrupt the linguistic system resulting in a disconnection syndrome characterized by an ability to speak and comprehend language but accompanied by an inability to repeat linguistic material. Although not as well documented, a similar syndrome is hypothesized for lesions affecting the right insular region (Ross, 1981) as affective components of language expression and comprehension may be disrupted.

As shown in Table 4.2 and Figure 4.3, a significant group effect emerged in the analysis suggesting that the insular length is bilaterally smaller in ADHD children. No significant hemispheric or group x hemispheric interactions were found, although an inspection of data in Figure 4.3 suggests that the ADHD children may have a slightly greater degree of asymmetry ($L > R$) than the normals who seem characterized by symmetrical insular length. Future studies will need to focus on more clearly articulating the importance of these group effects. It is also worth noting that a dyslexic group also showed this pattern, so the exact significance of this finding as it relates to children with ADHD is unclear (Hynd et al., 1989).

COMMENT AND IMPLICATIONS

What do these results suggest? First and foremost, they suggest that morphometric analysis of carefully selected ROI on MRI scans may be made in carefully diagnosed groups of children. As MRI is not invasive and because it is possible to make highly reliable measurements, significant differences in regional variation may be revealed if in fact they exist in the brains of these children. Consequently, neuroimag-

Table 4.2. MRI DATA: Insular Region—Means and Standard Deviations (cm)

| | Anterior* | | Posterior**[1] | |
	L	R	L	R
ADD/H	18.93 (2.06)	19.71 (1.65)	28.78 (3.75)	25.66 (3.49)
Normals	19.27 (2.48)	20.62 (2.71)	30.14 (3.98)	28.48 (4.19)

*Significant group effect ($F = 7.82, p < .007$). No significant hemisphere or group x hemisphere interaction effects.

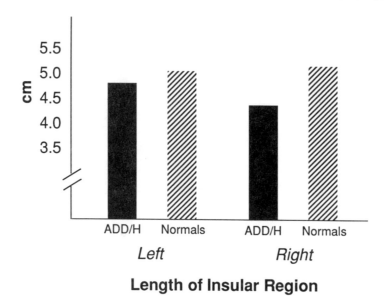

Length of Insular Region

Figure 4.3. Lengths of the left and right insular regions in normal control and ADHD children.

ing procedures, in this case employing MRI, may be theoretically useful in examining questions related to the neurological etiology of ADHD.

Do these results reveal anything about etiology? First, they suggest that the brains of ADHD children do not seem to evidence any significant indices of brain damage. This is consistent with developmental disorders. The brains look normal and, consistent with the results of Shaywitz et al. (1983), CT and MRI should not be expected to be revealing in children without a significant history of neurological trauma or neurological signs other than those associated with ADHD.

In this study, the bilateral posterior area seemed significantly smaller in ADHD children as did the length of the insular region. As there is good evidence that structural variation in brains is under significant genetic control (Oppenheim, Skerry, Tramo, & Gazzaniga, 1989), it might be hypothesized that these differences in the ADHD children are similarly related to genetic variation in fetal gestation. This is not an unreasonable hypothesis as the regions highlighted by this analysis initially develop between the 5th and 7th month of gestation. It might be hypothesized that fewer neurons migrate out from the periventricular matrix and that a normal rate of migration occurs, but there is a defect in maintaining

neuronal connectivity. Or a normal rate of neurons might migrate toward the cortex but a supranormal rate of cell death could occur, resulting in the smaller cortical area and insular length. These are only possibilities but they are the same issues facing researchers investigating variation in brain morphology in developmental dyslexia (Hynd & Semrud-Clikeman, 1989). If anything, these hypotheses need to be further investigated by those conducting developmental neurobiological and genetic studies.

Do these results correlate to or in some fashion reflect what is known about the behavioral symptomatology of ADHD? These morphometric differences did appear in carefully diagnosed ADHD children in comparison to normal control children. The more relevant question is whether they make conceptual sense based on what is known from the behavioral literature. As with any study that reports correlated findings, the issue of causality becomes important.

As previously noted, Voeller and Heilman (1988a, 1988b) have provided initial behavioral data suggesting that some children with ADHD may suffer from what they term a right hemispheric syndrome. Do the observed morphometric differences reported here correlate with this syndrome? There is at present no way to answer this question as the number of subjects included in this study was small and precluded an analysis of correlations with behavioral data acquired on these children. It is perhaps of interest to note that when the most hyperactive children were examined separately, (PIC Hyperactivity T scores > 70) a significant group effect emerged in the magnitude of the posterior area. As shown in Figure 4.2, it would appear that the significant effect may be due to the smaller right posterior area, although no group by hemisphere interaction was found. There clearly is a need for an examination of morphometric differences in the brains of ADHD children as they may relate to behavioral differences such as reported for children with a right hemisphere syndrome.

Do subcortical differences exist in the brains of ADHD children? While this study did not address this issue, research by Lou et al. (1984; 1989) does suggest that neurometabolic differences may exist in the striatum. Further, a recently completed study that examined morphometric differences in the corpus callosum of ADHD children and normals found that ADHD children's corpus callosum was significantly smaller than normal (Hynd, Semrud-Clikeman, Lorys, Novey, Eliopolus, & Lyytinen, 1989). This difference in the area of the corpus callosum seemed most evident in the region of the genu, splenium, and an area just anterior to the splenium. Fibers transversing these regions serve to interconnect the right and left anterior region, the inferior parietal and temporal areas, and the visual association cortex (Pandya & Seltzer, 1986). A static conceptualization of the role of the corpus callosum would suggest that these differences may simply reflect the smaller number of fibers that may interconnect the two cerebral hemispheres. Lassonde (1986), however, provides evidence that the corpus callosum could participate more actively in interhemispheric regulation, perhaps by exerting inhibitory or excitatory influences in modulating cerebral activation. If the corpus callosum is smaller in ADHD children, does that mean that it functions less effectively in modulating hemispheric activation or in establishing reciprocal patterns of interaction? At present there are no data addressing this possibility although the use of dichotic listening or visual half-field paradigms with ADHD children could reveal whether patterns of cerebral activation correlate to morphometric differences in the brains of these children.

SUMMARY

The etiological bases of ADHD are still not definitive or fully understood. Numerous hypotheses have been proposed involving specific and nonspecific neural substrata, singular neurotransmitters and combinations thereof, as well as environmental, psychosocial, and biologic factors. The literature is often contradictory and inconsistent, and a definitive answer may never be reached because of the multi-contributory nature of all possible factors. In addition, the consideration that ADHD is a behavioral diagnosis also plays a role in investigations of possible etiologies. It may be that a variety of medical and nonmedical conditions are manifested in similar behavioral pathology.

Neuroimaging studies may provide one window into how the brains of these children differ from those of normal children. It remains to be seen how these patterns of morphological variation may be distinguished from patterns observed in children with other developmental disorders. Also, the nature of the interrelationships between the behavioral deficits documented in these children and variation in brain morphology needs to be further explored so that a more comprehensive understanding of the etiology of this disorder may be achieved. Further research is necessary to more specifically differentiate the behavioral manifestations of this disorder before an accurate account of the etiology can be offered. It is hoped that etiological knowledge will influence and guide avenues of intervention for ADHD children.

REFERENCES

Aman, M., Mitchell, E., & Turbott, S. (1987). The effects of essential fatty acid supplementation by efamol in hyperactive children. *Journal of Abnormal Child Psychology, 15,* 75–90.

American Psychiatric Association. (1968). *Diagnostic and statistical manual of mental disorders (2nd ed.).* Washington, DC:

American Psychiatric Association. (1980). *Diagnostic and statistical manual of mental disorders (3rd ed.).* Washington, DC:

American Psychiatric Association. (1987). *Diagnostic and statistical manual of mental disorders–Revised (4th ed.).* Washington, DC:

Anisman, H. (1975). Time-dependent variations in aversively motivated behaviors: Nonassociative effects of cholernergic and catecholaminergic activity. *Psychological Review, 82,* 359–385.

Barkley, R. (1982). Guidelines for defining hyperactivity in children. In B. Lahey & A. Kazdin (Eds.), *Advances in clinical child psychology,* (Vol. 5). New York: Plenum Press.

Behar, D., Rapoport, J., Adams, A., Berg, C., & Cornblath, M. (1984). Sugar challenge testing with children considered behaviorally "sugar reactive". *Journal of Nutrition and Behavior, 1,* 277–288.

Beirman, C., & Furukawa, C. (1978). Food additives and hyperkinesis: Are there nuts among the berries? *Pediatrics, 61,* 932–933.

Bradley, C. (1937). The behavior of children receiving Benzedrine. *American Journal of Psychiatry, 94,* 577–585.

Broman, S., Brien, E., & Shaughnessy, P. (1985). *Low achieving children: The first seven years.* Hillsdale, NJ: Lawrence Erlbaum Associates.

Buchsbaum, M., & Wender, P. (1973). Average evoked responses in normal and minimally brain dysfunctioned children treated with amphetamine: A preliminary report. *Archives of General Psychiatry, 29,* 764–770.

Cantwell, D. (1972). Psychiatric illness in the families of hyperactive children. *Archives of General Psychiatry, 27,* 414–417.

Cantwell, D., & Baker, L. (1988). Issues in the classification of child and adolescent psychopathology. *Journal of the American Academy of Child and Adolescent Psychiatry, 27,* 521–533.

David, O. (1974). Association between lower lead concentrations and hyperactivity in children. *Environmental Health Perspectives, 7,* 17–25.

David, O., Clark, J., & Hoffman, S. (1979). Childhood lead poisoning: A reevaluation. *Archives of Environmental Health, 34,* 106–111.

David, O., Clark, J., & Voeller, K. (1972). Lead and hyperactivity. *Lancet, 2,* 900–903.

Davis, G. (1957). Effects of central excitant and depressant drugs on locomotor activity in the monkey. *American Journal of Physiology, 188,* 619–623.

Douglas, V. (1972). Stop, look, and listen: The problem of sustained attention and impulse control in hyperactive and normal children. *Canadian Journal of Behavioral Science, 4,* 259–282.

Douglas, V., & Peters, K. (1979). Toward a clearer definition of the attentional deficits of hyperactive children. In G. Hale & Lewis (Eds.), *Attention and the development of cognitive skills.* New York: Plenum Publishing.

Dykman, R., Ackerman, P., Clements, S., & Peters, J. (1971). Specific learning disabilities: An attentional

deficit syndrome. In H. R. Myklebust (Ed.), *Progress in learning disabilities* (Vol. 2). New York: Grune & Stratton.

Edelbrock, C., Costello, A., & Kessler, M. (1984). Empirical corroboration of attention deficit disorder. *Journal of the American Academy of Child Psychiatry, 23,* 285–290.

Eliason, M. (1986). Neurofibromatosis: Implications for learning and behavior. *Developmental and Behavioral Pediatrics, 7,* 175–179.

Feingold, B. (1973a). *Introduction to clinical allergy.* Springfield, IL: Charles C. Thomas.

Feingold, B. (1973b). Food additives and child development. *Hospital Practice, 8,* 11–12, 17–18, 21.

Feingold, B. (1975a). *Why your child is hyperactive.* New York: Random House.

Feingold, B. (1975b). Hyperkinesis and learning disabilities linked to artificial food flavors and colors. *American Journal of Nursing, 75,* 797–803.

Feingold, B. (1975c). *Hyperkinesis and learning disabilities (H-LD) linked to the ingestion of artificial food colors and flavors.* Paper presented to the U.S. Subcommittee on Health.

Feingold, B. (1976). Hyperkinesis and learning disabilities linked to the ingestion of artificial food color and flavors. *Journal of Learning Disabilities, 9,* 551–559.

Feingold, B., German, D., Brahm, R., & Simmers, E. (1973). *Adverse reaction to food additives.* Paper presented at the Annual Meeting of the American Medical Association, New York.

Fukuyama, U., Miyao, M., Ishizu, T., & Maruyama, H. (1979). Developmental changes in normal cranial measurements by computed tomography. *Developmental Medicine and Child Neurology, 21,* 425–432.

Fuxe, K., & Ungerstedt, U. (1970). Histochemical and functional studies of central monoamine neurons after acute and chronic amphetatmine administration. In E. Costa & S. Garattini (Eds.), *International symposium on amphe* amines and related compounds. New York: Raven Press.

Goldstein, S., & Goldstein, M. (1989). *Managing attention disorders in children.* New York: John Wiley & Sons.

Gorenstein, E., & Newman, J. (1980). Disinhibitory psychopathology in children. *Journal of Nervous and Mental Disease, 155,* 55–71.

Hagerman, R., Kemper, M., & Hudson, M. (1985). Learning disabilities and attentional problems in boys with the fragile X syndrome. *American Journal of Diseases of Children, 139,* 674–678.

Hazel, J., & Schumaker, J. (1988). Social skills and learning disabilities: Current issues and recommendations for future research. In J. Kavanaugh & T. Truss,

Jr. (Eds.), *Learning Disabilities: Proceedings of the National Conference.* Parkton, MD: York Press.

Heikkila, R., Orlansky, H., Mytilineous, C., & Cohen, G. (1975). Amphetamines: Evaluation of d- and l-isomers as releasing agents and uptake inhibitors for 3 H-dopamine and 3 H-norepinephrine in slices of rat neostriatum and cerebral cortex. *Journal of Pharmacology and Experimental Therapeutics, 194,* 47–56.

Hier, D. (1980). Learning disorders and sex chromosome aberrations. *Journal of Mental Deficiency Research, 24,* 17–26.

Huessy, H. (1984). Remarks on the epidemiology of MBD/ADD. In L. M. Bloomingdale (Ed.), *Attention deficit disorder: Diagnostic, cognitive, and therapeutic understanding.* Jamaica, New York: Spectrum Publications.

Hynd, G., Lorys, A., Semrud-Clikeman, M., Nieves, N., Huettner, M., & Lahey, B. (1991). Attention deficit disorder without hyperactivity (ADD/WO): A distinct behavioral and neurocognitive syndrome. *Journal of Child Neurology, 6,* 538–542.

Hynd, G., & Semrud-Clikeman, M. (1989). Dyslexia and brain morphology. *Psychological Bulletin, 106,* 1–36.

Hynd, G., Semrud-Clikeman, M., Lorys, A., Novey, E., & Eliopulos, D. (1990). Brain morphology in developmental dyslexia and attention deficit disorder/hyperactivity: *Archives of Neurology, 47,* 919–926.

Hynd, G., Semrud-Clikeman, M., Lorys, A., Novey, E., Eliopulos, D., & Lyytinen, H. (1991). Corpus callosum morphology in attention deficit hyperactivity disorder (ADHD): Morphometric analysis of MRI. *Journal of Learning Disabilities, 24,* 141–146.

Hynd, G., & Willis, G. (1988). *Pediatric neuropsychology.* Orlando, FL: Grune & Stratton Inc. [Allyn & Bacon].

Kahn, E., & Cohen, L. (1934). Organic drivenness. *New England Journal of Medicine, 210,* 748–756.

Kaplan, H., Wamboldt, R., & Barnhardt, R. (1986). Behavioral effects of dietary sucrose in disturbed children. *American Journal of Psychology, 7,* 143.

King, C., & Young, R. (1982). Attentional deficits with and without hyperactivity: Teacher and peer perceptions. *Journal of Abnormal Child Psychology, 10,* 483–496.

Kinsbourne, M. (1984). Beyond attention deficit: Search for the disorder in ADD. In L. M. Bloomingdale (Ed.), *Attention deficit disorder: Diagnostic, cognitive, and therapeutic understanding.* Jamaica, NY: Spectrum Publications.

Knobel, M., Wolman, M., & Mason, E. (1959). Hyperkinesis and organicity in children. *AHA Archives of General Psychiatry, 1,* 310–321.

Kornetsky, C. (1970. Psychoactive drugs in the immature organism. *Psychopharmacologia, 17,* 105–136.

Kostowski, W. (1980). Noradrenergic interactions among central neurotransmitters. In W. B. Essman (Ed.), *Neurotransmitters, receptors, and drug action.* New York: Spectrum Publications.

Lahey, B., Pelham, W., Schaughency, E., Atkins, M., Murphy, H., Hynd, G., Russo, M., Hartdagen, S., & Lorys-Vernon, A. (1988). Dimensions in types of attention deficit disorder. *Journal of the American Academy of Child and Adolescent Psychiatry, 27,* 330–335.

Lahey, B., Schaughency, E., Hynd, G., Carlson, C., & Nieves, N. (1987). Attention deficit disorder with and without hyperactivity: Comparison of behavioral characteristics of clinic-referred children. *Journal of the American Academy of Child and Adolescent Psychiatry, 26,* 718–723.

Lahey, B., Schaughency, E., Frame, C., & Strauss, C. (1985). Teacher ratings of attention problems in children experimentally classified as exhibiting attention deficit disorders with and without hyperactivity. *Journal of the American Academy of Child and Adolescent Psychiatry, 24,* 613–616.

Lahey, B., Schaughency, E., Strauss, C., & Frame, C. (1984). Are attention disorders with and without hyperactivity similar or dissimilar disorders? *Journal of the American Academy of Child Psychiatry, 23,* 302–309.

Lassonde, M. (1986). The facilitatory influence of the corpus callosum on interhemispheric processing. In F. Lepore, M. Ptito, & H. Jasper (Eds.), *Two hemispheres—One brain.* New York: Alan R. Liss.

Laufer, J., Denhoff, E., & Solomons, G. (1957). Hyperkinetic impulse disorder in children's behavior problems. *Psychosomatic Medicine, 19,* 38–49.

Le Moal, M., Cardo, B., & Stinus, L. (1969). Influence of ventral mesencephalic lesions on various spontaneous and conditioned behaviors in the rat. *Physiology and Behavior, 4,* 567–574.

Le Moal, M., Galey, D., & Cardo, B. (1975). Behavioral effects of local injection of 6-hydroxydopamine in the medial ventral tegmentum in the rat: Possible role of the mesolimbic dopaminergic system. *Brain Research, 88,* 190–194.

Le Moal, M., Stinus, L., & Galey, D. (1976). Radiofrequency lesion of the ventral mesencephalic tegmentum: Neurological and behavioral considerations. *Experimental Neurology, 50,* 521–535.

Le Moal, M., Stinus, L., Simon, H., Tassin, J., Thierry, A., Blanc, G., Glowinski, J., & Cardo, B. (1977). Behavioral effects of a lesion in the ventral mesencephalic tegmentum: Evidence for involvement of A10 dopaminergic neurons. In E. Costa & G. Gessa (Eds.), *Advances in biochemical psychopharmacology* (vol. 16, pp. 237–245). New York: Raven Press.

Lordon, J., Rickert, E., Dawson R., & Pellymounter, M. (1980). Forebrain norepinephrine and the selective processing of information. *Brain Research, 190,* 569.

Lou, H., Henriksen, L., & Bruhn, P. (1984). Focal cerebral hypoperfusion in children with dysphasia and/or attention deficit disorder. *Archives of Neurology, 41,* 825–829.

Lou, H., Henriksen, L., Bruhn, P., Borner, H., & Nielsen, J. (1989). Striatal dysfunction in attention deficit and hyperkinetic disorder. *Archives of Neurology, 46,* 48–52.

Mason, S. (1979). Noradrenalin and behavior. *TINS, 2,* 82–84.

Mason, S. (1980). Noradrenalin and selective attention: A review of the model and the evidence. *Life Sciences, 27,* 617–631.

Mason, S., & Fibiger, H. (1978). Noradrenalin and spatial memory. *Brain Research, 156,* 382–386.

Mason, S., & Fibiger, H. (1979). Noradrenalin and selective attention. *Life Sciences, 25,* 1949–1956.

Mikkelson, E., Lake, C., Brown, G., Ziegler, M., & Ebert, M. (1981). The hyperactive child syndrome: Peripheral sympathetic nervous system function and the effect of d-amphetamine. *Psychiatry Research, 4,* 157–169.

Mintz, L., & Collins, B. (1985). Qualitative influences on the perception of movement: An experimental study. *Journal of Abnormal Child Psychology, 13,* 143–153.

Nichols, P., & Chen, T. (1981). *Minimal brain dysfunction: A prospective study.* Hillsdale, NJ: Lawrence Erlbaum Associates.

Oades, R. (1982). Search strategies on a hole-board are impaired in rats with ventral-tegmental damage: Animal model for tests of thought disorder. *Biological Psychiatry, 17,* 243–258.

Oppenheim, J., Skerry, J., Tramo, M., & Gazzaniga, M. (1989). Magnetic resonance imaging morphology of the corpus callosum in monozygotic twins. *Annals of Neurology, 26,* 100–104.

Pandya, D., & Seltzer, B. (1986). The tomography of commissural fibers. In F. Lepore, M. Ptito, & H. Jasper, (Eds.), *Two hemispheres—One brain.* New York: Alan R. Liss.

Paul, S. (1983). *Neurotransmitter receptor plasticity.* Paper presented at the 15th Annual Taylor Manor Hospital Psychiatric Symposium, Ellicott City, MD.

Pennington, B., & Smith, S. (1983). Genetic influences on learning disabilities and speech and language disorders. *Child Development, 54,* 369–387.

Pieniadz, J., & Naesar, M. (1984). Computed tomo-

graphic scan cerebral asymmetries and morphologic brain asymmetries. *Archives of Neurology, 41,* 403–409.

Pribam, K. (1971). *Language of the brain: Experimental paradoxes and principles in neuropsychology.* Englewood Cliffs, NJ: Prentice-Hall.

Rosenthal, R., & Allen, T. (1978). An examination of attention, arousal, and learning dysfunctions of hyperkinetic children. *Psychological Bulletin, 85,* 689–715.

Ross, D., & Ross, S. (1982). *Hyperactivity: Current issues, research & theory.* New York: John Wiley & Sons.

Ross, E. (1981). The aprosodias: Functional-anatomic organization of the affective components of language in the right hemisphere. *Archives of Neurology, 38,* 561–569.

Routtenberg, A. (1968). The two-arousal hypothesis: Reticular formation and limbic system. *Psychological Review, 75,* 51–80.

Rummo, J., Routh, D., Rummo, N., & Brown, J. (1979). Behavioral and neurological effects of symptomatic and asymptomatic lead exposure in children. *Archives of Environmental Health, 34,* 120–124.

Satterfield, J., & Braley, B. (1977). Evoked potentials and brain maturation in hyperactive and normal children. *Electroencephalography and Clinical Neurophysiology, 43,* 43–51.

Satterfield, J., Cantwell, D., Lesser, L., & Podosin, R. (1972). Physiological studies of the hyperkinetic child: I. *American Journal of Psychiatry, 128,* 1418–1424.

Satterfield, J., & Dawson, M. (1971). Electrodermal correlates of hyperactivity in children. *Psychophysiology, 8,* 191–197.

Satterfield, J. H., Cantwell, D. P., & Satterfield, B. T. (1974). Pathophysiology of the hyperactive child syndrome. *Archives of General Psychiatry, 31,* 839–844.

Shader, R., & Jackson, A. (1975). Approaches to schizophrenia. In R. I. Shader (Ed.), *Manual psychiatric therapeutics.* Boston: Little-Brown.

Shaywitz, S., & Shaywitz, B. (1988). Attention deficit disorder: Current perspectives (pp. 369–498). In J. Kavanaugh & T. Truss, Jr. (Eds.), *Learning disabilities: Proceedings of the National Conference.* Parkton, MD: York Press.

Shaywitz, B., Shaywitz, S., Byrne, T., Cohen, D., & Rothman, S. (1983). Attention deficit disorder: Quantitative analysis of CT. *Neurology, 33,* 1500–1503.

Shaywitz, B., Yager, R., & Klopper, J. (1976). Selective brain dopamine depletion in developing rats: An experimental model of minimal brain dysfunction. *Science, 191,* 305–308.

Solanto, M. (1984). Neuropharmacological basis of stimulant drug action in attention deficit disorder with hyperactivity: A review and synthesis. *Psychological Bulletin, 95,* 387–410.

Still, G. (1902). The Coulstonian Lectures on some abnormal physical conditions in children. *Lancet, 1,* 1008–1012, 1077–1082, 1163–1168.

Strauss, A., & Lehtinen, L. (1947). *Psychopathology and education of the brain-injured child.* New York: Grune & Stratton.

Strecker, E., & Ebaugh, F. (1924). Neuropsychiatric sequelae of cerebral trauma in children. *Archives of Neurology and Psychiatry, 12,* 443–453.

Taylor, E. (1986). Attention deficit. In E. Taylor (Ed.), *The overactive child* (pp. 73–106). Philadelphia: J. B. Lippincott.

Voeller, K. K. (1986). Right-hemisphere deficit syndrome in children. *American Journal of Psychiatry, 143,* 1004–1009.

Voeller, K., & Heilman, K. (1988a). Motor impersistence in children with attention deficit hyperactivity disorder: Evidence for right hemisphere dysfunction. *Annals of Neurology, 24,* 333.

Voeller, K., & Heilman, K. (1988b). Attention deficit disorder in children: A neglect syndrome? *Neurology, 38,* 806–808.

Wender, P. (1971). *Minimal brain dysfunction in children.* New York: John Wiley & Sons.

Wender, P. (1972). The minimal brain dysfunction syndrome in children. *Journal of Nervous and Mental Disease, 155,* 55–71.

Wender, P. (1974). Some speculations concerning a possible biochemical basis of minimal brain dysfunction. *Life Science, 14,* 1605–1621.

Wender, P. (1975). The minimal brain dysfunction syndrome. *Annual Review of Medicine, 26,* 46–52.

Wender, P. (1976). Hypothesis for a possible biochemical basis of minimal brain dysfunction. In R. M. Knights & D. J. Bakker (Eds.), *Neuropsychology of learning disorders.* Baltimore, MD: University Park Press.

Wender, P. (1984). Remarks on the neurotransmitter hypothesis. In L. M. Bloomingdale (Ed.), *Attention deficit disorder: Diagnostic, cognitive, and therapeutic understanding.* Jamaica, New York: Spectrum Publications.

Wender, E. H. (1986). The food additive-free diet in the treatment of behavior disorders: A review. *Developmental and Behavioral Pediatrics, 7,* 35–42.

Wender, P., Epstein, R., Kopin, I., & Gordon, E. (1970). Urinary monoamine metabolites in children with minimal brain dysfunction. *American Journal of Psychiatry, 127,* 1411–1415.

Werner, E., & Smith, R. (1977). *Kauai's children come of age.* Honolulu: University of Hawaii Press.

Wolf, M., Bally, H., & Morris, R. (1986). Automaticity, retrieval processes, and reading: A longitudinal study in average and impaired readers. *Child Development, 57,* 988–1000.

Zametkin, A., & Rapoport, J. (1986). The pathophysiology of attention deficit disorder with hyperactivity: A review. In B. Lahey & A. Kazdin (Eds.), *Advances in clinical child psychology* (vol. 9). New York: Plenum Publishing.

Zametkin, A., Karoum, F., Rapoport, J., Brown, G., & Wyatt, R. (1984). Phenylethylamine excretion in attention deficit disorder. *Journal of the American Academy of Child Psychiatry, 23,* 310–314.

CHAPTER 5

METHODOLOGY

Ralph Mason Dreger

What is to be resisted is the notion that the cultivation of methodology is either necessary or sufficient for successful scientific endeavor.—Abraham Kaplan, *The Conduct of Scientific Inquiry*

This chapter is on methodology, the study of method. It dwells in considerable detail on sound method, as it ought to, more than on specific techniques. Nevertheless, also included in this chapter is practical advice for use of techniques, so that the reader should be able to come away with an understanding of what constitutes a good technique and a sense of how to use it. In composing this part of the Handbook, I have tried to keep from boring the expert and at the same time not confusing those who are rather inexperienced in methodology and research design. This task has been most difficult.

In the early years of my practice, teaching, and research, I took over the direction of what was then called a child guidance clinic in Jacksonville, Florida. One of my first tasks as a member of the psychological staff was to make psychological assessments of about 15 to 20 children referred from a cerebral palsy (CP) clinic; the cases of these children had been accumulating awaiting the arrival of the new measurement specialist.

These CP children were the most difficult ones with whom I had had to deal. And frankly, they were among the most difficult with whom I have ever dealt in subsequent years. Perhaps it was the concentration of so many youngsters of this type all at one time that was so impressive. But in actuality, it was not so much the quantity as the *quality* of the hyperactivity of the children which made so strong an impact. These were not ordinary "hyperactives." For one thing there was a much larger proportion of females than normally found, so "his" was not appropriate as a pronoun for the group. More substantively, however, these were not youngsters who could be described merely as "always having the motor running." They were at the extreme of what DSM-III-R (American Psychiatric Association, 1987) ranks as Severe ADHD. They "climbed the walls." They ran in the halls virtually uncontrollably. They ran in the examination room. None of the effects in this room, including tests and test supplies, which ordinarily did not suffer from children's handling, was safe from these children. They were hyperactive hyperactives.

By dint of great firmness and a God-given ability to relate to children on my part, the evaluations were completed with some more or less valid estimates of general (academic) intellectual levels of intelligence and a moderate amount of distinguishing personal characteristics. Quite by accident, actually out of desperation as to what to do with some of the most obstreperous youngsters, I discovered the paradoxical effect on them of a playroom equipped with a host of toys and a sandbox. Whereas these children just could not be tested in the examination room, when they were placed (literally *placed*) in the playroom which should by all logic have been more distracting than the examination room, they calmed down so that even while they were playing with one toy or another they could respond to examination questions quite sensibly.

What do these experiences have to do with methodology? These interactions have served as a background for studying (a) the methods people have used to identify for either clinical or research purposes which children are hyperactive, (b) what methods they have used to determine etiologies of the symptoms of hyperactivity, and (c) what methods have been adopted to treat the symptoms and/or the underlying disorder.

In respect to (a), determination of just which child is hyperactive has sometimes been confused by lack of clarity in terminology and criteria. To be sure, one could adopt the position of Schrag and Divoky (1975) who call "hyperactivity" a "myth," by which they mean that labeling such a large proportion of children as "hyperactive" is principally a means of controlling children, inviting medical rather than psychological means; however, these authors object to much of the latter control mechanisms as well. They raise a larger issue of "behavioral control," an issue beyond the scope of this chapter. Nevertheless, even though we can admit the reality of hyperactivity, cautions raised by Schrag and Divoky should not be set aside as irrelevant to children's welfare which is after all the reason for engaging in any kind of diagnostic classification or therapeutic intervention. If we do accept its reality, what is "it"?

Is "it" hyperactivity or ADD (attention deficit disorder) or ADD-H (attention deficit disorder with hyperactivity) (American Psychiatric Association, 1980, 1987), or ADHD (attention deficit hyperactivity disorder) or MBD (minimal brain damage or disorder or dysfunction—your choice)? Further, does "it" involve conduct disorder or anxiety? What relation is there between CP and/or brain damage and/or educable mental retardation (EMR) and "it"? These are all questions raised in the literature, answers to some of which and other questions as well are found in this Handbook. Here, it is only necessary to call attention to the problems posed by differing criteria and nomen-

clature. As one reads the literature on hyperactivity, it seems that at times apples and oranges are being compared as each set of authors defines hyperactivity in their own way. For purposes of this chapter, it is accepted that "hyperactivity" must be identified by multiple criteria from sources that are reasonably independent. DSM-III-R requires multiple criteria but does not require independent sources, although in its discussion mention is made of "at home" and "with peers." Use of both Conners' teacher and parent rating scales satisfies "reasonable independence."

Often, the methods used to diagnose a child as "hyperactive" have failed to take account of hyperactivity levels. Children have been labeled hyperactive when they are within the limits of normal overactivity, say, below two standard deviations on the Conners' teacher's scale (although one must be certain as to which scale is used [Ullmann, Sleator, & Sprague, 1985]). Conclusions from research have been false to the extent that they lump together a wide variety of children with the same label, so that the within-group variance is too large for testing true differences, a type II error.

In respect to (b) etiologies of the disorder, the presuppositions (some of which are discussed below) of practitioners and researchers have often determined what etiological bases they adopt. Some have decided that all hyperactivity has purely biochemical origins, so social or familial causation has been neglected. Some have decided that biochemical concomitants are just that, so that the social or familial roots are overemphasized.

Treatment considerations (c) follow right along with those concerning diagnosis or identification and etiologies. In this connection, distinction sometimes has not been made between behaviors that are *actually* uncontrollable from those that can come under voluntary control. My experience with the CP children tended to demonstrate the differences. Even though the playroom behaviors were calmer than those in a different environment, there were degrees of activity from child to child that showed some who seemed quite capable of controlling their hyperactivity within societal norms and others whose fidgeting and sometimes aimless motions appeared to be beyond their control. There was no clearcut line between the two groups; emphasis is made here on the *degrees* which at the extremes were a difference of *kind*.

The changing concepts of diagnosis, etiology, and treatment have been reflected in the literature on hyperactivity, all having an interactive, virtually transactional, relation to methodology. In the first DSM (American Psychiatric Association, 1952), there was *no mention* of hyperactivity as such. By a stretch of the imagination, the disorder could be subsumed under "Conduct disturbance," which along with "Habit disturbance" and "Neurotic traits" constituted the basic diagnostic categories for children's disorders.

It can hardly be supposed that hyperactivity had not been observed before DSM-I. Wickman (1928) included among his frankly arbitrary classification of "undesirable behaviors," "Violations of classroom rules: disorderliness (playing with pencil, disorderly lines, unnecessary noise, etc.), restlessness, interruptions, too social [!], whispering, lack of supplies, etc." And Ackerson (1931, 1942) likewise in his listing of children's behavior problems had one logical category that can be denominated "Irritable restlessness." Other evidence that hyperactivity had been noted by professionals (parents recognized it all along) prior to DSM-I is found in the review of classification of children and their problems in Dreger (1981a,b). DSM-I failed not only to recognize hyperactivity; it failed to recognize most children's problems.

By 1968, however, this lack of recognition had changed, influenced considerably by Richard L. Jenkins, a pioneer researcher in child psychiatry. In that year DSM-II (American Psychiatric Association, 1968) published a more extended list of problem categories, including one specifically designated "Hyperkinetic reaction of childhood (or adolescence)." Note that this is a descriptive category, not an etiological one, evidently meant purposely to avoid causative inference, for in the interim between the two DSMs the popular designation was "minimal brain dysfunction" or MBD (Clements, 1966). This designation with its implied physiological basis of hyperactivity continued beyond the publication of DSM-II (Conners, 1972; Sisk, 1981; U.S. Department of Health, Education, & Welfare, 1969). As readers of this Handbook are no doubt aware, terminology in DSM-III, "Attention deficit disorder

with hyperactivity" and DSM-III-R, "Attention deficit hyperactivity disorder" (though differently subcategorized) continues to be descriptive, except for brief paragraphs suggesting etiology: ". . . in which neurologic disorders are thought to be predisposing factors," and ADHD "is believed to be more common in first-degree biologic relatives."

These changing concepts of diagnosis and etiology have corresponded with changing modes of treatment of hyperactive children; some of these, of course, have been utilized throughout regardless of supposed causation, especially medication, behavior therapy, and diet alteration. These aspects of hyperactivity are dealt with in other chapters of this volume. The main emphasis here is that methodological considerations are involved not alone in *research* on hyperactivity but in all phases of diagnosis, etiology, and treatment. The CP children described above brought to a focus my prior training in research methodology, but also forced me to recognize the need to study method in all functioning of the disciplines concerned with hyperactivity.

SCIENTIFIC METHODS IN RESEARCH AND PRACTICE

The reason for using the quotation from Kaplan (1964) to begin this chapter is not to disparage methodology, but to raise the question of whether science or practice needs methodology in order to proceed in an effective manner. The answer to the query is both yes and no. Kaplan (1964, p. 23) differentiates between methodology as "very general philosophical principles" which underlie all scientific endeavor, and methodology as "concerned with very special scientific techniques." The former, as demonstrated below, includes examination of science's presuppositions, of the logical and sometimes epistemological and metaphysical aspects of the most concrete applications of scientific methods, and of the short- and long-term consequences of scientific results. As to whether science needs methodology of this first sort to carry on scientific endeavor, the answer is clearly no. Study of principles and techniques that work, the second kind of methodology, keeps science from having to reinvent the wheel. Nevertheless, again as Kaplan asserts, methodology of the first sort, the philosophical bases and consequents of scientific endeavor, is necessary for *understanding* what science is all about. "Esthetics does not produce art," Kaplan writes, "but it frees both artist and audience from constraints that stand in the way of its creation and appreciation" (Kaplan, 1964, p. 24).

I would go further than Kaplan in maintaining that methodology in the larger sense is essential in the last analysis to the *continued* existence of science. Science like every human endeavor carries within itself the seeds of its own destruction. Therefore, unless scientific endeavor is viewed from a larger perspective than science itself, philosophic and even possibly religious, in its myopic frenzy of production without larger goals, it may fling itself to pieces. The science of ancient Babylonia disappeared into the deserts of Persia, and the science of Aristotle into the oblivion of the Dark Ages, kept alive only in the Arabian world with a different philosophy from that in Europe.

While addressing general issues in methodology, one consideration must be advanced. That is, most of the chapter deals with quantitative research and practice insofar as the latter uses the results of quantitative research. In recent decades, however, there has been a renewed emphasis on qualitative research (e.g., Polkinghorne, 1983; Taylor & Bogdan, 1984). Influenced in part by developments in the physical and biological sciences and in part by dissatisfactions within the human sciences themselves, qualitative research has revived to some extent: theory construction as a basis for ordering phenomena, the interaction of observer and observed, models and methods of observation, and the idiographic (literally, characteristic signatures or trademarks, more specifically, the one-only personality pattern of each individual) nature of entities, especially people. A somewhat abbreviated summary of what qualitative research is and what it implies is found in Searight (1989). Reflections of this qualitative research trend can be seen in this chapter; I do not regard quantitative and qualitative research as antithetical, but complementary.

Setting forth what good scientific methods are here should enable the reader to judge the literature in her or his field from the standpoint of methodology and also judge against a good standard the research

or practice in which the reader engages. It must be recognized that the outline of research methods below *is not the only one that could be presented*. It is only one very good example of scientific methods. Further, as extensive as it is, it is only a bare sketch; whole books do not encompass all there is to know about scientific methods. Although Cohen and Nagel (1934) speak of the "scientific method," their definition implies that within that rubric a number of different ways of pursuing it are almost required. They state that science demands the "best available evidence" which is the realm of logic. "Scientific method is thus the persistent application of logic as the common feature of all reasoned knowledge. From this point of view scientific method is simply the way in which we test impressions, opinions, or surmises by examining the best available evidence for and against them" (p. 192). (Classic texts to be consulted are Brown and Ghiselli, 1955; Churchman, 1948; Cohen and Nagel, 1934; Feibleman, 1972; and Kaplan, 1964.) Nevertheless, an outline of this sort can be utilized as a reference for both practice and research. (Professor Milton Metfessel of the University of California is given full credit here for the basic outline of this section, as presented in a seminar in the summer of 1950. Although I have searched diligently, I can find no reference to Dr. Metfessel's having published this outline. It seemed at the time of the seminar, and still seems today, the single most succinct overview of a general research method with which I am acquainted and should not repose solely in notes hidden in a file cabinet. The substance in the text, filling in the outline, is mine, but with minor exceptions the outline is Metfessel's.)

I. Pre-investigative Considerations

In the following section, "presupposition" and "assumption" are used interchangeably, though some technical differences exist between them. Although all of the following considerations are linked under the rubric of "presuppositions," some of them will seem more like dicta than prior assumptions; they need to be considered somewhere, and thus are grouped here under "Pre-investigative Considerations."

A. *It must be recognized that before seeing a client or patient or before the start of any research we already hold numerous general scientific presuppositions, that is, those elements in the investigatory situation that are not being tested.* Among these presuppositions are two interrelated ones:

1. There is a general uniformity to nature. No matter how unpredictable a hyperactive youngster may be, we still assume that he (mostly, he, with males constituting a far larger percentage of diagnosed cases than females) is not operating outside of nature, and apart from random error, given the same variables impinging on his behavior, the same (general) behaviors will occur. In the world beyond the concerns of this Handbook, we assume that water runs downhill, that a red shift from the Crab Nebula means the same thing as a red shift anywhere within the astral system, and so forth.

The uniformity of nature does not mean that the "laws of nature" are immutable, but only that within certain boundary conditions they are probabilistically true, as indicated in the following paragraphs.

2. Events are determined. In the present understanding of the philosophy of science, determinism is quite removed from that of the 17th or even the 19th century. For the former views, everything in the universe was rigidly fixed in its course. For a newer view, groups of events are determined to a high degree of precision, but single events often are not predictable. A well-known example is that of the Wilson cloud chamber, where the electron stream can be ascertained by observers to a high degree of precision, but the path of any single electron is virtually unpredictable.

Putting these two presuppositions together, we can judge that by the first one we should not expect the child to take off and fly, despite our inability to predict his exact behaviors. By the second presupposition we expect a group of hyperactive children to show all the symptoms of ADHD as a group, even though no one youngster shows all of them (though one might).

3. As many as a dozen general presuppositions can be adduced relating to logical inference and mathematical propositions. For instance, in scoring a test or using a computer, does not the reader assume that $1 + 1 = 2$ under ordinary circumstances? But what about $1 + 1 = 10$, to the base 2? Mathematics consists of a series of axioms and deductions from those axioms that are essentially assumptions. And there are different systems of mathematics built up on different sets of axioms. So where one arrives depends upon where one begins, at certain presuppositions.

One assumption, generally accepted in science, is the honesty of the scientist. Indeed, one of the most famous psychologists of the first part of this century, McDougall (1926), wrote, "We accept all scientific conclusions on the strength of the moral improbability that men of science have entered into a conspiracy to deceive the rest of the world." McDougall probably overstated the case even for his day, yet a generation or so later this writer could state that the last thing attacked even in the most vituperative scientific debate is the character of the scientist (Dreger, 1962). The instances in which scientists have deliberately deceived the world are few, like Lysenko's attempting to prove the inheritance of acquired characteristics by touching up photographs with India ink and Cyril Burt's manufacturing intelligence data. Possibly, with the tremendous pressure placed on scientists to publish (or perish), there may be more instances of dishonesty than there were earlier, as recorded in the pages of the journal *Science* (e.g., Norman, 1988). On the other hand, such instances make news because they are so contrary to the usual acceptance of the assumption of honesty among scientists.

B. *Both science and practice are bounded by a cultural framework often challenged by the findings of visitors to other lands, and especially by the results of anthropological and cross-cultural psychological research.*

1. With some regret because of Margaret Mead's beautiful poetic prose, it must be acknowledged that some of her findings have not been supported by further research. However, if any major portion of Mead's (1949) observations on maleness and femaleness have verity at all, some of our presuppositions about male and female are peculiar to Western culture. Research on cultural factors in understanding and assessing psychopathology (Butcher, 1987), reported in the special series of the *Journal of Consulting and Clinical Psychology,* illustrates how our diagnostic categories and the very diagnoses we make are bound by Western cultural patterns to an appreciable extent.

2. Back of our systems of classification of most phenomena lie centuries highly influenced by Aristotle and relatively more recently by Galileo (Lewin, 1935) and Linnaeus (Dreger, 1968). Just as our classification systems are culture-bound, so those of nonliterate societies have systems based on their own presuppositions (e.g., Campbell, 1974; Price-Williams, 1967; Diamond, 1966) and useful for their own purposes in life.

Rather than belabor further the point which has been amply demonstrated particularly by anthropology, it is sufficient to state that before scientific undertakings and practice based on such undertakings are begun, cultural presuppositions are operative which distort investigations often to an unknown degree. One brief, edited text on *Assessing Minority Group Children* (Oakland & Phillips, 1973, gathers together data that could be valuable for any professional working with children to ponder and to question his or her own cultural presuppositions.

An instance from Matluck and Mace (1973) exemplifies this important point. They set forth this thesis concerning Mexican-American children: While other influences are important in the Standard English–deficient speech production of these children, probably the main problem is that *these children do not hear some English sounds*. The magnitude of the problem has gone unrecognized because investigators untrained in linguistics have not reported phonological errors and because teachers and others have so concentrated on *production* of sounds, and with little success, that they have lost sight of the larger problem of *perception*. Until the Spanish-speaking child has been trained to do otherwise, he hears, for example, "watch" and "wash" or "ran" and "rang" as identical words. The authors present convincing evidence to support their thesis (this summary is a verbatim excerpt from the review of Oakland and Phillips' book [Dreger, 1973]).

Similar phenomena can be observed in Louisiana. For instance, "Cajun" (Acadian) speakers, even intelligent persons, often use "aks" for "ask"; from informal inquiry, the only conclusion one can reach is that they hear others saying "aks" and think when they use the distorted term that they are saying what others are saying.

C. *An unspoken assumption of science is that only those macro variables that can be assessed by* *"scientific" instruments need be taken into account.* How many scientists attempt to take into account the "stars in their courses"? Yet in the annals of history there is ample evidence that by far a larger proportion of humankind *has* endeavored to take into account the influence of the stars than that proportion who have not regarded their motions and positions as having any direct bearing on our destinies (e.g., Campbell, 1974). Only those astral variables that can be measured like X-rays, radio waves, and physical light rays are admissible to science. Although extrasensory perception (ESP) has been accorded some status in science, a generally accepted principle is that natural causes must be given precedence before one attempts to take cognizance of other variables. Some, including this writer, are willing to admit that there may be variables beyond those we can presently admit, but investigations of those we can admit must be exhausted before others which now are included in "experimental error" should be given attention.

D. *Humane practices are assumed to be the norm in science.* The revulsion that scientists, along with most other Westerners, felt on learning of ghoulish Nazi medical experiments and in general the Nazi destruction of human beings—Jews, Gypsies, Poles, Russians, and others—was in keeping with humane cultural presuppositions of Western society. Nazi physicians were not castigated for their being unscientific, for before Hitler's Final Solution began German science was acknowledged as among the best in the world; it was the violation of the unexpressed assumption of humanity that caused scientists to condemn German doctors.

An example closer to home is one of the most well-known experiments ever done in social psychology on obedience. Milgram (1963) in a supposed learning situation had naive subjects administer "shocks" that were really nonexistent to a "learner" to determine, again supposedly, how much "shock" it would take to bring about learning a list of words. Although told that the shocks might be painful to the "learner" (an accomplice of the experimenter), they would cause no tissue damage. However, as the "shocks" became more "dangerous," the presumed learner began to protest more and more until he pounded on the wall and finally gave no answers. When the subject protested, the experimenter told him he was required to carry on, that he had no choice. Despite the evident distress of the learner, 26 of 40 subjects continued to the end, eight giving "shocks" labeled "Extreme Intensity Shock," one even administering shocks labeled on the "shock" machine "Danger: Severe Shock."

The extreme distress of the subjects in this obedience experiment is illustrated by the description one of the observers gave of what may have been the most affected subject, although all subjects evidently showed great signs of tension:

> I observed a mature and initially poised business-man enter the laboratory smiling and confident. Within 20 minutes he was reduced to a twitching, stuttering wreck, who was rapidly approaching a point of nervous collapse. He constantly pulled on his earlobe, and twisted his hands. At one point he pushed his fist into his forehead and muttered: "Oh God, let's stop it." And yet he continued to respond to every word of the experimenter, and obeyed to the end. (Milgram, 1963, p. 377)

After the experimental session, the subjects were interviewed and tested, "dehoaxed" in the report's terms. Then, the report continues,

> After the interview, procedures were undertaken to assure that the subject would leave the laboratory in a state of well being. A friendly reconciliation was arranged between the subject and the victim, and an effort made to reduce any tensions that arose as a result of the experiment (p. 374).

The deep revulsion felt by many after reading Milgram's report was matched only by the incredulity of some over the almost unbelievable naiveté of the experimenter. Here, people had been "used" in the name of science, humiliated, shamed, feeling forced to go against the norms of society, their human dignity violated, engaging in what they knew amounted to torture of the victim whom they had seen strapped into an "electric chair." How could anyone, and especially a psychologist, think that a simple debriefing could overcome the effects of what may well have been the most traumatic experience of their lives? It would take more time than I am willing to devote to the task to know if any attempt has been made to follow up the subjects, who were the real victims of this unconscionable experiment; but I would be willing to hazard a supposition that immediately or as

a delayed reaction a fair percentage of the subjects became as shattered emotionally as the man described above.

The fundamental moral norms of society have been developed over countless generations and are remarkably similar in the great philosophical and religious systems (Dreger & Barnert, 1969). Science is not free to violate them.

E. *All relevant specific demographic variables within a culture must be accounted for*. A major methodological argument is used to challenge findings: "But Jones did not allow for the influence of X and Y variables which Smith has shown to account for 10% of the variance in such-and-such." In respect to hyperactivity, it is disturbing that sometimes the assumption here goes unrecognized. Some writers will attempt to take account of some demographic variables, like sex, race, socioeconomic status, and intellectual level (e.g., Abikoff, Ganelas, Reiter, Blum, Foley, & Klein, 1988; Conners & Wells, 1986; McGee, Williams, Moffitt, & Anderson, 1989; Moffitt & Silva, 1988). Others give a partial account of demographic variables (e.g., van der Meere & Sergeant, 1988). Still others make little pretense of covering demography except for one or two variables (e.g., Gordon, Di Niro, & Mettelman, 1988; Smeets & Streifel, 1988). As the reader undoubtedly knows, differing etiologies have been suggested for ADHD, some involving genetics, others proposing prenatal and perinatal events, neurotoxic conditions, gender experiences, and so on. If an investigator does not take account of demographic variables, it is not clear that his or her procedures constitute a test of these variables or of the hypotheses set up to be tested. And investigation that does not attempt to account for such variables *presupposes* that they are not important.

F. *Behavior is a resultant of interactions between genes and environment*. Even the most ardent hereditarians and most ardent environmentalists make this assumption.

Assuredly, not all pre-experimental considerations have been included in this section. If, however, the reader has gained the solid impression that neither a research project nor assessment of a client starts *de novo* as if there were no factors to be taken into account prior to the investigation, the author's purpose will have been accomplished.

II. Experimental and/or Practice Considerations

In this section further assumptions are reviewed. Unlike those discussed in the previous section, which are often unconsciously assumed, these on the whole are assumptions a knowledgeable researcher or practitioner is fully capable of recognizing and specifying. In most instances, it is possible to state these presuppositions and to explain how they affect the method utilized and what limitations they place on the results obtained, either in the laboratory, school, or clinic.

A. *Tests, scales, statistics, and computer printouts are fallible guides to truth.*

1. Every test or scale has limits to its validity and reliability. The distinction between "test" and "scale" is that the former is more comprehensive than the latter. Test is derived from the Latin *testum* for a cupel or porous earthen vessel, used in refining of metals, especially precious ones. Thus, a test can be any refining process for sifting out the precious from the undesirable, as automobiles are tested at a "testing ground." Scale is derived from the Latin *scala* (or the Scandinavian term for a drinking bowl which came to be used for a bowl on a balance), which means a ladder or a flight of steps. The relation between the regular divisions of these objects and those of a measuring instrument of almost any sort is obvious. A scale thus is a form of test. While sometimes the two terms, *test* and *scale,* are used interchangeably, the distinction should ordinarily be kept in mind, as asking how tall a child can stretch is a test but not a scale. To be sure, in the latter instance a scale of centimeters or inches could be used. When employing test instruments in an investigation, whether acknowledged or not, the assumptions of the test or scale are involved. If the validity (for the purpose of the investigation) is relatively satisfactory, then the investigator is not testing the test but is testing the hypotheses of the study. Although all forms of validity can be shown (Messick, 1988) to be just "validity," it is important to know whether a test is valid in a particular situation; thus, one can speak of "validities" for this purpose.

One frequent methodological error I have encountered in many years of reviewing manuscripts is what I call the "circular error." An investigator determines the characteristics of a test she or he has constructed and possibly standardizes it; all well and good. Then, utilizing the *same* data on which the test was standardized, the test creator draws inferential conclusions, such as making comparisons between two subgroups of the population. This is a fallacy: One cannot legitimately make inferences of this sort, because inferential use of a test *has to assume the characteristics of the test such as already established validity and reliabilities*. Only an entirely new set of data, representing the same population on which the test was standardized, can be used to draw inferences about that population. Use of a test or scale then in an investigation *assumes* the predetermined characteristics of that instrument, else one cannot be sure one is testing the designated hypothesis or the test.

2. Computers can compound mistakes. The adage, "To err is human, but it takes a computer to really foul things up," makes even more sense in this day of packaged programs. Even though the producers of manuals (for BMDP, SAS, SPSS, et al.) include references to texts which explain the theory of individual statistics, so that those unfamiliar with the particular statistic can know its limitations and pitfalls, evidently not all users of a program bother to consult the texts. Not only do misunderstandings of a statistic occur; sometimes those not familiar with a substantive field accept results of the neatly formatted printout without realizing the results are completely false.

One egregious example is the failure to specify a reasonable number of components (in component analysis) or factors (in factor analysis) to retain. It was more common in an earlier day to read, "Seven factors were retained and rotated," with no explanation of criteria for the choice; yet that choice may have been crucial to the entire enterprise being carried out. In more recent times, greater sophistication has led writers to report, "Seven factors were retained by the Scree test or the eigenvalue-of-one criterion." There may still be questions whose answers are vital: Was there only one Scree break? Does not the eigenvalue-of-one criterion yield more components or factors than it ought to on theoretical grounds? Guttman's (1954) classic paper on the minimum rank of a correlation matrix with unities in the diagonal showed that that minimum is greater than or equal to 1.00. But that criterion generally yields too many retained components (Tucker, Koopman, & Linn, 1969). The caution in the Statistical Analysis System STAT/GUIDE (1987) should be kept in mind:

> No computer program is capable of reliably determining the optimal number of factors since the decision is ultimately subjective. You should not accept blindly the number of factors obtained by default; instead, use your own judgment to make a decision. (p. 127)

Computer programs, whether individual or packaged, (Fowler, 1969) require the *informed* judgment of the user. This principle is a specific case of a more general one—that whatever the calculating medium, the user must be knowledgeable in the substantive field in which the medium is to serve. It is not simply "Garbage in—garbage out" in respect to the one medium, the computer, but the recognition that even very good data can be made to generate ridiculous results (and produce them almost instantaneously by computer).

Currently, an additional assumption has been made that may prove more or less false (Davis & Cowles, 1989; Groth-Marnat & Schumaker, 1989): that tests administered by computer achieve results comparable to those administered conventionally. A review of studies comparing automated and conventionally administered tests (Mazzeo & Harvey, 1988) must give pause to both practitioners, researchers, and companies with on-line services for computer test administration (and scoring). Mean scores from computer administration tend to be lower than those from conventional administration. Items are more likely to be omitted in the first case than in the second. Speeded tests result in differences in the means of the two types of administration in some instances. For both the Minnesota Multiphase Personality Inventory (MMPI) and California Psychological Inventory (CPI), effect sizes (computer mean minus conventional mean) were found in two studies by the same team to be virtually all minus. The signal exception was the MMPI Cannot Say (?), with a huge positive (computer mean higher) effect size. However, there were contradictory results in some cases; and correlations, which do not take account of levels of mean scores, only of rank order and dispersion of scores, are generally high. The *Guide-lines for Computer-Based Tests and Interpretations* (American Psychological Association, 1986) warns that the equivalence of scores derived from computerized testing should be established before one uses norms or cutting scores from conventional tests.

3. *Statistics also have assumptions* (Snedecor & Cochran, 1980, Ch. 15). This fact is to be regarded seriously, especially with the present use (and abuse) of packaged computer procedures for multivariate statistics. Sometimes violations of statistical assumptions may vitiate the results of an investigation by either researcher or practitioner. As long ago as 1961, Carroll (1961) stressed that the choice of a correlation coefficient may make considerable difference to the interpretation of results, especially in factor analyses. Rarely does one read in books or articles that any consideration has been given to the Pearson r's assumption of linearity (in the parameters) of regression. The analysis of variance as an instance of the general linear model (GLM) has a similar assumption. (Draper and Smith, 1981, state the assumptions of regression succinctly.)

The violation of statistical assumptions may or may not, however, imply that an investigation is necessarily invalidated. In the 1950s, Norton (1952) utilized empirically derived distributions of differing forms and variances and compared the resulting F's (ms_g/ms_w) with tabled F values. *Generally*, F's derived from any of these comparisons, even for those with considerably different forms (J-shaped, rectangular, etc.) and variances were not markedly different from the theoretically derived tabled values. However, leptokurtic and rectangular distributions yielded too-large values, especially with small degrees of freedom.

At the beginning of research with behavioral instruments such as that developed for the Children's Behavioral Classification Project (Dreger, 1981a,b; Dreger & Dreger, 1962), statistical authorities were unanimous in agreeing that dichotomous distributions with p-values of .10 or less were not legitimate for use with the Pearson r. Because a fair number of items in an instrument for assessing psychopathology are bound to be very highly skewed (.005 or less at times), the research team assumed that those items generating distributions with proportions of less than .10 would require logical categories to supplement the dimensions that a factor analysis would produce.

However, when all items, regardless of distributions were analyzed, these items identified appropriate factors. No statistical authority the team has consulted has been able to give a satisfactory explanation of the anomaly.

The research team was computer-naive and did not know that items with very low p values could be omitted by formatting and retained them in the analyses, with fortunate results, as it turned out. Although these results have been known for many years, instruments are still being constructed by omitting items that are rarely endorsed; because these are usually the highly pathognomonic ones, the range of such instruments is definitely restricted.

The qualifications implied above are not intended to suggest that statistical assumptions are unimportant. The user of statistics should be aware of their assumptions even if in particular instances it may not be necessary to assure oneself that none are being violated. Nevertheless, a principle that I have stressed over and over in the use of any statistics must be invoked here: The investigators should know their fields thoroughly, so that if results turn out to be nonsensical or deviant from what they expect, they should immediately question whether violation of the assumptions of the statistics has been responsible for the results.

B. *Any investigation in research or practice involves specific presuppositions and cautions.* Some of these considerations may seem too obvious to state; but rather than have them overlooked, they are given here.

1. *The level of training necessary for administering standardized instruments or qualitatively complex nonstandardized tests must be observed.* This stricture applies to both research and practice. The *Standards for Educational and Psychological Testing* (American Psychological Association, 1985) emphasizes" that test users should have a sound technical and professional basis for their actions" (p. 3). And yet, tests that require the highest level of such training and experience are sold to and are being used (abused) by unqualified persons, physicians and others, who have never had even an elementary course in tests and measurements. At times, decisions are made affecting life goals by those who are not familiar with the errors that may occur in test development and use, with statistical ranges of confidence, or with computer distortions, and with the potential disasters that might come from misinterpretations of test data. Though the writer was one of the first to call attention to the potentials of computer interpretation of tests (Dreger, 1966), his enthusiasm has waned as publishers have allowed unqualified users to employ their most complicated tests which should be used only by highly trained experts. These dangers must be noted in particular in ADHD research and practice where decisions are made for prescribing (or withholding) medications on possibly false psychological test results (Ullmann & Sleator, 1985).

2. *The instructions accompanying a test are to be followed as closely as possible.* Sometimes gross departures from these instructions have invalidated the results of an examination. Terman and Merrill (1937) stressed that an examiner has to be flexible in administering tests, taking account of the immediate circumstances; if, for example, someone inadvertently walks in on an examination when a child has been given an otherwise unrepeatable item but is startled, the examiner has to make a judgment about repeating the item or perhaps giving an alternate item. An examiner who is alert to the condition of her or his examinee knows when the latter is fatigued and introduces an activity or rest period not scheduled in the examination booklet. But the proper interpretation of test results *presumes* that the administration will follow instructions as closely as possible.

In group testing, correct distribution of test booklets, verbatim repetition of instructions, and correct scoring and interpretation (in most cases involving comparison with norms) are presumed. An advantage of computer testing, tailored or straightforward, is that the computer does not misread, skip, or alter instructions, though the examinee may do so even then, except when verbalizations are produced by the computer.

3. *The conditions of examination must be conducive to concentration by the examinee, in either research or practice.* Anastasi (1976) cites evidence to the effect that students using desks scored significantly higher on a test than those using chairs with desk arms. She notes likewise that examiners sometimes use the wrong answer sheets. In several parts of the country, clinics and schools have been found

with no facilities adequate for individual testing, especially for hyperactive children. If an office has to be used for testing, let it be as uncluttered as possible. A clinic I designed did use an office for testing, the desk equipped with top front overlap so older children and adults could sit right up to the desk top; the walls bare except for a license and diploma; the only chairs being one for the examiner, one for the examinee, and a simple armchair for interviewing; and no telephone. (For *genuine* emergencies a secretary knocked on the door; *very* few emergencies occurred.)

From the experience described at the beginning of this chapter came a lesson for test administration for children: A playroom equipped with a wide variety of toys and a sandbox is a very useful adjunct for testing and observation. After sometimes active, even wild, exploration, a child settles down to one or a few toys. The manner in which the child manipulates objects, especially the degree of creativity, eye-hand coordination, large and small muscle usage, and accompanying verbalizations allow not only for rough estimates of intellectual level but also judgments of basic temperament patterns. And these observational opportunities apply to normally active as well as underactive and hyperactive children. For preschool children, the sandbox has been a regular tool for testing, with some children able to respond meaningfully to up to 200 items in one session. (Cf. Cattell and Dreger, 1974, for a more extended description of playroom testing.)

The main point of this discussion is that accurate and truthful results of an investigation, diagnostic or experimental, require conditions conducive to eliciting accurate and truthful responses.

This is an appropriate place to introduce a concept that helps to answer the question raised by the previous paragraph: What are accurate and truthful responses? The concept is "redundant validity." It means that no important conclusion concerning an individual client or subject is to depend on one piece of evidence only. For example, in the very diagnosing of hyperactivity, to depend solely on the ADD-H Comprehensive Teacher's Rating Scale (ACTeRS; Ullman, Sleator, & Sprague, 1988) or either of Conners' scales is not sufficient to identify a child as hyperactive (Ullmann & Sleator, 1985). Even though the 93-item Conners' parent scale includes the same items (substantially) as the Abbreviated Teacher Rating Scale, so that use of the ATRS might seem superfluous, common sense if not scientific consideration suggests that data from a different source adds to a "truthful" picture of the child.

Going beyond diagnosis or classification, redundant validity calls for more than one estimate of intellectual level. Early in my research (Dreger, 1953) IQs up to 52 points' difference were found between two well-standardized tests given by the same trained administrator to a single child. In my practice, up to 70 points' difference was obtained. Since the subjects in the controlled experiment were nonclinical, it seems safe to say that a single estimate of intelligence with either clinical or nonclinical subjects may be wide of the mark. The same principle of redundant validity holds for testing of temperament ("personality") characteristics. Redundant validity enables the clinician, teacher, or researcher to approximate the truth more adequately than use of the commonly accepted "incremental validity" (Meehl, 1959), which allows only those test instruments to be used that add to prediction over base rates. Whatever one's definition of "truth" may be, human endeavor can only approximate it, anyway. The principle of redundant validity provides a useful tool for such approximation.

4. *In any particular investigation, there are variables that may differentially influence results:* (a) Determine which of these can be presumed to be irrelevant (but make sure about this irrelevancy), for example, phases of the moon or sunspots, room temperature, amount of light, intensity of distracting stimuli outside the room, the comfort of examinees' chairs, and so forth. (b) Ask what controls will be exerted for those variables that cannot be presumed to be differentially influential, for example, masking white noise for distracting stimuli or making simple adjustments of chair height for children of different height.

A few words are required in connection with pre-investigative and experimental considerations: Why, the reader may well ask, has so much attention been paid in these sections to assumptions. Is not methodology a study of *method*? But thus far very little has been devoted to *methods* of research, though some space has been given to methods of practice.

In response, it must be stated, if the message has not come through clearly: *Most investigations that falter or fail do so not because of their methods or techniques per se but because of neglecting the presuppositions of the investigations.* If the reader will think back over failures in diagnosis or in research, he or she will see from the results of the diagnosis or critiques of the research that in most instances failures were in lack of attention to presuppositions.

III. Methods and Designs for Research and Practical Investigations

We come now to discussion of methods of gathering and utilizing data in practice and/or research. The "and/or" in the last sentence signifies my belief, supported by experience from practice, that research can be done through practice (Dreger, 1990). The reality is that most research and most practice are carried on separately from each other. Thus, what is usually designated "research design" is treated here as if applicable only to research; but the same basic principles apply to practice in school or clinic as to research, with only minor adaptations.

A. When the term *research design* was utilized in earlier days, it referred almost exclusively to analysis of variance (Feinstein, 1988) as interpreted by R. A. Fisher (1966), Federer (1955), Lindquist (1953), and in the late 1970s by Kennedy (1978). Among the few who resisted the trend to equate research design with analysis of variance (ANOVA) was Sidman (1960) who elaborated on the essential principles of experimental design. Sidman's statement pertaining to design of investigations is still worth quoting and heeding:

> I could make the trite statement that every rule has its exception, but this is not strong enough. Nor is the more relaxed statement that the rules of experimental design are flexible, to be employed only where appropriate. The fact is that *there are no rules of experimental design.*
>
> Every experiment is unique. Experiments are made to find out something we do not yet know.
> . . . In our search for new information we must be prepared at any point to alter our conception of what is desirable in experimental design. Nature

does not yield its secrets easily, and each new problem of investigation requires its own techniques. Sometimes the appropriate techniques will be the same as those which have been employed elsewhere. Often the known methods will have to be modified, and, on occasion, new principles of experimental design and procedure will have to be devised. There is no rule to inform an experimenter which of these eventualities he will meet. (p. 214).

Although it is not necessary to adopt Sidman's extreme position, his statements can serve as an antidote to the notion that science consists of following rigid rules. When analysis of variance *was* research design for most, all that seemed necessary was to select an apparently appropriate ANOVA design and fill in the cells with data. The modern adaptation of analysis of variance as represented by the General Linear Model sometimes seems to fall into the same trap with the use of computers. GLM is essentially extended regression analysis which does expand the concept of research design beyond ANOVA. But here, too, the temptation is to let the computer do the thinking so that all the researcher needs to do is to supply the computer some numbers.

In truth, science is more than specific research designs and more than some "approved" method. In years gone by, Murray and his colleagues (1938) at the Harvard Psychological Clinic wrote in *Explorations in Personality,* "We tried to design methods appropriate to the variables which we wished to measure; in case of doubt, choosing those that crudely revealed significant things rather than those that precisely revealed insignificant things" (p. 33). Thus, to repeat Sidman in slightly revised version, there is no one research method, no one set of research designs to be followed slavishly. Therefore, in the outline of one method of investigation below, no assertion is made that it is *the* experimental method; it happens to be one which I regard as rather comprehensive and helps in the ordering of data. It should not be followed rigidly, either!

B. Below is an eight-point coordinated experimental design.

1. *A statement of the theoretical and/or practical background of the investigation is given.*

a. The nature of the theory or practical problem to be investigated should be made explicit.

Is the theory suspect in some way that some parts or all of it need to be tested against a set of data? Or is there need to confirm all or parts of the theory? If it is a practical problem to be investigated, the problem should be stated succinctly but fully enough so that the reader of a report will understand what the investigation is intended to answer.

b. Specify what changes in the theory or knowledge about the practical problem *any* outcome of the investigation would bring about. Suppose the results should turn out contrary to expectation, or partially in confirmation and partially in contradiction? Is it clear in the mind of the investigator what the significance of *any* positive or negative outcome would be?

2. *A statement of the question(s) to be asked of the data is to be expressed in such a way as to be testable.*

a. The question(s) must be phrased so that answers are

(1) Exclusive—Sometimes hypotheses are stated so as to make any outcome confirmatory, as "The means of Group A and Group B will be significantly different from each other." Which way? If Group A's mean is "significantly higher" than that of Group B, the hypothesis is confirmed. If Group B's mean is higher, the hypothesis is likewise confirmed! This example may seem simplistic, and it is; but a fair number of manuscripts I have reviewed have just such illogical hypotheses that do not force an exclusive answer.

(2) Exhaustive—Insofar as possible, all potential outcomes should be set forth. To be sure, it is probably impossible to foresee all such outcomes. Yet, someone who knows the specific field well should not ordinarily be surprised when the results are in. Surely, we are trying to find new information by an investigation; but science cannot advance if research constantly produces new, utterly unforeseen results.

(3) Mutually exclusive and exhaustive— When different possible answers are stated to the question(s), they must be nonoverlapping as well as exhaustive (insofar as possible). Take the two following statements: "CP children will improve by one standard deviation on the Attention scale of the ACTeRS under treatment A" and "CP children will improve by one-half standard deviation on the At-

tention scale under treatment A." Most overlappings are subtler than this very obvious example.

b. The question(s) must be answerable in terms of observable events or in operational terms if the events are nor directly observable. Behavioral inventories provide items relating directly to observable events, like "Cries out in sleep" or "Faints, passes out, 'falls out,' or blacks out." On the other hand, inventories attempting to assess a person's attitudes, feelings, and emotional states seek to operationalize these inner states by items purporting to relate to them. Such instruments are subject to many errors, although Wilde (1978) has shown that they are about as reliable as performance measures. Meehl (1945) maintained that "a 'self-rating' constitutes an intrinsically interesting bit of verbal behavior, the nontest correlates of which must be discovered by empirical means" (p. 277). For Meehl, then, responses to a questionnaire can be directly observable events. While this usage is possible, the manner in which questionnaires are commonly used makes them but operational measures of unobservable events.

3. *Alternative hypotheses should be stated.*

a. A formal statement of hypotheses is helpful because it clarifies what the possible answers are. Some investigators can keep these alternative hypotheses and answers in mind or jotted down on the backs of envelopes. Most of us have something in more tangible or organized form.

b. Whether a formal statement of hypotheses is actually written down, as this author thinks it should be, even informally stated, the aim is to relate certain classes of variables (independent or predictor) with certain classes of other variables (dependent or criterion). Someone familiar with such a technique as factor analysis (in any of its varieties) may say that there are no independent or dependent variables, for all of them are just put together in a correlation or covariance matrix without distinction. On the contrary, factor analysis is a very clear case of relating two classes of variables. The factor analysis model closely parallels a regression model. For component analysis, the equation is:

$$z_j = a_{j1}F_1 + a_{j2}F_2 + \ldots + a_{jn}F_n,$$

where z_j is the standard score on variable j, $a_{j1} \ldots a_{jn}$ are conponent weights, and $F_1 \ldots F_n$ are the components. For classical factor analysis, the model is only slightly different. In any case, a class of dependent variables, z_j, is related to a class of latent or independent variables, F_i.

      c. Hypotheses are implied whether stated or not. Some researchers declare that they do not have and do not need hypotheses, but examination of what they do will almost always reveal that they do have them. A young colleague came to me for help in designing an experiment. Quite naively, I asked, "What are your hypotheses?" "Oh," the other replied, "I don't have any." He was seen immediately to have been trained by methodologists with the philosophy another colleague expressed, "I just gather a lot of material together and see what the hell comes of it." Thus, I did not challenge the statement the young man made, but only suggested, "Tell me what you intend to do in the experiment." At that, this man began to describe in some detail what he would do and *how he expected it to turn out.* I did not have the heart to point out to him that his very clear statement of expectations constituted hypotheses.

The very selection of variables to be investigated is an implicit statement of a hypothesis, relating one set of variables to another. In simple regression, each set or class may consist of only one variable. In canonical correlation, the generalization of multiple regression, both sets contain more than one variable. It must also be said that in virtually every case involving statistics the null hypothesis is also involved. On the other hand, as Cohen (1988) points out, attention to a null hypothesis should not obscure the even more important size of the effect. The latter is assessed by power analysis, a subject beyond the scope of this chapter.

    4. *Observable specifications of the design are identified and measures of control described.*

      a. These specifications include observable events, subjects, and objects which or who are used as referents of the classes specified in the hypotheses. If the hypothesis reads, "Hyperactive children will respond with reduced activity to administration of Ritalin (methylphenidate)," what first is meant by the class of children called "hyperactive"? Will they be identified as such by parental report, pediatric diagnosis, teacher report, a standardized scale such as the Hyperactivity scale of the Children's Behav-

ioral Classification Project (also dubbed "Nuisance aggressiveness"). What levels of any of these indicators will be accepted to identify "hyperactive children?" Administration of Ritalin seems rather straightforward. Ritalin is a class of objects, but what dosage will be used? Who is responsible for administration and what controls will be exerted to assure that the prescribed regimen is carried out? Likewise "reduced activity" is a class of events. What base rate will be used and how measured? What will constitute "reduced activity" from the base rate and how will it be measured? And what statistical tests will be utilized for making the comparison?

If the child is her or his own control, that is, the base rate is taken on each child before the administration of the medication and then the final rate is taken on the same child, the questions asked above may seem to be answered fairly easily. However, if the study is a comparison between one hyperactive group and another, the control group, the one getting the treatment and the other not during a specified time period, everything is more complicated. Whereas the first "own-control" experiment is an instance of J. S. Mill's (1843) first canon of experimental inquiry (that of Agreement), the two-group study is an example of the second canon (that of Difference). (See pages 81–82 below.) We must assume that in such studies the single change in the situation is administration of the medication, so that any change in the behavior of the child or children results from the drug administration. This assumption is weak, as is evident from application of the questions in the preceding paragraphs to either type of study.

Even a simple two-group design requires an additional class in the hypothesis and elaboration of the statistical portion of the design. A multiple-group design calls for additional class specifications and further elaboration of the single hypothesis into several hypotheses that take account of interactions among the independent variables or among both independent and dependent variables in a multivariate design.

      b. Controls should be specified which will be exerted to eliminate the influence of those variables that are unavoidably present but for which no presupposition of irrelevance can be made.

        (1) Simple randomization. Presupposed randomness is often not sufficient to ensure proper

control. In the fatal poll of voters taken before the presidential election in 1936 by the *Literary Digest*, fatal because it caused the demise of the magazine, two million voters expressed their presidential preferences and the *Digest* reported with great emphasis that Franklin Delano Roosevelt would lose the election. But as the event turned out, he won by a large margin. What happened was that the magazine polled people who owned telephones and automobiles; a very great many who actually voted, however, did not in that day own telephones or automobiles. The presumption was that with so massive a number of respondents surely the voters polled were representative of all voters. Unfortunately, the *Digest* pollsters' presumed randomness was just not there.

In other words, some definite steps must be taken to assure randomness. The principle is that every member of a specified population has to have the same chance of being selected. That principle can be carried out by having all members of the population numbered just as they come and using a table of random numbers found in some statistics texts to select participants. In connection with the topic of this Handbook, it cannot be assumed that any one group of hyperactive children are representative of all hyperactive children. Unless prior information is available which allows that assumption, it is incumbent on the investigator to make direct attempts to get a group that is a sample from the specified population, else the limits imposed by a nonrepresentative sample must be thoroughly explained.

(2) Manipulative randomization. Statistics and research design texts describe a number of ways that randomness may be achieved. One extension of the fundamental principle is that, when different levels or degrees of an independent variable are set off from one another, or fixed values such as sex are used to separate subjects, every member of the population potential for each cell has an equal chance of being selected for that cell.

This *stratified random sampling* is, however, the ideal which in some cases is impossible to fulfill. For instance, if an investigator wishes to compare hyperactive children of both sexes on some other variable, the population of girls is rather meager. It may be that to have reliable data, all of the girls available are required for the cell(s) for female sex. Or in order to accommodate school classrooms, it might be necessary to take all the children rather than just the ones who are required to fill cells; yet, having all the children from rooms with differing numbers of children would require an unbalanced design which the investigator would like to avoid. This second instance is more easily handled than the first; all that is necessary is to select randomly from the entire group in a room the number required by the design. The first instance, on the other hand, requires recognition and a clear statement of the limitations imposed by having to utilize all the potential subjects: There can be no presupposition that this particular sample is representative of the population of all girls with specified types and levels of hyperactivity.

(3) Controls should be exerted for removing, blocking out, or masking unwanted stimuli. In standardizing the Preschool Personality Questionnaire (Dreger, Lichtenstein, & Cattell, 1986) the examiners found that with the assistance of a teacher and/or aide, 6-year-old children could be tested together in ordinary classroom-sized groups. Five-year-olds could be tested in groups of up to 15. But although initially small group testing was attempted with 4-year-olds, it was soon determined that they had to be tested individually. In other words, any other children in the vicinity of the 4-year-old proved too distracting and had to be removed as stimuli, the actual process being removal of the target child to a separate room. With hyperactive children, other stimuli may have to be removed or blocked as well if results are to be valid. The paradoxical effect of placing such children in a playroom with a host of apparently distracting stimuli, as described in the introduction to this chapter, serves as a reminder that the ultimate arbiter of what proves to be distracting or not is empirical, not theoretical. Some external stimuli are equally stimulating to both or all groups, like planes overhead or traffic noise. But if these or others should possibly be differentially stimulating, arrangements must be made to render them equal or eliminate them altogether.

5. *Specifications respecting causal, limiting, correlational, and/or functional relations are identified.* Boundary conditions imposing limits on the scope of the proposed investigation are covered here. Just what are the expected relations among the chosen variables? For the most part, research in the human

sciences does not deal with causal relations but primarily with functional or correlational ones.

a. In the last several decades, a new kind of logical and statistical modeling has come into prominence (e.g., Bentler, 1989; Jöreskog & Sörbom, 1989). This methodological innovation was first known as "path analysis" and more recently by a more general term, "structural equation modeling." This latter has been embodied in one computer program, among other similar programs, called LISREL (LInear Structural RELations) which in its several versions (number VII as of this writing) has revolutionized thinking in the social sciences. Originated by Karl Joreskog and Dag Sorbom when they worked with others at the Educational Testing Service, to some enthusiasts LISREL is the answer to every problem or relations among variables. However, some statisticians have advanced cautions to the effect that no equation that ultimately depends on covariance demonstrates causation.

It is impossible in this chapter to cover any significant part of structural equation modeling; thus, only a few sentences can be devoted to a rough and too-simple description of what it is. Such modeling is a form of latent variable analysis (including latent class analysis) (Bartholomew, 1987; Everitt, 1984; Langeheine, 1988) in which observed variables are regarded as manifestations of "true" latent variables. In reliability theory, for example, the "true" reliability of a test can be estimated by the intercorrelations among the variables making up the test,

$$r_{tt} = k\bar{r}_{ij}/(1 + (k-1)\bar{r}_{ij}),$$

where r_{tt} is the "true" reliability, k is the number of variables, and $\bar{r}_{ij}$ is the mean of all correlations between any two variables (Nunnally, 1978). The component analysis model, given on page 78, represents another instance of utilizing manifest variables to estimate latent variables, the factors. Emphasis in recent years has been more on *confirmatory factor analysis* than on *exploratory factor analysis* which is what most such analyses have been. Other multivariate models have been developed.

Once again, with these high-powered techniques for establishing relations among variables, latent or manifest, the expertise of the investigator must be the ruling consideration, not the sophistication of the techniques. Even the most comprehensive text on the use of LISREL (Hayduk, 1987) emphasizes that the program will be most beneficial to those scientists who are most thoroughly grounded in the substance of their fields. And a text which, while not underestimating the value of structural equation modeling for equating structures or for confirmatory analyses, protests at an overemphasis on the latter and states simply, "It is our belief that much of the original intuitive geometrical appeal of exploratory factor analysis as a technique of scientific discovery has been diminished over the years by excessive emphasis on the detailed mathematical and statistical aspects of the model" (Yates, 1987, p. 5ff.).

b. It is easy to roll off the tongue the familiar terms, *necessary, sufficient,* and *necessary and sufficient conditions*. It is far harder to specify these for any particular investigation. Yet it is worth trying for it may help to clarify a research design.

In a study of what was then called minimal brain dysfunction, comparing MBD, brain-damaged, and normal children, Sisk (1981) attempted to ascertain the relation of life-history variables to MBD, BD, and normality. From previous research (Fitch, 1976), Sisk amassed a list of 51 life-history variables that had been presumably linked in some way to MBD, all the way from pregnancy through infancy to early childhood. "Linked in some way" is purposely vague, but each of the 51 events was regarded by some authority as causative of MBD. Although not expressed directly as necessary, sufficient, or both, none of the variables was regarded as necessary or sufficient alone; only in some combination was it anticipated that these variables would be sufficient to cause MBD. Suffice it to say here that certain combinations of life-history variables *did* distinguish significantly among MBD, BD, and normal children, mostly as sufficient but not necessary causation. Generally, only very highly controlled experimental studies can claim that they have identified necessary, sufficient, or both conditions. Nevertheless, trying to do so may prove surprisingly fruitful.

c. No chapter on methodology should be complete without at least summary reference to J. S. Mill's (1963, orig. 1843) methods of experimental inquiry, called "canons" by Mill. The first canon is *If two or more instances of the phenomenon under investigation have only one circumstance in common, the circumstance in which alone all the instances agree, is the cause (or effect) of the given phenomenon.* This is the weakest method of inquiry, that of Agreement, although sometimes the only one available in natural settings. The adage, "Correlation does not mean causation," is applicable to this method.

The second canon is *If an instance in which the phenomenon under investigation occurs, and an instance in which it does not occur, have every circumstance in common save one, that one occurring only in the former, the circumstance in which alone the instances differs, is the effect, or the cause, or an indispensible part of the cause, of the phenomenon.* This canon, that of Difference, is much stronger than that of Agreement, though both are methods of elimination. Agreement indicates that what can be eliminated is not connected to the phenomenon; Difference indicates that what cannot be eliminated is connected.

The third canon is the Joint Method of Agreement and Difference: *If two or more instances in which the phenomenon occurs have only one circumstance in common, while two or more instances in which it does not occur have nothing in common save the absence of that circumstance, the circumstance in which alone the two sets of instances differ, is the effect, or the cause, or an indispensable part of the cause, of the phenomenon.* An example illustrating the increased power of this method over the first two methods can be drawn from a study of hyperactivity and otitis media (especially, with effusions, OME; Hagerman & Falkenstein, 1987). Children were either patients of or followed by the child development unit of a children's hospital. Twenty-seven of the 67 children were identified by three measures as hyperactive: a score of at least 15 on each of Conners' parent and teacher rating scales, and diagnosis of ADD with hyperactivity by DSM-III criteria. The control group of nonhyperactives was matched with the experimental children on age and IQ on the WISC-R, but socioeconomic status (SES) differed significantly between the two groups. Otitis media infections were determined by parent reports and physicians' records, and were considered verified if they had been treated with antibiotics for at least 10 days.

If this were a pure third canon design, the otitis media would be the circumstance (independent variable) and hyperactivity the phenomenon (dependent variable). We can disregard other variables temporarily and report a significant (actually, the obtained level was $p . < 00001$) association between otitis media and hyperactivity. Specifically, in more than one instance (a fair number of children) the circumstance of otitis media occurred together with the phenomenon of hyperactivity; and in more than one instance (a fair number of children) the circumstance of otitis media did not occur and hyperactivity was absent as well. (This bare outline assumes that all other variables were equal between the two groups, a condition that was not met.)

The authors of the study recognize that the association between otitis media and hyperactivity does not necessarily represent a causal link and in fact calls for research to establish an etiological relation (if any exists). This study does, however, provide an opportunity for discussion of some important methodological points. First, by reporting numbers of subjects precisely the authors obviate one criticism of some studies from which it is impossible to tell how many subjects there are and often how many enter into experimental and control groups. Further, by using Mill's third canon (though not expressly stating so), the authors made use of a fairly powerful research design. And by reporting procedures fully enough for others to build on their work, the investigators followed accepted scientific reporting standards which help to make science an incremental endeavor rather than sets of unrelated activities.

There are, however, some negative points that need to be expressed in respect to this study. The most notable of these is the lack of discussion of the possible mediating influence the SES variable(s) might have on both otitis media and hyperactivity. The reader will recall that a significant difference held between the two groups; Hollingshead and Redlich (1958) scores are inversely related to social class, so that hyperactive children came from lower SES backgrounds. Although an attempt was made to separate the influence of SES scores from other independent variables in a logistic regression analysis (incidentally, using a statistical test meant for *large* numbers of subjects), merely entering numbers representing SES status does not take into account the conditions represented by those numbers, conditions that could well underlie both otitis infections and hyperactivity.

Another problem with the report of the study is that the description of subjects is rather unclear. As indicated above, the numbers in toto and in each group are given, a plus for the report; but the description of subjects leaves something to be desired: "Sixty patients were white, one was black, one was of mixed black/white parentage, three were Hispanic, one was Oriental, and one was native American" (p. 254). Aside from the ambiguity of racial identification (Dreger & Miller, 1968), the children are not identified by group. How does one match for experimental control one black, one of black/white parentage, one Oriental, and one native American?

A fairly common error to which attention is paid later in this chapter is not fatal but is misleading, that is, reporting results in percentages when the total N is much below 100, in this case, 67. For example, 50% of nonhyperactives = 20; 74% of hyperactives = 20; 89% of hyperactives = 24; and so on. Numbers accompany these percentages in the text, yet use of the percentages is unjustified. A further difficulty is found in the figure that presumably is meant to clarify the relation between the two main variables. It certainly does not fulfill the adage, "A picture is worth a thousand words," for it does not make clear the authors' intent. As the overall chi-square seems to have been done to generate a significance level of $p < .00001$, a much better, although simplified, presentation would convey the essential message of the study: a 2 × 2 table (Figure 5.1) for which the

numbers were gleaned from the Table 1 and Figure 1 of the report. The reader may wish to compute the chi-square, which will indeed be found to support the authors' significance level from the chi-square.

There is only one other minor point which nevertheless indicates a misunderstanding on the part of these authors and others in other studies. The first sentence of the Results begins, "In the entire study population, 27 children (40%) were rated hyperactive by two or more raters." What should have been stated was, "In the entire study *sample*, 27 children . . ." These children constituted a *sample* from the *population* of hyperactives, of which, with the rather careful selection procedures utilized, most likely they were representative.

The writer of this chapter does not wish to hold up the otitis media study as an example of poor methodology, for it is no worse than numerous other studies. In fact, in some ways it is superior to many of them; despite its shortcomings there is little doubt that the authors have proved with considerable certainty the main hypothesis: that there is a strong relation between otitis media and hyperactivity. They did not intend to show any more than that, leaving it for future investigation to establish causation.

The fourth of Mill's canons is known as the Method of Residues: *Subduct from any phenomenon such part as is known by previous inductions to be the effect of certain antecedents, and the residue of the phenomenon is the effect of the remaining antecedents.* As Mill points out, this is one of the most important methods of discovery. What the residue is may be so obscure among numerous other antecedents that one might not look for it spontaneously. A hypothetical but data-based example of this type of procedure is given in Dreger (1962). A very promising young man applies for pilot training in the military. His record is excellent in everything he has attempted—school, sports, social relations. His general intelligence is very high. From all kinds of interviews and records the selection board makes the unanimous judgment, "He'll make a good pilot." But this talented and capable young man "washes out" miserably. Among all the many circumstances which if they had been negative should have been the causes of failure, only one which might have seemed very obscure is responsible: the nearly complete lack of a trait called *Psychomotor Coordination I*, the ability

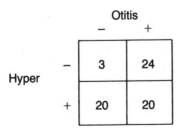

Figure 5.1   2 × 2 table.

to make fine, sensitive, and highly controlled adjustments in movements that are restricted in scope. This trait correlated .64 with Navy midshipmen's success in flight training when eliminations were due to flying deficiency. That trait was the "residue" that could easily be missed unless one knew where to look.

Finally, Mill's fifth canon is the Method of Concomitant Variations: *Whatever phenomenon varies in any manner whenever another phenomenon varies in some particular manner, is either a cause or an effect of that phenomenon, or is connected with it through some fact of causation.* The last clause is required, because mere concomitance does not prove causation. Further, the concomitance itself must be proved by the Method of Difference. Latent trait analysis which is touched upon above is an example of this method, although unlike Mill's original formulation the comcomitance is of a probability nature. The observed variables and the latent variables are regarded as in distributions, with the latent variable distribution conditional on the observed variable distribution (though arguably the *causal* relation is vice versa). This is as far as we shall go with this illustration of Mill's fifth canon.

A few cautions are in order in the use of this method. The correlation between two variables, which may indeed represent causation directly or indirectly, may hold only for a certain range of each variable. In other words, extrapolation from the measured range may be dangerous. Further, the fact of concomitance, without elimination of other variables, may mean that causation is so far removed from the two variables at hand that any causation involved is so tenuous as to be negligible. Here is a favorite example: It used to be said that the number of deaths by drowning and the amount of ice cream consumed are highly positively correlated. A hint as to the meaning of the statement can be given by stating that the fluctuations in ice cream consumption year round are probably considerably less, now that refrigeration is so widespread in this country. Finally, the size of a correlation coefficient does not guarantee either its statistical significance or logical importance. If N is very small, say 5, an r of over .75 is required to achieve significance at the .05 level. On the other hand, by increasing N indefinitely *any* coefficient except .00 can be made statistically significant. However, a practical usage of very small

but significant coefficients was made during World War II: Guilford (1948) and his co-workers found that with the very large N's with which they were dealing coefficients of from .10 to .20 contributed usefully to prediction of pilot training.

Mill's canons thus encapsulate the essence of scientific methods. It is not expected that every investigation will first undertake a "canonical" analysis. Yet, unless the investigator asks, "What will be the grounds of inferences I shall be making, however the results turn out?" it may be that there are logical holes in the design. And, be informed that if there are, there are critics who will expose these holes, sometimes quite unmercifully.

6. *The operational specifications, or what actually is to be done in the investigation, should be outlined.*

a. What instruments, tests, or apparatus will be used? For guidelines in the selection and uses of tests, the joint publication of the American Educational Research Association, the American Psychological Association, and the National Council on Measurement in Education, *Standards for Educational and Psychological Testing,* (1985) is a must. Insofar as possible, the discussion in this section is limited to methodological aspects of testing, since detailed assessment methods are found in Section Two of this Handbook.

b. For both practice and research, development of a standard battery of tests is recommended. This recommendation goes against a prevailing view that only those tests specifically required for a particular client should be utilized. For research that requires follow-up, a standard battery is a virtual necessity, unless all the initial and follow-up efforts are purely qualitative. But when I established a private practice called Psychological Research and Services, I instituted a standard battery for the first purpose, research, and found that its use proved to be the most valuable service that could be provided for many clients (Dreger, 1990). The professionals using the battery are free to add any instruments they deem necessary for adequate evaluation, but basically the standard battery if chosen carefully can ordinarily offer as much information as is needed (from tests, which are embedded in the entire evaluation process).

With the demand for testing instruments from

more traditionally trained professionals supplemented now by demands by behaviorally trained professionals who have come to realize that tests can provide information they need, there has been a burgeoning of new tests and restandardizing of old ones; and the publishing of tests has become big business. Thus, for the practitioner the need for careful selection of tests is even greater than previously, great as it was then. But similarly, that same need holds for researchers as well. The guidance given on pages 73–75 for selection and use of tests can be generalized to more than the one area covered by this Handbook.

Whatever one's choice of test for defined purposes within either research or service, general aims, administration, scoring, and interpreting are important operations to be considered initially and throughout the investigation. Even when collection of data, scoring, and some interpretation are automated, the one who has to make the final interpretation must know whether the results are reasonable. Procedures other than automated ones allow for clerical errors that can vitiate a whole complex assessment process.

Computer administration and interpretation of tests (Fowler, 1969) have introduced considerable alteration in specifying operations for either practice or research. Before the advent of computers into this field there was continual violation of the requirements of good psychological and educational testing principles, as persons untrained in psychometrics and statistics were administering and (mis)interpreting the most complicated tests. But, where it was once said that any intelligent person could give a test, no matter how unintelligible the results, now it does not even require an intelligent person to press keys on a keyboard. I stated almost three decades ago, "These new developments in test analysis call for even greater professional competence in the clinical psychologist than was called for in premachine days" (Dreger, 1966, p. 187). The need for professional competence is even greater now, to use and interpret tests in this computer age.

c. There are some very necessary operations in the conduct of an investigation that are not mentioned in texts of methodology; yet if proper attention is not paid to them, they can minimize the value of the research. A checklist of these operations may help:

- What arrangements must be made with the following?
    School system officials and research director in particular
    Mental health or special education authorities, state research supervisor, for example
    School principals, assistant principals, school secretaries
    Clinic or hospital administrators
    Teachers, teacher aides
    Mental health or special education professionals
    Parents and/or other caretakers
    Patients, clients, general public
- How are laboratory assistants, examiners, etc., recruited, trained, and supervised?
    Qualifications: Age, sex, race, etc.
    Recruitment: volunteer, paid
    Extent and type of training
    Supervisory procedures
- What physical facilities will be needed?
    Specially equipped rooms
    Ordinary classrooms
    Auditoria
- What equipment and supplies will be needed?
    Computer, keyboard, monitor, printer, diskettes, etc.
    Test materials, booklets, answer sheets, manual
    Information sheets, consent forms, instruction sheets
    Writing materials, pencils, styli, etc.
    Office supplies, furniture
    Special apparatus, stopwatch, etc.
- How are subjects to be recruited and instructed?
    Subject population
    Subject pool
    Volunteer or paid
    Anonymous or identified—confidentiality
    Preformal instructions, establishing rapport, for example
    Formal instructions: Know thoroughly but not memorize
    Posttest verbal and other behaviors
- How will research materials be handled?
    Numbering or other identification
    Method of distribution
    Method of collection
    Method of storing

Certainly, this checklist is incomplete, and each investigator will wish to add something she or he thinks essential. Yet, consideration of the items listed may prevent someone's forgetting a vital step.

    d. What measuring operations will be involved and what kind of scale will be used? Published objective tests and some projective tests virtually dictate their measuring operations by providing standard response forms. Beyond these standard operations, special situations call for special operations with handicapped persons, illiterate individuals, non-native-speaking individuals, and others. With children addressed in this Handbook, their very impulsiveness and fidgetiness call for special means of obtaining valid data from them. Aside from the suggestion already made for use of a playroom, these special operations are left to other chapters of the book.

The kind of scale utilized for measurement determines in part the kinds of analyses that can be carried out with the data collected. The familiar categorization of scales by S. S. Stevens (1951) appears to have been generally accepted. For completeness, it is summarized here:

Nominal. Here, entities (subjects, events, etc.) are labeled or categorized arbitrarily, as in the use of essentially meaningless numbers for clinical cases or experimental subjects, or categorized in such a manner as not to imply order, as sex or race identity. There is some question of whether nominal "scales" constitute measurement at all; certainly, they do not represent a scale (*scala* = ladder) in the same sense as the other varieties of scales. Nevertheless, certain statistics can be used with them: frequency counts, contingency coefficients in particular, and sometimes the mode.

Ordinal. Objects are rank ordered by some criterion or criteria with no suggestion of distance between any two objects or exact mapping of objects to numbers. If a teacher is asked to rank four children on degree of hyperactivity, she or he could most likely do so without much trouble; but if asked to assign numbers to indicate the *quantities* of hyperactivity each possesses, the teacher might find the task rather challenging. The statistics appropriate for use with ordinal scales are those suitable for nominal scales plus area-type transformations like percentiles, rank-order coefficients like Spearman's ρ, Kendall's

τ, but not usually Pearson's r, normalization statistics (though rather meaningless with very large discrepancies among objects, like countries—China and Surinam!). Such scales are said to be "invariant over a monotonic transformation."

Interval. In this case, the distances between numbers on a scale correspond (or are assumed to correspond) with distances from one object to another in the degree or quantity of an attribute. The numbers are said to be mapped to the objects. Rank ordering objects is assumed; therefore, an interval scale is also an ordinal scale. Accordingly, those statistics appropriate for the latter also are appropriate for an interval scale. Further, means, standard deviations (and other moments about the mean), and Pearson's r are usable with interval scales. The several estimates of r, like the tetrachoric, may or may not be applicable depending on the character of the distributions of the variables. Interval scales have an arbitrary zero point. Nunnally (1978) believes that usually no harm is done in the behavioral sciences if the mathematical and statistical methods used presuppose that most measurement methods lead to interval scales.

Ratio. There is in the case of a ratio scale a true zero for both the attribute being measured and the scale measuring it, and also equality of the rank orders and of the ratios formed from the intervals. In explanation of the last characteristic of a ratio scale, note that for a scale with a true zero and equality of rank orders, (a—b):(c–d)::(a'—b'):(c'—d'), the primes indicate the scale and the unprimed letters the attribute. Most physical measurements form ratio scales, and most psychological measurements do not. Nevertheless, Stevens (1951) and others have found ways to create ratio scales for psychological measurement; since neuropsychophysical measurement sometimes involves such scales, investigators into children's problems, including ADHD, need to become familiar with ratio scales.

    e. What are the units of measurement that will be used? Measurement consists of what logicians term "mapping," that is, assigning a set of symbols to a set of entities or variable quantities. A simple but useful mapping is to assign the symbols "M" and "F" to males and females. There is no need to convert these symbols to numbers, for they can be used as nominal categories, say, for application of a contingency coefficient: "1" and "2" can be used as categories just as well as letter symbols. Their use as quantitative indices is a different matter, implying ordering of the data to which they are mapped.

These considerations introduce a distinction that must be observed between two types of distributions that underlie our measurements and determine what we can do with data collected. Distributions are *discrete*, like the numbers of psychotic, conduct disorder, or ADHD children in a given population; or they are *continuous*, like the degree to which any disorder is found in individual children, the degrees varying along a continuum. To be sure, as Snedecor and Cochran (1980) explain, all quantitative measures are discrete *as recorded*, for they can take only a distinct series of numbers no matter how much we round them off. But the difference between discrete and continuous distributions has to be observed for some types of statistical manipulations. "Distribution-free" statistics do not call for the distinction discussed here. Yet the unit of measurement chosen is important for either parametric or nonparametric statistics.

Assuming an underlying continuum, Ullmann and her colleagues (Ullmann, Sleator, & Sprague, 1988) chose numbers 1 to 5 to map the terms *Almost Never,* to *Almost Always* for the presence of certain characteristics of hyperactivity. Dreger and his research team (Dreger, 1981b) utilized only "1" and "0" to map to *Present* or *Absent* in respect to aspects of general psychopathology including ADHD. In other words, even though different authorities choose different units of measurement, careful thought needs to go into their selection and the ones making the choice must be ready to defend their choice.

7. *Statistical specifications of the investigation should be set forth in sufficient specificity to guide collection of data.* At times students and others have brought massive amounts of data, laboriously gathered, to find out what can be done with them. After examination of the set of data, the writer is often tempted to say, "Chuck them in File 13. Nothing can be done with these data." For extensive as they are, the data have not been gathered with any idea as to what statistics will be used with them. Therefore, not only have assumptions of statistical methods been violated—and as pointed out above such violations have to be gross in order to vitiate results—but also the data are not in such form as to be conveniently amenable to any statistical procedure. An emphasis should be made on "conveniently," for in all cases except one, I have been able to salvage something by judicious selection or combination of subsets of the data. In some instances, though, a very large amount of the data had to be discarded.

It is easy these days with computers to "play around with the data" and derive some useful results. But how much more efficient it is to gather data with specific statistical techniques in mind. Even with the most careful planning, of course, investigators are encouraged to do some "playing" with the data. Nevertheless, when interesting results come from such activity, and more especially when the data were gathered without clear hypotheses, these results can only be considered helpful leads for *future* investigation.

a. Translation of experimental hypotheses into appropriate statistical concepts and methods is required. To demonstrate not only the mapping of statistics to a hypothesis but also a couple of other methodological points, one study on gifted children is cited. Duncan and Dreger (1978) hypothesized that well-adjusted gifted children would differ significantly in a socially acceptable direction on behavioral syndromes of psychopathology from well-adjusted average children matched with them on age, sex, race, and one SES indicator, father's occupation. If the presence or absence of giftedness, as measured by several criteria, could be related to a single "psychopathology" score, a simple t-test would have been suitable. To be realistic, however, no single score could represent all psychopathology, so the children had to be assessed on a number of syndromes (factors in this case). Again, each syndrome could have been taken singly and comparisons made between the means of two groups, and in fact such comparisons were made later. First, though, in terms of the interactions of syndromes one with another, the entire set of syndromes was investigated by the multivariate analysis of variance (MANOVA). That is, the independent variable was being gifted or not, and the dependent variables were the factor scores on the pathology syndromes. Since there were only two groups, Hotelling's T could have been used. The null hypothesis could not be rejected by the results of the MANOVA at the predetermined level of significance.

At this point, the analyses might have stopped. Nevertheless, the researchers decided to continue with further tests, not for definitive conclusions but for leads to future studies. Univariate F's were obtained for each syndrome, although t-tests would have been satisfactory. Post hoc (the Scheffé, for example) tests as such were not legitimate, for this was not a case of identifying *where* the differences lay, after a significant overall F, but of "playing with the data" after a nonsignificant F.

Now, however, a legitimate analysis was possible to help answer the main hypothesis. *Prior* to starting the investigation, the statistical design included carrying out a linear discriminant analysis, which it turned out correctly classified, on the basis of the entire set of measurements on the syndromes, 25 of 30 gifted children and 25 of 30 average children, a result which those who work with classification recognize as quite acceptable. Examination of the specific dimensions that enabled the discriminant function to separate the two groups revealed that the gifted children were perceived as behaving in more socially acceptable ways. This conclusion must be tempered by the findings of the MANOVA, even though the discriminant analysis was planned and executed independently.

b. Specific aspects of assumptions and uses of statistical methods should be kept in mind. One of the simplest of these is how many subjects are required for a specific technique to be used reliably. Statistics texts provide reverse equations to determine what N is necessary to assure that, when a desired power is to be reached (Cohen, 1988) or a pre-specified true difference is found between sample means, the probability is high that it is statistically significant (cf. Snedecor & Cochran, 1980, for example). However, simplest of all techniques is comparison of percentages or proportions. Yet quite often researchers fail consider that the percentages or proportions are based on Ns of 100 and make comparisons on far fewer numbers than 100, using their relatively small N's in percentage form. An article that was regarded for many years as a classic in its field and widely quoted turned out to base one of its most important conclusions on a percentage of 69. Examination of the original article revealed that that "percentage" in turn was based on an N of nine out of 13 individuals! It is well known that with small

expected frequencies in chi-square cells, various adjustments have to be made, including corrections for continuity. (Or in some cases Fisher's, 1966, exact test can be used; with computers and programs for that test, the tedious calculations for Fisher's test can handily be made.) This is no place to discuss all the requirements of statistics, only to put the reader on notice that they must be observed.

c. Selection of samples cannot be left to chance. When television or radio stations conduct polls on some current issue, they usually add a caution (probably not heeded by many listeners) to the effect that "This is not a scientific poll." And well they might, for usually only those who feel very strongly about the issue take the trouble to call in. However, polls like Gallup's, Roper's, or Yankelovitch's can estimate with only 3% or 4% inaccuracy what public opinion in general is from samples of from 1200 to 1500, usually by rather complex sampling by age, sex, race, geographical region, or other means of stratification. For practical purposes of ordinary research in schools, clinics, or other research settings, random samples can be obtained by use of random number tables. Modern computers have built-in randomization programs to accomplish the same purpose. A warning is necessary on this score, because with some of the programs *the same series of random numbers will be generated if the program is run a second time*, which defeats the purpose of randomization. In later versions of BASIC, like GWBASIC ("gee whiz" BASIC), prefacing the RND command with the command RANDOMIZE will result in different number series from trial to trial, even if the same "seed" number is used.

Stratification can be done with whatever process will decrease the within-sum of squares, thus increasing the power of F-tests. This result can be accomplished by grouping those individuals in separate cells according to a factor not being tested in the study. When, for example, impulsivity is being assessed in children for some other purpose than comparing them by age, the greater variance expected of younger children can be separated from that of older children so that wide differences between younger and older children in impulsivity are eliminated from the within-cell variance.

Once more, it is not so important in this place to elucidate on sampling techniques which occupy whole books in themselves as it is to make sure that sampling is not haphazard. That not enough attention is paid to this vital part of research has impressed itself over and over on the writer in both reviewing manuscripts for publication and reading published works. In one study which exemplifies this failure, the purpose was to study certain aspects of attentional deficits and learning problems. But the sample was limited to average and upper income children. If the authors had stated clearly that their results were applicable only to that limited population of children, the failure would not have been as great, even though one questions any study that would be so limited. However, nothing in the report noted that results were not applicable to the large proportion of attentional deficit and learning problem children of lower SES status.

After emphasizing so strongly the need to have appropriate sizes of samples for specific statistics, it might seem that no room is left for research with $N = 1$. Such is not the case, however. This type of research is especially applicable to behavioral analysis and treatment, but is also useful for other forms of assessment and therapeutic modalities. Take the most easily recognizable studies which fully conform to statistical assumptions and use, what is called P-technique research (Dreger, 1985; Dreger & Brabham, 1986). This technique uses factor analysis with occasions within a subject as the sample data, so that the population is the set of all occasions on which measurement of certain variables would be possible. It may be that a number of subjects are combined so that a study uses the usual number of subjects for group analysis. But the study using just an N of one fulfills statistical requirements.

Gordon Allport (1937) called for "idiographic" as well as "nomothetic" research, by the former meaning extensive and intensive study of the individual. And Kurt Lewin (1935) urged Galileian rather than Aristotelian research, meaning lawfulness for the individual as compared to lawfulness for a class or group. But the methodology for implementing such research was lacking, except for psychophysics (see below) whose methods were not available for study of personality to which both Allport and Lewin were addressing themselves; Allport's own research had to depend on nomothetic methods. In the latter part of this century, then,

methods began to be developed that are logical and legitimate for use with individuals. Campbell and Stanley (1966) provided research designs which, although intended primarily for groups, are applicable in part for single-case research. Chassan's (1979) *Research Designs in Clinical Psychology and Psychiatry* and Barlow and Hersen's (1984) *Single Case Experimental Designs* provide strategies for research with single individuals. The important element in such research is *control*, either with the subject's serving as his or her own control or with some control group. A case study without controls may be interesting, instructive, and evocative of hypotheses, but it is not science.

Caution needs to be observed at this point: "Idiographic" does not mean "idiosyncratic." It may be very therapeutic to institute a regimen of treatment, whether behavioral or psychoanalytic or whatever, which is successful with a single individual; but that fact does not constitute science at its best. The single case may be studied scientifically for its own sake, with hypotheses set up and tested against as objective data as possible under the circumstances. But to contribute to scientific advance, single cases must be studied as a group to ascertain common patterns that may be applicable to larger groups. This type of research is precisely that in which psychophysics engages. Very few subjects are employed for such research, yet results garnered from them are regarded as applicable to the larger population.

d. The number of trials or replications necessary to achieve stable statistics and *believability* should be planned. In either group or individual investigation, sufficient data need to be gathered to establish reasonably reliable means, standard deviations, and so forth. The word *reasonably* is included here to emphasize that the amount of data gathered does not depend solely on probability levels, even though allowances can be made for small cell numbers by various statistical or manipulative procedures, as suggested above, in determining the number of subjects necessary to achieve certain probabilities for differences between or among groups. And from a pragmatic viewpoint, the investigator with limited resources is under pressure to keep the trials or replications to a minimum. Nevertheless, even though the minimum is acceptable from a scientific standpoint, from a psychological standpoint it is more *convincing* to have just a few more trials or replications than required. This is one form of "redundant validity" which none of the methodology texts mention, but which in dealing with assessment of clinical clients has proved its worth. For science, increased N means greater reliability of the statistics, which even to scientists will not be rejected; for *appearance,* increased N adds to believability. This is not a methodological matter but a psychological one.

　　　e. Set the level of acceptable significance *prior to* conducting the study. On the basis of previous work done in a particular field, a level can be set suitable for the stage of the field in which the investigation is taking place. If the stage is early, then a more lenient level is called for, .10 or even .20, for example. A Type II error, accepting the null hypothesis when it is in fact false, is more costly at this stage than a Type I error, rejecting the null hypothesis when it is in fact true, because further investigation of promising leads might be prevented. On the other hand, when the field has reached the point at which "promising leads" are not the subjects of investigation, more stringent levels of significance are required, anywhere from .05 to .001, say, because type I errors are more costly. One of the problems of some hyperactivity research has been acceptance of causality hypotheses (rejection of the null hypothesis) which would not have been accepted if the probability demands had been stricter.

Note that "prior to" has been emphasized above. Even today with presumably greater methodological sophistication, one finds statements such as "The difference was statistically significant" with no indication of the level at which the difference was to be accepted. Those who may think it is not important to set the level before beginning the investigation (or at the very least, before examining the results) misunderstand the nature of significance or hypothesis testing. This testing involves drawing conclusions about a *population*, not just the *sample*. Therefore, ahead of time the researcher must set up a region (or regions in a two-tailed test) of *rejection* in the population's distribution. If the region is not determined beforehand, then any region of rejection can be arbitrarily decided by the investigator after the results are examined. Such a practice is not only

statistically unsound, but is logically a form of cheating.

Setting levels of significance a priori does not preclude wringing as much out of the data as computers can find. What it does preclude is accepting these later "findings" as scientifically proven. The same stricture holds for "results" that "approach significance," and especially when, as in some instances, substantive conclusions are drawn from these "nearly significant results." The rejection region(s) having been set (for rejecting the null hypothesis), anything not found in the rejection region(s) is not acceptable, period. A rubber yardstick is not a good measure.

This is the appropriate place to bring up a caveat expressed by Barlow and Hersen (1984). They speak of *statistical versus clinical significance,* arguing that for applied research establishing functional relations between independent and dependent variables is not enough. Establishing *meaningful* clinical or socially relevant relations is required. Their simple example is that if depression could be reliably measured on a scale of 0 to 100, treatment that improved each patient from 80 to 75 might be statistically significant if untreated controls remained at 75. But a clinician would not, or should not, be satisfied if 75 were still in the suicidal range. Often, however, both clinicians and researchers (we hope they are the same) accept a "significant" finding also to be clinically effective. Again, as expressed more than once in this chapter, the antidote to this kind of stereotypical thinking is sound knowledge of the field. Only then can one judge whether a *statistical* result is also an *important* one. This caveat is not to denigrate the use of statistical hypothesis testing, but only to place it in the context of logical thinking.

　　　8. *Critical analysis of existing research helps to clarify a research design.* This principle is applied to a New Zealand study of treatment of hyperactive children with essential fatty acid supplementation (Efamol). Aman, Mitchell, and Turbot (1987) carried out a double-blind design with placebo controls and crossing over of drug order administration and repeated measures treatment. That is, administration of Efamol was given to a random half of 31 children (15 or 16?) for four weeks, then following a week's "washout" period, comparable placebo capsules were

given for four weeks; the other half received the placebo first, then the Efamol capsules.

Although a clear hypothesis is not stated in this report, one can be reasonably inferred from introductory remarks: That supplementation of essential fatty acid (EFA) will improve behavior, learning, and motor performance of children selected for inattention and hyperactivity. So far so good, with only a small negative for not making an explicit statement of the hypothesis. Next, the massive amount of testing done with these children deserved a larger sample, just for the sake of appearances; but obtaining the cooperation of even 31 children and their parents over a period of at least 9 weeks is a feat in itself.

Further, it is not clear to whom the "double-blind" aspect applied, though it is stated in the Results section that the serum fatty acid levels were determined without knowledge of treatment conditions. One of the next comments is that the level of significance is not stated in the description of the research design where it should be. And the tabular presentation of results do not make clear what level(s) the investigators had in mind initially, for levels are listed as $p < .007, < .02, < .01, < .07, < .05, < .10$, and $< .001$. In one place, however, for the 42 behavioral measures used to monitor the effects of the drug, the alpha level was set at .05, bringing the probability level to .0012 for each measure, because the overall F test could not reject the null hypothesis at the .05 level for most of the main effects (and the few which are significant, at levels ranging from .10 to .001 are easily attributable to chance [Sakoda, Cohen, & Beall, 1954; Wilkinson, 1951].

Again, a less important but noticeable omission is that the *statistical design* is not given where it should be, but in the Results section. Whether the analysis of covariance for the psychomotor tests and rating scales (for parents and teachers) was the correct one to use depends on whether the repeated measures are regarded as dependent or independent variables. As the EFA was the primary independent measure, and the various tests and scales were used to assess the effects of EFA, it is almost certain that these tests and scales must be regarded as dependent variables. As such the repeated measures call for the use of multivariate analysis of variance (MANOVA) rather than a form of the analysis of variance (Bernstein, 1988).

Now, after making these rather negative comments, we can look at the larger picture and ask whether the study has contributed methodologically and substantively to the field of hyperactivity. I think it does, though if I had been a reviewer of the manuscript in the first place I would have insisted on a modified report. It was, first, a clearcut test of a fairly clear hypothesis. Previous work by the authors and others had promoted the possibility that EFA supplementation is a treatment for hyperactive children. Then, most of the subjects of the study were carefully chosen by two well-standardized behavioral instruments, Conners Teacher Questionnaire and the Revised Behavior Problem Checklist, while 5 were diagnosed using Attention Deficit Disorder from DSM-III (not III-R, of course), four of whom also scored above the 90th percentile on the two selection devices. Thus, it is virtually certain that the children were truly hyperactives. We have to take the authors' word that the experimental and control capsules were comparable; but assuming that they were, the design allowed for an efficient use of the number of subjects by having each subject serve as his or her own control, effectively doubling the N.

Further, by utilizing the most satisfactory measures of cognitive and motor behaviors as were possible under the circumstances—or in some cases, under any circumstances—and behavioral reports from significant others, the child's world, internal and external, was explored about as adequately as anyone could expect. Without expressing it overtly, the authors used the principle of "redundant validity" discussed earlier. For definitive decisions they did not depend on what methodologists call "incremental validity," or the idea that one adds another measure only if it increases the predictive validity appreciably.

Finally, whether the statistical design was entirely suitable, and the question is debatable, the overall results almost call for acceptance of the conclusion of the experiment: "The burden of proof lies with those who would advocate this form of therapy [EFA supplementation] first to establish its efficacy before claiming that it has a therapeutic role to play in treating hyperactive children" (Aman, et al., 1987, p. 88).

To close this long section on methodological specifications, a quotation from one of the greatest statisticians of this century is noteworthy; he applies it primarily to ANOVA, but think of it also in relation to the whole scientific enterprise:

> We would emphasize that the analysis of variance, like other statistical techniques, is not a mill which will grind out results automatically without care or forethought on the part of the operator. It is rather a delicate instrument which can be called into play when precision is needed, but requires skill as well as enthusiasm to apply to the best advantage. The reader who roves among the literature of the subject will sometimes find elaborate analyses applied to data in order to prove something which was almost obvious from careful inspection right from the start; or he will find results stated without qualification as "significant" without any attempt at critical appreciation. (Kendall, 1947, vol. 2, p. 245)

SUMMARY

A dramatic experience with a group of CP children who were very hyperactive led me to consider the issues of what criteria should be used to identify a hyperactive child; what presuppositions about etiologies mean to diagnosis of and research on hyperactivity; and how these issues reflect themselves in treatment. Changing concepts relating to these issues have been mirrored in successive editions of the DSM. On a more general level but still quite applicable to the subject of this Handbook, scientific methodology can be regarded as general philosophical principles and as specialized techniques, both of which are essential to the scientific enterprise. Although this chapter deals primarily with quantitative research, a renewed emphasis on qualitative research reminds us that science does not consist solely of numbers. Before beginning any investigation for either research or practice, numerous qualitative matters must be considered, chief of which are cultural and scientific presuppositions. In particular in the use of measuring instruments and computers, certain presuppositions if violated may invalidate the results of an investigation. For either research or practice, depth knowledge of the subject matter of the field and understanding of the needs of subjects or clients are required. In dealing with individuals, in contrast to dealing with groups, the principle of

"redundant validity" is a means of approximating the truth about such individuals.

There is no one correct method of doing scientific research, but guidance is given for doing research by elucidating one proven method, "an eight-point coordinated experimental design." The main points of this design are these: (1) A statement of the theoretical and/or practical background of the investigation is given. (2) A statement of the question(s) to be asked of the data is expressed in such a way as to be testable. (3) Alternative hypotheses are stated. (4) Observable specifications of the design are identified and measures of control described. (5) Specifications respecting causal, limiting, correlational, and/or functional relations are identified. (6) What actually is to be done in the investigation—the operational specifications—are outlined. (7) Statistical specifications of the investigation are set forth in sufficient specificity to guide collection of data. (8) Critical analysis of existing research helps to clarify a design.

Under the fifth point, J. S. Mill's "canons" of experimental inquiry are discussed. Under the sixth point, S. S. Stevens' categorization of measurement scales—nominal, ordinal, interval, and ratio—is described. And under the seventh point, strong emphasis is placed on planning what statistics will be used and setting a level of significance for rejecting the null hypothesis before an investigation is undertaken. Use of group statistics does not preclude research on an N of 1.

Throughout the chapter attention is directed to the twin requirements of good methods of investigation: substantive knowledge of the field and logical usage of the instruments of research and practice.

ADDENDUM

One of the most helpful steps I and my students have utilized in the initial stages of designing studies is simply making a list of all possibly relevant variables which might be influential in the study. Sometimes the design has risen out of the list almost visibly. Going over the list enables an investigator to determine which are the independent and which the dependent variables, which can be eliminated because their differential impact would be negligible or because they are too far removed from the vicinity of the study, and which ones most likely are interdependent. Also, alternative hypotheses are suggested when one sees relations among variables that might not be seen otherwise. It has been most fruitful to make the list on paper or computer and check each item as its usefulness or lack thereof becomes clear.

At least the following variables should be listed, some of which will be seen to be irrelevant immediately in any particular investigation:

- Sex
- Chronological age
- Mental age, or general intellectual level, or specific factor levels (Verbal Comprehension, Perceptual Speed, etc.)
- Educational level or training
- Socioeconomic status: caste or class
- Culture or ethnic status
- Native or adoptive citizenship status
- Family status: ordinal position, marital status, etc.
- Physical condition: health, normal/abnormal body structure, etc.
- Geographical location: urban, rural, suburban, etc., section of country
- Psychological condition: diagnosed or undiagnosed
- Variables specific to investigation

REFERENCES

Abikoff, H., Ganeles, D., Reiter, G., Blum, C., Foley, C., & Klein, R. G. (1988). Cognitive training in academically deficient ADDH boys receiving stimulant medication. *Journal of Abnormal Child Psychology, 16*, 411–432.

Ackerson, L. (1931). *Children's behavior problems* (Vol. 1). Chicago: University of Chicago Press.

Ackerson, L. (1942). *Children's behavior problems* (Vol. 2). Chicago: University of Chicago Press.

Allport, G. W. (1937). *Personality: A psychological interpretation*. New York: Henry Holt.

Aman, M. G., Mitchell, E. A., & Turbott, S. H. (1987). The effects of essential fatty acid supplementation by Efamol in hyperactive children. *Journal of Abnormal Child Psychology, 15*, 75–90.

American Psychiatric Association Mental Hospital Service. (1952). *Diagnostic and statistical manual: Mental disorders*. Washington, DC: Author.

American Psychiatric Association. (1968). *Diagnostic and statistical manual of mental disorders* (2nd ed.). Washington, DC: Author.

American Psychiatric Association. (1980). *Diagnostic and statistical manual of mental disorders* (3rd ed.). Washington, DC: Author.

American Psychiatric Association. (1987). *Diagnostic and statistical manual of mental disorders* (3rd ed. rev.). Washington, DC: Author.

American Psychological Association. (1985). *Standards for educational and psychological testing*. Washington, DC: Author.

American Psychological Association. (1986). *Guidelines for computer-based tests and interpretations*. Washington, DC: Author.

Barlow, D. H., & Hersen, M. (1984). *Single case experimental designs: Strategies for studying behavior change* (2nd ed.). Elmsford, NY: Pergamon Press.

Bartholomew, D. J. (1987). *Latent variable models and factor analysis*. London: Charles Griffin.

Bentler, P. M. (1989). EQS: *Structural equations program manual*. Los Angeles: BMDP statistical software.

Bernstein, L. H. (with C. P. Garbin & G. K. Teng). (1988). *Applied multivariate analysis*. New York: Springer-Verlag.

Brown, C. W., & Ghiselli, E. E. (1955). *Scientific method in psychology*. New York: McGraw-Hill.

Butcher, J. N. (Ed.), (1987). Special series: Cultural factors in understanding and assessing psychopathology. *Journal of Consulting and Clinical Psychology, 55*, 459–512.

Campbell, D. T., & Stanley, J. C. (1966). *Experimental and quasi-experimental designs for research*. Chicago: Rand McNally.

Campbell, J. (1974). *The mythic image*. Princeton, NJ: Princeton University Press.

Carroll, J. B. (1961). The nature of the data, or how to choose a correlation coefficient. *Psychometrika, 26*, 347–372.

Cattell, R. B., & Dreger, R. M. (1974). Personality structure as revealed in questionnaire responses at the preschool level. *Child Development, 45*, 49–54.

Chassan, J. B. (1979). *Research design in clinical psychology and psychiatry* (2nd ed., rev. & enlarged). New York: Halstead.

Churchman, C. W. (1948). *Theory of experimental inference*. New York: Macmillan.

Clements, S. D. (1966, 1969). *Minimal brain dysfunction*. Washington, DC: U.S. Department of Health, Education, and Welfare.

Cohen, J. (1988). *Statistical power analysis for the behavioral sciences* (2nd ed.). Hillsdale, NJ: Lawrence Erlbaum Associates.

Cohen, M. R., & Nagel, E. (1934). *An introduction to logic and the scientific method*. New York: Harcourt Brace.

Conners, C. K. (1972). *Psychological assessment of children with minimal brain dysfunction.* Paper presented at the Conference on Minimal Brain Dysfunction sponsored by the New York Academy of Sciences, March 20–22, 1972.

Conners, C. K., & Wells, K. C. (1986). *Hyperkinetic children: A neuropsychosocial approach: Vol. 7. Developmental clinical psychology and psychiatry.* Beverly Hills, CA: Sage Publications.

Davis, C., & Cowles, C. (1989). Automated psychological testings: Method of administration, need for approval, and measures of anxiety. *Educational and Psychological Measurement, 49,* 311–320.

Diamond, J. M. (1966). Zoological classification system of a primitive people. *Science, 151,* 1102–1104.

Draper, N. R., & Smith, H. (1981). *Applied regression analysis* (2nd ed.). New York: John Wiley & Sons.

Dreger, R. M. (1953). Different I.Q.'s for the same individual associated with different intelligence tests. *Science, 118,* 594–595.

Dreger, R. M. (1962). *Fundamentals of personality.* Philadelphia: J. B. Lippincott.

Dreger, R. M. (1966). Objective personality tests and computer processing of personality test data. In I. A. Berg & L. A. Pennington (Eds.), *An introduction to clinical psychology* (3rd ed.). New York: Ronald.

Dreger, R. M. (1968). Aristotle, Linnaeus, and Lewin, or the place of classification in the evaluative-therapeutic process. *Journal of General Psychology, 78,* 41–59.

Dreger, R. M. (1981a). First-, second-, and third-order factors from the Children's Behavioral Classification Project instrument and an attempt at rapprochement. *Journal of Abnormal Psychology, 90,* 242–260.

Dreger, R. M. (1981b). The classification of children and their emotional problems. *Clinical Psychology Review, 1,* 415–430.

Dreger, R. M. (1985). Real and random P-technique analyses of the State-Trait Anxiety Inventory and their relation to R-technique analysis. *The Southern Psychologist, 2,* 17–28.

Dreger, R. M. (1990). A research-oriented private psychological clinic: The potentiality and the actuality. *Multivariate Experimental Clinical Research, 9,* 131–143.

Dreger, R. M., & Barnert, M. (1969). Measurement of the custom and conscience functions of the superego. *Journal of Social Psychology, 77,* 269–280.

Dreger, R. M. & Brabham, J. L. (1986). Two clinical validation studies of the state form and types of reliability of the trait form of the State-Trait Anxiety Inventory. *Multivariate Experimental Clinical Research, 8,* 195–209.

Dreger, R. M., & Dreger, G. E. (1962). *Proceedings of the Technical Assistance Project.* Behavioral Classification Project Report No. 1. Jacksonville, FL: Behavioral Classification Project, Jacksonville University.

Dreger, R. M., Lichtenstein, D., & Cattell, R. B. (1986). Factor structure and standardization of the Preschool Personality Questionnaire. *Journal of Social Behavior and Personality, 1,* 165–181.

Dreger, R. M., Lichtenstein, D., & Cattell, R. B. (1989). *Manual for the Preschool Personality Questionnaire.* Champaign, Illinois: Institute for Personality and Ability Testing.

Dreger, R. M., & Miller, K. S. (1968). Comparative studies of Negroes and whites in the United States: 1959–1965. *Psychological Bulletin Monograph Supplement, 70,* 1–58.

Duncan, J. A., & Dreger, R. M. (1978). A behavioral analysis of gifted children. *Journal of Genetic Psychology, 133,* 43–57.

Everitt, B. S. (1984). *An introduction to latent variable models.* London: Chapman and Hall.

Federer, W. T. (1955). *Experimental design: Theory and application.* New York: Macmillan.

Feibleman, J. K. (1972). *Scientific method: The hypothetico-experimental laboratory procedure of the physical sciences.* The Hague: Nijhoff.

Feinstein, A. R. (1988). Scientific standards in epidemiologic studies of the menace of daily life. *Science, 242,* 1257–1263.

Fisher, R. A. (1966). *The design of experiments* (8th ed.). London: Oliver and Boyd.

Fitch, J. M. (1976). *A behavioral analysis of brain damaged children and children with minimal brain dysfunction.* Unpublished master's thesis, Louisiana State University.

Fowler, R. D., Jr. (1969). Automated interpretation of personality test data. In J. W. Butcher (Ed.), *MMPI: Research developments and clinical applications.* New York: McGraw-Hill.

Gordon, M., Di Niro, D., & Mettelman, B. B. (1988). Effect upon outcome of nuances in selection criteria for ADHD/hyperactivity. *Psychological Reports, 62,* 539–544.

Groth-Marnat, G., & Schumaker, J. (1989). Computer-based psychological testing. *American Journal of Orthopsychiatry, 59,* 257–263.

Guilford, J. P. (1948). Some lessons from aviation psychology. *American Psychologist, 3,* 3–11.

Guttman, L. (1954). Some necessary conditions for common-factor analysis. *Psychometrika, 19,* 149–161.

Hagerman, R. J., & Falkenstein, A. R. (1987). An association between recurrent otitis media in infancy and later hyperactivity. Special issue: Developmental and behavior disorders. *Clinical Pediatrics, 26,* 253–257.

Hayduk, L. A. (1987). *Structural equation modeling with LISREL: Essentials and advances*. Baltimore: Johns Hopkins University Press.

Hollingshead, A. B., & Redlich, F. C. (1958). *Social class and mental illness*. New York: John Wiley & Sons.

Jöreskog, K. G., & Sörbom, D. (1989). *LISREL 7: A guide to the program and applications*. Chicago: SPSS, Inc.

Kaplan, A. (1964). *The conduct of scientific inquiry*. San Francisco: Chandler.

Kendall, M. G. (1947). *The advanced theory of statistics* (2nd ed.). London: Griffin.

Kennedy, J. J. (1978). *An introduction to the design and analysis of experiments in education and psychology*. Washington, DC: University Press of America.

Langeheine, R. (1988). New developments in latent class theory. In R. Langeheine & J. Rost (Eds.), *Latent trait and latent class models*. New York: Plenum Publishing.

Lewin, K. (1935). *A dynamic theory of personality*. New York: McGraw-Hill.

Lindquist, E. F. (1953). *Design and analysis of experiments in psychology and education*. Boston: Houghton Mifflin.

Matluck, J. H., & Mace, B. J. (1973). Language characteristics of Mexican-American children: Implications for assessment. *Journal of School Psychology, 11,* 365–386.

Mazzeo, J., & Harvey, A. L. (1988). The equivalence of scores from automated and conventional psychological tests: A review of the literature. *College Board Report No. 88–8. ETS RR No. 88–21*. New York: College Entrance Examination Board.

McDougall, W. B. (1926). The "Margery mediumship." *Psyche, 7,* 15–30.

McGee, R., Williams, S., Moffitt, T., & Anderson, J. (1989). A comparison of 13-year-old boys with attention deficit and/or reading disorder on neuropsychological measures. *Journal of Abnormal Child Psychology, 17,* 37–53.

Mead, M. (1949). *Male and female*. New York: William Morrow.

Meehl, P. E. (1945). The dynamics of "structured" personality tests. *Journal of Clinical Psychology, 1,* 296–303.

Meehl, P. E. (1959). Some ruminations on the validation of clinical procedures. *Canadian Journal of Psychology, 13,* 102–128.

Messick, S. (1988). Validity. In R. L. Linn (Ed.), *Educational measurement* (3rd ed.). New York: Macmillan.

Milgram, S. (1963). Behavioral study of obedience. *Journal of Abnormal and Social Psychology, 67,* 371–378.

Mill, J. S. (1963). *A system of logic, ratiocinative and inductive*. Collected Works, Vol. VII. Toronto: Toronto University Press. (Original work published 1843).

Moffitt, T. E., & Silva, P. A. (1988). Self-reported delinquency, neurological deficit, and history of attention deficit disorder. *Journal of Abnormal Child Psychology, 16,* 533–569.

Murray, H. A. (1938). *Explorations in personality, a clinical and experimental study of fifty men of college age by the workers at the Harvard Psychological Clinic*. New York: Oxford University Press.

Norman, C. (1988). Stanford inquiry casts doubt on 11 papers. *Science, 242,* 659–661.

Norton, D. W. (1952). An empirical investigation of the effects of non-normality and heterogeneity upon the *F*-test of analysis of variance. *Dissertation Abstracts, 12,* 713. (Elaborated in Lindquist, 1953).

Nunnally, J. C. (1978). *Psychometric theory* (2nd ed.). New York: McGraw-Hill.

Oakland, T., & Phillips, B. N. (1973). *Assessing minority group children: A special issue of the Journal of School Psychology*. New York: Behavioral Publications.

Polkinghorne, D. (1983). *Methodology for the human sciences: Methods of inquiry*. Albany, NY: State University of New York Press.

Price-Williams, D. R. (1962). Abstract and concrete modes of classification in Nigeria. *British Journal of Educational Psychology, 32,* 50–61.

Sakoda, J. M., Cohen, B. H., & Beall, G. (1954). Tests of significance for a series of statistical tests. *Psychological Bulletin, 51,* 172–175.

SAS-STAT guide for personal computers Version 6 ed. (1987). Cary, NC: SAS Institute, Inc.

Schrag, P., & Divoky, D. (1975). *The myth of the hyperactive child*. New York: Dell.

Searight, H. R. (1989). Psychology's neglected child. *Journal of Social Behavior and Personality, 4,* 1–16.

Sidman, M. (1960). *Tactics of scientific research*. New York: Basic Books.

Sisk, G. B. (1981). An empirical analysis of brain damage and minimal brain dysfunction in school age children. *Dissertation Abstracts International, 41,* 1527B.

Smeets, P. M., & Striefel, S. (1988). Time-delay discrimination training with impulsive children: Self-monitoring nonwait responses and the dimensions of prompts. *Journal of Abnormal Child Psychology, 16,* 693–706.

Snedecor, G. W., & Cochran, W. G. (1980). *Statistical methods* (7th ed.). Ames: Iowa State University Press.

Stevens, S. S. (1951). *Handbook of experimental psychology*. New York: John Wiley & Sons.

Taylor, S. J., & Bogdan, R. (1984). *Introduction to qualitative research methods* (2nd ed.). New York: John Wiley & Sons.

Terman, L. M., & Merrill, M. M. (1937). *Measuring intelligence*. Boston: Houghton Mifflin.

Tucker, L. R., Koopman, R. F., & Linn, R. L. (1969). Evaluation of factor analytic research procedures by means of simulated correlation matrices. *Psychometrika, 34,* 421–460.

Ullmann, R. K., & Sleator, E. K. (1985). Attention deficit disorder children with or without hyperactivity. *Clinical Pediatrics, 24,* 547–551.

Ullmann, R. K., Sleator, E. K., & Sprague, R. L. (1985). A change of mind: The Conners Abbreviated Rating Scales reconsidered. *Journal of Abnormal Child Psychology, 13,* 553–565.

Ullmann, R. K., Sleator, E. K., & Sprague, R. L. (1988). *Manual for the ADD-H Comprehensive Teacher's Rating Scale: ACTeRS*. Champaign, IL: Meritrech.

U.S. Department of Health Education, and Welfare Public Health Service. (1969). *Minimal brain dysfunction in children*. Public Health Service Publication No. 2015. Washington, DC: U.S. Government Printing Office.

van der Meere, J., & Sergeant, J. (1988). Focused attention in pervasively hyperactive children. *Journal of Abnormal Child Psychology, 16,* 627–639.

Wickman, E. K. (1928). *Children's behavior and teachers' attitudes*. New York: The Commonwealth Fund.

Wilde, J. G. S. (1978). Trait description and measurement by personality questionnaires. In R. B. Cattell & R. M. Dreger (Eds.), *Handbook of modern personality theory*. New York: Hemisphere/Halstead.

Wilkinson, B. (1951). A statistical consideration in psychological research. *Psychological Bulletin, 48,* 156–158.

Yates, A. (1987). *Multivariate exploratory data analysis: A perspective on exploratory factor analysis*. Albany: State University of New York Press.

CHAPTER 6

PSYCHOSTIMULANT EFFECTS ON LEARNING AND COGNITIVE FUNCTION

Mark D. Rapport
Kevin L. Kelly

Psychostimulants effects on learning and cognitive function in children with attention deficit hyperactivity disorder (ADHD) are of interest for both heuristic and practical reasons. From a heuristic standpoint, understanding these effects may help to elucidate the underlying causes or specific handicapping conditions associated with ADHD—especially those that are pathognomonic to this population of children. Distinct drug response may portend different pathophysiologies underlying certain aspects of behavior, provide evidence regarding the validity of the syndrome, and help to define biological correlates of cognitive and motor effects. Readers interested in these areas are referred to Rapoport and Zametkin (1988) for a review regarding the relevance and contribution of drug treatment to the scientific study of ADHD.

The clinical and therapeutic reasons for studying psychostimulant effects on learning and cognition in children with ADHD are multifaceted and intertwined. Two of the most salient reasons are the chronic academic difficulties encountered and the widespread use of psychostimulants to treat the disorder. Academic difficulties usually manifest themselves in classroom behavior that may be described as "consistently inconsistent," with most children experiencing difficulties in at least three areas related to learning and cognition: maintaining attention or staying "on-task," completing academic assignments *correctly* on a regular basis, and using memory as it relates to problem solving, skill acquisition, and organization of strategic planning. Others have described these difficulties in the context of information processing factors (Douglas, 1988) and have attempted to differentiate structural from functional deficits of attention (Sergeant, 1988). Regardless of the terminology used, the correspondences among the amount of time a child spends "on-task," academic achievement (Berliner & Rosenshine, 1977), and mastery of academic skills (Cronbach, 1977; Gagne, 1977) have been reasonably well documented. The implications of these findings for children with ADHD are that more than 50% of affected children are estimated to have co-existing learning or achievement deficiencies (McGee & Share, 1988), and significant numbers of them fail academically as evinced by poor scholastic grades and grade-level retentions (Weiss & Hechtman, 1986, pp. 35–49).

The widespread use and appeal of psychostimulants as a therapeutic modality has several bases. Although much of their popularity may be attributed to established clinical efficacy and safety, an equally important factor has been the paucity of alternative therapies available for children with ADHD. Attempts to enhance the ADHD child's cognitive performance and problem-solving abilities by means of traditional forms of psychotherapy have been unequivocally futile. More recently, cognitive-behavioral therapies, heralded as the "silver lining," have been proposed as alternative or adjunctive treatments to medication therapy. The results of controlled outcome investigations, however, have shown no generalized or lasting therapeutic benefit of cognitive training with ADHD children, either alone (Abikoff, 1985; 1987; Brown, Borden, Wynne, Schleser, & Clingerman, 1986) or in combination with psychostimulant treatment (Abikoff et al., 1988; Abikoff & Gittelman, 1985; Brown et al., 1986). The more streamlined forms of behavior therapy (contingency management), which provide immediate consequences of both a positive and negative nature (e.g., response cost), have produced more impressive results on a short-term basis (Rosen, O'Leary, Joyce, Conway, & Pfiffner, 1984; Rapport, Murphy, & Bailey, 1982). These procedures, however, evoke an unacceptably high cost to treatment-benefit ratio owing to their limited applicability within and across days, and overreliance on professional monitoring to maintain treatment integrity and effectiveness (Rapport, 1983; 1988; Werry & Wollersheim, 1989).

As a first-line defense among treatment regimens, the psychostimulants represent a mainstay therapeutic modality for ADHD and are currently used in an estimated 600,000 children annually (Barkley, 1981). Their basic psychopharmacological properties and clinical usefulness in treating children with ADHD are well established (Conners & Werry, 1979; Rapport, 1990; Shaywitz & Shaywitz, 1988; Solanto, 1984; Werry, 1982; 1988). Basic efficacy and comparative treatment studies have been conducted and described (Conners & Eisenberg, 1963; Conners & Taylor, 1980;

Gadow, 1985; Pelham, Schnedler, Bologna, & Contreras, 1980; Rapport, 1983; 1988; Werry, Sprague, Weiss, & Minde, 1970). Psychostimulant effects on children's cognitive function, learning, and social deportment have been examined in several landmark investigations (Barkley, 1977; Barkley & Cunningham, 1979; Conners, Eisenberg, & Sharp, 1964; Douglas, 1988; Kinsbourne & Swanson, 1979; Sprague, Barnes, & Werry, 1970; Sprague & Sleator, 1973; 1977; Weiss, Werry, Minde, Douglas, & Sykes, 1968). And dose-response curves for different behavioral domains have been hypothesized (Kinsbourne & Swanson, 1979; Sprague, 1972; Sprague & Sleator, 1973; 1975; 1976) and tested empirically in a limited number of studies (Douglas, Barr, O'Neill, & Britton, 1986; Pelham, Bender, Caddell, Booth, & Moorer, 1985; Rapport, DuPaul, Stoner, & Jones, 1986; Rapport, Jones et al., 1987; Rapport, Stoner, DuPaul, Birmingham, & Tucker, 1985; Rapport, Stoner et al., 1988; Solanto & Conners, 1982; Sprague & Sleator, 1973, 1976, 1977; Swanson, Kinsbourne, Roberts, & Zucker, 1978; Werry & Sprague, 1974). Despite the wealth of information available on psychostimulant effects in children, the field continues to be stimulated by several, long-held misinterpretations and controversies, especially with regard to their effects on learning and cognitive performance.

In this chapter, several topical issues relevant to the study of psychostimulant effects on children's learning and cognitive function are reviewed. In the first section, the effects and dose-response nature of psychostimulants on performance as measured by clinic and laboratory-based neurocognitive instruments, are examined. The relationships among children's performance on a select number of these measures and their academic efficiency and behavior in school are addressed in the second section. The section focuses on both hypothesized and tested dose-response potency profiles across behavioral domains, and external validity. In the third section, the time course of psychostimulant effects on cognitive processing is examined critically, and methodological issues relevant to measuring these effects, discussed. Implications for developing a psychopharmacological model of psychostimulant effects on cognitive function in children with ADHD is presented in the final section.

MEASURING COGNITIVE AND LEARNING PERFORMANCE IN THE LABORATORY

Issues regarding the cognitive abilities of children with ADHD, and whether and how their performance differs from children considered "normal" (Douglas, 1984; 1988) or who suffer from other psychopathological conditions of childhood (Werry, Elkind, & Reeves, 1987), have been examined critically in recent years. The viewpoint that ADHD involves a generalized self-regulatory defect that impairs performance across divergent modalities (visual, motoric, auditory, perceptual-motor) is supported by over a decade of work from the independent laboratories of Douglas (1988), Kinsbourne (1984), and Henker and Whalen (1989). Their work has largely involved examining the performance of children with ADHD under different test or environmental conditions, in contrast to that of normal control children, or in some cases, to children with learning disabilities (see Douglas, 1988, for a comprehensive review). Recently, large-scale investigations making similar comparisons of cognitive performance among children with ADHD and relevant clinical controls (e.g., children with diagnosed conduct, oppositional, and anxiety disorders), indicate that many of the differences found previously may not be specific to ADHD, but common to several psychopathological conditions of childhood (Schachar, Logan, Wachsmuth, & Chajczyk, 1988; Werry et al., 1987). Firm conclusions regarding the utility of cognitive measures for differentiating childhood disorders must be held in abeyance, however, owing to a number of methodological concerns. These include the limited range in types of tasks used, as well as the within-task parameters employed in these studies (Carlson & Rapport, 1989). Thus, the age-old adage, "awaits further empirical study," can be aptly applied to the implications of this line of investigation for child psychopathology and clinical diagnosis.

Parallel to these studies, corresponding to a resurgence of the cognitive sciences and growth in computerized instrumentation, has been an increased interest in studying drug effects on learning and cognition. This area of inquiry diverges from the differential diagnosis line of investigation discussed above, although the two obviously share commonalities in regard to their methodologies and implications for understanding biological substrates or localizing areas of dysfunction associated with psychopathology. Its primary concerns have involved (a) defining more precisely the way in which drugs affect cognitive processes and learning as they relate to the acquisition of specific academic skills and school performance, and (b) promoting understanding of specific aspects of higher brain functions such as attention, information processing, memory, and intelligence. Herculean efforts in the latter area have been described recently and involve simultaneous measurement or yoking of performance on various cognitive tasks to physiological measures such as the electroencephalogram (EEG) (Callaway, 1983; Conners et al., 1984; Klorman et al., 1988; Peloquin & Klorman, 1986), or the use of new technologies such as magnetic resonance imaging (MRI) (Gaffney, Muilenburg, Sieg, & Preston, 1989). The remainder of this section focuses on the former area, by providing an overview of the findings gleaned from clinic- and laboratory-based, neurocognitive and learning instruments used in pediatric psychopharmacological research.

Overview of Neurocognitive Instruments

It is unlikely that the plethora of tests, tasks, and paradigms used to assess psychostimulant effects on children's cognitive function will yield to facile attempts at classification. Some have described them by emphasizing basic features or within-task parameters of the instruments, such as whether the task is child- versus experimenter-paced (Sykes, Douglas, Weiss, & Minde, 1971). Others have attempted to categorize them according to whether they can be completed in a more or less automatic fashion as opposed to necessitating "effortfulness" on the subject's behalf (Ackerman, Anhalt, Holcomb, & Dykman, 1986; Borcherding et al., 1988; Hasher & Zachs, 1979). Differences between instruments requiring divergent and convergent thinking have been drawn (Solanto & Wender, 1989). And attempts to order them on a dimension of complexity or difficulty, from low level to high level, have been proposed (Swanson, 1985; Weiss & Laties, 1962).

Most necessitate the use of multiple modalities that make it difficult to differentiate effects associated with the visual, auditory, and perceptual fields. The use of instructions and the ability to delay gratification (Rapport, Tucker, DuPaul, Merlo, & Stoner, 1986-b), motivation related to task characteristics (Firestone & Douglas, 1975; Kinsbourne, 1984; Sykes, Douglas, & Morgenstern, 1973), ensuing consequences (Douglas, 1984; Douglas & Peters, 1979), the presence of an adult (Draeger, Prior, & Sanson, 1986), and an endless array of testing parameters (Douglas, 1988) have been shown to alter the ADHD child's performance under controlled conditions. More disheartening, even when the same task is being used by different investigators (e.g., the CPT or Continuous Performance Test), it rarely entails identical task parameters. We have clearly learned that even minimal changes can affect children's test performance in a rather dramatic fashion.

Nevertheless, an attempt is made here to review the various cognitive instruments used in assessing psychostimulant effects in children with ADHD. The instruments are listed in Table 6.1 according to several parameters described below, with a corresponding brief insertion regarding the original citation, subjects, and medication conditions. Before discussing the table, two points should be noted. First, the task of locating *all* references in this area was a formidable one, owing in part to the sheer number of investigations conducted, but even more so to the range of journals in which these articles were published. Thus, we acknowledge and regret a priori the inevitable omission of some studies and hope that interested readers will bring these to our attention for future updates of this work. We have also elected to include only those investigations meeting the following characteristics because of the voluminous literature in pediatric psychopharmacology: (a) a placebo control was used; (b) methylphenidate (MPH) specifically was used (this represented in excess of 98% of the studies located; we excluded those studies in which other psychostimulants such as dextroamphetamine were used, as we sought to avoid compounding an already difficult task by wrestling with whether different drugs were equivalent at different doses with respect to their effect on cognitive function); (c) the subjects were described as hyperactive or hyperkinetic, or met more formal diagnostic criteria for ADDH and ADHD (excluded were a few earlier studies that described subjects only as "emotionally disturbed," while studies using "normals" were included and are indicated in Table 6.1 for comparative purposes); (d) the subjects were within the pediatric age range; (e) a cognitive, performance, learning or neuropsychological measure, instrument, task, or paradigm was used (excluded were studies that examined short- or long-term academic achievement or performance data, effects on standard intellectual tests, or data concerning conduct or behavior ratings); and (f) a determination could be made regarding experimental outcome. Several studies depicted results graphically and referred to "significant changes" from one condition to another but failed to document these changes with statistical analyses. An alarming number of studies also reported significant interaction effects but failed to conduct (or report) appropriate simple effects and post hoc analyses. They were included in Table 6.1 nonetheless, but tagged with question marks to indicate that specific results could not be determined from the data presented.

MPH Effects on Cognitive Function: General

Table 6.1 shows that an impressive array of tasks has been used to study psychostimulant effects on cognitive function in children with ADHD. A total of 84 studies were located. Of these, 49 met the aforementioned inclusionary/exclusionary criteria. Tasks were categorized initially according to whether they necessitated "convergent" or "divergent" thinking skills (see top and bottom of Table 6.1, respectively). Studies were placed in the convergent category if they required a specific, predesignated response or correct answer(s), and under the divergent category if the child was instructed to generate multiple responses representing different conceptual classes (e.g., Solanto & Wender, 1989).

Tasks were categorized subsequently under general headings such as Paired Associate Learning, Matching-to-Sample, Picture Recognition Tasks and so on, depending on the specific measure employed.

(text continues on page 114)

Table 6.1. Task by Dose Effects of Methylphenidate on Children's Cognitive and Learning Performance

CONVERGENT TASKS	CITATION	P/L	P/M	P/H	L/H	INT.	SAMPLE & MEDICATION CONDITIONS
Stimulus Equivalence Learning:							
Stimulus Equivalence Task	Vyse et al., (1989)						26 ADDH Base, Placebo, 5, 10, 15 & 20 mg MPH
%Correct. Test		NS	M	H	NS		
Correct per Min. Test		L	M	H	H		
Correct-per-Min Acqu.		NS	NS	H	NS		
Latency Acquisition		NS	NS	NS	NS		
Latency to Choice, Test		NS	NS	NS	NS		
Trials Acquistion		NS	NS	NS	NS		
Matching to Sample:							
MFFT (Cairns 20 Item)	Douglas et al., (1988)						19 ADDH Placebo, .15, .3 & .6 mg/kg MPH
Latency		NS	M				
Errors		L	M				
MFFT (Kagan 20 Item)	Sebrechts et al., (1986)						12 ADD w/ & w/o Hyperactivity Placebo, .3 mg/kg E.O.D., .3 mg/kg B.I.D. & .6 mg/kg E.O.D. MPH
Latency		NS	NS				
Errors		NS	M				
MFFT (Kagan-like 16 Item)	Tannock et al., (1989)						12 ADDH Placebo, .3 & 1.0 mg/kg MPH
Latency: Drug × Number of Variants						SIG	
Drug with 6 Variants		L		H			
Drug with 8 Variants		NS		NS			
Errors: Drug × Number of Variants						NS	
Errors Main Effect		NS		NS			
MFFT (Kagan 12 Item)	Rapport et al., (1988)						22 ADDH Base, Placebo, 5, 10, 15 & 20 mg MPH
Latency		NS	NS	NS	H		
Errors		NS	M	H	H		
MFFT (Kagan 12 Item)	Rapport et al., (1988)						12 ADD w/ & w/o Hyperactivity Placebo, .3 mg/kg E.O.D., .3 mg/kg B.I.D. & .6 mg/kg E.O.D. MPH
Latency		NS	M				
Errors		NS	NS				
MFFT (Kagan 12 Item)	Barkley et al., (1989)						37 Aggressive & 37 Nonaggressive ADHD Placebo, .3 & .5 mg/kg MPH
Latency		NS	NS				
Errors		NS	NS				
MFFT (Kagan 12 Item)	Brown et al., (1984)						8 Hyperactive Placebo, .15, .3 & .6 mg/kg MPH
Latency		L	NS				
Errors		L	NS				
MFFT (Kagan 12 Item)	Rapport et al., (1985-a)						14 ADDH Placebo, 5, 10 & 15 MPH
Error Percentiles		NS	M				
Latency Percentiles		NS	NS				

Continued

Table 6.1. Continued

CONVERGENT TASKS	CITATION	P/L	P/M	P/H	L/H	INT.	SAMPLE & MEDICATION CONDITIONS
MFFT (Kagan 12 Item)	Brown et al., (1979)						11 Hyperactives Placebo, .3 & .10 mg/kg MPH
Latency		NS			NS		
Errors		L			NS		
MFFT (Kagan 12 Item)	Conners et al., (1980)						60 Hyperactive Placebo & Mean = .41 mg/kg MPH
Latency		NS-O	NS-O				
Errors		NS-O	NS-O				
MFFT (Kagan 12 Item)	Campbell et al., (1971)						22 Hyperactive Base, Placebo & "Optimal" (5 to 50 mg B.I.D.)MPH
Latency				O			
Errors				O			
Figure Matching Task (MFF-Type)	Flintoff et al., (1982)						32 Hyperactive Placebo & Mean = 13.12 mg MPH
Errors: Responder Type × Drug × Sides						SIG.	
Drug × Sides						SIG.	
Drug @ Favorable Responders 8 Sides			0				
Drug @ Favorable Responders 12 Sides			0				
Drug @ Favorable Responders 16 Sides			0				
Drug @ Non-favorable Responders 8 Sides			NS-0				
Drug @ Non-favorable Responders 12 Sides			0				
Drug @ Non-favorable Responders 16 Sides			NS-0				
MFFT (Kagan 12 Item)	Gittelman et al., (1983)						66 Reading Disorder "Not Hyperactive" Placebo & Mean = 1.9 mg/kg, (Range = 10 to 60 mg/day) MPH
Latency				O			
Errors			NS-O				
Paired Associate Learning:							
PAL Task (Animals & Zoo City Names)	Gan et al., (1982)						20 ADDH Base, Yoked Placebo, .3, .5 & 1.0 mg/kg MPH
Omission Errors		NS	NS	NS	NS		
Commission Errors		L	NS	NS	NS		
PAL Task (Chinese & English Words)	Kupietz et al., (1988)						47 ADDH & Developmental Reading Dis. Base → Placebo, .3, .5 & .7 mg/kg MPH Groups
Errors: Drug Group × Reading Therapy						SIG	
Drug @ 2 Weeks (Before Therapy)		NS	NS	NS	NS		
Drug @ 27 Weeks (After Therapy)		NS	NS	H	H		
PAL Task (Animals & Zoo Numbers)[1]	Rapport et al., (1989)						42 ADHD Base, Placebo, 5, 10, 15 & 20 mg MPH
Trials to Criterion: No Exposure		L	M	H	NS		
Trials to Criterion: Partial Exposure		L	M	H	NS		
Trials to Criterion: Full Exposure		NS	NS	NS	NS		

102

Measure	L	M	H	O	Sig.	Citation	Sample
Percent Correct: No Exposure	NS	NS	NS				
Percent Correct: Partial Exposure	NS	NS	H				
Percent Correct: Full Exposure	NS	NS	NS				
PAL Task (Word Pairs) Errors	NS	NS				Douglas et al., (1989)	19ADDH Placebo, .15, .3 & .6 mg/kg MPH
PAL Task (Animals & N. S. E. W. Zoo) Errors	NS	NS				Sebrechts et al., (1986)	12 ADD w/ & w/o Hyperactivity Placebo, .3 mg/kg E.O.D., .3 mg/kg B.I.D. & .6 mg/kg E.O.D. MPH
PAL Task (Arbitrary Word Pairs) Number Correct	L					Douglas et al., (1986)	16 ADDH Placebo & .3 mg/kg MPH
PAL Task (Pictures and Numbers) Errors to Criterion	L					Stephens et al., (1984)	36 ADDH Placebo, 1.9 mg/kg Pemoline & .3 mg/kg MPH
PAL Task (Animals & N. S. E. W. Zoo) Errors: Drug × Order					NS	Dalby et al., (1989)	30 Hyperactive Favorable Responder Placebo & "Known Effective" Dose Mean = 11.8 mg MPH
Errors Main Effect					SIG.		
Presentation Rate Selection: Drug × Order				O	SIG.		
MPH, Placebo Order				NS-O			
Placebo, MPH Order				O			
Completed Trials: Drug × Order				NS-O	SIG.		
MPH, Placebo Order				O			
Placebo, MPH Order							
PAL Task (Animals & Zoo Numbers) Percent Correct Responses				O	???	Rapport et al., (1985-b)	12 ADDH Placebo, 5, 10 & 15 mg MPH
PAL Task (Animals & Zoos) Errors: Drug × Responder Status					???	Swanson et al., (1983)	11 Hyperactive Placebo & Optimal Dose (Range = 5 to 15 mg) MPH
Drug @ Favorable Responders				O			
Drug @ Non-favorable Responders				O			
PAL Task (Animals & Zoos)					SIG.	Swanson et al., (1978)	53 Mixed Hyperactive, Overanxious & Un-soc.-Agg. Base, Placebo & "Optimal Dose" MPH
Drug × Order × Resp. Stat.					???		
Drug × Order @ Each Resp. Stat.		???			???		
No Follow-up Analyses							
Drug × Reps. Stat @ Each Order		???			???		
No Follow-up Analyses							
PAL Task (Animals & N. S. E. W. Zoo) Drug × Order × Rate					SIG.	Dalby et al., (1977)	28 Hyperactive Favorable Responder Placebo & "Known Effective" Dose Mean = 13.8 mg MPH
No Follow-up Analyses		???			???		
Drug × Rate @ Each Order		???			???		
No Follow-up Analyses							

Continued

Table 6.1. Continued

CONVERGENT TASKS	CITATION	MEDICATION CONTRASTS					SAMPLE & MEDICATION CONDITIONS
		P/L	P/M	P/H	L/H	INT.	
Drug × Hours After Medication × Rate						SIG.	
Drug × Hours After Medication @ Each Rate			???			???	
No Follow-up Analyses							
Drug × Rate @ Each Hour After Medication			???			???	
No Follow-up Analyses							
Matching-of-Pairs (PAL-Like)	Thurston et al., (1979)						54 Hyperactive Distractible Placebo & Mean = 10 mg (Range = 5 to 20 mg)MPH
Task Scores			NS-O				
Proportions			O				
Efficiency			O				
PAL Task (Animals & Zoos) Percent Correct	Taylor et al., (1987)		NS-O				39 Disruptive Base, Placebo & "Optimal Dose" (Range = 5 to 30 mg) MPH
PAL Task (Digit & Symbol) Errors	Conners et al., (1964)						81 Deprived or Emotionally Disturbed Base → Placebo & 60 mg MPH Groups
PAL Task (?) Trials	Gittelman et al., (1983)			NS-O			66 Reading Disorder "Not Hyperactive" Placebo & Mean = 1.9 mg/kg, (Range = 10 to 60 mg/day) MPH
Spelling Tasks:							
Nonsense-word Spelling Errors: Drug × Phase	Stephens et al. (1984)					NS	36 ADDH Placebo, Pemoline 1.9 mg/kg & .3 mg/kg MPH
Drug Main Effect		L					
Nonsense-Word Spelling Errors: Drug × Reinforcement × Order	Pelham et al., (1986)					NS SIG.	25 ADDH, 4 ADD & 1 Other Placebo & .3 mg/kg MPH
Drug × Order		L					
P → MPH Order		NS					
MPH → P Order							
Drug × Reinf						NS	
Picture Recognition Tasks:							
Picture Recognition Task	Sprague et al. (1977)						20 Hyperactive Placebo, .3 & 1.0 mg/kg MPH
Accuracy: Drug × Matrix Size						SIG.	
Drug @ Small Matrix				NS	NS		
Drug @ Medium Matrix				NS	NS		
Drug @ Large Matrix			???	???	???		
Latency: Drug & Matrix Size						SIG.	
Drug @ Small Matrix				NS	NS		
Drug @ Medium Matrix				???	???		
Drug @ Large Matrix				NS	NS		

Measure	Reference							Sample / Dose
S. T. Memory Task (Picture Recognition)	Kupietz et al., (1988)							47 ADDH & Developmental Reading Dis. Base → Placebo, .3 .5 & .7 mg/kg MPH Groups
Latency to Correct		NS		NS	NS		SIG.	
Number Correct: Drug × Time								
Drug at Time-1		NS	NS	H	NS	NS		
Drug at Time-2		NS	NS	NS	NS	NS		
Sternberg Type Task	Sprague et al., (1970)						NS	12 "Emotionally Disturbed" Antisoc., Distrct., Hyp. Placebo, Thioridizine, .25 & .35 mg/kg MPH
Accuracy: Drug × Dose × Number of Stimuli		L						
Main Effect for Drug		L						
Reaction Time								
S. T. Recognition Memory (Picture Recognition)	Werry et al. (1975)							24 Hyperactive
Accuracy: Drug × Difficulty		???					SIG.	Placebo & .3 mg/kg MPH
No Follow-up Analyses								
Speed: Drug × Difficulty		NS					NS	
Drug Main Effect								
Latency: Drug × Difficulty		NS					NS	
Drug Main Effect								
S. T. Recognition Memory (Picture Recognition)	Werry et al. (1980)							30 Hyperactive
Speed		NS						Placebo & .4 mg/kg MPH
Accuracy		NS						
Picture Recognition Task	Sprague (1972)							9 Hyperactive Base, Placebo & .5 mg/kg MPH
Drug Differences		NS		NS				
Picture Recognition	Sprague et al., (1976)							23 Hyperactive Placebo, .1, .3 & .7 mg/kg MPH
Percent Correct		???		???				
Category Verification (Words and Pictures)	Reid et al., (1984)							12 Hyperactive Placebo & Mean = .44 mg/kg (Range = .3 to .87 mg/kg) MPH
Response Time		NS-O		NS-O				
Sternberg Memory Scanning Task (1966)	Peloquin et al., (1986)						SIG.	18 "Normals" (i.e., Not ADD) Placebo & .3 mg/kg MPH
Errors: Drug × Set Size								
Drug at Small Set		NS						
Drug at Large Set		L						
Reactiontime		NS						
Picture Recognition (Accuracy & Latency)	Sprague et al., (1971)						SIG.	16 "Emotionally Disturbed" Base, Placebo, .1, .2, .3 & .4 mg/kg MPH
Drug Main Effect (4 Low Levels)		L						
No Follow-up Analyses		???						

Continued

Table 6.1. Continued

CONVERGENT TASKS	CITATION	MEDICATION CONTRASTS					SAMPLE & MEDICATION CONDITIONS
		P/L	P/M	P/H	L/H	INT.	
Long/Short-term Recall Tasks							
Selective Reminding Rest (WordList Recall)	Evans et al., (1986)						14 ADD
Sum Recall: First Trial		NS	NS				Base, Placebo, .2, .4 & .6 mg/kg MPH
Delay Trial		NS	M				
Slope		NS	NS				
Word Sum		NS	NS				
Trials To Learn: 5 Words		NS	NS				
6 Words		NS	NS				
7 Words		NS	NS				
8 Words		NS	NS				
9 Words		NS	NS				
Long-term Storage:							
First Trial		NS	NS				
Delay Trial		NS	NS				
Slope		NS	M				
Word Sum		NS	M				
Trials to Learn: 5 Words		NS	M				
6 Words		NS	NS				
7 Words		NS	M				
8 Words		NS	M				
9 Words		NS	NS				
Long-term Recall							
First Trial		NS	NS				
Delay Trial		NS	NS				
Slope		NS	M				
Word Sum		NS	M				
Trials to Learn: 5 Words		NS	M				
6 Words		NS	NS				
7 Words		NS	M				
8 Words		NS	NS				
9 Words		NS	NS				
Consistent Long-term Retrieval							
First Trial		NS	NS				
Delay Trial		NS	M				
Slope		NS	M				
Word Sum		NS	M				
Trials to Learn: 5 Words		NS	NS				
6 Words		NS	M				
7 Words		NS	M				
8 Words		NS	NS				
9 Words		NS	NS				

Task / Measure	Result			Citation	Sample / Drug
Selective Reminding Task (Word List Recall)				Barkley et al., (1989)	37 Aggressive & 37 Nonaggressive ADHD Placebo, .3 & .5 mg/kg MPH
Recall	L				
Long-Term Storage	NS				
Consistent Long-Term Retrieval	L				
Word Span (Word List Recall)				Reid et al., (1984)	12 Hyperactive Placebo & Mean = .44 mg/kg (Range = .3 to .87 mg/kg)MPH
Number of Words in Longest List	NS-O				
Free Recall of Stimulus Cards (Animals & Objects)				Thurston et al., (1979)	54 Hyperactive Distractible
Number Recalled: Drug × Responder ×			NS		
Type of Recall					
Drug × Type of Recall					Placebo & Mean = 10 mg (Range = 5 to 20 mg/day) MPH
Central Type		O			
Incidental Type		P	SIG.		
Digit Span				Sebrechts et al., (1986)	12 ADD w & w/o Hyperactivity Placebo, .3 mg/kg E.O.D., .3 mg/kg B.I.D. & .6 mg/kg E.O.D. MPH
No Statistics Reported	???	???			
Sentence Recall				Sebrechts et al., (1986)	12 ADD w & w/o Hyperactivity Placebo, .3 mg/kg E.O.D., .3 mg/kg B.I.D. & .6 mg/kg E.O.D. MPH
Recall Score	???	???			
Visual Sequential Memory Test				Gittelman et al., (1983)	66 Reading Disorder "Not Hyperactive" Placebo & Mean = 1.9 mg/kg (Range = 10 to 60 mg/day) MPH
Drug Group Differences			O		

Visual/Perceptual Acuity Tasks:

Task / Measure	Result			Citation	Sample / Drug
Self-ordered Pointing Task (Touch All Pics. Once)				Douglas et al., (1988)	19 ADDH
Errors (Representational)	NS				
Total Time (Representational)	NS				
Errors (Abstract)	NS				Placebo, .15, .3 & .6 mg/kg MPH
Total Time (Abstract)	NS				
Children's Embedded Figures Test (Karp, 1963)				Campbell et al., (1971)	22 Hyperactive
Drug Condition			NS-O		Base, Placebo & "Optimal" (Range = 5 to 50 mg B.I.D.) MPH
Children's Embedded Figures Test				Gittelman et al., (1983)	66 Reading Disorder "Not Hyperactive" Placebo & Mean = 1.9 mg/kg (Range = 10 to 60 mg) MPH
Group Differences			NS-O		

Stimulus Identification Tasks w/And w/o Distraction:

Task / Measure	Result		Citation	Sample / Drug
Selective Attention (Attention with Distraction)			Sebrechts et al. (1986)	12 ADD w & w/o Hyperactivity
Drug Differences	NS	NS		Placebo, .3 mg/kg E.O.D., .6 mg/kg E.O.D. MPH

Continued

Table 6.1. Continued

CONVERGENT TASKS	CITATION	P/L	P/M	P/H	L/H	INT.	SAMPLE & MEDICATION CONDITIONS
Posner Letter Matching: (AA, Aa Bc etc.) Errors: Drug × Order	Reid et al., (1984)					NS	12 Hyperactive Placebo & Mean = .44 mg/kg (Range = .3 to .87 mg/kg) MPH
Drug Main Effect			O				
Item Identification (Picture Naming) Mean Naming Times	Reid et al., (1984)		NS-O				12 Hyperactive Placebo & Mean = .44 mg/kg (Range = .3 to .87 mg/kg) MPH
Color Distraction Test Distractibility	Campbell et al., (1971)			NS-O			22 Hyperactive Base, Placebo & "Optimal" (Range = 5 to 50 mg B.I.D.) MPH
Interference				NS-O			
Complete Commission Errors				O			
Partial Commission Errors				O			
Omission Errors				NS-O			
Naming Animals Test Drug Conditions	Campbell et al., (1971)			NS-O			22-Hyperactive Base, Placebo & "Optimal" (Range = 5 to 50 mg B.I.D.) MPH
Speed of Color Naming Drug Conditions	Cambell et al., (1971)			NS-O			22 Hyperactive Base, Placebo & "Optimal" (Range = 5 to 50 mg, B.I.D.) MPH
Selective Listening (Selective Digit Span) Group Differences	Taylor et al., (1987)		NS-O				39 "Disruptive Boys" Base, Placebo & "Optimal Dose" (Range = 5 to 30 mg) MPH
Perceptual/Motor Acuity Tasks:							
Maze Tracking on "Etch-A-Sketch" Errors	Douglas et al., (1988)	L	M				19 ADDH Placebo, .15, .3 & .6 mg/kg MPH
Total Time		NS	NS				
Error Variability		???	???				
Motor Performance Task (???) Drug Differences	Sprague (1972)		NS				9 Hyperactive Base, Placebo & .5 mg/kg MPH
Rotary Pursuit Test Drug Condition	Sprague (1972)		NS				9 Hyperactive Base, Pladebo & .5 mg/kg MPH
Porteus Maze (Porteus, 1947) Age Score	Taylor et al., (1987)			NS-O			39 "Disruptive Boys" Base, Placebo & "Optimal Dose" (Range = 5 to 30 mg) MPH
Qualitative Score				NS-O			
Porteus Mazes IQ Score	Gittelman et al., (1983)			O			66 Reading Disorder "Not Hyperactive" Placebo & Mean = 1.9 mg/kg (Range = 10 to 60 mg/day) MPH
Qualitative Score		NS-O					

Stimulus/Reaction Time Tasks: (section continued)

Measure	Study				Sample
Visual Motor Integration		NS-O			
Raven's Matrices — Percentile Score	Gittelman et al., (1983)	O			66 Reading Disorder "Not Hyperactive" Placebo & Mean = 1.9 mg/kg (Range = 10 to 60 mg/day) MPH
Draw A Person — IQ Score	Gittelman et al., (1983)	NS-O			66 Reading Disorder "Not Hyperactive" Placebo & Mean = 1.9 mg/kg (Range = 10 to 60 mg/day) MPH
Purdue Pegboard — Right Hand	Gittelman et al., (1983)	NS-O			66 Reading Disorder "Not Hyperactive" Placebo & Mean = 1.9 mg/kg (Range = 10 to 60 mg/day) MPH
Left Hand		NS-O			
Both Hand		NS-O			
Left, Right & Both		NS-O			
Assembly		NS-O			
Stimulus/Reaction Time Tasks:					
Stopping Task (Go, No-Go Type)	Tannock et al., (1989)				12 ADDH Placebo, .3 & 1.0 mg/kg MPH
Inhibition Function: Drug × Signal Delay		???	???	SIG.	
Drug @ Each Signal Delay		NS	H		
Reaction Time: Signal Trials		L	???		
Non-Signal		L	H		
Variability		NS	NS		
Commission Errors on Discrimination					
Reaction Time, Delayed (w/Warn Signal)	Douglas et al., (1988)				19 ADDH Placebo, .15, .3 & .6 mg/kg MPH
Mean RT		L	M	H	
Variability		???	???	NS	
Anticipatory Response		L	M	NS	
Serial Reaction Time	Sykes et al., (1972)				23 Hyperactive Base, Placebo & "Optimal Dose" MPH
Correct Responses		O			
Incorrect Responses		O			
Choice Reaction time	Sykes et al., (1972)				23 Hyperactive Basde, Placebo & "Optimal Dose" MPH
Latencies		O			
Reaction Time @ 4 Difficulties	Reid et al., (1984)				12 Hyperactive Placebo & Mean = .44 mg/kg (Range = .3 to .87 mg/k)MPH
Reaction Time: Drug × Difficulty				NS	
Drug Main Effect		O			
Drug × Trial				SIG.	
Drug @ First Half		NS-O			
Drug @ Second Half		O			
Reaction Time Task	Solanto, et al. (1982)				10 Hyperactive Placebo & Mean of .3, .6 & 1.0 mg/kg MPH Scores
Latency		O			
Commission Errors		NS-O			

Continued

Table 6.1. Continued

CONVERGENT TASKS	CITATION	P/L	P/M	P/H	L/H	INT.	SAMPLE & MEDICATION CONDITIONS
Reaction Time (Auditory/Visual) Variability: Drug × Order	Cohen et al., (1971)					SIG.	22 Hyperactive Placebo & Titration from 5 to 100 mg/day MPH
Drug @ Each Order				???			
Redundant Motor Responses				O			
Latency				O			
Vigilance Tasks:							
CPT (Double Version)	Klorman et al., (1989)						24 ADHD Non-Agg., 19 ADHD AGG., 20 "Not Criterion" Base, Placebo & .3 mg/kg MPH
Accuracy		L					
Speed		L					
Misses		NS					
Reaction Time		NS					
CPT (Gordon 1-9 Version) Omission Errors	Rapport et al., (1987)	L	M	NS	NS		42 ADDH Placebo, 5, 10, 15 & 20 mg MPH
CPT (1-9 & 2-5 Versions) Omission Errors: Drug × Group	Barkley et al., (1989)					NS	37 Aggressive & 37 Nonaggressive ADHD Placebo, .3 & .5 mg/kg MPH
Drug Main Effect		L	M				
Commission Errors: Drug × Group						SIG.	
Drug (Non-Aggressives)		L	M				
Drug (Aggressives)		NS	NS				
CPT (Gordon 1-9 Version) Omission Errors	Rapport et al., (1986-a)	L	M				14 ADDH Placebo, 5, 10 & 15 mg MPH
Commission Errors		NS	M				
CPT (AX Version)	Kupietz et al., (1976)						20 Hyperactive and/or Aggressive Beh. Problems Base, Placebo, Elavil & Median = 40 mg (Range = 20 to 60 mg)
Omission Errors				O			
Commission Errors				O			
CPT (Type (3) × I.S.I. (2)) Absolute Score: Drug × I.S.I. × Version	Sykes et al., (1971)					???	40 Hyperactive Base & Placebo -or- "Optimal Dose" mode = 30 mg MPH
Drug × I.S.I. @ × Version				O			
Drug @ × Version						NS	
Drug × I.S.I. @ AX Version						NS	
Drug @ AX Version				NS-O			
Drug × I.S.I. @ Form Version						NS	
Drug @ Form Version				O			
Drug × Version @ Each I.S.I.						???	
No Follow-up Analyses				???			

Measure / Analysis			Study	Sample
Error: Drug × I.S.I. × Version		???		
Drug × I.S.I. @ × Version	???			
Drug @ × Version		SIG.		
Drug × I.S.I. @ AX Version	???			
Drug @ AX Version		NS		
Drug × I.S.I. @ Form Version	???			
Drug @ Form Version		NS		
Drug × Version @ Each I.S.I.	???	???		
No Follow-up Analyses				
CPT (× Version)			Klorman et al., (1988-b)	18 ADD; Placebo & .3 mg/kg MPH
Omission Errors	L			
Commission Errors	NS			
Reaction Time	L			
CPT (× Version)			Klorman et al., (1989)	24 ADHD Non-Agg., 19 ADHD AGG., 20 "Not Criterion"; Base, Placebo & .3 mg/kg MPH
Accuracy	L			
Speed	L			
Misses	NS			
Reaction Time	NS			
CPT (× Version)			Werry et al. (1980)	30 Hyperactive; Placebo & .4 mg/kg MPH
Omission Errors	L			
Commission Errors	L			
Latency	L			
CPT (× Version)			Werry et al (1975)	24 Hyperactive; Placebo & .3 mg/kg MPH
Omission Errors	L			
Commission Errors	L			
Correct Response Latency	NS			
Correct Response Speed	NS			
CPT (Pick the 7's out of 2 → 8)			Swanson et al., (1979)	36 DSM II Hyperactive; Placebo & "Optimal" -or- 10 mg MPH
Errors: Drug × Responder Type	O	SIG.		
Drug @ Favorable Resp.	NS-O			
Drug @ Non-favorable Resp.	NS-O			
Reaction Time: Drug × Responder Type		NS		
Drug Main Effect				

Continued

111

Table 6.1. Continued

CONVERGENT TASKS	CITATION	MEDICATION CONTRASTS					SAMPLE & MEDICATION CONDITIONS
		P/L	P/M	P/H	L/H	INT.	
CPT (× Versions (Auditory & Visual)) Correct Responses: Drug × Type (a/v) × Block	Sykes et al., (1972)					???	23 Hyperactive Base, Placebo & "Optimal Dose" MPH
Block No Follow-up Analyses Drug × Type @ Each Block						???	
No Follow-up Analyses Drug × Type			???			SIG.	
No Follow-up Analyses Drug × Block @ Each Type			???			???	
No Follow-up Analyses Drug × Block			???			SIG.	
No Follow-up Analyses Drug Main Effect			???				
Errors: Drug Main Effect Visual Version: Omission Errors			O				
Commission Errors			O				
Vigilance Task (3 Stim. CPT-Like) No Statistics Reported	Sebrechts et al., (1986)	???	???				12 ADD w & w/o Hyperactivity Placebo, .3 mg/kg E.O.D., .3 mg/kg B.I.D. & .6 mg/kg E.O.D. MPH
CPT (?) Omission Errors	Conners et al., (1980)	NS-O					60 Hyperactive Placebo & Mean = .41 mg/kg MPH
Commission Errors		NS-O					
CPT (?) All Dependent Variables	Sprague (1972)		NS				9 Hyperactive Base, Placebo & .5 mg/kg MPH
CPT (Double Version) d'	Peloquin et al., (1986)	L					18 "Normals" (i.e., Not ADD) Placebo & .3 mg/kg MPH
Misses		L					
False Alarms		NS					
Reaction Time		L					
Reaction Time Variability		L					
CPT (Double Version) Percent Correct	Taylor et al., (1987)		O				39 "Disruptive Boys" Base, Placebo & "Optimal Dose" (Range = 5 to 30 mg) MPH
Percent False Responses			NS-O				
CPT (?) Omission Errors	Gittelman et al., (1983)			O			66 Reading Disorder "Not Hyperactive" Placebo & Mean = 1.9 mg/kg, (Range = 10 to 60 mg/day) MPH
Commission Errors				O			

112

Divergent Tasks

Variable	Reference	MC1	MC2	MC3	SIG.	Sample & Medication Conditions
Cognitive Decision Task (Word Associations)						
Reaction Time: Drug × Decision Type × Visual Field	Malone et al., (1988)				SIG.	24 ADD; Placebo & Mean = 10.8 mg (Range = 5 to 20 mg) MPH
No Follow-up Analyses						
Drug × Decision Type @ Each Visual Field			???			
No Follow-Up Analyses						
Drug × Visual Field @ Each Decision Type			???			
No Follow-up Analyses						
General Statement Only		O	???			
Instances Test (Word Instances w/in a Class)	Solanto et al., (1989)					19 ADDH; Base, Placebo, .3, .6 & 1.0 mg/kg MPH (ADDH Group Only)
Instances Score		???	???	???		
Alternate Uses Test (Uses of Sample Items)	Solanto et al., (1989)					19 ADDH; Base, Placebo, .3, .6 & 1.0 mg/kg MPH (ADDH Group Only)
Classes		???	???	???		
Functional Responses		???	???	???		
Total Responses		???	???	???		
Unintended Items		???	???	???		
Word Association (Food & Animal Categories)	Sebrechts et al., (1986)					12 ADD w/ & w/o Hyperactivity; Placebo, .3 mg/kg E.O.D., .3 mg/kg B.I.D. & .6 mg/kg E.O.D. MPH
No Statistics Reported			???	???		
Word Discovery Task (Douglas, 1986)	Douglas et al., (1986)					16 ADDH; Placebo & .3 mg/kg MPH
Number of Words		NS				
Total Time Spent		NS				
Word Discovery Task (Douglas, 1986)	Douglas et al., (1988)					19 ADDH; Placebo, .15, .3 & .6 mg/kg MPH
Number of Words		L	M			
Total Time Spent		NS	NS			

Note 1: P = placebo, L = low dose range (0–10 mg or < 0.50 mg/kg), M = mid dose range (11–19 mg or 0.50 – 0.74 mg/kg), H = high dose range (> 19 mg or > 0.74 mg/kg); P/L = placebo/low dose range contrast; P/M = placebo/mid dose range contrast; P/H = placebo/high dose range contrast; L/H = low/high dose range contrast; L/M = low/mid dose range contrast; INT = interaction effect.

Note 2: Symbols shown under "Medication Contrasts" heading indicate that a contrast was performed between the dose conditions listed in the heading, and that the dose range specified in the body of the table was found to be significantly superior. "O" indicates that the study included children on different doses of medication (believed to represent their "optimal" medication level) and that the mean group dose range reported was within the range listed under the contrast heading. "NS" indicates that no significant differences were found between the contrasting dose conditions. "NS-O" indicates that no significant differences were found between an "optimal" mean group dose range and the contrasting dose range specified. Question marks (???) under the medication contrast heading indicate that either appropriate analyses were not reported, or were uninterpretable in the study.

Note 3: Dependent variables examined for a particular task are specified under each task listing.

Note 4: Tasks conducted with non-ADHD children or normals are shown under regular task category headings (see main text for explanation), but contained within a boxed border to highlight differences between subject groupings.

This sorting was done to facilitate between-dose comparisons both within and across tasks. Multiple listings of a particular study in the table thus correspond with the number of different instruments or tasks employed in that particular study. Task headings were then ordered in a hierarchical fashion based on the degree of complexity associated with the task, both within and between task categories. Determination of complexity was based on two factors: (a) descriptions provided by Weiss and Laties (1962), and (b) relation of the task to traditionally defined parameters characteristic of "fast" or "slow" human information processing research (Mulder, 1983). Tasks used in fast processing research typically are performed very quickly (i.e., on the order of milliseconds), without introspection, and rely on automatic or nearly automatic information processing (e.g., reaction time paradigms, overlearned motor responses). Those used in slow processing research, in contrast, are usually performed over an extended time course (minutes to hours), are accessible by introspection (i.e., rules or plans, characteristic of how the task was approached or solved, can usually be discerned), necessitate flexibility, and demand greater attention. A strictly "automatic" versus "effortful" dimension for categorizing tasks was not used here, as nearly all tasks necessitated serial rather than parallel processing (i.e., a child could not complete the task successfully while attending simultaneously to other tasks).

The ordering *within* a given task category was based on two criteria: complexity and range of doses administered. Tasks were ordered initially from most to least difficult (if such a determination could be made), then arranged in a hierarchical fashion according to whether multiple or single doses were administered. For example, under the heading, Vigilance Tasks, the double letter CPT (i.e., respond to each letter that immediately repeats itself) was ranked first, followed by the A–X or 1–9 numeral versions (e.g., respond to each X that is preceded immediately by an A), then by the single letter or numeral versions (e.g., respond to each X presented).

Several points are worth noting in the table. For example, of the 81 individual task listings for ADHD children, 57% of them were examined under single dose conditions, with 36% using an "optimal" or "known effective" dose as determined by task performance (usually on the same task being examined) or by clinical titration. The other 21% used a lone set dose (either fixed mg or mg/kg). Children's performance on the remaining 43% of total task listings were examined under two (32%) or three (11%) active dose conditions, respectively. Conclusions regarding *dose-response* relationships on cognitive function were severely limited as a result, and the belief that such studies are no longer necessary is grossly in error.

If one disregards task difficulty for the moment, a significant *overall* main effect for drug was found in 68% of the tasks examined (i.e., at least one dependent variable was significantly affected by active drug). No significant overall dose effect was reported in 23% of the tasks, and the findings in the remaining 9% were uninterpretable or not reported.

Of the 46 (57%) tasks in which cognitive performance was examined under a single dose, 62% and 59% of those using an "optimal" and "fixed" dose, respectively, reported a significant overall medication effect.

Of the 35 tasks in which two or more doses were administered, 24 or 69% reported significant *overall* medication effects. Low/high dose contrasts were performed in 37% of the studies in which two or more doses were administered (see Table 6.1). Of the low/high comparisons, 38% revealed significant *between-dose* differences, 100% of which favored the high dose condition. These findings may be artificially deflated, however, owing to the small number of tasks comparing low/high dose conditions relative to the total sample of tasks examined in the table (i.e., 16%). For example, significant overall drug effects were found on 100% of the tasks (whose findings were interpretable) in which cognitive performance was examined under three separate conditions as defined in the table. Of these, 43% reported a significant between-dose effect, 100% of which favored the high dose condition.

Note that the above descriptive statistics were based on the total number of "tasks," not "studies" in which psychostimulant effects were examined. Comparisons based on total studies produced similar results with one exception. The percentage of significant overall does effects increased from 68% (based on total tasks) to 95% (based on total studies). The finding provides strong support for the belief that cognitive function in children with ADHD is enhanced significantly as a function of MPH treatment. Caution is urged when interpreting this statistic, however, as simple box score tallies of published findings do not take into account the number of unpublished studies in which nonsignificant results are obtained.

Most tasks (94%) listed in Table 6.1 fell into the convergent category. MPH effects on tasks falling into the divergent category were largely uninterpretable, because of a failure to report simple effects and post hoc analyses. As a result, conclusions could not be drawn regarding the way in which MPH affected divergent thinking in children with ADHD or whether these effects differed from those obtained under the convergent task classification.

MPH Effects on Cognitive Function: Specific

A summary table was drawn to illustrate the dose-response effects MPH exerts on children's performance across categories of cognitive tasks (see Table 6.2). The percentage of tasks that were performed under one, two, or three distinct dose conditions (see Table 6.1 for defining attributes) are listed initially, followed by the percentage of tasks in which significant overall medication effects were

reported. The percentage of tasks in which low/high dose contrasts were examined is listed subsequently. The fourth heading indicates, for those tasks in which low/high contrasts were examined, the percentage finding (a) significant differences in favor of the "low" and "high" dose conditions, or (b) nonsignificant differences between the two conditions (NS). Unknown results (usually owing to a failure to conduct and/or report post hoc analyses) are indicated under the UK column.

Table 6.2 shows that the preponderance of studies examined cognitive performance under unitary dosage parameters. Conclusions from these studies tell us nothing about dose-response effects, but do yield valuable information regarding whether MPH improves different types of cognitive performance relative to inactive medication conditions. As noted previously, MPH improved performance relative to placebo conditions in over two-thirds of the tasks or 95% of the studies examined. The percentage of studies shown using one, two, or three doses must be interpreted with caution and in conjunction with the number of tasks examined in the particular category—especially in cases in which the n is small, as estimates become inflated.

Significant overall medication effects were reported in a majority of studies, forming a bimodal distribution according to task type. Performance on tasks listed at the high and low end of the cognitive

Table 6.2. MPH Dose-Response Effects Across Categories of Cognitive Tasks

| | (n) | % of Tasks Using Doses of | | | % Sign Med Effects | % Comparing Low/High Conditions | % Sign Between-Dose Difference | | |
		1	2	3			Low	NS/UK	High
Convergent Tasks:									
Stimulus Equivalance:	(1)	0	0	100	100	100	0	0/0	100
Matching to Sample:	(12)	25	67	8	83	25	0	33/0	67
Paired Associates:	(13)	62	15	23	85	23	0	67/0	33
Spelling:	(2)	100	0	0	0	100	0	0/0	0
Picture Recognition:	(8)	63	25	12	50	29	0	50/50	0
Long/Short Term Recall:	(6)	33	67	0	50	0	0	0/0	0
Visual/Perceptual:	(2)	50	50	0	0	0	0	0/0	0
Stimulus Identification:	(6)	83	17	0	33	0	0	0/0	0
Perceptual/Motor:	(3)	67	33	0	33	0	0	0/0	0
Reaction Time:	(7)	71	29	0	100	14	0	0/0	100
Vigilance:	(15)	73	20	7	80	7	0	100/0	0
Divergent Tasks:	(6)	33	33	34	33	33	0	0/100	0

Note: NS - not significant; UK = unknown.

spectrum (i.e., moving from the top to the bottom of Table 6.2) were improved by medication, whereas relatively few significant overall effects were reported for the more traditional, visual-perceptual search tasks listed in the middle of the table. This finding may be an artifact, however, as all the studies using tasks of this variety limited their comparisons to two or fewer dose conditions.

Comparatively few of the total tasks (13 of 81, or 16%) were examined under low/high dose conditions. These were spread across 6 of the 11 (55%) convergent category listings. A breakdown of the results from the 13 studies contrasting low to high MPH dose conditions revealed no significant between-dose differences in 38.5% of the tasks, significant between-dose differences favoring the high dose condition in 38.5% of the tasks, and uninterpretable findings in the remaining 23% of the tasks. The breakdown of post hoc findings are of special interest, owing to the commonly embraced hypothesis that children's cognitive performance and learning are optimized under low versus high doses of stimulant. As can be seen in Table 6.2, *low doses of MPH were not reported as significantly superior to high doses in enhancing cognitive performance in a single study reviewed*. Rather, performance tended to be superior under high dose conditions as a function of task difficulty and complexity, that is, primarily in those studies requiring higher order learning, problem solving, and combinations of these elements (tasks of the slow processing variety that require complex behavior). The lone exception was the single study investigating reaction time under low/high dose conditions.

Conclusions

Several conclusions can be drawn from the material reviewed in this section. There appears to be an inverse relationship between the number of studies investigating MPH effects on children's cognitive performance and our understanding of these effects. The most obvious reason for this predicament is that an overwhelming number of studies conducted to date examined effects under a unitary dose. This dose frequently represented the mean of a range of doses, which in turn, was based on one of two methods of individual titration. Regardless of the

number of doses under which performance was examined, the evidence strongly supports the contention that MPH facilitates cognitive function in children with ADHD.

Aside from the overall facilitative effect MPH exerts on cognitive function, the limited evidence available regarding task by dose effects suggests that the dose required for optimal performance may be related to task complexity and the type of information processing required by the task. The interplay among these and other variables is discussed in the final summary section, as are implications for the development of a psychopharmacological model of stimulant effects on cognition and learning. No evidence was found to support the contention that children's cognitive performance is optimized under low compared to high doses of MPH.

Only a handful of studies compared the cognitive performance of "normals" to children with ADHD using psychostimulant probes, and these were carried out under a limited range of experimental conditions. As shown in Table 6.1, for example, all normal comparison studies were conducted under low dose conditions and their effects were limited to tasks at the low end of the cognitive spectrum with regard to difficulty and complexity. Thus, the frequently cited notion that children with ADHD and normals react similarly to stimulant probes is conceptually in error and remains an important empirical question.

CLINIC-BASED TESTING AND ITS RELATIONSHIP TO CHILDREN'S BEHAVIOR AND ACADEMIC PERFORMANCE IN THE CLASSROOM

Low-Dose Learning, High-Dose Social Behavior Optimization Hypothesis

The question, "Do cognitive performance and social deportment represent domains that are optimized at widely discrepant doses of psychostimulants?" has been debated for over a decade. Aside from the intriguing notion that two or more mechanisms, and perhaps separate physiologic systems (Conners & Solanto, 1984), may be involved, the situation has broad implications for individual titration. Does one base dosage on improved conduct at the cost of reduced cognitive efficiency, or should disruptive behavior be tolerated at the cost of improved academic efficiency? If so, what are the long-term implications of optimizing one domain over another, and which should be targeted for intervention?

Before tackling this issue, it is imperative to examine the premise upon which it was based. In their landmark study, Sprague and Sleator (1977) used the Abbreviated Conners Teacher Rating Scale (ACTRS) and a short-term memory task (picture recognition) at three levels of increasing information load (3, 9, and 15 pictures) under placebo and two doses of methylphenidate (0.3 and 1.0 mg/kg) to indicate dose-related changes in the domains of social behavior and learning performance, respectively. Briefly, they found that learning performance was optimized under the low dose condition (0.30 mg/kg), whereas teacher ratings were most improved under the high (1.0 mg/kg) dose condition.

The implied insensitivity of classroom teachers in detecting dose effects that stemmed from this report, whether intentional or not, appears to be grossly undeserved. Although several of the study's findings are difficult to interpret because of omission of statistical results (e.g., incomplete reporting of simple effects tests and post hoc analyses), teachers were not asked to rate cognitive functioning or improvement relative to academic performance; their input was limited to a 10-item scale that requests information relative to gross motor activity, emotional lability, frustration tolerance, inhibitory control, and disturbance to others. The point that Sprague and Sleator (1977) appeared to be making regarding differential effects of dose was nonetheless a valid one. Most children with ADHD are referred because of their disruptive conduct, not their cognitive disabilities—although the two domains clearly influence one another in a reciprocal fashion. Thus, the admonition that learning may be impaired by titrating psychostimulants using improved conduct as the primary target symptom, should be taken literally.

Empirical Questions Regarding Dose-Response in Children

Regardless of one's interpretation of Sprague and Sleator's (1977) findings, empirical work was needed to address two questions inspired by their investigation: (a) whether the domains of learning or academic efficiency and social behavior are affected and perhaps optimized at widely discrepant doses of psychostimulants, and (b) whether the clinic and laboratory-based measures of psychopharmacological response are valid indices of the way in which children attend, complete academic assignments, and behave in school. To answer these and related empirical questions, we carried out a series of clinic-based validation studies that examined the relationship between the effects of MPH in ADHD children and their behavior in school. Children's performance on three commonly used clinic measures, the Continuous Performance Test (CPT), the Paired Associate Learning Task (PALT), and the Matching Familiar Figures Test (MFFT) were compared to the results of in vivo observations of their academic efficiency (AES), attention (on-task), and teacher ratings of classroom functioning in school.

Participants

Children meeting stringent DSM-III (*Diagnostic and statistical manual of mental disorders*, 3rd ed.; American Psychiatric Association [APA], 1980) diagnostic criteria for ADDH (Attention Deficit Disorder with Hyperactivity) participated in the study. Inclusion criteria was based on (a) semistructured interview (with parent and child interviewed separately); (b) independent diagnosis by a clinical psychologist and physician; (c) standardized information and ratings from multiple informants across settings (home and school); (d) careful and detailed review of historical information regarding development, medical history, chronicity, and course of behavioral disturbance; (e) direct observations of classroom functioning; and (f) consideration of appropriate exclusion criteria. In excess of 110 children participated in our planned, 6-week medication assessment study over the course of 5 years.

Experimental Design and Medication Protocol

A double-blind, placebo-control, within-subject (crossover) experimental design was used in which children received each of four MPH doses (5, 10, 15, and 20 mg) and a placebo (following baseline measures); each dose was administered for 6 consecutive days in a randomly assigned, counterbalanced sequence. Fixed doses (versus mg/kg) were used in our studies initially because of standard clinical titration practices in the United States and the flexibility it allows for examining comparative data sets. The practice was continued, however, because the results of a large-scale investigation failed to support the hypothesis of a relationship between children's gross body weight and behavioral response to MPH (Rapport, DuPaul, & Kelly, 1989). All medication was packaged in capsule form to avoid detection of dose and taste, with additional controls incorporated so that cognitive testing and all classroom observations and teacher ratings were conducted under strict double-blind conditions, and during active medication periods only.

Children were tested once weekly in the clinic using standardized procedures, under baseline and each of the counterbalanced conditions described above (placebo, 5, 10, 15, and 20 mg MPH). Testing began 60 to 90 minutes after oral ingestion, owing to the reported behavioral time-response of MPH (Swanson et al., 1978).

Assessment

Standard procedures were followed in administering the Paired Associate Learning task (PAL) (Rapport, Stoner et al., 1985-b; Rapport, Quinn, DuPaul, Quinn, & Kelly, 1989), Continuous Performance Test (CPT) (Rapport, DuPaul et al., 1986-a; Rapport, Jones et al., 1987), and Matching Familiar Figures Test (MFFT) (Rapport, DuPaul, Stoner, Birmingham, & Masse, 1985; Rapport, Stoner, 1988) as described elsewhere.

Classroom assessment for individual children involved 6 consecutive weeks of observation (three times per week) to correspond with the 6-week clinic testing period described above. All children were observed in their regular (non-special education)

classrooms during morning hours, approximately 1½ hours following ingestion of placebo or active medication (and at an equivalent time during baseline conditions), at a time in which they worked on regularly assigned academic seat work (usually arithmetic or language arts). Dependent measures were limited to morning hours and included (a) direct observations of attention (i.e., on-task) over 20 consecutive minutes 3 times weekly; (b) an academic efficiency score (AES), which was calculated as the weekly percentage of academic assignments completed correctly; (c) weekly teacher ratings that were based on behavior exhibited during the *morning* hours only, using the Abbreviated Conners Teacher Rating Scale (ACTRS) (Goyette, Conners, & Ulrich, 1978), Teacher Self-Control Rating Scale (TSCRS) (Humphrey, 1982), and ADD-H Comprehensive Teacher Rating Scale (ACTeRS) (Ullmann, Sleator, & Sprague, 1985).

Preliminary Results

For illustrative purposes, the results obtained from clinical testing and classroom observations for 36 children are presented here. All dependent measures with the exception of CPT omission errors were highly significant in the multivariate analysis of variance (MANOVA) and univariate follow-up analyses. Consistent with our previous findings, *school-based measures* of attention, academic efficiency (AES), and teacher ratings of self-control (TSCRS), social deportment (ACTRS), and attention (ACTeRS attention factor) were highly sensitive to both overall and between-dose MPH effects. Most *clinic-based measures*, however, were disappointingly insensitive in detecting *overall* and between-dose differences. PAL errors and CPT commission errors were highly susceptible to placebo and/or practice effects, and neither measure was improved significantly under active medication conditions. Changes in children's performance on the MFFT were consistent with earlier findings (Rapport, DuPaul et al., 1985-a; Rapport, Stoner et al., 1988), in that overall and between-dose differences were found for the MFFT under the higher MPH dose conditions, compared to baseline, placebo, and lower doses.

We elected to plot dose-response data for each variable using standard *(T)* scores to facilitate comparisons among direct observational measures of attention and academic efficiency, classroom teacher ratings, and clinic-based measures of cognitive tempo (MFFT), vigilance (CPT), and learning (PAL). In the scores, improvement is indicated by upward movement on the vertical axis for all dependent measures. To address the two empirical questions raised earlier in this section, the two classroom observational measures (on-task and AES) were contrasted directly with the three teacher rating scales and three clinic-based measures using six distinct, dose-response, miniplots (see Figure 6.1)

As expected, the direct observations of attention and academic efficiency showed similar between-dose changes, with increases of between 1.3 and 1.6 standard deviations (SD) from baseline and placebo conditions to 20-mg MPH. The three teacher ratings showed remarkably similar dose-related increments as a function of increased dose (see top three miniplots in Figure 6.1). When these curves were analyzed using appropriate analysis for trend, both observational measures and the ACTRS were found to contain significant quadratic components, indicated by a single change in slope. Post hoc analyses indicated that the significant change was due to a relatively marked improvement in observed and teacher-rated behavior between placebo and 10-mg, followed by continuing but less dramatic improvement as dose increased from 10-mg to 20-mg. The remaining two teacher ratings showed a significant, positive linear relationship between improvement and increasing dose.

Contrasting the miniplots of classroom observations with those of clinic-based testing yielded results dissimilar to the teacher ratings described above (see bottom three miniplots in Figure 6.1). Whereas the between-dose sensitivity of the MFFT and PAL task to changes in medication status were enhanced moderately and approached 1 SD, CPT omission (SD = 0.5) and commission (SD = 0.5) errors evinced minimal change and remained within a relatively constricted range. Unfortunately, the nearly one-half SD change evinced on the PAL task was due to improved performance between baseline and placebo conditions. These data suggest that the establishment of a stable baseline prior to using the traditional form of this measure in dose manipulation studies is critical, or that a learning measure with greater

test-retest stability is required. Changes in children's performance on the MFFT, on the other hand, suggest that the measure is sensitive to MPH effects, but that relatively high doses are required to enhance the type of visual problem solving inherent to this task.

To evaluate further the disparate reasons for the relative insensitivity of the clinic-based battery in assessing MPH effects, a matrix was constructed to depict the correlations between these measures and those obtained using direct observations in the classroom across experimental conditions (see Table 6.3). Several points relevant to our discussion are worth noting in Table 6.3—the most poignant one being that only 3 of 66 possible correlations emerged as significant among children's performance on the clinic measures and their attention and academic efficiency in school. The three found were among CPT errors, on-task, and academic efficiency at the two higher MPH doses. By themselves and with an absence of trend in the correlation matrices, we attribute the findings to chance occurrence. This finding held true across no-medication, inactive medication, and active medication conditions.

Although not shown in Table 6.3, all possible Measure X Medication matrices were generated. The results showed that the intra-task measures were highly correlated as would be expected (e.g., CPT omission and commission errors were significantly related to one another across experimental conditions), but that inter-task correlations were insignificant. This finding suggests that the tests appear to tap different aspects or dimensions of behavior and show surprisingly little similarity with or overlap between one another.

A last note of interest were the correlations between children's attention (on-task) and academic efficiency (AES) shown in Table 6.3 (see top portion of table). As expected, observations of children's attention showed that it was significantly related to their academic efficiency across all experimental conditions, with the exception of one. Under the higher 20-mg dose condition, the correlation between the two measures failed to reach significance. Results from a separate set of post hoc analyses revealed that children's attention continued to improve under the 20-mg dose, whereas academic efficiency peaked

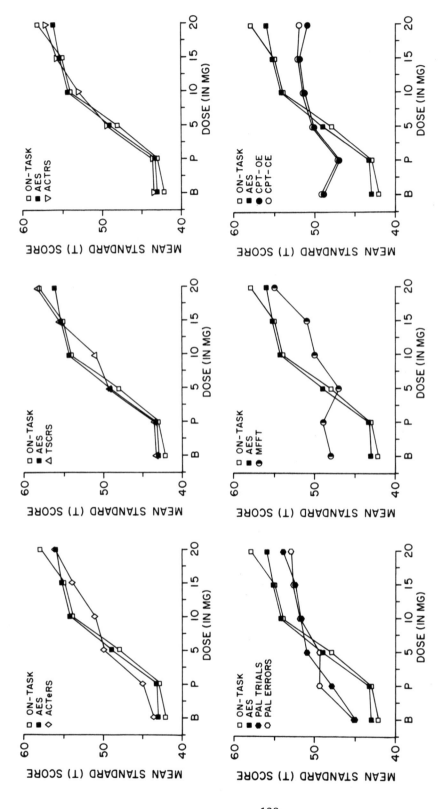

Figure 6.1. The mean group response frequencies plotted as dose-response curves are expressed as standard *T* scores for the clinic-based measures (see bottom three miniplots; and PAL) and teacher rating scales (see top three miniplots: ACTRS, ACTeRS, and TSCRS). Dose-response curves for the two direct observational measures (On-Task and AES) are shown on each miniplot for comparison purposes. Scores were derived based on the performance of the present sample (*N* = 36) aggregated across all conditions excluding baseline). Improvement on all dependent variables is indicated by upward movement on the vertical axis.

Table 6.3. Correlations Among Classroom and Clinic Measures Across Dose

	On-Task					
	Base	Placebo	5 mg	10 mg	15 mg	20 mg
DependentMeasure:						
CPT:						
OE	−.12	.08	−.19	.20	−.60[b]	−.23
CE	−.07	−.15	−.19	.06	−.56[a]	−.17
MFFT:						
Errors	−.34	−.03	−.11	−.32	−.20	.04
PAL:						
Trials	−.28	−.42	−.23	.29	−.20	.05
Errors	−.25	−.43	−.40	.26	−.36	−.04
AES	.70[b]	.64[b]	.88[b]	.48[a]	.63[b]	.09
	Academic Efficiency					
CPT:						
OE	−.26	.28	−.24	−.10	−.49[a]	−.60[b]
CE	−.24	−.37	−.25	.24	−.25	−.58[b]
MFFT:						
Errors	−.24	.05	−.24	−.06	.06	.09
PAL:						
Trials	.02	−.37	−.22	−.14	−.01	
Errors	−.06	−.40	−.32	.03	−.35	−.04

Note: Correlations shown are with dependent measures listed on left-hand ordinate, attention (top), and Academic Efficiency (bottom) across dose. CPT = Continuous Performance Test. MFFT = Matching Familiars Figure Test. PAL = Paired Associate Learning Task. AES = Academic Efficiency Score.

[a] $p < .01$
[b] $p < .001$

under the lower 15-mg dose and showed a plateau effect thereafter.

A final set of figures was constructed to address the relative insensitivity and lack of generalization between clinic and classroom measures. The two figures (Figures 6.2 and 6.3) show the percentage of possible improvement on each dependent measure from baseline conditions. Values were obtained by determining the range of possible change relative to baseline for each dependent measure in standard *(T)* score form, and calculating the percentage of change associated with each dose condition. Scores were converted in this manner so the measures could be placed on the same scale for comparison purposes, and to equate for differences in the degree or range of change possible across measures.

Inspection of Figure 6.2 indicates that two reasons for the apparent insensitivity of the clinic measures involve (a) practice or placebo effects, and (b) a failure to differentiate between low, intermediate, and high dose conditions. Changes due to the placebo and/or

practice effects are shown in the rectangular boxes labeled "placebo response" at the bottom of each of the three miniplots. Greater susceptibility to these effects are evinced as scores progress from a left to right position on the abscissa. As shown, PAL trials to criterion and errors evince approximately 10% and 16% of their total change from baseline performance conditions under placebo (see top plot in Figure 6.2). CPT omission (OE) and commission (CE) errors show an opposite pattern (see middle miniplot in Figure 6.2) and worsen under placebo conditions, as indicated by their movement from right to left of the "0" line in the bottom left-hand corner of the figure (Note: Children's CPT OE and CE actually showed a much greater worsening effect of 14% and 48%, respectively, but could not be plotted because of practical considerations in constructing the graph). The undesirable degree of instability inherent to these two instruments is consistent with clinical observations of improved PAL and worsened CPT performance over time under no-medication conditions.

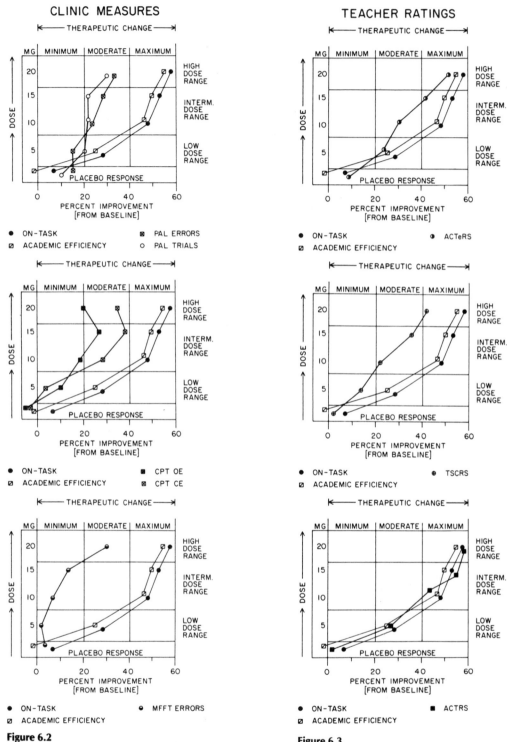

Figure 6.2

Figure 6.3

The dose-response curves shown in the three miniplots of Figure 6.2 also indicate that changes in the clinic-based measures from baseline to medication conditions are approximately 20% to 30%. This findings stands in direct contrast to the relatively broad range evinced in the two classroom measures of between 50% and 65%, and suggests that the measures are insensitive to dose-related changes in behavior and/or limited by attributes inherent to the tasks themselves (e.g., floor and ceiling effects). The shape and placement of the curves are also of interest. For example, consider the preponderance of Dose X Change data points falling within a single therapeutic range (minimum or intermediate windows) in Figure 6.2. Their placement indicates that one difficulty with the clinic-based measures is their failure to differentiate between low- and high-dose conditions, although the two requiring learning (PAL) and problem solving (MFFT) begin to move from a left (minimal change) to right (intermediate) position on the figure as a function of increasing dose. In contrast, the dose-response curves for CPT OE and CE begin to retreat toward baseline levels with increasing dose.

Comparisons between dose-response curves based on teacher ratings of attention (ACTeRS), social deportment (ACTRS), and self-control (TSCRS), and those derived from direct observations of attention and academic efficiency indicate a similar pattern and range of improvement across dose conditions. In contrast to the clinic measures, teacher ratings do not appear particularly susceptible to practice or placebo effects (see bottom of each miniplot labeled "placebo response" in Figure 6.3). Rather, they tend to change in a more or less linear fashion as a function of increasing dose, mirroring changes observed in children's attention and academic efficiency to a similar (ACTeRS and TSCRS) or near perfect degree (ACTRS).

Summary of Findings Regarding the Effects of MPH on Children's Functioning in Clinic and Classroom Settings

Our findings thus far indicate several tentative conclusions regarding MPH effects in children with ADDH:

1. The dose-response relationship between MPH and children's attention and academic efficiency in regular classroom settings is usually characterized (at a *group* level) by improved functioning with increasing dose in a linear and quadratic fashion, respectively. The quadratic relationship between AES and dose is not represented by the classic inverted U-shaped curve, but characterized by less dramatic improvement and eventually a plateau effect under doses between the intermediate to high dose range.

2. Significant decreases in classroom functioning under high dose conditions relative to low dose or no-medication conditions have not been found thus far. Thus, the ubiquitous hypothesis that children's cognitive performance, as it relates to everyday classroom functioning, is optimized under low versus high doses of MPH is unsupported by the findings reported herein. The issue of whether cognitive functioning is enhanced under a restricted range of doses is decidedly more complex and will be addressed in the summary section.

3. Children can and do exhibit a wide range of response to MPH (Barkley, 1981; Conners, 1971; Kinsbourne, 1984; Rapport, Jones, et al., 1987;

Figure 6.2 The mean percentage of improvement possible on each dependent measure relative to baseline conditions depicted as dose-response curves and expressed as standard T scores for the clinic (MFFT errors, CPT omission and commission errors, and PAL trials and errors) and classroom observational (on-task and AES) measures. Improvement on all dependent variables is indicated by left-to-right movement on the horizontal axis. Therapeutic "windows" highlight Dose by Change effects.

Figure 6.3 The mean percentage of improvement possible on each dependent measure relative to baseline conditions depicted as dose-response curves and expressed as standard T scores for the weekly teacher ratings (ACTRS, ACTeRS attention factor, and TSCRS) and classroom observational (On-Task and AES) measures. Improvement on all dependent variables is indicated by left-to-right movement on the horizontal axis. Dose is shown on the vertical axis. Therapeutic "windows" highlight Dose by Change effects.

Rapport, Stoner, et al., 1988; Rapport, Quinn, et al., 1989). As such, one should clearly avoid relying on statistical averages or single measures (including teacher ratings) for determining optimal treatment for a particular child. A systematic trial using multiple measures and a wide range of doses is recommended.

4. The external validity of the clinic-based instruments reported here for assessing children's cognitive functioning as it relates to academic performance in school remains unproven at present. Barkley (1989) has come to a similar conclusion in his review of the ecological validity of clinic-based instruments. This unfortunate situation appears to hold true under baseline as well as under a wide range of dose conditions. As such, no instrument described here can be recommended, alone or in combination, for the expressed purpose of clinically titrating MPH in children with ADHD.

TIME-RESPONSE STUDIES OF MPH EFFECTS ON CHILDREN'S COGNITIVE FUNCTION

MPH Time-Action Effects

Most laboratory-based instruments used to measure psychostimulant effects in children are timed to take a "snapshot" of behavior during an interval in which the drug is presumed to be potent, exerting its optimal therapeutic effect on behavior. Teacher and clinical ratings of psychostimulant effects, however, are usually based on observations of constantly changing medication states over extended periods of time, such as at the end of a week-long dosage trial. An understanding of the onset, time course, and eventual loss of behavioral and cognitive effect associated with the psychostimulants is thus of utmost consequence to issues bearing on both clinical titration and experimental methodology.

Although Bradley (1937) offered anecdotal comments regarding the time course of psychostimulants on children's behavior, experimental time-action studies were not conducted until nearly 35 years later. Nine of 17 subjects completed what appears to be

the first published report of a behavioral time-action study of psychostimulant effects in children, in which placebo and 0.50 mg/kg MPH were administered for 2 days each in the context of a crossover design (Sprague, 1972). Children were tested using a battery of cognitive tests (e.g., CPT, picture recognition) at premedication and at 6 distinct time intervals following ingestion. Heart rate was also assessed upon completion of each test session. The only statistically significant result reported by Sprague (1972) was that heart rate (HR) increased as a function of both MPH and time—a finding replicated by Kelly and colleagues (1988), who reported that moderate to higher doses of MPH were linearly related to increasing levels of HR, and that these effects were dependent upon *both* the initial HR value and the time course of the medication.

A Critical Review

The next series of behavioral time-action studies began appearing in journals approximately 6 years later. James Swanson and colleagues (1978) evaluated time-action effects of MPH in over 50 children, and it is on the basis of this and later reports (1979, 1983) that MPH was described as having a relatively brief "behavioral half-life" (i.e., the time taken for a 50% decline from the time of peak effect) of approximately 3 to 4 hours (Swanson et al., 1978). Their results have effected important changes in both experimental procedure and within-day clinical titration of MPH in children. MPH dose is administered routinely twice or three times daily using a 4-hour between-dose interval, and it is recommended that cognitive effects be assessed during the 1 to 3-hour postingestion time frame—the interval described as representing the time of "maximum effect" on cognitive performance (Swanson et al., 1978, p. 27). In their now classic series of time-action studies of MPH effects on Paired Associate Learning, Swanson and colleagues (1978, 1979, 1983, 1988) traditionally (a) use a within-day drug testing schedule (i.e., both drug and placebo are administered on the same day), (b) assess children under the dose in which their previous PAL performance was optimized, (c) analyze data based on the "average" group dose, (d) categorize children into groups of "favorable" and "adverse" responders using PAL performance as their criterion measure, and (e) express and analyze drug response as a percent change score from baseline or placebo conditions.

Unfortunately, interpretation of time-action effects on cognitive performance are difficult to discern from the results of these studies. For example, both pharmacokinetic (Gualtieri, Hicks, Patrick, Schroeder, & Breese, 1984; Shaywitz et al., 1982) and behavioral (Pelham et al., 1987; Swanson et al., 1978; Solanto & Conners, 1982) studies have shown that MPH effects may persist beyond 4 hours. Administering different doses of a short-acting stimulant using a within-day testing schedule across an 8-hour period will invariably result in some drug-order or carryover effects (e.g., see Figure 4 in Swanson et al., 1978). Similarly, changes in cognitive effects *within*, and not across days, must be used to assess and control for the hour-to-hour changes in PAL performance. This procedure is necessary owing to both the normal fluctuation observed under multiple within-day testing conditions (Swanson et al., 1978) and to the instability of PAL performance over repeat administration across days (Rapport, 1990). Assessing children's cognitive performance on a measure and under the one dose known to optimize test performance on that particular measure is also somewhat unorthodox. The influence these design factors exert on obtained results is difficult to discern. One is left wondering, for example, whether an "average" test dose of 12.5 mg is representative of a "low-dose" when the actual doses administered to the sample in the 1978 study ranged from 5 to 30 mg. Moreover, the practice of using a child's previous test performance under a particular dose and on an identical test to determine which dose to use in subsequent testing, and categorizing children as "favorable" and "adverse" responders based on obtained test performance, represent a serious threat to validity. Conclusions regarding time-action effects of psychostimulants on cognitive performance can be drawn only while maintaining experimental integrity between the independent and dependent variables.

A fourth point to consider in reviewing this series of studies is the use of percent change scores for purposes of graphical illustration and statistical analysis of results. Scores in drug and placebo conditions were typically expressed as a percent change from the initial baseline score (Swanson et al., 1978) or the average placebo score over time (Swanson, 1988). Use of this method not only assumes that PAL performance observed at a single premedication time interval is a valid index of performance at subsequent testing times, but also has the untoward effect of artificially inflating the degree of observed change. The following example will serve to illustrate this point. Assume that a child is required to learn 10 pairs of associations during each of 10 consecutively administered PAL trials as per standard instructions. Further, assume an initial error rate of 30% (i.e., 30 errors). This is fairly typical of children with ADHD and approximates the error frequency sought during initial level setting procedures to minimize ceiling and floor effects.

Finally, assume that the child makes 25, 10, 15, and 20 errors on the ensuing time-course trials during the day.

The decision to use the percent change from baseline or placebo as opposed to the percent of change in test scores (traditional method) affects the results in a rather dramatic fashion (see Figure 6.4) In the example offered, the transformation results in an inflated estimate in excess of 300% relative to scores obtained using the traditional method of calculating percent change. The result is that a quadratic-shaped but relatively flat time-action curve, that may not be significantly different from baseline or placebo levels of functioning, is transformed into one that suggests dramatic changes in cognitive performance as a function of time. Moreover, unless a priori transformations are performed, statistical analyses derived from assumptions of normal distribution theory are inappropriate for use with difference scores.

Two additional points pertaining to the PAL time-action series of investigations merit discussing. The first is that, based on their PAL performance, 41% of the sample who completed the initial time-action portion of the 1978 study were classified as "adverse responders." One reason for the disproportionately high percentage of poor responders may be the mixed diagnostic groups of children who participated in the study (Swanson et al., 1978, p. 22). By current standards, many would meet diagnostic criteria for overanxious disorder and solitary-aggressive conduct disorder in addition to ADHD.

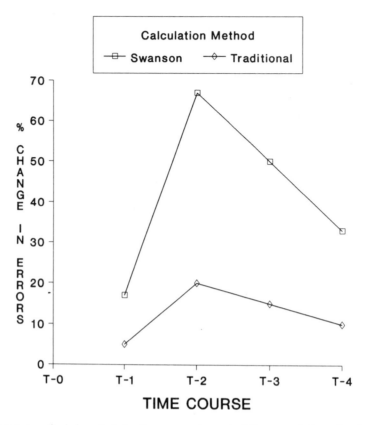

Figure 6.4. Shown are two methods for calculating the percent change in PAL errors relative to baseline or placebo conditions over multiple time intervals (T-0 . . . T-4), and their corresponding time-action curves . Traditional method is the calculation of a change score based on percent of total possible test errors. Swanson method is the calculation of change score based on percent of baseline or placebo error levels. Traditional method involves dividing the number of errors committed during test by the number of errors possible in test and multiplying by 100 to calculate error percentage. Error percentage scores obtained for each testing condition (T-1 . . . T-4) are subtracted from those obtained during baseline or placebo to derive "percentage change in errors." Swanson method involves subtracting the number of errors committed during baseline (or placebo) test from the number of errors committed in each subsequent test session (at T-1 . . . T-4), and dividing each "difference score" by the baseline (or placebo) score and multiplying by 100 to derive the "percentage change in errors."

A second point worth noting is that "trials to criterion" has been disregarded in both time-action and dose-response studies using PAL tasks. The implied assumption that percent correct provides the most useful information regarding a child's learning may be inaccurate, or at best, misleading. It could be argued, for example, that the rate at which a child learns a concept or association to a desired level of comprehension is, in the overall context of learning, as important as, or more important than, the degree of accuracy associated with a child's precriterion performance (Rapport, Quinn et al., 1989). It would

be prudent to examine both accuracy and rate of acquisition in future investigations.

Recent Studies

Despite the widespread and increasing use of MPH as a mainstay treatment for children with ADHD, until recently there were no published reports of its time-action effects on children's cognitive functioning using multiple measures *or* across a systematically delivered range of doses. Solanto and Conners

(1982) were the first to address this issue by assessing the response of 10 children with ADDH over the course of 5 hours and 50 minutes under placebo and three doses of MPH (0.3, 0.6, & 1.0 mg/kg) across days, using a repeated measures within-day testing schedule (5 sessions daily). The results of their time-action, dose-response paradigm on physiological (heart rate, finger temperature), gross motor (seat activity), and cognitive variables (reaction time, commission errors) revealed several findings. Although not directly relevant to our discussion here, it is noteworthy that the only significant changes in both physiological measures and seat activity occurred under active drug conditions at 50 minutes, the approximate time interval associated with the onset of behavioral and cognitive effects in children receiving MPH. The cognitive measure used in the study, a serial reaction time task, necessitated careful vigilance, but for a total duration of only 5 to 6 minutes per testing session. Commission errors alone showed a significant drug by time effect, with error reduction occurring at 50 minutes post ingestion under all MPH dose conditions.

A final study that has some bearing on the time-action course of MPH on children's cognitive performance was conducted by Pelham et al. (1987). Although designed to investigate the relative effects of standard (10-mg) and sustained release (SR-20 mg) formulation of MPH, the results revealed that, compared to placebo, CPT omission errors were significantly reduced at 2 and 3 hours post ingestion following a standard 10-mg dose.

Summary

Relatively little can be concluded at present regarding the time-action effects of MPH on children's cognitive performance, owing to the limited number of and methodological shortcomings associated with studies conducted to date. Readers unfamiliar with pediatric psychopharmacological research, however, should bear in mind that the conduct of this type of study involves a degree of methodological rigor, statistical analysis, and experimental control over a highly dysfunctional group of children, that is rarely encountered in mainstream clinical research. Few have been willing to commit the required resources, time, energy, and expertise.

Nonetheless, we will be unable to answer basic questions regarding time and dosage effects on children's cognitive performance until such studies are completed. The accumulated results thus far suggest that the onset of MPH effects on children's cognitive function is somewhere in the neighborhood of 50 to 60 minutes, with peak enhancement lasting 2 and 3 hours. This time interval applies only to a highly restrictive range of "cognitive tasks," most of which require minimal or no learning, or in the latter case, are of low to moderate task complexity. The potential interaction between dose, task complexity, and time has not been studied to date, but should prove to be one of the most informative and fruitful areas of research for building a psychopharmacological-cognitive model of stimulant effects in children. The yoking of physiological to cognitive measures using a Time by Dose by Task paradigm is a second avenue of research that should provide much needed information relevant to localization and dysfunction of brain activity, as well as having practical implications for clinical titration.

Finally, an "overdose response" and "cognitive impairment" have been offered as explanations in several dose-response and time-action studies in which cognitive performance is *judged* to be higher under low relative to high dose conditions. These interpretations are highly misleading and it is recommended that they be reserved for phenomena in which cognitive response is *impaired* relative to levels of *baseline* or placebo functioning. In future investigations it would also be prudent to incorporate appropriate statistical analyses, rather than graphical illustrations, to support interpretations regarding both overall and between-dose differences in cognitive functioning at single and multiple time intervals.

SUMMARY

Evidence derived from the dose-response studies reviewed herein suggest that the effects of MPH on children's cognitive function are interactive, interdependent, and highly complex. It would be naive, however, to expect a single dose or range of doses to optimize all types of cognitive functioning in all children. Werry and Aman (1975) arrived at a similar conclusion 15 years earlier and suggested that at least four factors influence the way in which drugs affect cognitive function: drug factors, organismic factors, task factors, and social environmental factors.

The same may be said regarding the time-action course of psychostimulants. Available evidence, as well as our own pilot work, suggest multiple time-action curves not only *among* behavioral domains, but *within* domains (e.g., attention, inhibition, motor). For example, optimal psychostimulant effects for tasks of a fast processing nature and that rely primarily on vigilance seem to appear at an earlier point on the time-action curve than those that require slow processing, learning, and higher levels of inhibition. Drug and dose effects also interact with time course and are influenced by a range of factors such as task complexity, social-environmental conditions, and psychological processes (e.g., motivational factors).

What may be of potential benefit to the field is the development of a model to guide systematically controlled investigations, rather than the "tail wagging the dog" atheoretical approach presently in vogue. For example, tasks that vary in difficulty and complexity along categorical and hierarchical dimensions, and that measure more specific aspects of cognitive processes may prove useful. Unfortunately, the tasks that are purest with respect to their ability to sample unitary dimensions of cognitive function are unrepresentative of the attentional and learning demands placed upon children in school. Tasks that necessitate higher levels of complexity, by design, draw upon multiple brain processes. The clarification or classification of these processes by means of cognitive task dissection may thus prove to be a difficult if not impossible feat. Nevertheless, others have expressed optimism regarding the possibility that the biological bases of automatic and effortful processing may be clarified (Posner & Presti, 1987) and have suggested that drug effects may depend upon the particular pattern of neuropsychological deficits associated with an individual child (Conners & Wells, 1986).

A preliminary psychopharmacological model of stimulant effects on children's cognitive function is offered below for two reasons: first, to place existing data into a conceptual framework that promotes more focused and sustained work in the field; second, to lay the groundwork for empirical testing of specific predictions with the hope of developing a more comprehensive model by which to guide research.

A Preliminary Psychopharmacological Model of MPH Effects on Children's Cognitive Function

The proposed hypothetical model of psychostimulant effects on cognitive function in children with ADHD requires several assumptions and extrapolations to be drawn, owing to the lacuna in existing knowledge. A primary assumption, albeit based upon preliminary empirical work, is that children differ in both their attentional and inhibitory capacities, and that different environmental conditions will minimize and antagonize these differences. It can also be assumed that these domains are mediated by different pathways or brain systems, but that they are interconnected and hence, interdependent and interactive. Thus, developing "pure" measures to differentiate system functioning, such as pharmacological probes or cognitive tasks, may not be possible. Arranging tasks (or pharmacological probes) on a continuum that samples more of one than the other, however, merits consideration. For reasons of parsimony, discussion will be limited to the attention and inhibition domains of behavior, as they are highly relevant to and moderately well studied phenomena in this population of children.

The tasks traditionally used in fast processing research necessitate primarily automatic versus controlled processes and are assumed to rely more on vigilance than inhibition. The reverse is assumed of slow processing or effortful tasks. Our review of the studies outlined in Table 6.1 also suggest that these two domains are affected differentially by dose. The hypothesized relationship between performance on these tasks and MPH dose are shown as three distinct dose-response curves in Figure 6.5.

Performance on tasks that rely primarily on heightened arousal and vigilance, and that can be completed in a near automatic or less effortful fashion, are postulated to be optimally enhanced under relatively low doses of stimulant in children with ADHD. This relationship is depicted in Figure 6.5 by the peak performance effect occurring in the dose range of approximately 0.2 to 0.4 mg/kg, and a leveling off, then drop-off in performance (relative to lower dose conditions, not baseline!) thereafter.

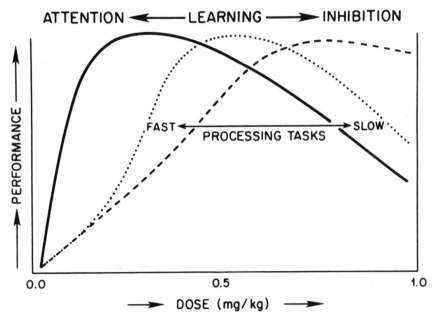

Figure 6.5. Hypothetical dose-response performance curves for the domains of attention, inhibition, and learning. The learning curve intersects the attention and inhibition curves at different points along the abscissa, depending upon the relationship among processing task variables, the degree of vigilance or inhibition demanded by the task, and dose.

Performance on tasks of the slow-processing variety that necessitate increased effort, behavioral inhibition, organization and strategic planning, on the other hand, are postulated to be optimally enhanced under mid to high doses of stimulant. Peak performance on the inhibition curve is estimated to occur in the dose range of approximately 0.7 to 0.9 mg/kg (see Figure 6.5).

The *learning* function is depicted as a curve in the middle of the figure and intersects the attention and inhibition curves at different points along the abscissa. The implication postulated is that the nature and inherent demands of a particular learning task play a critical role in determining the relationship between enhanced performance and dose. As one moves along the learning continuum, from tasks relying heavily on automatic processes and heightened vigilance to those of a slow-processing, effortful nature that place heavier demands on inhibition capabilities, the dose required to achieve optimal performance increases proportionately. Children's performance on reaction time and continuous performance type tasks should thus be optimally enhanced under low doses of stimulant (i.e., between 0.1 and

0.4 mg/kg), with minimal improvement or even a decrement evinced thereafter as a function of increasing dose. Performance on tasks requiring nearly equal degrees of vigilance and inhibition, and falling more or less in the middle of the learning curve (e.g., Paired Associate Learning, Picture Recognition tasks at middle to high information load), should be optimized in the dose range of between 0.3 and 0.7 mg/kg, with lesser effects observed bilaterally from these points as a function of task requirements. For the highly effortful tasks that require greater behavior inhibition, optimal performance should be realized in the dose range of between 0.6 and 0.9 mg/kg (e.g., Stimulus Equivalence Paradigm). It should be emphasized that the aforementioned discussion applies to cognitive performance at the group level. An individual child's basal ability, relative to vigilance and inhibitory control would be expected to interact with dosage in a similar manner, depending upon the profile status of the child—that is, to the degree to which the child experiences difficulties with attention and behavioral inhibition, and was able to compensate for said difficulties (e.g., by above average intelligence).

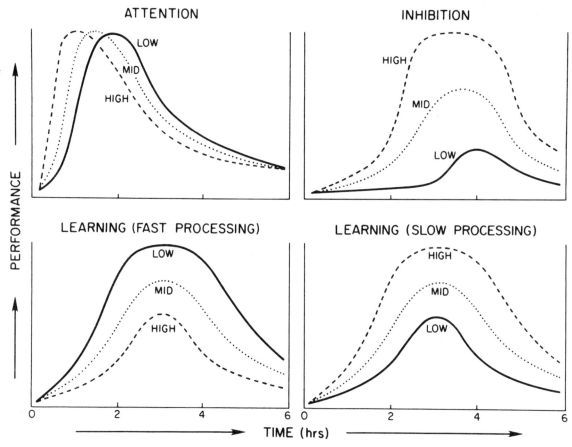

Figure 6.6. Hypothetical dose-response time-action curves for the domains of attention, inhibition, and learning are depicted as four distinct miniplots. Cognitive performance is influenced by a complex interaction among processing task variables, the degree of vigilance or inhibition demanded by the task, dose, and time course following ingestion.

Effortful tasks are carried out serially and thought to be more dependent on psychological processes involving motivation, self-regulation, and organization of strategies. As such, the introduction of variables ranging from increased task structure (e.g., instructions, feedback) to performance consequences (reward and punishment) should interact with the drug in such a manner that the level of drug needed to achieve optimal performance is lessened concomitant with the potency of these variables (e.g., Sprague & Sleator, 1977).

A second set of graphs was drawn to further illustrate the hypothesized Task by Dose relationships, but as a function of performance change over time (see Figure 6.6). Performance by Dose by Time

curves are shown separately for the domains of attention and inhibition (see upper left- and right-hand miniplots, respectively, in Figure 6.6). Hypothesized dose effects on these domains over a 6-hour time course are depicted separately on each miniplot and labeled "low," "mid" and "high." Consistent with the main graph depicted in Figure 6.5, the domains of attention and behavioral inhibition are postulated to be optimally affected at nearly opposite ends of the dose spectrum and in a more or less inverse fashion. Peak behavioral effects are also thought to occur at different points along the time-action continuum, with attention being affected much earlier than is inhibition.

The two learning functions shown in Figure 6.6

(see bottom left- and right-hand miniplots) suggest that time-action effects of the drug on both the fast- and slow-processing variety of tasks will be similar, with peak effects occurring from 2 to 4 hours post ingestion. It is also postulated that the total duration of time-action effects will be lengthened and drug potency increased as a function of dose, but in an inverse manner. The relationship will likely depend on the degree of vigilance and behavioral inhibition required by the specific learning task.

Preliminary Conclusions

Several tentative conclusions can be drawn with respect to the effects of MPH on cognitive function in children with ADHD:

1. Empirical evidence to date suggest that several types of cognitive function in children with ADHD are improved by MPH. Beneficial effects do not appear to be limited to only those areas in which initial deficits are found.

2. Beliefs in a unitary mechanism of defect and a corresponding assumption that MPH produces a unitary effect in the brain and/or on specific aspects of behavior are conceptually weak. Differences in dose-response effects on cognitive performance imply that biologically independent, or more likely, interdependent systems (or storage pools), are involved in the pathogenesis of ADHD.

3. The effects of MPH on cognitive function are interactive with and interdependent on a variety of variables such as dosage, time course, child characteristics, type of information processing required, performance variables, task factors, and prevailing social-environmental conditions. It is unclear whether these factors are secondary to a more central, core deficiency in attentional capacity, or to reduced numbers of interneuronal connections in the frontal regions necessary for complex problem solving.

4. The greatest cognitive deficits in this population of children appear to involve performance on effortful tasks that require slow processing, which may in turn, interact with task complexity, demand, and any number of psychological processes such as motivation in determining performance. Many of these factors may depend on the specific neurological deficits inherent to the child, but this awaits further study.

5. It may be more fruitful, as suggested by others (Conners & Solanto, 1984), to re-examine our dichotomies of children along more meaningful dimensions such as cognitive type, as opposed to overt behavioral disturbance.

6. Psychostimulant effects may be mediated by transient emotional states such as anxiety, whereby doses that had previously produced therapeutic effects may no longer do so, or in some cases result in agitation or even exacerbation of target symptoms. This area of investigation has been virtually ignored thus far.

REFERENCES

Abikoff, H. (1985). Efficacy of cognitive training interventions in hyperactive children: A critical review. *Clinical Psychology Review, 5,* 479–512.

Abikoff, H. (1987). An evaluation of cognitive behavior therapy for hyperactive children. In B. Lahey & A. Kazdin (Eds.), *Advances in clinical child psychology* (Vol. 10, pp. 171–216). New York: Plenum Publishing.

Abikoff, H., Ganeles, D., Reiter, G., Blum, C., Foley, C., & Klein, G. R. (1988). Cognitive training in academically deficient ADDH boys receiving stimulant medication. *Journal of Abnormal Child Psychology, 16,* 411–432.

Abikoff, H., & Gittelman, R. (1985). Hyperactive children treated with stimulants. Is cognitive training a useful adjunct? *Archives of General Psychiatry, 42,* 953–961.

Ackerman, P. T., Anhalt, J. M., Holcomb, P. J., & Dykman, R. A. (1986). Presumably innate and acquired automatic processes in children with attention and/or reading disorders. *Journal of Child Psychology and Psychiatry, 27,* 513–529.

American Psychiatric Association. (1980). *Diagnostic and statistical manual of mental disorders,* 3rd ed. Washington, DC: Author.

Barkley, R. A. (1977). The effects of methylphenidate on various types of activity level and attention in hyperkinetic children. *Journal of Abnormal Child Psychology, 5,* 350–369.

Barkley, R. A. (1981). *Hyperactive children: A handbook for diagnosis and treatment.* New York: Guilford Press.

Barkley, R. A. (1989). *The ecological validity of laboratory and analogue assessment methods of ADHD symptoms.* Paper presented at the international symposium on attention deficit hyperactivity disorder, Amsterdam, April, The Netherlands.

Barkley, R. A., & Cunningham, C. E. (1979). The effects

of methylphenidate on the mother-child interactions of hyperactive children. *Archives of General Psychiatry, 36,* 201–208.

Barkley, R. A., McMurray, M. D., Edelbrock, C. S., & Robbins, B. A. (1989). The response of aggressive and nonaggressive ADHD children to two doses of methylphenidate. *Journal of the American Academy of Child and Adolescent Psychiatry, 28,* 873–881.

Berliner, D. C., & Rosenshine, B. (1977). The acquisition of knowledge in the classroom. In R. C. Anderson, R. J. Spiro, & W. E. Montague (Eds.), *Schooling and the acquisition of knowledge* (pp. 375–396) Hillside, NJ: Lawrence Erlbaum Associates.

Borcherding, B., Thompson, K., Kruesi, M., Bartko, J., Rapoport, J. L., & Weingartner, H. (1988). Automatic and effortful processing in attention deficit hyperactivity disorder. *Journal of Abnormal Child Psychology, 16,* 333–345.

Bradley, C. (1937). The behavior of children receiving benzedrine. *American Journal of Psychiatry, 94,* 577–585.

Brown, R. T., Borden, K. A., Wynne, M. E., Schleser, R., & Clingerman, S. R. (1986). Methylphenidate and cognitive therapy with ADD children: A methodological reconsideration. *Journal of Abnormal Child Psychology, 14,* 481–487.

Brown, R. T., & Sleator, E. K. (1979). Methylphenidate in hyperkinetic children: Differences in dose effects on impulsive behavior. *Pediatrics, 64,* 408–411.

Brown, R. T., Slimmer, L. W., & Wynne, M. E. (1984). How much stimulant medication is appropriate for hyperactive school children? *Journal of School Health, 54,* 128–130.

Callaway, E. (1983). The pharmacology of human information processing. *Psychophysiology, 20,* 359–370.

Campbell, S. B., Douglas, V. I., & Morgenstern, G. (1971). Cognitive styles in hyperactive children and the effect of methylphenidate. *Journal of Child Psychology and Psychiatry, 12,* 55–67.

Carlson G. A., & Rapport, M. D. (1989). Diagnostic classification issues in attention deficit disorder. *Psychiatry Annals, 19,* 576–583.

Cohen, N. J., Douglas, V. I., & Morgenstern, G. (1971). The effect of methylphenidate on attentive behavior and autonomic activity in hyperactive children. *Psychopharmacologia, 22,* 282–294.

Conners, C. K. (1971). Drugs in the management of children with learning disabilities. In L. Tarnopol (Ed.), *Learning disorders in children: Diagnosis, medication, education* (pp. 287–293). Boston: Little, Brown.

Conners, C. K., Blouin, A. G., Winglee, M., Lougee, L., O'Donnell, D., & Smith, A. (1984). Piracetam and event-related potentials in dyslexic children. *Psychopharmacology Bulletin, 20,* 667–673.

Conners, C. K., & Eisenberg, L. (1963). The effects of methylphenidate on symptomatology and learning in disturbed children. *American Journal of Psychiatry, 120,* 458–464.

Conners, C. K., Eisenberg, L., & Sharpe, L. (1964). Effects of methylphenidate (Ritalin) on paired-associate learning and Porteus maze performance in emotionally disturbed children. *Journal of Consulting Psychology, 28,* 14–22.

Conners, C. K., & Solanto, M. V. (1984). The psychophysiology of stimulant drug response in hyperkinetic children. In L. M. Bloomingdale (Ed.), *Attention deficit disorder: Diagnostic, cognitive, and therapeutic understanding* (pp. 191–204) New York: Spectrum.

Conners, C. K., & Taylor, E. (1980). Pemoline, methylphenidate, and placebo in children with minimal brain dysfunction. *Archives of General Psychiatry, 37,* 922–930.

Conners, C. K., & Wells, K. C. (1986). Hyperkinetic children: A neuropsychosocial approach. In A. E. Kazdin (Ed.), *Developmental clinical psychology and psychiatry* (Vol. 7, pp. 1–160) Beverly Hills, CA: Sage Publications.

Conners, C. K., & Werry, J. S. (1979). Pharmacotherapy. In H. C. Quay, & J. S. Werry (Eds.), *Psychopathological disorders in childhood* (2nd ed.) (pp. 336–386). New York: John Wiley & Sons.

Cronbach, L. J. (1977). *Educational psychology* (3rd ed.) New York: Harcourt Brace Jovanovich.

Dalby, J. T., Kinsbourne, M., & Swanson, J. M. (1989). Self-paced learning in children with attention deficit disorder with hyperactivity. *Journal of Abnormal Child Psychology, 17,* 269–275.

Dalby, J. T., Kinsbourne, M., Swanson, J. M., & Sobol, M. P. (1977). Hyperactive children's underuse of learning time: Correction by stimulant treatment. *Child Development, 48,* 1448–1453.

Douglas, V. I. (1984). The psychological processes indicated in ADD. In L. M. Bloomingdale (Ed.), *Attention deficit disorder: Diagnostic, cognitive and therapeutic understanding* (pp. 147–162). Jamaica, NY: Spectrum Publications.

Douglas, V. I. (1988). Cognitive deficits in children with attention deficit disorder with hyperactivity. In L. M. Bloomingdale & J. Sergeant (Eds.), *Attention deficit disorder: Criteria, cognition, intervention* (pp. 65–81). Elmsford, NY: Pergamon Press.

Douglas, V. I., Barr, R. G., Amin, K., O'Neill, M. E., & Britton, B. G. (1988). Dosage effects and individual responsivity to methylphenidate in attention deficit disorder. *Journal of Child Psychology and Psychiatry, 29*, 453–475.

Douglas, V. I., Barr, R. G., O'Neill, M. E., & Britton, B. G. (1986). Short term effects of methylphenidate on the cognitive, learning and academic performance of children with attention deficit disorder in the laboratory and the classroom. *Journal of Child Psychology and Psychiatry, 27*, 191–211.

Douglas, V. I., & Peters, K. (1979). Toward a clearer definition of the attention deficit of hyperactive children. In G. A. Hale & M. Lewis (Eds.), *Attentional and cognitive development* (pp. 173–247). New York: Plenum Publishing.

Draeger, S., Prior, M., & Sanson, A. (1986). Visual and auditory attention performance in hyperactive children: Competence or compliance. *Journal of Abnormal Child Psychology, 14*, 411–424.

Evans, R. W., Gualtieri, C. T., & Amara, I. (1986). Methylphenidate and memory: Dissociated effects on hyperactive children. *Psychopharmacology, 90*, 211–216.

Firestone, P., & Douglas, V. I. (1975). The effects of reward and punishment on reaction times and automatic activity in hyperactive and normal children. *Journal of Abnormal Child Psychology, 3*, 201–215.

Flintoff, M. M., Barron, R. W., Swanson, J. M., Ledlow, A., & Kinsbourne, M. (1982). Methylphenidate increases selectivity of visual scanning in children referred for hyperactivity. *Journal of Abnormal Child Psychology, 10*, 145–161.

Gadow, K. D. (1985). Relative efficacy of pharmacological, behavioral, and combination treatments for enhancing academic performance. *Clinical Psychology Review, 5*, 513–533.

Gaffney, G. R., Muilenburg, J., Sieg, K. G., & Preston, D. (1989). *Brain imaging in attention-deficit hyperactivity disorder.* Paper presented at the 36th annual meeting of the American Academy of Child and Adolescent Psychiatry (October 11–15), New York.

Gagne, R. M. (1977). *The conditions of learning* (3rd ed.). New York: Holt Rinehart & Winston.

Gan, J., & Cantwell, D. P. (1982). Dosage effects of methylphenidate on paired associate learning: Positive/negative placebo responders. *Journal of the American Academy of Child Psychiatry, 21*, 237–242.

Gittelman, R., Klein, D. F., & Feingold, I. (1983). Children with reading disorders II. Effects of methylphenidate in combination with reading remediation. *Journal of Child Psychology and Psychiatry, 24*, 193–212.

Goyette, C. J., Conners, C. K., & Ulrich, R. F. (1978). Normative data on Revised Conners Parent and Teacher Rating Scales. *Journal of Abnormal Child Psychology, 6*, 221–236.

Gualtieri, C. T., Hicks, R., Patrick, K., Schroeder, S., & Breese, G. (1984). Clinical correlates of methylphenidate serum levels in children and adults. *Therapeutic Drug Monitoring, 6*, 379–392.

Hasher, L., & Zachs, R. T. (1979). Automatic and effortful processing in memory. *Journal of Experimental Psychology, 108*, 356–388.

Henker, B., & Whalen, C. K. (1989). Hyperactivity and attention deficits. *American Psychologist, 44*, 216–223.

Humphrey, L. L. (1982). Children's and teacher's perspectives on children's self-control: The development of two rating scales. *Journal of Consulting and Clinical Psychology, 50*, 624–633.

Kelly, K. L., Rapport, M. D., & DuPaul, G. J. (1988). Attention deficit disorder and methylphenidate: A multistep analysis of dose-response effects on children's cardiovascular functioning. *International Clinical Psychopharmacology, 3*, 167–181.

Kinsbourne, M. (1984). Beyond attention deficit: Search for the disorder in ADD. In L. Bloomingdale (Ed.), *Attention deficit disorder: Diagnostic, cognitive, and therapeutic understand*ing (pp. 133–162). New York: Spectrum Publications.

Kinsbourne, M., & Swanson J. M. (1979). Models of hyperactivity: Implications for diagnosis and treatment. In R. L. Trites (Ed.), *Hyperactivity in children: Etiology, measurement and treatment implications* (pp. 1–20). Baltimore, MD: University Park Press.

Klorman, R., Crumaghim, J. T., Coons, H. W., Peloquin, L., Strauss, J., Lewine, J. D., Borgstedt, A. D., & Goldstein, M. G. (1988). The contributions of event-related potentials to understanding effects of stimulants on information processing in attention deficit disorder. In L. M. Bloomingdale & J. Sergeant (Eds.), *Attention deficit disorder: Criteria, cognitive, intervention* (pp. 199–218). *Elmsford, NY: Pergamon Press.*

Klorman, R., Salzman, L. F., & Borgstedt, A. D. (1988). Brain event-related potentials in evaluation of cognitive deficits in attention deficit disorder and outcome of stimulant therapy. In L. M. Bloomingdale (Ed.), *Attention deficit disorder: New research in attention, treatment, and psychopharmacology* (pp. 49–80). Elmsford, NY: Pergamon Press.

Klorman, R., Brumaghim, J. T., Salzman, L. F., Strauss, J., Borgstedt, A. D., McBride, M. C., & Loeb, S. (1989). Comparative effects of methylphenidate on attention-deficit hyperactivity disorder with and without aggressive/noncompliant features. *Psychopharmacology Bulletin, 25*, 109–113.

Kupietz, S. S., Winsberg, B. G., Richardson, E., Maitinsky, S., & Mendell, N. (1988). Effects of methylphenidate dosage in hyperactive reading-disabled children: I. Behavior and cognitive performance effects. *Journal of the American Academy of Child and Adolescent Psychiatry, 27,* 70–77.

Kupietz, S. S., & Balka, E. B. (1976). Alterations in the vigilance performance of children receiving amitriptyline and methylphenidate pharmacotherapy. *Psychopharmacology, 50,* 29–33.

Malone, M. A., Kershner, J. R., & Seigel, L. (1988). The effects of methylphenidate on levels of processing and laterality in children with attention deficit disorder. *Journal of Abnormal Child Psychology, 16,* 379–395.

McGee, R., & Share, D. L. (1988). Attention deficit disorder-hyperactivity and academic failure: Which comes first and what should be treated? *Journal of the American Academy of Child and Adolescent Psychiatry, 27,* 318–325.

Mulder, G. (1983). The information processing paradigm: Concepts, methods and limitations. *Journal of Child Psychology and Psychiatry, 24,* 19–35.

Pelham, W. E., Bender, M. E., Caddell, J., Booth, S., & Moorer, S. H. (1985). Methylphenidate and children with attention deficit disorder. *Archives of General Psychiatry, 42,* 948–952.

Pelham, W. E., Milich, R., & Walker, J. L. (1986). Effects of continuous and partial reinforcement and methylphenidate on learning in children with attention deficit disorder. *Journal of Abnormal Psychology, 95,* 319–325.

Pelham, W. E., Schnedler, R. W., Bologna, N. C., & Contreras, A. (1980). Behavioral and stimulant treatment of hyperactive children: A therapy study with methylphenidate probes in a within subject design. *Journal of Applied Behavior Analysis, 13,* 221–236.

Pelham, W. E., Sturges, J., Hoza, J., Schmidt, C., Bijlsma J. J., Milich, R., & Moorer, S. (1987). Sustained release and standard methylphenidate effects on cognitive and social behavior in children with attention deficit disorder. *Pediatrics, 80,* 491–501.

Peloquin, L. J., & Klorman, R. (1986). Effects of methylphenidate on normal children's mood, event-related potentials, and performance in memory scanning and vigilance. *Journal of Abnormal Psychology, 95,* 88–98.

Posner, M. I., & Presti, D. E. (1987). Selective attention and cognitive control. *Trends in Neuroscience, 10,* 13–17.

Rapoport, J. L., & Zametkin, A. (1988). Drug treatment of attention deficit disorder. In L. M. Bloomingdale, & J. Sergeant (Eds.), *Attention deficit disorder: Criteria, cognition, intervention* (pp. 161–182). Elmsford, NY: Pergamon Press.

Rapport, M. D. (1983). Attention deficit disorder with hyperactivity: Critical treatment parameters and their application in applied outcome research. In M. Hersen, R. Eisler, & P. Miller (Eds.), *Progress in behavior modification* (pp. 219–298). New York: Academic Press.

Rapport, M. D. (1988). Attention deficit disorder with hyperactivity. In V. B. Van Hasselt, P. S. Strain, & M. Hersen (Eds.), *Handbook of developmental and physical disabilities* (pp. 295–315). Elmsford, NY: Pergamon Press.

Rapport, M. D. (1990). Controlled studies of the effects of psychostimulants on children's functioning in clinic and classroom settings. In C. K. Conners, & M. Kinsbourne (Eds.), Attention deficit hyperactivity disorder: ADHD; clinical, experimental and demographic issues. Germany: MMV, Medizin Verlag.

Rapport, M. D., DuPaul, G. J., & Kelly, K. L. (1989). Attention-deficit hyperactivity disorder and methylphenidate: The relationship between gross body weight and drug response in children. *Psychopharmacology Bulletin, 25,* 285–290.

Rapport, M. D., DuPaul, G. J., Stoner, G., Birmingham, B. K., & Masse, G. (1985-a). Attention deficit disorder with hyperactivity: Differential effects of methylphenidate on impulsivity. *Pediatrics, 76,* 938–943.

Rapport, M. D., DuPaul, G. J., Stoner, G., & Jones, J. T. (1986-a). Comparing classroom and clinic measures of attention deficit disorder: Differential, idiosyncratic, and dose-response effects of methylphenidate. *Journal of Consulting and Clinical Psychology, 54,* 334–341.

Rapport, M. D., Jones, J. T., DuPaul, G. J., Kelly, K. L., Gardner, M. J., Tucker, S. B., & Shea, M. S. (1987). Attention deficit disorder and methylphenidate: Group and single-subject analyses of dose effects on attention in clinic and classroom settings. *Journal of Clinical Child Psychology, 16,* 329–338.

Rapport, M. D., Murphy, H. A., & Bailey, J. S. (1982). Ritalin vs. response cost in the control of hyperactive children: A within subject comparison. *Journal of Applied Behavior Analysis, 15,* 205–216.

Rapport, M. D., Quinn, S. O., DuPaul, G. J., Quinn, E. P., & Kelly, K. L. (1989). Attention deficit disorder with hyperactivity and methylphenidate: The effects of dose and mastery level on children's learning performance. *Journal of Abnormal Child Psychology, 17,* 669–689.

Rapport, M. D., Stoner, G., DuPaul, G. J., Birmingham, B. K., & Tucker, S. (1985-b). Methylphenidate in hyperactive children: Differential effects of dose on academic learning and social behavior. *Journal of Abnormal Child Psychology, 13,* 227–243.

Rapport, M. D., Stoner, G., DuPaul, G. J., Kelly, K. L.,

Tucker, S. B., & Schoeler, T. (1988). Attention deficit disorder and methylphenidate: A multilevel analysis of dose-response effects on children's impulsivity across settings. *Journal of the American Academy of Child and Adolescent Psychiatry, 27,* 60–69.

Rapport, M. D., Tucker, S., DuPaul, G. J., Merlo, M., & Stoner, G. (1986-b). The influence of control over and size of rewards in delaying gratification. *Journal of Abnormal Child Psychology, 14,* 191–204.

Reid, M. K., & Borkowski, J. G. (1984). Effects of methylphenidate (Ritalin) on information processing in hyperactive children. *Journal of Abnormal Child Psychology, 12,* 169–186.

Rosen, L. A., O'Leary, S. G., Joyce, S. A., Conway, G., & Pfiffner, L. J. (1984). The importance of prudent negative consequences for monitoring the appropriate behavior of hyperactive students. *Journal of Abnormal Child Psychology, 12,* 581–604.

Schachar, R., Logan, G., Wachsmuth, R., & Chajczyk, D. (1988). Attaining and maintaining preparation: A comparison of attention in hyperactive, normal and disturbed control children. *Journal of Abnormal Child Psychology, 16,* 361–378.

Sebrechts, M. M., Shaywitz, S. E., Shaywitz, B. A., Jatlow, P., Anderson, G. M., & Cohen D. J. (1986). Components of attention, methylphenidate dosage, and blood levels in children with attention deficit disorder. *Pediatrics, 77,* 222–228.

Sergeant, J. (1988). From DSM-III attentional deficit disorder to functional defects. In L. M. Bloomingdale & J. Sergeant (Eds.), *Attention deficit disorder: Criteria, cognition, intervention* (pp. 183–198). Elmsford, NY: Pergamon Press.

Shaywitz, S. E., Hunt, R. D., Jatlow, P., Cohen, D. J., Young, J. G., Pierce, R. N., Anderson, G. M., & Shaywitz, B. A. (1982). Psychopharmacology of attention deficit disorder: Pharmacokinetic, neuroendocrine, and behavioral measures following acute and chronic treatment with methylphenidate. *Pediatrics, 669,* 688–694.

Shaywitz, S. E., & Shaywitz, B. E. (1988). Attention deficit disorder: Current perspectives. In J. F. Kavanagh, & T. J. Truss (Eds.), *Learning disabilities: Proceedings of the National Conference* (pp. 369–523). Parkton, MD: York Press, Inc.

Solanto, M. V. (1984). Neuropharmacological basis of stimulant drug action in attention deficit disorder with hyperactivity: A review and synthesis. *Psychological Bulletin, 3,* 387–409.

Solanto, M. V., & Conners, C. K. (1982). A dose-response and time-action analysis of autonomic and behavioral effects of methylphenidate in attention deficit disorder with hyperactivity. *Psychophysiology, 19,* 658–667.

Solanto, M. V., & Wender, E. H. (1989). Does methylphenidate constrict cognitive functioning? *Journal of the American Academy of Child and Adolescent Psychiatry, 26, 356–362.*

Sprague, R. L. (1972). Psychopharmacology and learning disabilities. *Journal of Operational Psychiatry, 3,* 56–67.

Sprague, R. L., Barnes, K. R., & Werry, J. S. (1970). Methylphenidate and thioridazine: Learning, reaction time, activity, and classroom behavior in disturbed children. *American Journal of Orthopsychiatry, 40,* 615–628.

Sprague, R. L., & Sleator, E. K. (1973). Effects of psychopharmacological agents on learning disabilities. *Pediatric Clinics of North America, 20,* 719–735.

Sprague, R. L., & Sleator, E. K. (1975). What is the proper dose of stimulant drugs in children? *International Journal of Mental Health, 4,* 75–104.

Sprague, R. L., & Sleator, E. K. (1976). Drugs and dosages: Implications for learning disabilities. In R. M. Knights & D. J. Bakker (Eds.), *The neuropsychology of learning disorders: Theoretical approaches* (pp. 351–366). Baltimore, MD: University Park Press.

Sprague, R. L., & Sleator, E. K. (1977). Methylphenidate in hyperkinetic children: Differences in dose effects on learning and social behavior. *Science, 198,* 1274–1276.

Sprague, R. L., & Werry, J. S. (1971). Methodology of psychopharmacological studies with the retarded. *International Review of Research in Mental Retardation, 5,* 147–219.

Stephens, R., Pelham, W. E., & Skinner, R. (1984). State-dependent and main effects of pemoline and methylphenidate on paired-associate learning and spelling in hyperactive children. *Journal of Consulting and Clinical Psychology, 52,* 104–113.

Swanson, J. M. (1985). Measures of cognitive functioning appropriate for use in pediatric psychopharmacological research studies. *Psychopharmacology Bulletin, 4,* 887–892.

Swanson, J. M. (1988). What do psychopharmacological studies tell us about information processing deficits in ADDH? In L. M. Bloomingdale & J. Sergeant (Eds.), *Attention deficit disorder: Criteria, cognition, intervention* (pp. 97–115). Elmsford, NY: Pergamon Press.

Swanson, J. M., Sandman, C. A., Deutsch, C., & Baren, M. (1983). Methylphenidate hydrochloride given with or before breakfast. I. Behavioral, cognitive, and electrophysiological effects. *Pediatrics, 72,* 49–55.

Swanson, J. N., Barlow, A., & Kinsbourne, M. (1979). Task specificity of response to stimulant drugs in laboratory tests. *International Journal of Mental Health, 8,* 67–82.

Swanson, J. M., Kinsbourne, M., Roberts, W., & Zucker,

K. (1978). Time-response analysis of the effects of stimulant medication on the learning ability of children referred for hyperactivity. *Pediatrics, 61,* 21–29.

Sykes, D. H., Douglas, V. I., & Morgenstern, G. (1972). The effect of methylphenidate (Ritalin) on sustained attention in hyperactive children. *Psychopharmacologia, 25,* 262–274.

Sykes, D. H., Douglas, V. I., & Morgenstern, G. (1973). Sustained attention in hyperactive children. *Journal of Child Psychology and Psychiatry, 14,* 213–220.

Sykes, D. H., Douglas, V. I., Weiss, G., & Minde, K. K. (1971). Attention in hyperactive children and the effect of methylphenidate (Ritalin). *Journal of Child Psychology and Psychiatry, 12,* 129–139.

Tannock, R., Schachar, R. L., Carr, R. P., Chajczk, D., & Logan, G. D. (1989). Effects of methylphenidate on inhibitory control in hyperactive children. *Journal of Abnormal Child Psychology, 17,* 473–491.

Taylor, E., Schachar, R., Thorley, G., Wieselberg, H. M., Everitt, B., & Rutter, M. (1987). Which boys respond to stimulant medication? A controlled trial of methylphenidate in boys with disruptive behavior. *Psychological Medicine, 17,* 121–143.

Thurston, C. M., Sobol, M. P., Swanson, J., & Kinsbourne, M. (1979). Effects of methylphenidate (Ritalin) on selective attention in hyperactive children. *Journal of Abnormal Child Psychology, 7,* 471–481.

Ullmann, R. K., Sleator, E. K., & Sprague, R. L. (1985). Introduction to the use of ACTeRS. *Psychopharmacology Bulletin, 21,* 915–920.

Vyse, S. A., & Rapport, M. D. (1989). The effects of methylphenidate on learning in children with ADDH: The stimulus equivalence paradigm. *Journal of Consulting and Clinical Psychology, 57,* 425–435.

Weiss, G., & Hechtman, L. (1986). *Hyperactive children grown up.* New York: Guilford Press.

Weiss, B., & Laties, V. G. (1962). Enhancement of human performance by caffeine and the amphetamines. *Pharmacological Reviews, 14,* 1–36.

Weiss, G., Werry, J. S., Minde, K., Douglas, V., &

Sykes, D. (1968). Studies on the hyperactive child V: The effects of dextroamphetamine and chlorpromazine on behavior and intellectual functioning. *Journal of Child Psychology and Psychiatry, 9,* 145–156.

Werry, J. S. (1982). An overview of pediatric psychopharmacology. *Journal of the American Academy of Child Psychiatry, 21,* 3–9.

Werry, J. S. (1988). Drugs, learning and cognitive function in children—An update. *Journal of Child Psychology and Psychiatry, 29,* 129–141.

Werry, J. S., & Aman, M. G. (1975). Methylphenidate and haloperidol in children: Effects on attention, memory and activity. *Archives of General Psychiatry, 32,* 790–795.

Werry, J. S., Aman, M. G., & Diamond, E. (1980). Imipramine and methylphenidate in hyperactive children. *Journal of Child Psychology and Psychiatry, 21,* 27–35.

Werry, J. S., Elkind, G. S., & Reeves, J. C. (1987). Attention deficit, conduct, oppositional, and anxiety disorders in children: III. Laboratory differences. *Journal of Abnormal Child Psychology, 15,* 409–428.

Werry, J. S., & Sprague, R. L. (1974). Methylphenidate in children: Effect of dosage. *Australian and New Zealand Journal of Psychiatry, 8,* 9–19.

Werry, J. S., Sprague, R. L., Weiss, G., & Minde, K. (1970). Some clinical and laboratory studies of psychotropic drugs in children: An overview. In W. L. Smith (Ed.), *Symposium on higher cortical function* (pp. 134–144). Springfield, IL: Charles C Thomas.

Werry, J. S., & Wollersheim, J. P. (1989). Behavioral therapy with children and adolescents: A twenty year overview. *Journal of the American Academy of Child and Adolescent Psychiatry, 28,* 1–18.

Zametkin, A. J., & Rapoport, J. L. (1987). Neurobiology of attention deficit disorder with hyperactivity: Where have we come in 50 years? *Journal of the American Academy of Child and Adolescent Psychiatry, 26,* 676–686.

CHAPTER 7

DIAGNOSIS

John S. Werry

The term *diagnosis* is used in different ways in child psychopathology but most imply a process of defining what the problem(s) is so as to allow the application of professional knowledge. In medicine, diagnosis has a more precise meaning of defining an abnormal state of function, disease, or disorder, by applying a classificatory name or label which serves as a point of entry or index to all the technical knowledge about that disorder. It is in this way that the term will be used here. Psychiatry is the medical specialty that deals with disorders of behavior and emotion, though in the case of children much of this role is also carried out by pediatricians and other medical specialists like neurologists. Not surprisingly, all these medical specialties carry with them the epistemological baggage of medicine including the concept of diagnosis.

It has become fashionable in many quarters to deride and deplore the notion of diagnosis in psychopathology especially with children, as "labeling" human beings in such a way as to elide their uniqueness and individuality as human beings, as emphasizing abnormality rather than health, as medicalizing what is human unhappiness or justifiable discomfort, hence treating it as abnormal, requiring it to be dealt with in the health system and leading to emphasis on physical methods of assessment and treatment. Much of this thinking is in fact erroneous but it will be the purpose of this chapter to review

the application of diagnosis to hyperactivity highlighting its strengths and weaknesses.

THE PURPOSE AND CHARACTERISTICS OF DIAGNOSIS

As noted, as used here, diagnosis a label that serves to identify a body of technical knowledge about a disease or disorder. The components of this knowledge include the following: (a) defining characteristics that must tell not only what the disorder is but what it is not—that is, it must have distinctiveness or specificity; (b) the epidemiology or distribution of the disorder in the population and various subgroups such as particular gender, cultural, ethnic, or ecological groups; (c) the associated symptomatology or features that indicate the kinds of other problems (e.g., learning disorders) which, though not essential to the diagnosis, are often part of it; (d) the etiology or cause of the disorder including the fundamental derangements of structure or function which give rise to the clinical picture as seen; (e) the course of the disorder over time and its outcome; (f) the treatment of the disorder; and (g) its prevention. The number of disorders in medicine in which the diagnostic label can provide information in all seven areas is much smaller than is generally believed, but in psychiatry, the hit rate falls much shorter of ideal for all disorders. Even more disturbing, what is known in any category is often only probabilistic, and the order of probability may only be somewhat above chance level. It may not be a great deal of help to know, for example that in 6% to 10% of cases the children of someone with schizophrenia may develop the disorder; the question is what is the situation for this child or children?

The question then must arise as to why diagnose at all in psychopathology? Several authors have tried to answer this (e.g., Cantwell & Baker, 1988; Gittelman, 1988; Rutter & Shaffer, 1980; Werry, 1985). The first purpose is to define a common language that can be shared by professionals (and/or clients), however imprecise. Thus, the term *hyperactive child* conjures up for all who use it a clinical picture that has strong elements of communality across persons, though there may be substantial variations in particular elements of the picture. Such a common language is even more essential for research, and whatever may be said about the precision or otherwise of *hyperactivity,* it indisputably has been a profound stimulus to research that has had spin-off far beyond the field of hyperactivity. For example, much of the methodology of abnormal child psychology has come out of research on hyperactivity. Many parents find comfort in the label of hyperactivity as it tells them that they are not the first parents to have such a child and it satisfies, however incompletely, the fundamental question put to every professional: "What is wrong with my child?" There are also now implications for commonly found correlates for treatment and for outcome (see below). As with any medical diagnosis, there are those who will overdiagnose and misapply treatments; but this argument is no more valid for discarding the diagnosis of hyperactivity than it would be for doing the same with the diagnosis of, say, bacterial infection and the consequent prescription of antibiotics just because a large proportion of such diagnoses and prescriptions in ambulatory practice are almost certainly viral not bacterial and hence beyond the reach of any medical treatment. The real question to be faced is what is the scientific status of the diagnosis of hyperactivity?

HISTORICAL VIEW

The first chapter in this monograph and several reviews have addressed the historical issue (Campbell & Werry, 1986; Ross & Ross, 1982 pp. 1–24; Weiss & Hechtman, 1986). Here, the focus is on the medical-diagnostic category. The notion of a diagnostic entity of hyperactivity, hyperkinesis, minimal brain damage or dysfunction as it was originally or subsequently called, began at least last century and even before. However, the real impetus in medicine seems to have begun in the second quarter of this century in the aftermath of the encephalitis epidemic and as a result of the seminal influence of the emigrant German pediatric neurologist Strauss who defined the "brain damage-behavior syndrome" in the late 1940s. Like an epidemic, in which the initial incubation period may take some time, there was only an occasional article in the 1950s (e.g., Laufer & Denhoff, 1957) to show that the idea of a diagnosis of hyperactivity was alive and spreading. However, by the 1960s the idea was in full flight, resulting in the famous monographs by Clements (1966) and probably the most influential of all, the convincing but scientifically not well-documented monograph by Wender (1972). The rest is too well known to need detailing. According to Ross and Ross (1982), the number of publications rose from 31 in the period from 1957 to 1960 to 700 in the three years from 1977 to 1980 and the rate is still climbing.

Prior to 1980, there was no universally agreed way to define hyperactivity and the field can only be described as chaotic (see Ross & Ross, 1982). In fact, some of the definitions of hyperactivity were so loose that practically anything that adults disliked about a child could be so encompassed. Barkley (1982) found that of 210 studies of hyperactivity, less than a third set out any diagnostic criteria at all and of these, most were below an acceptable level.

Reaction was not long in coming both publicly (as in Omaha, Nebraska) and professionally (e.g., Prior & Sanson, 1986; Rutter & Shaffer, 1980). Psychiatric conventions in the United States can now expect to be regularly picketed by opponents of the medical-diagnostic view of hyperactivity and its medical treatment. Despite the chaos, however, there were some emergent themes of how to diagnose, of which two eventually have become prepotent. The first is a traditional psychologist's approach, based on normative scores on Conners' behavior problem checklists, especially his Teacher Questionnaire (see Conners, 1985), and is discussed in more detail elsewhere. The other, which is the subject of this review, is a medical one derived from literature on "the hyperkinetic syndrome" (Laufer & Denhoff, 1957). Like most medical diagnoses it required a particular pattern of symptoms—in this case, hyperactivity, impulsivity, short attention span, and distractibility with variable contributions of aggressivity—in typical medical fashion. The presence of this pattern was defined largely by the eye of the diagnostician rather than in precise terms as in the competing psychologist approach. With the appearance in 1980 of DSM-III (American Psychiatric Association [APA], 1980), which embodied the medical view, much of the diagnostic chaos seems to have disappeared, though this should not be taken as automatically meaning that from a scientific point of view, things are necessarily in fine fettle. Also, DSM-III certainly has not replaced the psychologist method, as recent issues of the *Journal of Abnormal Child Psychology* well illustrate.

DIAGNOSTIC SYSTEMS IN ABNORMAL PSYCHOLOGY

In his comprehensive review, Quay (1986a) describes two main classification systems, the medical-categorical and the dimensional.

Dimensional Classifications

The dimensional classification is discussed in detail in chapter 6 by Dyckman, but briefly, it describes children along a set of dimensions and yields a profile which, if there are several dimensions, is unique to that child. All children are scored on all dimensions. The usual method by which such dimensional systems are derived is from behavior symptom checklists completed by parents or teachers and subjected to empirical multivariate statistical analyses, most commonly factor analysis.

In practice however, profiles seem to be rather unpopular and Quay, for example, slides impercepti-

bly from dimensions or profiles into talking of categories of children such as "conduct disordered" or "anxious-withdrawn," while those who follow Achenbach talk of externalizers or internalizers (see Quay, 1986a).

The principal dimensional system used in hyperactivity is derived from Conners Teacher Questionnaire (Conners, 1985) which is referred to frequently throughout this book. As noted, abnormality is in terms of deviations from population norms (1.5–2) and is discussed elsewhere. Suffice it to say here that such a method of establishing a category is radically different from the medical one in that it makes assumptions about the frequency of a disorder in the population derived from the normal distribution curve rather than from some independent way of demonstrating the frequency or validity of the disorder. It is thus based on normal variation rather than abnormality. In practice, too, it has nearly always been unidimensional or unifactorial, though in some cases low scores on other dimensions such as conduct problem and high scores on two dimensions such as inattention and hyperactivity have been necessary for category definition (e.g., Raport, Tucker, DuPaul, Merlo, & Stoner, 1986).

One should clearly understand that this diagnostic system is not synonymous with the medical ones that follow as the underlying assumptions and the data base are dissimilar. It is likely, however, that there is some degree of overlap in diagnoses made by both systems.

Medical or Categorical Systems

In contrast, medical systems are categorical or, put another way, one either has the disorder or does not, though there are degrees of severity once the disorder is said to be present. Unlike the gradation in a dimensional system, all degrees of the diagnosis are ipso facto abnormal so that a diagnosis always implies abnormality. The process by which diagnostic classifications are derived also differs in that these classifications are still, and certainly always used to be, based on a derivative of "visual inspection" in which a pattern of symptoms were said to hang together in such a way that the pattern was unique and meaningful. Few of the categories in medicine have been subjected to formal statistical analysis to determine the degree to which this "eyeball" pattern is empirically real. Unlike diagnoses in psychiatry, however, most physical diagnoses, to survive, have had to show that they had some degree of validity or utility, at least in terms of pathology, treatment, or outcome. Further, for all its pretensions to science, medicine was, and to some degree still is, an authoritarian system; status rather than science was the test of whether a diagnosis should be accepted into a classification system. In many ways DSM-III typified the authoritarian tradition in medicine as its scientific base was far too slender to justify many of its categories (see Quay 1986a; Rutter & Shaffer, 1980) and its acceptance derived as much from the authority of the body espousing it (the large and powerful American Psychiatric Association) as to anything else.

There are two main medical diagnostic classification systems. These are discussed in the following sections.

International Classification of Diseases (ICD)

As the name suggests, the International Classification of Diseases is the official system for all countries that belong to the United Nations. It is published by a UN body, the World Health Organization. The current version of the ICD is the ninth revision or ICD-9 which contains several categories of relevance to hyperactivity. With few exceptions, however, the ICD-9 has never been widely accepted, especially in the serious research literature on hyperactivity. It will be replaced shortly by the next revision, which is rumored to be radically different. The ICD-9 classification is discussed by Quay (1986a) and Werry (1985), for those who are interested in obtaining further details, but it will not be discussed further here.

Diagnostic and Statistical Manual (DSM-III)

The publication of the American Psychiatric Association's *Diagnostic and Statistical Manual of Mental Disorders,* 3rd ed. (DSM-III; American Psychiatric Association [APA], 1980) in 1980 proved

to be one of the most important events in the history of psychiatry. Useful reviews of it can be found in Quay (1986a) and Cantwell and Baker (1988). DSM-III was instantaneously successful and virtually swept aside all other classifications (including ICD-9) in most countries. This success, however, was not based on any scientific foundation for the taxonomic system; rather, it seems the DSM-III offered what the vast majority of psychiatrists seemed to want—a diagnostic system that was comprehensive and explicit, complete with a handbook that set out the main features of each disorder and the rules by which the diagnosis was to be made. Dissident voices and proponents of alternative systems (see Achenbach, 1980; Quay 1986a; Rutter & Shaffer, 1980) who attempted to draw attention to the shortcoming of DSM-III—such as the unwarranted and untested number of categories and subcategories—had little impact.

In the area of hyperactivity, DSM-III reduced chaos almost overnight and there are now few papers that do not use DSM-III or its derivative DSM-III-R criteria for diagnosis, if they hold to a medical categorical system. In order to escape the nosological chaos and make a clean start, and in sharp contrast ot ICD-9, which retained the term *hyperkinetic syndrome,* DSM-III accepted Virginia Douglas's (1972) long-standing contention that the real problem was not hyperactivity but a cognitive disorder of inattention, and named it "attention deficit disorder with hyperactivity" (ADDH) in which hyperactivity was relegated to second place. In setting out the diagnostic criteria, DSM-III formalized what had become almost customary medical practice in diagnosing hyperactivity or hyperkinesis (e.g., Laufer & Denhoff, 1957) by defining the disorder as having three necessary symptom-domains: inattention, impulsivity, and hyperactivity. Where DSM-III differed from previous medical practice was in its attempt to define what it meant by each of the key symptoms-domains by providing a "menu" of behavioral symptoms for each domain together with the minimum number of these symptoms necessary to declare it present. While this was an improvement over the previous situation, it tended to mask the reality that there was still a great deal of subjectivity and imprecision in the diagnostic judgments about each symptom. Also novel were the requirements that the condition be chronic (duration greater than 6 months) and have onset before the patient was 7 years old. Although these features were also derived from previous medical thinking, they were less stringent, as there had been a tacit acceptance previously that, except where there was some obvious major brain insult such as encephalitis postnatally, the disorder first appeared in early life, usually when the child first began to walk. DSM-III also had a category of attention of deficit disorder without hyperactivity (ADD) which differed from ADDH only in not having hyperactivity as one of its symptom-domains and in having a "residual" category where the patient once had ADDH but now had lost the hyperactivity though retaining sufficient inattention and impulsivity to be impaired. Not only was DSM-III unique in setting out precise diagnostic criteria but it also had exclusionary criteria of which the most important was severe or profound mental retardation.

It is also important to emphasize that DSM-III had one other feature that events would show was seldom observed in practice, and that was to make as many diagnoses as all the symptoms required. Nevertheless, unitary diagnoses were common and it was not until the late 1980s that the concept of "comorbidity" or the coexistence of more than one diagnosis became generally accepted. This failure makes for considerable diffficulties in interpreting many studies of ADDH because of the common association between ADDH and conduct/oppositional disorder (see Werry, Reeves, & Elkind, 1987a). A similar problem is now emerging in childhood depression (Anderson et al., 1987) and anxiety disorders (Werry, in press), where comorbidity is also common.

Despite seeing ADDH as a genuine advance, Barkley (1982) drew attention to some major problems primarily the absence of any specified ways to determine, measure, or norm the symptoms, and it comments on how severe (pervasive) the symptoms must be (a major argument of the English school; see Schachar, Sandberg & Rutter, 1986). He also disagreed with the age of onset (too late) and the duration (too short). It should also be added that there is considerable reason to doubt that the domain of impulsivity is valid or discrete from hyperactivity (Campbell & Werry, 1986; Dienske & Sanders-Woudstra, 1988; Gittelman, 1988).

DSM-III-R

In 1987, the American Psychiatric Association published its revised *Diagnostic and Statistical Manual of Mental Disorders,* third edition (DSM-III-R), to a startled and often disgruntled world (see Rey 1988; Werry, 1988c). The cause of this disaffection lay primarily in the very strong feeling that there had been insufficient time to do studies of DSM-III which would have allowed the changes made in DSM-III-R to have occurred on the basis of sufficient hard data about its defects instead of by what seemed to be quite arbitrary means. The DSM-III-R manual and a review by two of those involved (Cantwell & Baker, 1988) provides both a catalog of the changes and some of the rationale.

ADDH was now relabeled "attention deficit hyperactive disorder" to bring back hyperactivity to at least equal status; but the most important change lay in the defining characteristics. Although the preamble reaffirmed the triad of symptom-domains of inattention, impulsivity, and hyperactivity, the way of determining the diagnosis was now "polythetic" or on the basis of a single list or menu of 14 symptoms of which 8 were needed. The reason given for this was (American Psychiatric Association, 1987, p. 411) that in field trials of several hundred children, the single list, the symptoms and the threshold (8 symptoms) gave better sensitivity and specificity, especially with respect to conduct and oppositional disorder. The parentage of the 14 symptoms is not hard to divine. Some, perhaps a third, bear close resemblances to items in Conners Teacher Questionnaire, some are direct from DSM-III, and others seem to be a sharpening and operationalizing of DSM-III items. There was no change in the age of onset or duration of symptoms and the only exclusionary diagnosis was now pervasive developmental disorder, with mental retardation simply meriting a caution that the symptoms must be assessed against the patient's developmental rather than chronological level. ADD without hyperactivity was dropped as a specific category (though a new, less specific one, "undifferentiated attention deficit disorder," was added) on grounds that in the DSM-III-R field trials of "several hundred children" this diagnosis was seldom made. The move may yet prove premature as there are now a number of studies that do find this category and there is some evidence to support it as distinct from ADDH (Cantwell & Baker, 1988; Lahey, et al., 1988). The residual category was also removed as a specific category and now simply put in parentheses after ADHD. The reason given was that hyperactivity sometimes persists into adulthood and thus presumably, its specific exclusion from the residual category in DSM-III was felt unnecessarily to limit the use of the residual category. A dimension of severity was added along a 3-point scale, but did not reflect Barkley's (1982) or the English view (Schachar et al., 1986) that pervasiveness rather than severity was essential.

Attempting to evaluate these changes is difficult, as no figures are given as to reliability or validity, and there are no references to some of the statements. Cantwell and Baker (1988), who participated in the field trials, go so far as to say that, in their opinion, the trials failed to meet proper standards and the results do not correspond with their own. Some criticism of the polythetic or menu approach as opposed to the medical symptom-domain or construct area approach, comes from Shaffer, Campbell, Cantwell, Bradley, Carlson, Cohen, et al. (1989) who argue that it is liable to result in more marked clinical heterogeneity; that by making the criteria more restrictive, it increases the problem of threshold; and that it takes no account of developmental changes in the symptomatology. Of these three criticisms, the last is best argued. The first, of clinical heterogeneity, would be valid if the items re not highly inter-correlated, and the second, of threshold, would have merit if all the items are not of equal power. A proper psychometric analysis needs to be done of these 18 items, though the DSM-III-R manual suggests that in the field trials, items were found to differ in sensitivity and specificity. Further, as Lahey et al. (1988) point out, the evidence from empirical statistical studies shows that hyperactivity and inattention load on different factors, suggesting that the polythetic model that lumps them flies in the face of established fact. Their own study added further proof of this fact.

DSM-IV and ICD-10

ICD-10 is due to appear in 1991, the DSM-IV in 1993. According to Cantwell and Baker (1988),

ICD-10 will continue to be significantly different from DSM though it seems there may have been some revisions more toward DSM-IV since (see Shaffer et al., 1989). DSM-IV is well underway and the principles that guide its revision are rather interesting (Shaffer et al., 1989). All changes from DSM-III-R are to be conservative, on the basis of empirical data rather than expert opinion, and to be properly documented and referenced in a "source book." Whether this will prove to be so as far as ADHD is concerned remains to be seen, but it is to be hoped for. However, since Shaffer et al. (1989) are actually the members of the DSM-IV Children's Disorders Subcommittee, their obvious distaste for the polythetic method of DSM-III-R suggests that substantial changes in ADHD in DSM-IV are likely. It is also clear that they favor reintroduction of ADD without hyperactivity. Second, an effort will be made to match ICD-10 as much as possible without any sacrifice of distinctions felt by the DSM-IV committee to be more valid. A third criterion makes for the widest possible consultation including attention to "theoretical orientations" which may be necessary politically but scientifically is unsound.

DIAGNOSTIC METHODS FOR MEDICAL TYPE CLASSIFICATIONS

The reliability and validity of any diagnosis depends as much on the method of data capture as on the psychometric properties of the diagnostic systems or category. Medicine has always relied primarily on the history (what is recounted by patient or caretaker) and examination (what is observed by professionals). Both history and examination have been expected to cover as many of the areas and in as much detail as are relevant to the illness. Over the years, medical history taking and examination have gradually acquired a fair degree of structure but nothing like that seen in intelligence tests or some psychological questionnaires. Even more important, there has been little psychometric study of their reliability or validity. However, history taking is now increasingly backed by a set of very precise and valid laboratory, organ-imaging and other high-tech methods and highly specific treatment methods that offer validation and are having a feedback effect on history taking and examination.

Just as in the rest of medicine, in the child psychiatric field, the traditional way has always been based on interview and examination of both parent and child. Unlike medicine, however, these techniques have remained unstructured and largely clinician driven. The reliability and validity of this diagnostic method has been seldom examined but is seriously open to question (Young, O'Brien, Gutterman, & Cohen, 1987). However, when some structure is injected, it is possible to achieve good reliability (Young et al., 1987), and the last few years have seen the development of a number of structured interviews aimed specifically at generating DSM-III diagnoses including ADDH (see Orvaschel, 1985; Young et al., 1987), most of which have been adapted to DSM-III-R. A number of these now exist in microcomputer-administered or -diagnosed form.

Until very recently, most literature on hyperactivity has not used such structured interviews, though many studies were assisted by the use of Conners Teacher Questionnaire and other scales. It is often difficult to tell exactly how the use of such scales was integrated into the clinical interview data. Further, the Conners scales yield scores on dimensions, not DSM-III or other medical categorical diagnoses, and even requiring high scores on both dimensions of hyperactivity and inattention does not give an exactly comparable diagnosis to DSM-III. There is some evidence to support the view that the medical method, which relies on multisourced-multimodal data, is more reliable and valid than the much-vaunted Conners or other questionnaires used alone (e.g., Milich, Loney, & Landau, 1982). However, until and unless studies begin to use established structured diagnostic interview and other data-capture methods, the possibility of considerable variation in diagnosis across studies is likely to continue (Barkley, 1982).

As noted above, medicine increasingly relies on laboratory methods to arrive at a final diagnosis. While there are a number of special techniques that have been applied to the diagnosis of ADHD, none of these has yet achieved anything approaching a specific role.

Psychological tests, electroencephalograms (EEGs), and neurological, biochemical, or organ-im-

aging techniques have all been applied with enthusiasm to hyperactivity. While abnormalities are often found in all of these, none is highly enough associated nor specific enough to ADHD to allow their use to clinch a suspected diagnosis (see Campbell & Werry, 1986; Reeves & Werry, 1987; Reeves et al., 1987; Ross & Ross, 1982; Werry et al., 1987a; Werry, Elkind, & Reeves, 1987b; Whalen, in press; Zametkin & Rapoport, 1987). However, it is important to keep clearly in mind that it is the role of these tests in diagnosis that is being questioned, *not their role in assessment of the individual child or in management planning*.

In summary, then, the diagnosis of ADHD is made on clinical symptomatological and historical grounds alone, and this is quite clear from the DSM manuals. The use of information from parent and teacher behavior symptom checklists, and behavioral observations, all described in more detail elsewhere in this book, may be extremely valuable in assisting the diagnoser to judge whether there is a disorder (i.e., abnormality) and if so whether the critical symptoms (now 8 of 14) are present and in sufficient degree of severity to warrant the diagnosis. But in the end, it is up to the diagnostician to decide which data are relevant, how to weight them, and how to aggregate them into a final judgment.

RELIABILITY OF MEDICAL DIAGNOSES OF HYPERACTIVITY

In spite of all the criticisms of hyperactivity as a diagnosis (e.g., Prior & Sanson, 1986), there is evidence that it is possible to achieve at least modest reliability across diagnosers (Anderson et al., 1987; Horn, Wagner, & Ialongo, 1989; Lahey et al., 1988; Quay, 1986a; Reeves, Werry, Elkind, & Zametkin, 1987). Nevertheless, some caveats apply. Most of the good data in this respect stem from DSM-III on and much of them are tied to structured diagnostic methods, so application to older literature and more informal studies needs to be most cautious. Also, training is necessary, and researchers are more reliable than clinicians (Prendergast, Taylor, Rapoport, Bartko, Donnelly, Zametkin et al., 1988). Suffice it to say, that given properly structured diagnostic data-capture and decision methods, and properly trained diagnosers, the DSM-III and DSM-III-R diagnoses can be made reasonably reliably.

VALIDITY

There are various ways of looking at validity, but in keeping with the question "why diagnose" posed at the beginning of this chapter, here it is addressed in terms of the seven aims of the ideal diagnosis.

Specificity

In reviewing reliability, it was concluded that the diagnosis can be made reliably, given certain conditions. However, this statement is only partly true in the sense that what ADHD *was* could be diagnosed reliably; what is *was not or what was not it* offered much more of a problem. This dilemma centered primarily on its distinctiveness from conduct disorder with British child psychiatrists holding that what was called hyperactivity, ADDH, or ADHD in the United States was more properly called conduct disorder (CD). This area has been reviewed by a number of authors and has been the subject of intense research recently (Anderson et al., 1987; Reeves et al., 1987; Werry et al., 1987a, 1987b; Werry, 1988b; Whalen, in press).

In DSM-III and DSM-III-R, conduct disorder is characterized by social behavior that systematically exploits and violates the rights of others in antisocial ways. There is an implicit notion of deliberate nastiness to this behavior suggestive of a lack of feeling for other human beings, but there is evidence that this distinction from the putatively involuntary disruptiveness of some of the behaviors of ADHD is not so easy to make, especially in those who, like teachers, are at the receiving end of hyperactive behaviors (e.g., Schachar et al., 1986). Further evidence of the difficulty of making this distinction in practice can be seen in the irregular but rather persistent tendency of hyperactivity to appear on the same dimension as conduct problem items in empirical statistical studies (see Dienske & Sanders-Woudstra, 1988; Quay, 1986a).

In the end, the problem of discriminating CD from ADHD seems to have turned out to be rather simple

to me—at least conceptually. It is necessary to accept that CD is strongly associated with ADHD in some way but the reverse is not true, especially once one steps outside psychiatric clinic samples where cases of pure ADHD apparently abound (e.g., Anderson et al., 1987; Reeves et al., 1987). It is easy to see why psychiatric clinics should find a strong association between ADHD and CD since it is less likely that a child who has no problems except ADHD would be referred, though the same argument would not apply, say, to a clinic specializing in children with learning problems. It does not, however, explain why pure CD, which certainly exists, is so infrequent though there are few studies of nonclinic samples (e.g., Anderson, et al., 1987). It is therefore necessary to postulate that ADHD greatly increases vulnerability to CD or even that CD is unlikely to occur unless ADHD is first present. It is also possible that the reverse relationship exists, though if currently favored hypotheses of a congenital biological role in ADHD and a social learning one in CD (see Werry et al., 1987a) are valid, they would suggest that ADHD would come first. An alternative hypothesis of course is that whatever causes ADHD can also cause CD. Whatever the cause, this association—or comorbidity, to use the new buzz word—will have the following result if the current tendency to make only one diagnosis persists: If the diagnoser has a set toward ADHD, as in the United States, that is the diagnosis that will be made, whereas if the focus is on the conduct-type symptoms, as in the United Kingdom, the diagnosis will be CD. There is now proof of this in the US/UK collaborative studies (Prendergast et al., 1988).

One of the further revelations of this latter study was that UK diagnosers, when using the unfamiliar to them DSM-III, had a greater tendency to make more than one diagnosis per child. Put another way, if researchers since 1980 had followed the instructions of the DSM-III properly and had made all the diagnoses which the data suggested instead of just one, the current confusion between what is ADHD and what is CD would have diminished considerably. Psychiatric researchers and journals seem now to have accepted comorbidity as a fact of life, but nonmedical researchers (e.g., Van der Meere & Sergeant, 1988; Benezra & Douglas, 1988) continue to do studies, and even more inexcusably, journals continue to accept studies that ignore the association of CD with ADHD. This present and past tendency makes nonsense of much of the research purporting to be of ADHD since it is quite unclear as to which of the findings is true of ADHD and which attributable to coexistent CD. To sum up, ADHD and CD are difficult to differentiate diagnostically, though it can be done. Coexistence of the two conditions is common, and acceptance of this by diagnosticians would lead to a better standard of research and hence, of knowledge.

Epidemiology

There are clear gender differences in ADHD (which is overwhelmingly a male disorder) not present in other disorders including CD (Werry et al., 1987a). On other demographic variables, there is as yet far too little epidemiological data, especially of ADDH or ADHD, to make any conclusions beyond the fact that it is probably not uncommon, especially in minor or subclinical degrees (Anderson et al., 1987; Whalen, in press). One study (Anderson, 1988) suggests that there may be some link with social disadvantage. ADHD is not confined to Western culture (e.g., Luk, Leung, & Lee, 1988) though the criteria used in non-Western studies were not always DSM in type.

Associated Features

A large number of studies suggest that ADHD is commonly associated with learning problems, minor EEG, psychophysiological, and neurological abnormalities (principally poor coordination and tics), perinatal abnormalities, and of course, with conduct-type symptoms. Unfortunately, most of these studies are methodologically less than robust, especially in their diagnostic rigor, and use normal (often biased) rather than other diagnostic (especially CD) groups as controls. When these errors are corrected and proper comparisons are made across diagnostic groups, the only associated features that remain are cognitive impairment and CD (Reeves & Werry, 1987; Werry et al., 1987a, 1987b), though there are also other possibilities (e.g., with tics/Tourettes [Comings & Comings, 1987; Riddle, Hardin, Soo

Churl, Woolston, & Leckman, 1988]). All efforts so far to define the nature of this cognitive impairment have remained elusive and conflicting (Campbell & Werry, 1986; Douglas, 1988; McGee, Williams, Moffitt, & Anderson, 1989; Van der Meere & Sargeant, 1988; Whalen, in press). It is just that ADHD children do not perform as well as they should on intelligence and a wide variety of laboratory, achievement, and classroom tasks. This observation is also reflected in the long-term outcome of occupational underachievement (Weiss & Hechtman, 1986). The addition of CD to ADHD simply magnifies the degree of social handicap (Anderson, Williams, McGee & Silva, 1989; Reeves et al., 1987; Werry, et al., 1987a, 1987b).

ETIOLOGY

There is a longstanding belief that the etiology of ADHD is biological and usually congenital. However, there is so far no definitive proof of this (Prior & Sanson, 1986; Werry et al., 1987a; Whalen, in press), though it would be fair to say that there is plenty of smoke suggestive of fire below. Some of this suggestive evidence is biochemical (Zametkin & Rapoport, 1987), genetic (though there is better evidence of this relating to activity level than ADHD) (Ross & Ross, 1982; Whalen, in press), toxicological (Fergusson, Fergusson, Horwood, & Kinzett, 1988) and neurodevelopmental (Werry et al., 1987a). Evidence that ADHD is not caused by family factors, life events, and other psychological processes is conflicting (Whalen, in press), but when there is a careful separation of ADDH/ADHD from CD, the evidence becomes somewhat stronger (Reeves et al., 1987; Werry et al., 1987a).

COURSE OVER TIME

There is quite a substantial body of research now about course but it is hampered by its failure to use other diagnostic groups and clearly to separate out CD, and there are other methodological problems as well (see Thorley, 1984). However, some tentative conclusions may be drawn (Weiss & Hechtman, 1986). First, in a substantial minority, ADHD becomes subclinical—especially excessive motor activity—by high school, but blind behavior observers can still detect differences in the cardinal symptoms of hyperactivity and inattention. Second, in an unknown but substantial minority, ADHD is still clinically present in adulthood (Weiss & Hechtman, 1986; Wender, 1987). Third, occupational adjustment suggests that underachievement continues after school, but because of the changed social demands, it now ceases to be perceived as a central problem. Fourth, in a significant number, there are problems of antisocial behavior, and alcohol and drug abuse. It is hard to interpret the latter finding as some of the best predictors of this outcome are aggression and other conduct-type problems and poor family ecology in childhood, all of which suggest that they are associated with an undiagnosed or associated CD which has such an outcome (Quay, 1986b) rather than ADHD which probably does not. According to Werry et al. (1987a), studies on CD almost disappeared in the period when studies of hyperactivity mushroomed, and evidence that this may have resulted in significant misdiagnosis can be seen in the follow-up study by Gittelman, Mannuzza, Shenker, and Bonagura (1985) in which over 25% were rediagnosed as having CD at outcome. Also, the distinction from CD may be particularly difficult at young ages, as the follow-up study by Campbell, Breaux, Ewing, and Szumowski (1986) suggests.

In summary, then, the diagnosis of ADHD seems to have definite implications as to outcome, though findings are muddied by the failure properly to diagnose coexistent conduct disorder. It appears that for many, the course will be chronic, though the degree of social disability and personal discomfort probably lessens as academic demands are replaced by occupational ones that are more attuned by simple job market forces to the actual level of performance than to theoretical ability. It seems likely, too, that if there is an associated conduct disorder or possibly, a high residual level of ADHD, that the outcome will be worse and there will be more antisocial and substance abuse problems.

TREATMENT

The topic of treatment is covered extensively elsewhere in this volume and here only the specific indications that follow from the diagnosis of ADHD are discussed. Here, there is a clear and obvious treatment indication—namely the use of stimulant drugs, the value of which in the reduction of symptoms of inattention and hyperactivity is well established (Werry, 1988a); this finding may be equally true of adolescents (Klorman, Brumaghim, Coons, Peloquin, Strauss, Lewine, et al., 1988) and adults with ADHD (Mattes, Boswell, & Oliver, 1984; Wender, Reimherr, Wood, & Ward, 1985). However, it is also true that these benefits are largely drug-dependent and proof of long-term benefit is lacking. Also, currently contentious is whether drugs produce anything cognitively other than simply elevating performance of that which is already known (Werry, 1988a). The negative findings in outcome and new learning, however, may reflect the complexity of assessing this relationship (see chapter 6 by Rapoport and Kelly) rather than produce a definitive result.

Some will argue that this treatment indication is not absolute as not all children will respond, nor should administration of drugs seen as automatically necessary. Also, that the drug effects seen are not specific to ADHD as the same are found in normal children and adults (Rapoport, Buchsbaum, Zahn, Weingartner, Ludlow, & Mikkelson, 1978; Werry & Aman, 1984). Neither have stimulants yet been tried in other disorders such as CD. All these qualifications may be true but even so the facts are that so far, only ADHD is a well-established indication for the use of stimulants in child psychopathology.

Another treatment that was claimed as specific to ADHD, namely the Meichenbaum cognitive behavioral technique, has proven ineffective, (Abikoff, Ganeles, Reiter, Blum, Foley, & Klein, 1988). Equally, the whole area of dietary intervention is much more poorly anchored than current popularity suggests (Whalen, in press).

While other treatments such as behavior therapy are helpful in ADHD, they cannot be classified as specific though, as other reviews in this volume show, they are well enough demonstrated that they could be regarded as treatment indications that flow from the diagnosis. Thus, it can be said that the diagnosis of ADHD has some specific and some adjunctive treatment indications.

PREVENTION

The ultimate aim in medicine is to prevent the disorder from ever occurring. In order to achieve this, a good understanding of etiology is essential. Because we lack this level of knowledge, prevention becomes elusive at this stage. However, there are few areas where prevention may still be carried out at an empirical level. Reduction of lead levels appears one of the more plausible (Fergusson et al., 1988), though it is unlikely to account for more than a small proportion of cases of ADHD. If on the other hand ADHD is a complex interaction between biologically determined preexisting vulnerability in the child and a mismatched family and social ecology, as suggested by Whalen (in press), then it would make good sense to engage in social engineering. In my opinion, such a view is too vague and too expensive to be viable at the moment. In any case, the most compelling argument for attempting to optimize each child's environment stems from simple humanism, not from ADHD, and seems to be little different in the end from such well-intentioned failures of the past as the Mental Hygiene movement.

CONCLUSIONS

At the beginning of this review the question "why diagnose ADHD" was posed. I hope I have answered this question by showing that such a diagnosis is meaningful in describing a clinical picture, can be made reliably if care is taken with methods and diagnosers, and that useful technical knowledge stems from the diagnosis in the areas of correlates, treatment, and outcome. The diagnosis has also proven to be most heuristic in research as any survey of the history of the concept from hyperkinesis to ADHD shows. One of the greatest benefits has been in the development of research methodology and clinical techniques that have applications far beyond ADHD, reaching into childhood psychopathology in general. Also, hyperactivity ADDH/ADHD first exposed the problem of comorbidity, which now can be seen as a serious issue affecting nearly all the childhood disorders in DSM-III-R (Anderson et al., 1987; Werry, in press). Clearly, hyperactivity research has contributed to the study of CD even if this was at first quite unwitting. But there have been

some costs, too. There is no doubt that in the United States particularly, but also in other parts of the world, clinicians have sometimes abused the diagnosis and the specific treatment with stimulant drugs; but as stated earlier, this is true of every medical diagnosis and treatment and is a problem for medical education and practice to grapple with. It is also clear that some clinicians, teachers, and parents use the diagnosis to explain all of a child's behavior. ADHD is a diagnosis that concerns only certain areas of function, notably cognition and motor activity, and then only tendencies that are strongly influenced by different environments. In these days in which "holistic" medicine is fashionable, it may seem out of tune to have to say that ADHD explains a disorder; it does not explain the child who has the disorder.

REFERENCES

Abikoff, H., Ganeles, D., Reiter, G., Blum, C., Foley, C., & Klein, R. (1988). Cognitive training in academically deficient ADDH boys receiving stimulant medication. *Journal of Abnormal Child Psychology, 16,* 411–432.

Achenbach, T. M. (1980). DSM-III in the light of empirical research on the classification of childhood psychopathology. *Journal of the American Academy of Child Psychiatry, 19,* 395–412

American Psychiatric Association. (1980). *Diagnostic and statistical manual of mental disorders* (3rd ed.). Washington, DC: Author.

American Psychiatric Association. (1987). *Diagnostic and statistical manual of mental disorders* (3rd ed., rev.). Washington, DC: Author.

Anderson, J. C., Williams, S., McGee, R. O., & Silva, P. A. (1987). The prevalence of DSM-III disorders in a large sample of pre-adolescent children from the general population. *Archives of General Psychiatry, 44,* 69–81.

Anderson, J. C., Williams, S., McGee, R. O., & Silva, P. A. Social correlates of DSM-III disorders in preadolescent children. *Journal of the American Academy of Child & Adolescent Psychiatry, 28,* 830–846.

Barkley, R. A. (1982). Guidelines for defining hyperactivity in children. In B. B. Lahey & A. E. Kazdin (Eds.), *Advances in clinical child psychology* (Vol. 5, pp. 137–180). New York: Plenum Publishing.

Benezra, E., & Douglas, V. I. (1988). Short-term serial recall in ADDH, normal reading disabled boys. *Journal of Abnormal Child Psychology, 16,* 511–526.

Campbell, S. B., Breaux, A. M., Ewing, L. J., &

Szumowski, E. K. (1986). Correlates and predictors of hyperactivity and aggression: A longitudinal study of parent-referred problem preschoolers. *Journal of Abnormal Child Psychology, 14,* 217–235.

Campbell, S. B., & Werry, J. S. (1986). Attention deficit disorder (hyperactivity). In H. C. Quay & J. S. Werry (Eds.), *Psychopathological disorders of childhood* (3rd ed., pp. 111–155). New York: John Wiley & Sons.

Cantwell, D. P., & Baker, L. (1988). Issues in the classification of child and adolescent psychopathology. *Journal of the American Academy of Child and Adolescent Psychiatry, 27,* 521–533.

Clements, S. (1966). *Minimal brain dysfunction in children.* Washington DC: U.S. Government Printing Office.

Comings, D. E., & Comings, B. (1987). Tourettes and ADDH. *Archives of General Psychiatry, 44,* 1023–1025.

Conners, C. K. (1985). Parent and Teacher Questionnaires. *Psychopharmacology Bulletin, 21,* 823–831.

Dienske, H., & Sanders-Woudstra, J. S. R. (1988). A critical and conceptual consideration of attention deficit and hyperactivity from an ethological point of view. In L. M. Bloomingdale & J. A. Sargeant (Eds.), *Attention deficit disorder: Criteria, cognition, intervention* (pp. 43–64). Oxford: Pergamon Press.

Douglas, V. I. (1972). Stop, look and listen: The problem of sustained attention in hyperactive and normal children. *Canadian Journal of Behavioural Science, 4,* 259–281.

Douglas, V. I. (1988). Cognitive deficits in children with ADDH. In L. M. Bloomingdale & J. A. Sargeant (Eds.), *Attention deficit disorder: Criteria, cognition, intervention* (pp. 65–78). Oxford: Pergamon Press.

Fergusson, D. M., Fergusson, J. E., Horwood, L. J., & Kinzett, N. G. (1988). A longitudinal study of dentine lead levels on intelligence, school performance and behaviour: Part III—Dentine lead levels and attention/activity. *Journal of Child Psychology & Psychiatry, 29,* 811–824.

Gittelman, R. (1988). The assessment of hyperactivity: The DSM-III approach. In L. M. Bloomingdale & J. A. Sargeant (Eds.), *Attention Deficit Disorder: Criteria, cognition, intervention* (pp. 9–28). Oxford: Pergamon Press.

Gittelman, R., Mannuzza, S., Shenker, R., & Bonagura, N. (1985). Hyperactive boys almost grown up. *Archives of General Psychiatry, 42,* 937–947.

Horn, W. F., Wagner, A. E., & Ialongo, N. (1989). Sex differences in school-aged children with pervasive attention deficit disorder. *Journal of Abnormal Child Psychology, 17,* 109–125.

Klorman, R., Brumaghim, J. T., Coons, H. W., Peloquin,

L.-J., Strauss, J., Lewine, J. D., Borgstedt, A. D., & Goldstein, M. G. (1988). The contribution of event-related potentials to the understanding of stimulants on information processing in attention deficit disorder. In L. M. Bloomingdale & J. A. Sargeant (Eds.), *Attention deficit disorder: Criteria, cognition, intervention* pp. 199–218). Oxford: Pergamon Press.

Lahey, B. B., Pelham, W. E., Schaughency, E. A., Atkins, M. S., Murphy, H. A., Hynd, G., et al., (1988). Dimensions and types of Attention Deficit Disorder. *Journal of the American Academy of Child and Adolescent Psychiatry, 27,* 330–335.

Laufer, M., & Denhoff, E. (1957). Hyperkinetic behavior syndrome in children. *Journal of Pediatrics, 50,* 463–474.

Luk, S. L., Leung, P. W. L., & Lee, P. L. M. (1988). Conner's Teacher Rating Scale in Chinese children in Hong Kong. *Journal of Child Psychology & Psychiatry, 29,* 165–174.

McGee, R. O., Williams, S., Moffitt, T., & Anderson, J. (1989). A comparison of 13-year-old boys with attention deficit and/or reading disorder on neuropsychological measures. *Journal of Abnormal Child Psychology, 17,* 37–54.

Mattes, J. A., Boswell, L., & Oliver, H. (1984). Methylphenidate effects on symptoms of attention deficit disorder in adults. *Archives of General Psychiatry, 41,* 1059–1063.

Milich, R., Loney, J., & Landau, S. (1982). Independent dimensions of hyperactivity and aggression: A validation with playroom observations. *Journal of Abnormal Psychology, 91,* 183–198.

Orvaschel, H. (1985). Psychiatric interviews suitable for research with children and adolescents. *Psychopharmacology Bulletin, 21,* 737–745.

Prendergast, M., Taylor, E., Rapoport, J. L., Bartko, J., Donnelly, M., Zametkin, A., Ahearn, M. B., Dunn, G., & Wieselberg, H. M. (1988). The diagnosis of childhood hyperactivity: A U.K. cross-national study of DSM-III and ICD-9. *Journal of Child Psychology & Psychiatry, 29,* 289–300.

Prior, M., & Sanson, A. (1986). Attention deficit disorder with hyperactivity: A critique. *Journal of Child Psychology & Psychiatry, 27,* 307–320.

Quay, H. C. (1986a). Classification. In H. C. Quay & J. S. Werry (Eds.), *Psychopathological disorders of childhood* (3rd ed., pp. 1–34). New York: John Wiley & Sons.

Quay, H. C. (1986b). Conduct disorders. In H. C. Quay & J. S. Werry (Eds.), *Psychopathological disorders of childhood* (3rd ed. pp. 34–72). New York: John Wiley & Sons.

Rapoport, J., Buchsbaum, M., Zahn, T., Weingartner, H.,

Ludlow, C., & Mikkelson, E. J. (1978). Dextroamphetamine cognitive and behavioral effects in normal prepubertal boys and adults. *Science, 199,* 560–563.

Raport, M. D., Tucker, S. B., DuPaul, G. J., Merlo, M., & Stoner, G. (1986). Hyperactivity and frustration: The influence of control over and size of rewards in delaying gratification. *Journal of Abnormal Child Psychology, 14,* 191–204.

Reeves, J. C., & Werry, J. S. (1987). Soft signs in hyperactivity, In D. E. Tupper (Ed.), *Soft neurological signs* (pp. 225–246). New York: Grune & Stratton.

Reeves, J. C., Werry, J. S., Elkind, G. S., & Zametkin, A. (1987). Attention deficit, conduct, oppositional and anxiety disorders in children: II—Clinical characteristics. *Journal of the American Academy of Child & Adolescent Psychiatry, 26,* 144–155.

Rey, J. M. (1988). DSM-III-R.: Too much, too soon. *Australian & New Zealand Journal of Psychiatry, 22,* 173–182.

Riddle, M. A., Hardin, M. T., Soo Churl, C., Woolston, J. L., & Leckman, J. F. (1989). Desipramine treatment of boys with ADHD and tics: Preliminary clinical experience. *Journal of the American Academy of Child & Adolescent Psychiatry, 27,* 811–814.

Ross, D. M., & Ross, S. A. (1982). *Hyperactivity: Current issues, research and theory* (2nd ed.). New York: John Wiley & Sons.

Rutter, M., & Shaffer, D. (1980). DSM-III: A step forward or a step backward in terms of classification of childhood disorders. *Journal of the American Academy of Child Psychiatry, 19,* 371–394.

Schachar, R., Sandberg, S., & Rutter, M. (1986). Agreement between teachers' ratings and observations of hyperactivity, inattentiveness, and defiance. *Journal of Abnormal Child Psychology, 14,* 331–345.

Shaffer, D., Campbell, M., Cantwell, D., Bradley, S., Carlson, G., Cohen, D., Denckla, M., Allen, F., Garfinkel, B., Klein, R., Pincus, H., Spitzer, R. L., Volkmar, F., & Wediger T. (1989). Child and adolescent disorders in DSM-IV: Issues facing the child psychiatry work group. *Journal of the American Academy of Child & Adolescent Psychiatry, 28,* 830–835.

Thorley, G. (1984). Review of follow-up and follow-back studies of childhood hyperactivity. *Psychological Bulletin, 96,* 116–132.

Van Der Meere, J., & Sargeant, J. (1988). Focussed attention in pervasively hyperactive children. *Journal of Abnormal Child Psychology, 16,* 627–640.

Weiss, G., & Hechtman, L. T. (1986). *Hyperactive children grown up.* New York: Guilford Press.

Wender, P. H. (1972). *Minimal brain dysfunction in children.* New York: John Wiley.

Wender, P. H. (1987). *The hyperactive child, adolescent and adult; Attention deficit disorder during the lifespan.* New York: Oxford University Press.

Wender, P. H., Reimherr, F. W., Wood, D. W., & Ward, M. A. (1985). A controlled study of methylphenidate in attention deficit disorder residual type in adults. *American Journal of Psychiatry, 142,* 547–552.

Werry, J. S. (1985). ICD-9 & DSM-III: Diagnosis for the clinician. *Journal of Child Psychology & Psychiatry, 26,* 1–6.

Werry, J. S. (1988a). Drugs, learning and cognitive function in children. *Journal of Child Psychology & Psychiatry, 29,* 129–142.

Werry, J. S. (1988b). Differential diagnosis of attention deficit from conduct disorder. In L. M. Bloomingdale & J. A. Sargeant (Eds.), *Attention deficit disorder: Criteria, cognition, intervention* (pp. 83–86). Oxford: Pergamon Press.

Werry, J. S. (1988c). In memoriam, DSM-III. *Journal of the American Academy of Child & Adolescent Psychiatry, 27,* 138–139 (letter).

Werry, J. S. (in press). Overanxious disorder—A taxonomic review. *Journal of the American Academy of Child & Adolescent Psychiatry.*

Werry, J. S., & Aman, M. G. (1984). Methylphenidate in hyperactive and enuretic boys. In B. Shopsin & L. Greenhill (Eds.) *The psychobiology of childhood: A profile of current issues.* Jamaica, NY: Spectrum.

Werry, J. S., Reeves, J. C., & Elkind, G. S. (1987a). Attention deficit, conduct, oppositional and anxiety disorders in children: I—A review of research on differentiating characteristics. *Journal of the American Academy of Child & Adolescent Psychiatry, 26,* 133–143.

Werry, J. S., Elkind, G. S., & Reeves, J. C. (1987b). Attention deficit, conduct, oppositional and anxiety disorders in children: III—Laboratory differences. *Journal of Abnormal Child Psychology, 15,* 409–428.

Whalen, C. K. (in press). Attention deficit and hyperactivity disorders. In T. H. Ollendick & M. Hersen (Eds.), *Handbook of child psychopathology* (2nd ed.). New York: Plenum Publishing.

Young, J. G., O'Brien, J. D., Gutterman, E. M., & Cohen, P. (1987). Research on the clinical interview. *Journal of the American Academy of Child & Adolescent Psychiatry, 26,* 613–630.

Zamtkin, A. J., & Rapoport, J. L. (1987). The neurobiology of attention deficit disorder with hyperactivity: Where have we come in 50 years? *Journal of the American Academy of Child & Adolescent Psychiatry, 26,* 676–686.

CHAPTER 8

BEHAVIORAL ASSESSMENT OF ATTENTION DEFICIT HYPERACTIVITY DISORDER

Typical Charaecs of Disorder

David C. Guevremont
George J. DuPaul
Russell A. Barkley

Attention deficit hyperactivity disorder (ADHD) (American Psychiatric Association [APA], 1987) is currently considered a developmental disorder of age-appropriate attention span, impulse control, rule compliance, and motor restlessness or overactivity (APA, 1987; Barkley, 1981). Moreover, a large literature exists that shows ADHD children to experience a wider range of behavioral, social, emotional, and educational difficulties than those suggested by the core diagnostic features alone (Breen & Barkley, 1985; Loney & Milich, 1982; Safer & Allen, 1976). Most investigators endorse a biological predisposition for behavioral problems, yet the severity of the child's actual problems, the emergence of secondary behavioral and emotional difficulties, and the longer term outcomes are believed to be strongly related to environmental factors (Weiss & Hechtman, 1986).

The purpose of this chapter is to present a multimethod assessment approach for the evaluation of ADHD. Because of the complexity of this disorder the evaluation necessitates two distinct but interre-lated processes: (a) clinical assessment for the purpose of yielding a diagnosis and (b) behavioral assessment of specific problems and their causes for the purpose of selecting target behaviors for treatment. The evaluation process to be described borrows from a traditional medical and psychiatric model of diagnosis that attempts to establish that criteria for a syndrome are met and that its manifestation is not accounted for by other medical, psychological, or psychosocial conditions.

The evaluation also utilizes methods derived from behavioral assessment that emphasize an objective, scientific, and multimethod approach to data collection. A core assumption of behavioral assessment is that, regardless of the originating conditions, identified problems are best understood in the context of current organismic and environmental conditions that maintain or exacerbate symptoms. Thus, assessment of behavioral difficulties is approached without the assumption that these problems are uniformly consistent across situations. Furthermore, behavioral assessment emphasizes a sampling of behavior that may exist as a subset of actual behavior to be targeted for change. In this regard, information derived from interviews is viewed as only one source of data, and additional data sources are necessary to enhance the ecological validity of the assessment process. Empirically validated methods are utilized and replace traditional psychological models of assessment, such as projective techniques which view disturbed behavior as a sign of underlying psychological disturbance. Finally, assessment measures are employed that are sensitive to developmental factors, thereby placing the child's problems in the context of social and age-related norms.

PRIMARY SYMPTOMS AND SITUATIONAL VARIATIONS

Each of the symptoms constituting ADHD are believed to be multidimensional rather than unitary, although research has been conflicting as to precisely which dimensions are the most distinguishing deficits in the disorder. Nonetheless, most research suggests that ADHD children have their greatest difficulties with sustained attention or vigilance (Douglas, 1983). Referral complaints often concern incomplete work, off-task behavior, daydreaming, distractibility, or rapid shifting of activities. Both the frequency and severity of problems usually fluctuate across settings, activities, and caregivers (e.g., Tarver-Behring, Barkley, & Karlsson, 1985; Zentall, 1984). Poor sustained attention may become more pronounced in the context of dull tasks, repetitive or effortful activity, or tasks with little intrinsic appeal (Barkley, 1989; Luk, 1985). These problems may dissipate in severity under conditions of continuous and immediate reinforcement as opposed to partial and delayed schedules of reinforcement (Douglas & Parry, 1983), self-paced tasks, intrinsically interesting activities (e.g., video games), and under novel conditions or in unfamiliar settings (Barkley, 1977, 1989; Luk, 1985). The situational fluctuations suggest that sustained attention of ADHD children is highly interactive with and influenced by the current environmental context (Barkley, 1981, 1989; Zentall, 1984).

Impulsivity is also believed to be multidimensional in nature (Milich & Kramer, 1985) and may show variability across different environmental and reinforcement arrangements (Douglas & Parry, 1983). Impulsivity has been characterized as a pattern of rapid, inaccurate responding (Brown & Quay, 1977) and poor ability to delay immediate gratification (Rapport, Tucker, DuPaul, Merlo, & Stoner, 1986). Frequent referral complaints by parents or teachers include problems waiting for a turn, blurting out answers prematurely, rushing through work carelessly, and interrupting the activities of others.

Numerous studies have shown ADHD children to be more active, restless, and fidgety than normal children (Barkley & Cunningham, 1970; Porrino et al., 1983), although motor restlessness may also vary depending on the situation. Factor analytic studies suggest further that overactivity represents a distinct symptom cluster from measures of inattention in ADHD children (Edelbrock, Costello, & Kessler, 1984; Lahey et al., 1988). Thus, children may display inattention but not hyperactivity. This non-hyperactive but inattentive group appears to correspond to the diagnosis of attention deficit disorder without hyperactivity (APA, 1980), where a sluggish cognitive tempo, higher prevalence of anxious and depressive features, social withdrawal, and a greater incidence of learning disabilities have been reported (Carlson, 1986; Lahey, Schaughency, Hynd, Carlson, & Nieves, 1987).

Poor compliance to instructions and rules may also represent a primary deficit of ADHD (APA, 1987; Barkley, 1981, 1982). Like other primary ADHD symptoms, governance by rules and instructions may vary across caregivers, situations, and reinforcement arrangements. Nonetheless, most ADHD children demonstrate significant problems with compliance to parental and teacher commands (Barkley, 1985; Whalen, Henker, & Dotemoto, 1980), with experimental instructions when the experimenter is not present (Draeger, Prior, & Sanson, 1986), and with prohibitions to defer gratification (Rapport et al., 1986). Although such problems may be a byproduct of poor impulse control and attention, researchers have observed that ADHD children are primarily contingency-shaped rather than rule-governed in their behavior and, as such, seem to be influenced more so by the immediately available contingencies rather than the previously given or implicit rule (Barkley, 1981, 1987a, 1989). Not surprisingly, common referral complaints often center upon problems complying with adult directives and rules (Barkley, 1981).

In addition to the core symptoms of ADHD, the evaluation process necessitates a thorough assessment of secondary problems that may coexist with ADHD. Among these problems are sleep disturbances, enuresis, motor incoordination, academic underachievement, and learning disabilities (Hart sought & Lambert, 1985; Ross & Ross, 1982; Safer & Allen, 1976; Stewart, Thach, & Friedin, 1970). Peer relationship problems may be found in as many as 60% of ADHD children (Campbell & Paulauskas, 1979; Johnston, Pelham, & Murphy, 1985; Milich & Landau, 1982) while poor self-esteem and mild forms of depression may emerge as problems of later childhood (Barkley, 1981; Breen & Barkley, 1985; Weiss & Hechtman, 1986). Finally, oppositional-defiant behavior and conduct problems, found in up to 70% of clinic samples (Loney & Milich, 1982), are carefully evaluated because of the poorer prognosis associated with these problems where they coexist with ADHD. Recognition of the numerous associated problems experienced by some ADHD children and the variability of behavior across situations necessitates a comprehensive assessment model that will ultimately lead to the clarification of specific treatment needs.

THE ASSESSMENT PROCESS

The assessment process may begin as a broad-based screening for the presence of ADHD symptoms. The most recent guidelines for diagnosing ADHD appear in the revised *Diagnostic and Statistical Manual of Mental Disorders*, 3rd ed. (DSM-III-R) (APA, 1987) presented in Table 8.1.

A cutoff score of at least eight symptoms was established through a clinical field trial as the score with the greatest accuracy in correct classification among several different diagnostic groups. Additional guidelines for establishing a diagnosis have been suggested by Barkley (1982) and include (a) documentation of the developmental deviance of symptoms, (b) duration of symptoms for at least 12 months, (c) onset by 6 years of age, (d) symptoms established as significantly pervasive across settings, and (e) symptoms that are not accounted for by delays in intellectual development.

Table 8.1. Criteria for Diagnosing Attention Deficit Hyperactivity Disorder from DSM-III-R

A. A disturbance of at least 6 months during which at least eight of the following are present:
  (1) often fidgets with hands or feet or squirms in seat (in adolescents, may be limited to subjective feelings of restlessness).
  (2) has difficulty remaining seated when required to do so
  (3) is easily distracted by extraneous stimuli
  (4) has difficulty awaiting turn in games or group situations
  (5) often blurts out answers to questions before they have been completed
  (6) has difficulty following through on instructions from others (not due to oppositional behavior or failure of comprehension), for example, fails to finish chores
  (7) has difficulty sustaining attention in tasks or play activities
  (8) often shifts from one uncompleted activity to another
  (9) has difficulty playing quietly
  (10) often talks excessively
  (11) often interrupts or intrudes on others, for example, butts into other children's games
  (12) often does not seem to listen to what is being said to him or her
  (13) often loses things necessary for tasks or activities at school or at home (e.g., toys, pencils, books, assignments)
  (14) often engages in physically dangerous activities without considering possible consequences (not for the purpose of thrill seeking), that is, runs into street without looking
B. Onset before the age of 7
C. Does not meet criteria for pervasive developmental disorder

Note: From the *Diagnostic and Statistical Manual of Mental Disorders* (3rd ed. rev.) by the American Psychiatric Association, 1987, Washington, DC: Author.

Based on diagnostic criteria appearing in DSM-III and DSM-III-R and methods derived from behavioral assessment, Barkley (1981, 1987a) has outlined parameters that may be used in a comprehensive multimethod assessment of ADHD. First, measurement of primary symptoms (e.g., sustained attention, impulsivity) should allow age-related comparisons via adequate normative data to establish the developmental deviance of these symptoms. Second, other psychiatric, learning, or emotional disorders must be ruled out as the primary cause of the referral concerns. Third, the presence of coexisting problems (e.g., oppositional-defiant behavior, learning disabilities) should be thoroughly assessed. Fourth, the situational variations of problems dictate that multiple sources of information be obtained from diverse settings. Fifth, the persistence of symptoms across childhood and into adolescence necessitates the use of methods that are sensitive to a wide age range. And sixth, specific and narrowly defined target behaviors must be delineated for treatment.

Four general methods of assessment are employed as part of the clinical protocol: interview, standardized child behavior rating scales, direct observation, and clinic test measures.

Interviews

An in-depth interview with the parent is indispensable for establishing that certain diagnostic criteria are met and that conditions other than ADHD are not primarily responsible for the child's current behavior. Five broad domains are assessed: (a) details of the referral concerns, (b) medical and developmental history, (c) school and educational background, (d) family history and psychosocial functioning, and (e) psychiatric history and status of the child. Such information provides a foundation for differential diagnosis and identification of coexisting problems. The examiner must be familiar with the diagnostic features of ADHD as well as other childhood disorders, as some may mimic or overlap with ADHD (e.g., schizotypal personality or pervasive developmental disorders).

The referral concerns are elucidated through specific questioning about recent examples of problem behavior and the age of onset of problems. For the purpose of identifying potential target behaviors for treatment, parents are also questioned about the frequency and pervasiveness of problems across caregivers and situations (e.g., home, school, in public), possible factors maintaining problem behaviors, and the nature of previous attempts to correct problems. An estimate of the age and gender-appropriateness of symptoms that the parent reports is considered by the examiner. Parental expectations, tolerance, and knowledge of normal child development will influence reporting of symptoms.

A general medical and developmental history is also obtained, including information pertaining to pre- and perinatal conditions, obstetrical complications, early milestones (e.g., walking, talking), chronic and acute medical conditions (e.g., allergies, seizures) and physical disabilities (e.g., vision, hearing). Questions about the child's school history emphasize the age of onset of school difficulties, chronicity of problems, and whether academic or intellectual deficits have been assessed. Educational and psychological testing are often advised in order to rule out low intellectual functioning or the presence of learning disabilities that could account for underachievement.

A psychiatric interview is used to assess the presence of anxiety, thought disruptions, perceptual disturbances, developmental disorders, social deficits, language and communication development, motor peculiarities, and other domains needed to rule out more serious psychiatric disabilities and/or to determine whether other disorders coexist with ADHD. A thorough family history regarding prevalence of psychiatric, conduct, learning, and developmental disorders is obtained to aid in the differential diagnosis and to determine risk factors and psychosocial conditions that may contribute to the child's behavior patterns. Questions pertaining to current functioning of family members is also needed to assess factors such as marital disharmony, parental depression, and alcohol abuse, as such problems are more common in families of ADHD children (Beferra & Barkley, 1985).

Finally, an interview with the child allows further specification of basic language and social skills and may alert the examiner to gross oddities in motor, social, thinking, or communication abilities that were not viewed as significant by others. The presence and degree of motor restlessness, inattention, impulsivity, and noncompliance with instructions can also be gauged during the interview with the child, although extreme caution is necessary when drawing conclusions about ADHD symptomology on the basis of such observations. As noted previously, ADHD symptoms will often dissipate in structured and novel situations, particularly those involving one-on-one attention (Barkley, 1981; Sleator & Ullmann, 1981). Judgments about behavior in contrived settings (e.g., interviewers' offices) can lead to false conclusions about the child's diagnostic status.

Behavior Rating Scales

Standardized, well-normed parent and teacher behavior rating scales with adequate psychometric properties have become an indispensable part of the behavioral assessment process. They provide a means of objectifying the occurrence of behaviors across multiple settings and informants and help establish the developmental deviance of problem behaviors by comparing scores with available norms. A detailed review of child behavior rating scales is available in Barkley (1987a). Several scales with excellent psychometric properties and normative data are useful in the evaluation of ADHD.

Parent Rating Scales

Several parent rating scales have proven especially valuable in the assessment of ADHD. These scales are designed to obtain information about ADHD symptoms, other common forms of child psychopathology, and the situational variation of behavior problems in the home setting.

The Child Behavior Checklist (CBCL) (Achenbach & Edelbrock, 1983) provides a thorough screening of child psychopathology through the 113-item Behavior Problems Scale. Profiles were derived for boys and girls, using factor analyses, for three age groups: 3 to 5, 6 to 11, and 12 to 16. Based on factor scores, common dimensions of childhood disorders (e.g., aggressive, social withdrawal) can be plotted on profiles containing normative data for the age and gender of the child. This allows the examiner to determine the dimensions, if any, on which the child is depicted as developmentally or statistically deviant. A hyperactivity factor score correlates highly with the likelihood of a psychiatric diagnosis of ADHD derived via interviewing (Edelbrock & Costello, 1988).

The Social Competence Scale of the CBCL allows a general screening of gross social deficits. The CBCL is one of the few scales available that includes items pertaining to adaptive behavior and social competence. The psychometric properties of the CBCL are excellent (Barkley, 1987a) and it discriminates ADHD from normal and other clinic-referred groups of children (Breen, 1986; Mash & Johnston, 1983).

The Conners Parent Rating Scale-Revised (CPRS-R) (Goyette, Conners, & Ulrich, 1978) is a second useful device for assessing ADHD symptoms within a developmental context. It is the most extensively employed scale in research on ADHD. The revised 48-item questionnaire has the most satisfactory normative data among the different versions of the scale and yields five factor scores: Conduct Problems, Learning Problems, Psychosomatic, Impulsive-Hyperactive, and Anxiety. Although many of the items overlap with the CBCL, the CPRS-R includes a separate Hyperactive Scale for 3- to 5-year-olds, which is not available on the CBCL. The CPRS-R is also briefer and may be more useful when readministration of the scale is anticipated for evaluating treatments. Normative data on the CPRS-R were obtained from a sample of 750 3- to 17-year-olds and its psychometric properties are adequate. The measure also discriminates ADHD from non-ADHD children and is sensitive to stimulant medication and parent training interventions (Barkley, 1987a).

The Home Situations Questionnaire (HSQ) (Barkley, 1981) supplements rating scales that assess problem behavior by evaluating the specific home situations in which these problems may occur. The HSQ allows assessment of the situational variation in behavior as well as the pervasiveness and severity of behavioral difficulties. The HSQ contains 16-items about common situations occurring at home (e.g., while playing alone) and in public (e.g., while in stores). Parents indicate whether problems exist in each situation and provide a severity rating using a scale from 1 (mild) to 9 (severe). The scale yields two scores: number of problem situations and mean severity. Normative data on the HSQ are available for 4- to 12-year-olds (Barkley & Edelbrock, 1987). The scale has been found to differentiate ADHD from normal children and is sensitive to parent training and stimulant medication (Barkley, Karlsson, Pollard, & Murphy, 1985; Befera & Barkley, 1985; Pollard, Ward, & Barkley, 1983).

Teacher Behavior Ratings

Teacher behavior ratings on well-normed scales are an essential part of the behavioral assessment of ADHD. Teacher ratings provide necessary information about the child's behavior in the school setting, provide information from a second informant, and are particularly valuable because they can provide judgments of a child's behavior in the context of his or her similar aged peers. A number of teacher-completed rating scales are available; these measure a variety of dimensions of psychopathology in children (see Barkley, 1987a, for review). The three counterparts of the parent-completed scales also have sound psychometric properties and normative data, and allow ratings of ADHD symptoms as well as additional behavior problems.

The Child Behavior Checklist–Teacher Report Form (CBCL–TRF) (Achenbach & Edelbrock, 1983) has many of the same items that appear on the parent version and also includes scales measuring adaptive behavior as well as child psychopathology. The Adaptive Functioning Scale produces five scores pertaining to general school performance, effort, behavior, learning, and the child's apparent happiness. The 118-item Behavior Problem Scale yields factor scores (e.g., Anxious, Obsessive-Compulsive) which are plotted on profiles containing normative data available for both sexes and for two age groupings: 6 to 11 and 12 to 16. The Inattentive and Nervous-Overactive factors provide separate scores for attention and hyperactivity. The CBCL-TRF discriminates ADHD from other psychiatric problems (Edelbrock et al., 1984).

The Conners Teacher Rating Scale (CTRS) (Conners, 1969; Goyette et al., 1978) is a 39-item counterpart to the parent version. There is also a 28-item revised version that overlaps with the longer version but is completed more quickly. The revised CTRS is well normed and provides factor scores relevant to ADHD, including Hyperactive, Inattentive-Passive, and Conduct Problem factors. The scale appears to load heavily on problems in conduct, however, and may not be as useful as the CBCL for evaluating other areas of psychopathology. The CTRS has adequate test-retest reliability (Edelbrock, Greenbaum, & Conover, 1985), discriminates ADHD children from other children, and is sensitive to stimulant medication effects (Barkley, 1987a).

The School Situations Questionnaire (SSQ) (Barkley, 1981) assesses the types of situations in which problem behaviors occur in the school setting. The SSQ provides an estimate of how circumscribed or pervasive behavioral difficulties of the child are at school. The scale contains 12 school-related situations (e.g., while teacher is lecturing) sampling across a variety of structured and unstructured situations. Teachers indicate whether the situation is a problem for the child and rate the severity of the problem on a scale from 1 (mild) to 9 (severe). The number of settings in which problems occur and a mean severity rating are obtained. Norms are contained in Barkley and Edelbrock (1987). The SSQ discriminates ADHD from normal children and is also sensitive to the effects of stimulant medication (Barkley, Fischer, Newby, & Breen, 1988). Both the HSQ and the SSQ have recently been revised to assess the situational pervasiveness of attention problems across home and school settings (DuPaul & Barkley, 1991). Normative data are available in the text by Barkley (1990).

ADHD Rating Scales

Several behavior rating scales have been developed to assess ADHD symptoms in children more specifically. The Attention Deficit Disorder Comprehensive Teacher Rating Scale (ACTeRS) (Ullmann, Sleator, & Sprague, 1984) was developed to evaluate attention deficit disorders and responses to treatment. There are four separate subscales: Oppositional Behavior, Attention, Hyperactivity, and Social Problems; these generate results that can be compared to normative data on a large sample of 5- to 12-year-olds. The ACTeRS differentiates ADHD from normal and learning disabled children (e.g., Ullmann, Sleator, & Sprague, 1984). The ACTeRS has not yet been as extensively researched as other available rating scales.

The Edelbrock Child Attention Profile (CAP) was derived from the lengthier CBCL (see Barkley, 1987a) and designed specifically to assess stimulant drug responses of ADHD children. The five items loading highest on the Overactivity scale but lowest on Inattention and the seven loading highest on the Inattention scale but lowest on Overactivity of the CBCL-TRF were selected for this scale. The CAP scale is shown in Figure 8.1. The CAP is especially useful for classifying ADHD children according to the subtypes with hyperactivity and without hyperactivity. Normative data are based on scores obtained

CAP Rating Scale

Child's Name: _____

Today's Date: _____

Filled Out By: _____

FOR OFFICE USE ONLY

Below is a list of items that describe pupils. For each item that describes the pupil *now* or *within the past week*, check whether the item is Not True, Somewhat or Sometimes True, or Very or Often True. Please check all items as well as you can, even if some do not seem to apply to this pupil.

	Not True	Somewhat or Sometimes True	Very or Often True
1. Fails to finish things he/she starts	[ ]	[ ]	[ ]
2. Can't concentrate, can't pay attention for long	[ ]	[ ]	[ ]
3. Can't sit still, restless, or hyperactive	[ ]	[ ]	[ ]
4. Fidgets	[ ]	[ ]	[ ]
5. Daydreams or gets lost in his/her thoughts	[ ]	[ ]	[ ]
6. Impulsive or acts without thinking	[ ]	[ ]	[ ]
7. Difficulty following directions	[ ]	[ ]	[ ]
8. Talks out of turn	[ ]	[ ]	[ ]
9. Messy work	[ ]	[ ]	[ ]
10. Inattentive, easily distracted	[ ]	[ ]	[ ]
11. Talks too much	[ ]	[ ]	[ ]
12. Fails to carry out assigned tasks	[ ]	[ ]	[ ]

Please feel free to write any coments about the pupil's work or behavior in the last week.

Figure 8.1. The Edelbrock Children's Attention Problems (CAP) Scale for obtaining teacher ratings. Copyright © by Craig S. Edelbrock. Reprinted with permission.
Reprinted with permission of Craig S. Edelbrock.

from 1,100 male and female children, 6 through 16 years of age (Barkley, 1990) and are shown in Table 8.2. Preliminary studies indicate that the CAP is sensitive to stimulant drug effects (Barkley, McMurray, Edelbrock, & Robbins, 1989).

Finally, the Self-Control Rating Scale (SCRS) (Kendall & Wilcox, 1979) contains 33 items pertaining to children's ability to follow rules, inhibit behavior, and control impulses. The scale yields a single summary score representing self-control and discriminates ADHD from normal children and those with other psychiatric disorders. The scale is also sensitive to cognitive-behavioral treatment (Barkley, 1988; Kendall & Wilcox, 1979)

and correlates significantly with direct observation measures of off-task behavior and "bugging others" in the classroom (Kendall & Braswell, 1982). The SCRS has not been as extensively studied in evaluating ADHD and currently has a small normative sample, which may limit its widespread use.

Self-Report Ratings

With older children and adolescents, it may also be of some value to have self-report ratings completed as a general indication of the child's own perceptions of his or her problems. Self-report ratings

Table 8.2. Normative Cutoff Points for the Inattention, Overactivity, and Total Scores for the Edelbrock CAP Scale

Cutoff Points	Total (1100)	Boys (550)	Girls (550)
	Inattention[b]		
Median	1	2	0
69 Percentile	3	4	2
84 Percentile	6	7	5
93 Percentile	8	9	7
98 Percentile	11	12	10
	Overactivity		
Median	0	1	0
69 Percentile	1	2	1
84 Percentile	4	4	2
93 Percentile	6	6	5
98 Percentile	8	8	7
	Total Score		
Median	2	4	1
69 Percentile	6	7	4
84 Percentile	10	11	8
93 Percentile	14	15	11
98 Percentile	19	20	16

[a]Numbers in parentheses are sample sizes.

[b]Inattention score is the sum of items 1, 2, 5, 7, 9, 10, and 12.

The Overactivity score is the sum of items 3, 4, 6, 8, and 11.

Table entries are raw scores that fall at or below the designated percentile range. The 93rd percentile is the recommended upper limit of the normal range. Scores exceeding this cutoff are in the clinical range. All scores are based on teacher reports.

may also reveal covert antisocial behaviors unknown to other informants or depressive symptoms not gauged through the interview or other behavior ratings. The Youth Self-Report Form of the Child Behavior Checklist (Achenbach & Edelbrock, 1987) offers a comprehensive self-report rating scale for children or adolescents to complete. As part of the assessment of adolescents, we have also found it useful to obtain parent ratings on the type, frequency, and severity of conflictual issues by using the Issues Checklist and Interaction Behavior Questionnaire (see Robin & Foster, 1989 for a complete discussion and normative data derived from these instruments). These rating scales may also be completed by the adolescent and provide information on the extent of parent-adolescent conflicts and the specific issues that provoke such conflicts.

Where parent reports via interviews or scales serve as the sole source for information on ADHD symptoms, it may be useful to collect parent self-report ratings of depression and marital discord. This suggestion is founded on emerging evidence that depressed or maritally discordant parents may report, possibly in an exaggerated manner, greater symptom deviance in their children on rating scales than may actually be true (Forehand & McMahon, 1981; Griest, Wells, & Forehand, 1979). Likewise, assessment of parental psychopathology may provide useful information on the child's psychosocial environment and weigh heavily in the selection of treatments. We have found the following instruments useful in our clinical protocol: Symptom Checklist 90-Revised (Derogatis, 1986), Beck Depression Scale (Beck, Rush, Shaw, & Emory, 1979), and the Locke-Wallace Marital Adjustment Scale (Locke & Wallace, 1959). In our own clinic, we routinely refer seriously depressed or overly distressed parents for individual treatment prior to initiating parent training.

Direct Observation

Several observational systems appear promising in the assessment of ADHD. Direct observational procedures, like rating scales, also have to be judged according to their psychometric properties, adequacy of sampling, amount of training necessary for their reliable use, and the availability of resources before being considered in a protocol for assessing ADHD.

Abikoff, Gittleman-Klein, and Klein (1977) developed a direct observational code for assessing ADHD symptoms in the classroom. Fourteen categories reflecting ADHD behaviors (e.g., off-task, movement about the classroom) are scored on an interval basis. Twelve of these 14 codes differentiate ADHD and normal children. The Hyperactive Behavior Code (Jacob, O'Leary, & Rosenblad, 1978) may also be used to assess ADHD symptoms in a classroom setting. Six behavior codes (e.g., change of position, daydreaming) are recorded on an interval system and collapsed to yield a single summary score. The summary score discriminates ADHD from normal children in classroom situations and correlates highly with teacher ratings of ADHD behaviors on the CTRS.

To address some of the practical constraints encountered when attempting to use direct observational procedures in the natural environment, clinical analogue observational procedures have been developed. Roberts (1979) developed a clinic playroom observational procedure to assess ADHD behavior. The system was validated by Milich and his associates (e.g., Milich et al., 1982; Milich, 1984). Using this system, children are observed in two 15-minute situations: free play and restricted academic periods. During free play, children are allowed to play with available toys while six ADHD behaviors are recorded (e.g., fidgeting, vocalizations) using an interval recording system. In the restricted academic period, the child is instructed to remain seated, complete a series of worksheets, and not play with any of the toys in the room. The child's behavior is again recorded on an interval basis using the six observation codes and two additional categories: time spent touching toys and number of worksheet items completed. The system discriminates ADHD children from other psychiatric disorders, and ADHD from children with aggressive behavior problems only and from those who are both ADHD and aggressive. The measure is also stable over time and correlates significantly with behavior ratings and other laboratory measures of ADHD (Barkley, 1991).

This observational system was adapted by Barkley (e.g., Barkley, 1990; Barkley et al., 1988) for use in the clinical assessments of ADHD children and to evaluate stimulant drug responses. It uses only the restricted academic period, in which the child is instructed to complete a set number of mathematics problems selected from workbooks for the child's grade level. The child's behavior is recorded by an observer behind a one-way mirror. The initial occurrence of five behaviors are recorded during each 30-second interval. The coding form is presented in Figure 8.2. The following behaviors are measured: off-task, fidgets, vocalizes, out of seat, and plays with objects. Definitions for the five behavior codes are provided in Table 8.3. The percentage of occurrence of each of the behaviors is summarized. The overall percentages of behavior may also be collapsed to yield a total summary score of ADHD behavior. The system discriminates ADHD from normal children (Breen, 1986) and is sensitive to stimulant drug dose effects (Barkley et al., 1988).

Clinic Test Measures

Standardized clinic tests with adequate normative data may supplement other assessment methods that attempt to measure ADHD symptoms directly. Recently, normative and validity data have been established on several of these tests, allowing their inclusion in a multimethod assessment protocol.

Attention Span

One of the most widely used measures for direct assessment of attention span or vigilance is the Continuous Performance Test (CPT). Most of these measures require a child to observe a screen while stimuli (e.g., numbers, letters) are rapidly projected. The child is instructed to press a button when a certain stimulus or pair of stimuli appear in sequence. The task may last between 9 and 15 minutes and requires continuous attention for maximum performance.

Total correct responses, number of stimuli missed (omissions), and the number of stimuli to which the child incorrectly responded (commissions) are recorded. The total number correct and omission scores are used as measures of sustained attention while commission scores are assumed to measure impulsivity and possibly sustained attention as well. The CPT discriminates ADHD from normal children (Douglas, 1983) and correlates with other measures of attention-span (e.g., behavior ratings) (Klee & Garfinkel, 1983). Several computer software programs and a commercially available solid-state computerized device (The Gordon Daagnostic System [GDS]) for assessing sustained attention and impulsivity have recently become available (Swanson, 1985). The GDS is a small, solid-state computerized device that has normative data on over 1,000 children aged 3 to 16 years. It has been shown to discriminate ADHD and normal children (Gordon, 1979, 1983, 1985) and may also be sensitive to stimulant drug responses (Barkley et al., 1988).

Impulsivity

Clinic tests may also be used to measure impulse control. The GDS (described above), for example, includes a test of impulsivity called the Delay Task. The task requires the child to delay or inhibit responding to earn points. The Delay Task yields three measures: number of correct responses, total number of responses, and the ratio of correct responses to the total number. Each of these measures has tentatively been found to discriminate ADHD and non-ADHD clinic-referred children and to correlate with behavior ratings of ADHD (Gordon, 1979). Barkley et al. (1988) recently found that scores on the Delay Task were not sensitive to stimulant drug effects.

The Matching Familiar Figures Test (MFFT) (Kagan, 1965) is one of the most widely used tests of impulsivity in children. The MFFT is a match-to-sample task in which the child is presented with a sample picture and is instructed to select the same picture from an array of highly similar pictures.

The amount of time taken to the first response (response latency) and the number of errors are recorded. The average response latency and total number of errors can then be compared to normative data available on 2,846 5- through 12-year-olds. Scores that deviate from age and gender norms are believed to reflect an impulsive cognitive response style. Both response latency and error scores discriminate ADHD and normal children (Campbell, Douglas, & Morganstern, 1971) and correlate with observational measures of ADHD behaviors (activity, attention) (Milich et al., 1981). Both scores are also sensitive to stimulant drug effects, although this has been a somewhat inconsistent finding (Barkley, 1977).

Activity Level

Clinic tests may be used to assess activity level in children. The actometer and pedometer, for example, are devices that can be attached to the child's body (e.g., wrist, ankle) to measure movement mechanically. These instruments are commonly used in research but have not been widely employed in clinical assessments of ADHD. Their limited use may be related to the absence of normative data, questionable reliability of scores, and practical limitations that arise in attempts to use specialized instrumentation. Also, the relationship of scores obtained using such devices to other well-founded measures of ADHD has been somewhat weak (Barkley & Ullmann, 1975; Milich, Loney, & Landau, 1982). Their inclusion in a clinical protocol would necessitate cautious interpretation of scores.

In general, most of the clinic tests and analogue assessment measures reviewed are able to discriminate ADHD from normal groups of children. A recent review of these assessment methods (Barkley, 1991), however, suggests that clinic and analogue methods are less consistent in discriminating ADHD children from other clinical populations. Thus, further research is needed before the ecological validity of these methods can be considered sound. In the meantime, such assessment methods are best included as part of a multimethod approach and interpreted in the context of information derived from other sources and assessment methods.

ACADEMIC SITUATION CODE SHEET

Interval #:	1	2	3	4	5	6	7	8	9	10	11	12	13	14	15	16	17	18
Off-Task																		
Fidgeting																		
Vocalizing																		
Plays w/Obj.																		
Out of Seat																		

Interval #:	19	20	21	22	23	24	25	26	27	28	29	30	Total				Scoring	
Off-Task														/30	=		=	
Fidgeting														/30	=		=	
Vocalizing														/30	=		=	
Plays w/Obj.														/30	=		%	
Out of Seat														/30	=		%	

Total ADD Beh. _____ /150 = _____

Child's Name _____ Coder Initials _____

Session: Init. Wk1 Wk2 Wk3   Is this a reliability check? YES Date: _____

If so, with whom? _____ NO

Comments:

Figure 8.2. The behavior coding sheet for the Restricted Academic Playroom Situation

160

Table 8.3. Coding Procedures for the Restricted Academic Situations Test

Instructions for Conducting Observations:

Place the child in a playroom having a one-way mirror and intercom facilities, a small table and chair at which the child will work, and a number of toys. Instruct the child to sit at the small table and work on grade level arithmetic problems presented on worksheets. Instruct the child to work on the math problems, remain in his or her seat, and not to touch any objects in the room.

Begin observing the target child using a stopwatch or audiotape that cues interval changes. This tape merely contains voice prompts indicating the beginning of each 30-second interval (i.e., Begin 1 . . ., Begin 2 . . ., Begin 3 . . ., Begin 30 . . .). When the tape sounds the interval number, the coder proceeds to that column on the observation form and places a check mark in that block corresponding to each behavior category. Each category is scored only once during a 30-second interval, regardless of how often it may occur. When the tape recorder sounds the next interval number, the coder moves to the next column and begins marking any behavior categories which occur in that interval.

The following behavior categories are recorded: off-task, fidgeting, vocalizations, plays with object, and out of seat. It *is* possible to score a child as showing any or all of these behavior categories within any 30-second interval.

There are 30 intervals to be coded (15 minutes × 2 intervals each minute). The following definitions are used for each behavior category.

Definitions of Behavior Categories:

1. *Off-task:* This category is checked if the child interrupts his attention to the tasks to engage in some other behavior. Off-task behaviors are looking around the room, playing with the pencil, talking to another person, or any other behavior where the child is not looking at his task. A child can hum or whistle while working, kick his legs, and even stop using his pencil and still remain "on-task" as long as he maintains eye contact with the task. It is essentially the breaking of eye-contact with the task that constitutes "off-task" behavior.

2. *Fidgeting:* Any repetitive, purposeless motion of the legs, arms, buttocks, or trunk. The movement must occur at least twice in succession to be considered repetitive *and* it should serve no purpose. Examples: swaying back and forth, kicking one's legs back and forth, shuffling feet from side to side, shifting one's buttocks about in the chair, tapping one's pencil on the desk.

3. *Vocalization:* Any vocal noise or verbalization made by the child. Examples: talking aloud, humming, whistling, throat clearing, clicking one's teeth together, singing.

4. *Plays with Objects:* If the child manually touches any other object in the room that is not related to the task (pencil, paper, and desk) or his body (including clothing), it is scored in this category. Playing with one's own body parts or clothing is not scored here.

5. *Out of Seat:* Any time the child's buttocks break contact with the flat surface of the seat in which he is sitting, it is coded in this category.

Scoring Dependent Measures

The score for each category is derived by counting the number of check marks for that category and dividing by 30 to yield a percent occurrence.

IDENTIFYING TARGET BEHAVIORS AND MAINTAINING CONDITIONS

The multimethod assessment approach just described yields information about the child's diagnostic status with respect to ADHD as well as information about associated problems that may coexist with ADHD. Also, the severity and pervasiveness of problems across settings will have been delineated. The diagnostic phase within behavioral assessment is conducted with the expectation that the information derived will also lead to treatment recommendations. Thus, the final phase of the behavioral assessment includes a selection of relevant target behaviors for treatment as well as the specification of possible conditions maintaining problem behavior.

Target Behaviors

A primary assumption of the behavioral assessment of ADHD stems from the position that one will not directly treat the disorder in a curative sense. ADHD is usually chronic and there is no known cure. Instead, the child's family is assisted in selecting specific and meaningful behaviors that may be alterable. Target behaviors selected for treatment usually have one or more key characteristics: (a) the behavior produces maladaptive consequences for the child or others; (b) the behavior, if changed, is likely to be reinforced, so that it will be maintained or supported by natural contingencies; (c) the behavior is viewed as essential and is consistent with developmental or local norms for performance; (d) the behavior is known to be associated with a poor long-term prognosis (e.g., aggression) (Robins, 1966).

In behavioral assessment, target behaviors are operationally defined according to specific and, perhaps, observable actions. Vague descriptions of problems are translated into more specific accounts of behavior. Parents' complaints concerning "his bad attitude" may be more specifically defined as "he frequently whines and cries when he does not get his way" or concerns that "she has no manners" operationalized as "she interrupts me constantly when I'm on the phone." Primary symptoms of ADHD, such as overactivity and short attention span, are often deemphasized as target behaviors. This is often, in part, because (a) these symptoms may be largely unchangeable through nonpharmologic means, (b) they merely represent broad characteristics of the child rather than specifically defined behavior problems, and (c) behaviors that develop secondary to ADHD (e.g., noncompliance, peer rejection) are often more related to and predictive of later life maladjustment than the ADHD symptoms themselves (Loney & Milich, 1982; Satterfield, Satterfield, & Cantwell, 1981).

Instead, informants are assisted in delineating what problems are produced by the child's hyperactivity, inattention, or poor impulse control. Specific examples may include "leaving the table excessively while having dinner," "not finishing a chore," "taking too long to get dressed in the morning," and "blurting out answers in the classroom." Such be-

haviors may be byproducts of inattention, impulsivity, or overactivity but they represent more concrete and specific behaviors that may be targeted as part of a treatment program. The selection of target behaviors also necessitates a consideration of associated behavioral problems and the child's functioning across situations and settings. Much of this information would have been derived through the multimethod evaluation. Target behaviors may be found in the context of peer interactions (e.g., hits or pushes others), classroom behavior (e.g., leaves his seat without permission), academic achievement (e.g., rarely completes her work), sibling relations (e.g., constantly teases his brother), or parent-child interactions (e.g., has to be told five times to do something).

Barkley (1981, 1987a) has argued that noncompliant behavior in ADHD children should be thoroughly assessed as a possible target behavior because (a) it represents one of the most frequent referral complaints; (b) it may have indirect effects on general family functioning (e.g., completion of chores) and the child's own psychological and social development; (c) it is a significant predictor of later maladjustment in the adolescent and young adult years; and (d) noncompliance constitutes a large class of problematic behavior, all of which may be treatable via parent behavior management training. Specific examples of noncompliant behaviors are presented in Table 8.4.

Parent behavior ratings and the initial interview may be sufficient for determining the extent to which noncompliance is a problem for an individual child. Several behavioral observation systems (Mash, Terdal, & Anderson, 1973; Barkley, 1981; Patterson, 1982) have been developed to assess noncompliant behavior in parent-child interactions. One system that may be used in clinical settings was developed by Forehand and McMahon (1981). A simplified version of this system to assess the interactions of parents and their ADHD children is found in Barkley (1987a).

As noted earlier, it is essential that the examiner carefully assess how realistic a parent's expectations may be in light of the child's age and the limitations imposed on him or her by ADHD. Oftentimes the family will need assistance in understanding these limitations and focusing their treatment efforts on manageable behavior problems.

Table 8.4. Types of Noncompliant Behaviors Common in Children Referred for Attention Deficit Hyperactivity Disorder

Yells	Steals	Physically resists
Whines	Lies	Destroys property
Complains	Argues	Fights with others
Defies	Humiliates	Fails to complete homework
Screams	Teases	Disrupts others' activities
Throws tantrums	Ignores requests	Ignores self-help tasks
Throws objects	Runs off	
Talks back	Cries	
Swears	Fails to complete chores	

Note: Adapted from Barkley (1987a), *Defiant Children: A Clinician's Manual for Parent Training.* New York: Guilford Press. Adapted with permission.

Maintaining Conditions

After target behaviors are selected for treatment, the behavioral assessment turns to a delineation of possible conditions maintaining problem behavior. The term *maintaining conditions,* as used here, refers to any environmental condition (e.g., structure of the classroom, parental disciplining practices) that may account, at least in part, for the continuation of the problem behavior. With behavioral interventions, treatment ultimately involves introducing modification in the current environmental conditions maintaining or aggravating these problem behaviors. Although any number of conditions may serve to maintain problem behavior for an individual child, we have found it clinically useful to assess and address three common environmental conditions that may maintain problem behavior among ADHD children: (a) deficient reinforcement arrangements, (b) escape and avoidance learning, and (c) the "goodness of fit" between environmental demands and the child's capacities. Each of these potential maintaining conditions are briefly discussed.

With respect to *deficient reinforcement arrangements,* evidence was previously reviewed that suggests that ADHD children, in comparison to normal controls, show an idiosyncratic response to reinforcement schedules. That is, the child's performance (e.g., attention span, accuracy) may be poorer than same-aged peers when reinforcement is delivered on a partial rather than continuous schedule and when reinforcement is delayed rather than more immediate. Moreover, there is some evidence that ADHD children may habituate to reinforcers more rapidly than their normal peers and that appropriate behavior is extinguished more quickly when reinforcement is no longer delivered. Under continuous and immediate reinforcement schedules and when reinforcers are periodically rotated, problems ascribed to ADHD may dissipate considerably.

These phenomena have recently been discussed as a "motivation deficit" (Barkley, 1989; Haenlein & Caul, 1987). This proposed deficit is not meant to suggest the presence of defective personality characteristics, whereby ADHD children are inherently "lazy." In contrast, most investigators endorse a biologic-neurologic predisposition explanation for these findings and suggest that ADHD is best understood in the context of an interactional model (Barkley, 1981, 1989). Stated simply, the ADHD child's performance would be expected to vary according to the particular reinforcement arrangements present in the immediate environment. Thus, what may represent adequate performance incentives for most children may be grossly insufficient for the ADHD child. An analysis of the reinforcement arrangements in situations where performance deficits (e.g., incomplete school work) exist may lead to alteration of these potential maintaining conditions, namely, by increasing the rate, immediacy, and "richness" of reinforcement available for desired behavior.

A second major locus of maintaining conditions involves *escape and avoidance learning.* Escape and avoidance learning is occasioned by negative reinforcement. For those not well versed in behavioral terminology, negative reinforcement is said to occur when a child is subjected to an unpleasant or aversive situation and behaves in such a way as to terminate the situation. If the situation is successfully terminated (avoided or escaped from) the child will be more likely to employ similar avoidant tactics again in the future. Over time, overly passive or even coercive behavior may be used by the child in an attempt to "get out of" the situations or tasks that are experienced as unpleasant. This potential maintaining condition has been well studied by Patterson (1982) with aggressive children and we have found this to be a very common occurrence in ADHD children.

In many ways, the development of escape and avoidance behavior on the part of ADHD children is understandable. First, poor sustained attention may result in greater difficulties in completing tasks within the time frame generally provided. Second, if the conditions of reinforcement are insufficient (secondary to a motivational deficit), the child may find routine work demands more taxing than most children and lacking meaningful incentive. An ADHD child, for example, may find homework responsibilities especially unpleasant because, perhaps, there is little intrinsic interest in the task and the child needs far more time to complete the work than do his or her peers. Attempts to escape and avoid such an aversive situation may include the child's protesting vehemently about having to do homework and frequently returning home without the necessary assigned material. If these tactics are intermittently successful, it is likely that the child will employ similar tactics in the future.

Analysis of escape and avoidant learning as maintaining conditions for problem behavior may suggest the necessity of working with parents, and perhaps teachers, to block successful avoidance of necessary responsibilities. Parent training, classroom management training, and home-school based communication systems have been successfully employed to address such problems (see Barkley, 1981, and Barkley, 1987b, for a description of these interventions). Generally, when attempts are made to prevent escape or avoid activities, mild punishment is often necessary (Patterson, 1982). As noted, it is often understandable why ADHD children may engage in avoidant behavior when one considers the limitations imposed upon the child's developmental capacities for sustained performance. Therefore, it is useful to consider one

final environmental condition that may contribute to or maintain problem behavior.

The "goodness of fit" between the child's innate capacities and environmental demands represents a third potential maintaining condition for problem behavior. This "fit" refers to the extent to which the requisite skills are available to the child to consistently perform successfully. Where demands and expectations regarding performance outweigh the child's capacities for consistently meeting those standards, deficient or highly inconsistent performance may occur. Moreover, secondary emotional responses, such as passivity, aggression, or increased emotionality may emerge, perhaps as a function of frustration or because of punitive tactics that may begin to dominate intervention efforts. Where a poor goodness of fit exists it is unlikely that modifications in the reinforcement contingencies or the blocking of escape and avoidance behavior alone will be sufficient. Instead, altering the maintaining conditions may include attempts to restructure the child's environment or the introduction of compensatory strategies. Such modifications may include, for example, reducing the amount of work required at school and/or for homework, extending the amount of time for completing tests, using posted "cue cards" at home to prompt better rule compliance, and breaking down work tasks into smaller and more manageable units.

The introduction of environmental restructuring and compensatory techniques may initially sound somewhat like a contradiction between recommendations to "block" escape and avoidance behavior. One could argue that changing the demands and expectations for performance may, in fact, encourage avoidance behavior. Undoubtedly, the assessment and modification of maintaining conditions will include a carefully balanced treatment plan that considers each of these potential maintaining conditions in the context of the child's overall psychological profile, available resources, and sound clinical judgment.

Finally, altering maintaining conditions for problem behavior is unlikely to have a curative effect. That is, it is frequently the case that such changes will need to be continued for long periods of time. Should previously problematic maintaining conditions resurface, it is likely that problem behavior will also reemerge. For this reason, altering problematic maintaining conditions and introducing techniques that result in successful behavior for ADHD children may be viewed as an attempt to create a prosthetic environment that maximizes the child's ability to perform successfully (Barkley, 1981, 1987). Maintenance of this prosthetic environment may be essential in preventing maladaptive behavior for a number of years.

SUMMARY

Attention deficit hyperactivity disorder is currently viewed as a developmental disorder with primary deficits in the domains of sustained attention, rule compliance, impulse control, and motor restlessness. It is usually chronic and pervasive or cross-situational. Although most investigators endorse a biological predisposition for these core deficits, ADHD symptoms appear to be interactive with the environment and show considerable variability and fluctuation across settings, tasks, caregivers, and reinforcement arrangements. In addition to these primary symptoms, ADHD children show a greater prevalence of associated problems in emotional, behavioral, social, and academic domains.

This chapter has described a diagnostic and assessment protocol for evaluating ADHD in children, borrowing from both a medical-psychiatric model and methods derived from behavioral assessment. A multimethod approach to assessment was emphasized. The current status of the field suggests that an assessment protocol rely on multiple methods, utilizing several different sources of information obtained from different settings and informants (Barkley, 1981, 1988). The inclusion of parent and teacher interviews, standardized parent and teacher behavior ratings, several clinic test measures of sustained attention and impulsivity, and direct observation can provide information pertaining to the onset of symptoms, their chronicity, pervasiveness, developmental deviance of primary symptoms, coexisting behavior difficulties, and the requirement that other conditions (e.g., psychiatric, medical) be excluded.

The diagnostic and assessment process described leads to the selection of target behaviors for treatment. Target behaviors are defined as concrete and observable instances of behavior rather than as broad characteristics of the child or ADHD symptoms per se. Maintaining conditions for these problem behaviors are sought in the external environment and are often found to be related to deficient reinforcement arrangements, escape and avoidance learning, and a poor "goodness of fit" between the child's innate capacities and the demands and expectations imposed on the child by others. Modification of these maintaining conditions may help to create a prosthetic environment that maximizes the child's abilities and adaptive behavior.

REFERENCES

Abikoff, H., Gittelman-Klein, R., & Klein, D. (1977). Validation of a classroom observation code for hyperactive children. *Journal of Consulting and Clinical Psychology, 45*, 772–783.

Achenbach, T. M. & Edelbrock, C. (1983). *Manual for the child behavior checklist and revised child behavior profile*. Burlington, VT: Thomas Achenbach.

Achenbach, T. M. & Edelbrock, C. (1987). *Manual for the Child Behavior Checklist Youth Self-Report*. Burlington: University of Vermont, Department of Psychiatry.

American Psychiatric Association. (1980). *Diagnostic and statistical manual of mental disorders* (3rd ed.). Washington, DC: Author.

American Psychiatric Association. (1987). *Diagnostic and statistical manual of mental disorders* (3rd ed. rev.). Washington, DC: Author.

Barkley, R. A. (1977). A review of stimulant drug research with hyperactive children. *Journal of Child Psychology and Psychiatry, 18*, 137–165.

Barkley, R. A. (1981). *Hyperactive children: A handbook for diagnosis and treatment*. New York: Guilford Press.

Barkley, R. A. (1982). Specific guidelines for defining hyperactivity in children (attention deficit disorder with hyperactivity). In B. Lahey & A. Kazdin (Eds.), *Advances in clinical child psychology* (Vol. 5, pp. 137–180). Elmsford, NY: Pergamon Press.

Barkley, R. A. (1985). The social interactions of hyperactive children: Developmental changes, drug effects, and situational variation. In R. McMahon & R. Peters (Eds.), *Childhood disorders: Behavioral-developmental approaches* (pp. 228–243). New York: Brunner/Mazel.

Barkley, R. A. (1987a). Child behavior rating scales and checklists for research in child psychopathology. In M. Rutter, H. Tuma, & T. Lann (Eds.), *Diagnosis and assessment in child and adolescent psychopathology*. New York: Guilford Press.

Barkley, R. A. (1987b). *Defiant children: A clinician's manual for parent training.* New York: Guilford Press.

Barkley, R. A. (1988). The problem of stimulus control and rule-governed behavior in children with attention deficit disorder with hyperactivity. In J. Swanson & I. Bloomingdale (Eds.), *Research on attention deficit disorders* (Vol. IV). New York: Plenum Publishing.

Barkley, R. A. (1990). *Attention deficit hyperactivity disorder: A handbook for diagnosis and treatment.* New York: Guilford.

Barkley, R. A. (1991). The ecological validity of laboratory and analogue assessment methods of ADHD symptoms. *Journal of Abnormal Child Psychology, 19,* 149–178.

Barkley, R. A., & Cunningham, C. E. (1979). The effects of Ritalin on the mother-child interactions of hyperactive children. *Archives of General Psychiatry, 36,* 201–208.

Barkley, R. A., & Edelbrock, C. (1987). Assessing situational variations in children's behavior problems: The Home and School Situations Questionnaires. In R. Prinz (Ed.), *Advances in behavioral assessment of children and families* (Vol. 3, pp. 157–176). Greenwich, CT: JAI Press.

Barkley, R. A., & Ullman, D. G. (1975). A comparison of objective measures of activity and distractibility in hyperactive and nonhyperactive children. *Journal of Abnormal Child Psychology, 3,* 231–244.

Barkley, R. A., Fischer, M., Newby, R., & Breen, M. (1988). Development of a multimethod clinical protocol for assessing stimulant drug responses in ADD children. *Journal of Clinical Child Psychology, 17,* 14–24.

Barkley, R., Karlsson, J., Pollard, S., & Murphy, J. (1985). Developmental changes in the mother-child interactions of hyperactive boys: Effects of two dose levels of Ritalin. *Journal of Consulting and Clinical Psychology, 52,* 750–758.

Barkley, R. A., McMurray, M., Edelbrock, C., & Robbins, K. (1989). The response of aggressive and nonaggressive ADHD children to two doses of methylphenidate. *Journal of the American Academy of Child and Adolescent Psychiatry, 28,* 873–881.

Beck, A. T., Rush, A. J., Shaw, B. F., & Emery, G. (1979). *Cognitive therapy for depression.* New York: Guilford Press.

Befera, M., & Barkley, R. A. (1985). Hyperactive and normal boys and girls: Mother-child interaction, parent psychiatric status, and child psychopathology. *Journal of Child Psychology and Psychiatry, 26,* 439–452.

Breen, M. (1989). Cognitive and behavioral differences in AdHD boys and girls. *Journal of Child Psychology and Psychiatry, 30,* 711–716.

Breen, M., & Barkley, R. A. (1985). Psychological adjustment in learning disabled, hyperactive, and hyperactive/learning disabled children using the Personality Inventory for Children. *Journal of Clinical Child Psychology, 13,* 232–236.

Brown, R. T., & Quay, L. C. (1977). Reflection-impulsivity of normal and behavior-disordered children. *Journal of Abnormal Child Psychology, 5,* 457–462.

Campbell, S. B., & Paulauskas, S. (1979). Peer relations in hyperactive children. *Journal of Abnormal Child Psychology, 20,* 233–246.

Campbell, S. B., Douglas, V. I. & Morganstern, G. (1971). Cognitive styles in hyperactive children and the effect of methylphenidate. *Journal of Child Psychology and Psychiatry, 12,* 55–67.

Carlson, C. (1986). Attention deficit disorder without hyperactivity: A review of preliminary experimental evidence. In B. Lahey & A. Kazdin (Eds.), *Advances in clinical child psychology* (Vol. 9, pp. 153–176). New York: Plenum Publishing.

Conners, C. K. (1969). A teacher rating scale for use in drug studies with children. *American Journal of Psychiatry, 126,* 884.

Derogatis, L. (1986). *Manual for the symptom checklist-90, revised (SCL-90R).* Baltimore MD: Author.

Douglas, V. I. (1983). Attention and cognitive problems. In M. Rutter (Ed.), *Developmental neuropsychiatry* (pp. 280–329). New York: Guilford Press.

Douglas, V. I. & Parry, P. A. (1983). Effects of reward on delayed reaction time task performance of hyperactive children. *Journal of Abnormal Child Psychology, 11,* 313–326.

Draeger, S., Prior, M., & Sanson, A. (1986). Visual and auditory attention performance in hyperactive children: Competence or compliance. *Journal of Abnormal Child Psychology, 14,* 411–424.

DuPaul, G. J., & Barkley, R. A. (1991). *Situational variability of attention problems: Psychometric properties of the Revised Home and School Situations Questionnaires.* Unpublished manuscript, University of Massachusetts Medical Center.

Edelbrock, C., & Costello, A. J. (1988). Convergence between statistically derived behavior problem syndromes and child psychiatric diagnoses. *Journal of Abnormal Child Psychology, 16,* 219–231.

Edelbrock, C., Costello, A., & Kessler, M. D. (1984). Empirical corroboration of attention deficit disorder. *Journal of the American Academy of Child Psychiatry, 23,* 285–290.

Edelbrock, C., Greenbaum, R., & Conover, N. C. (1985). Reliability and concurrent relations between the teacher version of the Child Behavior Profile and the Conners Revised Teacher Rating Scale. *Journal of Abnormal Child Psychology, 13,* 295–304.

Forehand, R. L., & McMahon, R. J. (1981). *Helping the*

noncompliant child: A clinicians' guide to parent training. New York: Guilford Press

Gordon, M. (1979). The assessment of impulsivity and mediating behaviors in hyperactive and non-hyperactive children. *Journal of Abnormal Child Psychology, 7*, 317–326.

Gordon, M. (1983). *The Gordon Diagnostic System*. Boulder, CO: Gordon Systems.

Gordon, M. (1985, August). *Assessment of ADD/hyperactivity: Research on the Gordon Diagnostic System*. Symposium presented at the American Psychological Association. Los Angeles, CA.

Goyette, C. H., Conners, C. K., & Ulrich, R. F. (1978). Normative data for Revised Conners Parent and Teacher Rating Scales. *Journal of Abnormal Child Psychology, 6*, 221–236.

Griest, D., Wells, K. C., & Forehand, R. (1979). An examination of predictors of maternal perceptions of maladjustment in clinic-referred children. *Journal of Abnormal Psychology, 88*, 227–281.

Haenlein, M., & Caul, W. F. (1987). Attention deficit disorder with hyperactivity: A specific hypothesis of reward dysfunction. *Journal of the American Academy of Child and Adolescent Psychiatry, 26*, 356–362.

Hartsough, C. S., & Lambert, N. M. (1985). Medical factors in hyperactive and normal children: Prenatal, developmental, and health history findings. *American Journal of Orthopsychiatry, 55*, 190–201.

Jacob, R. G., O'Leary, K. D., & Rosenblad, C. (1978). Formal and informal classroom settings: Effects on hyperactivity. *Journal of Abnormal Child Psychology, 6*, 451–458.

Johnston, C., Pelham, W. E., & Murphy, H. A. (1985). Peer relationships in ADDH and normal children: A developmental analysis of peer and teacher ratings. *Journal of Abnormal Child Psychology, 13*, 89–100.

Kagan, J. (1965). Reflection-impulsivity: The generality and dynamics of conceptual tempo. *Journal of Abnormal Psychology, 71*, 17–24.

Kendall, P. C., & Braswell, L. (1982). Cognitive-behavioral self-control therapy for children: A component analysis. *Journal of Consulting and Clinical Psychology, 50*, 672–689.

Kendall, P. C., & Wilcox, L. E. (1979). Self-control in children: Development of a rating scale. *Journal of Consulting and Clinical Psychology, 47*, 1020–1029.

Klee, S. H., & Garfinkel, B. D. (1983). The computerized continuous performance task: A new measure of attention. *Journal of the American Academy of Child Psychiatry, 11*, 487–496.

Lahey, B. B., Pelham, W. E., Schaughency, E. A., Atkins, M. S., Murphy, H., Hynd, G., Russo, M., Hartdagen, S., & Lorys-Vernon, A. (1988). Dimen-sions and types of attention deficit disorder. *Journal of the American Academy of Child and Adolecent Psychiatry, 27*, 330–335.

Lahey, B. B., Schaughency, E. A., Hynd, G. W., Carlson, C. L., & Nieves, N. (1987). Attention deficit disorder with and without hyperactivity: Comparison of behavioral characteristics of clinic-referred children. *Journal of the American Academy of Child and Adolescent Psychiatry, 26*, 718–723.

Locke, H. J., & Wallace, K. M. (1959). Short marital adjustment and prediction tests: Their reliability and validity. *Journal of Marriage and Family Living, 21*, 251–255.

Loney, J., & Milich, R. (1982). Hyperactivity, inattention, and aggression in clinical practice. In M. Wolrich & D. Routh (Eds.), *Advances in behavioral pediatrics* (Vol. 2, pp. 113–147). Greenwich, CT: JAI Press.

Luk, S. (1985). Direct observations studies of hyperactive behaviors. *Journal of the American Academy of Child Psychiatry, 24*, 338–344.

Mash, E. J., & Johnston, C. (1983). Parental perceptions of child behavior problems, parenting self-esteem, and mothers' reported stress in younger and older hyperactive and normal children. *Journal of Consulting and Clinical Psychology, 51*, 68–99.

Mash, E. J., Terdal, L. G., & Anderson, K. (1973). The response class matrix: A procedure for recording parent-child interactions. *Journal of Consulting and Clinical Psychology, 40*, 163–164.

Milich, R. (1984). Cross-sectional and longitudinal observations of activity level and sustained attention in a normative sample. *Journal of Abnormal Child Psychology, 12*, 261–276.

Milich, R., & Kramer, J. (1985). Reflections on impulsivity: An empirical investigation of impulsivity as a construct. In K. Gadow & I. Bialer (Eds.), *Advances in learning and behavioral disabilities* (Vol. 3, pp. 117–150). Greenwich, CT: JAI Press.

Milich, R. S., & Landau, S. (1982). Socialization and peer relations in hyperactive children. In K. D. Gadow & I. Bialer (Eds.), *Advances in learning and behavior disabilities* (Vol. 1). Greenwich, CT. JAI Press.

Milich, R., Landau, S., & Loney, J. (1981, August). *The interrelationships among hyperactivity, aggression, and impulsivity*. Paper presented at the meeting of the American Psychological Association, Los Angeles.

Milich, R., Loney, J., & Landau, S. (1982). The independent dimensions of hyperactivity and aggression: A validation with playroom observation data. *Journal of Abnormal Psychology, 91*, 183–198.

Patterson, G. R. (1982). *Coercive family process*. Eugene, OR: Castalia.

Pollard, S., Ward, F. M., & Barkley, R. A. (1983). The

effects of parent training and Ritalin on the parent-child interactions of hyperactive boys. *Child and Family Behavior Therapy, 5,* 51–69.

Porrino, L. J., Rapoport, J. L., Behar, D., Sceery, W., Ismona, D. R., & Bunney, W. E. (1983). A naturalistic assessment of the motor activity of hyperactive boys. *Archives of General Psychiatry, 40,* 681–687.

Rapport, M. D., Tucker, S. B., DuPaul, G. J., Merlo, M., & Stoner, G. (1986). Hyperactivity and frustration: The influence of control over and size of rewards in delaying gratification. *Journal of Abnormal Child Psychology, 14,* 191–204.

Roberts, M. (1979). *A manual for the Restricted Academic Playroom Situation.* Iowa City, IA: Author.

Robin, A. L., & Foster, S. L. (1989). *Negotiating parent adolescent conflict: A behavioral-family systems approach.* New York: Guilford Press.

Robins, L. N. (1966). *Deviant children grown up,* Baltimore, MD: Williams & Wilkins.

Ross, D. M., & Ross, S. A. (1982). *Hyperactivity: Current issues, research, and theory* (2nd ed.). New York: John Wiley.

Routh, D. K. (1978). Hyperactivity. In P. Magrab (Ed.), *Psychological management of pediatric problems* (pp. 3–48). Baltimore, MD: University Park Press.

Safer, R., & Allen, D. (1976). *Hyperactive children.* Baltimore, MD: University Park Press.

Satterfield, J. H., Satterfield, B. T., & Cantwell, D. P. (1981). Three year multimodality treatment study of 100 hyperactive boys. *Journal of Pediatrics, 98,* 650–655.

Sleator, F. K., & Ullmann, R. A. (1981). Can the physician diagnose hyperactivity in the office? *Pediatrics, 67,* 13–17.

Stewart, M. A., Thach, B. T., & Freidin, M. R. (1970). Accidental poisoning and the hyperactive child syndrome. *Diseases of the Nervous System, 31,* 403–407.

Swanson, L. M. (1985). Measures of cognitive functioning appropriate for use in pediatric psychopharmacological research studies. *Psychopharmacology Bulletin, 21,* 887–890.

Tarver-Behring, S., Barkley, R. A., & Karlsson, J. (1985). The mother-child interactions of hyperactive boys and their normal siblings. *American Journal of Orthopsychiatry, 55,* 202–209.

Ullmann, R. K., Sleator, F. K., & Sprague, R. I. (1984). A new rating scale for diagnosis and monitoring of ADD children. *Psychopharmacology Bulletin, 20,* 160–164.

Whalen, C. K., Henker, B., & Dotemoto, S. (1980). Methylphenidate and hyperactivity: Effects on teacher behaviors. *Science, 208,* 1280–1282.

Weiss, G., & Hechtman, I. (1986). *Hyperactive children grown-up.* New York: Guilford Press.

Zentall, S. (1984). Context effects in the behavioral ratings of hyperactivity. *Journal of Abnormal Child Psychology, 12,* 345–352.

CHAPTER 9

ACADEMIC ASSESSMENT OF ADHD CHILDREN

Liam K. Grimley

Young children who are hyperactive are usually initially identified because of their excessive gross motor activity. By the time these children reach school age, however, other problems become apparent, most notably inappropriate impulsivity and inattention. In the classroom they often have difficulty remaining still in their assigned seats, blurt out answers before they are questioned, fidget frequently with their hands and feet, and are easily distracted by extraneous stimuli. Not surprisingly, therefore, these children are often described as having academic problems in school (Keogh & Barkett, 1980). Furthermore, problems with academic achievement and problem solving are not confined to the elementary school years but often persist into adolescence. In reviewing studies of the cognitive style of hyperactive adolescents, in comparison with normals, Sattler (1988) concludes that the ADHD group are more impulsive and field-dependent, are more likely to respond without thinking, and appear to be more easily distracted by compelling cues.

In the academic assessment of hyperactive children one must immediately confront the equivocal nature of the terms that are used. Prior to 1980, the terms *hyperactivity, hyperkinesis and hyperkinetic reaction* were commonly used. The revised third edition of the *Diagnostic and Statistical Manual of*

Mental Disorders (DSM-III-R) (American Psychiatric Association [APA] 1987) proposes the term *attention deficit hyperactivity disorder* (ADHD) to replace the earlier DSM-III term *attention deficit disorder with hyperactivity* (APA, 1980). The term attention deficit hyperactivity disorder (ADHD) is used throughout this chapter except when reporting findings from studies that have used other terms. Similar terms that have been used in the past include *hyperkinetic impulse disorder, hyperkinetic behavior disorder, hyperactive child syndrome, minimal brain dysfunction, central nervous system immaturity, development hyperactivity, developmental overload, organic drivenness* and *learning disability* (Conners, Denhoff, Millichap, & O'Leary, 1978).

There is an equally perplexing array of behavioral descriptors of these children including overactive, inattentive, distractible and impulsive (Delamater, Lahey, & Drake, 1981), school truant, disruptive, defiant, uncooperative, and easily discouraged (Brumback & Weinberg, 1977), inattentive, highly active, impulsive, and aggressive (Lambert & Sandoval, 1980).

The problem is compounded when professionals use the same terms but do not define them in a univocal way. Hence there have been wide variations in statistical estimates of the prevalence of hyperactivity in children. Among school-aged children as a whole, estimates of hyperactivity range from 3% to 20% (Cantwell, 1975), but in clinical populations of children the range is from 23% to 50% depending on the criteria used to define hyperactivity (Sattler, 1988).

When social-behavioral signs of hyperactivity are accompanied by poor achievement, the probability of identification of the problem is high. Although some authors claim that academic underachievement is found in most ADHD children (Sattler, 1988), the problem of sample bias must be taken into consideration. It has been found that identification of hyperactivity is more likely when it is accompanied by academic failure (Keogh & Barkett, 1980).

SOME MYTHS REGARDING ADHD CHILDREN

Before embarking on academic assessment of an individual ADHD child, it would be well to dispel some myths regarding ADHD children in general.

Myth #1. On academic tasks, ADHD children spend more time off-task (more "distractible") than normal children.

Myth #2. Psychostimulant medication will produce improved academic performance in ADHD children.

Myth #3. Improvement in the behavioral manageability of ADHD children due to psychostimulant medication will result in improved academic performance.

Myth #4. ADHD children respond to behavioral reinforcements in the same ways as nonhyperactive children.

Myth #5. Cognitive self-control changes that occur in ADHD children as a result of treatment will become generalized and durable.

With regard to Myth #1, Douglas and Peters (1979), in an extensive review of studies of distractibility in hyperactive children, have concluded that the findings may suggest a higher level of stimulus-seeking behavior rather than an inability to ignore task-irrelevant stimuli. With regard to Myths #2 and #3, it is important for the examiner to ascertain,

before beginning the academic assessment process, if the ADHD child is receiving any medication. Later in this chapter we will discuss findings that indicate that academic performance of ADHD children does not improve as a result of medication. We will also discuss findings related to Myth #4 which indicate differences between hyperactive and nonhyperactive children in the ways in which they respond to both positive and negative reinforcement. Some recent efforts aimed specifically at generalizability and durability of treatment effects (Myth #5) have met with partial success. More program development and research is needed, however, to establish both generalization and maintenance (Meichenbaum, 1986).

REFERRAL

Referral of ADHD children for academic assessment is usually made by the child's parents, teacher, or physician. In reviewing the referral information it is important to keep two questions in mind: (a) Are there descriptive samples of behavior including frequency, duration, antecedents, and consequences? (b) Is there direct evidence of academic problems?

Before assessment begins the parents, the teacher, and often the physician must be involved in specifying the nature of the referral problem. In working with parents it is important to determine the nature of the parents' realistic or unrealistic expectations for their child, their awareness of the activity level and academic performance that is typical for the child's age, and situational factors that may contribute to the child's problems. Likewise, in working with teachers, it is important to keep in mind that different teachers set different codes for acceptable classroom behavior. What one teacher describes as disruptive impulsivity, another may describe as desirable spontaneity in a child. In working with physicians, it must be remembered that hyperactive children are not likely to exhibit their most problematic behaviors in the one-to-one setting of a physician's office. While physicians often have helpful insights into the hyperactive child's problems their diagnosis is frequently based on second-hand information gathered from parents and/or teachers.

Some very normal children are sometimes referred for hyperactive behavior because of intolerant attitudes of parents or teachers. On the other hand, some hyperactive children are never referred for assessment and treatment because of more convivial environments. It is important, therefore, for the clinician to supplement referral information with data gathered from behavioral checklists, interviews, and direct observations related both to the ADHD child and to the environments in which problems reportedly occur.

BEHAVIORAL CHECKLISTS

The major advantage of behavioral checklists is that they provide a systematic method for gathering quantifiable information about a wide range of behaviors. They can generally be administered and scored easily. Their main weaknesses are their limited predictive validity and their susceptibility to respondent misperceptions and biases. It is important to obtain data about the child from a variety of sources. There may be marked differences in the way one teacher rates a child compared with another teacher or in the way a father and mother perceive the same ADHD child's behavior.

The Conners Parent Rating Scale (Conners, 1985) is a rating scale that has been carefully researched and widely used in the assessment of hyperactive children. The longer form contains 93 items that yield eight factors (Conduct Disorder, Fearful-Anxious, Restless-Disorganized, Learning Problem-Immature, Psychosomatic, Obsessional, Antisocial, and Hyperactive-Immature). A factor analytic study of the shorter 48-item form by Goyette, Conners, and Ulrich (1978) yielded five factors (Aggression-Conduct Problems, Inattention-Learning Problems, Psychosomatic Problems, Impulsivity-Hyperactivity Problems, and Anxiety Problems). Items are scored on a 4-point scale (0–3) ranging from "not at all" to "very much." Research studies indicate that the Conners Parent Rating Scale has adequate reliability and validity. Sex-by-age normative data are available for the 48-item form. In addition, the Abbreviated Parent Questionnaire, sometimes referred to as the hyperactivity index, consists of the 10 items on the scale that are scored for hyperactivity. This 10-item scale with separate norms for boys and girls, aged 3 to 17 years, is useful for initial screening or for follow-up monitoring of treatment.

Another well-standardized parent rating scale with adequate reliability and validity is the Child Behavior Checklist developed over the past 20 years by Achenbach and his associates (Achenbach & Edelbrock, 1986a). The version for children aged 4 to 16 years contains 113 items that describe a wide variety of problems experienced by children in this age group. The respondent indicates if the item is very true or often true (score of 2), somewhat or sometimes true (score of 1), or not true (score of 0) in describing the child now or within the past 6 months. This version also provides separate norms for boys and girls aged 4 to 5, 6 to 11, and 12 to 16 years. Based on factor analysis, separate scales have been developed within each of these age groups. For example, for the 6 to 11 age group, the nine factors are Schizoid, Depressed, Uncommunicative, Obsessive-Compulsive, Somatic Complaints, Withdrawn, Hyperactive, Aggressive, and Delinquent. These factors may also be grouped into two major factors: Internalizing and Externalizing. Children who are internalizers appear to be less egocentric, are better able to cope with stress, are better able to conform to rules, are generally brighter, good readers, and exhibit better overall school adjustment (Cohen, Gotlieb, Kershner, & Wehrspann, 1985).

C. Keith Conners has also developed the Conners Teacher Rating Scale (Conners, 1985). Various forms of the scale are available, of which the most widely used and extensively researched is the 39-item version. Normative data are available for this version based on a sample of 9,853 Canadian children aged 4 to 12 years (Trites, Blouin, & Laprade, 1982). This version yields six factors (Hyperactivity, Conduct Problem, Emotional Overindulgent, Anxious Passive, Asocial, and Daydream-Attention Problem). As with the parent rating scale, items are scored on a 4-point scale (0–3) ranging from "not at all" to "very much." Research studies indicate that this scale has adequate reliability and validity (Conners, 1985; Schachar, Sandberg, & Rutter, 1986). The abbreviated Teacher Questionnaire, sometimes referred to as the hyperactivity index, consists of the same 10 items that are scored for hyperactivity. It is not only useful for initial screening and for follow-up monitoring of treatment, but it also provides a basis for comparison between parent and teacher ratings of the same symptoms in different environments.

Another well-standardized teacher's rating scale

is the Teacher's Report Form (Achenbach & Edelbrock, 1986b) which also has adequate reliability and validity. The 113-item form yields eight scales (Anxious, Socially Withdrawn, Unpopular, Self-Destructive, Obsessive-Compulsive, Inattentive, Nervous-Overactive, and Aggressive). Separate norms are provided for boys and girls aged 6 to 11 years and 12 to 16 years.

While behavioral checklists provide a systematic method for gathering data it is possible that important information may sometimes be overlooked on these scales. For that reason interviews with the parents, teacher, and child are an important next step in the assessment process.

PARENT, TEACHER, AND CHILD INTERVIEWS

Parents, teachers, and children generally have very different perceptions of the academic problems of an ADHD child. These discrepancies usually become evident during the interview process. The major goal of the academic assessment interview is to acquire relevant information that will contribute to academic program decision making. For that reason these interviews must be both focused and flexible. In academic assessment the focus must be on the specific nature of the hyperactive child's academic problems. At the same time the interviews must be sufficiently flexible to ensure that no relevant important data are overlooked.

The parent interview can be most helpful in identifying unique strengths and weaknesses of the ADHD child. In the home, the ADHD child's inattentive and impulsive behavior may result in sudden shifts from one activity to another, frequent fidgeting with hands or feet, inappropriate blurting out of remarks, and failure to follow instructions or complete chores. On the other hand, this same child may not appear to be more easily distracted than his peers in some situations such as, for example, while watching a television show. While ADHD children appear to exhibit many similar problems, it is extremely important to identify the unique characteristics of each individual ADHD child. Prior to the parent interview it is important to review not only the referral information but also

data gathered by other means such as behavior checklists. In this way clarification may be obtained about different aspects of the problem including (a) internal discrepancies, (b) external discrepancies between one rater and another, and (c) unusual or unanticipated responses.

Parents are usually the best available source of information about the ADHD child's developmental and medical history, which may be obtained either by interview or by case history questionnaire. It is important to obtain information also about family structure and dynamics including marital status, educational level and occupation of parents, number of children, ordinal position, as well as information about play and recreational activities of the family.

During the interview, parents' perceptions of their ADHD child's academic problems need to be clarified. Any previous intervention efforts should be discussed including situational factors that appeared to contribute to success or failure. The parents' expectations of the assessment and treatment process should be carefully explored. Their ability and willingness to participate in future intervention efforts should also be evaluated.

The ADHD child's teacher is a most important source of information about the child's specific academic problems. In the classroom, the ADHD child is likely to show signs of restlessness, to fail in awaiting his turn in group activities, to blurt out answers at inappropriate times, and to give the impression of not listening to instructions. Besides these behavioral manifestations, an ADHD child's academic performance is generally characterized by great unevenness (Keogh & Barkett, 1980). This unevenness in academic performance is also to be found in the subgroup of ADHD children who are also learning disabled (Lambert & Sandoval, 1980).

Prior to the interview, the teacher should complete a behavioral checklist. Based on the problems identified, the teacher should specify the extent of the problem behaviors by documenting their frequency and timing, the social context in which they occur, and other relevant situational factors. Interventions that have been attempted in the classroom, including changes in the ADHD child's physical or social environments should also be documented indicating which interventions were successful and which ones were not.

During the teacher interview it is important to determine as specifically as possible the interventions that were focused specifically on improvement of the ADHD child's academic skills. Keogh and Barkett (1980) have noted that few classroom interventions with hyperactive children have been directed specifically at improvement of academic skills. Most of the interventions focus on reducing restlessness, distractibility, and inattentiveness, or improving social behaviors with an underlying assumption that these interventions will have a beneficial effect on general school performance.

There is some evidence to suggest that classroom structure has an effect on the identification and treatment of ADHD children. Flynn and Rapoport (1976), in a study of hyperactive children in open and traditional classroom environments, reported that although levels of activity and achievement scores were found to be similar in both environments, hyperactive children were less likely to be perceived by teachers as distinctive and disruptive in the open classroom than in the traditional classroom. In a study by Baldwin (1976), elementary school-aged hyperactive boys did not differ from a nonhyperactive control group in either length of attention span or in the number of stimuli to which they attended. The difference was in the focus of attention, with hyperactive boys more likely to focus on nonacademic stimuli. Douglas (1972) and her associates have suggested that these children, rather than being engaged in daydreaming or aimless activity, focus their attention on activities other than those prescribed by the teacher. Their work also indicates that these children are capable of performing as well as their nonhyperactive peers when they are helped to focus their attention prior to the presentation of the task and are allowed to work at their own rate. Ross and Ross (1982) provide well-documented clinical and research evidence that indicates that the hyperactive child possesses the requisite skills for academic performance but does not make consistent use of these skills.

Because of unevenness in academic performance the ADHD child may fail to master basic academic skills needed for learning in subsequent school years. There is indeed evidence to document the persistence of the academic problems of these children (Douglas, 1974). There is often a marked discrepancy between their measured intellectual potential and level of academic achievement, a discrepancy that generally widens as the child progresses through school with an increasing backlog of unmastered academic skills (Ross & Ross, 1982).

One of the most effective ways to identify the unique characteristics of each ADHD child is by means of the child interview. Kirby and Grimley (1986) have outlined a four-part child interview procedure that focuses on (a) the child's perception of the problem, (b) the child's attributional style, (c) the child's awareness of attentional variables, and, if appropriate, (d) the child's view of medication.

The first part of the interview consists of general interview questions about home and school. Once good rapport has been established with the child, It is possible to probe specific problem areas previously identified either by the parent or teacher. It should be noted that the ADHD child's perceptions will often be quite different from those of the adult. Knowledge about the child's level of awareness and insights into his problems will likely be particularly helpful later in designing effective intervention strategies.

The second part of the child interview deals with the child's attributional style. It consists of the locus of control scale for children developed by Nowicki and Strickland (1973) as well as some interview questions concerning the child's attributions of success or failure in academic and social situations. The rationale for including attributional style in the ADHD child's interview is because these children have been found to respond in atypical, and often unpredictable, ways to reinforcement contingencies (Douglas, 1984; Kinsbourne, 1984).

The third part of the interview deals with the child's awarenes of attentional variables. This part of the interview begins with open-ended questions derived from the work of Miller and Bigi (1979) to assess the child's general understanding of the concept of paying attention. These questions are followed by more specific multiple-choice interview questions to assess the child's awareness of the influence of situational variables, such as noise level or distracting stimuli, on attentional behavior.

The fourth part is intended only for ADHD children who are currently or have been on medication. The questions are based on work by Whalen and Henker (1980) to explore the child's perceptions and knowledge about the effects of medication.

The three interviews, with parents, teacher, and child, are a most important element in the assessment of the ADHD child's academic problems. Observation of the speech, tone of voice, and nonverbal behaviors of the interviewee, as well as any evidence of positive or negative feelings, may provide important diagnostic information related to the child's social, emotional, and cognitive functioning.

Observation

Direct observation of the ADHD child in a variety of settings should always be a part of the academic assessment process. These observations should focus not only on the individual child but also on the environmental settings in which academic problems occur. Porges and Smith (1980) have noted that hyperactivity is in part "a dysfunction of adaptation to adult-defined constraints and expectations" (p. 81). Understanding the academic problems of the ADHD child requires observation not only of the individual child's characteristics but also of the interactions between the child and his environment. These interactional observations will later be a crucial component in designing effective individualized intervention strategies.

Some observational studies have indicated that the behaviors of the ADHD child have a general detrimental effect on teacher-student interactions in the classroom which, in turn, adversely impacts the ADHD child's subsequent behavior. Campbell, Endman, and Bernfeld (1977), for example, noted in the course of an observational study that the behaviors of a hyperactive child had a negative impact on the classroom environment, which resulted in more controlling and demanding behavior by the teacher. As the teacher imposes more controlling restraints, the ADHD child is likely to become more active, inattentive, and impulsive.

The ADHD child has been found to function better on tasks that are self-paced rather than ones that are teacher paced (Douglas, 1972). Jacob, O'Leary, and Rosenblad (1978) conducted classroom observations of hyperactive children in both formal and informal classroom settings. While hyperactive children behaved similarly in both types of settings, it was more

difficult for them than for nonhyperactive children to change from an informal to a formal situation. Whalen, Henker, Collins, McAuliffe, and Vaux, (1979) found that hyperactive children have difficulty grasping the ground rules of a new activity. They are likely to function better on familiar straightforward tasks than on new challenging tasks.

Some studies have found that measurements of direct observation appeared to be unrelated to the ratings of parents and/or teachers (e.g., Klein & Gittelman-Klein, 1975). Cross-validation is needed before inferences may be made based on observations or ratings alone. It has also been found that instruments that successfully distinguished hyperactive from nonhyperactive subjects in some studies, failed to do so in other studies (Sandoval, 1977). Inconsistencies in research findings related to overactive behavior of ADHD children as well as a better understanding of underlying factors have resulted in a shift of focus in recent years from study of mere motor activity to studies of the related problems of inattention and impulsivity (Kirby & Grimley, 1986).

Attentional problems in the classroom are generally manifested by the ADHD child's having difficulty organizing work, staying on task, and completing assigned work. Bremer and Stern (1976) conducted a study in which hyperactive and nonhyperactive boys read stories under distracting and nondistracting conditions. They found that the hyperactive group attended more often than the control group to the distracting stimuli, such as the ringing of a telephone. The work of Virginia Douglas and her associates at McGill University suggests that findings such as these must be interpreted very carefully (Douglas, 1984). Their work indicates that the attention which hyperactive children pay to extraneous events may suggest stimulus-seeking behavior rather than an inability to ignore task-irrelevant stimuli.

Although Douglas and her colleagues used the term *attention deficit disorder* long before it was adopted by the American Psychiatric Association in DSM-III (1980), Douglas now cautions that this label could result in an unnecessarily constricted conceptualization of the problems of these children (Douglas, 1984). Observations of the ADHD child that merely record "time off-task" are inadequate without information about other related variables, such as the nature of the task, the nature of positive or negative reinforcement, and other relevant situational conditions and demands.

As more diagnostic information about the ADHD child is obtained, observational methods may be changed, supplemented, or combined in a different manner. Too often in the past, behavioral observations have been made in a brief and routine manner merely to identify an appropriate test battery for the child or to design an immediate intervention program (Gerken, 1985). In the case of the ADHD child such brief and routine observations are not only inadequate but may frequently be misleading. What is needed is a comprehensive observational plan that encompasses observations of the ADHD child performing a broad array of tasks under a variety of environmental conditions.

SOME GENERAL CONSIDERATIONS ABOUT TESTING ADHD CHILDREN

The purpose of academic assessment of the ADHD child is to generate hypotheses that will guide intervention rather than to attach a once-and-for-all-time label. Furthermore, this assessment needs to be perceived as being part of an ongoing assessment-intervention-assessment process, rather than merely as a preintervention procedure. We will discuss some of the issues that make the academic assessment of ADHD children particularly difficult.

The research literature pertaining to academic assessment of ADHD children is complex because of confounding and often contradictory findings. One explanation for this confusion, as already noted, is the lack of a common definition of the problems investigated in research studies. It has also been customary to interpret anomalies in terms of human-related factors, such as variables related to the examiner and/or examinee, when apparently similar tests, which purported to measure the same skills, produced significantly different results. Seldom has sufficient attention been paid to the significant differences in test scores that occur solely due to the psychometric characteristics of the instruments that are used. This aspect of the academic assessment of the ADHD child needs further elaboration.

Bracken (1988) has noted 10 psychometric reasons that similar tests produce dissimilar results. These reasons are (a) floor effects, (b) ceiling effects, (c) item gradients, (d) differences in norm table layout, (e) use of grade or age equivalents for comparisons, (f) reliability differences, (g) skill differences assessed across tests, (h) content differences across tests, (i) differences in publication dates, and (j) representativeness of the norming sample.

Floor effects refer to the significant differences that may occur between the scores on two similar tests if one or both of the instruments have limited floors. The Kaufman Assessment Battery for Children (K-ABC) (Kaufman & Kaufman, 1983) for example, has several subtests at a variety of age levels that have limited floors (Bracken, 1985). Similarly tests that have limited ceilings, because of insufficient items to measure superior abilities, can also result in significant discrepancies between scores on similar instruments. Item gradient refers to how steeply the level of item difficulty is arranged within a test. Tests with steep item gradients often fail to differentiate skill levels along an ability continuum. This can result in marked discrepancies between test scores. Norm-table layout is another factor that can account for apparently incongruous results. Bracken (1988), by an analysis of the McCarthy Scales of Children's Abilities examiner's manual (McCarthy, 1972), has provided a hypothetical example in which, with the child's raw scores remaining constant over a period of 2 days, the child's IQ equivalent could drop from 112 to 101 depending on which of the 2 successive days are used to calculate the corresponding scale scores in the norm-table layout.

A fifth psychometric reason that similar tests may produce dissimilar results is due to comparisons based on age or grade equivalents. Reynolds (1981) has pointed out that age and grade equivalents do not possess the psychometric properties of standard scores. When age or grade equivalents are used in comparing results from two or more tests, discrepancies between these measures will frequently be found. Another psychometric source of disparity between test scores is due to low reliabilities of some test instruments. Tests with low reliabilities produce larger measurement error. The problem is compounded when two such tests are compared with one another, resulting in a significant discrepancy between the scores.

Tests that purport to measure the same global skill, such as arithmetic or reading, may produce different test results because of differences in the specific skills assessed by the different tests. Similarly, different tests that assess the same global skill and sample the same content domain may produce different scores because of a lack of overlap in the content samples. This is particularly problematic with abbreviated tests when insufficient samples of the content domain may be used.

Another psychometric reason for significantly different scores between seemingly similar tests is purely a function of different publication dates. Performance scores on more recently normed tests are generally lower than on older tests (Bracken, 1981) and the longer the gap between publication dates, the greater will be the score differences between tests. Last, differences in the representativeness of the norming samples of different tests can result in different scores on otherwise similar tests. Bracken (1988) notes that "even the best efforts fail to sample important selection variables to an ideal degree" (p. 165). In selecting instruments for academic assessment of ADHD children careful consideration should therefore be given to the psychometric characteristics of these instruments.

In reviewing five frequently used group-administered achievement batteries, Salvia and Ysseldyke (1981) have pointed out that far more useful information may be obtained from normative and/or criterion-referenced analysis of data from these instruments than from most of the multiple-skill or single-skill achievement tests that are individually administered. In reviewing the literature on group versus individual tests, Gerken (1985) concluded that group tests are often technically superior to individual tests, include larger samples of behavior, and can generally be linked more directly to curriculum.

Even though a group-test instrument may be technically more adequate than an individually administered test it should be noted that the ADHD child will likely perform better on an individually administered test than on a group-administered test (Minde, Weiss, & Mendelson, 1972). This finding may be because in the individual test situation examiners generally elicit the child's attention before administering a test item and cease testing whenever there is a lapse of attention. For these reasons group tests are generally considered to underestimate the abilities of the hyperactive child (Keogh & Barkett, 1980).

Even on individually administered tests, such as individual intelligence tests, the scores of ADHD children may be more variable than those of normal children. Sattler (1988) has noted that lower scores may be obtained by ADHD children in particular on the Bender-Gestalt, Bruininks-Oseretsky Test of Motor Proficiency, the Developmental Test of Visual Perception, and the Draw-A-Person. These lower scores are generally attributed to the problems that ADHD children have in organizing their work, in inhibiting impulsive responses, and in focusing and sustaining attention.

SPECIFIC TEST INSTRUMENTS USED FOR ACADEMIC ASSESSMENT OF ADHD CHILDREN

Although the diagnostic label attention deficit hyperactivity disorder may appear to imply a uniform clinical picture, individual ADHD children differ greatly with regard to educational and psychological functioning. That is why there is no standard battery of test instruments that can be prescribed for the academic assessment of all ADHD children.

The task is to select, based on each individual ADHD child's referral problems, the most technically adequate instruments that will provide relevant information from which effective interventions may be developed. The link between assessment and intervention is crucial and the assessment process should always include a plan for evaluating the effectiveness of the interventions.

Although the quest is for technically adequate testing tools, it must be acknowledged that some technically sound instruments merely yield scores with little information relevant to direct intervention. What is often needed in the assessment of ADHD children is a combination of both formal and informal assessment techniques, with due recognition of the limitations of whatever techniques are used. We will briefly review some of the tests that are commonly used for academic assessment of ADHD children.

The Wechsler Intelligence Scales for Children

The Wechsler Scales—namely, the Wechsler Intelligence Scale for Children-Revised (WISC-R) and the more recent third edition of the Wechsler Intelligence Scale for Children (WISC-III)—are among the most commonly used measures of children's intelligence. Of particular interest in the assessment of ADHD children have been the three subtests, Arithmetic, Digit Span, and Coding, which Kaufman (1979) identified on the WISC-R as *Freedom from Distractibility*. Subsequent research, however, has had somewhat inconclusive findings. Ownby and Matthews (1985) have pointed out that the term Freedom from Distractibility may be an oversimplification because of the complex task strategies involved in the act of focusing or sustaining attention. Douglas and Peters (1979) have noted that there have been a surprising number of research studies that have failed to find hyperactive children more distractible than normal controls. In those cases where a high level of distractibility has been demonstrated, Douglas (1984) has argued that this may be attributable to one of four basic predispositions of ADHD children which she has posited, namely, (a) an unusually strong inclination to seek immediate gratification and/or stimulation; (b) an unusually weak inclination to invest attention and effort in demanding tasks; (c) an impaired ability to inhibit impulsive responding; and (d) an impaired ability to modulate arousal or alertness to meet situational demands.

If a child's subtest scores on Arithmetic, Digit Span, and Coding are not consistent, the interpretation of the Freedom from Distractibility factor is particularly problematic. Sattler (1988) cautions that while factor scores may be helpful in generating hypotheses about the child's performance they should not be included in a psychological report. Douglas (1972) has noted that hyperactive children perform relatively well on the Picture Completion subtest of the WISC-R, perhaps because the child's attention is elicited before each stimulus picture is presented,

only one item must be found in each picture, and the pictures are presented one at a time.

The effects of drugs such as methylphenidate on ADHD children's Wechsler subtest scores appear to be quite variable. In a study by Rie, Rie, Stewart, and Ambuel (1976), both parents and teachers rated medicated hyperactive primary grade children as improved in their behavior. However, the only WISC subtest on which change reached statistical significance was Comprehension, which yielded lower scores when the children were on medication. Whalen and Henker (1976) have reviewed some studies in which improvements were reported in Verbal IQ or in Performance IQ when the children were on medication as well as other studies in which little or no changes were found. The evidence of the effects of medication on hyperactive children's scores on intelligence tests, such as the Wechsler Scale, remains inconclusive.

Peabody Individual Achievement Test

The Peabody Individual Achievement Test (PIAT) (Dunn & Markwardt, 1970) is a norm-referenced individually administered screening measure of Mathematics, Reading Recognition, Reading Comprehension, Spelling, and General Information. It was designed for children in kindergarten through 12th grade. The median test-retest reliability for the Total Test was .89, with a retest interval of 1 month. Subtest-retest reliabilities were lower, ranging from .88 for Reading Recognition to .64 for Reading Comprehension. Kiefer and Golden (1978) and Sattler (1988) have indicated that the PIAT's multiple-choice format of some subtests makes this instrument useful for special populations. It should be noted, however, that ADHD children sometimes have particular difficulty on tests with multiple-choice format (Douglas & Peters, 1979; Hoy, Weiss, Minde, & Cohen, 1978).

In comparison with group tests of achievement, the PIAT has lower reliability coefficients and does not provide measures of science, social studies, or study skills (Lyman, 1971). On the other hand, the ADHD child is more likely to perform well on an individually administered test than on a test that is group administered. While the PIAT is useful as a screening measure of achievement, the test scores should be carefully compared with those of a group achievement test, though these scores should not be used interchangeably. For a more accurate measure of the ADHD child's level of achievement, a more comprehensive achievement test may be individually administered at a later time.

Wide Range Achievement Test-Revised

The Wide Range Achievement Test-Revised (WRAT-R) (Jastak & Wilkinson, 1984) is an individually administered screening test of word recognition, spelling, and arithmetic. The norm sample included 5,600 subjects, 200 in each of 28 groups ranging in age from 5–0 to 11 and stratified nationally on the basis of sex, race, geographic location, and metropolitan/nonmetropolitan residence. The manual does not include any information, however, about the socioeconomic composition of the standardization sample.

The WRAT-R is mentioned in this chapter because it is one of the most commonly used measures of achievement in studies of hyperactive children. Great caution should be used in interpreting results of this test. No validity information is provided for the revised edition and the reliability information is inadequate, with no indication, for example, of the test-retest interval. The popularity of this instrument appears to be largely due to the ease and quickness with which it yields test scores.

Matching Familiar Figures Test

The Matching Familiar Figures Test (MFFT) was designed by Jerome Kagan and his colleagues (Kagan, Rosman, Day, Albert, & Phillips, 1964) to measure conceptual tempo, namely, the cognitive style impulsivity-reflectivity.

Impulsivity is one of the essential features that characterizes the ADHD child. The MFFT is a 12-item match-to-sample type test in which the child seeks to select correctly from an array of six pictures the one picture that identically matches the stimulus picture. In this test impulsivity is operationally

defined in terms of fast response latencies in combination with high error scores. By contrast, reflectivity is defined in terms of slow response latencies in combination with low error scores. In a review of studies of reliability data on the MFFT, Messer (1976) reports test-retest reliabilities from .58 to .96 for latency scores and from .34 to .80 for error scores.

The MFFT is the most frequently used measure of impulsivity in studies of hyperactive children. In several studies the MFFT has been shown to differentiate hyperactive children from control children at different age levels (Campbell, Douglas, & Morgenstern, 1971; Schleifer, Weiss, Cohen, Elman, Cvejic, & Kruger, 1975). This instrument has also been found to be sensitive to the effects of methylphenidate on hyperactive children. High impulsivity scores on the MFFT have been found to correlate with poor performance on inductive and inferential reasoning and reading tasks. Highly impulsive children also have a high proportional representation among children diagnosed as learning disabled and mentally retarded (see Messer, 1976, for a review of these studies).

There has been much debate in recent years about defining conceptual tempo in terms of both latency and error scores (Egeland, Bielke, & Kendall, 1981). There has also been criticism of the adequacy of the norms and of the reliability coefficients of this test. In the absence of any better measure of impulsivity, it is likely that the MFFT will continue to be used with ADHD children because its relationship to hyperactivity has been well established (Messer, 1976). This instrument is particularly useful with ADHD children when it is administered in an interactive manner that can provide valuable samples of the individual child's cognitive style in problem solving (Kirby & Grimley, 1986).

Continuous Performance Test

The Continuous Performance Test (CPT) (Rosvold, Mirsky, Sarason, Bransome, & Beck, 1956) was originally designed as a measure of brain damage. Because inattention is an essential feature of attention deficit hyperactivity disorder, many studies have used visual or auditory forms of this test as experimental measures of vigilance of attention (Douglas & Peters, 1979; Levy & Hobbes, 1981;

Doyle, Anderson, & Halcomb, 1976; Kirby & Grimley, 1986). Moray (1969) defined a vigilance task as "a situation where nothing much is happening, but the observer is paying attention in the hope of detecting some event whenever it does happen" (p. 6). This particular vigilance task requires the identification of some infrequent sequences of events, such as sounding a buzzer when a 0 is followed by a 1, or when an A is followed by an X.

In many studies in which hyperactive children have been compared with normal control groups, they have been found to make more errors of commission (i.e., more "false alarms") and more errors of omission (i.e., more failures in correct detection) (Doyle, Anderson, & Halcomb, 1976; Sykes, 1969; Sykes, Douglas, & Morgenstern, 1973; Sykes, Douglas, Weiss, & Minde, 1971). Two other findings from the Sykes et al. (1973) study should be noted, namely, that the performance of the hyperactive group deteriorated markedly with time on the task while the performance of the control group did not, and that treatment with methylphenidate for hyperactive subjects resulted in fewer errors of commission and omission as well as less deterioration in performance over time.

The lack of normative data for this test should be noted. Plomin and Foch (1981) reported test-retest reliability of .33 for errors of omission and .47 for errors of commission. The consistent findings in studies of hyperactive children in which this experimental measure has been used lend support to the view that ADHD children represent a constellation of interrelated symptoms involving impulsivity, inattention, and hyperactivity problems.

Porteus Maze Test

The Porteus Maze Test (Porteus, 1959) is a standardized measure of a child's planning and organization abilities. It consists of a series of paper-and-pencil maze tasks that are arranged in ascending order of difficulty. The test yields two scores: a Test Quotient (TQ) score and a Qualitative (Q) score. The TQ score is derived from the highest maze level successfully reached and the number of trials needed to complete each maze. The Q score is derived from the number of qualitative errors committed, such as lifting the pencil, cutting corners,

and touching or crossing the maze alley lines. Douglas and Peters (1979) have noted that facilitative behaviors that enhance success on this test are (a) concentrating on finding a safe route to the goal and (b) conducting careful search at critical points to discover consequences of taking alternate routes. Inhibitory behaviors include (c) avoiding entering blind alleys and (d) inhibiting qualitative errors, such as cutting corners or crossing lines.

Riddle and Roberts (1974), in a review of the Porteus Maze Test, reported reliability coefficients ranging from .43 to .97. The Porteus Maze Test has been used to differentiate hyperactive from control subjects (Spring, Yellin, & Greenberg, 1976) and to evaluate the effects of cognitive-behavioral treatment (Douglas, Parry, Marton, & Garson, 1976; Kendall & Wilcox, 1980). Palkes, Stewart, and Kahana (1968) found that both the TQ and Q scores of hyperactive boys improved after training in verbal mediation aimed at inhibiting impulsive behavior. It has also been found that stimulant drugs improve the performance of hyperactive children on the Porteus Maze Test (Conners, Taylor, Meo, Kurtz, & Fournier, 1972; Sroufe, 1975). Since ADHD children appear to have particular difficulty in planning and organizing, the clinical use of the Porteus Maze Test will likely continue as a part of the efforts to gain new understanding of the academic problems of ADHD children.

Other Tests of Specific Abilities

The preceding assessment instruments have been widely used in studies that sought to gain new insights into the learning styles and problems of ADHD children. Those who have worked closely with these children have been increasingly aware that each ADHD child is a unique individual (Kirby & Grimley, 1986). Hence other tests of specific abilities are needed in the academic assessment of ADHD children. It must be stressed that the purpose of this assessment is to generate hypotheses related to educational programming that focuses on specific academic areas.

Tests of specific abilities that are used in academic assessment are so well known that they do not need detailed comment in this chapter. In the area of reading, for example, both the Durrell Analysis of

Reading Difficulty (Durrell & Catterson, 1980) and the Gray Oral Reading Tests-Revised (Wiederholt & Bryant, 1986) provide information that is useful for task analysis and for remedial treatment. Likewise, in the area of arithmetic abilities, both the Key Math Diagnostic Arithmetic Test (Connolly, Nachtman, & Pritchett, 1971) and the more recent Sequential Assessment of Mathematics Inventories (SAMI) (Reisman, 1985) provide assessment data that can be linked directly to remedial interventions. Both the Bender Visual Motor Gestalt Test (Bender, 1938) and the Developmental Test of Visual-Motor Integration (VMI) (Beery, 1982) are useful instruments for evaluating a child's visual-motor abilities. Sattler (1988) has pointed out that the performance of ADHD children on these measures of visual-motor ability and on the Bruininks-Oseretsky Test of Motor Proficiency (Bruininks, 1978), which measures gross and fine motor skills, may be quite variable with resultant lower scores.

Because of the complexities involved in the academic assessment of ADHD children, the examiner must proceed in an investigative manner that Kaufman (1979) has likened to a detective who gathers and integrates data from multiple sources, generates hypotheses, develops interventions, and evaluates the effectiveness of these remedial strategies.

THE ONGOING ASSESSMENT–INTERVENTION– ASSESSMENT PROCESS

It must be stressed that in working with ADHD children the process of assessment–intervention–assessment must be an ongoing one. In a review of research dealing with the use of assessment information to plan instructional interventions, Ysseldyke and Mirkin (1982) cite a four-type model of measurement by Van Etten and Van Etten related to directness and continuity of assessment: Type I is indirect and noncontinuous, Type II is indirect and continuous, Type III is direct and noncontinuous, and Type IV is direct and continuous. These authors conclude that the more direct and continuous the assessment process is, the more precise the teaching-learning strategies will become.

The necessity of ongoing academic assessment of the ADHD child is due both to the nature of the interventions commonly used with ADHD children and to the disparities that exist between measures of the effectiveness of those interventions. We will briefly discuss the impact on the ADHD child's academic performance of three common treatment methods, namely, psychostimulant medication, behavior modification, and cognitive-behavioral treatment.

Wide discrepancies have been found between parent or teacher reports and objective measures of academic achievement with regard to the short-term effects of psychostimulant medication. In a review of studies of this issue, Ross and Ross (1982) have noted that whereas parents and teachers viewed improvement in academic achievement as a major outcome of their child's stimulant medication regimen, more objective measures of achievement either failed to corroborate these reported gains or showed transitory gains that dissipated in a relatively short period of time. Various methodological weaknesses have been noted in some of the studies that used objective measures of achievement, such as the short duration of drug treatment, inappropriate drug dosages, and faulty assessment techniques (Ross & Ross, 1982; Sprague & Berger, 1982).

Improvements have been noted in children under medication in performance on visual processing tasks (Gittelman-Klein & Klein, 1976) and on some attentional and test-skill variables (Barkley & Cunningham, 1978). A few studies have reported improved performance by children under medication on more complex perceptual and cognitive tasks (Campbell, Douglas, & Morgenstern, 1971; Dalby, Kinsbourne, Swanson, & Sobol, 1977; Sroufe, 1975). But the overall major effect of psychostimulant medication on ADHD children appears to be improvement in social behavioral manageability rather than in academic performance (Barkley & Cunningham, 1979). There have been many diverse interpretations of these complex findings (cf. Douglas, 1984; Kinsbourne, 1984). Further research is clearly needed to assess the short-term and long-term effects of psychostimulant medication on the academic achievement of ADHD children.

A second frequently used treatment method with ADHD children is behavior management. Many different aspects of the use of reinforcement with hyperactive children have been studied including positive versus negative, contingent versus non-contingent, continuous versus partial, and withdrawal of rewards during extinction (cf. Douglas, 1983, for a review). The findings from these studies are quite complex. Hyperactive and nonhyperactive children have been found to differ, for example, in their responses to certain reinforcers, with hyperactive children tending to respond atypically to both positive and negative reinforcement. Reinforcement can have positive or negative effects on the performance of hyperactive children depending on the reinforcement contingencies used (Freibergs & Douglas, 1969; Parry, 1973). Hyperactive children were also found to react differently to partial reinforcement where the nonreward in a reinforcement condition appeared to be particularly frustrating (Ryan & Watson, 1968). Whereas normal children were found to perform better with stimulating teaching materials, the learning of hyperactive children was more impaired than when taught with less stimulating materials (Zentall, Zentall, & Booth, 1978).

There have been numerous interpretations of the reinforcement abnormality found in hyperactive children. Wender (1971, 1973) has suggested that hyperactive children may be underresponsive to both positive and negative reinforcement. A more likely explanation has been proposed by Douglas (1984), namely, that hyperactive children appear to be unusually responsive to reinforcement. In this view reinforcement becomes a highly salient aspect of the learning situation for the hyperactive child who attends more to the reinforcement itself than to what it was intended to reinforce.

Cognitive-behavior management (CBM) is a third important treatment approach to working with ADHD children (Kirby & Grimley, 1986). Verbal self-instruction, cognitive self-monitoring, and interpersonal cognitive problem solving are among the cognitive self-control strategies used. This approach is based in part on the cognitive mediation studies by the Russian psychologists Luria (1959) and Vygotsky (1962). Studies by Palkes, Stewart, and Kahana (1968) and by Palkes, Stewart, and Freedman (1971) provide support for the use of verbal training with hyperactive children. Meichenbaum and Goodman (1971) developed a treatment program aimed at teaching children to use covert self-instruction followed by self-reinforcement. Meichenbaum's ap-

proach has been used with some success in a number of studies of hyperactive children (for reviews see Keogh & Barkett, 1980; Ross & Ross, 1982). In summarizing these findings, Keogh and Barkett conclude that from an educational point of view, "cognitive control training is probably best viewed as an important, but not sufficient, intervention for children with learning problems" (p. 277).

Just as there is not one battery of assessment instruments that is equally applicable to all ADHD children, there is not one treatment approach that is exclusively effective with these children. Although the use of medication, behavior therapy, and cognitive-behavior modification have been discussed separately, there is evidence to suggest that the efficacy of any one treatment approach may be enhanced by the combination of two or more treatment methods (Kirby & Grimley, 1986).

SUMMARY

By the time most ADHD children are referred for academic assessment and treatment they generally present a complex array of problems that may be identified as primary, secondary, or tertiary (Ross & Ross, 1982). An effective assessment-intervention-assessment process will almost always be multidimensional to assess the complex interrelationships between inattention, impulsivity, and hyperactivity problems and the individual ADHD child's academic strengths and weaknesses. Ongoing educational assessment is always needed to monitor the complex interactions between specific therapeutic approaches and direct academic interventions with the ADHD child.

REFERENCES

Achenbach, T. M., & Edelbrock, C. S. (1986a). *Child Behavior Checklist and Youth Self-Report*. Burlington, VT: Author.

Achenbach, T. M., & Edelbrock, C. S. (1986b). *Teacher's Report Form*. Burlington, VT: Author.

American Psychiatric Association. (1980). *Diagnostic and statistical manual of mental disorders, DSM-III* (3rd. ed.). Washington, DC: Author.

American Psychiatric Association. (1987). *Diagnostic and statistical manual of mental disorders, DSM-III-R* (3rd. ed. rev.). Washington, DC: Author.

Baldwin, M. A. (1976). *Activity level, attention span, and deviance: Hyperactive boys in the classroom.* Unpublished doctoral dissertation, University of Waterloo, Canada.

Barkley, R. A., & Cunningham, C. E. (1978). Do stimulant drugs improve the academic performance of hyperkinetic children? *Clinical Pediatrics, 17,* 85–92.

Barkley, R. A., & Cunningham, C. E. (1979). The effects of methylphenidate on the mother-child interactions of hyperactive children. *Archives of General Psychiatry, 36,* 201–208.

Beery, K. E. (1982). *Revised administration, scoring, and teaching manual for the Developmental Test of Visual-Motor Integration.* Cleveland, OH: Modern Curriculum Press.

Bender, L. (Ed.). (1938). A Visual Motor Gestalt Test and its clinical use. *American Orthopsychiatric Association Research Monograph, No. 3.*

Bracken, B. A. (1981). McCarthy Scales as a learning disability diagnostic aid: A closer look. *Journal of Learning Disabilities, 14,* 128–130.

Bracken, B. A. (1985). A critical review of the Kaufman Assessment Battery for Children (K-ABC). *School Psychology Review, 14,* 21–36.

Bracken, B. A. (1988). Ten psychometric reasons why similar tests produce dissimilar results. *Journal of School Psychology, 26,* 155–166.

Bremer, D. A., & Stern, J. A. (1976). Attention and distractibility during reading in hyperactive boys. *Journal of Abnormal Child Psychology, 4,* 381–387.

Bruininks, R. H. (1978). *Bruininks-Oseretsky Test of Motor Proficiency.* Circle Pines, MN: American Guidance Service.

Brumback, R. A., & Weinberg, W. A. (1977). Relationship of hyperactivity and depression in children. *Perceptual and Motor Skills, 45,* 247–251.

Campbell, S. B., Douglas, V. I., & Morgenstern, G. (1971). Cognitive styles in hyperactive children and the effect of methylphenidate. *Journal of Child Psychology and Psychiatry, 12,* 55–67.

Campbell, S. B., Endman, M. W., & Bernfeld, G. (1977). A three-year follow-up of hyperactive preschoolers into elementary school. *Journal of Child Psychology and Psychiatry, 18,* 239–249.

Cantwell, D. P. (Ed.). (1975). *The hyperactive child: Diagnosis, management, current research.* New York: Spectrum.

Cohen, N. J., Gotlieb, H., Kershner, J., & Wehrspann, W. (1985). Concurrent validity of the internalizing and externalizing profile patterns of the Achenbach Child Behavior Checklist. *Journal of Consulting and Clinical Psychology, 53,* 724–728.

Conners, C. K. (1985). *The Conners Rating Scales: Instruments for the assessment of childhood psychopathology.* Unpublished manuscript. Washington, DC: Children's Hospital National Medical Center.

Conners, C. K., Denhoff, E., Millichap, J. G., & O'Leary, S. G. (1978). Take a slow approach to hyperkinesis. *Patient Care, 15,* 22–78.

Conners, C. K., Taylor, E., Meo, G., Kurtz, M. A., & Fournier, M. (1972). Magnesium pemoline and dextroamphetamine: A controlled study in children with minimal brain dysfunction. *Psychopharmacologia, 26,* 321–336.

Connolly, A. J., Nachtman, W., & Pritchett, E. M. (1971). *The KeyMath Diagnostic Arithmetic Test.* Circle Pines, MN: American Guidance Service.

Dalby, J. T., Kinsbourne, M., Swanson, J. M., & Sobol, M. P. (1977). Hyperactive children's underuse of learning time: Corrections by stimulant treatment. *Child Development, 48* 1448–1453.

Delamater, A. M., Lahey, B. B., & Drake, L. (1981). Toward an empirical sub-classification of "learning disabilities": A psychophysiological comparison of "hyperactive" and "non-hyperactive" subgroups. *Journal of Abnormal Child Psychology, 9,* 65–77.

Douglas, V. (1972). The problem of sustained attention and impulse control in hyperactive and normal children. *Canadian Journal of Behavioural Science, 4,* 259–282.

Douglas, V. A. (1984). The psychological process implicated in ADD. In L. M. Bloomingdale (Ed.), *Attention deficit disorder: Diagnostic cognitive and therapeutic understanding.* New York: Spectrum.

Douglas, V. I. (1974). Sustained attention and impulse control: Implications for the handicapped child. In J. A. Swets & L. L. Elliott (Eds.), *Psychology and the handicapped child* (DHEW Publication No. [OE] 73-05000). Washington, DC: U.S. Government Printing Office.

Douglas, V. I. (1983). Attentional and cognitive problems. In M. Rutter (Ed.), *Developmental neuropsychology.* New York: Guilford Press.

Douglas, V. I., Parry, P., Marton, P., & Garson, C. (1976). Assessment of a cognitive training program for hyperactive children. *Journal of Abnormal Child Psychology, 4,* 389–410.

Douglas, V. I., & Peters, K. G. (1979). Toward a clearer definition of the attentional deficit of hyperactive children. In G. A. Hale & M. Lewis (Eds.), *Attention and the development of cognitive skills.* New York: Plenum Publishing.

Doyle, R. B., Anderson, R. P., & Halcomb, C. G. (1976). Attention deficits and the effects of visual distraction. *Journal of Learning Disabilities, 9,* 48–54.

Dunn, L. M., & Markwardt, F. C., Jr. (1970). *Peabody*

Individual Achievement Test. Circle Pines, MN: American Guidance Service.

Durrell, D. D., & Catterson, J. H. (1980). *Durrell Analysis of Reading Difficulty* (3rd ed.). New York: The Psychological Corporation.

Egeland, B., Bielke, P., & Kendall, P. C. (1981). Achievement and adjustment correlates of the Matching Familiar Figures Test. *Journal of School Psychology, 18*, 361–372.

Flynn, N. M., & Rapoport, J. L. (1976). Hyperactivity in open and traditional classroom environments. *Journal of Special Education, 10*, 285–290.

Friebergs, V., & Douglas, V. I. (1969). Concept learning in hyperactive and normal children. *Journal of Abnormal Psychology, 74*, 388–395.

Gerken, K. (1985). Best practices in academic assessment. In A. Thomas & J. Grimes (Eds.), *Best practices in school psychology*. Kent, OH: National Association of School Psychologists.

Gittelman-Klein, R., & Klein, D. F. (1976). Methylphenidate effects in learning disabilities: Psychometric changes. *Archives of General Psychiatry, 33*, 655–664.

Goyette, C. H., Conners, C. K., & Ulrich, R. F. (1978). Normative data on revised Conners Parent and Teacher Rating Scales. *Journal of Abnormal Child Psychology, 6*, 221–236.

Hoy, E., Weiss, G., Minde, K., & Cohen, N. (1978). The hyperactive child at adolescence: Emotional, social, and cognitive functioning. *Journal of Abnormal Child Psychology, 6*, 311–324.

Jacob, R. G., O'Leary, K. D., & Rosenblad, C. (1978). Formal and informal classroom settings: Effects on hyperactivity. *Journal of Abnormal Child Psychology, 6*, 47–59.

Jastak, S., & Wilkinson, G. S. (1984). *Wide Range Achievement Test-Revised*. Wilmington, DE: Jastak Associates.

Kagan, J., Rosman, B. L., Day, D., Albert, J., & Phillips, W. (1964). Information processing in the child: Significance of analytic and reflective attitudes. *Psychological Monographs, 78*(1) (Whole No. 578).

Kaufman, A. S. (1979). *Intelligent testing with the WISC-R*. New York: John Wiley & Sons.

Kaufman, A. S., & Kaufman, N. L. (1983). *K-ABC: Kaufman Assessment Battery for Children*. Circle Pines, MN: American Guidance Service.

Kendall, P. C., & Wilcox, L. E. (1980). A cognitive-behavioral treatment for impulsivity: Concrete versus conceptual training in non-self-controlled problem children. *Journal of Consulting and Clinical Psychology, 48*, 80–91.

Keogh, B. K., & Barkett, C. J. (1980). An educational analysis of hyperactive children's achievement prob-

lems. In C. K. Whalen & B. Henker (Eds.), *Hyperactive children: The social ecology of identification and treatment*. New York: Academic Press.

Kiefer, D. M., & Golden, C. J. (1978). The Peabody Individual Achievement Test with normal and special school populations. *Psychological Reports, 42*, 395–401.

Kinsbourne, M. (1984). Beyond attention deficit: Search for the disorder in ADD. In L. M. Bloomingdale (Ed.), *Attention deficit disorder: Diagnostic, cognitive and therapeutic understanding*. New York: Spectrum.

Kirby, E. A., & Grimley, L. K. (1986). *Understanding and treating attention deficit disorder*. Elmsford, NY: Pergamon Press.

Klein, D. F., & Gittelman-Klein, R. (1975). Problems in the diagnosis of minimal brain dysfunction and the hyperkinetic syndrome. *International Journal of Mental Health, 4*, 45–60.

Lambert, N. M., & Sandoval, J. (1980). The prevalence of learning disabilities in a sample of children considered hyperactive. *Journal of Abnormal Child Psychology, 8*, 33–50.

Levy, F., & Hobbes, G. (1981). The diagnosis of attention deficit disorder (hyperkinesis) in children. *Journal of American Academy of Child Psychiatry, 20*, 376–384.

Luria, A. (1959). The directive function of speech in development. *Word, 15*, 341–352.

Lyman, H. B. (1971). Review of the Peabody Individual Achievement Test. *Journal of Educational measurement, 8*, 137–138.

McCarthy, D. A. (1972). *Manual for the McCarthy Scales of Children's Abilities*. San Antonio, TX: The Psychological Corporation.

Meichenbaum, D. (1986). Foreword. In E. A. Kirby, & L. K. Grimley, *Understanding and treating attention deficit disorder* (pp. xi–iii). Elmsford, NY: Pergamon Press.

Meichenbaum, D. H., & Goodman, J. (1971). Training impulsive children to talk to themselves: A means of developing self-control. *Journal of Abnormal Psychology, 77*, 115–126.

Messer, S. B. (1976). Reflection-impulsivity: A review. *Psychological Bulletin, 83*, 1026–1052.

Miller, P., & Bigi, L. (1979). The development of children's understanding and attention. *Merrill-Palmer Quarterly, 25*, 235–250.

Minde,. K. K., Weiss, G., & Mendelson, N. (1972). A 5-year follow-up study of 91 hyperactive school children. *Journal of the American Academy of Child Psychiatry, 11*, 595–610.

Moray, N. (1969). *Attention: Selective processes in vision and hearing*. London: Hutchinson Educational, Ltd.

Nowicki, S., & Strickland, B. R. (1973). A locus of

control scale for children. *Journal of Consulting and Clinical Psychology, 40,* 148–154.

Ownby, R. L., & Matthews, C. G. (1985). On the meaning of the WISC-R third factor: Relations to selected neuropsychological measures. *Journal of Consulting and Clinical Psychology, 53,* 531–534.

Palkes, H., Stewart, M., & Freedman, J. (1971). Improvement in maze performance of hyperactive boys as a function of verbal-training procedures. *Journal of Special Education, 5,* 337–342.

Palkes, H. S., Stewart, M. A., & Kahana, B. (1968). Porteus Maze performance of hyperactive boys after training in self-directed verbal commands. *Child Development, 39,* 817–826.

Parry, P. (1973). *The effect of reward on the performance of hyperactive children.* Unpublished doctoral dissertation, McGill University, Montreal.

Plomin, R., & Foch, T. T. (1981). Hyperactivity and pediatrician diagnoses, parental ratings, specific cognitive abilities, and laboratory measures. *Journal of Abnormal Child Psychology, 9,* 55–64.

Porges, S. W., & Smith, K. M. (1980). Defining hyperactivity: Psychophysiological and behavioral strategies. In C. K. Whalen & B. Henker (Eds.), *Hyperactive children: The social ecology of identification and treatment.* New York: Academic Press.

Porteus, S. D. (1959). *The Maze Test and clinical psychology.* Palo Alto, CA: Pacific Books.

Reisman, F. K. (1985). *Sequential Assessment of Mathematics Inventories.* San Antonio, TX: The Psychological Corporation.

Reynolds, C. R (1981). The fallacy of "two years below grade level for age" as a diagnostic criterion for reading disorders. *Journal of School Psychology, 19,* 350–358.

Riddle, M., & Roberts, A. H. (1974). *The Porteus Mazes: A critical evaluation.* Unpublished manuscript. Minneapolis: University of Minnesota, Department of Psychiatry. (Report Number PR-74-3)

Rie, H. E., Rie, E. D., Stewart, S., & Ambuel, J. P. (1976). Effects of methylphenidate on underachieving children. *Journal of Consulting and Clinical Psychology, 44,* 250–260.

Ross, D. M., & Ross, S. A. (1982). *Hyperactivity: Current issues, research, and theory.* New York: John Wiley & Sons.

Rosvold, H. E., Mirsky, A. F., Sarason, I., Bransome, E. D., & Beck, L. H. (1956). A continuous performance test of brain damage. *Journal of Consulting Psychology, 20,* 343–350.

Ryan, T. J., & Watson, D. (1968). Frustrated nonreward theory applied to children's behavior. *Psychological Bulletin, 2,* 111–125.

Salvia, J., & Ysseldyke, J. E. (1981). *Assessment in special and remedial education* (2nd ed.). Boston, MA: Houghton Mifflin.

Sandoval, J. (1977). The measurement of the hyperactive syndrome in children. *Review of Educational Research, 47,* 293–318.

Sattler, J. M. (1988). *Assessment of children* (3rd ed.). San Diego: Author.

Schachar, R., Sandberg, S., & Rutter, M. (1986). Agreement between teachers' ratings and observations of hyperactivity, inattentiveness, and defiance. *Journal of Abnormal Child Psychology, 14,* 331–345.

Schleifer, M., Weiss, G., Cohen, N., Elman, M., Cvejic, H., & Kruger, E. (1975). Hyperactivity in preschoolers and the effect of methylphenidate. *American Journal of Orthopsychiatry, 45,* 38–50.

Sprague, R. L., & Berger, B. D. (1982). Drug effects on learning performance: Relevance of animal research to pediatric psychopharmacology. In R. M. Knights & D. J. Bakker (Eds.), *Rehabilitation treatment and management of learning disorders.* Baltimore, MD: University Park Press.

Spring, C., Yellin, A. M., & Greenberg, L. (1976). Effects of imipramine and methylphenidate on perceptual-motor performance of hyperactive children. *Perceptual and Motor Skills, 43,* 459–470.

Sroufe, L. A. (1975). Drug treatment of children with behavior problems. In F. D. Horowitz (Ed.), *Review of Child Development Research* (Vol. 4). Chicago, IL: University of Chicago Press.

Sykes, D. H. (1969). *Sustained attention in hyperactive children.* Unpublished doctoral dissertation, McGill University, Montreal.

Sykes, D. H., Douglas, V. I., & Morgenstern, G. (1973). Sustained attention in hyperactive children. *Journal of Child Psychology and Psychiatry, 14,* 213–220.

Sykes, D. H., Douglas, V. I., Weiss, G., & Minde, K. K. (1971). Attention in hyperactive children and the effect of methylphenidate (Ritalin). *Journal of Child Psychology and Psychiatry, 12,* 129–139.

Trites, R. L., Blouin, A. G. A., & Laprade, K. (1982). Factor analysis of the Conners Teacher Rating Scale based on a large normative sample. *Journal of Consulting and Clinical Psychology, 50,* 615–623.

Vygotsky, L. (1962). *Thought and language.* New York: John Wiley & Sons.

Wechsler, D. W. (1974). *Wechsler Intelligence Scale for Children-Revised.* New York: Psychological Corporation.

Wechsler, D. W. (1991). *Wechsler Intelligence Scale for Children-Third Edition.* New York: Psychological Corporation.

Wender, P. H. (1971) *Minimal brain dysfunction in children*. New York: John Wiley & Sons.

Wender, P. H. (1973). Some speculations concerning a possible biochemical basis of minimal brain dysfunction. *Annals of the New York Academy of Sciences, 205,* 18–28.

Whalen, C. K., & Henker, B. (1976). Psychostimulants and children: A review and analysis. *Psychological Bulletin, 83,* 1113–1130.

Whalen, C. K., & Henker, B. (Eds.). (1980). *Hyperactive children: The social ecology of identification and treatment.* New York: Academic Press.

Whalen, C. K., Henker, B., Collins, B. E., McAulliffe, S., & Vaux, A. (1979). Peer interaction in structured communication task: Comparisons of normal and hyperactive boys and of methylphenidate (Ritalin) and placebo effects. *Child Development, 50,* 388–401.

Wiederholt, J. L., & Bryant, B. R. (1986). *Gray Oral Reading Tests Revised.* Austin, TX: Pro-Ed.

Ysseldyke, J. E., & Mirkin, P. K. (1982). The use of assessment information to plan instructional interventions: A review of the research. In C. R. Reynolds & T. B. Gutkin (Eds.), *The handbook of school psychology.* New York: John Wiley & Sons.

Zentall, S., Zentall, T. R., & Booth, M. E. (1978). *Within-task stimulation: Effects on activity and spelling performance in hyperactive and normal children. Journal of Educational Research, 71,* 223–230.

CHAPTER 10

A SCHOOL-BASED MEDICATION EVALUATION PROGRAM

Kenneth D. Gadow

Routine clinical procedures for assessing response to stimulant medication in hyperactive children have remained essentially the same for the past 30 years (i.e., anecdotal reports from careproviders). The most significant innovation has been the development of reliable and valid behavior rating scales for use by classroom teachers, one of the most famous and clinically useful being the Abbreviated Teacher Rating Scale (ATRS) developed by Keith Conners (1973). (There are several versions of teacher rating scales developed by Conners, but the ATRS is the one most commonly employed for assessing drug response.) Although behavior rating scales can be very useful when making dosage adjustment decisions (Sleator & von Neumann, 1974), survey studies of treatment practices show that they have not been widely adopted (Gadow, 1983).

Research on drug assessment procedures has progressed much more slowly than our efforts to describe and understand drug response. There are at least three reasons for this. One, the rationale for drug therapy remains as ambiguous, unattended, and controversial today as it was 30 years ago. There is no generally agreed upon set of target behaviors (symptoms), no clearly articulated reasons for treating them, and relatively little research on their psychosocial implications. Beyond being able to say

they are annoying to others or possibly detrimental to the child's development, we are unable to set them in any theory of treatment. Few target behavior-outcome relationships have been compellingly demonstrated or their relationship to effective pharmacotherapy. Second, the therapeutic index (toxic dose divided by the effective dose) for stimulants is relatively large (i.e., there is a wide margin of safety), and subsequently the fear of injury has not been an important impetus for research on treatment practices for this class of drugs as it has for others. In other words, if the optimal dose is off by 5 or 10 or even 15 milligrams, there is a general belief that not much harm will result from such an error. Third, research on clinical management issues is relatively low in the science hierarchy because it is atheoretical, completely unrelated to etiology, and secondary to the discovery of documentation of drug efficacy (even though certain treatment practices can enhance clinical response). The two exceptions to this rule are drugs that have a therapeutic window or can induce serious toxicity at or near clinical levels.

In the early 1970s, the use of methylphenidate for the treatment of hyperactive children received considerable media attention, much of it negative (Hentoff, 1970; Divoky, 1973). Two of the issues that were raised repeatedly in the popular press were overdiagnosis and consequently the overprescribing of methylphenidate and less than adequate supervision (monitoring) of the treatment regimen. Allegations that pharmacotherapy was being misused prompted a number of investigations into the prevalence and management of drug therapy (reviewed by Gadow, 1981). One treatment prevalence study found that 1% of the elementary school population in Baltimore County, Maryland, was receiving medication for hyperactivity in 1971 (Krager & Safer, 1974). The rate appeared to level off at approximately 2% by the late 1970s, only to show a dramatic increase to the 6% level by 1987 (Safer & Krager, 1988). One possible explanation for this increase was the formulation of the diagnostic construct, attention deficit disorder, by the American Psychiatric Association (1980), which broadened the symptom complex to include inattentive children who were not necessarily significant behavior management problems. As the net enlarged, referral patterns changed, more diagnoses were made, and subsequently more children were treated with medication.

Not surprisingly, treatment prevalence studies have shown that the prevalence of psychotropic drug therapy for behavior disorders is much higher for students in special education programs than for youngsters in regular classrooms (Gadow, 1986a). Safer and Krager (1988), for example, found that in the 1980s, 19% to 26% of learning disabled students in special education classes were receiving medication for hyperactivity.

Investigations into the management of drug therapy confirmed, in large part, what many care providers had experienced first hand (Bosco & Robin, 1976; Gadow, 1975, 1976, 1978; Loney & Ordoña, 1975; Robin & Bosco, 1973; Sandoval, Lambert, & Yandell, 1976; Solomons, 1973; Weithorn & Ross, 1975). Diagnostic practices were idiosyncratic and rarely based on operational definitions of symptoms or normative data. Dosage adjustment was at best, haphazard. Direct contact between the treating physician and the classroom teacher was uncommon. Structured instruments for evaluating drug response (e.g., behavior rating scales) at home or in school were rarely used (Gadow, 1982, 1983; Loney & Ordoña, 1975). The standard method for obtaining such information was through anecdotal reports from the parents. Many parents adjusted dosage on their own, sometimes with the doctor's approval (Gadow, 1983; Solomons, 1973). Teachers frequently questioned the appropriateness of the dose of medication (Gadow, 1983), and noted that important treatment decisions were often made unilaterally by the patient's parents. Unfortunately, the findings from more recent treatment management studies show that many of the problems identified previously are still with us (Bennett & Sherman, 1983; Brulle, Barton, & Foskett, 1983; Copeland, Wolraich, Lindgren, Milich, & Woolson, 1987; Jensen, Xenakis, Shervette, Bain, & Davis, 1989; Sindelar & Meisel, 1982). Research on ways to improve the clinical management of children receiving medication for behavior disorders that involve school personnel are limited. Examples of such efforts are the development of school-based medication counseling (Slimmer & Brown, 1985) and evaluation (Neisworth, Kurtz, Ross, & Madle, 1976; Newton, 1982) procedures.

In an attempt to circumvent some of the logistical problems associated with obtaining treatment response data from the school, there has and continues to be an intense interest in developing laboratory- or hospital-based diagnostic and treatment response assessment procedures. Almost without exception, laboratory analogue devices focus on some aspect of cognitive function of learning and rarely on conduct problems. This in turn has led to the formulation of theories of treatment in which cognitive impairment (e.g., short attention span and by inference academic underachievement) is the primary target symptom. In other words, if the etiology of the child's life adjustment and performance problems is an attentional deficit, some have concluded that dosage should be titrated against a laboratory task that measures this ability. To date, the track record for laboratory analogue devices has not been particularly encouraging. They often correlate poorly with important classroom behaviors or are basically insensitive to drug effects, at least at doses that are generally clinically acceptable. Nevertheless, this remains an exciting area of research. Two highly interesting applications of laboratory analogue devices for clinical management are the detection of behavioral toxicity (Sprague & Werry, 1971) and, in the case of stimulant medication, the determination of the minimal effective dose, that is, the dose at which additional increments produce only marginal improvement in symptoms (Sprague & Sleator, 1975).

Ironically, efforts in the development of drug response measures for use in public schools that are as methodologically elegant (i.e., precise, molecular, unbiased) as laboratory analogue devices have been limited. Some notable examples are the amount of schoolwork completed (Bradley & Bowen, 1940), the amount of accurate schoolwork completed (Allyon, Layman, & Kandel, 1975; Pelham, Bender, Caddell, Booth, & Moorer, 1985; Sulzbacher, 1973), the amount of time off-task (Sprague, Barnes, & Werry, 1970), and motor movement defined as out of seat (Sprague et al., 1970). With regard to the types of disruptive and aggressive behaviors that typically prompt medical referral, there appear to be only two published placebo-controlled studies of these behaviors conducted in public school classrooms (Sprague et al., 1970; Wolraich, Drummond, Salomon, O'Brien, & Sivage, 1978).

As so little progress has been made in formulating drug assessment procedures for use in public school settings, a model for such a procedure was developed within the context of a drug research protocol operated within the Child Psychiatry Outpatient Service at the State University of New York at Stony Brook (Gadow, Nolan, Sverd, Sprafkin, & Paolicelli, 1990; Gadow, Paolicelli, Sverd, Sprafkin, Nolan, & Schwartz, 1991). This assessment procedure, which is called the School-Based Medication Evaluation (SBME), employs both behavior rating scales and direct observations to evaluate therapeutic and untoward effects of short-acting stimulant drugs prescribed for the management of aggressive, disruptive, or oppositional hyperactive children. The purpose of this chapter is to describe the basic components of the SBME (and, when available, supporting data) and the day-to-day realities of trying to obtain drug response data in public school settings. The chapter begins with a description of the schedule of drug administration, use of placebos and double-blind conditions, drug assessment instruments, guidelines for determining the optimal dose, and interactions with school personnel. This is followed by two case studies that illustrate how data generated from the SBME procedure can be used to make dosage adjustment decisions. The chapter concludes with a brief dis-

cussion of the advantages and disadvantages of the SBME and alternative models of clinical management.

It is important to emphasize at the onset that the SBME is presented here simply as a model for future study and not as a recommendation for clinical practice for several reasons. First, although the basic elements of the SBME are certainly not new and have received empirical support from numerous researchers, there remain many technical features (e.g., number of days of observation, single vs. multiple ratings, schedule of drug administration, appropriateness of cutoff scores) for which face validity is the sole criterion for their adoption. Second, the SBME must be adapted for use with special treatment populations (e.g., moderate to severely mentally retarded, preschool-age, and autistic individuals) or with different types of drugs (e.g., tricyclic antidepressants, fenfluramine). Third, the theory of (rationale for) treatment that is implicit in the SBME procedure is restricted to a limited set of target behaviors.

COMPONENTS OF THE SBME

The SBME assesses the effects stimulant medication under placebo-controlled double-blind conditions in public school settings. It is designed for the evaluation of elementary school-aged hyperactive children, especially those whose primary target symptoms are aggressive, disruptive, or oppositional behavior. The dosage adjustment phase, which requires 6 weeks, is the primary focus of this discussion.

Initial School Contact

After the child psychiatrist has rendered a diagnosis of attention deficit hyperactivity disorder (ADHD), counseled the family about medication, and obtained written consent to participate in the SBME, a member of the SBME team contacts a school staff member (usually the classroom teacher) to explain the purposes of the evaluation and obtain conditional approval to observe in the classroom. Next, the principal is contacted to see if the SBME violates any districtwide regulations. Occasionally, approval from the school board and even the local teacher's union is required before the evaluation can proceed.

Once a tentative agreement to participate is reached, the SBME team goes to the patient's school and meets with the teacher, principal, school nurse, and other interested parties. All aspects of the SBME are explained in detail at this time. It is important to emphasize that it is the child's behavior that is being evaluated, and not the teacher's, and to explain the reason for using placebos and double-blind conditions. If one is completely candid about the placebos, how they are made, and why they are part of the evaluation, their importance is rarely questioned. Permission is obtained to observe classroom peers, anonymously, to determine in what way the target child differs from them. At this time, the observers meet the teacher in the classroom when the students are not present and identify places to sit when they are there and establish a schedule for the observations. A copy of the class schedule is very useful.

The SBME team also meets individually with the school nurse to describe the medication schedule. Many states have guidelines regarding the administration of medication in school (Gadow & Kane, 1983), and relevant forms and consent letters are obtained. Occasionally, the school nurse refuses to cooperate with the SBME because the procedure allegedly violates school guidelines for the administration of medication in school. Ironically, these same nurses appear to have few reservations about withholding treatment by refusing to administer medication. There are several ways to overcome this obstacle, two of which are noted here. Say, for example, the nurse refuses to administer placebos under double-blind conditions (even when an appropriate parent consent letter and doctor's instructions are provided). One possible solution is to compromise and modify the SBME procedure in such a way that its basic integrity is maintained. In this case, the clinician can give the school the identity of the specified dose in a sealed envelope to be opened only in "emergencies." Our clinic has had some success with this procedure. A second possibility is simply to switch to a mornings-only dose schedule (administered by parents). Often a dose that is administered right before the child boards the school bus will still be effective during key observation settings (i.e., classroom, lunch, recess).

For parents who have transportation problems getting to and from the clinic and who live closer to the school, the principal will typically make a room available to consult with them in school as the need arises. This may be particularly relevant for low income families.

A favorable impression during the initial school contact is the key to a successful SBME. In general, school personnel are both thrilled and shocked to see someone from the treatment facility actually "going to their school." Once the initial novelty of their presence wears off, the observers from the SBME team often come to be accepted by the school as part of the staff.

Dose and Schedule

The SBME employs two standardized doses of methylphenidate (0.3 mg/kg, 0.6 mg/kg) and placebo, each of which is administered for 2 weeks. Medication is given morning and noon (approximately 3.5 hours apart), 7 days a week. Although this schedule of drug administration requires maximal exposure to medication and at doses that may not actually be necessary for initial maintenance treatment, there are several important reasons for so doing.

First, both a low (0.3 mg/kg) and moderate (0.6 mg/kg) dose of medication are administered because it is not possible, at least at the present time, to predict optimal dose on the basis of the child's symptoms during the diagnostic evaluation. Weight distribution data for elementary school children indicate that, for most children, the low dose will be 5 or 10 mg. The moderate dose will, of course, be double this amount. A number of different treatment and case review studies have shown that the majority of hyperactive elementary school-age children can be maintained on individual doses of 5 to 15 mg of methylphenidate, which are often administered twice daily (e.g., Eichlseder, 1985; Safer & Allen, 1976). The upper limit for the 0.6 mg/kg dose is 25 mg. The primary reason for using two fixed doses (in this procedure, mg/kg) instead of all possible doses within the specified dosage range is to avoid having to extend the dosage evaluation procedure, which is costly and probably unnecessary. For example, a child whose 0.6 mg/kg dose is 20 mg would require

10 weeks of medication assessment (placebo, 5, 10, 15, and 20 mg; 2 weeks each). It is more sensible to select two doses and estimate the missing values. The social validation procedure, which is described later in the chapter, adds greatly in making these estimates.

One could, of course, shorten the duration of each dose condition from 2 weeks to 1 week and thereby accommodate twice as many doses. However, 2-week dose conditions appear to be preferable for several reasons. First, some somatic side effects (e.g., gastrointestinal upset, headache) are less common in the second than the first week of drug exposure (see Conners, 1971), which *may* have implications for evaluating the first dose in the sequence for some children. Second, placebo effects are generally believed to have a relatively short course of action, and, like somatic complaints, may confound the first dose condition if it is too brief. Third, many hyperactive children show considerable day-to-day variability in their behavior. In other words, a behavior rating scale completed on a 5-day sample of behavior may be a less accurate characterization of drug response than two sets of 5-day ratings. (The clinical significance of these three considerations is generally obscured by analyses of group data.) Lastly, the schedule of school observations is probably the biggest consideration in determining the duration of dose conditions. Whatever the time interval, one must be able to collect enough days of data and to schedule makeup days for situations beyond experimental control (e.g., patient absenteeism, substitute teacher, field trip, special testing day, special event, removal from the observation setting as a punishment).

The second reason for examining a range of therapeutic doses is cost effectiveness. A considerable amount of time and effort is required to obtain the necessary approval and cooperation to conduct a SBME. It is important, therefore, to obtain as much information as possible in a relatively short time period, otherwise the procedure is not practical. Suppose, the example, the treatment team evaluated only placebo and the 5 and 10 mg dose. They find the latter to be the most effective and initiate treatment with that dose. Later in the school year careproviders begin to question the efficacy of the drug, which is a not uncommon occurrence

(see Eichelsader, 1985). The treatment team is now placed in the position of having to evaluate the therapeutic and untoward effects of a dose (15 mg) that has not yet been administered. At this point, it is simply not practical for financial and sometimes logistical reasons to conduct another SBME, although a truncated version is certainly a possibility. It would seem more prudent simply to examine the therapeutic dosage range at the onset of the SBME so that dosage increments can be made with some confidence later in the treatment process.

The third reason for maximal medication exposure during the SBME pertains to parent involvement. Medication is administered on Saturday and Sunday during dosage evaluation (even if the parents are not requesting medication for the child's behavior at home) because it is important to let the parents see with their own eyes exactly what the drug is doing to their child. Not only does this allay some of their anxieties about pharmacotherapy, but parents can be very helpful in discovering signs of behavioral toxicity.

Placebos

The SBME uses placebos to maintain double-blind conditions. The placebos are prepared by Ciba Pharmaceuticals Inc. and are identical to the active product. Ciba has generally made these placebos (5 mg tablets) available to investigators who submit research protocols that have been approved by a human subjects research review committee. There are also reports that small amounts are made available to private practitioners (Ottinger, Halpin, Miller, Demian, & Hannemann, 1985). Ciba has, however, suspended production of placebo tablets on various occasions, and at this writing, they are not available. To determine the exact formulation of tablets for any given child, one needs to determine the highest study dose. For example, if the 0.6 mg dose is 20 mg, the child would receive four 5-mg tablets of methylphenidate for a total of 20 mg. The 10-mg dose consists of two 5-mg tablets of methylphenidate and two 5-mg placebo tablets. The placebo dose is four 5-mg placebo tablets. In this manner, the dose is disguised. The tablets for each dose are placed in dated envelopes. A 2-week supply is prepared because that is the duration of each treatment condition. Parents and school nurses are asked to return unused envelopes to assess compliance and to make sure the observations and ratings were completed when the child was on medication. Some researchers place the matching placebo tablets in capsules for ease of administratin and to disguise the taste of the pills.

Clinicians can prepare their own placebos with a relatively modest amount of effort. The simplest way is to purchase gelatin capsules through a pharmacy or a health food store. The medication tablet is broken into several pieces and inserted into the capsule along with powdered lactose, which can also be purchased from a pharmacy. Care must be taken to cover the tablet pieces with the lactose so they cannot be seen through the capsule if the latter is either transparent or translucent. The placebo capsule contains pure lactose. The primary drawback of this procedure is that the capsule can be taken apart by either the child or careproviders and the contents deciphered. This situation may sound farfetched, but if the truth be known, this is probably not uncommon. An early study by Baker and Thorpe (1957) illustrates the problem. Nurses in the hospital (who were also nuns) took apart the capsules in his placebo-controlled study and even dumped the contents into water in an attempt to discern differences in solubility! One way to avoid the problem is to crush the medication tablets into a powder. This process is more expensive (best done by a pharmacist) and time consuming. (It takes approximately 1 to 2 hours to make enough capsules for a 6-week medication evaluation). However, most patients will gladly pay the additional cost for the formulation of medication capsules knowing that their child will receive an unbiased evaluation.

Although the value of a controlled (i.e., double-blind) medication evaluation is compelling, there really has been very little research on its necessity for establishing an accurate minimal effective dose especially when direct observation data are being collected by trained observers. The findings from several studies indicate that direct observations are relatively unaffected when the observers know the identity of the treatment condition, that is, drug versus placebo (Towns, Singh, & Beale, 1984). It would also be very useful to examine the suitability of no-treatment controls as substitutes for placebos. If necessary, estimates of placebo reactivity can be generated by comparing baseline and placebo performance in drug studies and calculating the percentage of improvement for specific types of dependent measures. For a particular dose to be considered clinically effective over baseline levels, it would have to exceed the percentage of improvement obtainable with a placebo (see, for example, Safer & Allen, 1976). When using a no-treatment control condition (often referred to as a *baseline*) in lieu of a placebo, it may be prudent to repeat this condition at some time later in the dosage evaluation to confirm the presence of a treatment effect. (This is particularly important when rating-scale data are the sole bases for evaluating drug response *and* the first no-treatment condition is really the diagnostic-intake phase of the medical evaluation.) Much research remains to be done in this area to develop more practical and cost-effective medication evaluation procedures. As an aside, behavioral interventions are rarely given such close scrutiny, even in research settings.

Measures

Two types of instruments are used to assess drug effects in the SBME: behavior rating scales and direct observation codes. Each type of instrument has advantages and disadvantages. Behavior rating scales are extremely easy to use and score. The rater requires little prior experience to generate useful treatment response data. The behavior rating scales that are commonly used to assess hyperactive children are generally reliable and correlate moderately well with certain direct observation code categories, particularly negativistic behavior (Atkins, Pelham, & Licht, 1989; Sprafkin & Gadow, 1987). The primary drawback of behavior rating scales is their inherent ambiguity. One is never really certain exactly what aspects of the child's behavior the rater is responding to. Observation codes are difficult to use because they are time-consuming and generally require extensive training for observers to achieve satisfactory reliability. However, when properly designed, they generate precise, unambiguous descriptions of child behavior.

Rating Scales

The SBME uses three different parent-teacher rating scales. The first is a slightly modified version of the Parent-Teacher Abbreviated Teacher Rating Scales (Conners, 1973). The Abbreviated Teacher Rating Scale (ATRS) is the most widely used instrument of its kind to assess stimulant drug effects in hyperactive children. It is fairly robust in that it is useful for a wide age range (preschool through adolescence) and for the assessment of hyperactivity symptoms in diverse

patient populations such as mentally retarded and autistic individuals. Numerous investigators have shown that the ATRS can differentiate between drug and placebo conditions and even between doses of medication (e.g., Sleator & von Neumann, 1974). The findings from one such study are presented in Figure 10.1, which illustrates the teacher rating scale scores for 10 aggressive hyperactive children treated with placebo and two doses of methylphenidate (Gadow et al., 1990). These *group* data show a linear dose-response relationship for teacher ratings, at least for the

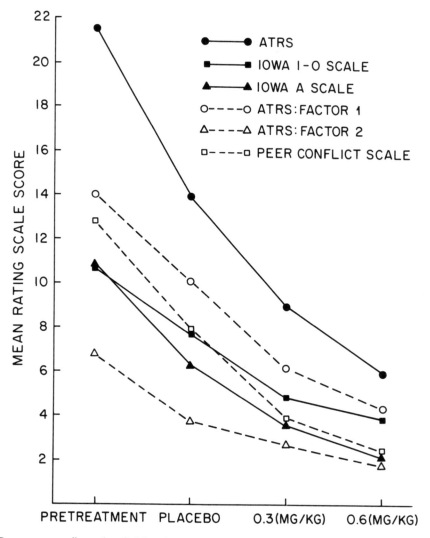

Figure 10.1.   Dose-response effects of methylphenidate on several teacher rating scales, where smaller numbers indicate better behavior. Copyright 1989 by K. D. Gadow. Reprinted by permission.

doses studied, with the greatest reduction in symptoms on the highest dose of medication.

Figure 10.1 illustrates another fairly common phenomenon associated with ATRS and other ratings, namely, a marked drop in symptom severity between pretreatment (often erroneously referred to as "baseline") and placebo ratings. (Bear in mind that the sequencing of the placebo condition in dose-response crossover studies is counterbalanced and only occasionally appears as the "first" dose in the dosage adjustment evaluation.) There are various explanations for this apparent "effect," one of which pertains to the rater's frame of reference. The first time that ATRS (or similar) ratings are typically obtained during clinical management is for the diagnostic (intake) evaluation. At this time, parents and teachers are asked to characterize the child's behavior in general or for the past several months. However, on subsequent occasions (i.e., during dosage adjustment), careproviders rate behavior for a specific, limited period of time (e.g., during a particular morning or day, during the past week). It is possible that this switch from general "traits" to specific "events" accounts for some of the decrease in symptom severity between diagnostic (intake) and placebo ratings. Our own research on this phenomenon is limited, but there is some evidence that ratings obtained during a second baseline following a dosage adjustment evaluation are less symptomatically severe than pretreatment ratings (Sverd, Gadow, & Paolicelli, 1989). It could be argued, of course, that the postdosage adjustment evaluation was "colored" by carryover treatment effects, a notion for which there is some empirical support (see Gadow, White, & Ferguson, 1986).

The ATRS has been factor analyzed on a large sample of special and regular education children and found to yield two factors (Epstein, Cullinan, & Gadow, 1986). Factor 1, which comprises the first six items, measures primarily hyperactivity symptoms. Factor 2 consists of items 7 through 10, which appear to assess emotional lability. At the present time there is very little research on the behavioral, cognitive, and affective correlates of these factors, but preliminary research does suggest a differential pattern of drug responsivity (see Figure 10.1).

The SBME uses an amended version of the ATRS (see Figure 10.2). Five items (11 through 15) were added to the rating scale to allow for the scoring of the Inattention-Overactivity (I-O) and Aggression (A) subscales of the IOWA Conners Abbreviated Teacher's Rating Scale (Loney & Milich, 1982). The I-O scale is composed of items 2, 4, 5, 6, and 11, and the A scale consists of items 10, 12, 13, 14, and 15. The wording of the overlapping ATRS items is essentially identical with the phrasing of the IOWA Conners Teacher's Rating Scale with the exception of item 1, which is simply called "Fidgeting" in the original I-O scale. This difference in phrasing occurs because the I-O scale is based on a modified verson of Conners' (1973) Teacher's Rating Scale and not the "original" verson that appeared in *Psychopharmacology Bulletin*.

Because the behavior rating scales commonly used to assess drug effects in hyperactive children contain few items that pertain to specific acts of peer aggression, the Peer Conflict Scale (Gadow, 1986b) was developed to evaluate treatment effects on peer-directed aggression. The Peer Conflict Scale contains 10 items that describe acts of physical and nonphysical aggression (see Figure 10.3), which are scored on a 4-point scale (0 = Not at all; 3 = Very much). This instrument is sensitive to stimulant dose effects (see Figure 10.1), and scores on the Peer Conflict Scale from teachers correlate moderately well with direct observations of nonphysical aggression in the classroom (Nolan, 1988).

Side effects are assessed two ways: anecdotal reports from careproviders and the Stimulant Side Effects Checklist (SSEC) (Gadow, 1986c). The SSEC, which contains 13 side-effect items, is presented in Figure 10.4. Each item is rated on a 4-point scale (0 = Not at all; 3 = Very much). For scoring purposes, items are grouped as follows: mood (items 1, 2, 3, 10), attention arousal (items 4, 5, 11, 12), physical complaints (items 6, 7, 9), and unusual motor movements (item 8).

Information about the psychometric properties of the SSEC is limited. In one study of 11 aggressive hyperactive boys treated with two doses of methylphenidate (0.3 and 0.6 mg/kg) and placebo (Gadow et al., 1990; Nolan, 1988), side-effect ratings completed by both parents and teachers were generally more favorable on days when medication rather than placebo was administered (see Table 10.1). Unlike teacher ratings of hyperactivity symptoms, the SSEC

Item	ATRS	IOWA Inattention-Overactivity Scale	IOWA Aggression Scale
1. Restless or overactive	X		
2. Excitable, impulsive	X	X	
3. Disturbs other children	X		
4. Fails to finish things he starts—short attention span	X	X	
5. Constantly fidgeting[a]	X	X	
6. Inattentive, easily distracted	X	X	
7. Demands must be met immediately—easily frustrated	X		
8. Cries often and easily	X		
9. Mood changes quickly and drastically	X		
10. Temper outbursts, explosive and unpredictable behavior	X		X
11. Hums and makes other odd noises		X	
12. Quarrelsome			X
13. Acts "smart"			X
14. Defiant			X
15. Uncooperative			X

Note: Response choices are as follows: Not at all(0), Just a little (1), Pretty much (2), and Very much (3).

[a]In the IOWA Conners Teacher's Rating Scale, this item is actually phrased "Fidgeting."

Figure 10.2. Items in the Conners (1973) Abbreviated Teacher Rating Scale (ATRS) and the IOWA Conners Teacher's Rating Scale.

Child's name: _____

Instructions:

Beside each item below, indicate the degree of the problem with a checkmark (√).
Please respond to all items. Evaluate the child's behavior on the following days:

_____

Item	Not at all	Just a little	Pretty much	Very much
1. Grabs things from other children				
2. Throws things at other children				
3. Smashes or destroys things				
4. Gives dirty looks or makes threatening gestures to other children				
5. Curses at or teases other children to provoke conflict				
6. Damages other children's property				
7. Hits, pushes, or trips other children				
8. Threatens to hurt other children				
9. Engages in physical fights with other children				
10. Annoys other children to provoke them				

Comments : _____

_____

_____

Name of person completing this form: _____

Dated: _____

Figure 10.3.   Peer conflict scale. Copyright 1986 by K.D. Gadow. Reprinted by permission.

Child's name: _____

Instructions:

      Beside each item below, indicate the degree of the problem with a checkmark (√).
      Please respond to all items. Evaluate the child's condition on the following days:

_____

Item	Not at all	Just a little	Pretty much	Very much
1. Irritable				
2. Unusually cheerful or happy				
3. Sad, weepy, cries, or unhappy				
4. Spaced out, blank stares				
5. Overly quiet				
6. Difficulty falling asleep (parent)				
7. Decreased appetite (parent)				
8. Tics, twitching, finger nail biting, unusual arm or leg movements				
9. Complains about headache, upset stomach, dizziness, and so forth				
10. Anxious				
11. Lethargic, drowsy				
12. Uninterested in others, stays by himself/herself				
13. Unusually talkative				
14. Other (please specify)				

Use the back of this form for additional comments.

List all illnesses (type and date) that occured on the specified days: _____

_____

Comments: _____

_____

Name of person completing this form: _____

Dated: _____

Figure 10.4.   Stimulant side effects checklist. Copyright 1986 by K. D. Gadow. Reprinted by permission.

Table 10.1. Means and Standard Deviations for Stimulant Side-Effects Checklist Scores for Placebo and Two Doses of Methylphenidate

	Placebo		0.3 mg/kg		0.6 mg/kg	
	M	SD	M	SD	M	SD
Teacher Ratings						
Mood index	2.4	2.75	1.9	1.43	1.7	2.15
Physical complaints index	0.3	0.49	0.2	0.19	0.3	0.48
Attention-arousal index	0.9	1.28	1.2	0.97	1.2	1.22
Unusual motor movements	0.5	0.96	0.9	1.59	0.2	0.42
Total score	3.7	3.51	3.6	2.04	2.2	2.04
Parent Ratings						
Mood index	3.1	2.92	3.1	1.64	2.8	2.98
Physical complaints index	1.4	0.96	1.5	1.14	1.5	1.29
Attention-arousal motor	1.2	1.83	1.3	1.57	1.7	3.27
Unusual motor movements	0.5	0.94	0.5	0.44	0.6	0.52
Total score	5.6	5.27	5.6	3.58	5.4	5.48

Note: From "The Effects of Methylphenidate on Aggression in ADD Boys" by E. E. Nolan, 1988, Unpublished doctoral dissertation, State University of New York, Stony Brook. Reprinted by permission.

dose effects (group data) are modest. There also appears to be some situational variability in side-effect evaluations. Parents are more apt to report side effects than teachers, possibly because children are more likely to complain to their parents about adverse drug reactions or parents are more inclined to inquire about the child's internal state. In addition to providing a standardized format for recording side effects, the SSEC is a useful instructional tool for alerting careproviders on what to look for and reassures them that some effort is being made to evaluate untoward effects.

Observation Codes

The Classroom Observation Code employed in the SBME is a modified version of the instrument used by Abikoff and Gittelman (1985a), which was designed to assess primary hyperactivity symptoms and found to be a highly sensitive indicator of stimulant drug response (Gittelman-Klein et al., 1976). Each of the following behavior categories in the Classroom Observation Code are scored once in any 15-second interval in which they occur:

Interference: making verbal statements, noises, or physical actions that are disturbing to other children

Motor movement: lifting at least one buttock off

desk seat or rocking back and forth (minor motor) or getting out of seat (gross motor)

Noncompliance: failing to follow teacher instructions or being reprimanded by the teacher

Nonphysical aggression: engaging in negative noncontact communication with (a) another child or (b) an adult

Off-task: not attending to the assigned task for 3 consecutive seconds

Physical aggression: engaging in negative physical contact with (a) another child or (b) an adult

In regular elementary school classrooms, physical aggression is an uncommon occurrence, as is nonphysical aggression directed toward adults. Although motor movement per se is rarely the primary reason for psychiatric referral, this behavior (as defined by the Classroom Observation Code) can be extremely helpful for establishing the existence of medication effects in difficult cases (e.g., mentally retarded, autistic, or preschool-aged children). A more detailed description of the Classroom Observation Code appears in Appendix 10.A.

The Classroom Observation Code has proven to be very sensitive to methylphenidate-induced changes in classroom behavior. The findings from one study (Gadow et al., 1990) of 10 aggressive-hyperactive boys are presented in Figure 10.5.

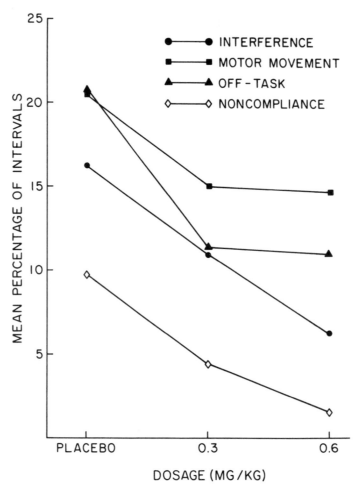

Figure 10.5.   Dose-response effects of methylphenidate on four categories of classroom behavior. Copyrightr 1989 by K. D. Gadow. Reprinted by permission.

Dose effects for all four behavioral categories were statistically significant. Post hoc analyses revealed significant differences between placebo and the 0.6 mg/kg dose for all four behaviors and between placebo and the 0.3 mg/kg dose for all behavioral categories except Noncompliance. As is clear from Figure 10.5, there appears to be a plateau effect (group data) for both the Motor Movement and Off-Task category. For these behaviors, the larger dose of methylphenidate did not produce superior group performance over the low dose. Drug response patterns for individual children are discussed later in this chapter.

The modified version of the Classroom Observation Code used in the SBME is relatively easy to learn. With trained observers, relatively high levels of interrater agreement can be achieved.

The direct observations in the lunchroom and on the playground are conducted using a modified version of the Code for Observing Social Activity (COSA) (Sprafkin, Grayson, Gadow, Nolan, & Paolicelli, 1986). The COSA was developed to evaluate aggressive and prosocial interactions between children. Each of the following behavior categories in the COSA are coded as being present or not present during 30-second intervals:

Appropriate social interaction: positive social interactions such as participating in cooperative play, conversing, or helping another child

Physical aggression: negative physical contact directed at another person using a body part (e.g., hitting, biting, kicking, tripping, pushing) or an implement (e.g., striking another child with an object)

Nonphysical aggression: noncontact negative social interaction directed at another person such as verbal aggression (e.g., threatening, teasing, name calling, tattling), symbolic aggression (e.g., chasing another child, making threatening gestures), and object aggression (e.g., damaging an object or throwing it forcefully on the floor)

Noncompliance: failure to follow directions or being reprimanded

Play aggression: physical force against another child in the context of play in which the aggressee is clearly participating and responds as though the aggressor is behaving appropriately

With regard to aggressive behaviors, aggression directed toward a child is coded separately from aggression directed toward an adult. A distinction is also made between an aggressive act that is initiated by the target child and an act that is emitted in response to (retaliatory) aggressive behavior initiated by another person. In public school lunchroom and playground settings, physical and nonphysical aggression (as defined by the COSA) directed toward adults is uncommon as is retaliatory physical aggression directed toward other children. The aggressive-hyperactive child is much more likely to be the initiator of physical aggression. For children who engage in relatively high rates of verbal aggression, it is useful to treat this subcategory of nonphysical aggression as a separate entity. A more detailed description of the COSA appears in Appendix 10.B.

In research situations, the COSA has proven to be useful in differentiating (a) the effects of viewing aggressive- and nonaggressive-content television on child behavior (Gadow & Sprafkin, 1987; Gadow, Sprafkin, & Ficarrotto, 1987; Sprafkin, Gadow, & Grayson, 1987, 1988), (b) behavior disordered and learning disabled children (Sprafkin & Gadow,

1987), and (c) the effects of methylphenidate and placebo on the behavior of aggressive-hyperactive children (Gadow et al., 1990) and their peers (Gadow et al., 1992). With a modest amount of training, reasonably high levels of interrater reliability can be achieved. The Nonphysical Aggression code category correlates in the low to moderate range ($r = .30$ to $r = .40$) with the Conduct Problem and Hyperactivity factors of the Teacher Rating Scale and the A scale from the IOWA Conners Teacher's Rating Scale (Sprafkin & Gadow, 1987).

Observation Procedure

Observations are conducted in three settings: classroom, lunchroom, and playground. The classroom has been and continues to be the traditional focus of school-based data collection efforts for several reasons. First, many people consider the primary purpose or function of elementary school education to be the acquisition of basic academic skills. Because many hyperactive children who are referred for medical assessment of their behavior problems are underachieving academically (but are not necessarily learning disabled), the classroom is typically perceived as the primary source of the child's problems. It is also commonly believed that structured, other-paced settings that require sustained attention are the most problematic for the hyperactive child. A related notion is that in unstructured free-play settings, hyperactive children are indistinguishable from their peers, at least with regard to activity level (Porrino, Rapoport, Behar, Sceery, Ismond, & Bunney, 1983).

Second, the teacher rating scales that figure prominently in the diagnosis of hyperactivity are based primarily on samples of classroom behavior (and to some extent, perhaps, the complaints of colleagues). In many schools, the teacher is not present during unstructured (playground), semi-structured (lunchroom), and different-structured (art and gym) nonacademic settings. Here, the hyperactive child may be just as annoying to peers as he is to the teacher in the classroom.

Third, hyperactivity is often perceived as being a type of learning disability. This was particularly true when the term *minimal brain dysfunction* was the popular label for both learning disabled and hyperactive children (Gadow, 1983). The notion that impaired learning ability and cognitive function are the primary features of hyperactivity and therefore are the bases for making dosage adjustment decisions is still popular (e.g., Swanson & Kinsbourne, 1978), but, from the author's perspective, somewhat mis-directed (Gadow, 1983, 1986a).

Direct observations of child behavior show that the classroom is an excellent setting in which to assess motor movement, off-task behavior, disturb-ing others, and noncompliance with teacher direc-tives and that the lunchroom and playground are more well-suited to evaluating the effects of medi-cation on social interactions with peers. The behav-ioral observations also add an extremely important dimension to the SBME, the assessment of behav-ioral toxicity. The rating scales do a fine job in determining whether the child's symptoms are less severe subsequent to the onset of treatment, but they provide essentially no information about adverse effects on adaptive behavior (e.g., appropriate social interaction). Even at relatively high clinical doses, the dose-response relationship for rating scale data remains linear, or, at the very most, plateaus (e.g., Sprague & Sleator, 1977). One can appreciate this relationship by performing a simple thought experi-ment. Examine Figure 10.1 and assume the investi-gator also studied the effects of an additional dose of medication that was at the very high end of the recognized dosage scale. Also assume that on this dose several of the children became catatonic, unable to move, speak, or work (these are *not* documented effects of methylphenidate). Now examine and com-plete the items in the ATRS (Figure 10.2). It should be readily apparent that, with the exception of item 4, these catatonic subjects would receive very low scores and the general linear trend in symptomatic improvement for the sample would continue.

Behavior observation codes also enable the doc-umentation of subtle treatment effects, which can be valuable when assessing difficult cases (e.g., hyper-active or inattentive children who are very young, mentally retarded, or autistic). Some children who appear, on the basis of clinical impression, to be nonresponders do in fact show decreases in some code behaviors that are generally considered to be symptoms of hyperactivity. Although medication is often not recommended for such children, the SBME

typically results in a much clearer specification of target symptoms.

Peers

The peer group that serves as the standard for normal behavior in the SBME consists of the three same-gender students who sit in closest proximity to the target child. The reason for selecting these children initially was to assess the potential spillover of treatment effects (Gadow et al., 1992). Other peer selection possibilities include students with average classroom behavior (Abikoff & Gittelman, 1985b), highly active or highly inattentive normals (e.g., Klein & Young, 1979), or a configuration of ideal, average, and overactive classmates (e.g., Loney, Weissenburger, Woolson, & Lichty, 1979). Given that the peers' behavior is the standard for normalcy and the basis for dosage adjustment decisions (see MED), it may be better to select students who represent the borderline normal end of the distribu-tion with regard to disruptive behavior in order to err on the conservative side in dosage selection. Peers in regular education classrooms who are receiving medication or who have disorders or disabilities that render them atypical are excluded. In special educa-tion classes, the selection of a peer comparison group is complicated by the possible distortion of the standard for normalcy (i.e., it may be inflated or deflated) because classroom peers also have learning and/or behavior disorders. Unfortunately, there does not appear to be any ready solution for this problem.

The selection of a suitable peer group in un-structured settings is also complicated by the fact that the makeup of the group of children in closest proximity to the target child changes on a day-to-day basis. In the lunchroom, however, the degree of variability in social organization is restricted to some extent because chidren are typically segregated by class (and sometimes self-segregate by gender) to sit at specific tables. The physical arrangement of the playground and the freedom to play with youngsters from other classes makes the procurement of peer data an extremely difficult, if not impossible, task. Because the behavior of the target child may (a) influence the behavior of peers and (b) change as a function of treatment status, the composition of a noncontact (with target child) peer group is also compromised when one of the peers interacts with the target child on a particular day. At the present time, the SBME uses only lunchroom peer observation data, but the composition of the peer group typically varies to some extent.

Social Validation

After observations of children were conducted in scores of regular and special education classrooms, it became apparent that there really was no good standard for normal conduct other than the behavior of classmates. Moreover, the standard for normalcy varied from one classroom to the next. Equally important was the observation that the teacher's behavior can greatly influence the magnitude of the child's symptoms, as illustrated in the following example. A learning disabled second grade boy in a fulltime special education classroom was referred to the Outpatient Clinic in late spring for evaluation of behavior problems in school. The mother did not see the son's behavior as being particularly troublesome at home or in the neighborhood. His teacher, however, rated his behavior as being clearly above cutoff on the IOWA I-O (13) and A (14) scales. She also stated that he was impulsive, noncompliant, distractable, and easily frustrated. Because the diagnostic evaluation was not completed until the end of the school year, his SBME was not scheduled until 6 weeks after the onset of the new academic year. Ratings completed by his third grade special education teacher indicated a very different symptom pattern. She scored his behavior on the I-O and A scales as 10 and 1, respectively. A SBME was conducted, and it revealed several important things about this boy and his environment. First, during a 6-week period (18 hours of observation), he committed only one act of physical aggression during the observation intervals. Second, he was well within the normal range (on the basis of peer behavior) in all code categories and all school settings studied. When the third grade teacher was questioned about the ratings from the previous year, she commented that his second grade teacher was known throughout the school as running the most disorganized classes in the building. This boy was not treated with medication. At 1-year followup (fourth grade), he was still doing satisfactorily.

Data on peer behavior in the classroom *and* during lunch and recess are an invaluable guide for making treatment decisions. *Normal* is defined as being within one standard deviation above or below the mean for the hyperactive child's peers. A behavioral symptom is said to be *normalized* by a particular dose of medication if it (a) is one standard deviation above the peer mean on placebo and (b) is brought within the normal range. In some instances, depending upon the dose of medication and the symptom profile of the child, treatment-induced improvements in behavior may exceed normal limits. When this occurs, the behavior is said to be *supranormalized*. Supranormalization pertains to both symptoms (behaviors that are abnormal) and collateral behaviors (i.e., behaviors that are within the normal range on placebo).

Minimal Effective Dose

The term *minimal effective dose* (MED) refers to the lowest dose of medication required to control the target behavior(s) (symptoms). The notion that the least amount of medication should be used in clinical management for the control of behavior disorders is embraced by most, but definitely not all, clinical psychopharmacologists and clinicians and is supported, in part, by research demonstrating dose-response relationships for most therapeutic effects and many untoward reactions. The term MED was popularized by Fielding, Murphy, Reagan, and Peterson (1980) who formulated a procedure for reducing neuroleptic drug levels in mentally retarded people in residential facilities in Minnesota. If not in fact, then at least in spirit, MED programs are the antithesis of research programs conducted in the early 1970s that explored the clinical utility of extremely high doses of neuroleptic medication for the treatment of schizophrenia, based on the belief that drug failure was often a product of underdosing (reviewed by Aubree & Lader, 1980). Some pediatric psychopharmacologists still believe that underdosing is a major clinical management problem among practitioners and even researchers.

In the hyperactivity area, credit for raising clinical consciousness about dose relationships between behavioral toxicity and suppression of target behaviors certainly goes to Robert Sprague, John Werry, Esther

Sleator, and their colleagues at the University of Illinois. They were able to demonstrate, with many other findings, that drug-induced *improvements* in adaptive behavior were compromised by doses that maximally suppressed target symptoms. Their index of adaptive behavior was a computer assisted short-term memory task, which at the time of its development purportedly measured an important component of learning (Scott & Scott, 1968). Their early research showed that the improvements in adaptive behavior observed at low to moderate doses of methylphenidate reached a plateau after a certain point (Sprague & Sleator, 1973), and with increasing dose, even deteriorated from maximal improvement levels, at least in some children (Sprague & Sleator, 1977). This finding, that after a certain dose level, additional increments in dose are unlikely to produce clinically *significant* gains in adaptive behavior, has been replicated by numerous investigators.

In the SBME, the procedure for establishing the MED is as follows: First, compare placebo and each dose and calculate the percent of improvement (i.e., the decrease in the target behavior). A dose is considered effective for a specific target behavior if it reduces the rate of occurrence by 30% or by one-half standard deviation of the peer mean. Second, if both doses are effective, the moderate dose is considered the superior dose if the magnitude of improvement between the low-moderate comparison is at least 30% or one-half standard deviation (of the peer mean) greater than the magnitude of the placebo-low dose comparison. When the peer's behavior covaries with the target child's behavior (i.e., the peer mean also decreases by 30% or more from placebo to medication conditions), consider the peer mean to be "artificially" inflated by the behavior of the target child. Disregard the 0.5 standard deviation of the peer mean criterion for determining whether a dose is effective and consider the behavior in question to be a target symptom (i.e., abnormal).

To determine the superior effective dose, examine the effective doses for all target symptoms. Typically, a fairly compelling pattern emerges indicating one dose over the other. The superior effective dose is then evaluated with regard to the supranormalization of target symptoms and collateral (i.e., normal) behaviors and behavioral toxicity (i.e., appropriate social interaction from the COSA and the Stimulant

Side Effect Checklist ratings). Ideally, the MED should produce significant clinical improvement but induce a limited degree of behavioral toxicity and supranormalization. As a general rule, when in doubt go with the lower dose, it can always be adjusted upward at a later time if necessary.

Postassessment Counseling Session

After the last set of ratings and observations are completed, the SBME team analyzes the drug response data and prepares a written report for the parents, and the school with parental approval, and for the clinic files. Even when a computer is used to analyze the data and prepare the report, a certain amount of time elapses between the last dose of the medication evaluation and the school and family counseling sessions. In order to avoid a break in treatment (which can be an extremely negative experience for a favorable responder), the lowest dose used in the medication evaluation is generally administered on a temporary basis. Adverse responders or nonresponders would of course be excluded from this consideration. When the SBME report is ready, separate counseling sessions are established for the family and the school. The following is a brief description of the content and goals of these meetings.

School

The findings in the SBME report are presented to school personnel who were involved in the medication evaluation during the postassessment counseling session. The objectives of this meeting are threefold. The primary objective is to describe what effect the medication has on specific target behaviors and to elicit additional observations about drug response from school staff members that may be relevant for determining the MED. In addition to presenting the percentage of change figures for specific target behaviors, a calendar indicating the dose for specific days is also reviewed, because school personnel (especially the child's teacher) are generally curious about the exact schedule of dosage manipulations. The second objective of the postassessment school meeting is to impress upon school personnel the significance of their involvement in the SBME and that with their assistance the treatment regimen has been established in an unbiased and scientifically sound manner. The third objective is to describe maintenance treatment and procedures for monitoring drug response. This objective is very important because school personnel generally do not have a very good idea of what should be done after a child is placed on medication. They know that treatment needs to be monitored, but are generally unclear as to exactly what is considered adequate according to current standards.

If the child is a serious conduct problem in school, the conversation invariably drifts to the home environment. Occasionally a school staff member offers a psychodynamic analysis of family interaction patterns, describes parental incompetencies, or reviews alleged environmental stressors. (At times one is struck by how public the lives of families with handicapped children really are.) Given the well-documented role of psychosocial factors in the etiology and maintenance of behavioral deviance, the treatment clinic must address these potential concerns beginning with the first day of diagnostic evaluation and establish channels of communication with appropriate school personnel. Sometimes the SBME team is confronted with the challenge to remediate these psychosocial problems, which may be presented with intense negative affect. At these moments it is important to note the efforts the clinic is making in this regard, the financial realities of health care to include psychological interventions, and the parents' right to refuse treatment if they so desire. Ironically, what starts out to be a meeting on the clinical management of the child can easily turn into a therapy session for school personnel.

Family

The objectives of the postassessment counseling session with the parents are similar to those for the school; that is, to describe drug response and the unbiased nature of the evaluation. The treating physician states his or her recommendation for the MED and the basis for that decision. The need for weekend doses is also discussed. Because the behavior rating scales completed by the parents are generally (but certainly not always) not as useful as

teacher ratings for assessing drug effects, anecdotal reports often become the basis for determining the schedule for weekend drug administrations. However, the direct observation data for the lunchroom and playground are also considered when making this decision if peer conflict is identified as a target symptom by the parents. In other words, drug response is presumed to generalize to the neighborhood setting. Maintenance therapy and monitoring procedures are reviewed. One of the intended salutary consequences of the parent counseling session is to enhance compliance with the recommended guidelines for drug administration.

CASE STUDIES

To demonstrate the SBME in action, two case studies are presented. Both boys are somewhat atypical, but they serve as good examples of the strengths and weaknesses of the SBME. The first case (Charlie) illustrates (a) the importance of direct observations for the identification of target behaviors, (b) symptom variability across settings, (c) the value of observational data for the lunchroom and playground, and (d) the convergence of teacher side-effect ratings and the supranormalization of certain classroom behaviors (motor movement, off-task). The second case (Quinn) is a boy who experiences extreme difficulty getting along with others in all settings. His case is interesting because of the (a) co-occurrence of hyperactivity symptoms and conduct problems, (b) mixed patterns of optimal doses, and (c) the clinical challenge of risk-to-benefit decision making. Both cases illustrate the impact of effective pharmacotherapy on the behavior of classmates.

Case #1 (Charlie)

Charlie was 10 years old when he was brought to the Outpatient Service by his parents at the urging of the school. According to his parents, he was quite a behavior problem. Under the supervision of a therapist, they had implemented behavior modification techniques to control Charlie's behavior with limited success over a 2-year period and saw medical intervention as being their last hope. Both parents were well educated and were successful in their respective professions. In school, Charlie had a long history of behavior problems and learning difficulties. He was held back in second grade due to immaturity and poor acedemic performance. His fraternal twin sister, who was perfect in every way, was also retained to minimize potential adverse psychological consequences to Charlie. There was one additional child in the family, a first grader, who was not symptomatic.

In the clinic, Charlie made an immediate and lasting impression as being an extremely annoying child. He scored well within the deviant range on all of our diagnostic instruments. He was clearly above cutoff on the IOWA I-O (13) and A (12) scales, the ATRS (19), and the teacher and parent ADD-H, Oppositional Disorder, and Conduct Disorder indicies of the Stony Brook Child Psychiatric Checklist-3 (Gadow & Sprafkin, 1986). Based on these rating-scale data and parent and child interviews, Charlie was diagnosed ADD-H by a child psychiatrist. Given the family's limited success with behavioral interventions, medication was suggested as a possible intervention. Although the parents were somewhat apprehensive about drug therapy, they were willing to "give it a try." The study doses were 10 mg (0.3 mg/kg) and 20 mg (0.6 mg/kg), which were administered morning and noon, 7 days a week for the duration of the medication evaluation. For this particular boy, the dose sequence was 0.6 mg/kg, placebo, and 0.3 mg/kg.

When the SBME team went to the school for their initial set-up meeting with the principal, classroom teacher, school nurse, and learning disabilities teacher, they learned that Charlie was at a point in his school career where something had to be done. Although he was above average intellectually, he was doing poorly academically, especially in reading. He was receiving "unofficial" help from the resource room teacher (i.e., had never been certified as being learning disabled). In the classroom, Charlie was unpopular. He would occasionally "take things" from other students without telling them. Subsequently, if anything was ever missing in the classroom, Charlie was always accused by the others in the classroom. Charlie's teacher was very concerned about his ability to handle the demands of fifth grade the following year.

The school agreed to the SBME program and were relieved to know that something was finally going to be done about Charlie. His teacher was also very supportive of the effort.

The findings from the SBME were both illuminating and surprising. To begin with, his behavior in the classroom was, for the most part, unremarkable (see Table 10.2). He was clearly within the normal range (defined as being within 1 standard deviation of the peer mean) for all four behavior categories when receiving placebo. Methylphenidate suppressed these behaviors, but given his initial-level normalcy, medication resulted in the supranormalization of two behaviors, particularly the moderate dose.

The lunchroom and playground analyses were most revealing because they illustrated the damaging consequences his symptoms had on peer interactions (lunchroom) and the profound impact methylphenidate can have on these behaviors. On placebo, Charlie engaged in extremely high rates of peer aggression (both physical and nonphysical) and, in the lunchroom, relatively low rates of appropriate social interaction. These behaviors were considered target symptoms because they were either one standard deviation above (antisocial) or below (prosocial) the peer mean. The observers described Charlie as a boy on the fringe of the social group, an annoying immature child whom the others went to great lengths to avoid. Methylphenidate suppressed Charlie's aggressive behavior, and to some extent, appropriate social interaction (low dose only).

The behavior of Charlie's peers in the lunchroom provides compelling insight into the disruptive nature of his social interactions. Treatment with methylphenidate not only resulted in a pronounced decrease in Charlie's level of aggression but led to a dramatic change in the behavior of his peers as well. These "spillover" effects dramatize the reciprocal nature of social interaction.

The teacher rating scale scores were in general agreement with the direct observation data. His ATRS scores were as follows: placebo (6.5), 0.3 mg/kg (1.0), and 0.6 mg/kg (2.0).

The two indices of behavioral toxicity (level of appropriate social interaction and the side-effect rating scale) were inconsistent. Although the moderate dose of methylphenidate *increased* the level of appropriate social interaction in the lunchroom,

Table 10.2. School Observations of Charlie and His Peers During Treatment with Placebo and Two Doses of Methylphenidate

Behavior Category	Placebo M	M	0.3 mg/kg (% change)	M	0.6 mg/kg (% change)	Peers M	SD
Classroom							
Interference							
Charlie	1.8*	2.2*	(+22)	0.6*	(−66)		
Peers	6.8	8.0		14.2		9.7	6.0
Motor movement							
Charlie	12.9	5.8	(−55)	1.9	(−85)		
Peers	13.3	19.5		5.4		12.7	12.0
Noncompliance							
Charlie	0.9	0.6	(−33)	0.6	(−33)		
Peers	0.0	0.0		1.1		0.4	1.1
Off-task							
Charlie	20.7	11.2*	(−46)	1.6*	(−92)		
Peers	22.7	15.0		22.7		20.1	6.2
Lunchroom							
Appropriate social							
Charlie	25.0*	14.0*	(−44)	38.0*	(+52)		
Peers	68.1	71.7		56.1		65.3	8.2
Noncompliance							
Charlie	6.3*	2.0*	(−68)	1.0	(−84)		
Peers	0.0	0.0		1.2		0.4	1.2
Nonphysical aggression							
Charlie	20.8*	0.0	(−100)	5.0	(−76)		
Peers	20.4	0.0		0.0		7.4	13.9
Physical aggression							
Charlie	8.3*	0.0	(−100)	0.0	(−100)		
Peers	7.5	1.8		0.0		3.1	5.2
Playground							
Appropriate social							
Charlie	54.2	44.4	(−19)	55.6	(+3)	NA	
Noncompliance							
Charlie	0.0	0.0		0.0		NA	
Nonphysical aggression							
Charlie	16.7	0.0	(−100)	1.9	(−89)	NA	
Physical aggression							
Charlie	4.2	0.0	(−100)	0.0	(−100)	NA	

Note: Figures in italics indicate the clinically optimal dose. Asterisk (*) indicates whether a specific behavior is more than one standard deviation above or below the peer mean.

which was good, it also resulted in higher teacher ratings on the Attention-Arousal index of the Stimulant Side Effects Checklist (see Table 10.3). Anecdotal reports from both teacher and principal give insight into this aspect of drug response. The teacher was concerned that his level of concentration was abnormally high. The principal commented that although Charlie's behavior was greatly improved, he was also "different" in some respects. For example, when the principal sat down next to Charlie in orchestra (as he had many times in the past), Charlie was not as spontaneous verbally as on previous occasions. He was polite and answered the principal's questions but did not elaborate. It is noteworthy that in more task-oriented situations, such changes in verbal behavior might be perceived in a positive light (reviewed by Gadow, 1986). This change in Charlie's spontaneity was sufficiently great enough to make the principal somewhat apprehensive about methylphenidate treatment.

The MED was determined using the aforementioned guidelines. Because both doses of methylphe-

Table 10.3. Charlie's Mean Stimulant Side-Effects Checklist Scores for Placebo and Two Doses of Methylphenidate

Side Effects	Placebo	0.3 mg/kg	0.6 mg/kg
Teacher Ratings			
Mood index	0.2	0.8	0.0
Physical complaints index	0.0	0.0	0.0
Attention-arousal index	1.2	3.2	3.0
Unusual motor movements	0.2	0.0	0.0
Total score	1.8	4.0	3.0
Parent Ratings			
Mood index	1.4	2.2	0.0
Physical complaints index	0.0	0.0	0.0
Attention-arousal index	1.4	1.5	0.0
Unusual motor movements	0.7	1.0	1.0
Total score	3.3	4.8	1.0

nidate improved the quality of Charlie's social interactions by decreasing many of his annoying behaviors, a decision had to be made as to which dose was most clinically desirable. Recall that an effective dose was operationally defined as one that normalized a target symptom (i.e., decreased the rate of occurrence to a level within the normal peer range). When two or more doses are effective, the lowest dose is considered to be the MED unless a higher produces a superior therapeutic response. To be deemed superior, the higher dose must further decrease the rate of occurrence by an additional 30% or by one-half standard deviation of the peer mean. As is clear from Table 10.2, the moderate dose was not superior to the lower dose in suppressing Charlie's antisocial behavior in the lunchroom. Because the collection of peer data on the playground is not currently part of the SBME, superior efficacy is determined on the basis of the magnitude of change. A percentile change of 30% or more over the low dose is considered clinically significant. In Charlie's case, the moderate dose did not lead to significantly greater improvements in his playground behavior.

Unfortunately, there was some indication that both doses were altering some aspects of Charlie's behavior that careproviders did not want changed. For example, in the classroom treatment with methylphenidate, particularly the moderate dose, resulted in unusually low levels (supranormalization) of certain behaviors (e.g., activity level, off-task). These changes in Charlie's behavior concerned school

personnel and in all probability account, in part, for the worsening in his teacher's SSEC ratings.

Taken together, the findings from the SBME seemed to indicate that the 20 mg dose was not clinically preferable to the 10 mg dose. Therefore, the initial MED recommendation was 10 mg twice daily.

Case #2 (Quinn)

Quinn was 6½ years old when he was evaluated by the Child Psychiatry Outpatient Service. His mother characterized him as an extremely hyperactive child and very difficult to manage. She stated that his hyperactivity first became a problem at the age of 3 years. He was enrolled in Head Start when he was 4 years old, and his teacher also characterized him as very hyperactive. He was currently attending a self-contained special education class in a regular elementary school and had been classified as learning disabled.

When the SBME team went to the school, the staff members were highly motivated to cooperate with the evaluation. In school Quinn was very aggressive (both verbally and physically) and was often sent to the office for misbehavior. His teacher maintained that behavior management techniques such as time out were not effective in controlling his inappropriate behaviors, which included hitting, spitting, yelling, and temper tantrums.

Quinn scored well above cut-off on all the hyperactivity–oppositionality–aggressivity teacher rating scales (e.g., IOWA I-O = 12; IOWA A = 13; ATRS = 26). Quinn also scored above cut-off on the ADD-H (parent and teacher versions), Oppositional Disorder (teacher version), and Conduct Disorder (parent version) of the Stony Brook Child Psychiatric Checklist-3. The mother was very concerned about Quinn's behavior at home. Based on the findings from the teacher and parent behavior rating scales, preliminary observations of classroom behavior, and diagnostic interviews with the mother, Quinn was diagnosed ADD-H by a child psychiatrist and scheduled for a methylphenidate evaluation. The study doses were 7.5 mg (0.3 mg/kg) and 15 mg (0.6 mg/kg), which were administered morning and noon, 7 days a week for the duration of the medication evaluation. For this particular boy, the dose sequence was 0.3 mg/kg, placebo, and 0.6 mg/kg.

The data from the classroom observations are presented in Table 10.4. Quinn was more noncompliant than his peers in the special class, and both doses of methylphenidate suppressed this behavior. Moreover, when Quinn's behavior improved, his peers engaged in less noncompliance and interference, which suggests a treatment spillover effect.

In the lunchroom and on the playground, he displayed relatively high rates of peer aggression (see Table 10.4). Treatment with low and moderate doses resulted in significant reductions in physical aggression initiated by Quinn and directed toward other children. Fortunately, improvements in antisocial behavior were associated with increased levels of appropriate social interaction.

Quinn's case also illustrates the convergence of teacher ratings and direct observations. For example, mean teacher ATRS ratings were as follows: placebo (18), 0.3 mg/kg (6), and 0.6 mg/kg (1). Not unexpectedly, parent ratings on a parallel version of this scale were not particularly drug sensitive: placebo (20), 0.3 mg/kg (15), and 0.6 mg/kg (23).

With regard to side effects, the teacher reported anecdotally that Quinn was lethargic and sometimes weepy when first receiving medication (which happened to be the 0.3 mg/kg dose). Both of these reactions were evidenced in the teacher SSEC rating for the Attention-Arousal (placebo = 0.3, low dose = 1.5, moderate dose = 0.3) and Mood (placebo = 0.0, low dose = 0.5, moderate 0.3) index, respectively. The mother, however, found Quinn to be more weepy and depressed on the moderate dose, and her Mood index scores were as follows: placebo = 6.0, low dose = 4.0, moderate dose = 9.0.

The MED for Quinn was somewhat difficult to determine for several reasons. First, although the superior dose (using the 30% reduction rule) was 7.5 mg for most behaviors, there were some "near misses" for the 15 mg dose (off-task, noncompliance) in the classroom and physical aggression on the playground. If these are counted as "hits," 15 mg is the superior dose. Second, it is noteworthy that the 15 mg dose resulted in the supranormalization of motor movement and noncompliance (and possibly off-task). The rate of appropriate social interaction was highest on the 7.5 mg dose, but the 15 mg dose was also beneficial (in the lunchroom). Fourth, after the first week of medication, side effects appeared to be minimal in the school. However, the mother observed that Quinn exhibited a depressed affect in the home on the 15 mg dose.

On the basis of the aforementioned analyses, the MED was determined to be 10 mg, twice daily, on school days and 5 mg, twice daily on weekends. Later in the same school year, Quinn's teacher stated that his behavior had worsened, and the week-day dose was raised to 15 mg, morning and noon.

LIMITATIONS OF THE SBME

The SBME generates precise, ecologically valid, and clinically meaningful information about child behavior in various settings, including some not currently assessed by popular caregiver rating scales. However, can such a program exist outside a specialized clinic and can it be financed in some way? The answer to both questions is a tentative yes. There does not seem to be any reason why licensed health care providers (e.g., psychologists, social workers, psychiatric nurses) or their supervisees could not conduct direct observations in collaboration with a community-based physician. The expenses incurred for such evaluations can be billed as part of the diagnostic workup (baseline) and treatment plan. Even in situations where insurance reimbursement is

Table 10.4. School Observations of Quinn and His Peers During Treatment with Placebo and Two Doses of Methylphenidate

Behavior Category	Placebo M	M	0.3 mg/kg (% change)	M	0.6 mg/kg (% change)	Peers M	SD
Classroom							
Interference							
Quinn	21.5	25.4	(+18)	15.4	(−28)		
Peers	22.5	21.9		15.4		19.9	8.5
Motor movement							
Quinn	38.0	19.8*	(−48)	23.0*	(−40)		
Peers	43.4	32.9		36.0		37.4	7.4
Noncompliance							
Quinn	13.2*	4.8	(−64)	0.1*	(−99)		
Peers	7.7	4.1		4.1		5.3	2.8
Off-task							
Quinn	5.4	3.3	(−39)	2.0*	(−63)		
Peers	4.8	4.4		19.7		9.6	8.4
Lunchroom							
Appropriate social							
Quinn	25.4*	53.8*	(+112)	42.1	(+66)		
Peers	50.8	46.0		32.2		45.0	6.4
Noncompliance							
Quinn	17.5*	7.6	(−57)	2.6	(−85)		
Peers	6.7	6.0		9.5		7.4	5.1
Nonphysical aggression							
Quinn	15.1	18.5	(+23)	11.8	(−22)		
Peers	12.4	7.4		18.6		12.8	9.6
Physical aggression							
Quinn	10.3*	1.7	(−83)	2.6	(−75)		
Peers	2.7	0.0		3.9		2.2	3.1
Playground							
Appropriate social							
Quinn	57.1	81.5	(+43)	53.8	(−6)	NA	
Noncompliance							
Quinn	0.0	0.0		0.0	(0)	NA	
Nonphysical aggression							
Quinn	14.3	25.9	(+81)	11.5	(−20)	NA	
Physical aggression							
Quinn	14.3	3.7	(−74)	0.0	(−100)	NA	

Note: Figures in italics indicate the clinically superior dose for target (abnormal) behaviors. Asterisk (*) indicates whether a specific behavior is more than one standard deviation above or below the peer mean.

not possible, many parents are more than willing to pay for such evaluations out-of-pocket.

Although the SBME provides decision rules for determining the optimal dose for specific target behaviors, a considerable amount of clinical judgement is still required for some cases. Notable examples are when the optimal dose varies across target behaviors and settings, side effects occur at the MED level, or the behavior of peers covaries with drug-induced changes in the patient's symptoms (i.e., treatment spillover effects). When spillover effects do occur, the best estimate of the peer mean and standard deviation is ambiguous.

The observation system of the SBME assesses drug effects on a relatively small number of target behaviors that are considered clinically important (i.e., its implicit theory of treatment). At present, it does not examine academic productivity, although others have shown academic productivity to correlate moderately well with observed levels of off-task (negatively) and disruptive (negatively) behavior in the classroom and clinical improvement (positively) on various teacher-completed behavior rating scales. Nor does the SBME evaluate the effects of stimulant medication on laboratory measures of cognitive performance, the patient's sense of well-being, behavior problems in the home environment (other than with parent rating scales). Because these and other aspects of child functioning have been identified as suitable targets for pharmacological intervention by various clinicians, the SBME must be considered somewhat limited in focus.

Last, behavior rating scales completed by care providers are relegated to a secondary role in the SBME for making dosage decisions. It is possible that these instruments provide a better picture of overall clinical response. However, because commonly used rating scales generally do not contain items that pertain to adaptive behavior or peer performance (although normative data may be available), their clinical utility is also limited.

ALTERNATIVE MEDICATION EVALUATION MODELS

Several clinical management models for evaluating stimulant drug response and adjusting dosage have been described in the literature during the past 15 years (e.g., Barkley, Fine & Jewesson, 1989; McBride, 1988; Neisworth et al., 1976; Ottinger et al., 1985; Pelham & Hoza, 1987; Rapport, in press; Safer & Allen, 1976; Sprague & Sleator, 1975; Swanson & Kinsbourne, 1978; Varley & Trupin, 1983; Yellin & Greenberg, 1981). Most are designed for specialized clinics, typically university-based research facilities. These treatment programs offer an exciting array of empirically based medication evaluation procedures, generate a wealth of scientific data, and provide excellent health care for patients who avail themselves of their services. The limited amount of research on clinical management is attested to by the tremendous differences among these studies with regard to the use of placebos, dose and schedule of stimulant medication, measures of therapeutic drug response and side effects, and their implicit theories of treatment. Furthermore, few treatment models have operationalized their dosage selection rules, clearly specified target behaviors, or established the ecological validity of their dose-re-

sponse measures. Only one involves direct observations of the patient's behavior in his or her community environment (Neisworth et al., 1976), but it is unknown whether this is necessary or even desirable. In this regard, it remains to be seen whether treatment models can even be meaningfully compared empirically because there is no consensus on the criteria for therapeutic improvement.

Research on various elements of treatment models has produced contradictory findings, or, at the very least, conflicting interpretations. Perhaps the best example of this is the role of cognitive performance tasks in determining optimal dose. One clinical research team has argued that one type of cognitive task (paired associate learning) should be the primary basis for selecting the optimal dose (Swanson & Kinsbourne, 1978), whereas another investigator has concluded that this task as well as others is not nearly so useful as the Abbreivated Teacher Rating Scale (Rapport, in press). Although contradictory research findings are discouraging, they are not an invitation for complacency when one is monitoring the effects of psychotropic medication. Most experts in the hyperactivity area believe that (a) behavior rating scales completed by the patient's teacher are an invaluable source of information, (b) there is a point at which further dosage increments produce trivial clinical gains, (c) bothersome side effects define the upper dosage limit, and (d) clinical response should be periodically reevaluated. Furthermore, with such a variety of drug response measures and assessment models to choose from (both community- and hospital-based), there is no defensible reason to explain why some type of scientifically valid medication evaluation procedure cannot be established for all clinical settings in which stimulant drugs are routinely prescribed for hyperactivity. The challenge for the next decade is to formulate a less ambiguous rationale for treatment and to "fine tune" clinical management.

CONCLUSIONS

The formulation of the SBME was based on a desire to provide an ecologically valid basis for making dosage adjustment decisions. Survey studies conducted during the past 20 years indicate that such decisions are generally made on the basis of anecdotal reports from the parents and much less frequently, behavior rating scales completed by the classroom teacher. Research psychologists have launched a vigorous campaign to develop treatment assessment programs in which computer-assisted tasks and laboratory playrooms often play an important role in diagnosing psychopathology and evaluating drug response. Unfortunately, the ecological validity of these procedures is often difficult to demonstrate. These efforts have also resulted in theories of treatment based on cognitive processes and, in some cases, learning ability or academic achievement. The SBME uses both rating scales and direct observation codes to assess behaviors that are considered to be the basis for psychiatric referral.

Much additional research is required to determine whether the SBME is truly effective in achieving its stated goals and whether its implicit theory of treatment is in fact valid from both a clinical and societal perspective. It is presented here as an alternative to the ever-growing popularity of laboratory analogue procedures and as a treatment model for future investigation. To be clinically comprehensive, the SBME must be expanded to include the diagnostic and follow-up phases of drug therapy.

Two case studies were presented to illustrate how the SBME can be used to make clinical decisions. Although its potential for determining the MED is promising, surprisingly little research has ever been directed toward this aspect of clinical management. There is of course a painful irony in this entire situation. The school, which has traditionally been conceptualized as the most clinically troublesome setting for hyperactive children, is only occasionally considered a potential source of answers to many of the hotly debated issues concerning the diagnosis and treatment of this disorder.

Acknowledgment: The development of the SBME would not have been possible without the assistance of the following dedicated colleagues: Edith Nolan, Lucia Paolicelli, Joyce Sprafkin, and Jeffrey Sverd. The author is also indebted to these people and to Howard Abikoff and John Pomeroy for many helpful comments on a preliminary draft of this chapter. The opinions expressed in this paper, however, are those of the author, and they are not necessarily shared by others working in this field of study.

REFERENCES

Abikoff, H., & Gittelman, R. (1985a). Classroom Observation Code: A modification of the Stony Brook Code. *Psychopharmacology Bulletin, 21,* 901–909.

Abikoff, H., & Gittelman, R. (1985b). The normalizing effects of methylphenidate on the classroom behavior of ADDH children. *Journal of Abnormal Child Psychology, 13,* 33–44.

American Psychiatric Association. (1980). *Diagnostic and statistical manual of mental disorders: DSM-III* (3rd ed.). Washington, DC: Author.

Atkins, M. S., Pelham, W. E., & Licht, M. H. (1989). The differential validity of teacher ratings of inattention/overactivity and aggression. *Journal of Abnormal Child Psychology, 17,* 423–435.

Aubree, J. C., & Lader, M. H. (1980). High and very high dosage antipsychotics: A critical review. *Journal of Clinical Psychiatry, 41,* 341–350.

Ayllon, T., Layman, D., & Kandel, H. J. (1975). A behavioral-educational alternative to drug control of hyperactive children. *Journal of Applied Behavior Analysis, 8,* 137–146.

Baker, A. A., & Thorpe, J. G. (1957). Placebo response. *Archives of Neurology and Psychiatry, 78,* 57–60.

Barkley, R. A., Fischer, M., Newby, R. F., & Breen, M. J. (1988). Development of a multimethod clinical protocol for assessing stimulant drug response in children with attention deficit disorder. *Journal of Clinical Child Psychology, 17,* 14–24.

Bennett, F. C., & Sherman, R. (1983). Management of childhood "hyperactivity" by primary care physicians. *Journal of Developmental and Behavioral Pediatrics, 4,* 88–93.

Bosco, J. J., & Robin, S. S. (1976). Ritalin usage: A challenge to teacher education. *Peabody Journal of Education, 53,* 187–93.

Bradley, C., & Bowen, M. (1940). School performance of children receiving amphetamine (Benzedrine) sulfate. *American Journal of Orthopsychiatry, 10,* 782–788.

Brulle, A. R., Barton, L. E., & Foskett, J. J. (1983). Educator/physician interchanges: A survey and suggestions. *Education & Training of the Mentally Retarded, 18,* 313–317.

Conners, C. K. (1971). Recent drug studies with hyperkinetic children. *Journal of Learning Disabilities, 4,* 476–483.

Conners, C. K. (1973). Rating scales for use in drug studies with children. *Psychopharmacology Bulletin* (Special Issue, Pharmacotherapy of children), 24–84.

Copeland, L., Wolraich, M., Lindgren, S., Milich, R., & Woolson, R. (1987). Pediatricians' reported practices in the assessment and treatment of attention deficit disorders. *Journal of Developmental and Behavioral Pediatrics, 8,* 191–197.

Divoky, D. (1973, March). Toward a nation of sedated children. *Learning,* pp. 6–13.

Eichlseder, W. (1985). Ten years of experience with 1,000 hyperactive children in private practice. *Pediatrics, 76,* 176–184.

Epstein, M. H., Cullinan, D., & Gadow, K. D. (1986). Teacher ratings of hyperactivity in learning-disabled, emotionally disturbed, and mentally retarded children. *Journal of Special Education, 20,* 219–229.

Fielding, L. T., Murphy, R. J., Reagan, M. W., & Peterson, T. L. (1980). An assessment program to reduce drug use with the mentally retarded. *Hospital & Community Psychiatry, 31,* 771–773.

Fine, S., & Jewesson, B. (1989). Active drug placebo trial of methylphenidate: A clinical service for children with an attention deficit disorder. *Canadian Journal of Psychiatry, 34,* 447–449.

Gadow, K. D. (1975, October). *Pills and preschool: Medication usage with young children in special education.* Paper presented at the meeting of the Illinois Council for Exceptional Children, Chicago. (Available from author)

Gadow, K. D. (1976, April). *Psychotropic and anticonvulsant drug usage in early childhood special education programs I. Phase One: A preliminary report: Prevalence, attitude, training and problems.* Paper presented at the annual meeting of the Council for Exceptional Children, Chicago. (ERIC Document Reproduction Service No. ED 125 198)

Gadow, K. D. (1978, May). *Drug treatment with children in programs for the trainable mentally handicapped.* Paper presented at the annual meeting of the Council for Exceptional Children, Kansas City. (ERIC Document Reproduction Service No. ED 153 398)

Gadow, K. D. (1981). Prevalence of drug treatment for hyperactivity and other childhood behavior disorders. In K. D. Gadow and J. Loney (Eds.), *Psychosocial aspects of drug treatment for hyperactivity* (pp. 13–76). Boulder, CO: Westview Press.

Gadow, K. D. (1982). School involvement in pharmacotherapy for behavior disorders. *Journal of Special Education, 16,* 385–399.

Gadow, K. D. (1983). Pharmacotherapy for behavior disorders: Typical treatment practices. *Clinical Pediatrics, 22,* 48–53.

Gadow, K. D. (1986a). *Children on medication (Vol. 1): Hyperactivity, learning disabilities, and mental retardation.* Boston, MA: College-Hill Press.

Gadow, K. D. (1986b). *Peer Conflict Scale.* State University of New York, Department of Psychiatry, Stony Brook, New York.

Gadow, K. D. (1986c). *Stimulant Side Effects Checklist.* State University of New York, Department of Psychiatry, Stony Brook, New York.

Gadow, K. D., & Kane, K. (1983). Administration of medication by school personnel. *Journal of School Health, 53,* 178–183.

Gadow, K. D., Nolan, E. E., Sverd, J, Sprafkin, J., & Paolicelli, L. (1990). Methylphenidate in aggressive-hyperactive boys: I. Effects on peer aggression in public school settings. *Journal of the American Academy of Child and Adolescent Psychiatry, 29,* 710–718.

Gadow, K. D., Paolicelli, L., Nolan, E. E., Schwartz, J., Sprafkin, J., & Sverd, J. (1992). Methylphenidate in aggressive-hyperactive boys: II. Indirect effects of medication treatment on peer behavior. *Journal of Child and Adolescent Psychopharmacology, 2,* 49–61.

Gadow, K. D., & Sprafkin, J. (1986). *Stony Brook Child Psychiatric Checklist-3.* State University of New York, Department of Psychiatry, Stony Brook, NY. (Available from author)

Gadow, K. D., & Sprafkin, J. (1987). Effects of viewing high versus low aggression cartoons on emotionally disturbed children. *Journal of Pediatric Psychology, 12,* 413–427.

Gadow, K. D., Sprafkin, J., & Ficarrotto, T. J. (1987). Effects of viewing aggression-laden cartoons on preschool-aged emotionally disturbed children. *Child Psychiatry and Human Development, 17,* 257–274.

Gadow, K. D., White, L., & Ferguson, D. G. (1986). Placebo controls and double-blind conditions. Placebo theory in experimental design. In K. D. Gadow & A. D. Poling (Eds.), *Advances in learning and behavioral disabilities (Suppl. 1): Methodological issues in human psychopharmacology* (pp. 41–83). Greenwich, CT: JAI Press.

Gittelman-Klein, R., Klein, D. F., Abikoff, H., Katz, S., Gloisten, A. C., & Kates, W. (1976). Relative efficacy of methylphenidate and behavior modification in hyperkinetic children: An interim report. *Journal of Abnormal Child Psychology, 4,* 361–379.

Hentoff, N. (1970, December). The drugged classroom. *Evergreen Review, 14,* 31–33.

Jensen, P. S., Xenakis, S. N., Shervette, R. E., Bain, M. W., & Davis, H. (1989). Diagnosis and treatment of attention deficit disorder in two general hospital clinics. *Hospital and Community Psychiatry, 40,* 708–712.

Klein, A. R., & Young, R. D. (1979). Hyperactive boys in their classroom: Assessment of teacher and peer perceptions, interactions, and classroom behaviors. *Journal of Abnormal Child Psychology, 7,* 425–442.

Krager, J. M., & Safer, D. J. (1974). Type and prevalence of medication used in the treatment of hyperactive children. *New England Journal of Medicine, 291,* 1118–1120.

Loney, J., & Milich, R. (1982). Hyperactivity, inattention, and aggression in clinical practice. In M. Wolraich & D. K. Routh (Eds.), *Advances in developmental and behavioral pediatrics* (Vol. 3, pp. 113–147). Greenwich, CT: JAI Press.

Loney, J., & Ordona, T. T. (1975). Using cerebral stimulants to treat minimal brain dysfunction. *American Journal of Orthopsychiatry, 45,* 564–572.

Loney, J., Weissenburger, F. E., Woolson, R. F., & Lichty, E. C. (1979). Comparing psychological and pharmacological treatments for hyperkinetic boys and their classmates. *Journal of Abnormal Child Psychology, 7,* 133–143.

McBride, M. C. (1988). An individual double-blind crossover trial for assessing methylphenidate response in children with attention deficit disorder. *Journal of Pediatrics, 113,* 137–145.

Neisworth, J. T., Kurtz, P. D., Ross, A., & Madle, R. A. (1976). Naturalistic assessment of neurological diagnoses and pharmacological intervention. *Journal of Learning Disabilities, 9,* 149–152.

Newton, J. (1982). Psychoactive medication in a large urban school district. *Journal of School Health, 52,* 495–497.

Nolan, E. E. (1988). *The effects of methylphenidate on aggression in ADD boys.* Unpublished doctoral dissertation, State University of New York, Stony Brook.

Ottinger, D. R., Halpin, B., Miller, M., Demian, L., & Hannemann, R. (1985). Evaluating drug effectiveness in an office setting for children with attention deficit disorders. *Clinical Pediatrics, 24,* 245–251.

Pelham, W. E., Bender, M. E., Caddell, J., Booth, S., & Moorer, S. H. (1985). Methylphenidate and children with attention deficit disorder: Dose effects on classroom academic and social behavior. *Archives of General Psychiatry, 42,* 948–952.

Pelham, W. E., & Hoza, J. (1987). Behavioral assessment of psychostimulant effects on ADD children in a summer day treatment program. In R. Prinz (Ed.), *Advances in behavioral assessment of children and families* (Vol. 3, pp. 3–34). Greenwich, CT: JAI Press.

Porrino, L. J., Rapoport, J. L., Behar, D., Sceery, W., Ismond, D. R., & Bunney, W. E. (1983). A naturalistic assessment of the motor activity of hyperactive boys. *Archives of General Psychiatry, 40,* 681–687.

Rapport, M. D. (in press). Controlled studies of the effects of psychostimulants on children's classroom behavior and academic functioning. In C. K. Conners & M. Kinsbourne (Eds.), *Attention-deficit disorder in children: Problems and prospects.* Munich: Munchner Medizinischer Verlag.

Rapport, M. D., Jones, J. T., DuPaul, G. J., Kelly, K. L., Gardner, M. J., Tucker, S. B., & Shea, M. S. (1987). Attention deficit disorder and methylphenidate: Group and single-subject analyses of dose effects on attention in clinic and classroom settings. *Journal of Clinical Child Psychology, 16,* 329–338.

Robin, S. S., & Bosco, J. J. (1973). Ritalin for school children: The teacher's perspective. *Journal of School Health, 43,* 624–628.

Safer, D. J., & Allen, R. P. (1976). *Hyperactive children: Diagnosis and management.* Baltimore MD: University Park Press.

Safer, D. J., & Krager, J. M. (1988). A survey of medication treatment for hyperactive/inattentive students. *Journal of the American Medical Association, 260,* 2256–2258.

Sandoval, J., Lambert, N., & Yandell, (1976). Current medical practice and hyperactivity. *American Journal of Orthopsychiatry, 46,* 323–334.

Scott, K. G., & Scott, M. S. (1968). Research and theory in short-term memory. In N. R. Ellis (Ed.), *International review of research in mental retardation* (Vol. 3). New York: Academic Press.

Sindelar, P. T., & Meisel, C. J. (1982). Teacher-physician interaction in the treatment of children with behavioral disorders. *International Journal of Partial Hospitalization, 1,* 271–277.

Sleator, E. K., & von Neumann, A. (1974). Methylphenidate in the treatment of hyperkinetic children. *Clinical Pediatrics, 13,* 19–24.

Slimmer, L. W., & Brown, R. T. (1985). Parents' decision-making process in medication administration for control of hyperactivity. *Journal of School Health, 55,* 221–225.

Solomons, G. (1973). Drug therapy: Initiation and follow-up. *Annals of the New York Academy of Sciences, 205,* 335–344.

Sprafkin, J., & Gadow, K. (1987). An observational study of emotionally disturbed and learning-disabled children in school settings. *Journal of Abnormal Child Psychology, 15,* 393–408.

Sprafkin, J., Gadow, K. D., & Grayson, P. (1987). Effects of viewing cartoons on the behavior of learning disabled children. *Journal of Child Psychology and Psychiatry, 28,* 387–398.

Sprafkin, J., Gadow, K. D., & Grayson, P. (1988). Effects of cartoons on emotionally disturbed children's behavior in school settings. *Journal of Child Psychology and Psychiatry, 29,* 91–99.

Sprafkin, J., Grayson, P., Gadow, K., Nolan, E. E., & Paolicelli, L. M. (1986). *Code for Observing Social Activity (COSA).* State University of New York, Department of Psychiatry, Stony Brook, New York.

Sprague, R. L., Barnes, K. R., & Werry, J. S. (1970). Methylphenidate and thioridazine: Learning, reaction time, activity, and classroom behavior in disturbed children. *American Journal of Orthopsychiatry, 40,* 615–628.

Sprague, R. L., & Sleator, E. K. (1973). Effects of psychopharmacologic agents on learning disorders. *Pediatric Clinics of North America, 20,* 719–735.

Sprague, R. L., & Sleator, E. K. (1975). What is the proper dose of stimulant drugs in children? *International Journal of Mental Health, 4,* 75–104.

Sprague, R. L., & Sleator, E. K. (1977). Methylphenidate in hyperkinetic children: Differences in dose effects on learning and social behavior. *Science, 198,* 1274–1276.

Sprague, R. L., & Werry, J. S. (1971). Methodology of psychopharmacological studies with the retarded. In N. R. Ellis (Ed.), *International review of research in mental retardation* (Vol. 5, pp. 147–219). New York: Academic Press.

Sulzbacher, S. I. (1973). Behavior analysis of drug effects in the classroom. In G. Semb (Ed.), *Behavior analysis and education-1972* (pp. 37–52). Lawrence: University of Kansas.

Sverd, J., Gadow, K. D., & Paolicelli, L. M. (1989). Methylphenidate treatment of attention-deficit hyperactivity disorder in boys with Tourette's syndrome. *Journal of the American Academy of Child and Adolescent Psychiatry, 28,* 574–579.

Swanson, J. M., & Kinsbourne, M. (1978). Should you use stimulants to treat the hyperkinetic child? *Modern Medicine, 46,* 71–80.

Towns, A. J., Singh, N. N., & Beale, I. L. (1984). Reliability of observations in a double- and single-blind drug study: An experimental analysis. In K. D. Gadow (Ed.), *Advances in learning and behavioral disabilities* (Vol. 3, pp. 215–240). Greenwich, CT: JAI Press.

Varley, C. K., & Trupin, E. W. (1983). Double-blind assessment of stimulant medication for attention deficit disorder: A model for clinical application. *American Journal of Orthopsychiatry, 53,* 542–547.

Weithorn, C. J., & Ross, R. (1975). Who monitors medication? *Journal of Learning Disabilities, 8,* 458–461.

Wolraich, M., Drummond, T., Salomon, M. K., O'Brien, M. L., & Sivage, C. (1978). Effects of methylphenidate alone and in combination with behavior modification procedures on the behavior and academic performance of hyperactive children. *Journal of Abnormal Child Psychology, 6,* 149–161.

Yellin, A. M., & Greenberg, L. M. (1981). Attention-deficit disorder: Monitored data-based assessment and treatment. *Minnesota Medicine, 64,* 487–490.

APPENDIX 10.A

Classroom Observation Code

I. *Interference* (I): This category is intended to detect any verbal or physical behaviors or noises that are disturbing to others. The object is to detect discrete and distinct behavior that does not necessarily persist and does not involve the forecul manipulation of objects.

A. Interruption of the teacher or another student during a lesson or quiet work period.

Examples:

1. Calling out during a lesson when the teacher or another student has the floor (includes ooh's and ahh's when raising hand).

2. Initiating discussion with another child during a work period.

NOTE:

(a) "Interference" is coded immediately within the interval in which it first occurs.

(b) If the child initiates a conversation that overlaps two intervals, code I only in the first interval.

(c) If conversation stops and then starts anew in the next interval, code that interval as I if it is initiated by the target child.

(d) If the child engages in a conversation overlapping two intervals that is initiated by another child, do not code I in either interval.

(e) Do not score the child as I if there is uncertainty as to whether the child initiated conversation or is only responding to another child.

(f) Do not score the child as I if there is any uncertainty as to whether or not a sound (e.g., "ooh") was made by the child.

B. Production of sounds

1. Vocalizations: for example, screams whistles, calls across room. Include operant coughs, sneezes, or loud yawns. 2. The child makes noises other than vocalization through the use of materials available: tapping ruler, foot tapping, hand clapping, and so on.

NOTE: Do not code I if a sound is made accidentally (e.g., the child drops a book, knocks over a chair, etc.).

Adapted from H. Abikoff and R. Gittelman, "Classroom Observation Code: A Modification of the Stony Brook Code," *Psychopharmacology Bulletin, 21,* 901–909, 1985.

C. Annoying Behavior—nonverbal interruption. The child interrupts another child during a teacher-directed or independent work lesson.

Examples:

1. Tapping lightly or making gentle physical movements or gestures toward another child.

2. Sitting on another's desk when that child is present at the desk.

3. Moving or lifting another's desk when the owner is present.

D. Clowning. The following behaviors are to be coded as I:

1. Mimicking the teacher or another child.

2. Kicking an object across the floor.

3. Engaging in or organizing games and other inappropriate activities during a work period (e.g., playing kickball in the class, throwing and catching a ball).

4. Showing off his or her own work when not called on by the teacher.

5. Making animal imitations.

6. Calling out a wildly inappropriate answer or making an obviously inappropriate public statement.

7. Shooting paper clips, airplanes, spitballs, etc. (If aimed at someone, this behavior is coded as "Physical Aggression Child," (PAc).

8. Standing on a desk, chair, or table when not requested to do so by the teacher, or in any other inappropriate situation.

9. Posturing (child acts to characterize an action, another object, or person).

10. Dancing in the classroom.

11. Play-acting

12. Making mock threats—if this does not occur in a clowning situation, then it is coded instead as "Nonphysical Aggression Child" (NPAc).

NOTE: If clowning involving vigorous gross motor movements (e.g., running, dancing) occurs while the child is out of his or her chair, then code both I and "Motor" (M).

II. *Off Task* (OFF): This category is intended to monitor behaviors where the child, after initiating the appropriate task-relevant behavior, attends to stimuli other than the assigned work. This includes manipulation and/or attending to objects, people, or parts of the body to the total exclusion of the task for three seconds.

Examples:

1. The child plays with a pencil for 3 seconds without visual orientation toward the assigned task.

2. The child engages in extended conversation while he or she is supposed to be working.

NOTE:

(a) When the child is doing something under the desk or where the observer cannot see, and is not attending to the task, assume it is inappropriate and code OFF.

(b) If the teacher is conducting a lesson at the blackboard, such that the task requires the child to look at the teacher or the board, score the child as OFF if he or she does not look at the teacher and/or the board for 3 full seconds.

(c) If the teacher or another student is lecturing, reading a story, issuing instructions, and so on, such that the child's task is to listen to the speaker, then code OFF if the child, by his or her behavior, indicates that he or she is not listening (e.g., head down on the desk, doodling in book, etc.). Do not code OFF if the child looks at the speaker.

(d) Do not code OFF if the child shows any visual orientation to the task. Do not code OFF if there is uncertainty as to his or her visual orientation.

(e) Do not code OFF if the child, by his or her behavior, indicates that he or she is listening (e.g., the child looks at the speaker, the child makes a verbal statement related to the speaker's subject matter).

(f) Do not code OFF if the child plays with or manipulates an object while attending to the task.

III. *Noncompliance* (NC): This category is intended to monitor behaviors that reflect a failure on the part of the child to follow teacher instructions or being reprimanded or reminded to follow an instruction. It is coded if the child fails to initiate appropriate behavior in response to a command or request from the teacher. This is to be distinguished from "OFF-Task" (OFF), which is coded when the child, after initiating task-relevant behavior, ceases this task-relevant behavior. Noncompliance includes either a reprimand by the teacher or a prompt for on-task behavior; this includes teacher repeating an instruction if it is intended to prompt on-task behavior.

Examples: After a command has been given by the teacher (e.g., "Copy the words on the board into your notebook"), the child has 1 full interval after the interval in which the command was given to initiate the request. If the child has not complied, begin coding NC and continue coding NC for each full interval that the child fails to initiate the task.

NOTE:

(a) If before initiating the task the child leaves the classroom for more than 1 full interval without permission, code NC and cross out the interval box. Continue coding NC as long as the child remains out of the room.

(b) The teacher will often issue commands that are not task related, but are instead related to the handling of materials (e.g., "Put down your pencils," "Put away your book"). If the child has not complied by the end of the first full interval following the interval in which the command was given, then code that interval as NC. Do not continue coding NC. If the teacher repeats the same command, code NC again and continue coding until the child complies.

IV. *Motor* (M): There are several aspects to this category:

A. Restlessness and fidgeting—buttock movements and rocking movements of the child when in his or her seat and/or buttock movements while in nonerect positions while out of his or her seat.

(i) The child engages in in-seat movements such that there is an observable movement of the lower buttock(s), that is, that part of the buttock(s) that is in contact with the seat of the chair.

Examples: The following pertain to movements of one or both buttocks.

1. Sliding in seat.

2. Twisting, turning, wiggling—coded only when accompanied by buttock movement.

3. Lifting one or both buttocks off the seat.

4. Buttock movement while kneeling or squatting in seat.

(ii) The child produces rocking movements of his or her body and/or the chair. Body rocking movements are defined as repetitive movements (at least two complete back and forth movements) where the child moves from the waist up in a back and forth manner. Movements of the chair are also coded when the child lifts two chair legs off the floor.

NOTE:

(a) Do not code if the child makes just one forward leaning movement. However, if this movement is accompanied by an observable buttock movement, then M should be coded.

(b) Code as M any movement which takes the child from a seated position into a kneeling, squatting, or crouching position, either in or out of seat.

(c) If the child is kneeling in or out of the seat, or leaning over a desk or table, then code as M any observable movements of the lower and/or upper buttocks, that is, that area from the upper thigh to the hip.

(d) If the child goes from a standing to a kneeling or squatting position, code this as M.

(e) Do not code M if the physical set-up is such that the child must move in order to work on a task. There are two specific situations where M should not be coded. (1) The position of the child's desk requires that he or she must move in order to work on a task (e.g., the child faces the side of the room and the blackboard is in front). In this situation, the child must move his or her buttocks in order to copy from the board. (2) While working on a task that requires his or her visual attention (e.g., copying from the board, watching the teacher), the child's view is obstructed, thereby requiring him or her to move in order to maintain visual contact.

(f) Do not code M if the child moves from a standing or kneeling position to a sitting position in the chair.

B. Motor activity which results in the child's leaving his or her seat and/or engaging in vigorous motor activity.

(i) Motor activity that results in the child's leaving his or her seat and standing on one or both legs (on the floor, chair, or desk) in an erect or semierect position such that the child's body from the waist up is at least at a 135-degree angle with the floor.

NOTE:

(a) Do not code M when the child has permission, specific or implied, to leave his or her seat (e.g., to sharpen a pencil, throw refuse away, get materials, go to the board, go to the teacher's desk, etc.). If the child leaves his or her seat without permission, then code M.

(b) Do not code M if the physical set-up is such that the child must move in order to work on a task. For example, while working on a task that requires visual attention (e.g., copying from the board, watching a demonstration), the child's view is obstructed, thereby requiring him or her to stand up in order to maintain visual contact. If there is uncertainty as to whether or not the child had to stand up, then code M.

(ii) Child engages in vigorous motor activity while not seated at his or her desk, or when the child leaves his or her seat in a sudden, abrupt, or impulsive manner.

Examples:

1. Jumping up out of seat.
2. Running away from seat.
3. Running in the classroom.
4. Crawling across the floor.
5. Twirling.
6. Acrobatics.
7. Swinging between two seats or desks.

V. *Physical Aggression* (PA): This category is intended to measure physical aggression directed at another person, or destruction of other's property. This behavior is coded regardless of the accuracy of the intended assault.

A. *Physical Aggression Child* (PAc): The child makes a forceful movement directed at another child, either directly or by utilizing a material object as an extension of the hand.

Examples:

1. Blocking someone with arms or body, tripping, kicking, or hitting another child.
2. Throwing objects at another child.
3. Pinching or biting another child.

NOTE:

(a) In all of the above examples, even if the child misses his or her goal, the behavior should be coded as PAc.

(b) Code PAc even when the physical aggression is initiated by another child and the target child defends his or her self.

B. *Physical Aggression Adult* (PAa):

Any of the above aggressive behaviors directed toward an adult.

VI. *Solicitation of Teacher* (S): This category monitors behaviors directed toward the teacher. It is important to note that this behavior is target-child initiated.

A. Behaviors directed at obtaining the teacher's attention.

Examples:

1. Leaving seat and going up to the teacher (this would be coded as S and "motor" (M); if the child speaks to the teacher, "Interference" (I) is also coded.
2. Raising hand.
3. Calling out to the teacher.

NOTE:

(a) These behaviors are coded as S whether or not the teacher recognizes the child.

(b) When a child calls out to the teacher by mentioning the teacher's name, or directs a question or statement specifically to the teacher while the teacher is attending to another child or addressing the class, then the behavior is coded as both S and "Interference" (I).

(c) If the child says "ooh," "ahh," and so on while raising his or her hand in response to a teacher's question, code this as "Interference" (I) but not S.

(d) If the observation begins while a teacher-interaction is taking place, assume that the teacher initiated the interaction and do not code S.

(e) If the child raises his or her hand in order to solicit the teacher, and keeps the hand raised for more than one interval, S is coded only in the first interval that it occurred.

(f) "Solicitation" and "Interference" (I) are coded if the child calls out an answer to the teacher when another child has the floor.

(g) S is not coded if the child raises his or her hand in response to a teacher's question.

(h) Solicitation is not coded if the child calls out in response to a teacher's question.

VII. *Nonphysical Aggression* (NPA):

1. *Nonphysical Aggression Child* (NPAc):

A. Destruction of other's materials or possessions, or school property.

Examples:

1. Tearing or crumpling other's work.
2. Breaking crayons, pencils, or pens of other children.
3. Misusing other's books (ripping out pages, writing in them, etc.).

4. Writing on another child or an another child's work.

NOTE:

(a) code NPAc even if the owner of the material is not at his or her desk.

(b) If the child engages in continuous destructive behavior then code NPAc only in the first interval that it occurs. If the child interrupts this destructive behavior and then returns to it, then code NPAc anew.

B. Verbalizations or physical gestures of children that are abusive or threatening. Encompasses all negative, noncontact communication. Includes stealing or taking the possessions of another person when the possessions are not on the victim's body.

C. Observed youth inflicts physical damage on an object by hitting, throwing, and so on. (Note: If the object is thrown at another person this is coded as physical aggression).

2. *Nonphysical Aggression Adult* (NPAa): Any of the above aggressive acts directed toward an adult. Includes destruction of school property.

Examples:

1. Writing on a school desk.
2. Writing in a school textbook.
3. Answering back to the teacher.

APPENDIX 10.B

Code for Observing Social Activity

I. *Appropriate Social* (APS): All appropriate verbal and nonverbal communication with peer or adult; playing a child-initiated game with another child or group of children.

Examples:

1. Child is talking to another child.
2. Child affectionately touches another child.
3. Child asks the teacher to help him or her.
4. Child is playing with another child in the sandbox.
5. Child is cooperating with another child by taking turns or by jointly building something.

© J. Sprafkin, P. Grayson, K. D. Gadow, E. E. Nolan, and L. M. Paolicelli, 1986. Reprinted by permission.

6. Child pats another child on the back in a congratulatory gesture.

NOTE:

(a) APS does *not* include parallel play. For example, if two children are using the same pool of blocks to build separate structures and are not communicating with one another, that would *not* be coded at all.

(b) Do *not* code as APS child's spontaneous verbalizations that are not directed at anyone in particular (i.e., child is talking to self).

(c) Do *not* code as APS if child is merely participating in a teacher initiated group activity (e.g., arts and crafts, kickball, storytime) unless s/he interacts verbally.

(d) Code as APS child's verbal replies to teacher's questions even if several youngsters reply simultaneously to a question posed to the whole class.

(e) The only nonverbal APS are (1) affectionate touches, and (2) cooperative play initiated by the children. Do *not* code as APS when a child complies nonverbally to a teacher request (e.g., "Hold this," "Clean up"). Do not code as APS if child is merely listening to another person.

II. *Physical Aggression* (PAg): Observed child hits, punches, bites, pushes, or kick another using body part or other implement and victim responds either neutrally or negatively (strikes back, grimaces, complains). Physical force used appropriately as part of play (e.g., football, wrestling, etc.) should be coded as Play Aggression (PLAg) unless the physical force exceeds acceptable limits, which is operationalized a negative reaction by the "victim."

Examples:

1. Observed youth impedes the motion of another youth with arm or other body part.
2. Observed youth throws something (e.g., sand, paper, toy) at another person. (*NOTE:* Object does *not* have to hit another child.)
3. Observed youth trips another child.
4. Observed youth punches another child even if he or she only taps child gently after winding up for a punch.
5. Observed youth jabs another child who does not appear to respond.
6. Child blows straw wrapper into face of nearby child.

NOTE:

(a) Tapping someone to get his or her attention is not PAg, but poking or jabbing to get attention is coded as PAg.

(b) If a child hurts another child accidentally, do *not* code at all.

A. *Physical Aggression Child* (PAc): Physical aggression directed toward another child.

(i) *Physical Aggression Child Initiated* (PAci): Physical aggression toward another child that is initiated by the target child.

(ii) *Physical Aggression Child Retaliatory* (PAcr): Target child responds to physical aggression initiated by another child, with physical aggression toward that child.

B. *Physical Aggression Adult* (PAa): Physical aggression directed toward an adult.

III. *Play Aggression* (PLAg): Physical force used against another person in the context of play in which the aggressee is clearly participating and responds as though the aggressor is behaving appropriately.

Examples:

1. Observed youth is playfighting with a willing peer during recess.

2. Observed youth is arm wrestling (or thumb wrestling) during lunch.

3. Observed youth sneaks up from behind and covers another child's eyes with his or her hands. The child giggles and tries to guess who is there.

4. Observed youth tickles another child who responds by trying to tickle back.

5. Observed youth pushes another child who responds by pushing back playfully.

NOTES:

a. Playfighting which is engaged in by two willing participants who respond playfully is coded as PLAg. The interaction involves PAg if either (1) one of the participants wants to withdraw and the other child keeps fighting, or (2) at least one of the children gets angry and the interaction no longer appears like play.

IV. *Verbal Aggression/Verbal Negative* (VAg): All negative verbal behavior. Includes attempts to hurt another person by nonphysical means such as verbally threatening, *tattling*, teasing, or name calling.

Examples:

1. Youth curses another person.

2. Youth teases another person by saying "You're stupid."

3. Youth responds negatively to request to share or do something.

4. Youth yells at another while tantruming.

5. Youth tattles on another child even if teacher requested information.

6. Observed child attempts to disrupt group activity in a verbal manner.

7. Youth instructs another child to hurt someone.

8. Youth threatens another child even if in the context of sticking up for a friend or for herself or himself (e.g., "Stop picking on her (him) (me). Pick on someone your own size.")

9. Child makes a negative statement to a peer or adult (e.g., complains, whines, teases, or curses).

NOTES:

a. VAg includes only words, not animal noises, grunts, etc.

b. Talking loudly is not sufficient to code as VAg.

A. *Verbal Aggression Child* (VAc): Verbal aggression directed toward another child.

(i). *Verbal Aggression Child Initiate* (VAci): Verbal aggression toward another child that is initiated by the target child.

(ii). *Verbal Aggression Child Respond* (VAcr): Target child responds to verbal aggression of another with verbal aggression.

B. *Verbal Aggression Adult* (VAa): Verbal aggression directed toward an adult.

V. *Symbolic Aggression* (SAg): Youth attempts to hurt or threaten another person or interfere with an individual or group activity in a nonverbal and noncontact manner. Included is chasing another child, waving fist in a threatening gesture, giving dirty looks, sticking out tongue, cheating in a game. Encompasses all negative, nonverbal, noncontact communication. Includes stealing or taking the possessions of another person when the possessions are not on victim's body.

Examples:

1. Observed youth chases another youth.

2. Observed youth gives aide dirty looks.

3. Observed youth makes animal noises to annoy another child.

4. Youth takes someone else's lunch

5. Youth takes someone else's art work (code as SAg) and ruins it (code as OAg).

6. Youth teases another child by taking his or her toy and holding it out of reach.

7. Child points his or her finger in a threatening gesture toward another child.

8. Youth annoys another child by deliberately putting his or her feet on the other child's toy.

9. Child turns off the lights in the classroom as a playful prank.

10. Child hides from teacher.

11. Observed child puts opened perfume bottle right up to another child's nose to annoy the child. (Note: If bottle touches child, code as PAg).

12. Child points his or her finger like a gun and says, "Bang-Bang."

NOTE:

a. If children are running and it's not clear whether they are just running around or actually chasing, wait until it's clear and then code. If they're running, code as APS; if they're chasing (even if part of a game), code as SAg.

b. If observed child is impeding a game by holding onto bat, ball, or other item, it could be coded as PAg or SAg depending on position of plaything. If plaything is being held by another child and observed child grabs or holds it, code as PAg or PLAg. If plaything is not being held by anyone and observed child withholds it from the group, code as SAg.

VI. *Object Aggression* (OAg): Observed youth inflicts physical damage on any object by hitting, throwing, and so on. (Note: If the object is thrown at another person this is coded as Physical Aggression).

Examples:

1. Youth throws crayon off desk.

2. Child chews on toy.

3. Observed youth destroys materials or possessions.

4. Child takes someone's cookie (SAg) and mashes it (OAg).

5. Child steps on ants.

6. Child picks leaves off tree or picks flowers.

7. Child kicks a chair or desk.

8. Child plays with his or her lunch and makes a mess of it.

9. Child crumples up paper containing assignment. (*Note:* If object is thrown at another person, code as PAg.)

VII. *Noncompliance* (NonC): (1) Observed youth is instructed or asked by aide or teacher directly and makes no effort to comply with the result by the end of the next 30-second period. (2) Teacher reprimands child or reminds child to follow earlier instructions.

Examples:

1. Aide instructs youth to clean up and observed youth does not initiate the requested action by the end of the next 30-second period. (NonC in the next 30-second interval.)

2. Teacher reminds child of a rule because she or he is breaking it. (Code NonC immediately.)

3. Teacher reprimands observed child, "Stop that, get away from there." (Code NonC immediately.)

NOTE:

a. We are considering only directives spoken to observed child (i.e., we're ignoring directives announced to the whole class). For example, if the teacher announces, "No talking," and observed child talks to neighbor, do *not* code NonC unless teacher reprimands child for talking.

b. code NonC in the present interval if teacher reprimands child.

c. Code NonC in the next 30-second interval if child was instructed to do something and makes no effort to do so by the end of the next interval. (For example, teacher tells a child to start cleaning up and she or he makes no effort to do so by the end of the next 30-second period.)

d. Code NonC once if child has not done what he was instructed to do.

VIII. *No Social Interaction:* Child is alone and does not interact, or is involved in parallel play without communication during the whole 30-second interval. Indicate by putting a slash through observation box.

CHAPTER 11

PHARMACOLOGICAL TREATMENT OF ATTENTION DEFICIT HYPERACTIVITY DISORDER

Josephine Elia
Judith L. Rapoport
James Kirby

Since Charles Bradley (1937) first reported that benzedrine helped behavior-disordered children, the efficacy of stimulants has been well established. Other medications have also been tried in children with attention deficit hyperactivity disorder (ADHD) in attempts to find alternative treatments, to gain a better understanding of the mechanism of action of these drugs, and possibly to learn the pathophysiology of ADHD. However, the stimulants, methylphenidate (MP), dextroamphetamine (d-amph), and pemoline, remain the drugs of choice for treating most cases of ADHD. They increase attention and reduce motor restlessness, impulsivity, aggression, and socially inappropriate behavior. Other medications such as the antidepressants have decreased symptoms; however, improvement has not always been sustained and side effects are usually more troublesome. Nonetheless, they can be of benefit to some children.

The decision to use medication is a clinical one based on the severity of symptoms as well as the ability of the child, parents, and school to cope with the problems of behavior. Given the complexity as well as the wide-ranging effects of behavioral problems in ADHD children, medication should be used only after careful diagnosis, with continuous monitoring, and within the context of a multimodal treatment plan (Dulcan, 1986). This chapter, however, is limited to drug treatment of ADHD, with other aspects of diagnosis and treatment covered elsewhere in this volume.

STIMULANTS

Methylphenidate and Dextroamphetamine

Methylphenidate (MP) and dextroamphetamine (d-amph) are the drugs of choice for the treatment of ADHD, followed by pemoline. Methylphenidate is a piperidine derivative, structurally related to amphetamine (see Table 11.1), which is readily absorbed after oral administration, reaching peak plasma concentration in about 2 hours, with a

Table 11.1. Structure and Dosages of Medications

Drug	Chemical Structure	Starting Dose	Max Dose Daily	Dose Range (mg/kg)
Methylphenidate (Ritalin)	OCH_3 / $O=C$ / CH, H (ring structures)	5 mg b.i.d.	90 mg	0.5–1.25 mg/kg b.i.d.
Dextroamphetamine (Dexedrine)	(ring)–CH_2–CH–CH_3 / NH_2	5 mg q.d. or b.i.d. (age 6 or older) 2.5 mg q.d. (ages 3–5)	45 mg	0.2–0.6 mg/kg b.i.d.
Pemoline (Cylert)	(ring) O, =NH, O N	37.5 mg q.d.	112.5 mg	0.5–2.0 mg/kg q.d.

half-life of 2 to 3 hours. Serum levels seem to correspond to the time course of clinical effects (Gualtieri, Wargin & Kanoy, 1982). Dextroamphetamine (d-alpha-methylphenethylamine) is structurally similar to norepinephrine. It is also well absorbed orally, achieves peak plasma levels in children in 2 to 3 hours, and has a half-life of 4 to 6 hours (with large individual variations) (Brown, Ebert, Mikkelson, Buchsbaum, & Bunney, 1979), although subjective clinical effects peak earlier than plasma levels, at approximately 1 to 3 hours (Ebert, van Kammen, & Murphy, 1976). It has central nervous system (CNS) stimulant and peripheral alpha and beta sympathomimetic action that may include elevations of systolic and diastolic blood pressure and weak bronchodilator and respiratory stimulant action. Both of these drugs are eliminated primarily by urinary excretion. Methylphenidate is mostly deesterified to ritalinic acid, with virtually none of the parent drug being found in the urine, whereas dextroamphetamine is metabolized by oxidative deamination to benzoic and hippuric acid, and one-third to one-half of the dose is excreted unchanged in the urine (Faraj et al., 1974).

Dosages for the stimulants for children aged 6 or older are given on Table 11.1. The usual beginning dosage of d-amph is 5 mg daily or twice a day, for MP it is 5 mg twice a day and for pemoline 37.5 mg daily. The medication is increased gradually every three to five days (weekly for pemoline) until therapeutic effects are achieved. Doses of up to 1.5 mg/kg/day for d-amph and 2.5 mg/kg/day for MP have been used (Borcherding, Keysor, Cooper, & Rapoport, 1989; Elia, Borcherding, Potter, Mefford, Rapoport, & Keysor, (1990).

The timing of doses is based on duration of drug action, which is relatively short for the standard preparations of methylphenidate and dextroamphetamine. Long-acting preparations of both of these drugs are available. Reports of their efficacy are few and conflicting, but Pelham et al. (*Pediatrics*, in press), in a placebo-controlled, double-blind, within-subject study, found the long-acting compounds (S-R Ritalin, pemoline, and Dexedrine spansule) to be comparable in efficacy to standard methylphenidate in a short-term treatment setting.

While both methylphenidate and dextroamphetamine produce striking clinical improvement, some clinical differences have been elucidated in a study comparing both drugs within the same population.

Methylphenidate, for example, was found to produce a greater decrease in motor activity than dextroamphetamine at supposedly comparable doses (Borcherding, Keysor, Cooper, & Rapoport, 1989). Individual children were also found to have a variable response to methylphenidate and dextroamphetamine, indicating that both of these stimulants should be tried, especially if optimal response is not obtained with the first one, or if adverse effects are severe. In a research setting, where compliance was assured and both medications were tried in a wide range of doses, most hyperactive children were found to respond to one or both (Elia, Borcherding, Rapoport, & Keysor, 1991).

Monitoring the efficacy of the medication is essential and can be done only by obtaining regular teacher and parental feedback, together with personal contact with the child and parent to assess both positive and negative drug effects. The dosage must also be reevaluated as the child grows. Weekend and summer "drug holidays" for the stimulants are routine, but exceptions can be made on an individual basis when behavioral problems at home are prominent and these improve dramatically on medication. The drugs should be discontinued at least once a year, preferably when teacher ratings are available, to assess the need for continued treatment. Following serum drug levels is not clinically useful.

The decision to discontinue stimulants is a clinical one. If treatment is just being initiated, lack of improvement after 2 weeks at maximum dosage of dextroamphetamine or methylphenidate, or 5 weeks of pemoline is indication to stop treatment with these preparations. Dosage can usually be reduced to minimize side effects, though more severe adverse effects might necessitate ending drug treatment, even when that treatment has been effective otherwise.

Even though medications significantly reduce the disruptive symptoms of ADHD, and children may be less hyperactive, more attentive, and less impulsive, they may still function poorly with respect to mood and social functioning. Combining medication with other treatments is therefore essential.

Stimulant response is not diagnostic of ADHD. Rapoport and colleagues (1978; 1980) demonstrated similar drug effects on motor activity and cognitive tasks in normal groups of boys and adult males.

The pharmacological mechanisms by which these drugs produce their clinical effects are unclear. Preclinical studies have shown that the stimulants both increase the release and inhibit the reuptake of dopamine and norepinephrine (Kuczenski, 1983). Amphetamine, and to a lesser extent methylphenidate, also have a weak monoamine oxidase (MAO) inhibitory activity (Axelrod, 1970).

Results of biochemical correlative studies in ADHD children have shown a decrease in urinary norepinephrine and more consistently its metabolite 3-methoxy-4-hydroxyphenylglycol (MHPG) following use of dextroamphetamine (Zametkin, Rapoport, Murphy, & Linnoila, 1985) but not methylphenidate (Elia et al., 1990; Zametkin & Hamburger, 1988). Homovanillic acid (HVA), the major metabolite of dopamine, does not seem to be significantly affected by either drug. Beneficial therapeutic effects of methylphenidate were not found to be accompanied by any alterations in platelet imipramine binding sites, thus minimizing the drug's therapeutic effects and possibly the pathophysiology of the disorder (Weizman, Bernhout, Weitz, Tyano, & Rehavi, 1988). Therefore, attempts at uncovering changes in a single neurotransmitter system are pointing to a much more complex mode of action. This direction is further indicated by the clinical effects produced by these drugs, whereby improvement on motor activity has been found to be independent from that on attention (Porrino, Rapoport, Behar, Ismond, & Bunney, 1983), and cognitive and behavioral improvements may also be independently produced from each other (Gittelman-Klein & Klein, 1976).

Brain-imaging studies may prove to be more fruitful. In a recent study, using xenon 133 inhalation and emission tomography to study cerebral blood flow distribution, hypoperfusion in the striatal regions of the brain was found in ADHD children. The administration of methylphenidate increased blood flow in these regions, and this increase correlated with definite clinical improvement (Lou, Henriksen, Bruhn, Borner, & Nielsen, 1989). Zametkin et al. (1985), using positron emission tomography, found cerebral glucose metabolism to be globally depressed by 8.2% in hyperactives, with the most significant difference occurring in the left premotor cortex.

Pemoline

Pemoline is a noneuphorigenic psychostimulant with actions similar to those of the amphetamines and methylphenidate, including CNS and respiratory stimulation and weak sympathomimetic activity. It has some advantages over the other preparations, such as once-daily dosing and lower abuse potential, but in some studies has been found to have relative disadvantages, such as slower onset of therapeutic effect and slightly lower effectiveness (Gittelman & Kanner, 1986). One recent study, however, found no significant difference in either the onset of its therapeutic effect or its overall efficacy when compared with other psychostimulants (Pelham, Swanson, Bender, & Wilson, 1980; Pelham et al., in press). Pemoline has been used in treating ADHD in the United States since 1975, with well-documented success (Conners & Taylor, 1980; Conners, Taylor, Meo, Kurtz, & Fournier, 1972; Stephens et al., 1984), but it is used in only about 2% of children medicated for ADHD (Safer & Krager, 1984).

Pemoline is an oxazolidinone derivative stimulant with a mean half-life of 7 hours in children and a wide variation ranging from 2 to 12 hours. This period is significantly shorter than the mean of 12 hours previously reported in adults and is probably due to the decrease in total body clearance of the drug with increasing age, a factor which should be considered during long-term drug therapy (Collier, Soldin, Swanson, Macleod, Weinberg, & Rochefort, 1985; Sallee, Stiller, Perel, & Bates, 1985). Pemoline and its metabolites are cleared almost totally by the kidney, with almost half the drug excreted unchanged in the urine and the rest metabolized in part by the liver to metabolites with much lower CNS stimulant activity. Cylert (made by Abbott Laboratories) is the only commercial preparation currently available. It has good oral absorption and achieves peak serum concentrations within 2 to 4 hours. As with the elimination half-life, there is wide variability in both the serum concentration following a given dose and the optimum therapeutic serum concentration. Thus, routine monitoring of pemoline serum concentration is not useful, and dosing regimens must be determined individually by clinical response (Collier et al., 1985).

The usual initial dosage of pemoline in children 6 years and older is 37.5 mg, administered as a single daily dose each morning. The dose may be increased by 18.7 mg at weekly intervals until full therapeutic response is achieved. The usual effective dosage ranges from 56.25 to 75 mg per day, with a maximum dosage of 112.5 mg daily in children. Although pemoline has been used safely in children under 6, there have been no controlled studies to confirm its safety or efficacy in this younger patient population. As opposed to methylphenidate and the amphetamines, therapeutic response to pemoline has been reported to be gradual, often taking up to 3–4 weeks before its beneficial effects become evident. However, there is increasing evidence that the onset of its action is similar to that of other stimulants (Pelham et al., in press). If the desired response is not achieved within 5 weeks at adequate dosages, treatment with pemoline should be discontinued. The response to treatment should be monitored with the usual objective measures, involving parents and teachers in assessing drug response, and with occasional drug holidays to verify the need for continued pharmacotherapy.

In a retrospective study, ADHD children with low whole-blood serotonin levels (below 90 ng/ml) were found to respond to pemoline while children with higher levels (above 100 ng/ml) did not benefit (Saul & Ashby, 1986). This finding however, needs to be replicated.

Pemoline's potential for abuse is very low, as confirmed by animal studies and clinical research (Langer, Sweeney, Bartenbach, Davis, & Menander, 1986). A review of the literature revealed no published case reports of euphoria, abuse, dependence, or withdrawal (with the exception of rare ingestions of high doses of pemoline by adults with a history of abusing other drugs). Following such excessive use, irritability, mental depression, and craving have occurred with abrupt cessation, but there are only four reported withdrawal reactions in the literature (Langer et al., 1986).

The mechanisms of action remain unknown. A decrease in turnover of brain catecholamines is suggested by preclinical studies (Moline & Orsingher, 1981). Zametkin, Linnoila, Karoum, & Sallee (1986) report no changes in urinary catecholamine excretion in a small sample of hyperactive boys, while phenylethylamine (PEA) and 5-hydroxy indoleacetic acid (5-HIAA) were significantly reduced and serotonin excretion was unchanged.

Adverse Effects of Stimulants

The most common short-term adverse effects of stimulants are anorexia and insomnia. Less common are weight loss, abdominal pain, nausea, headache, tremors, drowsiness, tachycardia, mydriasis, and dryness of mouth. These are generally short-lived and rarely require that the medication be stopped.

Suppression of weight and height has been found in short-term treatment with MP, d-amph, and pemoline (Gross, 1973; Gualtieri et al., 1982; Safer, Allen, & Barr, 1972). Decreases in height and weight percentiles with chronic treatment have been reported by some studies (Greenhill, 1981; Mattes & Gittelman, 1983) and not supported by others (Hechtman et al., 1984a & b). In a study by Gittelman-Klein Landa, Mattes, & Klein (1988), hyperactive children receiving long-term methylphenidate treatment were taken off medication during the summer months, and their height and weight were compared to a similar group of children whose treatment was not interrupted. After one summer, only weight was found to be higher in the group taken off medication. In contrast, two summers off medication led to a significantly greater growth rate. The ultimate stature of this same sample of children, however, was not found to be compromised (Gittelman-Klein & Mannuzza, 1988). These results indicate that if stimulant treatment is interrupted, there is no clinically significant decrement in height during adolescence due to long-term stimulant treatment in childhood. The physiological mechanisms underlying the temporary deleterious effect of stimulant treatment on height have not yet been identified.

Psychostimulants have been reported to exacerbate tics and other dyskinetic movements, and to precipitate symptoms of Tourette's disorder (Bachman, 1981; Mitchell & Matthews, 1980; Sallee, Stiller, Perel, & Everett, 1989; Sleator, 1980). Choreoathetoid movements of the face, limbs, and trunk have been reported both after acute exposure to the drugs and in chronically treated patients (Sallee et al., 1989).

Some patients receiving pemoline develop mild hepatic dysfunction, which appears to be a delayed hypersensitivity reaction and is reversible upon discontinuing the drug. This reaction is evident in elevations of SGOT (serum aspartate transaminase), SGPT (alanine transaminase), LDH (lactic dehydrogenase), and alkaline phosphatase that may occur after several months of therapy. Although there have been two reported deaths secondary to hepatic failure in patients being treated with pemoline, one of these cases occurred in a patient with preexisting primary biliary cirrhosis, and the other followed an overdose of pemoline (Jaffe, 1989). Nevertheless, monitoring hepatic function both prior to treatment and periodically during treatment is prudent.

Dysphoria has been reported in children receiving both dextroamphetamine and methylphenidate (Barkley, 1977; Bender & Cottington, 1942; Ounsted, 1955; Weiss, Minde, Douglas, Werry, & Sykes, 1971). Farmer (1983) reported an adolescent who developed significant depressive symptoms and escape from dexamethasone suppression following a trial of pemoline, conditions that remitted when the medication was stopped. In contrast, Brown, Borden, Spunt, & Medenis (1985) reported a case of depression following pemoline and methylphenidate withdrawal in a hyperactive 8-year-old child. In adolescents, methylphenidate has been reported to reduce subjective ratings of dysphoria (Klorman, Coons, & Borgstedt, 1987).

Mania has been found to be precipitated by methylphenidate in a prepubertal child (Koehler-Troy, Strober, & Malenbaum, 1986) and by pemoline (Sternbach, 1981) in a 20-year-old female. Both were being treated for an attention deficit disorder and both had a parent with bipolar disorder.

Psychosis, although rare, has occurred within the therapeutic dose ranges of these medications (Golinko, 1984; Young, 1981; Weiss, et al., 1971). Delusional thinking was the predominant feature in one 6-year-old ADHD child treated with methylphenidate (Bloom, Russel, Weisskopf, & Blackberry, 1988).

Contraindications of the use of stimulants are the presence of psychosis or a thought disorder, and hepatic dysfunction for pemoline. Relative contraindications are the presence of tics, extreme anxiety, or any medical condition such as hypertension, hyperthyroidism, or glaucoma which preclude the use of sympathomimetics. Also, they should not be used within 14 days following the administration of monoamine oxidase inhibitors (MAOIs).

Price

The average wholesale prices, as listed in the Red Book 1989–Annual Pharmacist's Reference, indicate that an equivalent dose of Dexedrine (d-amph) is half as expensive as Ritalin (MP), and even less expensive than generic methylphenidate. Long-acting formulations of dexedrine are approximately one-half more expensive than Cylert (pemoline), and a third more expensive than standard methylphenidate (Greenburg, Kreusi, & Grothe, in preparation). Given the questionable advantage of long-acting preparations of either dextroamphetamine or methylphenidate, and the lack of proven advantage of one standard preparation over another (except in individual cases of preferential response), cost should be an important consideration in prescribing stimulant drugs.

ANTIDEPRESSANTS

Numerous double-blind studies have demonstrated the efficacy of tricyclic antidepressants (TCAs) in ADHD (Biederman & Wright, 1987; Donnelly et al., 1986; Gross, 1973; Kupietz & Balka, 1976; Rapoport, Quinn, & Bradbard, 1974; Waizer et al., 1974; Werry, Aman, & Diamond, 1979; Winsberg et al., 1972; Yepes et al., 1977; Zametkin & Rappoport, 1983). Because side effects and adverse reactions are more common and potentially more serious with these medications than with the CNS stimulants, they are considered to be effective alternatives to stimulants, rather than first-line drugs for hyperactivity. There may be a subgroup of patients who respond better to TCAs, particularly when there are higher levels of anxiety and/or depression associated with ADHD (Pliszka, 1987; Rapoport et al., 1974). Those children with more severe aggressive behavior may not do as well on TCAs as with stimulants (Pallmeyer & Petti, 1979; Rapoport et al., 1974; Tec, 1983). Another situation in which a TCA may be preferable is the treatment of adolescents, who may pose an increased risk of stimulant abuse, either by the patient, his peers, or his family (though reported abuse by patients is extremely low). TCAs are also an important treatment

option in the patient with tics or a strong family history of Tourette's syndrome, which may be exacerbated or possibly precipitated by stimulant medications in susceptible children (Denckla, Bemporad, & MacKay, 1976, Donnelly et al., 1986; Golden, 1974, 1977; Lowe et al., 1982; Mitchell & Matthews, 1980; Riddle, Hardin, Cho, Wollston, & Leckman, 1988). Other TCA advantages include once-daily dosing for better compliance and elimination of "rebound" hyperactivity, elements that are often troublesome with methylphenidate and dextroamphetamine because of their short half-lives.

The mechanism of action of TCAs in the treatment of ADHD seems to be different from that of their antidepressant effects. Based on a study that looked closely at the time course of clinical effects in relation to plasma drug concentration and biochemical changes, TCAs produce their clinical effects in ADHD very early, sometimes as rapidly and as strikingly as do stimulants (Donnelly, et al., 1986). This speed is in contrast to an average response latency of 2–3 weeks in the treatment of depression. Also, just as the initial response is immediate, so is the return of symptoms when the drug is discontinued, again pointing to a different biochemical mechanism. Ordinarily, a therapeutic response in ADHD is achieved at comparatively low dosages and low serum drug concentrations relative to those reported for antidepressant effects. In some children with ADHD the response to a TCA unfortunately seems to wear off after about 6 weeks and does not respond to increasing dosages (Quinn & Rapoport, 1975; Waizer et al., 1974).

The vast majority of clinical experience with the use of TCAs in children has been with imipramine, both in the treatment of ADHD and other problems such as depression, nocturnal enuresis, and separation anxiety disorder. Desipramine has also been studied and was shown to be effective, but there are no definitive data addressing relative effectiveness of the two drugs. There has been some discussion in the literature comparing the effectiveness of low-dose imipramine versus high-dose imipramine (Werry et al., 1979), but there is very little evidence to support the use of dosages smaller than 1.0 mg/kg/day. The most effective dose range appears to be from 1.0 to 2.0 mg/kg/day, with a maximum dose of 150 mg/day. In extreme cases, dosages as high as 3.0 to 5.0 mg/kg/day have been used, but side effects may be severe, and very close monitoring, especially of cardiac status is essential. In order to reduce adverse effects, the initial dosage should be small (e.g., 25 mg), then gradually increased until the desired response is achieved. Following routine serum concentrations is not indicated unless there is a question of toxicity or a lack of treatment response on adequate doses.

The most commonly reported side effects of imipramine include mild tachycardia, increased diastolic pressure, orthostatic hypotension, drowsiness, constipation, dry mouth, and anorexia (Rapoport et al., 1974; Werry, Aman, & Diamond, 1979). An electrocardiogram (EKG) should be obtained prior to beginning treatment with a TCA because of the potential for adverse cardiac effects in children who have undiagnosed underlying cardiac conditions. Many clinicians continue to monitor periodically for EKG changes as dosages are increased. Side effects of TCAs are somewhat more prominent than with the stimulants, but the drugs are still generally well tolerated, although not as effective.

Monoamine oxidase inhibitors (MAOIs) have also been used successfully in the treatment of ADHD in children, though primarily in the research setting (Zametkin et al., 1985). They were originally used to help researchers better understand what mediates the antihyperactive effect of various drugs, by allowing them to evaluate the role of monoamines in this drug action. MAOIs, specifically tranylcypromine, parallel the drug effects of the stimulants more closely than any other agents, although they are less effective on some measures. They also seem to exert their clinical effects through multiple neurotransmitter systems. Similar to the TCAs, their response time is very rapid in ADHD, as opposed to their delayed antidepressant effects. One of the principal reasons that MAOIs are not more widely used is the serious concern that a child on this medication might unwittingly be given a stimulant, decongestant, or other drug that could produce a dangerous drug interaction. Compliance can also be a problem because of the need to keep the child on a fairly strict low-tyramine diet and to monitor blood pressure. Side effects have not been found to be troublesome, with mild drowsiness being the most common complaint. In selected cases, the administration of MAOIs for ADHD may be clinically useful but should be done judiciously, only after considering other alternatives and only when strict compliance is expected.

Bupropion, a novel antidepressant of the aminoketone class with weak dopamine-agonist activity, has achieved some positive results in preliminary studies treating children with ADHD (Casat, Pleasants, & Van Wyck Fleet, 1987; Simeon, Ferguson, & Van Wyck Fleet, 1986), but is still investigational at this time.

Nomifensine is an antidepressant with both dopaminergic and noradrenergic activity which was reported to be effective in preliminary studies in adults with residual ADHD, and anecdotally in children, but was recently taken off the market in the United States because of sensitivity reactions.

NEUROLEPTICS

Various antipsychotics such as haloperidol, chlorpromazine, and thioridazine have been used in the treatment of ADHD with limited success (reviewed by Winsberg & Yepes, 1978). They are, however, less effective than stimulants and have more troublesome side effects, including the risk of tardive dyskinesia, especially with long-term use. It is possible that some mentally retarded hyperactive patients may show a preferential reponse to neuroleptics. In the most severe cases of ADHD these drugs can also be a useful adjunct to stimulant treatment because of an additive effect that has been demonstrated when combined with methylphenidate (Gittelman-Klein, Klein, Katz, Saraf, & Pollack, 1976). Although mixing a dopamine agonist with a dopamine antagonist and getting an increased response does not make sense pharmacologically, its effectiveness demonstrates the complexity of the neurophysiology of this disorder and the mechanism of action of these drugs. Patients who benefit from neuroleptics usually respond in the low-dosage range.

MISCELLANEOUS DRUGS

Many different medications have been tried in the treatment of ADHD, some on an empirical basis due to their calming effects in adults, others as research tools because of their selective effects on specific neurotransmitter systems. Benzodiazapines (Millichap, 1973) and barbituates (Conners, 1972) are not effective in treating ADHD and often cause paradoxical excitation and agitation. Diphenydramine (Fish, 1975) and chloral hydrate are less likely to cause this paradoxical response and are sometimes useful as sedative-hypnotics for ADHD children. Caffeine (Conners, 1975) and deanol (Coleman, Dexheimer, DiMascio, Redman, & Finnery, 1976) have had only limited effectiveness in a few children, and are not commonly used today. Dopamine agonists such as carbidopa/levodopa (Langer, Rapoport, Brown, Ebert, & Bunney, 1982), piribedel (Brown, Ebert, Mikkelson, Buchsbaum, & Bunney, 1979), and amantadine (Mattes & Gittelman, 1979) were not found to be clinically useful. Serotonergic agents such as fenfluramine (Donnelly, Rapoport, Potter, Oliver, Keysor, & Murphy, 1989) and L-tryptophan are also ineffective. Other unsuccessful drug treatments include promethazine (Zametkin, Reeves, Webster, & Werry, 1986), tyrosine (Reimherr et al., 1987). D-phenylalanine (Zametkin, Karoun, & Rapoport, 1987), gamma linolenic acid (Arnold, Kleykamp, Lotolato, Taylor, Kontras, & Tobin, 1989), and mianserin (Winsberg, Camp-Bruno, Vink, Timmer, & Sverd, 1987). Lithium is not generally effective but may be useful in selected cases in which bipolar disorder is a strong diagnostic consideration (Whitehead & Clark, 1970; Greenhill, Rieder, Wender, Buchshaum, & Zahn, 1973).

A medication that seems promising based on initial clinical studies is the noradrenergic antihypertensive, clonidine (Hunt, 1987; Hunt, Minderaa, & Cohen, 1985). It has achieved results similar to those of methylphenidate and has a number of advantages such as convenient transdermal dosing, no evening rebound hyperactivity, and no abuse potential. Mild drowsiness was reported during the first 2–3 weeks of treatment, but it was otherwise well tolerated. In order to establish its usefulness as an alternative to the stimulants, further studies with clonidine are needed to validate these findings and investigate cognitive effects, preferential response of clinical subtypes, and correlation with serum drug concentrations.

SPECIAL PATIENT POPULATIONS

Preschoolers and Adolescents

Use of stimulants in preschool age children and adolescents has not been routine, though there are reports suggesting that these drugs are clinically effective in these groups (Schleifer, et al. 1975; Varley, 1983). A decrease in the use of maternal commands was recorded in ADHD preschoolers treated with low doses (0.15 mg/kg bid) of methylphenidate. At higher doses (0.50 mg/kg bid) there was an increase in on-task behavior, and the rate of compliance to maternal commands, as well as the length of sustained compliance to these commands, was found to improve (Barkley, 1988).

Follow-up studies of ADHD children indicate that symptoms of restlessness, impaired concentration, and impulsivity persist in as many as 70% of them as adolescents (Hechtman, 1985; Gittelman-Klein & Mannuzza, 1988). Although long-term studies have yet to be reported, positive short-term effects of stimulants in treatment of adolescents have been reported. Methylphenidate has been found to decrease inattention, overactivity, and noncompliance and to enhance cognitive functioning (Brown & Sexon, 1988; Klorman et al., 1987; Varley, 1983), as well as improve information processing among adolescents (Coons et al., 1987).

Research contradicts the likelihood of drug misuse for ADHD youths in the adolescent age range (Hechtman, Weiss, & Perlman, 1984a). Neither the use of stimulant medication nor the duration of treatment were associated with subsequent drug abuse in adolescence (Kramer & Loney, 1982) or in early adulthood (Hechtman, Weiss, & Perlman, 1984b). Drug use and dependence have not been shown to be any higher for this group than in the general population (Cantwell & Carlson, 1978; Gittelman, 1983; Goyer, Davis, & Rapoport, 1979). Cases of parental abuse of the drug have been reported (Fulton & Yates, 1988) and therefore caution should be used. A log of the amount of medication prescribed should be kept, requests to return unused medication should be made, and feedback from school and home on efficacy should be obtained to ensure compliance.

Tics and Tourette's Syndrome

Use of stimulants has been associated with the onset of exacerbation of tics, leading clinicians to discourage their use in patients with Tourette's syndrome (TS) and ADHD, as well as in children with a family history of tics or TS. There seems to be some association between the two syndromes, and as many as 25% of children with TS are likely to have received stimulants at some time.

Dextroamphetamine has been reported to increase the severity of tics in many patients with TS (Caine, Ludlow, Polinsky, & Ebert, 1984; Cohen et al., 1978; Feinberg & Carroll, 1979; Lowe, Cohen, Detlor, Kremenitzer, & Shaywitz, 1982). It decreased symptoms of ADHD while increasing the frequency of tics in a youngster with both ADHD and TS (Meyerhoff & Snyder, 1973).

The more numerous reports for methylphenidate show mixed effects, with several reporting the onset or worsening of tics after MP was started (Bremness, 1979; Denckla, Bemporad, & MacKay, 1976; Fras & Karlavage, 1977; Golden, 1977; Lowe, 1982; Pollack, Cohen, & Friedhoff, 1977; Sleator, 1980), while Rapoport (1982) found a heterogeneity of response in TS patients to dextroamphetamine and methylphenidate. Shapiro and Shapiro (1981), using a combination of methylphenidate and haloperidol, found no increased tics in patients with both hyperactivity and TS.

Sverd, Gadow, and Paolicelli (1989) reported worsening of tics in three children with ADHD and TS while they were receiving low doses of methylphenidate (5 mg per day), followed by an amelioration when higher doses (15 mg per day) were used.

There have been numerous case reports suggesting that the effects of pemoline on tics and TS are more prominent than with the other stimulants and sometimes persist following discontinuation of the drug (Bachman, 1981; Lowe, 1982; Mitchell, & Matthews, 1980; Rapoport, Nee, Mitchell, Polinsky, & Ebert, 1982).

In a retrospective study, Price and co-workers (1986) reported on six monozygotic twin pairs with TS, half of whom received stimulant treatment and half who did not. There was no significant difference in the age of onset of the symptoms between the treated twins and their untreated co-twins, who all developed the full syndrome. It it interesting that Comings and Comings (1984, 1987) actually reported a later onset for tics in ADHD children treated with stimulants (MP, d-amph, and pemoline) compared to those not treated, thus suggesting that stimulants do not precipitate the onset of tics but may actually delay it.

In summary, stimulants can still be effective treatments for attention deficit hyperactivity disorder in patients with TS, and it seems unlikely that they are etiologic in Tourette's syndrome. Methylphenidate's effect on tics appears to be heterogenous, while the few available reports suggest that pemoline may more consistently aggravate and/or precipitate tics.

Mentally Retarded Patients

Although mentally retarded children were included in early stimulant drug studies, they have not been part of more recent studies, presumably in part to decrease sample heterogeneity. Gadow's (1985) review of this topic suggests that stimulants are effective in this population, with the most severely retarded benefiting the least. In Aman's (1988) and Aman and Singh's (1982) double-blind placebo controlled, crossover study of methylphenidate and thioridazine in 30 intellectually subaverage hyperactive children, teachers reported consistent and significant improvement due to methylphenidate on a standardized teacher rating scale. However, parents failed to report consistent improvement with either of the active drugs. Mental age was found to be an important indicator of clinical response, with several variables showing MP-induced improvement for subjects of higher mental age (greater than 5 years old), and worsening or no change for children of low mental age children (less than 5 years of age). Two of the children, who were among those with the lowest IQs, showed increased agitation and stereotypy while receiving MP.

In a controlled trial of methylphenidate and dextroamphetamine in children with fragile X syndrome, improvement was found with both drugs; however, statistical significance for social improvement and attention were produced only by methylphenidate (Hagerman, Murphy, & Wittenberger, 1988).

Helsel, Hersen, and Lubetsky (1988) have reported adverse effects on social behavior with increasing dosages of stimulants in mentally retarded children, indicating a need for more research to clarify the effectiveness of these drugs in this undoubtedly heterogeneous population.

SUMMARY

Methylphenidate and dextroamphetamine remain the drugs of choice for treatment of ADHD. Since there is individual variability of response, both drugs should be tried in the same youngster, especially if suboptimal results or side effects occur with the first drug tried. Pemoline and the long-acting preparations of methylphenidate and dextroamphetamine should be considered in youngsters when compliance with multiple dosing is a problem, as well as when rebound effects are severe. Tricyclic antidepressants are the second-line treatment for ADHD, especially when anxiety or depressive symptoms are prominent. The use of neuroleptics and other miscellaneous drugs should be reserved for carefully selected atypical cases.

Monitoring the efficacy of the medication using teacher and parental feedback and using a multimodal approach to treatment are essential to assure maximal treatment response.

ADHD symptoms appear to respond to stimulants in children who have both Tourette's syndrome and ADHD. Precipitation and exacerbation of tics and other dyskinetic movements as well as delaying of tic development and amelioration of TS symptoms have been reported with stimulant treatment.

More research is needed to determine the efficacy of these medications in mentally retarded persons.

REFERENCES

Aman, M. (1988). The use of methylphenidate in autism [Letter]. *Journal of the American Academy of Child and Adolescent Psychiatry, 27,* 821–822.

Aman, M. G., & Singh, N. N. (1982). Methylphenidate in severely retarded residents and the clinical significance of stereotypic behavior. *Applied Research in Mental Retardation, 3,* 345–348.

Arnold, L. E., Kleykamp, D., Lotolato, N. A., Taylor, W. A., Kontras, S. B., & Tobin, K. (1989). Gamma-linolenic acid for attention-deficit hyperactivity disorder: Placebo-controlled comparison to D-amphetamine. *Biological Psychiatry, 25,* 222–228.

Axelrod, J. (1970). Amphetamine metabolism, physiolog-

ical disposition and its effect on catecholamine storage. In E. Costa, & S. Garratini (Eds.), *Amphetamines and related compounds* (pp. 207–216). New York: Raven.

Bachman, D. S. (1981). Pemoline-induced Tourette's disorder: A case report. *American Journal of Psychiatry, 138,* 1116–1117.

Barkley, R. A. (1977). A review of stimulant drug research with hyperactive children. *Journal of Child Psychology and Psychiatry, 18,* 137–165.

Barkley, R. A. (1988). The effects of methylphenidate on the interactions of preschool ADHD children with their mothers. *Journal of the American Academy of Child and Adolescent Psychiatry, 27,* 336–341.

Bender, L., & Cottington, F. (1942). The use of amphetamine sulfate (Benzedrine) in child psychiatry. *American Journal of Psychiatry, 99*(1), 116–121.

Biederman, J., & Wright, V. (1987). *Desipramine in the treatment of children and adolescents with attention deficit disorder.* Paper presented at the New Research Poster Section, 34th Annual Meeting of the American Academy of Child and Adolescent Psychiatry, Washington, DC.

Bloom, A. S., Russel, L. J., Weisskopf, B., & Blackberry, J. L. (1988). Methylphenidate-induced delusional disorder in a child with attention deficit disorder with hyperactivity. *Journal of the American Academy of Child and Adolescent Psychiatry, 27,* 88–89.

Borcherding, B. G., Keysor, C. S., Cooper, T. B., & Rapoport, J. L. (1989). Differential effects of methylphenidate and dextroamphetamine on the motor activity level of hyperactive children. *Neuropsychopharmacology, 2*(4), 255–263.

Bradley, C. (1937). The behavior of children receiving benzedrine. *American Journal of Psychiatry, 94,* 577–585.

Bremness, A. B., & Sverd, J. (1979). Methylphenidate-induced Tourette syndrome: Case report. *American Journal of Psychiatry, 136,* 1334–1335.

Brown, G. L., Ebert, M. H., Mikkelson, I., Buchsbaum, M. S., & Bunney, W. E., Jr. (1979). *Dopamine agonist piribedel in hyperactive children.* Paper presented at the annual meeting of the American Psychiatric Association.

Brown, R. T., Borden, K. A., Spunt, A. L., & Medenis, R. (1985). Depression following pemoline withdrawal in a hyperactive child. (Letter). *Clinical Pediatrics, 24,* 174.

Brown, R. T., & Sexon, S. B. (1988). A controlled trial of methylphenidate in black adolescents. *Clinical Pediatrics, 27,* 74–81.

Caine, E. D., Ludlow, C. L., Polinsky, R. J., & Ebert, M. H. (1984). Provocative drug testing in Tourette's syndrome: d- and l-amphetamine and haloperidol. *Jour-*

nal of the American Academy of Child and Adolescent Psychiatry, 23, 146–152.

Cantwell, D. P., & Carlson, G. A. (1978). Stimulants. In J. S. Werry (Ed.), Pediatric psychopharmacology: The use of behavior modifying drugs in children (pp. 171–207). New York: Brunner/Mazel.

Casat, C. D., Pleasants, D. Z., & Van Wyck Fleet, D. (1987). A double-blind trial of bupropion in children with attention deficit disorder. Psychopharmacology Bulletin, 23, 120–122.

Cohen, D. J., Shaywitz, B. A., Caparulo, B., Young, J. G., Bowers, M. B. Jr. (1978). Chronic multiple tics of Gilles de la Tourette's disease. Archives of General Psychiatry, 35, 245–250.

Coleman, N., Dexheimer, P., DiMascio, A., Redman, W., & Finnery, R. (1976). Deanol in the treatment of hyperkinetic children. Psychosomatics, 17, 68–72.

Collier, C. P., Soldin, S. J., Swanson, J. M., Macleod, S. M., Weinberg, F., & Rochefort, J. G. (1985). Pemoline pharmacokinetics and long term therapy in children with attention deficit disorder and hyperactivity. Clinical Pharmacokinetics, 10, 269–278.

Comings, D. E., & Comings, B. G. (1984). Tourette's syndrome and attention deficit disorder with hyperactivity: Are they genetically related? Journal of the American Academy of Child Psychiatry, 23, 138–146.

Comings, D. E., & Comings, B. G. (1987). A controlled study of Tourette syndrome. I. Attention deficit disorder, learned disorders and school problems. American Journal of Human Genetics, 41, 701–741.

Conners, C. K. (1972). Pharmacotherapy of psychopathology in children. In H. Quay & J. Werry (Eds.), Psychopathological disorders of childhood (pp. 316–348). New York: John Wiley & Sons.

Conners, C. K. (1975). A placebo-crossover study of caffeine treatment of hyperkinetic children. In R. Gittelman-Klein (Ed.), Recent advances in child psychopharmacology (pp. 136–147). New York: Human Sciences Press.

Conners, C. K., & Taylor, E. (1980). Pemoline, methylphenidate, and placebo in children with minimal brain dysfunction. Archives of General Psychiatry, 37, 922–930.

Conners, C. K., Taylor, E., Meo, G., Kurtz, M. A., & Fournier, M. (1972). Magnesium pemoline and dextroamphetamine: A controlled study of children with minimal brain dysfunction. Psychopharmacologia, 26, 321–336.

Coons, H. W., Klorman, R., & Borgstedt, A. D. (1987). Effects of methylphenidate on adolescents with a childhood history of attention deficit disorder: II. Information processing. Journal of the American Academy of Child and Adolescent Psychiatry, 26, 820.

Denckla, M. B., Bemporad, J. R., & MacKay, M. C. (1976). Tics following methylphenidate administration: A report of 20 cases. Journal of the American Medical Association, 235, 1349–1351.

Donnelly, M., Rapoport, J. L., Potter, W. Z., Oliver, J., Keysor, C. S., & Murphy, D. L. (1989). Fenflurimine and dextroamphetamine treatment of childhood hyperactivity. Clinical and biochemical findings. Archives of General Psychiatry, 46, 205–212.

Donnelly, M., Zametkin, A. J., Rapoport, J. L., Ismond, D. R., Weingartner, H., Lane, E., Oliver, J., Linnoila, M., & Potter, W. Z. (1986). Treatment of childhood hyperactivity with desipramine. Clinical Pharmacology and Therapy, 39, 72–81.

Dulcan, M. K. (1986). Comprehensive treatment of children and adolescents with attention deficit disorders: The state of the art. Clinical Psychology Review, 6, 539–569.

Elia, J., Borcherding, B. G., Potter, W. Z., Mefford, I. N., Rapoport, J. L., & Keysor, C. S. (1990). Stimulant drug treatment of hyperactivity: Biochemical correlates. Clinical Pharmacology and Therapeutics, 48, 57–66.

Elia, J., Borcherding, B. G., Rapoport, J. L., & Keysor, C. S. (1991). Methylphenidate and dextroamphetamine treatments of hyperactivity: Are there true nonresponders? Psychiatry Research, 36, 141–155.

Ebert, M. H., van Kammen, D. P., & Murphy, D. L. (1976). Plasma levels of amphetamine and behavioral response. In L. A. Gottschalk & S. Merlis (Eds.), Pharmacokinetics of psychoactive drugs: Blood levels and clinical response (pp. 157–169). New York: Spectrum.

Faraj, B. A., Israili, Z. H., Perel, J. M., Jenkins, M. L., Holtzman, S. G., Cucinelli, S. A., & Dayton, P. G. (1974). Metabolism and disposition of methylphenidate-14C: Studies in man and animals. Journal of Pharmacology & Experimental Therapy, 191, 535–547.

Farmer, P., Jr., Unis, A. S., & Hsu, G. (1983). Pemoline, depressive symptoms, and escape from dexamethasone. Journal of Clinical Psychopharmacology, 3, 331–332.

Feinberg, M., & Carroll, B. J. (1979). Effects of dopamine agonists and antagonists in Tourette's disease. Archives of General Psychiatry, 36, 979–985.

Fish, B. (1975). Drug treatment of the hyperactive child. In D. Cantwell (Ed.), The hyperactive child: Diagnosis, management, and current research. New York: Spectrum Publications.

Fras, I., & Karlavage, J. (1977). The use of methylphenidate and imipramine in Gilles de la Tourette's disease in children. American Journal of Psychiatry, 134, 195–197.

Fulton, A. I., & Yates, N. R. (1988). Family abuse of methylphenidate. American Family Physician, 38, 143–145.

Gadow, K. D. (1985). Prevalence and efficacy of stimulant

drug use with mentally retarded children and youth. *Psychopharmacology Bulletin, 21,* 291–303.

Gittelman, R. (1983). *Stimulants: Neurochemical, behavioral and clinical perspectives.* New York: Raven.

Gittelman, R., & Kanner, A. (1986). Psychopharmacotherapy. In H. Quay & J. Werry (Eds.), *Psychopathological disorders of childhood* (3rd ed., pp. 455–494). New York: John Wiley & Sons.

Gittelman-Klein, R., Klein, D. F., Katz, S., Saraf, K., & Pollack E. (1976). Comparative effects of methylphenidate and thioridazine in hyperkinetic children. *Archives of General Psychiatry, 33,* 1217–1231.

Gittelman-Klein, R., Landa, B., Mattes, J. A., & Klein, D. F. (1988). Methylphenidate and growth in hyperactive children. *Archives of General Psychiatry, 45,* 1127–1130.

Gittelman-Klein, R., & Mannuzza, S. (1988). Hyperactive boys almost grown up. *Archives of General Psychiatry, 45,* 1131–1134.

Golden, G. S. (1974). Gilles de la Tourette's syndrome following methylphenidate administration. *Developmental Medicine of Child Neurology, 16,* 76–78.

Golden, G. S. (1977). The effect of central nervous system stimulants on Tourette syndrome. *Annals of Neurology, 2,* 69–70.

Golinko, B. (1984). Side effects of dextroamphetamine and methylphenidate in hyperactive children—A brief review. *Progress in Neuropsychopharmacology and Biological Psychiatry, 8,* 1–8.

Goyer, P., Davis, G., & Rapoport, J. (1979). Abuse of prescribed stimulant medication by a 13-year-old hyperactive boy. *Journal of the American Academy of Child Psychiatry, 18,* 170–176.

Greenhill, L. L. (1981). Stimulant-related growth inhibition in children: A review. In M. Gittelman (Ed.), *Strategic interventions for hyperactive children* (pp. 39–63). Armonk, NY: ME Sharpe.

Greenhill, L., Rieder, R., Wender, P., Buchsbaum, M., & Zahn, T. (1973). Lithium carbonate in the treatment of hyperactive children. *Archives of General Psychiatry, 28,* 636–640.

Greensburg, J., Kreusi, M., & Grothe, D. (in preparation).

Gross, M. D. (1973). Imipramine in the treatment of minimal brain dysfunction in children. *Psychosomatics, 14,* 283–285.

Gross, M. D. (1976). Growth of hyperkinetic children taking methylphenidate, dextroamphetamine, or imipramine/desipramine. *Pediatrics, 58*(3), 423–431.

Gualtieri, C. T., Wargin, W., & Kanoy, R. (1982). Clinical studies of methylphenidate serum levels in children and adults. *Journal of the American Academy of Child and Adolescent Psychiatry, 21,* 19–26.

Hagerman, R. J., Murphy, M. A., & Wittenberger, M.

D. (1988). A controlled trial of stimulant medication in children with the Fragile X syndrome. *American Journal of Medical Genetics, 30,* 377–392.

Hechtman, L. (1985). Adolescent outcome of hyperactive children treated with stimulants in childhood: A review. *Psychopharmacology Bulletin, 21,* 178–191.

Hechtman, L., Weiss, G., & Perlman, T. (1984a). Hyperactives as young adults: Past and current substance abuse and antisocial behavior. *American Journal of Orthopsychiatry, 54,* 415–425.

Hechtman, L., Weiss, G., & Perlman, T. (1984b). Young adult outcome of hyperactive children who received long-term stimulant treatment. *Journal of the American Academy of Child and Adolescent Psychiatry, 23,* 261–269.

Helsel, W. J., Hersen, M., & Lubetsky, M. J. (1988). Stimulant medication and the retarded [Letter]. *Journal of the American Academy of Child and Adolescent Psychiatry, 28,* 138–139.

Hunt, R. D. (1987). Treatment effects of oral and transdermal clonidine in relation to methylphenidate: An open pilot study in ADD-H. *Psychopharmacology Bulletin, 23,* 111–114.

Hunt, R. D., Minderaa, R. B., & Cohen, D. J. (1985). Clonidine benefits in children with attention deficit disorder and hyperactivity: Report of a double-blind placebo-crossover therapeutic trial. *Journal of the American Academy of Child Psychiatry, 5,* 617–629.

Jaffe, S. L. (1989). Pemoline and liver function. *Journal of the American Academy of Child and Adolescent Psychiatry, 28,* 457–458.

Klorman, R., Coons, H. W., & Borgstedt, A. D. (1987). Effects of methylphenidate on adolescents with a childhood history of attention deficit disorder: I. Clinical findings. *Journal of the American Academy of Child and Adolescent Psychiatry, 26,* 363–367.

Koehler-Troy, C., Strober, M., & Malenbaum, R. (1986). Methylphenidate-induced mania in a prepubertal child. *Journal of Clinical Psychiatry, 47,* 566–567.

Kramer, J., & Loney, J. (1982). Childhood hyperactivity and substance abuse: A review of the literature. In K. Gadow & I. Bailer (Eds.), *Advances in learning and behavioral disabilities* (Vol. 1, pp. 225–259). Greenwich, CN: JAI Press.

Kuczenski, R. (1983). Biochemical actions of amphetamines and other stimulants. In I. Crease (Ed.), *Stimulants: Neurochemical, behavior and clinical perspectives,* (pp. 31–63). New York: Raven Press.

Kupietz, S., & Balka, E. (1976). Alterations in the vigilance performance of children receiving amitriptyline and methylphenidate. *Psychopharmacology, 50,* 29–33.

Langer, D. H., Rapoport, J. L., Brown, G. L., Ebert, M. H., & Bunney, W. E. (1982). Behavioral effects of carbidopa/levodopa in hyperactive boys. *American Academy of Child Psychiatry, 21,* 10–18.

Langer, D. H., Sweeney, K. P., Bartenbach, D. E., Davis, P. M., & Menander, K. B. (1986). Evidence of lack of abuse or dependence following pemoline treatment: Results of a retrospective survey. *Drug and Alcohol Dependency, 17,* 213–227.

Lou, H. C., Henriksen, L., Bruhn, P., Borner, H., & Nielsen, J. B. (1989). Striatal dysfunction in attention deficit and hyperkinetic disorder. *Archives of Neurology, 46,* 48–52.

Lowe, T. L., Cohen, D. J., Detlor, J., Kremenitzer, M. W., & Shaywitz, B. A. (1982). Stimulant medications precipitate Tourette's syndrome. *Journal of the American Medical Association, 247,* 1729–1731.

Mattes, J., & Gittelman, R. (1979). *A pilot trial of amantadine in hyperactive children.* Paper presented at the New Clinical Drug Evaluation Unit meeting, Key Biscayne, Florida.

Mattes, J. A., & Gittelman, R. (1983). Growth of hyperactive children on maintenance regimen of methylphenidate. *Archives of General Psychiatry, 40,* 317–321.

Meyerhoff, J. L., & Snyder, S. H. (1973). Gilles de la Tourette's disease and minimal brain dysfunction: Amphetamine isomers reveal catecholamine correlates in an affected patient. *Psychopharmacologia, 29,* 211–220.

Millichap, J. (1973). Drugs in the management of minimal brain dysfunction. *Annals of the New York Academy of Science, 205,* 321–334.

Mitchell, E., & Matthews, K. L. (1980). Gilles de la Tourette's disorder associated with pemoline. *American Journal of Psychiatry, 137,* 1618–1619.

Moline, V. A., & Orsingher, O. A. (1981). Effects of Mg-pemoline on the central catecholaminergic system. *Archives of International Pharmacodyn Therapy, 251,* 66–79.

Ounsted, C. (1955). The hyperkinetic syndrome in epileptic children. *Lancet, 268,* 304–311.

Pallmeyer, T. P., & Petti, T. A. (1979). Effects of imipramine on aggression and dejection in depressed children. *American Journal of Psychiatry, 136,* 1472–1473.

Pelham, W. E., Swanson, J., Bender, M., & Wilson, J. (1980, September). *Dose-response effects of pemoline on hyperactivity: Laboratory and classroom measures.* Paper presented at the American Psychological Association, Montreal.

Pelham, W. E., Greenslade, K. W., Vodde-Hamilton, M., Murphy, D. A., Greenstein, J. J., Gnagy, E. M., & Dahl, R. E. (in press). Relative efficacy of long-acting stimulants on ADHD children: A comparison of standard methylphenidate, Ritalin SR-20, Dexedrine Spansule, and pemoline. *Pediatrics.*

Pliszka, S. R. (1987). Tricyclic antidepressants in the treatment of children with attention deficit disorder. *Journal of the American Academy of Child and Adolescent Psychiatry, 26,* 127–132.

Pollack, M. A., Cohen, N. L., & Friedhoff, A. J. (1977). Gilles de la Tourette's syndrome: Familial occurrence and precipitation by methylphenidate therapy. *Archives of Neurology, 34,* 630–632.

Porrino, L. J., Rapoport, J. L., Behar, Ismond, D. R., & Bunney, W. E., Jr. (1983). A naturalistic assessment of the motor activity of hyperactive boys: II. Stimulant drug effects. *Archives of General Psychiatry, 40,* 688–693.

Price, R. A., Leckman, J. F., Pauls, D. L., Cohen, D. J., & Kidd, K. K. (1986). Gilles de la Tourette's syndrome: Tics and central nervous system stimulants on twins and nontwins. *Neurology, 36,* 232–237.

Quinn, P. O., & Rapoport, J. L. (1975). One year follow-up of hyperactive boys treated with imipramine or methylphenidate. *American Journal of Psychiatry, 132,* 241–245.

Rapoport, J. L., Buchsbaum, M. S., Zahn, T. P., Weingartner, H, Ludlow, C., Mikkelsen, E. J. (1978). Dextroamphetamine: Cognitive and behavioral effects in normal prepubertal boys. *Science, 199,* 560–563.

Rapoport, J. L., Buchsbaum, M. S., Weingartner, M., Zahn, T. P., Ludlow, C., et al. (1980). Dextroamphetamine: Cognitive and behavioral effects in normal and hyperactive boys and normal adult males. *Archives of General Psychiatry, 37,* 933–946.

Rapoport, J. L., Nee, L., Mitchell, S., Polinsky, M. R., & Ebert, M. (1982). Hyperkinetic syndrome and Tourette syndrome. In A. J. Friedhoff & T. N. Chase (Eds.), *Gilles de la Tourette syndrome* (pp. 423–426). New York: Raven Press.

Rapoport, J. L., Quinn, P. O., Bradbard, G., Riddle, D., & Brooks, E. (1974). A double-blind comparison of imipramine and methylphenidate treatments of hyperactive boys. *Archives of General Psychiatry, 30,* 789–793.

Reimherr, F. W., Wender, P. H., Wood, D. R., & Ward, M. (1987). An open trial of L-tyrosine in the treatment of attention deficit disorder, residual type. *American Journal of Psychiatry, 8,* 1071–1073.

Riddle, M. A., Hardin, M. T., Cho, S. C., Wollston, J. L., & Leckman, J. F. (1988). Desipramine and tics: Preliminary clinical experience. *Journal of the American Academy of Child and Adolescent Psychiatry, 27,* 811–814.

Safer, D., Allen, R. P., & Barr, E. (1972). Depression of growth in hyperactive children on stimulant drugs. *New England Journal of Medicine, 287,* 217–220.

Safer, D. J., & Krager, J. M. (1984). Trends in medication treatment of hyperactive school children. In K. D. Gadow (Ed.), *Advances in learning and behavioral disabilities* (Vol. 3, pp. 125–149). Greenwich, CT: JAI Press.

Sallee, F. R., Stiller, R. L., Perel, J. M., & Bates, T. (1985). Oral pemoline kinetics in hyperactive children. *Clinical Pharmacology and Therapy, 37,* 606–609.

Sallee, F. R., Stiller, R. L., Perel, J. M., & Everett, G. (1989). Pemoline-induced abnormal involuntary movements. *Journal of Clinical Psychopharmacology, 9,* 125–129.

Schleifer, M., Weiss, G., Cohen, N., Elman, M., Cvejic, H., & Kruger, E. (1975). Hyperactivity in preschoolers and the effect of methylphenidate. *American Journal of Orthopsychiatry, 45,* 38–50.

Shapiro, A. K., & Shapiro, E. (1981). Do stimulants provoke, cause, or exacerbate tics and Tourette syndrome? *Comparative Psychiatry, 22,* 265–273.

Simeon, J. G., Ferguson, H. B., & Van Wyck Fleet, J. (1986). Bupropion effects in attention deficit and conduct disorders. *Canadian Journal of Psychiatry, 6,* 581–585.

Sleator, K. E. (1980). Deleterious effects of drugs used for hyperactivity on patients with Gilles de la Tourette syndrome. *Clinical Pediatrics, 19,* 453–454.

Stephens, R. S., Pelham, W. E., & Skinner, R. (1984). State-dependent and main effects of methylphenidate and pemoline on paired-associate learning and spelling in hyperactive children. *Journal of Consulting and Clinical Psychology, 52,* 104–113.

Sternbach, H. (1981). Pemoline-induced mania. *Biological Psychiatry, 16,* 987–989.

Sverd, J., Gadow, K. D., & Paolicelli, L. M. (1989). Methylphenidate treatment of attention-deficit hyperactivity disorder in boys with Tourette's syndrome. *Journal of the American Academy of Child and Adolescent Psychiatry, 28,* 574–579.

Tec, L. (1983). Unexpected effects in children treated with imipramine. *American Journal of Psychiatry, 12,* 603.

Varley, C. K. (1983). Effects of methylphenidate in adolescents with attention deficit disorder. *Journal of the American Academy of Child Psychiatry, 22,* 351–354.

Waizer, J., Hoffman, S. P., Polizos, P., & Englehardt, D. (1974). Outpatient treatment of hyperactive school children with imipramine. *American Journal of Psychiatry, 131,* 587–591.

Weiss, G., Minde, K., Werry, J. S., Douglas, V., & Nemeth, E. (1971). Studies on the hyperactive child. 8. Five-year follow-up. *Archives of General Psychiatry, 24,* 409–414.

Weizman, A., Bernhout, E., Weitz, R., Tyano, S., & Rehavi, M. (1988). Imipramine binding to platelets of children with attention deficit disorder with hyperactivity. *Biological Psychiatry, 23,* 491–496.

Werry, J. S., Aman, M. G., & Diamond, E. (1979).

Imipramine and methylphenidate in hyperactive children. *Journal of Child Psychology and Psychiatry, 21,* 27–35.

Whitehead, P., & Clark, L. (1970). Effect of lithium carbonate, placebo and thioridazine on hyperactive chil- dren. *American Journal of Psychiatry, 127,* 824–825.

Winsberg, B. G., Bialer, I., Kupietz, S., & Tobias, J. (1972). Effects of imipramine and dextroamphetamine on behavior of neuropsychiatrically impaired children. *American Journal of Psychiatry, 128,* 1425–1431.

Winsberg, B. G., Camp-Bruno, J. A., Vink, J., Timmer, C. J., & Sverd, J. (1987). Mianserin pharmacokinetics and behavior in hyperkinetic children. *Journal of Clinical Psychopharmacology, 7,* 143–147.

Winsberg, B. G., & Yepes, L. E. (1978). Antipsychotics (major tranquilizers, neuroleptics). In J. S. Werry (Ed.), *Pediatric psychopharmacology: The use of behavior modifying drugs in children* (pp. 234–274). New York: Brunner/Mazel.

Yepes, L. E., Balka, E. B., Winsberg, B. G., & Bialer, I. (1977). Amitriptyline and methylphenidate treatment of behaviorally disordered children. *Journal of Child Psychology and Psychiatry, 18,* 39–52.

Young, J. (1981). Methylphenidate-induced hallucinosis: Case histories and possible mechanisms of action. *Journal of Developmental and Behavioral Pediatrics, 2,* 35–38.

Zametkin, A. J., & Hamburger, S. D. (1988). The effect of methylphenidate on urinary catecholamine excretion in hyperactivity: A partial replication. *Biological Psychiatry, 23,* 350–356.

Zametkin, A. J., Karoum, F., & Rapoport, J. L. (1987). Treatment of hyperactive children with D-phenylalanine. *American Journal of Psychiatry, 144,* 792–794.

Zametkin, A. J., Linnoila, M., Karoum, F., & Sallee, R. (1986). Pemoline and urinary excretion of catecholamines and indoleamines in children with attention deficit disorder. *American Journal of Psychiatry, 143,* 359–362.

Zametkin, A. J., Nordahl, T. E., Gross, M., King, C., Semple, W. E., Rumsey, J., Hamburger, S., & Cohen, R. (1990). Brain metabolism in hyperactive adults with childhood onset. *New England Journal of Medicine, 323,* 1361–1366.

Zametkin, A., & Rapoport, J. L. (1983). Tricyclic antidepressants and children. In G. D. Burrows, T. R. Norman, & B. Davies (Eds.), *Antidepressants* (pp. 129–147). Amsterdam: Elsevier.

Zametkin, A., Rapoport, J. L., Murphy, D. L., Linnoila, M., & Ismond, D. (1985). Treatment of hyperactive children with monoamine oxidase inhibitors. I. Clinical efficacy. *Archives of General Psychiatry, 42,* 962–966.

CHAPTER 12

SCHOOL-BASED PSYCHOLOGICAL TREATMENTS

Linda J. Pfiffner
Susan G. O'Leary

The array of difficulties hyperactive children exhibit in the classroom may be greater than in any other setting. Inattention, impulsivity, and overactivity, the cardinal symptoms of hyperactivity, often seem especially pronounced in the classroom setting. Teacher reports on standardized questionnaires, substantiated by direct observations in the classroom, indicate that these symptoms manifest themselves in the child's difficulty sitting still and concentrating, frequent interrupting and calling out, disorganization, and general disruption (Atkins, Pelham, & Licht, 1985; Klein & Young, 1979; Zentall, 1980).

The significance of these core problems notwithstanding, hyperactive children's school performance may be further jeopardized by a myriad of associated problems. Studies show that more than 50% of all hyperactive children have significant problems of an oppositional nature running the gamut from tantrums and defiance to serious social norm violations such as stealing, lying, and aggression (Hinshaw, 1987). Academic problems are also prevalent, as evidenced by frequent incomplete work and academic failure, as well as a high incidence of specific learning disabilities (Cantwell & Satterfield, 1978).

In addition to these problems, most hyperactive children have seriously disturbed peer relations. They are consistently rejected by their peers on sociometric indices (Milich & Landau, 1982), and observations and teacher reports indicate that their interactions with peers are typically intrusive and negative (Milich & Landau, 1982).

These problems pose many challenges for teachers. Perhaps in response to their difficult, disruptive behavior, teachers tend to be less positive and more interactive, commanding, and negative toward hyperactive than toward nonhyperactive children (Campbell, Endman, & Bernfield, 1977). In turn, hyperactive children often perceive significantly less acceptance and greater demands from their teachers than do their nonhyperactive peers (Peter, Allan, & Horvath, 1983).

The long-term impact of these predominantly negative interactions is not well studied, but theoretically may result in poor achievement, low motivation and self-esteem, and ultimately school failure. On the other hand, a positive teacher-student relationship may be of great benefit. In a long-term follow-up study of adults who had been hyperactive as children, Weiss and Hechtman (1986) found that very positive experiences with teachers or guidance counselors were reported as "turning points" by some of these individuals. A teacher's caring attitude, extra attention, and guidance were factors that the adults reported most helped them overcome their childhood problems.

The numerous problems faced by hyperactive children in school and the significance of school success in predicting later adjustment underscores the need to identify effective interventions to remediate their school problems early on. The present chapter reviews the range of behavioral and cognitive-behavioral interventions utilized in classroom settings. The chapter is divided into sections based on types of interventions. This approach has been adopted from previous excellent reviews of classroom management (see, for example: Barkley, 1981; Carlson & Lahey, 1988; Jones & Kazdin, 1981; O'Leary, & O'Leary, 1976; O'Leary & O'Leary, 1977).

The focus of this review is on studies evaluating the effects of these interventions with elementary-aged children identified as hyperactive (e.g., scoring at least one standard deviation above the mean on the hyperactivity factor of a standardized teacher- or parent-rating scale) or children having a diagnosis of attention deficit hyperactivity disorder (ADHD) (American Psychiatric Association [APA], 1987). In addition, selected studies of operant classroom management strategies are also included in cases where the children exhibited characteristics of hyperactivity but were not formally diagnosed. These studies are included because it is likely that many, if not most, of the children would have met the criteria for ADHD had they been diagnosed and because the studies are instructive regarding the range of management procedures that may be beneficial in treating hyperactive symptomatology.

TEACHER-ADMINISTERED INTERVENTION STRATEGIES

Teacher-administered positive and negative consequences are perhaps the behavioral interventions most commonly used with hyperactive children in the classroom. Positive consequences typically include positive teacher attention (e.g., praise), tokens, and tangible rewards. Negative consequences usually consist of ignoring, verbal reprimands, response-cost, and time-out. Many of the studies reviewed evaluated the separate effects of these procedures. In actual practice, however, classroom management programs typically involve a combination of these interventions.

Positive Teacher Attention

The effects of positive teacher attention were originally investigated in the context of classroom management in the 1960s with behavior problem children described as "acting out" but not formally diagnosed. For example, Madsen, Becker, and Thomas (1968) tested the effects of three teacher interventions—rules, praise, and ignoring—on the inappropriate behavior of two behavior problem children in a normal second grade class and one behavior problem child in a normal kindergarten class. The results in both classes indicated that, in the absence of praise, rules and ignoring were ineffective. Inappropriate behavior decreased only after praise was added. Thomas, Becker, and Armstrong (1968) also demonstrated the importance of praise in a regular elementary classroom. Specifically, whenever teacher approval was withdrawn, disruptive behaviors increased.

Studies of praise effects with hyperactive children have yielded somewhat different results. In a recent series of studies, Rosén, O'Leary, Joyce, Conway, and Pfiffner (1984) evaluated the relative impact of positive consequences (primarily praise) and negative consequences (primarily reprimands) in maintaining appropriate social and academic behaviors of second and third grade hyperactive children. Results from the first of four experiments revealed that children's on-task behavior and academic performance deteriorated when negative feedback was withdrawn but not when positive feedback was omitted. Students' on-task behavior remained very high even after 9 days of no praise from the teacher. These results were replicated in three subsequent experiments with a different class of hyperactive children, a different teacher, and conditions presented in a counterbalanced order.

The importance of praise in teaching classroom rules and appropriate behavior to hyperactive students was tested by withholding all positive consequences at the outset of a summer school class and using only reprimands for behavior management (Acker & O'Leary, 1987). Praise was then added after a week but did not improve the on-task rates achieved with reprimands. Dramatic deterioration in on-task behavior was observed when reprimands were subsequently withdrawn, even though the teacher was still delivering praise for appropriate behavior.

The lack of effects of praise on behavior and academic productivity in these studies stands in contrast to findings from the earlier studies with nonhyperactive children. These differences are consistent with recent theorizing that hyperactive children possess an elevated reward threshold that decreases the magnitude of reward they experience (Haenlein & Caul, 1987). In addition, work by Douglas and her colleagues (e.g., Douglas & Parry, 1983) shows that hyperactive children function as well as nonhyperactive children with a continuous schedule of reinforcement but perform significantly worse than nonhyperactives with a partial schedule of reinforcement, the schedule typically found in classrooms. Thus, hyperactive children may require more frequent and more powerful reinforcement programs than nonhyperactive children to achieve the same level of behavioral and academic performance. Nevertheless, praise may be important for other attributes including self-esteem, attitudes toward school, and persistence and motivation for academic work (e.g., Redd, Morris, & Martin, 1975).

Tangible Rewards and Token Programs

The effects of more powerful reinforcement systems with hyperactive children have been examined in numerous studies. Pfiffner, Rosén, and O'Leary (1985) compared the effects of an enhanced all-positive approach to classroom management to one in which either praise was the primary form of feedback or praise was combined with negative consequences. The enhanced positive procedure included a higher frequency of praise as well as more powerful, concrete rewards including special activities and privileges (e.g., songtime, posting work on "superstar" board, reading comic books, special recess activities). During one of the enhanced positive

conditions, an individualized reward program was also in effect wherein children selected their own rewards from a reward menu in addition to receiving the other enhanced positive consequences. The positive consequences were contingent on both appropriate behavior and complete, accurate academic work. Results indicated that in the absence of negative feedback, enhanced positive consequences were more effective in maintaining high rates of on-task behavior and academic productivity than an approach consisting mostly of praise. Children's functioning during the enhanced positives alone condition was also nearly as good as their functioning when both positive and negative consequences were delivered, particularly when children chose their own rewards. However, a subsequent study by Pfiffner and O'Leary (1987) showed that the use of an enhanced positive approach alone appeared to be successful only after negative consequences had been used to shape appropriate behavior and academic accuracy.

Token reinforcement systems have also been widely used to modify behaviors characteristic of children with hyperactivity. Two types of token systems are often used to reward appropriate behavior: one involves distribution of tokens and one involves recording of points, stars, or other symbols of reward. Tokens or points earned for desired behavior are later "spent" by children for desirable backup privileges, activities, or tangible objects. Privileges and activities are often preferred because they are more readily available in the school setting and may seem to be a more "natural" payoff for appropriate behavior.

The effectiveness of the token program in modifying children's classroom behavior has been well documented. In one of the earliest studies evaluating classroom management procedures, O'Leary, Becker, Evans, and Saudargas (1969) found that the use of a token program was necessary to reduce the disruptive behavior of six of seven second graders after a combination of rules, educational structure, praising, and ignoring had been unsuccessful with all but one child. The token program consisted of points exchangeable for daily backup reinforcers of differing values such as candy, dolls, toys, and comics. A more practical and less intensive procedure, involving the daily use of stars and weekly backup reinforcement (i.e., candy), was implemented after withdrawing the token program. This procedure resulted in maintenance of behavioral gains for most of the children. However, improvement did not generalize to school periods in which the contingencies were not in effect.

Some token systems involve group contingencies in which class members earn rewards based on the behavior of one or more of their classmates. These systems may be particularly useful when peer contingencies are competing with teacher contingencies. For example, Patterson (1965) applied a group reward program to a hyperactive child in which class rewards (M & M's and pennies) were contingent on his attending to task. Dramatic reductions in nonattending behavior occurred as a result of the intervention. Using a similar procedure, Coleman (1970) found an increase in working behavior and a decrease in talking aloud and out-of-seat behavior of four children having attentional and behavioral problems. Group contingencies involving consequence sharing have also been found to maintain academic and behavioral gains of a traditional token economy based on individual contingencies (Walker & Buckley, 1972).

A variation of group reward programs involves the use of team contingencies. For example, Barrish, Saunders, and Wolf (1969) implemented a program called the "good behavior game" to reduce disruptive behavior in a regular fourth grade class containing several behavior problem children. The children were divided into two competing teams. Disruptive behavior by any member of a team resulted in a mark being placed on the chalk-board indicating a possible loss of privileges (e.g., extra recess, special projects) by all members of that team. The game was first implemented during math period and later implemented during reading period. The team with the fewest marks at the end of the period earned the group privileges. In cases where both teams lost very few points, they both won the game and they both earned the privileges. This procedure resulted in significant reductions in out-of-seat and talking-out behavior of the students. In fact, both teams won the game (i.e., lost no more than a criterion number of points) more than 80% of the time.

Group token contingencies have been found to be as effective, if not more effective, than individual token contingencies. For example, Rosen-baum, O'Leary, and Jacob (1975) compared the effects of group rewards and individual rewards for an individual students' behavior. Ten hyperactive children from different classes were divided into two groups: one group worked for individual rewards and one group worked for group rewards. In both groups, target children earned a reward card at the end of each school hour if classroom rules had been followed. These cards were then exchanged for candy at the end of the day either for the child only (individual reward) or the child plus the entire class (group reward). Standardized teacher ratings of hyperactivity and ratings of specific target behaviors both indicated a significant treatment effect, although no difference was found between the two groups. However, the group reward resulted in somewhat better maintenance at a 1 month follow-up.

While the above studies have targeted disruptive behaviors thought to be interfering with educational goals, token programs have also been applied directly to academic achievement. Ayllon, Layman, and Kandel (1975) investigated the effects of a token reinforcement system contingent on academic accuracy on the behavior and academic performance of three diagnosed hyperactive children. The token system, implemented after the children had been withdrawn from medication, involved children's earning checks, recorded on an index card, for each correct academic response. The checks were exchanged for a large array of backup reinforcers (e.g., candy, free time, school supplies, picnics in the park) later in the day. Discontinuation of medication resulted in a dramatic increase in gross motor behaviors, disruptive noise, and disturbance of others across all three children. Subsequent implementation of the token program for academic performance sharply increased math and reading scores from a baseline level of 12% to a level of over 85% correct. Moreover, children's levels of hyperactive behaviors were reduced to a level similar to that observed in children on medication. It is important to note, however, that the generalizability of improvements in academic performance in this study to more challenging academic tasks may be limited. As Hinshaw and Erhardt (in press) pointed out, the academic tasks were relatively easy for the children to complete and it is not clear whether the results reflect improvement in academic achievement or simply greater on-task behavior.

Robinson, Newby, and Ganzell (1981) also evaluated the effects of applying a token reward system to the academic performance of hyperactive boys. Tokens were issued for successful completion of four tasks: two that involved learning to read and using new vocabulary words in sentences and two that involved teaching these tasks to another student. Tokens were exchangeable for access to a pinball machine or electronic "pong" game, both of which were located in the classroom. Using a reversal design, the token intervention program resulted in a ninefold increase in the mean number of tasks completed over the baseline level and significant improvement in performance on the school district's standardized weekly reading level exams. Although no specific contingencies were established for non-academic behavior, a reduction in disruptive behavior was also reported. This study is particularly noteworthy for demonstrating that a powerful token program with 18 hyperactive boys could be successfully administered by a single teacher.

Together, these as well as other studies (e.g., Ayllon & Roberts, 1974) indicate that token systems targeted to academic performance not only greatly improve academic performance but also indirectly decrease the inappropriate behavior of hyperactive students as well. The reverse has not always been true, pointing to the importance of targeting academic functioning in addition to targeting social or task-related behavior.

The dramatic improvements evidenced as a result of tangible rewards and token programs and their application to a wide range of problem behavior have led to their widespread use in school settings. However, not all children show maximal improvement as a result of these programs, and in those children who do respond positively, little evidence exists that treatment gains persist once the programs are terminated. In addition, token systems based on group contingencies may lead to undue peer pressure and some students may choose to subvert the system (O'Leary & Drabman, 1971). The success of these programs is also tempered by the amount of teacher time, effort, and material resources required for successful implementation, and the programs may require considerable modification for use in regular

classroom settings. As suggested by Carlson and Lahey (1988), attention also needs to be directed at ways to increase the practicality of these systems due to findings that teachers' acceptability of token systems are related to this issue (e.g., Witt, Martens, & Elliott, 1984).

Ignoring

Ignoring, defined as the withdrawal of teacher attention, is often used as one of the first interventions for mild misbehavior, especially in cases where children's misbehavior is maintained by teacher attention. Several studies with behavior problem children have reported that teacher ignoring of inappropriate behavior can produce dramatic reductions in disruptiveness and increases in on-task behavior when accompanied by praise for appropriate behavior (e.g., Becker, Madsen, Arnold, & Thomas, 1967; Hall, Lund, & Jackson, 1968; Madsen et al., 1968). However, it is noteworthy that teachers did not completely stop using negative consequences in any of these studies, despite instructions to do so. Thus, ignoring all inappropriate behavior may not be possible.

Furthermore, as reviewed earlier, several studies indicate that ignoring and praise alone are ineffective in shaping or maintaining high rates of on-task behavior and work productivity with hyperactive children (Rosén et al., 1984). Ignoring may be ineffective with hyperactive children because much of their misbehavior may be maintained by factors other than teacher attention (e.g., peer attention, physiological variables). Nevertheless, ignoring may be effective in maintaining appropriate behavior in the context of a more powerful reward program (e.g., Pfiffner, Rosén, & O'Leary, 1985). Ignoring may also be a viable procedure with hyperactive children when used as only one component of an overall classroom management program that also incorporates other negative consequences. However, no research currently exists addressing this issue.

Verbal Reprimand

The verbal reprimand is probably the most commonly utilized negative consequence in the classroom (White, 1975). Although early research suggested that reprimands may actually increase inappropriate behavior (Madsen, Becker, Thomas, Koser, & Plager, 1968; Thomas et al., 1968), more recent studies have documented that reprimands are not only effective but are also necessary with hyperactive children (Rosén et al., 1984). In fact, reprimands have been found to be more important than praise for maintaining appropriate behavior. The effectiveness of reprimands, however, appears to vary depending on a number of parameters associated with the delivery style.

A series of studies addressing this issue were conducted by S. O'Leary and her colleagues at Point of Woods Laboratory School, a full-day educational program for eight second and third grade children referred from regular classes because of inattention, overactivity, and conduct problems. In the first of these studies, the type of negative consequence issued by the teacher was directly manipulated (Rosén et al., 1984). Specifically, two multiple component reprimands, "prudent" and "imprudent," were compared in a reversal design. Prudent reprimands were immediate, unemotional, brief, and consistently backed up with time-out or loss of a privilege for repeated noncompliance. Imprudent reprimands were delayed, loud, and emotional, and concrete backup consequences were not utilized. The results strongly supported the beneficial effects of prudent reprimands.

Subsequent studies have examined the effects of a variety of individual parameters of negative consequences including length, timing, consistency, and intensity. Abramowitz, O'Leary, and Futtersak (1988) compared the effects of short and long reprimands in an alternating treatment design. Over the course of the study, short reprimands resulted in significantly lower off-task rates than long reprimands.

Hyperactive children also appear to respond differently to reprimands as a function of when they are delivered in the sequence of misbehavior. Abramowitz and O'Leary (1990) compared the effects of immediate and delayed reprimands on the off-task behavior of four hyperactive boys. Immediate reprimands resulted in much lower rates of off-task interactions with peers than did delayed reprimands. However, virtually no increase in off-task behavior

not involving peers (e.g., daydreaming) was observed when reprimands for those behaviors were delayed. The authors hypothesized that noninteractive off-task behavior may have been an avoidance response to difficult school work that was not affected by the timing of the teacher's reprimands, whereas the interactive off-task may have been reinforced by peer attention and thus more affected by the timing of the feedback. In fact, a subsequent study supported the hypothesis that peer attention mediated the timing effect on peer interactive off-task behavior (Abramowitz, 1988).

The consistency with which reprimands are delivered also appears to be important. Acker and O'Leary (1988) compared the effects of consistent reprimands and inconsistent teacher feedback on calling out, a behavior frequently exhibited by hyperactive children. In the inconsistent condition, the teacher reprimanded 25% of the time and "inadvertently" responded to called out as though children had raised their hands the rest of the time. Results showed clear superiority of consistent reprimands for minimizing children's calling out, highlighting the detrimental effect of mixing positive and negative feedback.

Pfiffner, O'Leary, Rosén, and Sanderson (1985) examined consistency when conceptualized in terms of the percentage of misbehaviors that are followed with reprimands versus those that are ignored. Overall, reprimands were not particularly effective in managing off-task behavior. Furthermore, reprimanding every instance of off-task behavior did not prove to be any more effective than reprimanding only one-quarter of the instances of misbehavior. Thus, in cases where reprimands are not sufficiently powerful, increased consistency does not appear to enhance their efficacy.

A recent study also suggests that the level of intensity or aversiveness of the initial delivery of reprimands may be a critical factor with hyperactive children (Futtersak, O'Leary, & Abramowitz, 1989). In this study, children were exposed to teachers who delivered either consistently strong reprimands from the outset (immediate, brief, firm, and in close proximity to the child) or reprimands that increased in severity over time. Results supported the hypothesis that gradually strengthening initially weak reprimands was less effective for suppressing off-task behavior than the immediate introduction and maintenance of "full strength" reprimands. Moreover, gradually increasing the strength of reprimands resulted in a greater frequency of negative feedback than initially applying "full strength" reprimands over the course of the study.

Together, these studies suggest that reprimands are most effective when they are consistent, immediate, brief, and of sufficient intensity at the outset. Reprimands also appear to be more effective when delivered with eye contact and in close proximity to the child (Van Houten, Nau, MacKenzie-Keating, Sameoto, & Colavecchia, 1982). These dimensions may be particularly critical with hyperactive children who may be sensitive to these stylistic features. However, verbal reprimands may not always be sufficiently powerful to manage the behavior of hyperactive children. As Barkley (1981) notes, hyperactive children are often exposed to the ineffective use of negative feedback at home, which likely reduces the overall effectiveness of reprimands. More powerful backup consequences, including response cost and time-out, may be necessary in these cases.

Response Cost

Response cost has been widely used to manage the disruptive behavior of hyperactive children. This procedure involves the loss of a reinforcer contingent upon inappropriate behavior. Lost reinforcers are typically privileges, activities, tokens, or similar conditioned reinforcers (e.g., point, chip) in a token economy.

Response cost has been applied in a variety of different ways in the classroom and a substantial body of research documents its effectiveness (Kazdin, 1982). In a single subject design with two hyperactive children, Rapport, Murphy, and Bailey (1982) compared the effects of response cost and stimulant medication on task-related behavior. The boys lost 1 point, which translated to a loss of 1 minute of recess, every time the teacher saw them not working. The boys were notified immediately of their point losses following off-task behavior and were kept apprised of their points on a continual basis. The response cost procedure resulted in significant increases in both on-task behavior and

academic performance. Furthermore, stimulant medication was noticeably less effective than the response cost procedure. Pfiffner, O'Leary, Rosén, & Sanderson (1985) also found that response cost (i.e., loss of recess time) was more effective than reprimands in maintaining on-task behavior in a class of eight hyperactive children.

Response cost has been compared to reward programs in several studies. Iwata and Bailey (1974) examined the responses of students in a special education class who exhibited high rates of off-task and disruptive behavior to response cost and reward procedures. In the reward condition, students received tokens contingent on following rules; in the response cost condition, students received tokens at the beginning of each day and were fined for not following rules. Both conditions resulted in a twofold increase in academic output, a reduction in inappropriate classroom behavior and a corresponding increase in on-task behavior. In addition, children did not show a differential preference for either the reward or response cost procedure. Other studies have also found comparable improvement in behavior-problem children's classroom behavior and academic output through the use of reward and response cost programs (e.g., Hundert, 1976).

A recent study examined the differential maintenance of treatment gains achieved with reward and response cost token programs with a group of five hyperactive and five learning-disabled children in the primary grades (Sullivan & O'Leary, 1990). The reward and cost programs were implemented in each of two classes, with one program in effect in reading and the other in effect during math. Consequences consisted of praise, reprimands, and check marks exchangeable for recess minutes or stickers. Within-subject analyses revealed that both the reward and response cost programs had large and equivalent treatment effects. However, differential effects of the two programs resulted during the fading procedure. Specifically, all children maintained treatment gains during the fading of the cost program. However, children rated as hyperactive or aggressive appeared to maintain treatment gains better during fading and withdrawal of the response cost program than the reward program. This difference may be due to the greater sensitivity hyperactive children may have to the differences in discriminability of the change when the reward procedure was faded than when the cost procedure was faded.

Overall, response cost programs appear to be useful with hyperactive children for several reasons: (1) they seem to be as effective as reward procedures in improving children's behavior (e.g., Iwata & Bailey, 1974), (2) they may result in superior maintenance of treatment gains of hyperactive children when faded (e.g., Sullivan & O'Leary, 1990), (3) response cost may be used as a valuable adjunct to cognitive-behavioral treatment programs for impulsive children (see Kendall & Braswell, 1985), (4) both teacher and child attitudes about response cost appear to be as positive as they are for reward programs (Iwata & Bailey, 1974), and (5) response cost may require relatively little teacher time and effort (e.g., Rapport et al., 1982), possibly because of the often greater salience and lesser frequency of inappropriate than appropriate behavior in a regular class. Nevertheless, the effectiveness of response cost is dependent on the selection of appropriate behavioral goals that afford the child success. Unreasonably stringent standards may lead to excessive point or privilege losses that threaten the success of the program.

Time-Out

Time-out from positive reinforcement is frequently recommended for hyperactive children as a consequence for aggressive or disruptive behavior. Time-out involves the withdrawal of environmental sources of positive reinforcement upon the occurrence of the unwanted behavior. In the classroom, this commonly translates into the removal of materials, adult or peer attention. In more severe cases, the student may be removed from the classroom situation. The latter procedure, often referred to as social isolation, was carefully evaluated by Drabman and Spitalnik (1973) in a classroom for emotionally disturbed children between the ages of 9 and 11. Social isolation involved removal from the classroom and placement in a small empty room for 10 minutes contingent on aggression and out-of-seat behavior. Social isolation was clearly effective in reducing the rates of these two behaviors. Other studies have also found social isolation to be effective in reducing aggression (Webster, 1976)

and obscene language (Lahey, McNees, & McNees, 1973).

Isolation time-out has been increasingly criticized over the years due to ethical concerns and difficulty implementing the procedure correctly (Gast & Nelson, 1977). Thus, nonexclusionary time-out procedures that are less controversial and less restrictive than social isolation have been utilized (Brantner & Doherty, 1983). In nonexclusion time-out, a child is not isolated but is removed from the area of reinforcement or the opportunity to earn reinforcement. In the classroom, this may involve having the child sit facing a corner or wall while staying in the classroom. This procedure has been effective for reducing a variety of disruptive and aggressive behaviors (LeBlanc, Busby, & Thomson, 1973; Porterfield, Herbert-Jackson, & Risley, 1976). It is important to note, however, that exclusionary time-out (e.g., removal from the classroom) may be required initially as a backup for noncompliance with the nonexclusionary time-out procedure.

In one of the few studies of time-out effects with a child formally identified as hyperactive, Kubany, Weiss, and Sloggett (1971) used a nonexclusionary time-out procedure and group reinforcement to reduce inappropriate behavior. The procedure involved use of a good behavior clock. Rewards (e.g., penny trinkets, candy) were earned for the child and his class contingent upon the clock running for a specified period of time. The clock ran whenever the child was seated and working quietly, but was stopped for at least 15 seconds when the child was noisy or out of his seat without permission. This procedure resulted in dramatic decreases in disruptive behavior.

In some cases, extremely disruptive hyperactive children may fail to comply with the standard procedure, either by refusing to go to time-out or not remaining in the time-out area for the required duration. Pelham and Bender (1982) described a time-out system that may be useful in such cases. This system involves a hierarchy of time-outs that increase in aversiveness as the child fails to comply (e.g., length of time-out increases, time-out is served in principal's office, child is sent home for time-out). The system also allows a child to earn time-off for complying with the time-out procedure (i.e., length of original time-out is reduced). Unfortunately, this procedure has not yet been empirically validated.

The effectiveness of time-out is well established. Further research is needed to identify parameters associated with the success of time-out with hyperactive children in the school setting. A host of factors may potentially relate to time-out effectiveness, but at this point, implementation of time-out seems to be based more on clinical experience and judgment than scientific findings. Potential factors include such problems as how to strategically select target behaviors and time-out administration procedures that do not provide unintended escape or reward for a child, warnings and allowable time for compliance, length and location of time-out, procedures for handling noncompliance to time-out, and use of time-out in conjunction with other interventions (e.g., positive reinforcement). From both an ethical and legal standpoint, caution in using time-out has also been recommended by investigators in this area (e.g., Branther & Doherty, 1983; Gast & Nelson, 1977) owing to the many possible deleterious effects associated with the misuse of the procedure. It is generally good practice, if not a legal requirement, to keep a running log of time-out. This not only provides documentation that time-out was delivered for an appropriate interval and in an ethical manner but it also provides the behavior analyst with important information about the settings and time of day in which time-outs occur.

PEER-ADMINISTERED CONTINGENCIES

The use of peers as change agents for producing and maintaining their classmates' appropriate behavior has been promoted due to the substantial influence peers have on one another. Unfortunately, children often promote and/or maintain the problem behavior of their peers rather than encouraging their display of appropriate behavior (Solomon & Wahler, 1973). This may be particularly true in the case of hyperactive children. The disruptive, intrusive quality of these children's interactions often disrupts other children who may respond in a provocative, retaliatory fashion, further perpetuating the problem behavior. Furthermore, as Whalen and Henker (1985)

pointed out, hyperactive children may find it particularly difficult to develop positive peer relations due to the mismatch between their need for frequent and consistent reinforcement and the typically low rates of reinforcement children provide for one another.

The ability for peers to serve as positive change agents and induce desirable changes in their disruptive classmates has been demonstrated in several studies. In one of the earliest studies examining this issue, Solomon and Wahler (1973) trained children to praise appropriate behavior and ignore disruptive acts of their classmates. Following training, substantial reductions in deviant behavior and increases in prosocial behavior occurred. It is noteworthy that the trained children were more successful in ignoring problem behavior than they were in rewarding appropriate behavior. Thus, changes in target children's behavior were probably more a result of a reduction in peer attention to inappropriate behavior rather than an increase in attention to appropriate behavior.

Peer reinforcement effects were observed in a later study (Grieger, Kauffman, & Grieger, 1976) in which children were encouraged to publically praise and provide happy-face badges to peers for cooperative behavior during sharing time each day. In this case, peer reinforcement resulted in increases in cooperative play and immediately reduced aggressive acts. During a reversal phase, children were told to report unfriendly rather than cooperative actions of their peers. This procedure was clearly less effective than peer's reporting on positive behavior and resulted in a decrease in cooperation and increase in aggressive acts.

The child change agents involved in the Solomon and Wahler (1973) study were selected because they were responsible and popular and in the Grieger et al. (1976) study children were from regular classes. However, emotionally handicapped children in special education classes have also been taught successfully to reduce teasing and ridiculing from their "normal" peers through ignoring and reinforcement (Graubard, Rosenberg, & Miller, 1971) and kindergarten-aged children with serious behavior and learning problems have also been able to implement a token program effectively under a teacher's supervision (Carden-Smith & Fowler, 1984). Drabman (1973) further demonstrated that peers could do just as well as teachers in reducing disruptive behavior through a token program.

Peer-mediated programs offer several advantages over teacher-mediated programs. As O'Leary and O'Leary (1977) pointed out, peers may be in a better position to observe and prompt appropriate behavior in their classmates than the teacher, especially in environments where adult supervision is minimal (e.g., recess) or absent. Training problem children to alter their interactions with peers can also have positive effects for the children who serve as "behavior modifiers" (e.g., Graubard et al., 1971). By changing their own behavior, these problem children may be in the position to experience more successful interaction with others which may then serve to maintain their positive behavior changes (O'Leary & O'Leary, 1977). Such an outcome would seem to be particularly beneficial for hyperactive children who are at such a great risk for poor peer relations.

Findings by Grieger et al. (1976) and Solomon and Wahler (1973) indicate that children can effectively reward their peers' positive behavior or ignore inappropriate behavior, but they should probably not be used as agents to report or punish negative behavior. Strategic ignoring of inappropriate behavior may be especially important since differences in disruptive, inappropriate behavior between hyperactive and nonhyperactive children may be more salient and more important than differences in prosocial behavior (see Whalen & Henker, 1985). However, further research is necessary to compare various peer interventions and their effects on specific target behaviors and sociometric indices. Perhaps ignoring is more effective for reducing disruptive, off-task behaviors and reinforcement is more important for increasing specific instances of prosocial acts.

Clearly, the success of peer reinforcement programs depends on the ability and motivation of children to learn and accurately implement the program. As O'Leary and O'Leary (1977) discussed, the possibility exists that children might use reward systems in a coercive or punitive fashion. On the other hand, children may be overly lenient in their implementation of the system. They may reward too liberally or withhold reward too infrequently out of fear of peer rejection, more lenient definitions of misbehavior, or because of pressure from their peers

to give excessively high ratings. Careful selection, training, and supervision of the peer monitors by the teacher as well as use of contingencies for accurate ratings may help minimize these problems (O'Leary & O'Leary, 1977), although doing so will clearly increase the cost of the program in terms of teacher time, effort, and resources. Further research is necessary to determine whether the time involved in implementing peer programs is actually greater than that required for teacher-administered programs, and if so, whether the advantages of peer programs (in terms of child attitude or behavior changes) outweigh the costs. In addition, most of the studies involving peer monitors have been conducted with children who have characteristics of hyperactivity but who are not formally identified as "hyperactive." Further research is needed to determine whether hyperactive children can effectively serve as peer monitors or respond favorably to other children serving as monitors.

HOME-BASED CONTINGENCIES

Home-based contingency programs have proved useful for modifying a wide array of school problems often exhibited by hyperactive children. The typical home-based program involves the teacher providing a written report indicating the degree to which a child has performed appropriately at school. Often this report is simply a checklist of several target behaviors. Parents then provide contingencies in the home depending on the teacher's report. Home-based programs typically begin with a note being sent home on a daily basis. In some cases, notes are sent home only when a child has met the behavioral or academic goals for that day. In other cases, a note is sent home on both "good" and "bad" days. Either way, the daily reports can readily be faded to twice weekly, weekly, biweekly, monthly, and finally to the reporting intervals typically used in the school (Barth, 1979).

Several studies have shown that hyperactive children are quite responsive to home-based programs. For example, O'Leary, Pelham, Rosenbaum, and Price (1976) implemented a home-based token program for nine hyperactive children in eight different classes. The program consisted of a daily report card indicating whether the child met his or her academic and/or prosocial goals (e.g., finished math assignment, cooperated with others). Praise and rewards were then provided by parents daily (e.g., extra television viewing, special dessert, time with parents) and weekly (e.g., dinner at a restaurant, special outing) for deserving students. This procedure resulted in significant reductions in teacher ratings of overall hyperactivity as well as in specific problem behaviors. Furthermore, the gains achieved with the note-home program were comparable to those obtained with medication. A similar home-based reward program has also been effective in maintaining behavioral gains following the withdrawal of stimulant medication (Pelham, 1977).

While these studies found that home-based rewards alone are effective, other programs incorporating both positive and negative consequences have been successful (e.g., Ayllon, Garber, & Pisor, 1975; Todd, Scott, Bostow, & Alexander, 1976) and at least one study found that a combination of positive and negative consequences may be more effective than the use of rewards alone (Rosén, Gabardi, & Miller, 1990). In addition, as with classroom-based programs, home-based programs targeting only academic performance have resulted in improvements in both academic and social behaviors (Witt, Hannifin, & Martens, 1983).

The many advantages of home-based programs (e.g., efficacy, practicality, frequent feedback, and reinforcement) have been cited repeatedly in the literature (e.g., Barkley, 1981; Carlson & Lahey, 1988; Jones & Kazdin, 1981). Overall, home-based reward programs can be as, if not more, effective than classroom-based programs (e.g., Ayllon et al, 1975). They generally require considerably less teacher time and effort than a classroom-based intervention and, as a result, teachers who have been unable to implement a classroom management program may be far more likely to implement a note-home program. Aside from their greater acceptability among teachers, these programs also afford parents more frequent feedback regarding their child's performance than would normally be provided. Furthermore, daily reports seem particularly well suited for hyperactive children since they often benefit from more frequent feedback than is usually provided at school. In addition, the type and quality of reinforcers

available in the home are typically far more extensive than those available in the classroom, a factor that may be critical with hyperactive children as reviewed earlier.

Despite the impressive success of note-home programs, several limitations are apparent. As pointed out by Barkley (1981), an accurate report of child behavior by the teacher and the consistent delivery of consequences at home are both necessary for the success of the program. Training in monitoring of child behavior, goal setting, and delivery of consequences may be sufficient for most teachers and parents to implement these programs effectively. In cases where such training is not possible or not sufficient, classroom aides or other school personnel may be utilized to implement the program (Barkley, 1989).

COGNITIVE-BEHAVIORAL INTERVENTIONS

Cognitive-behavioral interventions have been very popular in the treatment of hyperactivity since they were first introduced in the early 1970s. Conceptually, cognitive therapies, with their emphasis on self-control and self-regulation, seem particularly well suited for treating the impulsive, unorganized, and nonreflective manner in which hyperactive children approach their academic tasks and social interactions. Originally, these procedures were also expected to facilitate generalization and maintenance of treatment gains since children would be taught "portable" coping strategies to be used across situations and behaviors (Whalen, Henker, & Hinshaw, 1985).

Many different cognitive-behavioral procedures have been employed with hyperactive children in the classroom. Two such procedures, self-monitoring and self-reinforcement, typically have children monitor their own behavior and reward themselves based on those evaluations. These procedures have often been implemented toward the end of maintaining gains made from token reinforcement programs. For example, Drabman, Spitalnik, and O'Leary (1973) and Turkewitz, O'Leary, and Ironsmith (1975) established token economies in special classrooms of behavior-problem children and then faded the adult control of the programs by teaching children to evaluate and reward their own behavior. When children were reinforced if their ratings matched the teacher's ratings, behavioral gains made during the token program were maintained.

More recently, Hinshaw, Henker, and Whalen (1984a) evaluated the effects of reinforced self-evaluation on the peer interactions of hyperactive children. Twenty-four hyperactive boys were trained to monitor and rate their own behavior in comparison to predetermined behavioral criteria in playground environments. Reinforcement was provided for accurate self-evaluation, defined as matching the adult rating. Playground observations following training showed that reinforced self-evaluation was more effective than externally administered reinforcement in reducing negative and increasing prosocial peer contacts, such as cooperation, although the maintenance and generalization of these findings are not known.

Many cognitive training programs involve teaching children specific strategies such as self-instruction and problem-solving to promote self-control, in addition to the use of self-monitoring and self-reinforcement. The self-instructional program introduced by Meichenbaum and Goodman (1971) is often utilized in these programs. The first part of this procedure involves an adult trainer modeling the self-instructional process while performing a task. The process includes defining the task or problem, planning strategies, evaluating performance, self-reinforcing (usually in the form of positive self-statements), and correcting errors. The child then performs the same task under the verbal direction of the trainer. Next, the child performs the task while self-instructing aloud. These overt verbalizations are then faded to covert self-instructions. Reinforcement is typically provided to the child for following the procedure. The training tasks usually include a variety of psychoeducational tasks (e.g., reproducing designs, following sequential instructions, concept problems) and some studies also include academic and/or social relationship tasks.

A number of cognitive interventions with hyperactive children have been evaluated in terms of their effects on laboratory tests of attention and cognition, academic performance, and behavioral functioning. In general, the results of these studies have been inconsistent, with the most positive effects occurring on measures of attention and cognition (see Abikoff, 1985). However, some investigators have also found that the effects of cognitive training have generalized to academic performance. For instance, Douglas and her colleagues (Douglas, Parry, Marton, & Garson, 1976) provided cognitive training to eighteen 6- to 10-year-old hyperactive boys. The training involved 24 sessions over a 3-month period emphasizing the use of reflective problem-solving strategies (e.g., self-monitoring, modeling, self-verbalizations, self-reinforcement). Parents and teachers observed a portion of the training sessions and were encouraged to support the child's efforts in order to promote generalization at home and at school. Compared to a wait-list control group, the treated children demonstrated significantly greater improvement on several measures of reading achievement at posttest and at 3-month follow-up. However, improvement observed by the treated and control groups on a measure of arithmetic achievement and on teacher ratings of problem behavior at posttest and follow-up did not differ significantly.

Several other investigators have also found improvements in academic performance as a result of cognitive training (Cameron & Robinson, 1980; Kendall & Braswell, 1982; Varni & Henker, 1979). These improvements appear most consistently when external reinforcement is provided for self-evaluations. However, these improvements have often not generalized across academic subjects or to unsupervised settings (Varni & Henker, 1979). In addition, other studies have failed to find improvements in academic productivity as a function of cognitive training (Eastman & Rasbury, 1981; Friedling & O'Leary, 1979).

The use of predominantly nonacademic psychoeducational tasks during training has been blamed for the lack of academic improvement (Abikoff, 1985). In at least one study, academically relevant tasks facilitated generalization from the training sessions to academic performance in the classroom (Cameron & Robinson, 1980). However, findings from a recent study with academically deficient hyperactive boys are inconsistent with these results. In this study, Abikoff, Ganeles, Reiter, Blum, Foley, and Klein (1988) evaluated the effects of cognitive training focused exclusively on academic skills and tasks. The training program, which involved 2 hours of training for 16 weeks, incorporated problem-solving strategies as well as self-monitoring and self-reinforcement of problem-solving behavior and response accuracy. Contrary to expectations, cognitive training was not superior to remedial tutoring or medication alone on academic achievement or any of the other domains tested (i.e., cognitive functioning, school and home functioning, ratings of self-esteem, and attributional perceptions of academic functioning).

The impact of cognitive training on the classroom behavior of hyperactive children has been equally inconsistent. In general, however, training regimens that focus primarily on cognitive problem-solving with psychoeducational or academic tasks have failed to show improvement on teacher ratings of hyperactivity (Douglas et al., 1976) or on time spent on-task in the classroom (Eastman & Rasbury, 1981; Friedling & O'Leary, 1979). However, on-task behavior has been shown to increase when reinforcement for self-evaluations of academic work (Cameron & Robinson, 1980) or on-task behavior (Varni & Henker, 1979) is provided in conjunction with self-instructional training.

A multicomponent self-control training program including self-instructional training and reinforcement of children's self-evaluations was also examined in a study conducted by Barkley, Copeland, and Sivage (1980) with six 7- to 10-year-old hyperactive boys. Self-instructional training was provided in groups with training tasks, including academic and social problems. During individual seat work, children self-monitored and recorded their on-task behavior at signaled intervals. Accurate reports were rewarded with a token that could be exchanged for privileges. Results showed that on-task behavior improved only during individual seat work, pointing to the efficacy of self-monitoring and reinforcing children's evaluations of their own behavior. Training in self-instruction did not reduce misbehavior during the group lessons, presumably due to the lack of specific reinforcement contingencies for appropriate behavior during this period. In addition, behavioral improvements made

during individual seat work did not generalize to the regular classroom. Thus, the use of self-control skills appeared to be tied to the context in which they were taught and where contingencies were in effect for their use.

Most behavioral and cognitive-behavioral interventions have targeted classroom deportment and/or academic performance. More recently, the impact of cognitive-behavioral interventions on hyperactive children's interactions with their peers has been evaluated. The comparative and combined effects of cognitive-behavioral training and stimulant medication in controlling anger and aggression in 9- to 12-year-old hyperactive boys were evaluated by Hinshaw, Henker, and Whalen (1984b). The cognitive-behavioral treatment emphasized the use of social problem-solving skills and stress inoculation procedures that involved monitoring internal cues related to anger and aggression and rehearsing selected coping strategies under increasingly greater provocation from peers. A control treatment focused on social problem solving, perspective taking, and enhancement of empathy. Cognitive-behavioral treatment compared to the control training resulted in greater self-control and use of effective coping strategies in the face of verbal taunting and provocation from peers during a brief group interaction. Medication did not affect self-control, although it did reduce the intensity of the children's responses. Despite these promising results, it is not known from this study whether the beneficial effects found with cognitive training will generalize beyond the staged situation used in this study to more naturalistic encounters with peers.

In sum, the effects of cognitive therapy are often inconsistent. When positive effects are found, they are not as strong, as durable, or as generalizable as was once expected (Whalen et al., 1985). As suggested by Abikoff (1985), the lack of generalization of cognitive training effects to academic and behavioral measures may be due to the brevity of the training (often only a few hours), and to little or no overlap between the skills taught during training and the requirements of the classroom. Greater efforts at programming for generalization are needed. Few studies have assessed long-term maintenance of treatment gains, and those that have been conducted have yielded limited maintenance at best.

Aside from their questionable efficacy, cognitive-behavioral interventions frequently require an excessive amount of time and resources for proper implementation. These limitations are especially salient in the classroom setting and are particularly important since, as Barkley (1981) noted, the costs of implementing a cognitive-behavioral program may be greater than the costs of implementing a traditional behavioral program. Despite these concerns, continued revision and evaluation of cognitive-behavioral techniques may be justified on an experimental basis (see Whalen & Henker, 1987). As noted by Whalen and Henker (1987), however, cognitive-behavioral techniques should be viewed as adjuncts and not alternatives to procedures having documented efficacy with hyperactive children.

CLASSROOM CHARACTERISTICS AND TASK FACTORS

Early attempts to modify hyperactive behavior through alteration of the classroom environment focused on minimal stimulation programs. These programs were based on the premise that hyperactive children's poor school functioning was related to their distractibility or unusually high responsivity to environmental stimulation (Ross & Ross, 1976). As a result, the removal of as many visual distracters (e.g., pictures and posters, brightly colored walls and ceilings, attention-getting clothing and jewelry) and auditory distracters as possible was recommended. In some cases, desks were placed on corners facing the wall, and in other cases, the use of cubicles enclosed on three sides was recommended to reduce exposure to distracting stimuli. Despite initial claims of success, methodological shortcomings of studies evaluating the efficacy of these programs have precluded identification of clear, beneficial effects in the classroom (see Ross & Ross, 1976).

Recently, Zentall (1975) has posited that hyperactive children require more stimulation to achieve the point of optimal stimulation necessary for effective functioning than do nonhyperactive children. In

support of this theory, a series of laboratory studies (Zentall, Falkenberg, & Smith, 1985; Zentall & Meyer, 1987) suggests that extra and intratask novelty stimulation can reduce activity and improve performance of hyperactive children, especially on easy, repetitive tasks. Tasks requiring an active as opposed to a passive response may also allow hyperactive children to better channel their disruptive behaviors into constructive responses more efficiently (Zentall & Meyer, 1987). These findings may have implications regarding how best to structure academic assignments with hyperactive children (e.g., Barkley, 1989). However, research is required to verify whether academic assignments that are of greater interest or require an active response are actually more effective.

Whalen, Henker, Collins, Finck, and Dotemoto (1979) analyzed the effects of environmental and task variables in the classroom setting. They posited that hyperactivity is a function of the social and environmental context and may be best understood in terms of a child-by-situation interaction. Following this framework, they systematically examined the effects of auditory stimulation in the classroom and several task variables (e.g., task difficulty, self- vs. other-paced) on hyperactive children. Results of this work showed that, when children were unmedicated, a noisy environment was associated with less task attention and higher rates of negative verbalizations and other inappropriate behavior than was a quiet classroom. Tasks that were relatively difficult and paced by an outside source also resulted in greater rates of potentially inappropriate behavior. In fact, the performance of unmedicated children during quiet conditions with easy, self-paced tasks was equivalent to the performance of medicated and nonhyperactive children.

Identification of additional environmental factors affecting hyperactive children's classroom performance (e.g., size of class, ratio of hyperactive to nonhyperactive children, seating arrangements, open vs. closed classes, curriculum issues) requires further research. Although knowledge of such factors may lead to the development of low-cost intervention strategies, it is unlikely that these approaches will be sufficient for maximizing school performance without the use of traditional behavioral programs.

COMBINED EFFECTS OF BEHAVIORAL AND PHARMACOLOGICAL TREATMENTS

As indicated, a variety of different behavioral management strategies have been used with substantial success to modify the classroom behavior and academic performance of hyperactive children. Nevertheless, recent studies question the sufficiency of behavioral interventions for treating hyperactivity. Many children fail to show improvement with behavioral interventions (often due to the teacher's difficulty in implementing the program) and those who do usually continue to function outside the normal range (e.g., Abikoff & Gittelman, 1984; Pelham, et al., 1988). Furthermore, gains in behavioral programs are difficult to maintain and typically fail to generalize to other situations devoid of contingencies. As a result, investigators have begun examining whether medication can be used in conjunction with behavioral and/or cognitive-behavioral approaches to enhance treatment outcome.

Stimulant medication is currently the most prevalent form of treatment for hyperactivity. Numerous studies document significant improvement in treated children on measures of classroom deportment, academic productivity, and more recently, on measures of learning and social interaction on the playground (see chapter 11). However, like behavioral interventions, pharmacological approaches are not effective for all children, fail to normalize the academic and social functioning of those who do respond positively, lose their efficacy once they are discontinued, and do not improve long-term prognosis. Even though medication as a sole treatment is not sufficient, as is the case with behavioral approaches, the combination of the two has been predicted to be more effective than either alone due to interactive, complementary, and/or additive effects (Pelham & Murphy, 1986).

In a recent review of the literature in which a combination of behavioral and stimulant treatment was used with hyperactive children, Pelham and Murphy (1986) found that combined treatments were usually more effective than single interventions in terms of rank order, although not always in terms of

statistical significance. Nevertheless, treated children's gains in social, behavioral, and academic functioning have been found to approach the normal range only with a combined approach (Hinshaw et al., 1984; Pelham, Schnedler, Bologna, & Contreras, 1980; Pelham et al., 1988). It should be noted, however, that the superior effects of a combined approach appear to occur only during periods when medication is being administered. Several studies that withdrew medication during postassessments failed to find that the incremental effects were maintained.

The combination of behavioral and pharmacological treatments appears to be a more powerful treatment than the combination of cognitive-behavioral and pharmacological approaches. That is, the relatively weak effects of cognitive-behavioral approaches have generally not been enhanced with medication, particularly on measures of academic performance. However, recent work by Hinshaw, Buhrmester, and Heller (1989) suggests that medication may indeed facilitate the effects of cognitive-behavioral approaches on hyperactive children's self-control and interactions with peers.

In sum, combination treatments appear to hold much promise, but research in this area is still somewhat preliminary. Large individual differences exist in children's responses to the combined and singular interventions. The variables accounting for these differences are not known. Further research is also necessary to determine the importance of each treatment modality on specific target problems of hyperactive children. Poor maintenance and generalization with behavioral and cognitive-behavioral treatments were two of the most important factors associated with the initial call to combine medical and psychological treatments. Whether the combination will fulfill these goals awaits further research.

SUMMARY AND FUTURE DIRECTIONS

A wide variety of behavioral and cognitive-behavioral approaches have been implemented in the classroom to treat both the core problems (i.e., inattention, impulsivity, and overactivity) and associated problems (e.g., aggression, academic underachievement, peer difficulties) of hyperactive children. Many teacher-administered consequences have produced significant improvements in academic productivity, task attention, and social behavior. However, the combination of praising appropriate behavior and ignoring inappropriate behavior, which is often successful with nonhyperactive children, is not sufficient with these children. Hyperactive children seem to profit from more powerful and/or frequent incentives such as tangible rewards or token economies. They also seem to require prudent reprimands, backed up with a loss of privilege or time-out for severe behavior. Group contingencies and peer-administered consequences have been used less frequently with hyperactive children, but are promising, especially to the extent that they may indirectly improve peer status. Involvement of parents through home-based contingency programs has also resulted in substantial behavioral and academic improvement. An integration of home and school contingencies may be particularly effective (e.g., Ayllon et al., 1975; Pelham et al., 1980) and has been found to maintain appropriate classroom conduct following withdrawal of medication (O'Leary & Pelham, 1978).

Nevertheless, gains made as a result of these contingencies are often not clinically significant and most children continue to function outside the normal range. Furthermore, children's responses to behavioral contingencies are highly variable, with some children showing only limited improvement. Even in those children who do respond positively, the gains made seem to be limited to the situation in which contingencies are in effect. These limitations initially prompted the use of cognitive-behavioral therapies in conjunction with contingency management programs. For the most part, however, existing data have failed to demonstrate that these interventions lead to meaningful or generalizable gains in classroom conduct and academic achievement.

In light of these conclusions, one would expect that researchers would currently be exploring procedures to increase the efficacy of classroom interventions. However, surprisingly few studies examining behavioral or cognitive-behavioral interventions in schools have recently been conducted. Clearly, this is not a result of having found the curative or optimal intervention for hyperactivity. On the contrary, the long-term prognosis of these children continues to be poor.

Many potential reasons exist for the lack of current research in this area. The difficulty conducting large-scale classroom intervention studies in terms of time and resources is substantial. Many researchers may also have become disenchanted with behavioral and/or cognitive-behavioral approaches and, instead of perfecting these approaches, have sought alternative interventions such as stimulant medication. Along these lines, Hinshaw and Erhardt (in press) posit that the dearth of studies investigating behavioral interventions flows from the belief that stimulant medication is sufficiently effective that additional treatments are not necessary. Recent research, however, clearly disconfirms this belief. For instance, stimulant medication has not been shown to have a significant impact on academic skill acquisition and peer status. Moreover, stimulant medication has not been successful in altering the poor prognosis of hyperactive children.

Overall, a great need exists for research investigating school interventions, and the following recommendations are made. First, strategies are needed to improve the clinical significance of behavioral and cognitive-behavioral treatment outcomes as well as to facilitate the generalization and maintenance of treatment gains.

In terms of clinical significance, the potency of these interventions may need to be increased. To do so requires further understanding of the factors operative in behavioral change with hyperactive children. For instance, what are the critical aspects of a reward program with hyperactive children? Laboratory studies suggest that hyperactive children tend to seek direct, immediate rewards and respond best to a continuous as opposed to a partial reward schedule. These findings indicate that optimal functioning occurs with frequent positive feedback. However, they also suggest that the fading of reward programs through reductions in the frequency of feedback may thwart maintenance of treatment gains. Further research is necessary to determine whether and how reward programs should be faded. Group reward programs also deserve further study, not only because of their success in improving classroom functioning, but also because of their practicality and potential for improving peer relations.

Variables associated with the delivery of effective reprimands have recently been investigated, yet questions persist with regard to their optimal utilization in the context of reward programs, and how and when to implement more potent negative consequences such as response cost or time-out. Recent work suggests that fading of response cost programs results in better maintenance of treatment gains than fading of reward programs, although both procedures are equally effective in initially shaping children's behavior. Thus, in order to evaluate their overall efficacy, these procedures not only need to be evaluated in terms of their initial effects, but also in terms of the extent to which they can be faded successfully.

Effective behavioral programs necessarily involve contingencies that are based on a functional analysis of environmental cues, dispositional variables, and maintaining consequences. The same is true of cognitive-behavioral therapies, yet far too little research of these approaches has been based on such an analysis. For cognitive-behavioral approaches to be successful, it is necessary that they be based on a task analysis of the cognitive and problem-solving deficits that are responsible for the undesirable outcomes in the natural environment. In addition, it is unlikely that hyperactive children possess the high level of responsibility and motivation for change required for success in a cognitively based program. Thus, the concomitant use of behavioral interventions will likely be necessary. Indeed, when these factors are incorporated into cognitive-behavioral interventions, behavioral improvements have been found (e.g., Hinshaw et al., 1984).

Most classroom studies to date have limited their focus to outcome measures related to task attention and academic productivity. However, normalization of these children's behavioral gains also involves improvement in the critical areas of academic skill development and peer status. Greater research attention should be paid to treatments targeting these areas. Along these lines, cognitive-behavioral social skills training seems to hold promise for improving the interactions hyperactive children have with their peers. However, few studies have measured changes in peers' appraisal of hyperactive children (e.g., through sociometric measures) as a function of treatment. Given the importance of such measures

in predicting long-term adjustment, this would seem to be a fruitful area for more research.

It is interesting that many of the studies evaluating the effects of behavioral management programs have been conducted in special classes containing few children and with teachers who are well trained in behavioral procedures. However, hyperactive children are typically in mainstream classrooms containing up to 40 chidren and are taught by teachers who have little experience with behavioral procedures. Many of the programs implemented by teachers of small specialized classes are probably quite difficult to implement in larger classes. Short of providing extensive teacher training in behavior modification, many of these programs are apt to require some modification in terms of reduced time and resources in order to be implemented in mainstream classes. Although the modified procedures may be sufficient for some children, other children need special school placements in order to receive the intensive, individualized treatment that they need. Development and evaluation of multifaceted school-based treatment programs targeting the diverse array of problems evidenced by hyperactive children are important in this regard. At a minimum, such programs should include intensive behavioral classroom management systems, social skills training, and parent involvement in home-based contingency programs (see, for example, Swanson, 1988).

Pharmacological approaches have recently been found to be effective adjuncts to behavioral interventions. Combination treatments appear to be consistently more effective than singular interventions, especially in terms of normalizing children's behavior. Further research is necessary to determine how to optimize the combination of stimulant medication and behavioral approaches in individual children. The use of stimulant medication may be particularly advantageous if a low dose of medication can be shown to enhance the effects of less intensive, less complex behavioral programs. Such findings would suggest that hyperactive children could be successfully maintained in regular, mainstream classes.

Given the heterogeneity of hyperactive children and the individual variability in their response to behavioral and pharmacological interventions, meaningful treatment gains will most likely depend on the extent to which interventions can be individualized to meet the specific needs of each child. It seems unrealistic to expect that a relatively brief, circumscribed intervention in one classroom or academic period will generalize to the vastly different environment on the playground, needless to say to a different teacher and class the following year. The pervasiveness and durability of hyperactive children's problems necessitate broadly based, long-term interventions. Transfer of treatment effects needs to be carefully programmed and technologies developed to accomplish this goal. Studies are then needed to evaluate the success of these interventions in improving the long-term outcome of hyperactive children.

REFERENCES

Abikoff, H. (1985). Efficacy of cognitive training intervention in hyperactive children: A critical review. *Clinical Psychology Review, 5,* 479–512.

Abikoff, H., Ganeles, D., Reiter, G., Blum, C., Foley, C., & Klein, R. G. (1988). Cognitive training in academically deficient ADDH boys receiving stimulant medication. *Journal of Abnormal Child Psychology, 16,* 411–432.

Abikoff, H., & Gittelman, R. (1984). Does behavior therapy normalize the classroom behavior of hyperactive children? *Archives of General Psychiatry, 41,* 449–454.

Abramowitz, A. J. (1988). *Delayed vs. immediate reprimands in the classroom: The influence of competing peer reinforcers.* Unpublished doctoral dissertation, State University of New York at Stony Brook.

Abramowitz, A. J., & O'Leary, S. G. (1990). Effectiveness of delayed punishment in an applied setting. *Behavior Therapy, 21,* 231–239.

Abramowitz, A. J., O'Leary, S. G., & Futtersak, M. W. (1988). The relative impact of long and short reprimands on children's off-task behavior in the classroom. *Behavior Therapy, 19,* 243–247.

Acker, M. M., & O'Leary, S. G. (1987). Effects of reprimands and praise on appropriate behavior in the classroom. *Journal of Abnormal Child Psychology, 15,* 549–557.

Acker, M. M., & O'Leary, S. G. (1988). Effects of consistent and inconsistent feedback on inappropriate child behavior. *Behavior Therapy, 19,* 619–624.

American Psychiatric Association. (1987). *Diagnostic and statistical manual of mental disorders* (3rd ed., rev.). Washington DC: Author.

Atkins, M. S., Pelham, W. E., & Licht, M. H. (1985). A comparison of objective classroom measures and teacher ratings of attention deficit disorder. *Journal of Abnormal Child Psychology, 13,* 155–167.

Ayllon, T., Garber, S., & Pisor, K. (1975). The elimination of discipline problems through a combined school-home motivational system. *Behavior Therapy, 6,* 616–626.

Ayllon, T., Layman, D., & Kandel, H. J. (1975). A behavioral-educational alternative to drug control of hyperactive children. *Journal of Applied Behavior Analysis, 68,* 137–146.

Ayllon, T., & Roberts, M. (1974). Eliminating discipline problems by strengthening academic performance. *Journal of Applied Behavior Analysis, 7,* 71–76.

Barkley, R. A. (1981). *Hyperactive children: A handbook for diagnosis and treatment.* New York: Guilford Press.

Barkley, R. A. (1989). Attention deficit hyperactivity disorder. In E. J. Mash & R. A. Barkley (Eds.). *Treatment of Childhood Disorders* (pp. 39–72). New York: Guilford Press.

Barkley, R. A., Copeland, A. P., & Sivage, C. (1980). A self-control classroom for hyperactive children. *Journal of Autism and Developmental Disorders, 10,* 75–89.

Barrish, H. H., Saunders, M., & Wolf, M. M. (1969). Good behavior game: Effects of individual contingencies for group consequences on disruptive behavior in a classroom. *Journal of Applied Behavior Analysis, 2,* 119–124.

Barth, R. (1979). Home-based reinforcement of school behavior: A review and analysis. *Review of Educational Research, 49,* 436–458.

Becker, W. C., Madsen, C. H., Jr., Arnold, C. R., & Thomas, D. R. (1967). The contingent use of teacher attention and praise in reducing classroom behavior problems. *Journal of Special Education, 1,* 287–307.

Brantner, J. P., & Doherty, M. H. (1983). A review of timeout: A conceptual and methodological analysis. In S. Axelrod, & J. Apsche (Eds.), *The effects of punishment on human behavior* (pp. 87–132). New York: Academic Press.

Cameron, M. I., & Robinson, V. M. J. (1980). Effects of cognitive training on academic and on-task behavior of hyperactive children. *Journal of Abnormal Child Psychology, 8,* 405–419.

Campbell, S., Endman, M., & Bernfield, G. (1977). A three year follow-up of hyperactive preschoolers into elementary school. *Journal of Child Psychology and Psychiatry, 18,* 239–249.

Cantwell, D. P., & Satterfield, J. H. (1978). The prevalence of academic under achievement in hyperactive children. *Journal of Pediatric Psychology, 3,* 168–171.

Carden-Smith, L. K., & Fowler, S. A. (1984). Positive peer pressure: The effects of peer monitoring on children's disruptive behavior. *Journal of Applied Behavior Analysis, 17,* 213–227.

Carlson, C., & Lahey, B. (1988). Conduct disorders and attention deficit disorders. In Witt, Elliott, & Gresham (Eds.), *The handbook of behavior therapy in education* (pp. 653–677). New York: Plenum.

Coleman, R. A. (1970). A conditioning technique applicable to elementary school classrooms. *Journal of Applied Behavior Analysis, 3,* 293–297.

Douglas, V. I., & Parry, P. A. (1983). Effects of reward on delayed reaction time task performance of hyperactive children. *Journal of Abnormal Child Psychology, 11,* 313–326.

Douglas, V. I., Parry, P., Marton, P., & Garson, C. (1976). Assessment of a cognitive training program for hyperactive children. *Journal of Abnormal Child Psychology, 4,* 389–410.

Drabman, R. S. (1973). Child- versus teacher-administered token programs in a psychiatric hospital school. *Journal of Abnormal Child Psychology, 1,* 68–87.

Drabman, R. S., & Spitalnik, R. (1973). Social isolation as a punishment procedure: A controlled study. *Journal of Experimental Child Psychology, 16,* 236–249.

Drabman, R. S., Spitalnik, R., & O'Leary, K. D. (1973). Teaching self-control to disruptive children. *Journal of Abnormal Psychology, 82,* 10–16.

Eastman, B. G., & Rasbury, W. C. (1981). Cognitive self-instruction for the control of impulsive classroom behavior: Ensuring the treatment package. *Journal of Abnormal Child Psychology, 9,* 381–387.

Friedling, C., & O'Leary, S. G. (1979). Effects of self-instructional training on second and third grade hyperactive children: A failure to replicate. *Journal of Applied Behavior Analysis, 12,* 211–219.

Futtersak, M. W., O'Leary, S. G., & Abramowitz, A. J. (1989). *The effects of consistently and increasingly strong reprimands in the classroom.* Unpublished manuscript.

Gast, D. C., & Nelson, C. M. (1977). Timeout in the classroom: Implications for special education. *Exceptional Children, 43,* 461–464.

Graubard, P. S., Rosenberg, H., & Miller, M. B. (1971). Student applications of behavior modification to teachers and environments or ecological approaches to social deviancy. In E. A. Ramp & B. L. Hopkins (Eds.), *A new direction for education: Behavior Analysis 1971* (Vol. 1). Lawrence: University of Kansas.

Grieger, T., Kauffman, J. M., & Grieger, R. M. (1976). Effects of peer reporting on cooperative play and aggression of kindergarten children. *Journal of School Psychology, 14,* 307–313.

Haenlein, M., & Caul, W. F. (1987). Attention deficit disorder with hyperactivity: A specific hypothesis of reward dysfunction. *Journal of the Academy of Child and Adolescent Psychiatry, 26,* 356–362.

Hall, R. V., Lund, D., & Jackson, D. (1968). Effects of teacher attention on study behavior. *Journal of Applied Behavior Analysis, 1,* 1–12.

Hinshaw, S. P. (1987). On the distinction between attentional deficits/hyperactivity and conduct problems/aggression in child psychopathology. *Psychological Bulletin, 101,* 443–463.

Hinshaw, S. P., Buhrmester, D., & Heller, T. (1989). Anger control in response to verbal provocation: Effects of stimulant medication for boys with ADHD. *Journal of Abnormal Child Psychology, 17,* 393–407.

Hinshaw, S. P., & Erhardt, D. (in press). Behavioral treatment of attention deficit hyperactivity disorder. In V. B. Van Hasselt & M Hersen (Eds.), *Handbook of behavior therapy and pharmacotherapy for children: A comparative analysis.* New York: Grune & Stratton.

Hinshaw, S. P., Henker, B., & Whalen, C. K. (1984a). Cognitive-behavioral and pharmacological interventions for hyperactive boys: Comparative and combined effects. *Journal of Consulting and Clinical Psychology, 52,* 739–749.

Hinshaw, S. P., Henker, B., & Whalen, C. K. (1984b). Self-control in hyperactive boys in anger-inducing situations: Effects of cognitive-behavioral training and of methylphenidate. *Journal of Abnormal Child Psychology, 12,* 55–77.

Hundert, J. (1976). The effectiveness of reinforcement, response cost, and mixed programs on classroom behaviors. *Journal of Applied Behavior Analysis, 9,* 107.

Iwata, B. A., & Bailey, J. S. (1974). Reward versus cost token systems: An analysis of the effects on students and teachers. *Journal of Applied Behavior Analysis, 7,* 567–576.

Jones, R. T., & Kazdin, A. E. (1981). Childhood behavior problems in the school. In S. M. Turner, K. S. Calhoun, & H. E. Adams (Eds.), *Handbook of clinical behavior therapy* (pp. 568–588). New York: Wiley.

Kazdin, A. E. (1982). The token economy: A decade later. *Journal of Applied Behavior Analysis, 15,* 431–445.

Kendall, P. C., & Braswell, L. (1982). Cognitive-behavioral self-control therapy for children: A components analysis. *Journal of Consulting and Clinical Psychology, 50,* 672–689.

Kendall, P. C., & Braswell, L. (1985). *Cognitive behavioral therapy for impulsive children.* New York: Guilford Press.

Klein, A. R., & Young, R. D. (1979). Hyperactive boys in their classroom: Assessment of teacher and peer perceptions, interactions and classroom behaviors. *Journal of Abnormal Child Psychology, 7,* 425–442.

Kubany, E. S., Weiss, L. E., & Sloggett, B. B. (1971). The good behavior clock: A reinforcement/time out procedure for reducing disruptive classroom behavior. *Journal of Behavior Therapy and Experimental Psychiatry, 2,* 173–179.

Lahey, B. B., McNees, M. P., & McNees, M. C. (1973). Control of an obscene "verbal tic" through timeout in an elementary school classroom. *Journal of Applied Behavior Analysis, 6,* 101–104.

LeBlanc, J. M., Busby, K. H., & Thomson, C. (1973). The functions of timeout for changing aggressive behavior of a preschool child: A multiple baseline analysis. In R. E. Ulrich, T. S. Stachnik, & J. E. Mabry (Eds.), *Control of human behavior: Behavior modification in education* Vol. 3, pp. 358–364). Glenview, IL: Scott Foresman.

Madsen, C. H., Becker, W. C., & Thomas, D. R. (1968). Rules, praise, and ignoring: Elements of elementary classroom control. *Journal of Applied Behavior Analysis, 1,* 139–150.

Madsen, C. H., Becker, W. C., Thomas, D. R., Koser, L., & Plager, E. (1968). An analysis of the reinforcing function of "sit-down" commands. In R. K. Parker (Ed.), *Readings in educational psychology* (pp. 265–278). Boston: Allyn and Bacon.

Meichenbaum, D. H., & Goodman, J. (1971). Training impulsive children to talk to themselves: A means of developing self-control. *Journal of Abnormal Psychology, 77,* 115–126.

Milich, R., & Landau, S. (1982). Socialization and peer relations in hyperactive children. In K. D. Gadow & I. Bialer (Eds.), *Advances in learning and behavioral disabilities* (Vol. 1, pp. 283–339). Greenwich, CT: JAI Press.

O'Leary, K. D., Becker, W. C., Evans, M. B., & Saudargas, R. A. (1969). A token reinforcement program in a public school: A replication and systematic analysis. *Journal of Applied Behavior Analysis, 2,* 3–13.

O'Leary, K. D., & Drabman, R. S. (1971). Token reinforcement programs in the classroom: A review. *Psychological Bulletin, 25,* 379–398.

O'Leary, K. D., & O'Leary, S. G. (1977). *Classroom management: The successful use of behavior modification* (2nd ed.). Elmsford, NY: Pergamon Press.

O'Leary, K. D., Pelham, W. E., Rosenbaum, A., & Price, G. H. (1976). Behavioral treatment of hyperkinetic children: An experimental evaluation of its usefulness. *Clinical Pediatrics, 15,* 510–515.

O'Leary, S. G., & O'Leary, K. D. (1976). Behavior modification in the school. In H. Leitenberg (Ed.), *Handbook of behavior modification and behavior therapy* (pp. 475–515). Englewood Cliffs, NJ: Prentice-Hall.

O'Leary, S. G., & Pelham, W. E. (1978). Behavior therapy and withdrawal of stimulant medication in hyperactive children. *Pediatrics, 61,* 211–217.

Patterson, G. R. (1965). An application of conditioning techniques to the control of a hyperactive child. In L. P. Ullman & L. Krasner (Eds.), *Case studies in behavior modification* (pp. 370–375). New York: Holt, Rinehart, & Winston.

Pelham, W. E. (1977). Withdrawal of stimulant drug and concurrent behavioral intervention in the treatment of a hyperactive child. *Behavior Therapy, 8,* 473–479.

Pelham, W. E., & Bender, M. E. (1982). Peer relations in hyperactive children: Description and treatment. In K. D. Gadow & I. Bialer (Eds.), *Advances in learning and behavioral disabilities* (Vol. 1, pp. 365–436). Greenwich, CT.: JAI Press.

Pelham, W. E., & Murphy, H. A. (1986). Attention deficit and conduct disorders. In M. Hersen (Ed.), *Pharmacological and behavioral treatments: An integrative approach* (pp. 108–148). New York: John Wiley & Sons.

Pelham, W. E., Schnedler, R. W., Bender, M. E., Nilsson, D. E., Miller, J., Budrow, M. S., Ronnei, M., Paluchowski, C., & Marks, D. A. (1988). The combination of behavior therapy and methylphenidate in the treatment of attention deficit disorders: A therapy outcome study. In L. Bloomingdale (Ed.), *Attention deficit disorder* (Vol. 3, pp. 29–48). Elmsford, NY: Pergamon Press.

Pelham, W. E., Schnedler, R. W., Bologna, N. C., & Contreras, J. A. (1980). Behavioral and stimulant treatment of hyperactive children: A therapy study with methylphenidate probes in a within-subject design. *Journal of Applied Behavior Analysis, 13,* 221–236.

Peter, D., Allan, J., & Horvath, A. (1983). Hyperactive children's perceptions of teachers' classroom behavior. *Psychology in the Schools, 20,* 234–240.

Pfiffner, L. J., & O'Leary, S. G. (1987). The efficacy of all-positive management as a function of the prior use of negative consequences. *Journal of Applied Behavior Analysis, 20,* 265–271.

Pfiffner, L. J., O'Leary, S. G., Rosén, L. A., & Sanderson, W. C., Jr. (1985). A comparison of the effects of continuous and intermittent response cost and reprimands in the classroom. *Journal of Clinical Child Psychology, 14,* 348–352.

Pfiffner, L. J., Rosén, L. A., & O'Leary, S. G. (1985). The efficacy of an all-positive approach to classroom management. *Journal of Applied Behavior Analysis, 18,* 257–261.

Porterfield, J. K., Herbert-Jackson, E., & Risley, T. R. (1976). Contingent observation: An effective and acceptable procedure for reducing disruptive behavior of young children in a group setting. *Journal of Applied Behavior Analysis, 9,* 55–64.

Rapport, M. D., Murphy, H. A., & Bailey, J. S. (1982). Ritalin vs. response cost in the control of hyperactive children: A within-subject comparison. *Journal of Applied Behavior Analysis, 15,* 205–216.

Redd, W. H., Morris, E. K., & Martin, J. A. (1975). Effects of positive and negative adult-child interactions on children's social preferences. *Journal of Experimental Child Psychology, 19,* 153–164.

Robinson, P. W., Newby, T. J., & Ganzell, S. L. (1981). A token system for a class of underachieving children. *Journal of Applied Behavior Analysis, 14,* 307–315.

Rosén, L. A., Gabardi, L., & Miller, C. D. (1990). Home-based treatment of disruptive junior high school students: An analysis of the differential effects of positive and negative consequences. *Behavioral Disorders, 15,* 227–232.

Rósen, L. A., O'Leary, S. G., Joyce, S. A., Conway, G., & Pfiffner, L. J. (1984). The importance of prudent negative consequences for maintaining the appropriate behavior of hyperactive students. *Journal of Abnormal Child Psychology, 12,* 581–604.

Rosenbaum, A., O'Leary, K. D., & Jacob, R. G. (1975). Behavioral interventions with hyperactive children: Group consequences as a supplement to individual contingencies. *Behavior Therapy, 6,* 315–323.

Ross, D. M., & Ross, S. A. (1976). *Hyperactivity: Research, theory & action.* New York: John Wiley & Sons.

Solomon, R. W., & Wahler, R. G. (1973). Peer reinforcement control of classroom problem behavior. *Journal of Applied Behavior Analysis, 6,* 49–56.

Sullivan, M. A., & O'Leary, S. G. (1990). Maintenance following reward and cost token programs. *Behavior Therapy, 21,* 139–149.

Swanson, J. M. (1988). Discussion. In J. F. Kavanagh & T. J. Truss, Jr. (Eds.), *Learning disabilities: Proceedings of the national conference.* Parkton, MD: York Press.

Thomas, D. R., Becker, W. C., & Armstrong, M. (1968). Production and elimination of disruptive classroom behavior by systematically varying teacher's behavior. *Journal of Applied Behavior Analysis, 1,* 35–45.

Todd, D. D., Scott, R. B., Bostow, D. E., & Alexander, S. B. (1976). Modification of the excessive inappropriate classroom behavior of two elementary school students using home-based consequences and daily report-card procedures. *Journal of Applied Behavior Analysis, 9,* 106.

Turkewitz, H., O'Leary, K. D., & Ironsmith, M. (1975). Generalization and maintenance of appropriate behav-

ior through self-control. *Journal of Consulting and Clinical Psychology, 43,* 577–583.

Van Houten, R., Nau, P. A., MacKenzie-Keating, S. E., Sameoto, D., & Colavecchia, B. (1982). An analysis of some variables influencing the effectiveness of reprimands. *Journal of Applied Behavior Analysis, 15,* 65–83.

Varni, J. W., & Henker, B. (1979). A self-regulation approach to the treatment of three hyperactive boys. *Child Behavior Therapy, 1,* 171–192.

Walker, H. M., & Buckley, N. K. (1972). Programming generalization and maintenance of treatment effects across time and across settings. *Journal of Applied Behavior Analysis, 5,* 209–224.

Webster, R. E. (1976). A time-out procedure in a public school setting. *Psychology in the Schools, 13,* 72–76.

Weiss, G., & Hechtman, L. T. (1986). *Hyperactive children grown up: Empirical findings and theoretical considerations.* New York: Guilford Press.

Whalen, C. K. & Henker, B. (1985). The social worlds of hyperactive (ADDH) children. *Clinical Psychology Review, 5,* 447–478.

Whalen, C. K., & Henker, B. (1987). Cognitive behavior therapy for hyperactive children: What do we know? *Journal of Children in Contemporary Society, 19,* 123–141.

Whalen, C. K., Henker, B., & Hinshaw, S. P. (1985). Cognitive-behavioral therapies for hyperactive children: Premises, problems, and prospects. *Journal of Abnormal Child Psychology, 13,* 391–410.

Whalen, C. K., Henker, B., Collins, B. E., Finck, D., & Dotemoto, S. (1979). A social ecology of hyperactive boys: Medication effects in systematically structured classroom environments. *Journal of Applied Behavior Analysis, 12,* 65–81.

White, M. A. (1975). Natural rates of teacher approval and disapproval in the classroom. *Journal of Applied Behavior Analysis, 8,* 367–372.

Witt, J. C., Hannafin, M. J., & Martens, B. K. (1983). Home-based reinforcement: Behavioral covariation between academic performance and inappropriate behavior. *Journal of School Psychology, 21,* 337–348.

Witt, J. C., Martens, B. K., & Elliott, S. N. (1984). Factors affecting teachers' judgments of the acceptability of behavioral interventions: Time involvement, behavior problem severity, and type of intervention. *Behavior Therapy, 15,* 204–209.

Zentall, S. S. (1975). Optimal stimulation as theoretical basis of hyperactivity. *American Journal of Orthopsychiatry, 45,* 549–563.

Zentall, S. S. (1980). Behvioral comparison of hyperactive and normally active children in natural settings. *Journal of Abnormal Child Psychology, 8,* 93–109.

Zentall, S. S., Falkenberg, S. D., & Smith, L. B. (1985). Effects of color stimulation and information on the copying performance of attention-problem adolescents. *Journal of Abnormal Child Psychology, 13,* 501–511.

Zentall, S. S., & Meyer, M. J. (1987). Self-regulation of stimulation for ADD-H children during reading and vigilance task performance. *Journal of Abnormal Child Psychology, 15,* 519–536.

CHAPTER 13

PARENT TRAINING

Elizabeth A. Schaughency
Kathryn Vannatta
Jennifer Mauro

Parent training is a generally accepted component in the management of attention deficit hyperactivity disorder (ADHD) (Schaughency, Walker, & Lahey, 1988). (Although he acronyms, ADHD, ADD/H, and ADD have been used to refer to roughly the same population, different diagnostic terms are based, therefore, on different diagnostic criteria, thereby influencing sample composition. The terms used in this chapter reflect the diagnostic nosology used when the research was conducted.) While much of the current theory and research into the etiology of ADHD focuses on possible biological bases of the disorder, the literature also suggests a role for environmental factors and provides a rationale for parent training as one mode of intervention with children experiencing ADHD (Barkley, 1985, 1987).

Barkley (1987) presents a number of reasons for enlisting parents in treating this disorder. First, as noted elsewhere in this volume, the effects of clinic-based interventions conducted with the child have limited generalizability to other settings. Training adults who are involved in the child's day-to-day care to implement intervention programs should facilitate generalization to the natural environment.

Second, as was seen in the chapter on pharmacological interventions with ADHD, the effects of medication are limited as well. Some children do not respond favorably to medication; some are prescribed medication only during school hours, thereby necessitating alternative intervention strategies in the after-school at-home hours. Moreover, medication typically does not ameliorate all the behavioral difficulties displayed by children with ADHD, especially conduct problems developed or maintained by coercive social interaction patterns. Finally, as described below, parents of children with ADHD often experience stress associated with parenting a difficult child and lack confidence in their parenting skills. Treatment directly targeting the child does not provide parents with the skills and resources necessary to cope with a difficult child, whereas parent training provides a mechanism to address these issues.

This chapter begins with an overview of the literature establishing a rationale for intervention at the parent/family level; next is a review of the literature of parent training with parents of children with ADHD. The chapter concludes with a discussion of clinical implications of this work and directions for future research in this area.

HOME ENVIRONMENTAL CORRELATES OF ADHD AS A RATIONALE FOR PARENT TRAINING

Although a number of adverse home environmental circumstances have been found to be associated with ADHD, current views typically do not consider these factors to be causal in the development of ADHD; they may, however, be clinically important in developmental course and prognosis. Research discussed in this section focuses on three general areas of home environmental circumstances: parental and family pathology, parent-child interactions, and stress and coping.

Parental and Family Pathology

Parent Pathology

Historically, a high prevalence of sociopathy, alcoholism, and hysteria among the adult relatives of hyperactive children has been suggested (Cantwell, 1972; Morrison & Stewart, 1971). In the early 1980s, however, investigators began to question whether these relationships were specific to hyperactivity, noting a similar pattern of findings in other samples of children with behavior problems (August & Stewart, 1983; Hechtman, 1981; Stewart, DeBlois, & Cummings, 1980; Weiss & Hechtman, 1986). These researchers wondered whether these associations might instead be a general phenomenon seen in families of clinic-referred children or an artifact of the presence of conduct problems in the hyperactive samples.

Over the past 10 years a number of studies have explored these issues. Research examining parental pathology in samples of children with hyperactivity, conduct disorder, and codiagnoses of hyperactivity and conduct disorder has generally yielded consistent results: Mothers of children with conduct disorder, alone or with hyperactivity, are typically more likely to exhibit the triad of antisocial personality disorder, substance abuse, and somatization disorder, and fathers of these children are also likely to exhibit antisocial personality disorder or to abuse substances (Biederman, Munir, & Knee, 1987; Lahey et al., 1988; Reeves, Werry, Elkind, & Zametkin, 1987; Stewart et al., 1980; Werry et al., 1987).

In contrast, ADD/H in the absence of conduct disorder is typically not found to be associated with these parental disorders (Biederman et al., 1987; Lahey et al., 1988; Reeves et al., 1987). Research on hyperactive children has compared those whose parents have a history of antisocial behavior with those whose parents do not exhibit this behavior. The results have shown that hyperactive children—and their siblings—were more likely to develop conduct problems when their parents had a history of antisocial behavior (August & Stewart, 1983; Weiss & Hechtman, 1986). The presence of parental maladjustment in general, and antisocial behavior in particular, appears to be associated with an increased risk for antisocial outcomes in hyperactive children (Weiss & Hechtman, 1986).

Taken together, these findings suggest that ADHD per se is not associated with the parental antisocial triad of antisocial personality disorder, substance/alcohol abuse, and somatization disorder. However, the presence of these disorders may be clinically relevant to the conceptualization of the troubling overlap of ADHD and conduct disorder. Indeed, this dual diagnosis has been found to be associated with more antisocial outcomes than either diagnosis alone for both parents and children: Fathers of children with both ADD/H and conduct disorder are markedly more likely to have a history of aggression, arrest, and imprisonment (Lahey et al., 1988), with their children similarly exhibiting the greatest amount of physical aggression and other serious lawbreaking behavior (Walker, Lahey, Hynd, & Frame, 1987).

While these research findings suggest that the antisocial triad is not linked to ADHD, other research has indicated that parents of children with ADHD may experience adjustment difficulties. Hechtman (1981) found that parents of hyperactive boys were more likely to experience a "mild neurotic condition" than were parents of a normal control sample. In other studies an increase in depression among parents, particularly mothers, was found in samples of hyperactive children relative to normal controls (Beck, Young, & Tarnowski, 1990; Befera & Barkley, 1985; Biederman, Faraone, Keenan, Knee, &

Tsuang, 1990; Biederman et al., 1986; Brown & Pacini, 1989; Cunningham, Benness, & Siegel, 1988). Beck et al. (1990) compared depression of mothers of children with pervasive hyperactivity, children with situational hyperactivity, and normal controls. The authors found that, while mothers in both hyperactive groups had higher ratings of depression than mothers in the normal control group, only the difference between the mothers of the pervasive hyperactives and controls reached significance.

To determine whether increased depression is specific to parents of children with hyperactivity, several studies compared the adjustment of parents of children with hyperactivity to parents of other clinical samples, with mixed results. Brown and Pacini (1989) compared parents of children with ADD/H to parents of a clinical control sample of children diagnosed with specific learning disability or developmental disorder, excluding from both groups all children meeting diagnostic criteria for either conduct disorder or oppositional disorder. Results indicated a higher frequency of depressive symptomatology among parents of children with ADD/H. Similarly, Biederman et al. (1990) compared the prevalence of psychiatric disorders in relatives of children diagnosed with ADD (with or without hyperactivity) and in parents of a clinical control sample of children diagnosed as having affective disorder, anxiety disorder, pervasive developmental disorder, or Tourette's disorder. Biederman and colleagues again found an increased risk of mood disorders in relatives of the hyperactive group compared to relatives of psychiatric controls. Breen and Barkley (1988) compared depression in mothers of boys with ADD/H, girls with ADD/H, a clinic control group of girls with diagnoses of oppositional disorder, conduct disorder, pervasive developmental disorder, thought disorder, specific developmental disorders, or attention deficit disorder without hyperactivity, and a normal sample of girls. In this study, the authors found that only the mothers of clinical control girls experienced a higher rate of depression than the mothers of the normal control girls.

Although seemingly inconsistent, these results are not necessarily contradictory. Breen and Barkley (1988) interpreted their results as suggesting that

maternal distress is generally associated with externalizing behavior problems. Brown and Pacini (1989) excluded children with other externalizing behavior problems from their clinic control group, that is, the children in their ADD/H group were the only children in this study who exhibited externalizing behavior problems. The clinic control group in the Breen and Barkley (1988) study, on the other hand, included girls with diagnoses of oppositional disorder and conduct disorder.

While Breen and Barkley (1988) did not include a comparison between boys with ADD/H and a sample of clinic control boys, other research conducted with boys would be consistent with the interpretation that maternal distress is generally associated with externalizing behavior problems, rather than unique to ADHD. First, maternal depression and anxiety have been found to be associated with child behavior problems in general in clinical settings (cf. Griest, Forehand, Wells, & McMahon, 1980). Second, when the psychological adjustments of mothers of hyperactive, aggressive, hyperactive and aggressive, and nonproblem boys were compared, mothers of all three of these externalizing behavior problem groups were found to experience more psychological symptoms (unspecified) than the nonproblem controls, but they did not differ from each other (McGee, Williams, & Silva, 1984).

The diagnosis that does seem to be specifically related to ADHD is that diagnosis itself—namely ADHD. Biederman and colleagues found a higher prevalence of ADD in relatives of children with ADD than in relatives of both normal (Biederman et al., 1986) and clinical samples (Biederman et al., 1990). In research comparing biological and adoptive parents of hyperactive and normal control children, the biological parents of hyperactive children were found to exhibit attentional difficulties (Alberts-Corush, Firestone, & Goodman, 1986). Such findings have several clinical implications. Clinicians working with parents of children with ADHD should be alert to the possibility that the child's parent(s) may have experienced—or are experiencing—difficulties similar to those of their child. The clinician should be sensitive not only to the psychological issues that might arise for these parents but also to the potential ramifications such difficulties present for treatment implementation.

Family Characteristics

The research on the demographics and functioning of families of children with ADHD is scattered and mixed. In terms of demographic characteristics, Hartsough and Lambert (1982) reported that children identified as hyperactive by parent, teacher, and physician differed significantly from nonproblem controls on a number of family background characteristics, including father's occupation and number of times the family moved since the child was born. The occupational level of the fathers, as assessed by the Hollingshead Index, was found to be significantly higher in the nonproblem control group than in the hyperactive group. Unfortunately, the authors do not report the mean occupational levels of the two groups, so it is unknown whether hyperactivity was associated with economic adversity. The nonproblem control group was also found to have experienced fewer moves (an average of one or two moves) than children in the hyperactive group. The authors do not report the average number of moves for the hyperactive group." When this hyperactive group was compared to a group of children who scored comparably only on teacher ratings of hyperactivity, these differences disappeared, however. Moreover, in evaluating factors contributing to the diagnosis of hyperactivity, Lambert and Hartsough (1984) found that the contribution of the above family variables was outweighed by the contributions of constitutional factors such as parental history of hyperactivity and infant temperament, as well as home environmental values factors such as parental press for achievement, parent-child activities and discipline, which are described in the following section.

Hartsough and Lambert (1982, 1984) did not differentiate between those children in their hyperactive group who did and did not exhibit other externalizing behavior problems. Thus, it is possible that the differences in family characteristics that they identified are more generally associated with externalizing behavior problems than with hyperactivity per se. This possibility is supported by their findings that when the hyperactive group was compared to the behavior problem control group, no between group differences were found. Previous research suggests that groups identified as hyperactive by one method only contain a high false positive rate (cf. Schaughency & Rothlind, 1991), with aggressive behavior problems increasing the likelihood that a child will be inappropriately rated as inattentive or hyperactive (Schacher, Sandberg, & Rutter, 1986).

In their examination of hyperactivity and antisocial behavior in Great Britain, Taylor, Schachar, Thorley, and Weiselberg (1986) found antisocial behavior, but not hyperactivity, to be associated with lower socioeconomic status (SES). Werry, Reeves, and Elkind (1987) reviewed the literature comparing children with attention deficit, conduct, oppositional, and anxiety disorders, and, noting that the data on SES and family adversity are conflicting, concluded that no clear relationship exists between these factors and specific childhood disorders. In a subsequent paper, Reeves et al. (1987) compared the social ecology of children with attention deficit disorder with hyperactivity (ADD/H), with or without conduct or oppositional disorder, to children with anxiety disorders or normal controls. When no coexisting conduct or oppositional disorder was present, no differences in family characteristics were found among children with ADD/H, children with anxiety disorders, or normal controls. When ADD/H was coupled with a conduct or oppositional disorder, however, the children were more likely to have experienced family adversity and to have been placed in care outside the home (e.g., residential schools for the emotionally disturbed).

Thus, while family adversity does not appear to be uniquely linked to ADHD, it may be associated with behavior problems in general and the more serious combination of ADHD and conduct problems. Some support for the hypothesis that social adversity may be negatively linked with prognosis comes from the longitudinal work of Campbell and colleagues (Campbell, Breaux, Ewing, & Szumowski, 1986a). These authors have been following children identified with behavior problems suggestive of ADHD and a nonproblem comparison group since the chidren were 2 or 3 years old. The authors found that SES contributed to the prediction of childhood hyperactivity and aggression concurrently at age 2–3 and continued to contribute to this prediction at age 4. At age 6, SES continued to contribute to the prediction of hyperactivity but not to aggression. However, other variables contributed to these predictions as well, including family stress and parent-child interactions as discussed below.

The research on marital status and functioning of parents of children with ADHD is similarly mixed. In their study comparing parents of children with ADD/H and those of a clinical control group of children with learning or developmental disorders, Brown and Pacini (1989) found a higher frequency of divorce and separation in the ADD/H group. When parents of boys who were aggressive, hyperactive, and both aggressive and hyperactive were compared with parents of normal control boys, however, parental separation and single parenting were found to be associated only with childhood aggression (McGee et al., 1984). Based on their review of the literature comparing children with attention deficit, conduct, oppositional, and anxiety disorders, Werry et al. (1987) concluded that there is no clear pattern associating broken homes and childhood diagnosis.

With regard to marital functioning, Befera and Barkley (1985) compared the parents of children with hyperactivity to those of normal controls and found more marital discord in the parents of hyperactive children. However, other studies comparing the parents of similar groups report no differences in marital functioning between the two sets of parents (Breen & Barkley, 1988; Hechtman, 1981; Prinz, Myers, Holden, Tarnowski, & Roberts, 1983; Reeves et al., 1987).

When other clinical groups are included in the comparisons, the association between marital difficulties and ADHD becomes even more tenuous. In comparing the parents of children with ADD/H with or without a coexisting conduct or oppositional disorder, parents of children with anxiety disorders, and parents of normal controls, Reeves et al. (1987) found no differences in marital satisfaction among the groups. Similarly, Werry et al. (1987) found no clear pattern of association between marital conflict and child diagnosis in their review of the literature comparing children with attention deficit, conduct, oppositional, or anxiety disorders. In their study comparing parents of boys with ADD/H, girls with ADD/H, a mixed diagnostic group of clinic control girls, and normal control girls, Breen and Barkley (1988) found that only the parents of the clinic control group experienced significantly more marital distress than the normal control girls.

Researchers have generally found an association between marital discord and behavior problems in boys (Emery, 1982). The results of the work by Breen and Barkley (1988) are consistent in suggesting that marital distress is associated with children's externalizing behavior problems. However, the lack of association between marital satisfaction and ADHD in a number of studies cautions against assuming that this relationship holds in this population (cf. Prinz et al., 1983).

A number of studies examined the emotional climate in families of children with ADHD. Studies comparing families of hyperactives and those of normal controls yielded mixed results. Hechtman (1981) found that the emotional climate of the home, referring to the degree of positive versus negative interactions among family members, was considerably worse in the families of hyperactives. Similarly, two studies found families of hyperactives to have poor interpersonal relationships as assessed by the Family Environment Scale than families of controls (Moos & Moos, 1981; see also Brown & Pacini, 1989; McGee et al., 1984). However, a recent study using the Family Assessment Device (Epstein, Baldwin, & Bishop, 1983) failed to find significant differences between families of children with ADD/H and normal controls (Cunningham, Benness, & Siegel, 1988).

Research comparing the functioning of families of children with ADHD to other clinical groups is sparse, and the data that are available are mixed. Brown and Pacini (1989) found families of children with ADD/H to have poorer interpersonal relationships than families of a clinic control group of learning and developmentally disabled youngsters. In their study comparing boys who were hyperactive, aggressive, and both hyperactive and aggressive, McGee et al. (1984) found that families of all three groups had poor family relationships. Finally, in their study of hyperactivity and antisocial behavior in Great Britain, Taylor et al. (1986) found that antisocial behavior, but not hyperactivity, was associated with impaired family relationships. Thus, once again a pattern is emerging in which negative family circumstances appear to be related to externalizing problems in general, and conduct problems in particular, but do not appear to be uniquely associated with ADHD.

Parent-Child Interactions

Given that parent training aims to achieve its effects via alterations in the parents' interactions with the child, perhaps the literature most directly relevant to this endeavor is that which examines the interactions of children with ADHD and their parents. Indeed, research examining the relationship between family correlates such as maternal depression and SES and child behavior problems at a microsocial level finds that the effects of these variables are mediated by the parent's *parenting behavior* (cf. Patterson, 1982).

Over the past 2 decades, a few investigators have undertaken the task of trying to describe the correlates of ADHD at this microsomal level. As reviewed by Barkley (1985), pioneering work conducted in the 1970s suggested that hyperactive boys were more negative and less compliant with their mothers, and in turn, their mothers were more directive and negative with them. Since that time, research has examined the parameters of these interaction patterns.

The majority of research in this area evaluated the interactions of school-age hyperactive boys and their mothers by comparing them to the interactions of normal boys and their mothers. To date, only one study has examined the interactions between hyperactive boys and their fathers. Tallmadge and Barkley (1983) compared the parent-child interactions of mothers and fathers with hyperactive and normal boys. Consistent with previous research, hyperactive boys were generally less compliant and their parents were more directive than were boys and parents in the nonproblem parent-child dyads. These differences were most pronounced in structured tasks as opposed to free-play situations. Interestingly, although both fathers and mothers increased their directiveness in the task situation, the hyperactive boys increased their negative and competing behaviors only in response to commands from their mothers. As noted by the authors, these results lend some credence to the frequently heard complaint that hyperactive boys tend to behave better for their fathers.

In contrast to studies comparing the interactions of parents with hyperactive boys to interactions of parents with nonproblem children, Tarver-Behring,

Barkley, and Karlsson (1985) compared the interactions of mothers with their hyperactive and their nonhyperactive sons. The results indicated that hyperactive boys were less likely to respond to their mothers and more likely to engage in competing behaviors than their nonhyperactive brothers during free play and to be less compliant during the task situation. Such differences are consistent with the child's diagnosis of hyperactivity. Interestingly, no differences were found in the behavior of mothers toward their hyperactive and nonhyperactive sons.

As is true with research in ADHD in general, much of the parent-child interaction research has been limited to studies of hyperactive boys. In one of the few studies including hyperactive girls, Befera and Barkley (1985) compared the parent-child interactions of hyperactive and normal boys and girls and their mothers. Observations during free time failed to yield significant effects for either group or sex. During the task situation, however, hyperactive boys and girls were less compliant, engaged in more competing behaviors, and were more negative than normal children. These results are consistent with previous research suggesting that differences between normal and hyperactive children are more pronounced during task situations. In addition, this study suggests that parent-child interactions are similar for hyperactive girls and boys.

Recently, research has focused on the developmental course of the interactions between children with ADHD and their parents. As noted earlier, Campbell and colleagues have been involved in longitudinal research following children with problems suggestive of ADHD at ages 2 to 3. Campbell, Breaux, Ewing, Szumowski, and Pierce (1986b) compared the mother-child interactions of these problem and nonproblem preschoolers at initial assessment and at 1-year follow-up. At initial assessment, the authors found significant differences between the two groups in mother, but not child, behavior. Preliminary analyses suggested that mothers of problem preschoolers provide more suggestions of alternative activities and make more negative control statements. Qualitative ratings of these interactions suggested that the mother-child interactions of the problem group were characterized by less positive affect, more conflict, and less appropriate directiveness than were the interactions of control dyads. However, further analyses revealed that many of these variables were significantly related to SES. When the effects of SES were statistically controlled, the only significant difference remaining was increased maternal redirectiveness (diverting the child's attention away from an ongoing activity to an alternative activity) in the problem group. In addition, the authors found significant sex differences in mother-child interactions when the children were 3 years old. Boys were less compliant than girls, and mothers provided more structure and redirection with their sons. No group-by-sex interactions were found, consistent with Befera and Barkley's (1985) study of school-age hyperactive boys and girls.

Campbell et al. (1986a) extended this research by conducting multiple regression analyses to evaluate potential predictors of hyperactive and aggressive behavior in these children. The authors found that, in addition to SES and family stress, maternal negative and directive behavior contributed to the concurrent prediction of both hyperactive and aggressive behavior when the children were 3 years old.

At follow-up, Campbell et al. (1986b) found that mothers intervened less often in their children's play. Mothers of both problem children and controls had decreased their frequency of structuring and negative control statements. The number of negative control statements had decreased more substantially, however, among the mothers of control children; these mothers made significantly fewer negative control statements than mothers of problem children at follow-up. Mothers of problem children had decreased their redirectiveness to a level no different from the redirectiveness of control mothers. Also, mothers of boys showed greater decreases in maternal structuring and redirectiveness at follow-up, compared with mothers of girls.

Multiple regression analyses indicated that family SES and observed maternal behavior at intake, but not stress, continued to predict hyperactivity and aggression in the child at age 4 (Campbell et al., 1986a). Both these variables continued to predict hyperactivity at age 6, although only maternal behavior when the child was 3 was found to be a predictor of the child's aggression at this age. Unfortunately, these longitudinal analyses did not take into account the child's initial levels of hyperactivity and aggression.

In an investigation of hyperactive kindergartners, Cohen and Minde (1983) compared the mother-child interactions of the following: (a) children who were identified by parent and teacher as hyperactive and exhibited hyperactive behaviors during clinic assessment (pervasive hyperactives), (b) children who were identified by parent and teacher as hyperactive but did not exhibit hyperactive behaviors during clinic assessment ("clinically diagnosed" hyperactives), (c) children who were identified only by either parent or teacher (situational hyperactives), (d) and normal controls. The authors found that mothers of pervasive hyperactives gave more approval and negative feedback to their children than did mothers of situational hyperactives, but about the same amount as mothers of the clinically diagnosed hyperactives. The mothers of situational hyperactives, on the other hand, gave more disapproval than mothers of either clinically diagnosed hyperactives or normal controls. In sum, although the nature of the differences between the hyperactive groups is unclear, all three groups of hyperactive kindergartners experienced more parent-child interactional difficulties than their nonhyperactive peers.

Using a cross-sectional design, Mash and Johnston (1982) compared the mother-child interactions of younger ($\bar{x}$ age = 4.11) and older ($\bar{x}$ age = 8.4) hyperactive and normal children of comparable age groups. Consistent with previous research, mothers of hyperactive chidren were more directive and negative, and less positive, interactive, and responsive to their children's behavior. Post-hoc comparisons revealed that the mothers of younger hyperactives were less responsive and more negative than mothers in the other three groups.

The comparisons of child behavior indicated that hyperactive children asked more questions, displayed more negative behavior, and were more likely to initiate interaction with their mothers when their mothers were not interacting with them than were the normal controls. In addition, they were less compliant and responsive to their mothers than were normal controls. Specific comparisons revealed that younger hyperactive children initiated the most interactions, were more negative, and were less compliant and responsive to their mothers, compared to the other three groups.

Using a more stratified cross-sectional design,

Barkley, Karlsson, and Pollard (1985a) examined the effects of age on the mother-child interactions of ADD/H and normal boys at ages 5, 6, 7, 8, and 9. During free play, several main effects for group, but not age, were found. Consistent with previous research, the authors found that ADD/H boys were more likely to play independently of their mothers than were normal boys. Mothers of ADD/H boys were found to initiate fewer interactions, to give more commands, and to be less responsive to their sons' initiations than were mothers of normal boys.

Similar to previous research, results indicated that in the task situation ADD/H boys were less compliant with maternal commands, less able to sustain their compliance, off-task more often, and more negative with their mothers, compared to normal boys. Likewise, mothers of ADD/H boys gave more commands, were less likely to respond positively to their sons' compliance, and were more likely to respond with more control to their sons' compliance or off-task behavior; they also initiated fewer interactions with their sons than did mothers of normal boys. A main effect for age suggested that older boys in both groups were better able to sustain their compliance to commands than were younger boys. Mothers of older boys gave fewer commands, responded with less control to their boys' compliance, and spent more time passively observing their boys than did mothers of younger boys.

In sum, the research examining the interactions of parents and their ADHD children suggests the following: Consistent with the research conducted in the 1970s, research continues to suggest that hyperactive children are more negative and less compliant with their parents, and in turn, their parents are more directive and negative with them when compared with normal children and their parents. These differences in the parent-child interactions between normative and ADHD groups appear to be more pronounced in structured rather than free-play situations, with mothers rather than fathers, and with younger children. Although the interactions of parents and ADHD children improve over time, as do the interactions of parents and normal children, some differences still remain. Moreover, even though there are some nonsignificant differences between boys and girls with ADHD in their interactions with their parents, the interactional patterns of both sexes are similar.

Taken together, this research suggests that children with ADHD and their parents may experience interactional difficulties. However, this research does little to inform us about the direction of influences in these interactions (Barkley, 1985; Campbell, 1986a). On the one hand, such results could be interpreted to suggest that directive, negative, and controlling behaviors lead to the development of the child's hyperactivity and poor self-control. Or, they may suggest that parents become more negative and controlling in response to the high rates of their child's behavior. In fact, there are data to support both views.

Several studies suggest a possible contributory role for directive, controlling, or intrusive discipline. Hartsough and Lambert (1982) found that the parents of boys identified as hyperactive by parent, teacher, and physician used both rational/social control and physical discipline more frequently than did parents of nonproblem boys. They also used rational/social control discipline more frequently than did parents of teacher-identified boys, but did not differ from parents of teacher-identified boys in frequency of physical discipline. Multiple regression analyses indicated that the home environment, including these parent-child interaction variables, along with constitutional factors (i.e., parental history of hyperactivity, infant temperament) contributed significantly to the likelihood that a child would be identified as hyperactive (Lambert & Hartsough, 1984).

In a prospective longitudinal study, Jacobvitz and Sroufe (1987) found that two early caregiver variables, coupled with the constitutional variable of motor maturity assessed at 7 and 10 days of age, differentiated between children identified in kindergarten by teacher ratings as hyperactive and their nonhyperactive peers. The authors found that maternal interference, or the extent to which the mother disrupted the baby's ongoing activity rather than adapting her interactions to the baby's state, at 6 months, and maternal overstimulation at 42 months distinguished between the two groups.

In another longitudinal, prospective study, Olson, Bates, and Bayles (1990) investigated predictors of impulsivity at age 6 from a sample of children identified through published birth notices and recruited when the subjects neared 6 months of age. Correctional analyses revealed that high rates of positive verbal interaction at age 2 were associated with good performance on an index of delay ability and task orientation. Other findings were sex specific. Nonrestrictive, clear, consistent, and nonpunitive discipline at age 2 was related to high scores on a composite index of impulse control for boys, but not girls, at age 6. Similarly, highly secure mother-infant attachment relationships correlated with positive performance on measures of impulse control, delay of gratification, and task orientation for boys, but not girls. Girls who were more highly task oriented and compliant at age 6 had experienced high maternal responsiveness and intellectual stimulation at ages 13 and 24 months. Multiple regression analyses further indicated that responsive, cognitively stimulating parent-child interactions in the second year predicted laboratory indices of impulsivity at age 6.

The child's cognitive competence at age 2 was also associated with performance on measures of impulsive control at age 6, however, and parent-child interaction and child cognitive competence were intercorrelated. To determine whether early mother-child interaction made an independent contribution to the variance in age 6 outcomes, the authors conducted further hierarchical multiple regression analyses and found that parent-child interaction measures made significant independent contributions to the variance beyond that shared with child cognitive competence.

Taken together, the results of these studies suggest that nonresponsive, intrusive discipline may play a role in the development of behavioral difficulties such as those seen in ADHD. This notion would be consistent with the approach taken by developmental researchers interested in the coordination between parent-child interaction. As described by Westerman (1990), this approach investigates specific sequences of interactions and examines whether and in what way the behaviors of one person coordinate with the behaviors of another. With children, parents assume most of the responsibility for coordination, and research is beginning to suggest that such maternal responsiveness is related to child compliance (Westerman, 1990).

Using a cross-sectional design, Westerman (1990) compared the parent-child interactions of preschoolers with compliance problems to those of nonproblem preschoolers on a block building task. Westerman (1990) hypothesized that the mothers of nonproblem preschoolers alter their degree of directiveness with the child's performance on the task, becoming more directive when the child is experiencing difficulty, less so when the child is making progress independently. Results indicated that there were no significant differences between the groups in the frequency of maternal interventions or child performance. When analyses examined the coordination between maternal and child behavior in terms of conditional probabilities and in sequential analyses, both including and excluding mean level of specificity as a covariate, however, significant between-group differences emerged. Mothers in the nonproblem group shifted their behavior as a function of their child's success or failure, becoming more specific when the child failed and more general when the child was successful.

While these results are suggestive, they are inconclusive. Even though the studies by Lambert and Hartsough (1984), Jacobvitz and Sroufe (1987), and Olson et al. (1980) suggested that parenting variables predict behaviors suggestive of ADHD at a later age, these studies found early child characteristics that were predictors as well. Moreover, the study by Westerman (1990) used noncompliant preschoolers, not specifically children with ADHD, suggesting that this interactional pattern may not be unique to ADHD.

There are also data to suggest that parental behavior is, in part, a response to the child's behavior. Mash and Johnston (1983) investigated predictors of mothers' behavior with their hyperactive children during play and task situations. The authors found that the amounts of interaction, control, and nonresponding exhibited by mothers during play and task situations were significantly correlated with their children's behavior. Multiple regression analyses similarly revealed that child behavior during these situations predicted maternal behavior.

The possibility that parent-child interactional patterns are in response to child behavior is given further support by studies investigating the parent-child interactions of ADHD children receiving stimulant medication. As discussed by Barkley (1985), stimulant medication is fast acting with pronounced short-term behavioral effects in children who respond favorably to the medication. If parent behavior were driving the interactional difficulties observed between children with ADHD and their parents, stimulant medication effecting within-child behavior change would not be expected to change parent behavior. However, if parent behavior were in response to child behavior, changes in child behavior should be accompanied by changes in parental behavior.

The developmental parameters of this issue have been the focus of a series of studies by Barkley and colleagues. Barkley (1988) examined the effects of two dosages of methylphenidate (Ritalin) (0.15 mg/kg and 0.50 mg/kg b.i.d.) on the interactions of preschool children with ADHD and their mothers using a double-blind, placebo-controlled crossover design. Few drug effects were observed during the free-play situation. During the task situation, however, significant differences emerged, with children displaying a significant reduction in noncompliance and off-task, or competing, behavior in the high dose versus the placebo condition. An interesting but not statistically significant finding was that mothers also tended to be less controlling and negative and to be more positive with their children on medication than when their children were on placebo.

More pronounced effects were seen in two other studies examining the effects of age and methylphenidate dosage on the interactions between mothers and hyperactive children. Barkley, Karlsson, Strezelecki, and Murphy (1984) compared the mother-child interactions of three nonoverlapping age groups of hyperactive children (4 years, 0 months to 5 years, 11 months; 6 years, 0 months to 7 years, 11 months; 8 years, 0 months to 9 years, 11 months) during a double-blind drug placebo evaluation of two doses of methylphenidate (0.3 mg/kg and 1.0 mg/kg daily dose) in both free-play and task settings. As in the Barkley (1988) study, Barkley et al. (1984) found few drug or age effects on parent-child interactions during free play. During the task situation, however, both age and drug effects emerged, with no significant age by drug interactions. As with other studies examining the developmental changes in interactions of mothers and their hyperactive children, Barkley et al. (1984)

found that children increased their compliance and decreased their negative behavior with age and that their mothers decreased their levels of control and management of the children. With regard to drug effects, both dosages of methylphenidate increased child compliance, but mothers significantly decreased their control and negative behavior toward their children only under the high dose condition.

Using a more stratified design, Barkley, Karlsson, Pollard, and Murphy (1985b) compared the mother-child interactions of hyperactive children at five age levels (ages 5, 6, 7, 8, and 9) during free-play and task situations in a double-blind drug-placebo evaluation of two dose levels of methylphenidate (0.3 and 0.7 mg/kg b.i.d.). As in the previous two studies, Barkley et al. (1985b) again found no age or drug effects in the play situation and significant effects for both age and drug during the task situation for both child and mother behavior, with no age by drug interaction.

Taken together, these studies replicate the results of research examining the developmental changes of parent-child interactions, showing increasing child compliance and sustained attention with age and corresponding decreases in maternal direction and control. Development research suggests that differences in the parent-child interactions of hyperactive and normal children still remain, however. The effects of methylphenidate appear to continue to improve parent-child interactions in a normalizing fashion.

Because the effects of methylphenidate directly change only child behavior, these results suggest that the controlling, negative parent behavior observed in parent-child interactions may, to some degree, be a response to child behavior. Further, support for this notion comes from a recent study examining changes in parent-child relationships in families in which the child responds favorably to methylphenidate and those in which the child does not (Schachar, Taylor, Weiselberg, Thorley, & Rutter, 1987). Consistent with the work of Barkley and colleagues, Schachar et al. (1987) found that, among responders, there was increased maternal warmth, decreased maternal criticism, greater frequency of maternal contact, and fewer negative encounters with siblings. These changes were not observed in families of nonresponders, however, suggesting that the obtained changes were not a nonspecific effect of participating in a medication trial.

Findings that parental behavior may, in part, be a response to child behavior does not suggest that there are not other, nonchild factors influencing parental behavior. In their study examining predictors of maternal behavior, Mash and Johnston (1983) found that maternal behavior was significantly correlated with maternal self-esteem and stress in the parenting role as well as with child behavior. Moreover, the authors found that these maternal variables added to the prediction of maternal behavior in the task situation beyond that contributed by child behavior alone.

Because the child's behavioral difficulties are typically more pronounced in structured task situations, the mother's negative learning history with her child may have led to the increased role of these maternal variables in task situations. Although these cognitive/affective variables may again be in part a response to child behavior, they may also contribute uniquely to parent behavior with the child and may be important considerations for a clinician when working with children with ADHD and their parents.

Research investigating parent-perceptions and attributions regarding their children with ADHD is limited. A recent study sought to examine the attributions regarding child behavior of parents of children with ADD/H and non-ADD/H children (Sobol, Ashbourne, Earn, & Cunningham, 1989). Sobol et al. (1989) compared the reasons provided for noncompliance and compliance by parents of children with ADD/H and non-ADD/H children in six different situations. Parental attributions were rated on Weiner's (1979) dimensions of locus, stability, and controllability. The authors found that, in general, mothers rated attributions for noncompliance to be more external than did fathers. Mothers of children with ADD/H, in particular, viewed the causes of their children's behavior to be more unstable than did mothers of control children. In addition, parents of children with ADD/H had lower expectations for achieving future compliance from their child than did parents of non-ADD/H children, suggesting that parents of children with ADHD may have negative or pessimistic, although perhaps accurate, expectations of their children.

Consistent with this notion, Hartsough and Lam-

bert (1982) found that parents of hyperactive boys identified by parents, teachers, and physicians differed from nonproblem controls in three areas of achievement press: press for early learning (attainment of preacademic skills prior to school entry), parent evaluation of the child's academic competence, and parent aspiration for the child's success. These parents also differed from parents of boys idehtified by teacher only in press for early learning and aspiration for success. They did not differ from parents of teacher-identified boys in terms of evaluation of their sons' academic competence, however.

In keeping with these differences in expectations, Hartsough and Lambert (1982) also found differences in provisions for early learning. Parents of pervasive hyperactives perceived their children to be less interested in reading activities than did parents of nonproblem boys or teacher-identified boys; they were also less involved in reading activities with their children than were parents of nonproblem boys. Parental involvement with reading activities did not differ between pervasive or teacher-identified boys. Multiple regression analyses revealed that these aspects of the home environment, achievement press, and provision for early learning, along with parent-child interactions and constitutional factors, contributed significantly to the prediction that a child would be identified as hyperactive (Lambert & Hartsough, 1984).

Taken together, these findings suggest that parental perceptions may be an important component of the home environment of children with ADHD. A recent study examined whether parent and child affective attitudes (expressed emotion) and interaction covaried. Marshall, Longwell, Goldstein, and Swanson (1990) compared the expressed emotion and parent-child interaction in families of children with ADHD and ADHD plus oppositional defiant disorder or conduct disorder (ADHD + ODD/CD). The authors found a remarkable degree of reciprocity for parental and child expressed emotion, independent of symptom group. They also found the main correlate of parent, but not child, interactional behavior to be level of expressed emotion. No differences were found in interactions of parents of ADHD boys versus ADHD + ODD/CD boys. In contrast, the presence of ODD/CD was the major significant variable associated with more negative and less positive child interactive behavior. These results support the notion that parent's affective attitudes may influence their behavior with their children and that these attitudes may be independent of child behavior.

Although medication has been found to improve mother-child interactions by altering child behavior, other aspects of parenting may not change. Schacher et al. (1987) found no changes in the frequency of paternal contact, efficiency of parental coping, and interparental consistency in the parents of boys who responded favorably to methylphenidate. The fact that these aspects of parenting did not change as a result of improvements in child behavior suggests that these issues may need to be targeted directly if change is to be achieved.

In sum, the literature on interactions of parents and children with ADHD suggests a complex interplay of parent and child behavior, influenced by both intra-individual characteristics (e.g., child's attention span, parent's attributions) and the other's behavior. Work in the area of parent training with conduct problem children has taught us that the unidirectional model (i.e., parent behavior → child behavior) is insufficient. This research suggests that contextual factors such as parental cognitive/affective, marital, and social variables mitigate successful treatment of children with behavior problems and provides evidence that successful treatment must include treatment of other areas of family functioning (Griest & Wells, 1983). Although we cannot assume that all research with conduct problem children necessarily applies to children with ADHD, research examining the interactions of parents and their ADHD children suggests a need for an appreciation of these contextual factors as well.

The research reviewed thus far has found that cognitive/affective variables such as depression and negative or pessimistic expectations may be associated with ADHD. Moreover, it has been suggested that this association is bidirectional, that it, these factors may be a result of child behavior and may influence parent behavior toward the child. The remaining section of this discussion of family circumstances associated with ADHD is labeled "Stress and Coping." It more directly examines the psychosocial variables associated with parenting a child with ADHD.

Stress and Coping

Research examining psychosocial factors associated with ADHD is scattered and yields mixed results. In their comparison of children diagnosed with attention deficit, conduct, oppositional, and anxiety disorders, Reeves et al. (1987) found that parents of children with ADD/H with or without conduct disorder experienced more distressful life events than parents of normal controls. Campbell et al. (1986a) also found family stress, along with SES and maternal behavior, to contribute to the child's ratings of hyperactivity and aggression at age 3, but stress failed to contribute to the prediction of continued problems with hyperactivity and aggression at ages 4 to 6.

Beck et al. (1990) compared the perceived stress of mothers of pervasive hyperactive, and situational hyperactive, and normal boys. Mothers of both pervasive and situational hyperactive boys reported more maternal stress than did mothers of normal controls. When compared to mothers of controls, mothers of pervasively hyperactive boys rated themselves more depressed, less competent, more restricted, and more frustrated. They also experienced significantly more overall stress than mothers of situational hyperactive boys.

In their study of family functioning of parents of children with ADD/H, Cunningham et al. (1988) found that families of children with ADD/H did not differ substantially from normal control families. The authors did find, however, that families of ADD/H children reported fewer extended family contacts than did mothers of normal children and described these as less helpful.

Taken together, these results suggest that parental psychopathology and adverse family circumstances may not be necessarily linked to ADHD. However, they do suggest that parents of children with ADHD, particularly mothers, may be at risk for experiencing stress and isolation in the parenting role. The recent emergence of support groups for parents of children with ADHD is consistent with this conclusion. While the cognitive/affective and social contextual variables associated with parenting a child with ADHD certainly merit further investigation, the present findings should alert the clinician to be sensitive to these potential factors in working with a given case.

PARENT TRAINING WITH PARENTS OF CHILDREN WITH ADHD

Parent training is frequently recommended as a treatment option for children with ADHD (cf. Schaughency et al., 1988). However, there are only a few empirical studies that systematically evaluate the effectiveness of this treatment approach with this population. The majority of studies conducted in the area of parent training focus primarily on oppositional or conduct disordered children and not specifically on children with ADHD. Although many children with ADHD exhibit noncompliance and other behavior problems, it may not be prudent to assume that one program would work for all groups of children with disruptive behavior disorders. Indeed, the symptoms of ADHD may present a unique challenge to both therapists and client. This discussion focuses on the limited research that has specifically examined parent training with parents of ADHD children. For further information on parent training in general, the reader is referred to Forehand and McMahon (1981) and Griest and Wells (1983).

Research examining parent training as a treatment strategy with ADHD began to appear in the 1970s. Early reports by Dubey and Kaufman (1978) and Schaefer, Palkes, and Stewart (1974) suggested that educating parents of children with ADHD in social learning principles held promise in treating home behavior problems. O'Leary, Pelham, Rosenbaum, and Price (1976) published one of the first reports of the use of a home-based school-behavior management system with hyperkinetic children, with positive results.

Building on this work, Gittelman and colleagues conducted a series of studies to examine the relative efficacy of methylpenidate and behavior therapy with hyperkinetic children (Abikoff & Gittelman, 1984; Gittelman et al., 1980; Gittelman-Klein, Klein, Abikoff, Gloisten, & Kates, 1976). As described by Gittelman and co-workers, the parent management component of treatment consisted of a combination of parent education in behavioral principles and a home-reinforcement program such as that reported by O'Leary et al. (1976). Initial results published by Gittelman-Klein et al. (1976) suggested that all treatments reduced teacher ratings of behavior problems. However, methylphenidate resulted in greater reduction in teacher ratings than behavior therapy alone, and behavior therapy failed to add significantly to the treatment effects of methylphenidate. No significant between-group differences were found in mothers' ratings of treatment effects.

Unfortunately, Gittelman-Klein and colleagues did not include a normal comparison group in their initial report. Subsequently, no conclusions can be drawn about the degree to which the treatments were successful in bringing their child-clients' behaviors within normal limits. Although treatment effects were reported to be statistically significant, it is not known whether the obtained results were clinically significant.

These issues were addressed by Gittelman and colleagues in their more recent work (Abikoff & Gittelman, 1984; Gittelman et al., 1980). Abikoff and Gittelman (1984) found that behavior therapy was unsuccessful in normalizing the behaviors characteristic of ADHD (inattentiveness, impulsivity, and activity level). Methylphenidate, on the other hand, was found to have a considerable normalizing effect on many of these behaviors, while behavior therapy was found to reduce aggressive behavior within normal limits (Abikoff & Gittelman, 1984). Gittelman et al. (1980) found continued behavior difficulties with either treatment alone. The combined-treatments group, however, did not differ from their normal classmates on any of the behavioral measures, suggesting that the combined treatment approach had a normalizing effect on symptoms.

Taken together, these studies suggested that behavior therapy holds promise as an adjunct to methylphenidate, particularly with respect to treatment of coexisting conduct problems. The conclusions that we are able to draw about the particular contribution of parent training to treatment in these studies are limited by two factors, however. First, results are presented in terms of group data. Thus, we are unable to discern the effects of individual differences in response to treatment, an issue of particular importance when discussing response to methylphenidate (cf. Pelham & Hoza, 1987). Second, outcome is measured largely in terms of behavioral functioning within the classroom and does not examine treatment effects within the family. Although classroom functioning is an appropriate and important outcome variable (cf. Schaughency et al., 1988), parent training primarily targets behavior management within the home, thus making treatment effects within the home setting a prudent first step in evaluating this treatment modality.

To address this first concern, Pelham and colleagues evaluated behavior therapy, with a parent training component, and methylphenidate using within-subject methodology (Pelham, 1977; Pelham, Schnedler, Bologna, & Contreras, 1980). Consistent with the results of Gittelman and co-workers, Pelham et al. (1980) found that, although both stimulant medication and behavior therapy increased on-task behavior, levels of on-task behavior comparable to those of nonhyperactive classmates were achieved only with the combination of methylphenidate and behavior therapy. Group data suggested that normal levels of classroom behavior were reached only when children received the high dose of methylphenidate (0.75 mg/kg) after 13 weeks of behavioral intervention. Examination of individual response to treatment, however, revealed that two children reached this level on the low dose, one child reached this level without medication, and one never did achieve this level.

Pelham (1977) reported the results of a case study of a child who had previously received treatment with medication only (20 mg after breakfast, 10 mg at 3:00 p.m.) but continued to exhibit behavior problems at home and school. In this study, behavioral interventions were implemented at home and at school. Although the afternoon dose of medication was discontinued when treatment began, the child continued to receive medication during the school day. Teacher reports indicated that the child was "too good" on the combination of 20 mg of methylphenidate and behavior therapy, as reflected by teacher ratings of behavior problems well below average. A randomized, blind medication evaluation was subsequently undertaken utilizing placebo, and 10 mg and 20 mg of methylphenidate. Based on this medication trial, the child's dose was reduced to 10 mg qam. A medication-free trial was subsequently undertaken. Results indicated that the child continued to show improvement after medication was withdrawn. At termination, teacher ratings were reduced from greater than two standard deviations above the mean at pretreatment (medication only) to slightly above the mean. Parent ratings were also reduced, although effects were not as dramatic.

In general, these studies using within-subject methodology continue to suggest that behavior therapy can be a useful adjunct to medication, helping to bring the behavior of children with ADHD within normal limits. The findings that the most efficacious treatment regimen varies from child to child highlights the importance of this methodology in treatment evaluation. Indeed, these data suggest that, for some children with ADHD, behavior therapy may be an appropriate alternative to medication.

The study by Pelham et al. (1980) also begins to address the issue of the effects of parent training on the child's behavior within the family. Pelham and colleagues conducted in-clinic observations of parent-child interactions in addition to obtaining parent ratings of child behavior. All the children demonstrated positive change on both observational measures and rating scales. Research examining medication effects on parent-child interactions suggests that medication alone may result in improved child behavior in these settings, however (cf. Barkley, 1985); the authors did not report whether the children were on medication at the time of assessment (Pelham et al., 1980). Thus, whether the observed effects are a result of parent training, medication, or both is unknown.

In a multiple-baseline across-subjects design, Pollard, Ward, and Barkley (1983) assessed the effects of parent training alone and in combination with methylphenidate on the interactions of parents and three hyperactive boys. In general, either treatment alone decreased the number of commands given by the mother, sustained the child's compliance with commands, and improved parent ratings of deviant child behavior in the home. Only parent training, however, resulted in increases in the mother's use of positive attention following the child's compliance. Examination of specific results revealed that the combination of treatments increased treatment effects in one case.

Firestone, Kelly, Goodman, and Davey (1981) reported the results of a 3-month intervention study comparing stimulant medication alone, stimulant medication plus parent training, and parent training plus placebo. Similar to the early results of Gittel-man-Klein et al. (1976), initial results of 73 subjects (medication only: n = 30; parent training + placebo: n = 21; parent training + medication: n = 22) suggested that stimulant medication resulted in greater improvement in classroom behavior, attention, and impulse control than did parent training (Firestone et al., 1981).

In a subsequent report, however, Firestone and Witt (1982) noted that 83 subjects had initially been offered parent training. Of these, 20 rejected the offer of treatment, 22 accepted treatment but terminated prior to the last session, and 40 families completed all requirements of parent training (49% of those offered). Between-group analyses indicated that the children did not differ in severity of symptoms of ADHD or other behavior problems. Instead, results indicated that children in the dropout group were significantly younger and more likely to be girls than the chidren in the other groups, who did not differ from each other. Mothers in the dropout group also reported more psychological symptoms on the Minnesota Multiphasic Personality Inventory (MMPI), seemed less traditional in their female roles, experienced more somatic complaints and idiosyncratic thoughts, and were more suspicious than other mothers.

Children whose parents completed therapy obtained significantly higher scores on a measure of receptive vocabulary than did children in either of the other two groups, who did not differ from each other. Similarly, parents who completed training were older and obtained higher scores on a measure of cognitive functioning. Both mothers and fathers who completed therapy responded in a more defensive or socially desirable manner than those who did not.

In a similar vein, Firestone (1982) examined the factors associated with compliance with the medication condition of their outcome research. Of the 73 subjects initially qualifying for treatment, 9 families rejected any form of treatment, and 11 declined treatment with stimulant medication but were willing to consider parent training as an alternative. Of those subjects who did undergo treatment with stimulant medication, 80% continued to take medication at the conclusion of the intervention study, with no differential dropout rate between the medication only or

medication plus parent training condition. By the end of 10 months, however, the proportion of children continuing on medication had dropped to 44%. Again there was no difference in dropout rates between the two groups, and in the majority of cases, families discontinued medication without consulting either project staff or their physician.

Comparisons of those who discontinued medication and those who continued suggested that neither side effects nor lesser symptom reduction could account for nonadherence to medication. The major reasons cited for discontinuing medication were that parents were uncomfortable with medication as a treatment modality and that the children disliked the medication.

Further between-group analyses largely replicated Firestone and Witt's (1982) findings with respect to attrition in the parent training condition. Again, younger children, especially girls, with younger parents were more likely to discontinue medication treatment (Firestone, 1982).

Very few investigators have attempted to examine the long-term effects of parent training with parents of children with ADHD, with the exception of Firestone and colleagues. Firestone, Crowe, Goodman, and McGrath (1986) reported the results of a 2-year outcome study of this work. Of the original 73 subjects, only 30 were included in the follow-up analyses. Of the remaining 43, missing data caused 21 to be omitted. The other 22 were omitted because of changed treatment conditions resulting from clinical considerations (e.g., initiation or cessation of medication).

When analyzed on the basis of initial group assignment, pre-post results replicated the findings of Firestone et al. (1981), as would be expected, and this pattern of results continued to be found on the 1-year follow-up (Firestone et al., 1986). By the time of the 2-year follow-up, however, no differences were found between the three treatment conditions.

Noting that some of the children had actually changed treatment conditions, Firestone and colleagues conducted subsequent analyses comparing those children who remained in the medication only group, in the parent-training only group in the combined treatment group, and those who were switched from parent-training only to the combined condition. When examined in this way, all apparent between-group differences disappeared.

Once again, these results highlight the issue of matching the treatment regimen to the particular child. Earlier results suggested the superiority of medication to parent training, and, indeed, medication appears to have been indicated for some children originally assigned to the parent-training only condition. However, when those children were removed from that condition, parent training appears to have been an equally effective treatment modality.

The issue of matching treatment modality to individual cases is perhaps even more poignantly highlighted by Firestone and colleagues' description of those families who were lost to treatment. These findings suggest that neither parent training nor medication is reaching all families with children with ADHD. We can hope that by examining characteristics associated with attrition, clinicians and clinical researchers can develop ways to intervene more successfully with these families.

This approach is exemplified by a recent study comparing the relative effectiveness of two behavioral parent training programs. Knapp and Deluty (1989) compared parent training via modeling and role-playing to parent training via readings, tests, and discussions with mothers from middle and lower socioeconomic (SES) backgrounds whose 3- to 8-year-old children presented with behavioral problems. Middle SES mothers reported significantly greater child behavior change from pretraining to posttraining than did lower SES mothers. However, a significant training model by SES interaction indicated that, even though middle-class mothers in both training conditions increased their positive behaviors to a similar extent over time, the results differed for the lower SES mothers. Lower SES mothers who participated in the role-play training increased their positive behaviors significantly over time, while lower SES mothers in the more verbal discussion condition did not. These results are instructive in suggesting that differing treatment modalities may be needed with families with differing characteristics. In addition, although this research was not conducted with parents of children with ADHD per se, an early study with parents of children with hyperactivity incorporated video taping parent-

child interactions and used the tapes to provide feedback to parents in parent training with positive results (Furman & Feighner, 1973). These findings suggest that a behavioral, less verbal approach may be effective with this population.

The results of the developmental research reviewed earlier suggested that the preschool period may be particularly difficult. In addition, less pronounced positive effects of medication on parent-child interaction were also found during this period (Barkley, 1988). These results, coupled with the findings by Firestone and colleagues that parents of younger children were more likely to drop out of treatment, suggest that parent training treatment research may need to address the particular needs of this population. Two studies have been conducted evaluating parent training with parents of preschool children with ADHD.

Pisterman et al. (1989) evaluated the outcome of parent training with parents of preschoolers with ADD/H by comparing the treatment group to a wait-list control. The authors found positive treatment results on measures of compliance, parental style of interaction, and management skills. Further analyses indicated that these specific treatment results were maintained at a 3-month follow-up, but indicated no generalization to nontargeted child behaviors.

Based on the assumption that many parents may lack developmental knowledge, Campbell (1985) reported the results of work with her sample of preschoolers with suspected attentional and/or behavioral difficulties. Her study compared a parent-training program geared solely to teaching behavior management skills, one that also provided parents with information about the developmental tasks of toddlerhood and the early preschool years (autonomy, exploration and mastery, self-control, language development, peer relationships) and a wait-list control group. Campbell (1985) also noted problems with treatment noncompliance and attrition, making data interpretation difficult. At posttest, parents in both treatment programs rated their children as displaying fewer problems with no change in parent ratings of the control group. By 1-year follow-up, however, all between-group differences disappeared. Taken together, these findngs suggest that parent training with preschool children may hold promise but also may present particular challenges with attrition, maintenance, and generalization.

The majority of research reviewed thus far has compared behavioral parent training to medication or a no-treatment control. Recently research has begun to examine behavioral parent training in comparison, or in conjunction, with other psychological interventions.

Dubey, O'Leary, and Kaufman (1983) compared the effects of a 9-week program teaching either behavioral principles, as in their earlier work (Dubey & Kaufman, 1978), or communication skills (Parent Effectiveness Training (PET) (Gordon, 1970) to parents of hyperactive children; both treatment groups were also compared to a wait-list control. Results indicated that both treatments were more effective than no treatment in reducing ratings of behavior problems. Parents receiving behavior management training, however, rated their children as more improved than parents receiving PET; the behavior management parents were also more willing to recommend the program to a friend, felt the program was more applicable to them, and were less likely to drop out of treatment. Nine-month follow-up indicated that treatment parents continued to view their children more positively than did parents in the wait-list group.

Although parent perceptions of behavior problems decreased for the treatment groups, no differences were found in observed parent-child interactions for any of the three groups. As noted by the authors, the observations might not have been sensitive to treatment effects. Or, conversely, these results could indicate that the verbally oriented general discussion format for both treatment conditions was insufficient to achieve behavior change. In any event, the discrepancy between outcome measures highlights the need for multimethod outcome assessment. Parent behavior ratings are indices of parent perception and may in part reflect parental satisfaction. However, some form of external criterion, such as behavioral observation, may be needed to assess whether improvement in the form of behavior change did indeed occur.

Additional recent work has compared the effects of parent training to other forms of intervention with the child. Henry (1987) used a within-subject design to examine the effects of peer modeling alone and

with parent training on six children diagnosed with ADD/H who were receiving stimulant medication. The authors found that the peer modeling condition, which involved the children observing videotaped sequences of same sex and age models complying with parental commands, was of limited effectiveness in improving their compliance, compared with medication alone. Phase one of parent training, focusing on attending skills, rewarding appropriate behaviors, and ignoring inappropriate behaviors, was more effective than peer modeling alone in improving the chidren's compliance. Phase two of parent training, integrating a time-out procedure for noncompliance, was most effective, with maintenance of treatment effects suggested at 6-month follow-up.

In two studies, Horn and colleagues recently examined the effects of parent training and cognitive-behavioral self-control therapy, alone and in combination, with children diagnosed as having ADD/H. Horn, Ialongo, Popovich, and Perdotto (1987) found that all groups showed significant improvement over time, but the group receiving self-control instruction only showed a greater decrease in parent ratings of hyperactivity at the 1-month follow-up. Although maintenance of this change was significant at 1-month follow-up, there was no evidence of generalization to the classroom. Analyses again suggested a differential response to treatment: The greatest behavioral improvements were shown by mothers with greater perceived extrafamilial and community social support and children who were better able to reflect on problems, admitted to greater self-control problems, and had a more internal locus of control. Horn, Ialongo, Greenberg, Packard, and Smith-Winberry (1990) subsequently found that the combined treatment produced significantly more responders at follow-up than either treatment alone, but they continued to find no between-group differences in generalization to the school.

In an effort to increase the generalization of self-control treatment, Guevremont, Tishelman, and Hull (1985) involved mothers as adjunct therapists. Using a multiple-baseline design, Guevremont et al. evaluated a self-control training program tailored to the specific behavioral difficulties of the subjects and targeting work completion in the classroom. Mothers were trained as adjunct therapists and conducted a home training program. Results showed a substantial improvement in the children in percentage of daily classroom work completed, increased self-control and decreased disruptive behavior as reported by mothers and teachers, and higher grades at the end of treatment.

Szymula, Doll, Schleser, and Van Egeren (1989) similarly evaluated the effectiveness of training parents to administer self-instructional training to boys diagnosed with ADHD using an ABC design with extended follow-up. Results were promising, with limitations consistent with other studies reviewed thus far. There again appeared to be a greater impact on home behavior and parent ratings than on teacher ratings, and a greater impact was found when parent-administered consequences were added to the self-instructional program.

Bloomquist, August, and Anderson (1989) compared the effectiveness of methylphenidate versus placebo combined with cognitive-behavioral intervention with children alone or with their parents, using a between-groups design. The authors found that the combined parent and child cognitive-behavioral intervention resulted in significantly higher maternal ratings of improvement compared with the child-only cognitive-behavioral intervention and that the addition of methylphenidate to the combined parent and child treatment yielded significantly better results over the other three treatment groups. These results were not maintained at a statistically significant level at follow-up, although mothers in the combined parent and child groups continued to rate significantly more improvements in the parent-child relationship compared with the child-only groups. The authors found no consistent relationship between child self-report measures of locus of control and the parent-child relationship, however. Methylphenidate, which resulted in significantly more improvement on laboratory tests of attention when compared to placebo, also resulted in increases in child self-report ratings of global self-worth.

In sum, the limited research that has been conducted examining parent training specifically with children with ADHD offers some support for this treatment modality with the ADHD population, with promising findings emerging from studies combining parent training with other treatment strategies. This review also points to the clear need for further research addressing the topic. The present review provides the basis for the considerations for future work in thie area which are presented in the following section.

CONSIDERATIONS IN THE EVALUATION OF PARENT TRAINING AS A TREATMENT FOR ADHD

At the beginning of this chapter, empirical efforts were reviewed which examined the role of family factors in attentional disorders. Although limitations certainly exist, this body of work provides a rationale for including family interventions in the management of ADHD. The association of family functioning with attentional disorders can be conceptualized best in interactive or transactional terms. The evidence to date does not indicate that family interactions are of primarily etiological significance in ADHD. That is, the presence or absence of the commonly recognized core symptoms of ADHD—inattention, impulsivity and overactivity—does not rely heavily on environmental influences within the family. Rather, family interactions, either preexisting or responsive to child difficulties with attention and acitivty level, may mitigate the long-term prognosis of children exhibiting ADHD symptoms. More specifically, family processes may play an important role in determining the risk of co-morbid difficulties, such as conduct disorder, which predict poor long-range outcome. Secondary symptoms, such as noncompliant and aggressive behavior, may, in at least some cases, emerge when parents are unprepared to meet the elevated needs of their ADHD children for structure and consistency. Biological links between parents and children may also result in parents with affective, attentional, or impulsivity difficulties, which interfere with their execution of parental functions needed to manage behavioral difficulties.

Observational studies suggest that parent-child interactions improve with the direct treatment of ADHD core symptoms via stimulant medication. It would not, however, be realistic to view this as evidence that family interventions, such as parent training, are not necessary. It is unclear whether the effects of pharmacological interventions on family

symptoms are evident in settings outside the laboratory or clinic. It is conceivable that under circumstances existing at home, when different stimulus
cues exist and family members are unobserved,
medication effects on child symptoms may exert a
less powerful influence on family interactions. Furthermore, there is no evidence to suggest that
stimulant medication has any effect upon parent-child
interactions beyond the well-recognized, brief window of medication effectiveness. These considerations are of importance because children often do
not receive medication during hours that they have
the most contact with parents, such as evenings and
weekends. Furthermore, many children are not can-
didates for pharmacological treatment because of
parental reservations or undesirable side effects of
the medication.

In evaluating alternative treatment options, it is
important to consider their long-range impact on
child and family functioning. Longitudinal research
indicates that family characteristics and secondary
symptoms associated with family functioning (e.g.,
aggressive behavior), may be among the strongest
predictors of long-term outcome among ADHD
children (Weiss & Hechtman, 1986). Therefore, it
is possible that parent training interventions, which
target such behavioral patterns, may be useful in
improving the long-range prognosis of children with
attentional difficulties. This possibility not only
warrants further attention but should be a particular
focus in the implementation and evaluation of parent
training interventions.

As shown by the preceding review, there is an
emerging body of research investigating the efficacy
of parent training interventions for children with
ADHD. Although these studies generally converge to
support the use of these treatment efforts, it is
surprising that a larger number of studies has not been
conducted. Certainly it is unclear whether sufficient
data exist to justify using parent training as a "best
available treatment" control condition in empirical
evaluations of the effectiveness of alternative treatments, as was done by Horn and colleagues (1987).
It is likely that popular support for parent training
interventions in the management of ADHD is based
largely on successful studies of children with other
externalizing behavior disorders (e.g., oppositional
defiant disorder) as well as on anecdotal evidence.

Among the existing body of studies examining
ADHD children, there are methodological factors,
such as sample characteristics, measurement issues,
and design factors, which limit the conclusions that
may be drawn at the current time. As with efforts
examining other treatment modalities and disorders,
research examining the use of parent training in the
management of ADHD has generated many complicated questions, as yet unanswered. Empirical
efforts that simply investigate whether parent training
"works" are not sufficient to delineate the place of
such interventions within a comprehensive treatment
program. Additional research is needed to assess
specifically which symptoms are most responsive to
parent training at what point in time, for whom it is
most effective, and how parent training brings about
and maintains such changes.

Methodological Limitations

Evidence regarding the effectiveness of parent
training interventions for children diagnosed with
ADHD is currently inconclusive, in part because of
the methodological limitations of many existing
studies. These limitations provide some useful guidelines for future research endeavors. First, careful
attention needs to be paid to the selection criteria
used in constructing samples of children with ADHD
diagnoses. As noted above, relatively few investigations of parent training included children with clear
diagnoses of ADHD rather than other externalizing
behavioral disorders. Of those that do exist, comparison is often complicated by alterations in how
professional organizations and clinical researchers
defined and operationalized diagnostic criteria. In
addition to the criteria employed, researchers varied
in their reliance on observational, teacher report,
and/or parent report data. There is an obvious need
for multimodal assessment of carefully defined diagnostic criteria for ADHD in selecting subjects for
future research.

Second, sufficient numbers of subject must be
included to support statistical analyses of interest.
In general, previous studies included too few subjects for fair testing of the outcome of parent
training interventions. The limitations in statistical
power resulting from small sample sizes substantially increase the risk of type I errors or false

negative conclusions about group differences. In some cases, researchers conducted more analyses or group comparisons than were justified given their limited number of subjects. When treatment and control groups were compared on relatively many dependent variables, "significant differences" are likely to have occurred by chance. In addition to larger sample sizes, researchers may need to examine the significance of multivariate group differences before examining individual outcome variables to control for error rates or false positive findings. To the extent that small samples resulted from subject attrition, issues of generalizability become a primary concern. In fact, several initial reports suggested that premature termination of treatment is far from a random occurrence (Firestone, 1982; Firestone & Witt, 1982).

Third, there is a continuing need for carefully constructed control groups in future investigations. Previous researchers often compared parent training to other treatment approaches without the benefit of comparison subjects who received no active intervention efforts (e.g., Gittleman-Klein et al., 1976; Horn et al., 1987). The lack of adequate control comparisons makes it difficult to ascertain whether pre-post treatment differences are clinically meaningful as well as statistically significant. The impact of parent training with parents of children diagnosed with ADHD is certainly not understood sufficiently to warrant elimination of control groups in future research.

Expansion of Research Questions

Issues regarding selection criteria, sample size, and control groups are important to consider in any research efforts documenting the impact of parent training interventions in the treatment of ADHD. In addition to meeting stricter methodological criteria, empirical efforts are needed to exmine questions beyond *whether* parent training is or is not effective with this population. Future studies will need to examine how different clusters of symptoms respond to parent training, with whom these changes are most likely to occur and be maintained, and how parent training efforts bring about such changes.

What Are the Appropriate Targets of Parent Training?

Children with diagnosed ADHD display a wide range of behavioral symptoms. Characteristic patterns in parent-child interactions and parental cognition have also been identified. It is unrealistic to expect that any single intervention will be successful in altering all of these potential treatment targets. It is becoming increasingly clear that combinations of strategies may be necessary to achieve multidimensional treatment objectives. Previous research indicates that parent training interventions may be most effective in reducing levels of aggressive and noncompliant behavior (Abikoff & Gittleman, 1984; Gittleman et al., 1980; Pisterman et al., 1989) rather than the primary or core symptoms of ADHD: inattention, impulsivity, and overactivity, per se. Existing research does not, however, provide a clear picture of which indicators of these behavior problems are altered for ADHD children as a result of parent training efforts. For example, Dubey and colleagues (1983) found that parent training altered parent perceptions of behavior problems but did not seem to affect observed mother-child interactions in the laboratory. Even when observational methods have detected improvement with parent training (Pisterman et al., 1989), it has remained unclear whether these changes would generalize from the clinic or laboratory to the home setting. Clearly, future research will need to include multimethod assessment of behavioral targets in multiple settings (clinic, home, school) in order to address these issues.

What Is the Long-Range Impact of Parent Training?

The majority of parent training outcome studies with families of ADHD children focused on their immediate, posttreatment impact on child functioning. There is an obvious need for studies that include long-range follow-up assessments of children using the multimethod assessment approach advocated above. While some positive results were noted up to 3 to 9 months post treatment (Pisterman et al., 1989; Dubey et al., 1983), declines in group differences at 1 to 2 years posttreatment were reported (Firestone et al., 1986). It is difficult to compare existing studies with follow-up assessments directly because of differences in their samples, outcome variables, and quality or intensity of parent training protocol. It would seem that the question of *whether* parent training has long-range benefit for ADHD children is too simplistic. Rather, as with examination of immediate outcomes, researchers will need to examine the impact of sample characteristics (e.g., symptom profile, age), treatment protocols (e.g., content of the intervention, number of sessions), and intervening variables (e.g., continuation of parent behaviors learned in session) on the maintenance of immediate treatment gains (e.g., improved behavior ratings) as well as long-term prognostic indices (e.g., dropping out of school, delinquency).

Who Benefits Most from Parent Training?

The question of whether parent training interventions are differentially effective for subgroups of children with ADHD diagnoses remains an interesting area of research. Efforts addressing this issue need to examine the characteristics of children as well as their parents, which are associated with desired alterations in child behavior and parent-child interactions.

As parent training may be an effective treatment component for decreasing levels of aggressive and oppositional behavior often displayed by children diagnosed with ADHD, parent interventions may be most indicated when children possess co-morbid diagnoses of conduct or oppositional defiant disorders. Research has yet to be conducted that compares the relative impact of parent training interventions with children given diagnoses of ADHD alone, CD or ODD alone, and both ADHD and either CD or ODD. In conducting such investigations, it would be important to consider the long-range as well as immediate functioning of subgroups receiving and not receiving treatment. Such a design would help determine whether teaching parents behavior management techniques has any preventive effect. That is, could parent training with the parents of young ADHD children help reduce their risk of developing coexisting conduct disturbances?

Additional factors that might mitigate the success of parent training efforts could include parental educational or socioeconomic level, family structure variables (e.g., number of siblings, presence of more than one parent), parent or child cognitive variables (exceptions, attributions, perceived efficacy). Clearly there is no shortage of variables that could effect the impact parent training efforts have on parent-child interactions and child behavior problems. A strong deterrent to future studies of parent training's differential effectiveness is likely to be the size of samples that would be needed for adequate testing of these hypotheses.

Given that successful intervention outcomes should at least include completion of therapy, studies identifying predictors of subject attrition may be thought of as examinations of differential treatment effectiveness. Firestone and colleagues have identified families of younger and female ADHD children as more likely than others to drop out of treatment; however, this observation may not be specific to parent training interventions (Firestone, 1982; Firestone & Witt, 1982). In addition, these researchers have reported that socioeconomic status correlates positively with treatment completion, suggesting that higher SES children may benefit more from parent training efforts with their parents. Knapp and Deluty (1989) reported that middle SES mothers reported greater pre-post parent training effects than did lower SES mothers participating in the same parent intervention.

How Do Parent Training Interventions Work?

Efforts to identify how parent training programs work must address a wide range of clinical issues regarding the content and process of such interventions. Several good resources exist for describing the components of model parent training programs in general (Forehand & McMahon, 1981) and those for ADHD children specifically (Barkley, 1987). However, very few empirical efforts have been devoted to identifying the relative utility of different behavior management techniques (the content of parent training programs) with families of ADHD children. A second issue regarding how parent training programs work is the relative effectiveness of different methods for teaching behavioral techniques (the process of parent training programs). Finally, an understanding of how parent training programs impact ADHD children must include investigation of the association between outcome measures and theoretically based intervening variables.

It is important to recognize that parent training programs, in research and clinical practice, include a wide range of target skills and instructional techniques. In fact, there is wide variability in what skills are taught, how this is done, and the success with which the information is utilized by parents. This variability makes comparison of treatment outcome studies difficult at best. Parent training interventions typically include some combination of training in attending skills, effective command giving, selective attention or active ignoring, contingent reinforcement, and punishment techniques (e.g., time out from reinforcement). In a recent study, Henry (1987) reported data suggesting that ADHD children received incremental benefits from reinforcement and punishment techniques taught sequentially to their parents. Several researchers have helped parents promote generalization of cognitive interventions with their ADHD children by teaching them to implement self-control or instructional training methods at home (Guevremont et al., 1985). Szymula and colleagues (1989) reported increased effectiveness from teaching parents to administer consequences as well as self-instructional trainung at home with their ADHD sons. A somewhat different approach investigated by Campbell (1985) failed to find any incremental utility in providing parents with developmental information in addition to behavior management skills.

A separate issue from *what* should be taught in parent training programs is *how* these skills are best presented to parents. What format best promotes skill acquisition and usage? Systematic research has yet to be conducted on the relative efficacy of parent training interventions varying along structural dimensions such as the number and frequency of sessions or use of individual family versus multifamily group formats. In addition to considering these basic format issues, future research is needed to identify the intervention techniques that best promote acquisition of target skills. At least two initial existing reports suggest that skill acquisition may be best enhanced by active, hands-on approaches (e.g., role-playing,

video feedback) rather than purely verbal instruction (Furman & Feighner, 1973), particularly with lower SES families (Knapp & Deluty, 1989). Additional investigations of the efficacy of instructional techniques and their interaction with family characteristics is definitely needed. These efforts should include exploration of techniques that may promote generalization (e.g., home-practice assignments) and maintenance (e.g., booster sessions) of treatment effects.

A final issue regarding how parent training works is the role of intervening variables or processes. Theoretically, parent training interventions affect child behavior because they alter the behavior management strategies used by parents, which in turn promote positive behaviors and discourage negative behaviors. Numerous researchers have attempted to incorporate parent-child interaction assessments in their investigations of parent training interventions with the parents of ADHD children (e.g., Pisterman et al., 1989). Unfortunately, these efforts focused almost exclusively on laboratory observations. It is unclear whether improvements in child behavior ratings would be associated with altered parent behavior and parent-child interactions at home. Demonstrations of altered parent-child interactions in the laboratory or clinic may best be thought of as a behavioral "test" of what parents have learned in treatment. It seems reasonable to expect that improvements in children's long-range functioning would be associated with the ongoing implementation of behavior management techniques and altered parent-child interactions in the home. Alternative intervening variables warranting examination might be changes in parental cognition including expectations and attributions of child behavior.

CONCLUSION

This chapter reviewed research that found family correlates of ADHD to suggest a rationale for parent training with this population. Research examining this treatment modality with ADHD was then reviewed, followed by a discussion of considerations when evaluating parent training with this population. It was concluded that family variables, and subsequently parent training, are likely clinically important with this population, and further research in this area is clearly warranted.

REFERENCES

Abikoff, H., & Gittelman, R. (1984). Does behavior therapy normalize the classroom behavior of hyperactive children? *Archives of General Psychiatry, 41,* 449–454.

Alberts-Corush, J., Firestone, P., & Goodman, J. T. (1986). Attention and impulsivity characteristics of the biological and adoptive parents of hyperactive and normal control children. *American Journal of Orthopsychiatry, 56,* 413–423.

August, G. J., & Stewart, M. A. (1983). Familial subtypes of hyperactivity. *Journal of Nervous and Mental Disease, 171,* 362–368.

Barkley, R. A. (1985). The social behavior of hyperactive children: Developmental changes, drug effects, and situational variation. In R. J. McMahon & R. DeV. Peters (Eds.), *Childhood disorders: Behavioral-developmental approaches* (pp. 218–239). New York: Brunner/Mazel.

Barkley, R. A. (1987). What is the role of group parent training in the treatment of ADD children? In J. Loney (Ed.), *The young hyperactive child: Answers to questions about diagnosis, prognosis, and treatment* (pp. 143–152). New York: Haworth Press.

Barkley, R. A. (1988). The effects of methylphenidate on the interactions of preschool ADHD children and their mothers. *Journal of the American Academy of Child and Adolescent Psychiatry, 27,* 336–341.

Barkley, R. A., Karlsson, J., & Pollard, S. (1985a). Effects of age on the mother-child interactions of ADD/H and normal boys. *Journal of Abnormal Child Psychology, 13,* 631–637.

Barkley, R. A., Karlsson, J., Pollard, S., & Murphy, J. V. (1985b). Developmental changes in the mother-child interactions of hyperactive boys: Effects of 2 dose levels of Ritalin. *Journal of Child Psychology and Psychiatry and Allied Disciplines, 26,* 705–715.

Barkley, R. A., Karlsson, J., Strezelecki, E., & Murphy, J. V. (1984). Effects of age and Ritalin dosage on the mother-child interactions of hyperactive children. *Journal of Consulting and Clinical Psychology, 52,* 750–758.

Beck, S. J., Young, G. H., & Tarnowski, K. J. (1990). Maternal characteristics and perceptions of pervasive and situational hyperactives and normal controls. *Journal of the American Academy of Child and Adolescent Psychiatry, 29,* 558–565.

Befera, M. S., & Barkley, R. A. (1985). Hyperactive and normal girls and boys: Mother-child interaction, parent psychiatric status and child psychopathology. *Journal of Child Psychology and Psychiatry and Allied Disciplines, 26,* 439–452.

Biederman, J., Faraone, S. V., Keenan, K., Knee, D., & Tsuang, M. T. (1990). Family-genetic and psychosocial risk factors in DSM-III attention deficit disorder. *Journal of the American Academy of Child and Adolescent Psychiatry, 29,* 526–533.

Biederman, J., Munir, K., & Knee, D. (1987). Conduct and oppositional disorder in clinically referred children with attention deficit disorder: A controlled family study. *Journal of the American Academy of Child and Adolescent Psychiatry, 26,* 724–727.

Biederman, J., Munir, K., Knee, D., Haberlow, W., Armentano, M., Autor, S., Hoge, S. K., Waternaux, C. (1986). A family study of patients with attention deficit disorder and normal controls. *Journal of Psychiatric Research, 20,* 263–274.

Bloomquist, M. L., August, G. J., & Anderson, D. (1989). *Cognitive behavioral therapy for attention-deficit hyperactivity disordered children: Additive effects of parent involvement and methylphenidate.* Paper presented at the Association for the Advancement of Behavior Therapy Convention, Washington, DC.

Breen M. J., & Barkley, R. A. (1988). Child psychopathology and parenting stress in girls and boys having attention deficit disorder with hyperactivity. *Journal of Pediatric Psychology, 13,* 256–280.

Brown, R. T., & Pacini, J. N. (1989). Perceived family functioning, marital status, and depression in parents of boys with ADD. *Journal of Learning Disabilities, 22,* 581–587.

Campbell, S. B. (1985). Hyperactivity in preschoolers: Correlates and prognostic implications. *Clinical Psychology Review, 5,* 405–428.

Campbell, S. B., Breaux, A. M., Ewing, L. J., & Szumowski, E. K. (1986a). Correlates and predictors of hyperactivity and aggression: A longitudinal study of parent-referred problem preschoolers. *Journal of Abnormal Child Psychology, 14,* 217–234.

Campbell, S. B., Breaux, A. M., Ewing, L. J., Szumowski, E. K., & Pierce, E. W. (1986b). Parent-identified problem preschoolers: Mother-child interaction during play at intake and 1-year follow-up. *Journal of Abnormal Child Psychology, 14,* 425–440.

Cantwell, D. P. (1972). Psychiatric illness in the families of hyperactives. *Archives of General Psychiatry, 27,* 414–417.

Cohen, N. J., & Minde, K. (1983). The "hyperactive syndrome" in kindergarten children: Comparison of children with pervasive and situational symptoms.

Journal of Child Psychology and Psychiatry and Allied Disciplines, 24, 443–455.

Cuningham, C. E., Benness, B. B., & Siegel, L. S. (1988). Family functioning, time allocation, and parental depression in the families of normal and ADDH children. *Journal of Clinical Child Psychology, 17,* 169–177.

Dubey, D. R., & Kaufman, K. F. (1978). Home management of hyperkinetic children. *Pediatrics, 93,* 141–146.

Dubey, D. R., O'Leary, S. G., & Kaufman, K. F. (1983). Training parents of hyperactive children in child management: A comparative outcome study. *Journal of Abnormal Child Psychology, 11,* 229–246.

Emery, R. E. (1982). Interparental conflict and the children of discord and divorce. *Psychological Bulletin, 92,* 310–330.

Epstein, N. B., Baldwin, L. M., & Bishop, D. S. (1983). The McMaster Family Assessment Device. *Journal of Marital and Family Therapy, 9,* 171–180.

Firestone, P. (1982). Factors associated with children's adherence to stimulant medication. *American Journal of Orthopsychiatry, 52,* 447–457.

Firestone, P., Crowe, D., Goodman, J. T., & McGrath, P. (1986). Vicissitudes of follow-up studies: Differential effects of parent training and stimulant medication with hyperactives. *American Journal of Orthopsychiatry, 56,* 184–194.

Firestone, P., Kelly, M. J., Goodman, J. T., & Davey, J. (1981). Differential effects of parent training and stimulant medication with hyperactives. *Journal of the American Academy of Child Psychiatry, 20,* 135–147.

Firestone, P., & Witt, J. (1982). Characteristics of families completing and prematurely discontinuing a behavioral parent training program. *Journal of Pediatric Psychology, 7,* 209–222.

Forehand, R., & McMahon, R. J. (1981). *Helping the noncompliant child: A clinician's guide to parent training.* New York: Guilford Press.

Furman, S., & Feighner, A. (1973). Video feedback in treating hyperkinetic children: A preliminary report. *American Journal of Psychiatry, 130,* 792–796.

Gittelman, R., Abikoff, H., Pollack, E., Klein, D. F., Katz, S., & Mattes, J. (1980). A controlled trial of behavior modification and methylphenidate in hyperactive children. In C. K. Whalen & B. Henker (Eds.), *Hyperactive children: The social ecology of identification and treatment* (pp. 221–243). New York: Academic Press.

Gittelman-Klein, R., Klein, D. F., Abikoff, H., Katz, S., Gloisten, A., & Kates, W. (1976). Relative efficacy of methylphenidate and behavior modification in hyperkinetic children: An interim report. *Journal of Abnormal Child Psychology, 4,* 361–379.

Gordon, T. (1970). *Parent effectiveness training.* New York: Peter H. Wyden.

Griest, D. L., Forehand, R., Wells, K. C., & McMahon, R. J. (1980). An examination of differences between nonclinic and behavior-problem clinic-referred children and their mothers. *Journal of Abnormal Psychology, 89,* 497–500.

Griest, D. L., & Wells, K. C. (1983). Behavioral family therapy with conduct disorders in children. *Behavior Therapy, 14,* 37–53.

Guevremont, D. C., Tishelman, A. C., & Hull, D. B. (1985). Teaching generalized self-control to attention-deficient boys with mothers as adjunct therapists. *Child and Family Behavior Therapy, 7,* 23–37.

Hartsough, C. S., & Lambert, N. M. (1982). Some environmental and familial correlates and antecedents of hyperactivity. *American Journal of Orthopsychiatry, 52,* 272–287.

Hechtman, L. (1981). Families of hyperactives. *Research in Community and Mental Health, 2,* 275–292.

Henry, G. K. (1987). Symbolic modeling and parent behavioral training: Effects on noncompliance of hyperactive children. *Journal of Behavior Therapy and Experimental Psychiatry, 18,* 105–113.

Horn, W. F., Ialongo, N., Greenberg, G., Packard, T., & Smith-Winberry, C. (1990). Additive effects of behavioral parent training and self-control therapy with attention deficit hyperactivity disordered children. *Journal of Clinical Child Psychology, 19,* 98–110.

Horn, W. F., Ialongo, N., Popovich, S., & Peradotto, D. (1987). Behavioral parent training and cognitive-behavioral self-control therapy with ADD-H children: Comparative and combined effects. *Journal of Clinical Child Psychology, 16,* 57–68.

Jacobvitz, D., & Sroufe, L. A. (1987). The early caregiver-child relationship and attention-deficit disorder with hyperactivity in kindergarten: A prospective study. *Child Development, 58,* 1496–1504.

Knapp, P. A., & Deluty, R. H. (1989). Relative effectiveness of two behavioral parent training programs. *Journal of Clinical Child Psychology, 18,* 314–322.

Lahey, B. B., Placentini, J. C., McBurnett, K., Stone, P., Hartdagen, S., & Hynd, G. (1988). Psychopathology in the parents of children with conduct disorder and hyperactivity. *Journal of the American Academy of Child and Adolescent Psychiatry, 27,* 163–170.

Lambert, N. M., & Hartsough, C. S. (1984). Contribution of predispositional factors to the diagnosis of hyperactivity. *American Journal of Orthopsychiatry, 54,* 97–109.

McGee, R., Williams, S., & Silva, P. A. (1984). Background characteristics of aggressive, hyperactive, and aggressive-hyperactive boys. *Journal of the American Academy of Child Psychiatry, 23,* 280–284.

Marshall, V. G., Longwell, L., Goldstein, M. J., & Swanson, J. M. (1990). Family factors associated with aggressive symptomology in boys with attention deficit hyperactivity disorder: A research note. *Journal of Child Psychology and Psychiatry and Allied Disciplines, 31,* 629–636.

Mash, E. J., & Johnston, C. (1982). A comparison of the mother-child interactions of younger and older hyperactives and normal children. *Child Development, 53,* 1371–1381.

Mash, E. J., & Johnston, C. (1983). The prediction of mothers' behavior with their hyperactive children during play and task situations. *Child and Family Behavior Therapy, 5,* 1–14.

Moos, R. H., & Moos, B. S. (1981). *Family environment scale manual.* Palo Alto, CA: Consulting Psychologists Press.

Morrison, J. R., & Stewart, M. A. (1971). A family study of the hyperactive child syndrome. *Biological Psychiatry, 3,* 189–195.

O'Leary, K. D., Pelham, W. E., Rosenbaum, A., & Price, G. H. (1976). Behavioral treatment of hyperkinetic children: An experimental evaluation of its usefulness. *Clinical Pediatrics, 15,* 510–515.

Olson, S. L., Bates, J. E., & Bayles, K. (1990). Early antecedents of childhood impulsivity: The role of parent-child interaction, cognitive competence and temperament. *Journal of Abnormal Child Psychology, 18,* 317–334.

Patterson, G. R. (1982). *Coercive family process.* Eugene, OR: Castalla.

Pelham, W. E. (1977). Withdrawal of a stimulant drug and concurrent behavioral intervention in the treatment of a hyperactive child. *Behavioral Therapy, 8,* 473–479.

Pelham, W. E., & Hoza, J. (1987). Behavioral assessment of psychostimulant effects on ADD children in a summar day treatment program. In R. J. Prinz (Ed.), *Advances in behavioral assessment of children and families* (Vol. 3, pp. 3–34). Greenwich, CT: JAI Press.

Pelham, W. E., Schnedler, R. W., Bologna, N. C., & Contreras, J. A. (1980). Behavioral and stimulant treatment of hyperactive children: A therapy study with methylphenidate probes in a within-subject design. *Journal of Applied Behavioral Analysis, 13,* 221–236.

Pisterman, S., McGrath, P., Firestone, P., Goodman, J. T., Webster, I., & Mallory, R. (1989). Outcome of parent-mediated treatment of preschoolers with attention deficit disorder with hyperactivity. *Journal of Consulting and Clinical Psychology, 57,* 628–635.

Pollard, S., Ward, E. M., & Barkley, R. A. (1983). The effects of parent training and Ritalin on the parent-child interactions of hyperactive boys. *Child and Family Behavior Therapy, 5,* 51–69.

Prinz, R. J., Myers, deR., Holden, E. W., Tarnowski, K. J., & Roberts, W. A. (1983). Marital disturbance and child problems: A cautionary note regarding hyperactive children. *Journal of Abnormal Child Psychology, 11,* 393–399.

Reeves, J. C., Werry, J. S., Elkind, G. S., & Zametkin, A. (1987). Attention deficit, conduct, oppositional, and anxiety disorders in children: II. Clinical characteristics. *Journal of the American Academy of Child and Adolescent Psychiatry, 26,* 144–155.

Schachar, R., Sandberg, S., & Rutter, M. (1980). Agreement between teacher ratings and observations of hyperactivity, inattentiveness, and conduct problems. *Journal of Abnormal Child Psychology, 14,* 331–345.

Schachar, R., Taylor, E., Weiselberg, M., Thorley, G., & Rutter, M. (1987). Changes in family functioning and relationships in children who respond to methylphenidate. *Journal of the American Academy of Child and Adolescent Psychiatry, 26,* 729–732.

Schaefer, J. W., Palkes, H. S., & Stewart, M. A. (1974). Group counseling for parents of hyperkinetic children. *Child Psychiatry and Human Development, 5,* 89–94.

Schaughency, E. A, & Rothlind, J. (1991). Assessment and classification of attention deficit hyperactive disorders. *School Psychology Review, 20*(2), 197–202.

Schaughency, E. A., Walker, J., & Lahey, B. B. (1988). Attention deficit disorder and hyperactivity: Psychological therapies. In J. L. Matson (Ed.), *Handbook of treatment approaches to childhood psychopathology* (pp. 195–214). New York: Plenum Publishing.

Sobol, M. P., Ashbourne, D. T., Earn, B. M., & Cunningham, C. E. (1989). Parents' attributions for achieving compliance from attention-deficit-disordered children. *Journal of Abnormal Child Psychology, 17,* 359–369.

Stewart, M. A., DeBlois, C. S., & Cummings, C. (1980). Psychiatric disorder in the parents of hyperactive boys with and without conduct disorder. *Journal of Child Psychology and Psychiatry and Allied Disciplines, 21,* 283–292.

Szymula, G., Doll, M., Schleser, R., & Van Egeren, L. (1989). *Parents as therapists: The effects of parent administered self-instructional training on the home and school behavior of AD-HD boys.* Paper presented at the Association for the Advancement of Behavior Therapy, Washington, DC.

Tallmadge, J., & Barkley, R. A. (1983). The interactions of hyperactive and normal boys with their fathers and mothers. *Journal of Abnormal Child Psychology, 11,* 565–579.

Tarver-Behring, S., Barkley, R., & Karlsson, J. (1985). The mother-child interactions of hyperactive boys and their normal siblings. *American Journal of Orthopsychiatry, 55,* 202–209.

Taylor, E., Schachar, R, Thorley, G., & Weiselberg, M. (1986). Conduct disorder and hyperactivity: I. Separation of hyperactivity and antisocial conduct in British child psychiatric patients. *British Journal of Psychiatry, 149,* 760–777.

Walker, J. L., Lahey, B. B., Hynd, G. W., & Frame, C. L. (1987). Comparison of specific patterns of antisocial behavior in children with conduct disorder with or without coexisting hyperactivity. *Journal of Consulting and Clinical Psychology, 55,* 910–913.

Weiner, B. (1979). A theory of motivation for classroom experiences. *Journal of Educational Psychology, 71,* 3–25.

Weiss, G., & Hechtman, L. T. (1986). *Hyperactive children grown up: Empirical findings and theoretical considerations.* New York: Guilford Press.

Werry, J. S., Reeves, J. C., & Elkind, G. S. (1987). Attention deficit, conduct, oppositional, and anxiety disorders in children: I. A review of research on differentiating characteristics. *Journal of the American Academy of Child and Adolescent Psychiatry, 26,* 133–143.

Westerman, M. A. (1990). Coordination of maternal directives with preschoolers' behavior in compliance-problem and healthy dyads. *Developmental Psychology, 26,* 621–630.

CHAPTER 14

NUTRITION

Lee A. Rosén
Dionne Schissel
Susan Taylor
Linda Krein

In 1973, Dr. Benjamin Feingold announced to the annual convention of the American Medical Association that many of the hyperactive children seen in his practice were suffering from the effects of food additives, preservatives, and salicylates (Feingold, German, Brahm, & Simmers, 1973). This pronouncement was widely reported by the media and quickly popularized the notion that diet can affect behavior—especially the behavior of hyperactive children. Because of the publicity and controversy surrounding this issue, the public began to search for dietary causes of children's behavior problems in all sorts of common foods ranging from milk to soft drinks. In addition, this event precipitated some of the most concerted and creative research in all of psychology. Since Feingold's report, scores of studies have been conducted examining the effects of not only additives but also caffeine, sugar, aspartame, and other specific foods as well. Following is a review of the literature pertaining to the effects of diet and nutrition on the behavior of hyperactive children.

FOOD ADDITIVES

One of the many theories regarding the etiology of hyperactivity posits that artificial food additives

and food coloring can cause and/or exacerbate hyperactivity in children. This theory was proposed in the 1970s by B. F. Feingold, a pediatrician and allergist who noticed parallels between an increase in additives in typical American diets and the increase in learning disabilities and hyperactivity (Feingold, 1975a). His early investigations focused on the similarity in chemical structure between aspirin and salicylates (naturally occurring compounds found in many foods). Feingold (1975b) observed that people who have an intolerance to aspirin are adversely affected by ingestion of natural salicylates as well, with many of these reactions being physical and mental disturbances (Feingold, 1975a; Lipton, Nemeroff, & Mailman, 1979; Stare, Whelan, & Sheridan, 1980). Likewise, the chemical structure of many artificial flavors is similar to that of salicylates (Stare et al., 1980). Therefore, Feingold hypothesized that similar adverse reactions may be found in children who are genetically predisposed to toxic reactions to salicylates and food additives, and as a result demonstrate an increase in hyperactive behaviors (Beall, 1973; Conners, 1980; Feingold, 1975a). Specifically, Feingold stated that synthetic flavors and colors "are a common cause of adverse reactions affecting most body systems. . . . The most important and most dramatic adverse reactions produced by synthetic colors and flavors are behavioral disturbances" (Feingold, 1975a, p. 799).

Following from his hypothesis, Feingold proposed a diet that eliminated foods containing natural salicylates and food additives (colors and flavors). This diet, he claimed, would lead to improved behavior, better sleeping patterns, and freedom from hyperactive symptoms particularly among younger children (Beall, 1973). Feingold (1975b) noted improvements to be extreme in 40% to 50% of the children he treated. In his book entitled *Why Your Child Is Hyperactive,* Feingold (1975b) recommended that foods—convenience foods, most fruits and some vegetables—be eliminated because they contain salicylates, food coloring, and/or artificial flavoring (Beall, 1973; Conners, 1980; Feingold, 1975a, 1975b; Lipton, Nemeroff, Mailman, 1979). It was his recommendation that, once the diet was shown to be effective in reducing negative behavioral reactions in a child, eliminated foods be gradually reintroduced into the child's diet (Lipton et al., 1979).

Feingold's Evidence

Feingold derived his evidence from the nonscientific analysis of cases he saw in his own medical practice. Anecdotal evidence was provided by Feingold in his address to the American Medical Association (Feingold, German, Brahm, & Simmers, 1973). He reviewed 25 cases involving children considered to be hyperactive and who had been placed on his special diet. He reported that within 1 to 4 weeks on the diet, children displayed behavioral changes and could be freed of behavior modifying drugs. He also described recurrence of impaired behavioral patterns within 2 to 4 hours when patients violated the diet regimen. Finally, in a report to Congress on the efficacy of his diet, Feingold (Beall, 1973) cited three examples of clinical cases in which children showed marked improvement in disruptive, hyperactive behaviors and scholastic achievement after being placed on a salicylate-free diet.

Criticisms of Feingold's Diet

In 1975, the Nutrition Foundation along with the food industry formed the National Advisory Committee on Hyperkinesis and Food Additives to investigate the legitimacy of Feingold's diet. Preliminary reports of this investigation addressed several criticisms that were echoed by many scientists in the field. The major concerns focused on (a) the lack of controlled, scientific studies demonstrating the effects of an elimination diet, (b) the absence of confirmed significant improvement in hyperactive behavior, and (c) the need for further investigations.

Additional criticisms were also expressed by several researchers regarding the restrictiveness of the diet. Stare et al. (1980) hypothesized that the diet regimen outlined by Feingold alters the structure and dynamics of the family which, in turn, accounts for the effects on behavior seen by Feingold. In many of the cases cited by Feingold, the family was aware of the special diet; thus, patients and family members may have responded to demand characteristics and thus reported improved behaviors (Levine & Liden, 1976; Werry, 1976). Furthermore, Conners (1980) pointed out that, in many cases, the children's response to the diet resembles that of children placed on placebo diets.

Another concern of the diet itself is the potential for nutritional compromise resulting from the extensive number of foods (fruits and vegetables) eliminated because of their salicylate concentration (Conners, 1980; Lipton et al., 1979; Stare et al., 1980; Stine, 1976; Taylor, 1979). Conners, Goyette, Southwick, Lees, and Andrulonis (1976) reported a poorer intake of nutrients when children were on the Feingold diet compared to pretreatment baseline and a control diet. This condition was particularly true regarding vitamin C intake. While children were still receiving nutrient intakes exceeding the recommended daily allowance (RDA), the researchers warned against long-term effects of this restrictive diet.

Furthermore, the diet has been criticized for eliminating foods that do not have significant and measurable amounts of salicylates, thus not warranting their removal from the diet (Harley, Ray, et al., 1978). Finally, several researchers have questioned and criticized the scientific methodology (or lack of) utilized by Feingold and his fellow clinicians that have documented positive results of the Feingold diet (e.g., Coo, & Woodhill, 1976). Specifically, these reports have been criticized for their selection of subjects and qualifying criteria, lack of control subjects, inconsistent findings, and minimal use of objective measures (Conners, 1980; Levine & Liden, 1976; Taylor, 1979; Werry, 1976).

Investigations of the Feingold Diet

In response to the claims made by Feingold, and to the concerns brought forth by the National Advisory Committee on Hyperkinesis and Food Additives, a plethora of studies have been conducted attempting to determine more precisely the effect of the Feingold diet on hyperactive behaviors. These investigations have been of predominantly three types: uncontrolled studies, double-blind crossover studies, and challenge studies.

Uncontrolled studies closely resemble, in format, those clinical case studies presented by Feingold (e.g., Beall, 1973). Physicians and pediatricians provide anecdotal accounts of clinical observations they have made following the prescription of the diet to a pediatric patient (Conners, 1980). These informal observations and reports most often are presented in support of the diet's effectiveness in eliminating disruptive behaviors in hyperactive children (e.g., Cook & Woodhill, 1976).

Double-blind crossover studies utilize more rigorous experimental design when establishing the effectiveness of an elimination diet. The general procedure is as follows (Lipton et al., 1979): Children are first identified as being hyperactive and then are placed on one of two comparable diets, either the Feingold diet or a diet containing natural salicylates and artificial food flavors and coloring. Subjects, their families, and observers are "blind" as to which diet is being implemented, and behavioral reactions to the diet are recorded. After a period of time on one diet, the subject is crossed over to the other diet, to control for order effects. Harley and colleagues utilized the double-blind crossover design in their studies (Harley, Ray, et al., 1978).

The third type of study used by researchers (e.g., Conners, 1980) is the challenge design. In a challenge study experiment, children who have demonstrated responsiveness to the Feingold diet are selected and placed alternatively in test and control groups in a crossover design. When in test conditions, subjects are placed on the Feingold diet and, at various times over the course of several weeks, are "challenged" with foods containing salicylates (typically specially manufactured cookies) while subjects in control conditions are given identical food items that contain no salicylates. Following administration of the challenge, subjects are measured on one or more behaviors (Stare et al., 1980). In both double-blind crossover and challenge studies, subjects are typically removed from stimulant medication prior to the onset of the experiment

Uncontrolled Studies

The majority of clinical case studies examining the use of Feingold's diet support the diet's effectiveness in alleviating problematic behaviors among hyperactive children. One such observation was made by Cook and Woodhill (1976). They developed a comparable diet that accommodated foods available in Australia and prescribed it to 15 children aged 10 months to 13 years old. Based on informal assessments by the subjects' parents, the diet appeared to be effective for 10 children (i.e., decreased hyperactive symptoms), while three parents were "fairly certain" that the diet was effective. Parents also reported that hyperactive behavior returned if their child violated the diet regimen.

Personal observations of two preschool boys diagnosed as hyperactive were made by Stine (1976) after they were placed on the Feingold diet. Although early observations indicated minimal, if any, behavioral changes, results eventually showed mild to marked improvements in hyperactive behavior over time in home and school settings for both subjects. As noted by Stine (1976), this was not a statistically valid or scientifically controlled study.

Although Feingold suggests that generally predisposed children have toxic reactions to certain foods and artificial food additives, a number of clinicians specify allergic reactions in children when prescribing an elimination diet such as the Feingold diet. Following a procedure outlined by Hawley and Buckley (1974) designed to test children for food allergies, Salzman (1976) selected 18 children who tested positive for food allergies; 15 of these were subsequently placed on the Feingold diet. Fourteen of the 15 subjects showed significant improvement in behavior as measured by a questionnaire provided to parents. Specific changes were detected in impulsivity, excitability, overactivity, distractibility, atmosphere at home, sleep problems, and enuresis.

Crook (1980) treated 182 children for hyperactivity by examining their diets and eliminating foods they appeared to be allergic to. Improvements in behavior on elimination of certain foods or the reemergence of behaviors on challenge with specific foods were reported by 78% of the parents surveyed. Brenner (1977) also found marked responsiveness to the diet in approximately one-third of the children (aged 6 to 14) he placed on the Feingold diet.

Results from these clinical case reports must be interpreted with caution, as most uncontrolled studies present major methodological concerns. The lack of objective measures is a drawback in the Cook and Woodhill (1976), Crook (1980), Brenner (1977), and Stine (1976) reports. Strict compliance with the diet has not always been ensured; therefore, an exact interpretation of the diet's effectiveness is impossible (e.g., Cook & Woodhill, 1976). Similarly, the placebo effects of being on a special diet cannot be ruled out as a possible reason for improved behavior in several studies, as subjects and their families were not "blind" to the special diet regimen (e.g., Brenner, 1977). Finally, uncontrolled studies, by definition, lack the use of control groups found in experimental designs. These concerns are important enough to turn to scientific investigations to determine the effectiveness of the Feingold diet.

Double-Blind Crossover Studies

Conners et al. (1976) examined responsiveness to the Feingold diet of hyperactive children using a controlled double-blind experiment. Fifteen children, aged 6 to 12 years old and defined as hyperactive, were observed for 2 weeks by their teachers and parents and were rated on scales of behavioral symptoms. Subjects were randomly assigned to either the Feingold diet or a control diet and later crossed over to the other diet. Teachers reported a significant reduction in symptoms among subjects on the Feingold diet when compared to the control diet. Parents and teachers both reported significant improvement in behaviors between baseline and Feingold diet

periods, but not between baseline and control diet periods. While attempts were made to control for demand characteristics, there was no guarantee that mothers were blind to the use of the Feingold diet and they may have communicated a bias to their children favoring it. Furthermore, effects of the order in which the diets were received were present; those subjects receiving the control diet first demonstrated greater diet effects.

One of the most rigorous investigations focusing on the association between food additives and hyperactivity was that of Harley, Ray et al. (1978). In this study, thirty-six hyperactive boys (ages 6 to 12 years) were randomly assigned to either the Feingold diet or a comparable control diet containing salicylates. They were rated on several objective measures, including parent and teacher ratings, laboratory observations, and neuropsychological testing. At no time were subjects or their parents aware of which diet the children were on. Following a specified period of time, subjects were switched to the other diet in accordance with the counterbalanced design procedures. This experiment was unique and attractive in the manner in which strict compliance to the diet was maximized. Food purchased prior to the onset of the experiment was removed from each subject's home and the family was completely supplied with the diet-specific foods, including foods needed for special occasions. Results indicated that frequencies of inattentive, disruptive, and restless behaviors were greater for hyperactive subjects than for control subjects in classroom settings. In both classroom and standardized laboratory observations, these hyperactive children displayed more hyperactive behaviors. The effects of the experimental diet on these behaviors were not significant. Positive effects of the diet were indicated only by subjective parent ratings of behavior and not by teacher ratings. Among a sample of preschool boys (ages 3 to 5) tested in a separate phase of this study, parents indicated a positive response to the diet, an observation that again was not replicated in laboratory observations.

Challenge Studies

Goyette, Connors, Petti, and Curtis (1978) conducted a pair of challenge studies that demonstrated responsiveness to the Feingold diet. In the first study, 16 hyperactive children who had demonstrated a 25% reduction of symptoms while on the elimination diet were selected to participate. These children ranged in age from 4 to 11 years. In alternating fashion, the children received challenge and placebo cookies over an 8-week experimental period. While parents indicated 57% reduction in behavior problems on objective rating scales compared to a 34% reduction reported by teachers, statistically significant differences on double-blind tests were not found.

Closer examination of results (Goyette et al., 1978) and a retesting of a limited number of subjects revealed that younger children demonstrated a more pronounced response to the challenge and that effects of the challenge were greatest 1 hour after ingesting a cookie than after 2 or 3 hours. Based on these results, the researchers conducted a follow-up study with 13 hyperactive and borderline hyperactive children aged 3 to 10 years. Daily ratings were conducted by parents and teachers for specific 3-hour periods following ingestion of the challenge cookies. Results of the 2-week single crossover trial demonstrated a significant difference between the active and placebo challenge periods. Subjects were observed sooner after ingestion of the challenge food in this study than in the previous study a difference that may account for inconsistent findings. It was suggested, however, that the group effects may be deceptive in that the average difference between conditions is relatively small, while four subjects' differences were extreme, thus impacting the group results. Conners (1980) suggested that only a few subjects were highly responsive to the diet and that most effects may be placebo effects. Approximately half the subjects were responsive to the diet, but only a few demonstrated adverse effects of adding a forbidden food back into their diet.

Challenge studies conducted by Swanson and Kinsbourne (1980) and Rose (1978) also support the Feingold hypothesis. In a laboratory study measuring performance on paired-associate learning tasks, Swanson and Kinsbourne (1980) found that children diagnosed as hyperactive who received high doses of food dyes demonstrated impaired performance on learning tasks, particularly when measures were taken within a short period of time (½ hour) following ingestion of the food dye.

This study examined subjects' ability to sustain attention, however, and not the behaviors that Feingold suggested would be affected by artificial food coloring (Wender, 1980). Swanson and Kinsbourne (1980) have also been criticized for the large and excessive doses of food dyes they used in an attempt to induce hyperactive behaviors (Wender, 1980). Rose (1978) challenged two 8-year-old children diagnosed as hyperactive with artificial food coloring and found positive effects of the diet as measured by out-of-seat and on-task behaviors.

Most hyperactive children who participated in studies on the effects of food additives on their hyperactivity were removed from any medication used to alleviate hyperactive symptoms. Williams, Cram, Tausig, and Webster (1978), however, chose to study the relative effects of medication and an elimination diet on hyperactive behavior. Twenty-six children, aged 5 to 12 years, who had been diagnosed as hyperactive and had demonstrated responsiveness to stimulant medication, were selected to participate in the investigation. All subjects were placed on the Feingold diet and were crossed over into all four treatment conditions (stimulant medication vs. placebo medication and challenge cookies with additives vs. control cookies without additives). Results from parent and teacher ratings indicated that stimulant medication had a significant main effect on reducing hyperactive behaviors regardless of the diet it was paired with. Effects of diet, however, were inconsistent. Teacher ratings indicated that when coupled with stimulants, the Feingold diet produced minimal positive effects, but when coupled with placebo medication, the Feingold diet produced significant behavioral improvements in the children. No diet effects were found according to parent ratings.

Harley, Matthews, and Eichman (1978) conducted a challenge investigation similar to that of Conners (1980), examining the effects of the challenge on nine school-age diet-responsive boys and a matched control group. According to parent and teacher ratings, classroom observations, and neuropsychological testing, no significant difference between active and placebo conditions were found for the hyperactive subjects.

Among the challenge studies that have failed to support Feingold's hypothesis are those conducted by Levy and colleagues. Levy, Dumbrell, Hobbes, Ryan, Wilton, and Woodhill (1978) challenged children, judged to be hyperactive, with tartrazine, a common food coloring. After the initial four weeks of the elimination diet, mothers reported significant improvements in behavior. This effect was not substantiated by more objective tests and was not found in teacher or clinician scores on the same scale. Furthermore, when placebo and challenge periods were compared for the entire sample of subjects, significant differences were not found in mothers' ratings, teachers' ratings, or objective tests. A subgroup of children, demonstrating a 25% reduction of hyperactive symptoms while on the Feingold diet, were further analyzed. Results of this analysis showed a significant increase in hyperactive symptoms during challenge periods compared to behavior during placebo periods.

Levy and Hobbes (1978) also used a tartrazine challenge in a study of eight children exhibiting a 25% reduction in symptoms on the Feingold diet. Effects, as measured by mothers' scores on a rating scale, failed to reach significance and mothers were unable to distinguish active challenge from placebo cookies.

Similar investigations by Mattes and Gittelman (1981) and Mattes and Gittelman-Klein (1978), in which diet-responsive children were challenged with high doses of food coloring, also yielded negative results. For a sample of 11 children, parent and teacher response to a behavior rating scale, psychiatric evaluations, and results of psychological tests failed to demonstrate significant differences between placebo and challenge periods (Mattes & Gittelman, 1981). An intensive single-case study of a 10-year-old boy (Mattes & Gittelman-Klein, 1978) reported no increase in the boy's hyperactive behaviors while he was challenged with active cookies, as indicated by either teacher or parent ratings.

Finally, in a survey study by Palmer, Rapoport, and Quinn (1975) questionnaires were administered to parents of 56 hyperactive boys and to parents of a control group of 23 boys in order to ascertain their dietary habits. All subjects ranged in age from 6 to 12 years. No significant difference was found in the diets of these two groups and there was no difference in the amount of food additives consumed by the two groups.

Conclusions

It is quite apparent that Feingold's hypothesis and subsequent diet have generated considerable interest among parents, physicians, and psychologists. Some have responded out of hope for an alternate to medication in treating hyperactivity and some have reacted out of skepticism regarding the contentions Feingold has made. While many anecdotal and clinical case reports indicate favorable outcomes from use of the Feingold diet, scientifically controlled endeavors are inconsistent in their findings. Studies that have been highly controlled for placebo effects and demand characteristics, and whose investigators have ensured strict compliance to diet regimens (e.g., Harley et al., 1978) have not consistently demonstrated significant positive effects of the Feingold diet. The positive effects reported with the Feingold diet have been largely derived from subjective reports provided by parents and have not been substantiated by laboratory or teacher observations, nor by objective measures (e.g., Goyette et al., 1978; Harley, Ray, et al., 1978; Levy & Hobbes, 1978).

Some limited evidence suggests that preschool children may be more responsive to the Feingold elimination diet than their school-age counterparts (Goyette et al., 1978; Harley, Ray, et al., 1978). One must be careful, however, to interpret this information with caution until further investigations can provide clearer information.

Parents and medical professionals have naturally been attracted to this diet because of the possibility that their children and patients could be removed from stimulant medication treatments. Endorsements of the diet, however, were clearly premature (Levine & Liden, 1976). The majority of controlled studies have failed to show that the Feingold diet is an effective treatment for hyperactivity among children.

CAFFEINE

Caffeine has been suggested as both a cause of and treatment for hyperactivity. Although the behavioral effects of caffeine have been of interest for many years, relatively few studies have directly investigated the effects of caffeine on the behavior of children.

Dietary Sources

Caffeine, a xanthine derivative, is a naturally occurring central nervous system stimulant reported to be the most widely consumed behaviorally active drug in the world (Griffiths & Woodson, 1988). Consumption rates among children, however, vary widely; surveys have reported average day doses for high consumers ranging from 3.0 mg/kg to 11.0 mg/kg (Elkins et al., 1981; Food and Drug Administration, [FDA], 1978). A national survey by Morgan, Stults, and Zabik (1982) found an average intake for children of 1.1 mg/kg. In addition, Morgan, Stults, and Zabik (1982) reported that although intake among children (5 to 18 years old) increases with age, average mg per kg dosage remains fairly stable. An extensive investigation of dietary caffeine intake patterns in children indicated that caffeine consumption often begins early in life (Arbeit, Nicklas, Frank, Webber, Miner, & Berenson, 1988). The most frequent sources of caffeine among the infants and children studied were carbonated beverages, chocolate-containing foods, and tea. Significant racial and gender differences in caffeine intake were noted, with whites consuming more caffeine than blacks. This trend was seen among individuals as young as 1 year of age and continued to age 17. Among 15- and 17-year-olds, girls consumed more caffeine than boys both in total milligrams and in milligrams/kilogram body weight. Significant gender differences in intake were not noted among the younger aged groups which included 6 month-, 1 year-, 2 year-, 3 year-, 4 year-, 10 year-, and 13-year-olds (Arbeit et al., 1988).

Caffeine occurs naturally in coffee and tea (Clementz & Dailey, 1988; Neims & Borstel, 1983; Rall, 1985), and in cocoa and carob products (Wells, 1984). In addition, caffeine is frequently found in many over-the-counter medications either as an additive or as the principal ingredient. A review and analysis of literature pertaining to mood and behavioral effects of caffeine by Wells (1984) includes a summary of caffeine sources and consumption as well as a review of physiological properties of the drug.

Psychophysiological Effects

The literature related to the physiological and psychological effects of caffeine is extensive and contains diverse descriptions. Individual response to caffeine varies considerably as a function not only of differences in age and physiological sensitivity, but also as a function of frequency of use and amount consumed (Clementz & Dailey, 1988; Goldstein, Kaizer, & Whitby, 1969; Kuznicki & Turner, 1986; Rapoport et al., 1981).

Among the physiological and psychological effects of caffeine most frequently reported are nervousness, irritability, agitation, wakefulness, increased vigilance and decreased reaction time, diuresis, cardiac muscle stimulation and a resultant increase in heart rate (tachycardia), bronchodilation, headache, increase in gastric secretions and gastrointestinal disturbances including nausea, heartburn, and loose stools (Clementz & Dailey, 1988; Griffiths & Woodson, 1988; Neims & Borstel, 1983; Rall, 1985). Excessive intake of caffeine (caffeinism) has been shown to produce symptoms that closely resemble clinical anxiety disorders (Clementz & Dailey, 1988; Gilbert, 1976; Greden, 1981).

In a recent study of the acute autonomic nervous system effects of caffeine on normal prepubertal boys, Zahn and Rapoport (1987) demonstrated physiological effects partially similar to those seen in clinical anxiety states. Increases in electrodermal activity noted in the study support an anxiogenic hypothesis of caffeine effect. In contrast, the decrease in heart rate and motor activity noted with lower doses of caffeine (3 mg/kg) are inconsistent with stress and anxiety. Evidence of improved attention on caffeine was also noted. Thus, the response to caffeine cannot be described simply as sympathetic nervous system arousal.

CAFFEINE AS A TREATMENT ALTERNATIVE

In 1973, Schnackenberg reported the results of a pilot study in which 11 hyperactive children who had previously been treated successfully with dextroamphetamine and methylphenidate responded to caffeine as a substitute treatment. Because of the potentially adverse side effects associated with stimulant medication, the possibility of effective treatment of hyperactivity with caffeine represented a favorable alternative. Clinical support for the efficacy of caffeine treatment was found in several subsequent investigations (Firestone, Poitras-Wright, & Douglas, 1978; Harvey & March, 1978; Reichard & Elder, 1977). Many carefully controlled studies, however, have not found caffeine to be effective in the treatment of hyperactive behavior. Garfinkel, Webster, and Sloman (1975) demonstrated methylphenidate to be superior to both placebo and caffeine with no significant difference between placebo and caffeine treatment. Dosages used in this study were approximately half those used by Schnackenberg; however, Huestis, Arnold, and Smeltzer (1975) reported that caffeine in doses equal to those given in Schnackenberg's study were significantly less effective than either methylphenidate or dextroamphetamine. In addition, Gross (1975) reported no benefit from 100 to 400 mg/day of caffeine administered to 25 hyperactive children compared to treatment with imipramine, methylphenidate, and dextroamphetamine. Negative findings for the efficacy of caffeine have also been reported by Arnold, Christopher, Huestis, and Smeltzer (1978); Conners (1975); and Firestone, Davey, Goodman, and Peters (1978).

To summarize, although initial research suggested that caffeine might be used to treat hyperactivity, the majority of evidence indicates that caffeine is less reliable than and inferior to stimulant medications.

Behavioral Effects

As a part of a series of studies on the behavioral effects of common dietary substances in children by the Secton on Child Psychiatry of the National Institute of Mental Health, Rapoport and her associates examined the effects of caffeine in grade school children (Rapoport et al., 1981). Effects of a single low (3 mg/kg) or high (10 mg/kg) dose of caffeine on normal children and adults have been studied. Autonomic measures of arousal after caffeine intake were similarly affected for both children and adults; however, adults generally reported side effects whereas children did not. In addition, side effects were more prominent for adults with low habitual caffeine intake patterns. Children in this study were not selected on the basis of a dietary caffeine history of low or high daily caffeine intake patterns. Children who received the higher single dose of caffeine demon-

strated more objective changes than adults, with increases in motor activity and speech rate, and decreases in reaction time. The lower single dose of caffeine produced relatively few effects for either children or adults. Also noted in this study were the differential effects of caffeine and amphetamine, indicating distinctive actions of the two stimulants (Rapoport et al., 1981).

Findings consistent with those of Rapoport et al. (1981) were reported in a study that compared the effects of caffeine and dextroamphetamine on normal prepubertal boys (Elkins et al., 1981). Caffeine in single 10 mg/kg doses produced increased vigilance, increased motor activity, and decreased reaction time. Low doses (3 mg/kg) had little or not acute effect. Both of the studies described above (Rapoport et al., 1981, and Elkins et al., 1981) were conducted in the laboratory. In addition, caffeine was administered in a normally noncaffeinated soft drink, suggesting the possibility that caffeine may have been confounded with the effects of sugar, if any.

Differential behavioral effects of caffeine on high and low consumers have been observed by Rapoport et al. (1984). At the end of the 2-week (5 mg/kg, twice a day) caffeine challenge, children who were habitually low consumers of caffeine were reported by their parents to be more emotional, inattentive, and restless, while behaviors in children identified as habitually high caffeine consumers were not rated as changed unless they were deprived of their typical caffeine intake.

Caffeine effects also differed for adults identified as low (less than 100 mg/day) versus high (more than 300 mg/day) consumers (Rapoport et al., 1981). These findings were consistent with those of Goldstein et al. (1969) who also noted differences in caffeine reactivity between low and high consumers.

From these studies it appears that caffeine may increase motor activity, restlessness, and attention in children. In a recent study, however, which attempted to address methodological inconsistencies noted in previous studies, Baer (1987) investigated the effects of caffeine on the behavior of normal children in a kindergarten setting. Caffeine was observed to exert only a minimal and inconsistent effect on classroom behaviors, thus raising further questions on the importance of caffeine as a dietary variable influencing children's behavior.

Conclusions

Although further research is needed to clarify the incidence and extent of the behavioral effects of caffeine in normal children, past studies suggest that habitual level of dietary consumption is an important variable in predicting caffeine's effects. In most studies it has been found that nonusers or individuals whose typical consumption of caffeine is low show a significantly higher incidence of behavioral side effects when caffeine is consumed than do individuals whose level of consumption is higher. Conversely, individuals who regularly consume moderate to heavy amounts of caffeine may show signs of caffeine withdrawal syndrome (irritability, nervousness, restlessness, inefficiency, headache, nausea, and lethargy) when deprived of their usual intake (Clementz & Dailey, 1988).

In single dose laboratory studies, caffeine has been shown to affect speech rate, attention, motor activity, and reaction time to a greater extent in children than in adults (Rapoport, 1982/1983). However, recent direct observations in a natural setting of individual children who consumed doses of caffeine typical of a single serving showed that they demonstrated minimal behavioral effects (Baer, 1987).

SUGAR

Frequently, both parents and teachers of hyperactive children report that foods containing large amounts of refined sugar (sucrose) produce negative effects on these children's behavior. In one survey of parents of hyperactive children, most indicated their belief that ingestion of sugar was the number one cause of their child's behavior problems (Crook, 1975). Parents commonly report increased activity level and irritability, as well as impairment in the ability to sustain attention and inhibit impulses following ingestion of sugar. In addition, the general public has been exposed to several articles and books popularizing the presumed detrimental effects of sugar—such as *Sugar Blues* (Duffy, 1975). Scholarly journals have also been a forum for unfounded pronouncements regarding sugar's effects. For instance, Buchanan (1984), in a comment in the *American Psychologist,* labeled sugar "the most uniquitous toxin." Fortunately the number of well-

controlled studies examining this important issue has increased dramatically in the past few years. To date there are at least 10 well-designed studies examining the effects of sugar on children's behavior (see Milich, Wolraich, & Lindgren, 1986).

Uncontrolled Studies

An important correlational study, conducted by Prinz, Roberts, and Hantman (1980) examined the association between the ingestion of sugar and "hyperactive" behavior. These investigators discovered that although hyperactive children did not consume more sugar than did normal children, for hyperactive children "the amount of sugar products consumed, ratio of sugar products to nutritional foods, and ratio of carbohydrates to protein were all significantly associated with amounts of destructive-aggressive and restless behaviors observed during free play" (p. 760). In addition, the ratio of carbohydrates to protein was also correlated with restless behavior in normal children. Interpretation of these results is tempered, however, by the usual concerns associated with correlational research (i.e., it is impossible to determine from these results whether ingestion of sugar led to destructive-aggressive and restless behaviors or whether destructive-aggressive and restless hyperactive children simply eat more sweets). More recently, Prinz and Riddle (1986), also found a relationship between sugar ingestion and a measure of attention with normal 5-year-olds.

The Prinz et al. (1980) study has been criticized for flaws in basic methodology by Barling and Bullen (1985) who question the manner in which hyperactive behaviors were assessed, the alpha level set, and the use of grams rather than portions as an index of food consumption. In their replication, which corrected for these errors, they failed to find any significant relationships between sugar consumption and hyperactivity or aggression. Similarly, Wolraich, Stumbo, Milich, Chenard, and Schultz (1986), in their reply, criticized the Prinz group's (1980) methods. They noted that the measure of sugar consumption was calculated on the basis of the weight of the food rather than the weight of the nutrients. They argue that the more accepted and proper assessment is that based on nutrient weight. Using this method, they found results consistent with Prinz et al. regarding overall similarity in the dietary habits of hyperactive and normal children. In addition, they reported significant positive correlations between some "symptomatic" hyperactive behaviors and sugar intake. They caution, however, that this was true of only 4 of the 37 behavioral measures and that these were different from those obtained by Prinz et al. (1980) They conclude that, given the results of controlled experiments, it is most likely that the more hyperactive a child, is the more sugar he or she is likely to consume, rather than sugar ingestion's being the cause of the hyperactive behavior.

A recent study by Kaplan, McNicol, Conte, and Moghadam (1989) reinforces the original finding by Prinz et al. (1980) in again finding no differences in overall nutrient intake between hyperactive children and normal children. In addition, they found that a small number of children from both groups showed idiosyncratic sensitivities to sugar ingestion.

Finally, glucose tolerance tests have also been examined in an attempt to assess sugar's effects on children. Langseth and Dowd (1978) reported that a large percent of the hyperactive children they studied showed abnormal reactions on glucose tolerance tests. This study, like the studies by Crook (1975, 1976), has also been criticized for faulty research design (Conners, 1984; Prinz et al., 1980).

Controlled Experiments

Fortunately, a number of true experiments, those actually manipulating the amount of sugar ingested, have recently been conducted. One of these, reported by Conners and Blouin (1982), found that sugar caused an increase in total movement and a decrease in appropriate behavior for 13 children hospitalized with various behavior disorders. Following a high protein breakfast, these children received 50 grams of sucrose, fructose, or regular orange juice (containing a lower amount of sugar) on alternating days in a modified Latin Square Design. The authors were quick to note the preliminary nature of their results—given the small sample size, lack of control for increased calorie intake, and inconsistency of findings across measures. For example, in contrast to the observational findings, analysis of the behavioral

ratings made by both the teachers and ward nurses failed to detect significant differences between the sugar and control conditions.

Further controlled experimentation, documenting adverse effects of refined sugar, has been conducted by Goldman, Lerman, Contois, and Udall (1986). They reported that, in the eight normal preschool children they studied, the sugar condition (2 gm/kg of sucrose) relative to control condition (aspartame) caused an increase in inappropriate behavior, locomotion, and distractibility, and a decrease in attention. This study is noteworthy for its examination of normal children, for the large effects reported, and for the examination of effects at various time periods. However, in a recent replication and expansion of this study, with 12 normal preschoolers, Roshon and Hagen (1989) failed to obtain significant differences on any of the dependent measures.

In contrast to the experiments by Conners and Blouin (1982) and Goldman et al. (1986) reported above, many recent studies have failed to find any evidence that the ingestion of sugar produces hyperactive behaviors in either normal or hyperactive children. Behar, Rapoport, Adams, Berg, and Cornblath (1984) found that sugar produced a slight, but significant, *decrease* in motor activity for both hyperactive and normal children. The 21 boys examined in this study were all considered by their parents to be adversely affected by the ingestion of foods containing high amounts of refined sugar. The experiment took place over 3 days (a minimum of 48 hours apart) during which each child received one of each of the following three conditions—a drink sweetened with 1.75 gm/kg of sucrose, 1.75 gm/kg of glucose, or a taste-equivalent amount of saccharin. Each child received the drink at breakfast time; no other foods were given (the children had been fasting since 10:00 the night before). Following ingestion of the experimental drink, several behavioral and physiological measures were collected over a 5-hour period. Although there was a slight decrease in motor activity at 3 hours postingestion, no significant changes were seen on the behavioral ratings or on the memory and attention tasks. The authors conclude that these results "cast doubt on the clinical significance of sugar intake in the etiology of behavioral disturbance" (Behar et al., 1984, p. 277). Unfortunately sugar's effects on the hyperactive children were not examined separately from its effects on the normal children.

Conners et al. (1985) have also reported that, in 37 pediatric psychiatric patients they examined, sugar (both sucrose and fructose, 1.25 gm/kg) reduced activity level in the classroom and speeded reaction time. In addition, Ferguson, Stoddart, and Simeon (1986), after studying the behavior of 8 normal school-aged children (given sucrose, 1.5 gm/kg) and 18 normal preschool children (given sucrose, 1.8 gm/kg), concluded that "sucrose ingestion by children is not a common cause of behavior or learning problems" (p. 3). Similarly, the study by Rosén, Booth, Bender, McGrath, Sorrell, and Drabman, (1988) of 45 preschool and elementary school children concluded that sugar was not a cause of hyperactive behavior in normal children. Using a double-blind within-subject challenge design they provided each child with a basic breakfast that included a challenge drink containing either 50 g of sucrose, aspartame (as a placebo), or a very small amount of sucrose. The results indicated some slight effects of sugar on the teachers' ratings of the children's activity level, and on the cognitive performance of the girls. Sugar also appeared to have more of an effect on the preschoolers in general (relative to the elementary school children). These effects, however, were quite small and were not clinically meaningful. Sugar did not produce the major changes in behavior that parents and teachers often report.

"Sugar reactive" preschool children were solicited by Krusei et al. (1987) for their study of sugar on aggression and activity in children. Double-blind crossover challenges were conducted using 1.75 g of sucrose and glucose, with aspartame and saccharin as placebos. The results indicated no significant effect of either type of sugar on the rate of aggression or the activity level of these 18 children. The authors concluded that children labeled "sugar-responsive" by their parents may simply represent "a group with chronic behavioral disturbance for whom families are searching for understanding and help" (p. 1490).

Two studies have specifically examined the effects of sugar on diagnosed hyperactive chidren; Wolraich, Milich, Stumbo, and Schultz (1985) and Milich and Pelham (1986) reported that sucrose ingestion produced no changes in the behavior of the hyperactive children they examined. Wolraich et al. (1985) used a challenge design to examine the behavior of 32 hyperactive boys. On 3 successive days the children were admitted to a clinical research center and fed a sucrose-free diet. Following a day of baseline assessment, the children were served either 1.75 gm/kg of sucrose or a placebo in a challenge drink. A counterbalanced design was used to expose each child to each condition. The results showed no differences between the sugar and placebo on any of the 37 behavioral or cognitive measures. The authors conclude that "the findings undermine the hypothesis that sucrose plays a major role in accounting for the inappropriate behavior of hyperactive children" (p. 1). Milich and Pelham (1986) also studied diagnosed hyperactive children. In their study of 16 hyperactive boys, a crossover challenge design was employed to examine the effects of ingesting 1.75 g of sucrose or a placebo drink following an overnight fast. Results indicated no evidence that sugar affects the behavior or learning of hyperactive boys.

Conclusions

With only a few exceptions, the vast majority of controlled experimental studies have failed to demonstrate that sugar produces or exacerbates hyperactive behavior in children. Given the number of well-designed experiments, the variety of children studied, the different doses of sucrose used, and the variety of cognitive and behavioral measures employed, it is unlikely that further research will appreciably alter this basic conclusion. In addition, sorely missing from the research in this area are appropriate theoretical explanations concerning possible mechanisms for sugar's supposed effects. Until we have a clear and comprehensive explanation of the possible biochemical and neurophysiological mechanisms governing any hypothesized effect, it is unlikely that research will progress in any meaningful fashion. An important step in this direction is the outstanding methodological and theoretical review by Spring, Chiodo, and Bowen (1987).

ASPARTAME

Since its introduction to the marketplace in the early 1980s, aspartame, a common substitute for sugar now found in many food products, has come under scrutiny as a substance that may induce hyperactivity in children. To date, however, research has not demonstrated any definitive relationship between aspartame and hyperactivity.

Properties

Aspartame, a nutritive artificial sweetener, was approved for use as a sugar substitute by the Food and Drug Administration (FDA) for dry foods in 1981, and for carbonated beverages and carbonated beverage syrup bases in 1983. Aspartame is a dipeptide comprised of two amino acids, L-phenyl-alanine and L-aspartic acid, with a methyl group esterified to the carboxyl group of the phenylalanine. Both amino acids occur naturally in certain foods and, as necessary components of protein, are processed through normal metabolic pathways. The sole source of phenylalanine is dietary, whereas aspartic acid can be obtained either through dietary means or synthesized by the body. Methyl esters are a natural component of many fruits, vegetables, and wine.

In its pure form, aspartame appears as a white, odorless powder that is soluble in both water and acids. It is approximately 180 to 200 times sweeter than sugar (Harper, 1975; Roak-Foltz & Leveille, 1984). Marketed under the brand name NutraSweet, aspartame is currently found in a wide variety of foodstuffs. A complete listing of products containing NutraSweet can be obtained by contacting the manufacturer, the G. D. Searle Company.

Extimated Daily Intake

Maximum daily intake of aspartame for adults is estimated to be 20 mg/kg body weight (Potts, Bloss, & Nutting, 1980). Other researchers have estimated a total daily intake ranging from 500 to 870 mg (Harper, 1975; Horowitz & Bauer-Nehrl-ing, 1983; Roak-Foltz & Leville, 1984) with equivalent amounts of phenylalanine, aspartic acid, and methanol being 280–433 mg, 226–347 mg, and 54–87 mg, respectively. At the lower end of the estimate, the amounts of phenylalanine and aspartic acid are similar to levels found occurring naturally in either a 6-ounce glass of milk or in 3 ounces of

beef. Eight ounces of fruit or vegetable juice would provide the approximate amount of methanol, a metabolite of a methyl ester group (Harper, 1975).

Consumer Complaints

Pardridge (1986) reported that consumer complaints about aspartame fall into three general categories: those involving (a) the central nervous system, (b) the gastrointestinal tract, and (c) the female reproductive system. Problems relating to the CNS were insomnia, mood changes, and seizures. Gastrointestinal side effects included abdominal pain, nausea, and diarrhea. Gynecologic symptoms were limited to irregular menses. Janssen and van der Heijden (1988) reported that by 1986, 2,800 complaints had been received by the Centers of Disease Control (U.S. Public Health Service) and the Center for Food Safety and Applied Nutrition (Federal Drug Administration). These can be categorized as follows: CNS—neurological seizures (100), headaches (832), dizziness (383), change in mood (310), gastrointestinal (387), and allergic (239). The failure in identifying a distinct constellation of symptoms clearly related to aspartame, however, led to the conclusion by the Centers for Disease Control and for Food Safety and Applied Nutrition that ingestion of the substance did not pose any widespread public health hazard (cited in Janssen & van der Heijden, 1988). Wurtman (1983) cautioned that persons most likely to experience functional or behavioral changes following high doses of aspartame are those with conditions such as hypertension, Parkinson's disease, insomnia, hyperkinesia, or those taking drugs that interact with plasma phenylalanine or tyrosine (e.g., L-Dopa, or monoamine oxidase inhibitors).

Biochemical Changes in the Brain

Several investigators (e.g., Pardridge, 1986) have suggested that levels of phenylalanine in the brain following aspartame ingestion should be measured not only in isolation but also in comparison to levels of other amino acids (e.g., tyrosine, leucine, iso-leucine, valine, tryptophan, histidine, methionine). These amino acids must compete for sites on the same carrier molecule, responsible for transportation across the blood brain barrier. According to Pardridge (1986), the amino acid transport system has the highest natural affinity for phenylalanine. If phenylalanine is ingested in disportionally high amounts compared to other amino acids, then the latter may be unable to compete successfully for carrier molecule sites and subsequent access to the brain. Tryptophan, the precursor of the neurotransmittor serotonin, may in particular be affected. Tryptophan and serotonin levels normally increase when a meal high in carbohydrates is consumed. Wurtman (1983), however, found that when rats were fed aspartame prior to consumption of a carbohydrate meal, the expected increases in tryptophan and serotonin were almost completely blocked. One known effect of serotonin is that it is an anticonvulsant. A decrease in its concentration has the potential to lower the threshold for seizure activity. A review of animal studies by Garattini (cited in Janssen & van der Heijden, 1988) shows some evidence for lowering seizure threshold in mice and rats with high doses (1000 mg/kg body weight) of aspartame, but a review of seizure activity in humans by Schomer (cited in Janssen & van der Heijden, 1988) points out that animal models do not accurately represent epilepsy in humans.

Animal Studies

Experiments with Rodents

Potts et al. (1980) administered intragastric doses of aspartame to mice at 550 times the expected human daily intake and found no clinically significant biological effect on motor coordination, analgesic activity, hexobarbital-induced sleep time, anticonvulsant activity, antidepressant activity, or learning behavior. These researchers also administered acute doses of aspartame to rats for 13 weeks and noted no significant changes in activity level or learning behavior, with one exception. In male rats given a 13-week diet that was 9% aspartame by weight (or 550 times the expected daily human intake), there was a significant reduction in time required to respond to a conditioned avoidance response task.

Experiments with Primates

Both learning ability (i.e., object discrimination, pattern discrimination, object discrimination learning set, and oddity learning set) and hearing were assessed in stumptail macaques. At 1 ½ years of age, following a 9-month diet of elevated doses of aspartame or phenylalanine, these animals showed no deficits (Suomi, 1984). Although a control group was not included in this study, learning ability and hearing did not differ from levels reported for normal stumptail macaques of a comparable age. Reynolds, Bauman, Stegink, Filer, and Naidu (1984) also used stumptail macaques to examine the effects of both aspartame and phenylalanine on general developmental growth. Aspartame and phenylalanine given to neonatal macaques over a 9-month period in dosages ranging from 1–3mg/kg body weight, represented 50 to 150 times the estimated daily intake for humans. The assessment included measurements of feeding habits and physical growth, blood urine analysis, an electroencephalogram, and behavioral milestones. No significant differences were found between the experimental and control groups of monkeys on any of these measures.

Human Studies

Healthy Children and Adolescents

Wolraich (1987) has stated that evidence for effects of aspartame on behavior should be limited to those studies that are double-blind. Only by making a study double-blind can the power of suggestion in children, parents, teachers, and clinicians be eliminated as a confounding variable. Therefore, all the studies reviewed herein are double-blind unless noted otherwise.

In a study conducted by Frey (1976), 126 healthy children and adolescents, ranging from 2 to 21 years old and distributed in five age groups, were given either sucrose or aspartame (30–77 mg/kg body weight/day) for 13 weeks. Aspartame was ingested via dietary supplements to their regular diet. Dependent measures included a physical exam, an eye exam, and laboratory values reflecting liver and renal functioning, hematologic status, and plasma levels of phenylalanine and tyrosine. In addition, a record of subjective complaints was kept. With no resulting significant differences between the sucrose and aspartame group on any of the measures, the author concluded that aspartame appears to be a safe sweetening agent for children of any age.

In a crossover study, Goldman and colleagues (1986) used aspartame as a control to evaluate normal preschool children ingesting sucrose for ability to (a) sustain attention, and (b) inhibit fine or gross motor movement. Children were given orange juice with the artificial sweetener Equal® (250 mg/kg), in which aspartame is the active ingredient. The children given sucrose were judged to be significantly more impaired than their aspartame counterparts in both the attention and motor areas.

Ferguson, Stoddard, and Simeon (1986), using a crossover design, gave normal preschoolers either sucrose or aspartame (10.1 mg/kg) to evaluate specific behaviors. These behaviors were rated separately by parents, teachers, and experimenters. In addition, experimenters assessed fine and gross motor coordination, developmental drawing skills, and level of activity using an actometer. No evidence was found to suggest that aspartame had a detrimental effect on any of the measurements.

Rosén et al. (1988) conducted a 15-day within-subject challenge study with preschoolers and elementary school children using aspartame (122 mg) as a control to examine the effects of sucrose on behavior. Dependent variables included two measures of activity evaluated by teachers, target behaviors rated by trained observers, and two cognitive measurements: a paired association task and a matching task. Compared to a low-sugar and a high-sugar condition, aspartame did not have any effect on teacher ratings of activity, target behaviors, or cognitive measures.

Hyperactive Children

Ferguson and colleagues (1986) studied eight 5- to 13-year-old children believed by their parents to be "sugar responders" (i.e., children who respond to ingestion of sugar with hyperactivity). Following a psychiatric exam and medical history, five of these children were diagnosed as having attention deficit disorder, one as having a psychophysiological disorder, and two with no diagnosable disorder. These children were challenged with either sugar or one of three dosages of aspartame (2.78 mg–5.65 mg–8.33 mg/kg), all less than half of what is estimated to be the average daily intake. No change in any child due to aspartame was noted from baseline on measurements of vital signs, activity level as measured by an actometer, or cognitive functioning as measured by a continuous performance test, a paired association test, a memory task, and a matrix task.

In two challenge studies conducted by Wolraich, Milich, Stumbo, and Schultz (1985), 7- to 12-year-old boys diagnosed as hyperactive and given either sucrose or aspartame were evaluated for behavior change (playroom observations) and learning deficits (continuous performance test, paired associate learning test, draw-a-line test, and matching familiar figures test). Measurements were taken for a 2½ hour period beginning ½ hour after ingestion. In the first study, the challenge drink (6.4 to 8.8 mg aspartame/kg body weight) was given an hour after lunch, and in the second study it was given in the morning after an overnight fast. Neither study demonstrated a significant change in behavior or learning ability from baseline levels for aspartame or sucrose, or a significant difference in behavior or learning between aspartame and sucrose.

Milich and Pelham (1986) looked at the effects of aspartame and sugar on the behavior of sixteen 6- to 9-year-old hyperactive boys in a classroom environment using a challenge study. No statistical difference was found to exist between the sugar and aspartame conditions for academic productivity and accuracy, noncompliance with adult requests, and positive and negative peer interactions.

Conners et al. (1985) followed child psychiatric inpatients with diagnoses of conduct disorder, anxiety disorder, or hyperactivity; the children were given diets containing aspartame, sucrose, or fructose. Aspartame was not found to have any notable effects on autonomic, cortical, or behavioral responses.

Of the aforementioned studies with aspartame and hyperactive children, none exceeded dosages of 10 mg/kg body weight. Two studies, however, used amounts more closely approximating or even surpassing the estimated average daily intake. The first, carried out by Kruesi et al. (1987) examined preschool boys, 18 of whom were classified by their parents as "sugar responders" and 12 nonresponders.

Of the 18 "sugar responders," 11 had psychiatric diagnoses: attention deficit disorder with hyperactivity (4), oppositional disorder (2), conduct disorder (2), adjustment disorder with disturbed conduct (1), and separation anxiety disorder (1). Among the nonresponders, 11 had no diagnosis, and one had a diagnosis of borderline intellectual functioning. Effects of aspartame (30 mg/kg) were tested, as well as the effects of sucrose, glucose, and saccharin. Interpersonal aggression, hyperactivity, and emotional reactivity were assessed by trained observers and teachers in a playroom setting and by parents at home. General activity level was measured using an actometer. The only significant result attributed to aspartame was a lower level of general activity as measured by the actometer, although this difference was not detected by any of the observers. In addition, Zametkin, Karoum, & Rapoport (1987) conducted a crossover study using D-phenylalanine (20 mg/kg) to treat 6- to 12-year-old boys diagnosed with attention deficit disorder with hyperactivity. Previous work by Zametkin suggested that monoamine oxidase inhibitors have therapeutic effects in hyperactive children. Therefore, it was postulated that phenylalanine, as a precursor of tyrosine, dopamine, and norepinephrine, could potentially have the same ultimate effect as a monoamine oxidase inhibitor—increasing catecholamine activity in nerve synapses. Zametkin collected data on parent and teacher ratings of behavior and cognitive functioning as well as blood and urine measures of norepinephrine, amino acids, and trace amines. The results yielded no statistically significant changes in behavior or cognitive functioning from baseline measures. It is not known, however, whether the D isomer of phenylalanine used in this study is bioequivalent to the L form used in aspartame.

Conclusions

The results of research have not shown a causal relationship between aspartame and hyperactivity in children. All studies in humans, however, have been relatively short term and, therefore, have not assessed chronic ingestion. Given the numerous food products sweetened artificially with aspartame, and today's sugar-conscious public, chronic ingestion represents a realistic situation. At this point, however, there seems to be no evidence that aspartame is responsible for causing hyperactivity in children.

OTHER FOODS AND HYPERACTIVITY

A number of other foods have been implicated as causes of hyperactivity in children; among them are milk, chocolate, onions, cabbage, pork, eggs, fish, shellfish, tomatoes, nuts, apples, corn, wheat, potatoes, soy, beef, chicken, grapes, peanuts, pineapple, carrots, oats, rice, and lettuce (Crook, 1980; Davison, 1949; Rapp, 1978a). In most cases, the term *allergy* has been used to describe the behavioral symptoms thought to be caused by these foods. Atkins (1986), however, cautions that it should be reserved for reactions to substances in which the immunologic system is clearly involved; otherwise he advises using the term *food intolerance*. Allergic reactions involving the immune system can be immediate or delayed, but both are associated with classic gastrointestinal symptoms such as nausea, vomiting, cramping, flatulence, diarrhea, and edema and/or tingling of oropharyngeal tissue. Other symptoms associated with immediate allergic reactions are flushing, eczema, urticaria, rhinitis, laryngeal edema, and bronchospasms. Atkins (1986) also clarifies a number of other terms, such as *food sensitivity, food toxicity,* and *metabolic food reaction,* that are loosely applied to reported reactions in persons consuming various foods.

The bulk of information regarding reactions of children to these foods has come from anecdotal reports rather than empirical research. As clinicians, both Crook (1980) and Davison (1949) kept records of subjective symptoms reported to them by their patients. Common complaints with possible neurological components included headaches, bedwetting, irritability, depression, emotional lability, difficulty in concentrating, nightmares, and insomnia. Crook (1980) stated that hyperactivity would subside in 80% of the cases if children used an elimination diet for 5 to 7 days, with the remaining 20% resolving themselves after 3 weeks.

A case study of a 9-year-old boy with milk sensitivity presented by Rapp (1978b) met at least some of these criteria. The boy had been diagnosed as hyperactive at age 5, and given methylphenidate since age 8. Diet elimination and double-blind milk challenges demonstrated a sensitivity to milk that included symptoms of irritability and emotional lability. He also responded well to sublingual (under the tongue) milk therapy, which provided a confirmation of milk sensitivity when given in a double-blind fashion. Rapp (1978a) also conducted a double-blind study of 24 children with a mean age of 10 who were given either a mixture of milk, wheat, egg, cocoa, sugar, cornstarch, and corn syrup or a placebo consisting of prune juice. No differences were noted on either a timed visual-motor coordination task of a motor accuracy test, yet nurses and parents concurred 81% of the time that activity level increased slightly to moderately in 11 of 24 children.

Akins (1986), however, pointed out that a causal relationship between these foods and hyperactivity is nonconclusive because of lack of a scientific approach, and emphasized the need to measure symptoms objectively as well as to administer foods so that neither the researcher nor the subject is aware of the specific product being given. Atkins' suggestions for conducting future research in this area include doing a physical examination on subjects, gathering a comprehensive medical history, confirming food sensitivity with laboratory tests and elimination diets, and use of a double-blind format. Ideally, research would be conducted by a team of medical investigators such as an allergist, a psychiatrist, a psychopharmacologist, and a nutritionist.

Overall, however, the data are largely anecdotal and do not confirm a causal relationship between hyperactivity and any particular food substance.

DRUG EFFECTS ON NUTRITION

Central Nervous System Stimulants

The most commonly reported adverse reactions relevant to nutritional effects of central nervous system stimulants include anorexia, weight loss, and stomach pain (Committee on Children with Disabilities and Committee on Drugs, 1987; Conners, Taylor, Meo, Kurtz, & Fournier, 1972; Golinko, 1984;

Millichap, 1968; Murray, 1987; Scarnati, 1986; United States Pharmacopeial Convention, 1989). While no drug is completely free of side effects, when given in moderate doses, stimulant drugs are considered to be relatively safe ("Methylphenidata," 1988; Murray, 1987).

Among physicians, central nervous system stimulants are typically the treatment of choice for hyperactive children (Bennett & Sherman, 1983; Donnelly & Rapoport, 1985; Gadow, 1982; Gittleman, 1980; Ross & Ross, 1982; Winsberg, Yepes, & Bialer, 1976). Currently, the most frequently and effectively used stimulants are methylphenidate hydrochloride (Ritalin), dextroamphetamine sulfate (Dexedrine), and magnesium pemoline (Cylert) (Committee on Children with Disabilities and Committee on Drugs, 1987). A recent tabulation listed Ritalin among the top 200 new prescriptions most frequently dispensed in the United States community pharmacies in 1987 and 1988 (Pharmacy Data Service, 1989).

In general, weight loss and secondary effects on nutrition caused by appetite loss and gastrointestinal disturbance tend to be greater at treatment onset and in most cases dissipate after 1 to 2 weeks of treatment (Arnold, Christopher, Huestis, & Smeltzer, 1978; Golinko, 1984; "Methylphenidata," 1988; Ross & Ross, 1982; Winsberg, Yepes, & Bialer, 1976). It has been suggested that anorexia can usually be managed by taking prescribed stimulants just before meals (Gadow, 1982). Some researchers have found weight loss and slowed growth to occur even when anorexia was not present (Ross, 1982; Safer & Allen, 1973). These findings constitute the basis for concern that precipitated subsequent growth suppression research.

Growth Suppression

Because central nervous system stimulants frequently produce loss of appetite, stomachache, and weight loss, there has been concern regarding the long-term effects of their use on growth. Safer, Allen, and Barr (1972) and Safer and Allen (1973) evaluated gains in weight and height for hyperactive children taking either dextroamphetamine or methylphenidate. Long-term use of dextroamphetamine (defined as 2 or more years) was shown to suppress gains in weight and height significantly whereas less growth suppression was noted with methylphenidate and only when doses were over 20 mg. Tolerance developed to weight suppression effects of dextroamphetamine but not to inhibition of gains in height. Safer and Allen (1973) noted that the less stimulant medication the hyperactive child received, the less likely growth was to be suppressed. A later study by Safer, Allen, and Barr (1975) demonstrated a growth rebound effect when stimulant medication was discontinued; this effect compensated for depressed growth rates while the child was on medication. Other studies of children receiving low to moderate doses (0.3 mg/kg to 0.5 mg/kg) of methylphenidate have not shown growth suppression effects (Golinko, 1984; Kalachnik, Sprague, Sleator, Cohen, & Ullman, 1982; McNutt, Boileau, Cohen, Sprague, & von Neumann, 1977).

In a review of the literature on possible growth-suppression effects of stimulant medications in the long-term treatment of hyperactive children, Roche, Lipman, Overall, and Hung (1980) concluded that there is evidence of temporary slowing in the rate of growth in weight and suggestion of slowing in growth in stature in children taking "high-normal" doses (0.5 mg/kg to 0.8 mg/kg) of stimulant medication. However, no effect on eventual adult weight or height was noted. Roche et al. (1980) suggested that the temporary effect on growth in the first few years of treatment appears to be related to the dosage level given and the presence or absence of drug holidays.

In a more recent statement by the Committee on Children with Disabilities and Committee on Drugs (1987), the concerns surrounding growth suppression which generated a great deal of research in the mid to late 1970s are acknowledged briefly and in the past tense. "There was fear that stimulant medications would lead to growth retardation; however, growth suppression is only minimally related to stimulant dosage. . . . No growth suppression occurred at doses of methylphenidate up to 0.8 mg/kg during a prolonged period" (p. 759).

Comparison of Nutrition-Related Side Effects

A direct comparison of the side effects of methylphenidate, dextroamphetamine, and pemoline is difficult because of differences in comparisons and variables measured across reported studies. Nevertheless, some generalizations concerning nutritional effects are possible. Among the most commonly prescribed stimulants, methylphenidate has been reported to have fewer side effects overall, and to suppress appetite to a lesser degree than does dextroamphetamine (Conners, 1971; Golinko, 1984; Murray, 1987). In a comparison of efficacy, side effects, and safety of magnesium pemoline and dextroamphetamine, side effects (insomnia and anorexia) did not differ significantly for the two drugs (Conners et al., 1972). Differences among the central nervous system stimulants typically used to treat hyperactivity appear to be minimal and subject to individual differences in response. Methylphenidate, however, generally causes less weight loss and appetite suppression than do either dextroamphetamine or pemoline.

Tricyclic Antidepressants

Although central nervous system stimulants are the medical treatment of choice, other drugs have been used to treat hyperactivity when cases have not been responsive to stimulants or have shown severe side effects, and with adolescent and adult populations when the potential for abuse of stimulants increases. Imipramine hydrochloride (Tofranil) is the tricyclic antidepressant most widely used as an alternative to stimulant medication (Ross & Ross, 1982). The documented side effects of tricyclic antidepressants relevant to nutrition include weight gain and increased appetite for sweets (United States Pharmacopeial Convention, 1989). Weight gain has been reported during treatment in about one-third of adults treated with imipramine (Berken, Weinstein, & Stern, 1984; Fernstrom, Krowinski, & Kupfer, 1986). Nutrition-related side effects of imipramine in children, however, may differ from those observed in adults, in that decreased appetite and weight loss has been noted in some studies conducted with children (Biederman, Gastfriend, & Jellinek, 1986; Rapoport, Quinn, Bradbard, Riddle, & Brooks, 1974).

Conclusions

Although side effects of drug treatment for hyperactivity are relatively minor and transient, careful monitoring is indicated in the use of stimulant and antidepressant drugs in children. Anorexia and weight loss are common and dose dependent. Stimulants have been shown to suppress growth in weight; however, their effect on growth in stature is less certain. Recent studies indicate that any growth depression that occurs during treatment is compensated for by rebound growth when medication is discontinued. Evidence of growth suppression is not present in adulthood. Finally, any effects of prescribed medications on nutrition appear to be short term and secondary to loss of appetite and gastrointestinal disturbances induced by the drugs.

TREATMENT CONSIDERATIONS

The vast majority of controlled studies examining the effects of diet on behavior have failed to demonstrate any relationship between hyperactivity and nutrition. The exception is caffeine. The laboratory evidence shows that normal children who are unaccustomed to caffeine become more emotional, restless, and inattentive after consumption of large amounts. However, children who typically consume high doses of caffeine become more anxious and restless when deprived of their usual intake. These results are tempered by evidence showing the lack of a significant caffeine effect in a natural setting using a typical single-serving dose (8 oz of a soft drink) (Baer, 1987). There is no reason to believe that these results are not also applicable to hyperactive children. Therefore, we believe it is prudent for parents to monitor their children's access to caffeine. If it appears to be much beyond one can of soft drink a day and they observe the effects noted above, then it would be wise to restrict consumption. Otherwise it is unlikely that restriction will have much effect on the child's behavior. This notion is contrary to the position of some parents who believe caffeine can be given as a substitute for stimulant medication; but the results of a number of studies have already shown that caffeine is at best a poor substitute.

Understandably, most parents and teachers have not read the research reporting the lack of a diet-behavior connection and they have no doubt been influenced by the popular idea that diet exerts a major influence on behavior, especially on the behavior of hyperactive children. In fact, physicians have also been influenced by these popular notions. Bennett and Sherman (1983) reported finding that 45% of the pediatricians and family practitioners they surveyed have recommended a low-sugar diet for at least some of the hyperactive children they treated.

When working with hyperactive children whose parents insist that diet is playing a major role, we recommend a five-step approach (Rosén & Beyers, 1990). First, conduct a thorough behavioral assessment of all relevant variables affecting the child's behavior. Second, question the parents about their reasons for thinking that the child's behavior is being influenced by nutritional factors; get specific examples. Many times we find that there is clear alternative explanations for the behavior, such as an association between high sugar consumption and Halloween; the relevant functional variable is just as likely the lack of structure inherent in the holiday festivities as it is the increased sugar intake. Next, discuss with the parents the results of your assessment regarding the most likely maintaining variables. In addition, explain to them the conclusions of the numerous diet-behavior studies, and point out the alternative explanations for the diet-behavior connections they report for their child.

Many parents find it extremely taxing to rear their hyperactive child and are desperate for answers. Unfortunately, the popular notion has offered a key, diet change, which does not work. We recommend being honest with parents about this and letting them know that we all wish it were as easy as simply changing the child's diet. In fact, however, it is not. Our final step, therefore, is to discuss with the parents the treatment approaches that have been proven to be successful—approaches such as those reviewed in this volume. The argument we find most persuasive is to ask the parents if they truly think they could totally eliminate the suspect food(s) from the child's diet "at all times, in every situation." We then ask them whether, if it were possible to change their child's behavior without changing his or her diet (even if dietary factors were playing a role), they would be willing to "give it a try." This line of reasoning appears to make sense to most parents and allows us to initiate some proven psychological interventions that have a much better likelihood of helping the child than dietary change would have.

Some parents, however, continue to insist that the child's diet is at the root of the problem. In these cases we recommend "a complete physical examination specifically aimed at uncovering allergic disorders, a full allergy history, skin-prick testing, a dietary history, and, if prudent a double-blind challenge assessment using the substance in question" (Rosén & Beyers, 1990). It is because this course is expensive, lengthy, and unlikely to be fruitful that we recommend it only as a last resort.

GENERAL CONCLUSIONS

Despite the prevalence and tenacity of opinions to the contrary, there is little scientific evidence supporting dietary variables as either causative or exacerbating factors of hyperactivity in children. Food additives, sugar, aspartame, and other specific foods have not been found to have great effect children's behavior—hyperactive or otherwise. In addition, the effects of stimulant medications on the nutritional status of hyperactive children are typically short-term side effects that dissipate after a few weeks. The one substance for which the research does indicate consistent behavioral effects is caffeine. It is unlikely, however, that restriction will have much effect on the child's behavior if the consumption is within the normal range of about one can of cola a day. In general, it is *not* recommended that diet restriction or alteration be considered a part of a therapeutic approach to the treatment of hyperactive children.

Finally, there is a clear need for better public education concerning the findings of diet-behavior research. Hyperactivity is a serious and widespread condition, affecting not just the child but the family and school as well; sadly, there are no simple cures. What is gravely unfortunate is that, in their attempts to find answers, many parents and teachers of hyperactive children have been led to believe that diet is the key. No matter how appealing this may sound, it simply is not the truth.

REFERENCES

Arbeit, M. L., Nicklas, T. A., Frank, G. C., Webber, L. S., Miner, M. H., & Gerenson, G. S. (1988). Caffeine intakes of children from a biracial population; The Bogalusa Heart Study. *Journal of the American Dietetic Association, 88,* 466–471.

Arnold, L. E., Christopher, J., Huestis, R., & Smeltzer, D. J. (1978). Methylphenidate vs. dextroamphetamine vs. caffeine in a minimal brain dysfunction. *Archives of General Psychiatry, 35,* 463–473.

Atkins, F. M. (1986, May). Food allergy and behavior: Definitions, mechanisms and a review of the evidence [Supplement]. *Nutrition Reviews, 44,* 104–113.

Baer, R. (1987). Effects of caffeine on classroom behavior, sustained attention, and a memory task in preschool children. *Journal of Applied Behavior Analysis, 20,* 225–234.

Barling, J., & Bullen, G. (1985). Dietary factors and hyperactivity: A failure to replicate. *Journal of Genetic Psychology, 146,* 117–123.

Beall, J. G. (1973, October 30). Food additives and hyperactivity in children. *Congressional Record,* 519736.

Behar, D., Rapoport, J. L., Adams, A. J., Berg, C. J., & Cornblath, M. (1984). Sugar challenge testing with children considered behaviorally "sugar reactive." *Nutrition and Behavior, 1,* 277–288.

Berken, G. H., Weinstein, D. O., & Stern, W. C. (1984). Weight gain: A side effect of tricyclic antidepressants. *Journal of Affective Disorders, 7,* 133.

Bennett, F. C., & Sherman, R. (1983). Management of childhood "hyperactivity" by primary care physicians. *Journal of Developmental and Behavioral Pediatrics, 4,* 88–93.

Biederman, J., Gastfriend, D. R., & Jellinek, M. S. (1986). Desipramine in the treatment of children with attention deficit disorder. *Journal of Clinical Psychopharmacology, 6,* 359–363.

Brenner, A. (1977). A study of the efficacy of the Feingold diet on hyperkinetic children. *Clinical Pediatrics, 16,* 652–656.

Buchanan, S. R. (1984). The most ubiquitous toxin. *American Psychologist, 11,* 1327–1328.

Clementz, G. L. (1988). Psychotropic effects of caffeine. *American Family Physician, 37,* 167–172.

Clementz, G. L., & Dailey, J. W. (1988). Psychotropic effects of caffeine. *American Family Physician, 37,* 167–172.

Committee on Children with Disabilities and Committee on Drugs (1987). Medication for children with an attention deficit disorder. *Pediatrics, 80,* 758–760.

Conners, C. K. (1971). Recent drug studies with

hyperkinetic children. *Journal of Learning Disabilities, 4,* 476–483.

Conners, C. K. (1975). A placebo-crossover study of caffeine treatment of hyperkinetic children. *International Journal of Mental Health, 4,* 132–143.

Conners, C. K. (1980). *Food Additives and Hyperactive Children,* New York: Plenum Publishing.

Conners, C. K. (1984). Nutritional therapy in children. In J. R. Galler (Ed.), *Nutrition and behavior* (pp. 159–192). New York: Plenum Publishing.

Conners, C. K., & Blouin, A. G. (1982). Nutritional effects on behavior of children. *Journal of Psychiatric Research, 17,* 193–201.

Conners, C. K., Caldwell, J., Caldwell, L., Schwab, E., Kronsberg, S., Wells, K. C., Leong, N., & Blouin, A. G. (1985, February). *Experimental studies of sugar and aspartame on autonomic, cortical and behavioral responses of children.* A paper presented at a symposium on Diet and Behavior: A Multi-Disciplinary approach sponsored by the American Medical Association and the International Life Sciences Institute, Arlington, VA.

Conners, C. K., Goyette, C. H., Southwick, D. A., Lees, J. M., & Andrulonis, P. A. (1976). Food additives and hyperkinesis: A controlled double-blind experiment. *Pediatrics, 58,* 154–166.

Conners, C. K., Taylor, E., Meo, G., Kurtz, M. A., & Fournier, M. (1972). Pemoline and dextroamphetamine: A controlled study in children with MBD. *Psychopharmacologia, 26,* 321–336.

Cook, P. S., & Woodhill, J. M. (1976). The Feingold dietary treatment of hyperkinetic syndrome. *Medical Journal of Australia, 2,* 85–90.

Crook, W. (1975). Food allergy—The great masquerader. *Pediatric Clinics of North America, 22,* 227–238.

Crook, W. (1976). *Learning disabilities and hyperactivity in children due to foods.* Paper presented at the International Food Allergy Symposium, Toronto, Canada.

Crook, W. G. (1980). Can what a child east make him dull, stupid, or hyperactive? *Journal of Learning Disabilities, 13,* 53–58.

Davison, H. M. (1949). *Southern Medical Journal, 42,* 712–716.

Donnelly, M., & Rapoport, J. L. (1985). Attention deficit disorders. In J. M. Wiener (Ed.), *Diagnosis and psychopharmacology of childhood and adolescent disorders,* (pp. 179–197). New York: John Wiley & Sons.

Duffy, W. (1975). *Sugar blues.* Radnor, PA: Chilton.

Elkins, R. N., Rapoport, J., Zahn, T., Buchsbaum, M., Weingartner, H., Kopin, I., Langer, D., & Johnson, C. (1981). Acute effects of caffeine in normal, prepubertal boys. *American Journal of Psychiatry, 138,* 178–183.

Feingold, B. F. (1975a). Hyperkinesis and learning disabilities linked to artificial food flavors and colors. *American Journal of Nursing, 75,* 797–805.

Feingold, B. F. (1975b). *Why Your Child Is Hyperactive,* New York: Random House.

Feingold, B. F., German, D. F., Brahm, R. M., & Simmers, E. (1973). *Adverse reaction to food additives.* Paper presented at the Annual Meeting of the American Medical Association, New York.

Ferguson, H. B., Stoddart, C., & Simeon, J. G. (1986). Double-blind challenge studies of behavioral and cognitive effects of sucrose-aspartame ingestion in normal children. *Nutrition Reviews, 44,* 144–150.

Fernstrom, M. H., Krowinski, R. L., & Kupfer, D. J. (1986). Chronic imipramine treatment and weight gain. *Psychiatry Research, 17,* 269.

Firestone, P., Davey, J., Goodman, J. T., & Peters, S. (1978). The effects of caffeine and methylphenidate on hyperactive children. *Journal of the American Academy of Child Psychiatry, 17,* 445–456.

Firestone, P., Poitras-Wright, H., & Douglas, V. (1978). The effects of caffeine on hyperactive children. *Journal of Learning Disabilities, 11,* 133–141.

Frey, G. H. (1976). Use of aspartame by apparently healthy children and adolescents. *Journal of Toxicology and Environmental Health, 2,* 401–415.

Gadow, K. D. (1982). *Children on medication: A primer for school personnel* (pp. 14–32). Reston, VA: Council for Exceptional Children.

Garfinkel, B. D., Webster, C. D., & Sloman, L. (1975). Methylphenidate and caffeine in the treatment of children with minimal brain dysfunction. *American Journal of Psychiatry, 132,* 723–728.

Gilbert, R. (1976). Caffeine as a drug of abuse. In R. J. Gibbine (Ed.), *Research advances in alcohol and drug problems* (pp. 49–176). New York: John Wiley & Sons.

Gittleman, R. (1980). Childhood disorders. In D. Klein, R. Gittleman, F. Quitkin, & A. Rifkin (Eds.) *Drug treatment of adult and childhood psychiatric disorders.* Baltimore, MD: Williams and Wilkins.

Goldman, J. A., Lerman, R. H., Contois, J. H., & Udall, J. N. (1986). Behavioral effects of sucrose on preschool children. *Journal of Abnormal Child Psychology, 14,* 565–577.

Goldstein, J. A., Kaizer, S., & Whitby, O. (1969). Psychotropic effects of caffeine in man: IV. Quantitative and qualitative differences associated with habituation to coffee. *Clinical Pharmacological Therapy, 10,* 489–497.

Golinko, B. E. (1984). Side effects of dextroamphetamine

and methylphenidate in hyperactive children: A brief review. *Progress in Neuro-Psychopharmacology and Biological Psychiatry, 8,* 1–8.

Goyette, C. H., Connors, C. K., Petti, T. A., & Curtis, L. E. (1978). Effects of artificial colors on hyperkinetic children: A double-blind challenge study. *Psychopharmacological Bulletin, 14,* 39–40.

Greden, J. (1981). Caffeinism and caffeine withdrawal. In J. Lowinson & P. Ruiz (Eds.), *Substance abuse* (pp. 274–286). Baltimore, MD: Williams & Wilkins.

Griffiths, R. R., & Woodson, P. P. (1988). Caffeine physical dependence: A review of human and laboratory animal studies. *Psychopharmacology, 94,* 437–451.

Gross, M. (1975). Caffeine in the treatment of children with minimal brain dysfunction or hyperkinetic syndrome. *Psychosomatics, 16,* 26–27.

Harley, J. P., Matthews, C. G., & Eichman, P. (1978). Synthetic food colors and hyperactivity in children: A double-blind challenge experiment. *Pediatrics, 62,* 975–983.

Harley, J. P., Ray, R. S., Tomasi, L., Eichman, P. L., Matthews, C. G., Chun, R., Cleeland, C. S., & Traisman, E. (1978). Hyperkinesis and food additives: Testing the Feingold hypothesis. *Pediatrics, 61,* 818–828.

Harper, A. E. (1975). Aspartame. *In sweetners: Issues and uncertainties* (pp. 182–188). Washington, DC: National Academy of Sciences.

Harvey, D. H. P., & March, R. W. (1978). The effects of decaffeinated coffee versus whole coffee on hyperactive children. *Developmental Medicine and Child Neurology, 20,* 81–86.

Hawley, C., & Buckley, R. (1974). Food dyes and hyperkinetic children. *Academic Therapy, 10,* 27–32.

Horowitz, D. L., & Bauer-Nehrling, J. D. (1983). Can aspartame meet our expectations? *Research, 83,* 142–146.

Huestis, R. D., Arnold, L. E., & Smeltzer, D. J. (1975). Caffeine versus methylphenidate and d-amphetamine in minimal brain dysfunction: A double-blind comparison. *American Journal of Psychiatry, 132,* 868–870.

Janssen, P. J. C. M., & van der Heijden, C. A. (1988). Aspartame: Review of recent experimental and observational data. *Toxicology, 50,* 1–26.

Kalachnik, J. E., Sprague, R. L., Sleator, E. K., Cohen, M. N., & Ullman, R. K. (1982). Effect of methylphenidate hydrochloride on stature of hyperactive children. *Developmental Medicine and Child Neurology, 24,* 586–595.

Kaplan, B. J., McNicol, J., Conte, R. A., & Moghadam, H. K. (1989). Overall nutrient intake of preschool

hyperactive and normal boys. *Journal of Abnormal Child Psychology, 17,* 127–132.

Kruesi, M. J. P., Rapoport, J. L., Cummings, E. M., Berg, C. J., Ismond, D. R., Flament, M., Yarrow, M., Zahn-Waxler, C. (1987). Effects of sugar and aspartame on aggression and activity in children. *American Journal of Psychiatry, 144,* 1487–1490.

Kuznicki, J. T., Turner, L. S. (1986). The effects of caffeine on users and non-users. *Physiology and Behavior, 37,* 397–408.

Langseth, L. N., & Dowd, J. (1978). Glucose tolerance and hyperkinesis. *Federal Journal of Cosmetic Toxicology, 16,* 129–133.

Levine, M. D., & Liden, C. B. (1976). Food for inefficient thought. *Pediatrics, 58,* 145–148.

Levy, F., Dumbrell, S., Hobbes, G., Ryan, M., Wilton, N., & Woodhill, J. M. (1978). Hyperkinesis and diet: A double-blind crossover trial with a tartrazine challenge. *Medical Journal of Australia, 1,* 61–64.

Levy, F., & Hobbes, G. (1978). Hyperkinesis and diet: A replication study. *American Journal of Psychiatry, 135,* 1559–1560.

Lipton, M. A., Nemeroff, C. B., & Mailman, R. B. (1979). Hyperkinesis and food additives. In R. J. Wurtman & J. J. Wurtman, *Nutrition and the Brain* (pp. 1–27). New York: Raven Press.

Mattes, J., & Gittelman, R. (1981). Effects of artificial food colorings in children with hyperactive symptoms. *Archives of General Psychiatry, 38,* 714–718.

Mattes, J., & Gittelman-Klein, R. (1978). A crossover study of artificial food colorings in a hyperkinetic child. *American Journal of Psychiatry, 135,* 987–988.

McNutt, B. A., Boileau, R. A, Cohen, M. N., Sprague, R. L., & von Neumann, A. (1977). The effects of long-term stimulant medication on growth and body composition of hyperactive children. *Psychopharmacology Bulletin, 12,* 13–15.

Methylphenidata revisited. (1988). *Medical Letter on Drugs and Therapeutics, 30,* 51–52.

Milich, R., & Pelham, W. E. (1986). Effects of sugar ingestion on the classroom and playgroup behavior of attention deficit disordered boys. *Journal of Consulting and Clinical Psychology, 54,* 714–718.

Milich, R., Wolraich, M., & Lindgren, S. (1986). Sugar and hyperactivity: A critical review of the empirical findings. *Clinical Psychology Review, 6,* 493–513.

Millichap, J. G. (1968). Drugs in management of hyperkinetic and perceptually handicapped children. *Journal of the American Medical Association, 206,* 1527–1530.

Morgan, K., Stults, V., & Zabik, M. (1982). Amount of dietary sources of caffeine and saccharin intake by individuals ages 5 to 18 years. *Regulatory Toxicological Pharmacology, 2,* 296–307.

Murray, J. B. (1987). Psychophysiological effects of methylphenidate (Ritalin). *Psychological Reports, 61,* 315–336.

Neims, A. H., & von Borstel, R. W. (1983). Caffeine: Metabolism and biochemical mechanisms of action. *Nutrition and the Brain, 6,* 1–30.

Palmer, S., Rapoport, J. L., & Quinn, P. O. (1975). Food additives and hyperactivity. *Clinical Pediatrics, 14,* 956–959.

Pardridge, W. M. (1986). Potential effects of the dipeptide sweetener aspartame on the brain. In R. J. Wurtman (Eds.), *Nutrition and the brain: Vol. 7. Food constituents affecting normal and abnormal behaviors* (pp. 199–245). New York: Raven Press.

Pharmacy Data Service. (1989). The top 200 Rx drugs of 1988. *American Druggist, 199,* 38–52.

Potts, W. J., Bloss, J. L., & Nutting, E. F. (1980). Biological properties of aspartame: I. Evaluation of central nervous system effects. *Journal of Environmental Pathology and Toxicology, 3,* 341–353.

Prinz, R. J., & Riddle, D. B. (1986). Associations between nutrition and behavior in five-year-old children [Supplement]. *Nutrition Reviews, 44* 151–157.

Prinz, R. J., Roberts, W. A., & Hantman, E. (1980). Dietary correlates of hyperactive behavior in children. *Journal of Consulting and Clinical Psychology, 48,* 760–769.

Rall, T. W. (1985). Central nervous system stimulants: The methylxanthines. In A. G. Goodman (Ed.), *Goodman and Gilman's the pharmacological basis of therapeutics* (7th ed., pp. 589–601). New York: Macmillan.

Rapoport, J. L. (1982/1983). Effects of dietary substances in children. *Journal of Psychiatry Research, 17,* 187–191.

Rapoport, J. L., Berg, C. J., Ismond, D. R., Zahn, T. P., & Neims, A. (1984). Behavioral effects of caffeine in children. *Archives of General Psychiatry, 41,* 1073–1079.

Rapoport, J. L., Jensvold, M., Elkins, R., Buchsbaum, M. S., Weingartner, H., Ludlow, C., Zahn, T. P., Berg, C. J., & Neims, A. H. (1981). Behavioral and cognitive effects of caffeine in boys and adult males. *Journal of Nervous and Mental Disease, 169,* 726–732.

Rapoport, J. L., Quinn, P. O., Bradbard, G., Riddle, K. D., & Brooks, E. (1974). Imipramine and methylphenidate treatments of hyperactive boys. *Archives of General Psychiatry 30,* 789–793.

Rapp, D. J. (1978a). Does diet affect hyperactivity? *Journal of Learning Disabilities, 11,* 57–62.

Rapp, D. J. (1978b). Double-blind confirmation and treatment of milk sensitivity. *Medical Journal of Australia, 1,* 571–572.

Reynolds, W. A., Bauman, A. F., Stegink, L. D., Filer, L. J., & Naidu, S. (1984). Developmental assessment of infant macaques receiving dietary aspartame or phenylalanine. In L. D. Stegink & L. J. Filer (Eds), *Aspartame: Physiology and biochemistry* (pp. 405–424). New York: Marcel Dekker.

Reichard, C. C., & Elder, S. T. (1977). The effects of caffeine on reaction time in hyperactive and normal children. *American Journal of Psychiatry, 134,* 144–148.

Roak-Foltz, R., & Leveille, G. A. (1984). Projected aspartame intake: Daily ingestion of aspartic acid, phenylalanine, and methonol. In L. D. Stegink L. J. Filer (Eds.), *Aspartame: Physiology and biochemistry* (pp. 201–205). New York: Marcel Dekker.

Rose, T. L. (1978). The functional relationship between artificial food colors and hyperactivity. *Journal of Applied Behavior Analysis, 11,* 439–446.

Roche, A. F., Lipman, R. S., Overall, J. E., & Hung, W. (1980). The effects of stimulant medication on the growth of hyperkinetic children. *Psychopharmacology Bulletin, 16,* 13–17.

Rosén, L. A., & Beyers, J. A. (1990). Allergies: Behavioral effects and treatment implications. In A. Gross & R. Drabman (Eds.), *The Handbook of Clinical Behavioral Pediatrics.* New York: Plenum Publishing.

Rosén, L. A., Booth, S. R., Bender, M. E., McGrath, M. L., Sorrell, S., & Drabman, R. S. (1988). Effects of sugar (sucrose) on children's behavior. *Journal of Consulting and Clinical Psychology, 56,* 583–589.

Roshon, M. S., & Hagen, R. L. (1989). Sugar consumption, locomotion, task orientation, and learning in preschool children. *Journal of Abnormal Child Psychology, 17,* 349–357.

Ross, D. M., & Ross, S. A. (1982). *Hyperactivity: Current issues, research, and theory* (2nd ed.), New York: John Wiley & Sons.

Safer, D. J., & Allen, R. P. (1973). Factors influencing the suppressant effects of two stimulant drugs on the growth of hyperactive children. *Pediatrics, 51,* 600–667.

Safer, D. J., Allen, R., & Barr, E. (1972). Depression of growth in hyperactive children on stimulant drugs. *New England Journal of Medicine, 287,* 217–220.

Salzman, K. (1976). Allergy testing, psychological assessment, and dietary treatment of the hyperactive child syndrome. *Medical Journal of Australia, 2,* 248–251.

Scarnati, R. (1986). An outline of hazardous side effects of Ritalin (methylphenidate). *International Journal of Addiction, 21,* 837–841.

Schanckenberg, R. C. (1973). Caffeine as a substitute for Schedule II stimulants in hyperkinetic children. *American Journal of Psychiatry, 130,* 796–798.

Spring, B., Chiodo, J., & Bowen, D. J. (1987). Carbohydrates, tryptophan, and behavior: A methodological review. *Psychological Bulletin, 102,* 234–256.

Stare, F. S., Whelan, E. M., & Sheridan, M. (1980). Diet and hyperactivity: Is there a relationship? *Pediatrics, 66,* 521–525.

Stine, J. J. (1976). Symptom alleviation in the hyperactive child by dietary modifications: A report of two cases. *American Journal of Orthopsychiatry, 46,* 637–645.

Suomi, S. J. (1984). Effects of aspartame on the learning test performance of young stumptail macaques. In L. D. Stegink & L. J. Filer (Eds.), *Aspartame: Physiology and biochemistry* (pp. 424–445). New York: Marcel Dekker.

Swanson, J. M., & Kinsbourne, M. (1980). Food dyes impair performance of hyperactive children on a laboratory learning test. *Science, 207,* 1485–1487.

Taylor, E. (1979). Food additives, allergy, and hyperkinesis. *Journal of Child Psychology and Psychiatry, 20,* 357–363.

United States Pharmacopeial Convention, Inc. (1989). *USP Dispensing Information for the Health Care Professional* (9th ed.). Rockville, MD: Author.

Wells, S. (1984). Caffeine: Implications of recent research for clinical practice. *American Journal of Orthopsychiatry, 54,* 375–389.

Wender, G. (1980). New evidence on food additives and hyperkinesis. *American Journal of Diseases of Children, 134,* 1122–1124.

Werry, J. S. (1976). Food additives and hyperactivity. *Medical Journal of Australia, 2,* 281–282.

Williams, I. J., Cram, D. M., Tausig, F. T., & Webster, E. (1978). Relative effects of drugs and diet on hyperactive behaviors: An experimental study. *Pediatrics, 61,* 811–817.

Winsberg, B. G., Yepes, L. E., & Bialer, I. (1976). Pharmacologic management of children with hyperactive/aggressive/inattentive behavior disorders. *Clinical Pediatrics, 15,* 471–477.

Wolraich, M. (1987). Aspartame and behavior in children. In R. J. Wurtman & E. Ritter-Walker (Eds.), *Proceedings of the First International Meeting on Dietary Phenylalanine and Brain Function* (pp. 201–206). Cambridge, MA: Charitable Trust.

Wolraich, M., Milich, R., Stumbo, P., & Schultz, F. (1985). The effects of sucrose ingestion on the behavior of hyperactive boys. *Journal of Pediatrics, 106,* 675–682.

Wolraich, M. L., Stumbo, P. J., Milich, R., Chenard, C., & Schultz, F. (1986). Dietary characteristics of hyperactive and control boys. *Journal of the American Dietetic Association, 86,* 500–504.

Wurtman, R. J. (1983). Neurochemical changes following high-dose aspartame with dietary carbohydrates. *New England Journal of Medicine, 309,* 429–430.

Zahn, T. P., & Rapoport, J. L. (1987). Acute autonomic nervous system effects of caffeine in prepubertal boys. *Psychopharmacology, 91,* 40–44.

Zametkin, A. J., Karoum, F., & Rapoport, J. L. (1987). Treatment of hyperactive children with D-phenylalanine. *American Journal of Psychiatry, 144,* 792–794.

CHAPTER 15

COLLABORATION OF DISCIPLINES

Nirbhay N. Singh
Dean X. Parmelee
Aradhana A. Sood
Roger C. Katz

Hyperactivity and its various aliases (e.g., hyper-kinesis, minimal brain dysfunction, attention deficit hyperactivity disorder) is one of the most talked about, common, and controversial of all the child-hood behavior disorders (see Carlson & Rapport, 1989; Rapport, 1983). During the past quarter century, hyperactivity has captured the interest of countless researchers and clinicians, producing an increasing number of scientific publications as well as trade books for parents and teachers who interact with hyperactive children on a regular basis. As can be seen from the table of contents of this book alone, the scope and depth of the study of hyperactivity is impressive, and the many scholarly contributions from different disciplines (psychiatry, psychology, psychopharmacology, education) force one to wonder how the data can be integrated appropriately. This book is an attempt to give an up-to-date, multidisciplinary perspective on the problem of hyperactivity. In this chapter, our goal is to describe an integrative model for practice and research—one that can synthesize salient findings from the various disciplines that come together around this problem.

The epidemiology of hyperactivity in children leads to some critical notions in designing a model

that will enhance interdisciplinary care. First, hyperactivity as a diagnostic disorder (using the DSM-III-R [*Diagnostic and Statistical Manual of Mental Disorders,* 3rd ed., rev.; American Psychiatric Association (APA), 1987] criteria) appears to have stability over at least a 4–5 year period (Cantwell & Baker, 1989) and in adulthood often is associated with significant psychiatric or antisocial pathology (Hechtman, 1989). Second, follow-up studies indicate that some interventions produce better long-term outcomes than others (Satterfield, Satterfield, & Cantwell, 1981). In fact, it appears that some treatment effects reverberate throughout the behavioral repertoire of the hyperactive child for long periods of time (Weiss & Hechtman, 1986). Third, there are situation-specific factors in the environments of hyperactive children that can elicit, maintain, or terminate symptomatic behavior (August & Garfinkel, 1989; Drager, Prior, & Sanson, 1986). Fourth, it is likely that there are several subtypes of hyperactivity that include acquired and non-acquired types (August & Garfinkel, 1989; Rapport, 1983).

Hyperactive children usually have multiple problems (Barkley, 1981a; Henker & Whalen, 1989) and, for that reason, it is our view that future progress in assessing and treating the disorder will require a well-integrated multidisciplinary approach. Such an approach should not use a narrow time span to evaluate interventions. Furthermore, it should be predicted on the assumption that hyperactivity does not result from a single cause, and that its behavioral and cognitive manifestations occur via interdependent pathways.

CURRENT MODELS

The DSM-III-R (APA, 1987) provides a phenomenological description of hyperactivity without regard to its diverse and often conflicting theories of etiology. In addition, the chasm between theories of etiology and models of treatment is such that practitioners often are guided by their training, clinical lore, and intuition rather than empirical findings. In this section, we briefly consider prevailing theories of etiology and ways of treating hyperactivity. In doing so, we suggest the need for an ecobehavioral model that will provide a rapprochement between research and practice, and will facilitate greater collaboration between the disciplines.

Although numerous variables (e.g., brain damage, neurologic immaturity, genetics, chemical toxins, family stressors, diet) have been implicated as causes of hyperactivity, most of the causes can be subsumed under three broad etiological models: the *deficit* model, the *delay* model, and the *difference* model (Kinsbourne, 1975; Rapport, 1983). The deficit model, which is based on observations of hyperactivity in postencephalitic children, assumes that hyperactivity is the manifestation of deficits (e.g., motor control, attention, impulse) resulting from early brain damage. The delay model (Kinsbourne, 1973) postulates that hyperactivity is associated with immaturity in development, and that the behavioral and cognitive characteristics of hyperactivity eventually will disappear as the child grows older. The difference model (Kinsbourne & Swanson, 1979), or the *personal-historical* model (Aman & Singh, 1983), proposes that hyperactive children are similar to their nonhyperactive peers but on an extreme end of the behavioral and cognitive continuum. They have not acquired certain skills because

of personal attributes (e.g., temperament) and/or environmental factors.

While no single etiological model has been able to explain hyperactivity in its entirety, some models do a better job than others. For example, there is little support for the deficit and delay models. It is well established that some hyperactive children are neither brain damaged (Anastopoulos & Barkley, 1988; Carparulo, Cohen, Rothman, Young, Katz, Shaywitz, & Shaywitz, 1981) nor do they outgrow their problems (Hechtman, 1989; Hechtman, Weiss, Finkelstein, Werner & Benn, 1976; Hechtman & Weiss, 1983; Hechtman, Weiss & Perlman, 1984; Henker & Whalen, 1989; Mannuzza, Gittelman, Bonagura, Konig, & Shenker, 1988). The difference model enjoys the most support because it tends to be most consistent with the data (Rapport, 1983).

There are three major models for treating hyperactivity: medical, psychodynamic, and behavioral. Although a family systems model is currently in vogue, the few reports available in the literature do not provide much basis for its evaluation. Indeed, the applicability of family systems therapy may be limited, considering the finding that only some hyperactive children come from dysfunctional families (Piacentini, Lahey, & Hynd, 1986; Weiss, 1983).

Medical Model

The medical model views hyperactivity like any other childhood disorder. It assumes that eventually a specific cause will be found, such as a faulty gene or clustering of genes, that leads to a biochemical abnormality and results in hyperactivity. This model engages clinicians and researchers in the study of the disorder's etiology, pathogenesis, signs, symptoms, diagnosis, and treatment. The physician elicits the history of the child, searching for a group of symptoms consistent with the current diagnostic criteria (e.g., DSM-III-R, ICD-9 [International Classification of Diseases; World Health Organization (WHO), 1977]). Once the diagnosis is made, treatment usually consists of some type of psychotropic medication (e.g., methylphenidate) as the primary intervention. Some physicians combine pharmacotherapy with parent counseling or psychotherapy, and recommend intensive school-based interventions for children with comorbidity, such as a learning disabilities (Bennett & Sherman, 1983; Greenhill, 1989; Sandoval, Lambert, & Sassone, 1981).

Psychodynamic Model

Derived from psychoanalytic theory, the psychodynamic model views hyperactivity and its attendant distractibility and impulsiveness as the manifestation of anxiety resulting from an underlying neurotic conflict. The diagnostic component is aimed at understanding the child's psychodynamics. Treatment consists of a combination of individual psychotherapy, play therapy, and parent guidance. Psychotherapy is aimed at interpreting the transference neurosis that develops between the child and the therapist. This treatment provides a vehicle through which the child's insight and ego controls are enhanced. Parent guidance also may be used to help parents understand their children's motivations and improve parent-child relationships. In general, there is little scientific data to support the efficacy of this model for treating hyperactivity but, nonetheless, many practitioners continue to use it (Heavilon, 1980).

Behavioral

Although there is no single behavioral model of hyperactivity, proponents of this approach advocate a *functional analysis* as the key to understanding hyperactive behavior. Functional analysis is one of the main methods used by behavior therapists for identifying the environmental events (antecedents and consequences), behaviors, and organismic variables of which hyperactivity, or any other behavior problem for that matter, is a function. For example, a child's hyperactivity might be related functionally to his teacher's classroom management style, peer interaction patterns, deficits in self-control, parent-child interactions, family stressors, and so on. That these variables can operate at different times or in different situations is only one reason for a multidisciplinary approach to assess and treat the problem. From the standpoint of therapy, the emphasis is on modifying events in the current environment to produce changes in the child's behavior. Treatment follows directly from assessment, which is ongoing

to ensure that desired results are achieved. In this regard, the system is self-correcting. The more common behavioral interventions include contingency management programs, which can be implemented by parents and teachers, as well as cognitive behavioral approaches to improve the child's self-control and problem-solving skills (Abikoff, 1985; Barkley, 1981a).

Summary

Clearly, there is a disparity between what is known about hyperactivity and the methods used to treat it. In addition, there is a tendency among some professionals to be elitist in their approach, which interferes with interdisciplinary communication and, in the long run, can undermine the efficacy of therapy. Given the range of problems experienced by hyperactive children (poor peer relationships, school failure, conflict with parents, low self-esteem, aggression, and delinquency), it is clear that this disorder is not unidimensional; moreover, a complete understanding of the problem can be achieved only through the combined effort of different disciplines. What is needed, therefore, is an empirically based conceptual framework that can provide a vehicle for a multidisciplinary effort in the assessment and treatment of hyperactivity. The ecobehavioral model that we describe below is one such approach.

ECOBEHAVIORAL MODEL

This overview of conceptual models leads us to the conclusion that different disciplines can make a useful contribution to the assessment and treatment of hyperactive children. In the past, the field has been dominated by discipline-specific research and treatment modalities. One consequence of this approach is that it leads to a conceptual and professional polarization that is detrimental to scientific progress, and ultimately, to the welfare of patients. We should be aware that our best efforts at assessing and treating hyperactivity can be limited by the confines of our specialty.

The call for closer collaboration among psychologists, child psychiatrists, and educators who treat hyperactive children has increased dramatically over the past decade (e.g., Bennett & Sherman, 1983; Dulcan, 1986; Greenhill, 1989; Sandoval et al., 1981; Shaywitz & Shaywitz, 1984). Other specialists, such as those in child neurology, pediatrics, speech therapy, special education, and audiology, also should be considered as important contributors for selected children. In addition, we consider the parents of hyperactive children to be a valuable source of diagnostic information and active participants in the therapeutic process (Johnson & Katz, 1972). In this chapter, our use of the term *professional* includes parents.

The major advantage of a multidisciplinary approach is the ability of the treatment team to draw on its collective expertise in assessing the problem and developing an appropriate intervention. This is especially important considering the multitude of problems that hyperactive children typically display. A multidisciplinary approach broadens the perspective by focusing attention on a larger range of variables. This approach also lessens the likelihood that any one clinician will take on responsibilities for which they are poorly trained. In both cases, quality of care should be enhanced. According to this perspective, the hyperactive child's behavior is the result of a combination of interacting variables—some genetically and biochemically mediated, others in the external environment, and still others that are "person centered," such as the child's self-perception, attributional style, and expectations. All these factors need to be considered because they all affect what the child does.

We propose an ecobehavioral model that provides a comprehensive framework for assessing and treating hyperactivity and that also has heuristic value for future research. The ecobehavioral approach focuses on the study of individuals within their social and physical contexts and provides a methodology to describe the interactions and interrelationships that occur among individuals' behavior, their physical and social settings, and their internal state. It combines the concerns of ethologists and ecological psychologists with environment-behavior interrelationships (e.g., Barker, 1968) and the descriptive assessment strategies within the behavior analytic framework (Martens & Witt, 1988; Rogers-Warren & Warren, 1977). As eloquently stated by Bijou and Baer (1978),

The interaction between the child and the environment is continuous, reciprocal, and interdependent. We cannot analyze a child without reference to an environment, nor is it possible to analyze an environment without reference to a child. The two form an inseparable unit consisting of an interrelated set of variables, or an interactional field. (p. 29)

One of the assumptions of an ecobehavioral approach is that any one professional, regardless of discipline, can serve as the primary therapist or case manager. The major requirement is that this person be able to coordinate the duties of the different team members, and act as liaison with parents and professionals in an effective manner. Often this role will be filled by a psychologist or child psychiatrist because these professionals have traditionally been the ones who are given the task of diagnosing the problem and/or prescribing treatment. However, this need not be the case for all referrals.

A basic assumption of the ecobehavioral model is that hyperactivity is a multifaceted problem that defies explanation by any single theory of etiology. As a first step, any useful model must take into account environment-behavior interactions that are involved in the pathogenesis and maintenance of the disorder. The ecobehavioral model recognizes this interaction by emphasizing the study of individuals in an environmental context. Both the physical and social environment are assessed, as is the cognitive environment, because factors such as intelligence can have bearing on the problem. Furthermore, the ecobehavioral model provides a methodology for describing interactions that occur between person and situational variables (Singh & Aman, 1990). The former include cognitive and emotional factors (e.g., intellectual competencies, values, expectancies), while the latter include events in the external environment, such as ambient levels of distraction, consequences for positive and negative behavior, and modeling influences. Environment-behavior interactions can be viewed as setting events (Bijou & Baer, 1961; Singh & Repp, 1988; Wahler & Fox, 1981) and can be assessed through a multidisciplinary approach.

Assessment within an ecobehavioral model is multidisciplinary and requires the collaboration of child psychiatrists, psychologists, psychometricians, teachers, parents, school nurses, and professionals from related fields (e.g., language and speech pathologists, audiologists). The model encourages a comprehensive assessment of the problem. It eschews discipline-specific approaches in favor of multimethod approaches and provides a framework for synthesizing information from the different disciplines.

The initial assessment uses tools from various disciplines to construct a comprehensive data base— one that addresses the history of the disorder, antecedents, consequences, prior treatments, and family and school situation as well as other relevant variables that are thought to play a role in the child's behavior. For example, the child psychiatrist might be responsible for conducting a diagnostic interview and obtaining a thorough medical and family history. Similarly, the psychologist may be given the task of observing the child at home or school to obtain behavioral measures on which a functional analysis can be performed. The psychologist also is responsible for obtaining psychometric data (e.g., IQ and achievement test results) to confirm the diagnosis or identify other problems that the child may have. Such data can indicate the need for additional disorder-specific assessment, depending on the type of comorbidity suspected. Input from parents and teachers can be obtained through the use of rating scales or questionnaires that have been developed for that purpose (e.g., the Conner's Symptom Checklist or Child Behavior Checklist).

Once a diagnosis has been made and the particulars of the disorder have been described (e.g., severity, comorbidity), the case manager is responsible for initiating and coordinating a treatment plan. This is achieved in two ways, both of which can be carried out in the child's natural environment, using parents and teachers as the primary agents of change. First, by altering certain antecedent conditions (e.g., learning to provide clear and specific directives, making appropriate curricula changes, using reminders to prompt desired behavior, providing structured opportunities to "blow off steam"), the problem behaviors of many hyperactive children can be reduced to more manageable levels. In other cases, the consequences of the behavior may have to be modified. This can be done by selectively reinforcing

appropriate behavior or using a brief period of "time-out" when the child misbehaves. Sometimes it is helpful to link performance at school with reinforcers at home. This can be done by sending home daily "report cards" of the child's in-class behavior and having the parents provide consequences at home. One of the benefits of this approach is that reinforcement is relatively immediate and ongoing. The system also keeps parents informed of their child's academic progress while ensuring greater consistency in the way behavior is consequated in the two environments. Another useful though somewhat controversial technique (Abikoff, 1985) involves the use of cognitive interventions to enhance the child's self-control skills. There is ample evidence that methods such as these can be effective with many hyperactive children (Jones, Lattimore, Ulicny, & Risley, 1986; Schroeder, 1990). It is also noteworthy that they confer few risks or side effects and are compatible with pharmacological approaches should they be needed.

Children requiring assistance for multiple problems can be referred elsewhere (e.g., to an audiologist if a central auditory processing problem is suspected) or treated by the primary case manager. The choice to refer or not depends on the nature of the presenting problems and the expertise of the clinician. The format for treatment is the same regardless of the number of problems present: (a) a problem list and treatment priorities are established (Katz & Woolley, 1975); (b) each problem is assessed carefully so that controlling variables are identified; (c) an appropriate intervention is selected, which is based on empirical considerations about its efficacy for similar problems and subjects; and (d) the intervention is implemented and data are collected in an ongoing fashion so that the treatment's effectiveness can be monitored. This monitoring requires a reliable feedback system (e.g, direct behavioral observations or behavior ratings furnished by the child's caretakers) so that accountability is assured. Note that the ecobehavioral approach is neutral with respect to the type of therapy used or the person providing it. Psychological, educational, and pharmacological treatments fit into the model equally well.

As noted above, the ecobehavioral model involves training parents and teachers in behavior management techniques, particularly the use of antecedent manipulations and positive reinforcement practices. Given the limited knowledge of most teachers about the effects and side effects of stimulant medication (Singh, Epstein, Leubke, & Singh, 1990), it may be instructive to provide them with training on this topic as well. In addition, teachers should be informed about how their interactional patterns can affect the child's behavior (Whalen, Henker, & Dotemoto, 1980), and how medication may change the dynamics of those interactions (Abikoff & Gittelman, 1985). The way that the child's caretakers perceive alternative approaches can affect treatment outcome (Reimers, Wacker, & Koeppl, 1987). In the ecobehavioral model, professionals not only measure this aspect of caretakers, but may have to modify it through appropriate educational experiences (Singh & Katz, 1985).

Summary

This overview has shown how professionals from different disciplines can come together to provide more comprehensive care for children with hyperactivity. The model does not emphasize one discipline or professional over another; instead, it uses the child's clinical needs as the basis for determining what type of assessment and treatment modalities are appropriate. To be effective, this approach requires the active collaboration of professionals from different disciplines, and in the following sections, we discuss how this may be achieved.

ASSESSMENT

In the ecobehavioral model, assessment of the hyperactive child is not discipline specific because the emphasis is always on obtaining a broad range of data from different sources of information to provide a comprehensive picture of the child and his environment. While the emphasis is on the type of data collected rather than by whom, there are numerous tests and assessments that are usually undertaken by certain professionals because of their formal training and clinical experience in their specialties. In this respect, the model recognizes and, indeed, capitalizes on the strengths of clinicians representing

different disciplines. Thus, the ecobehavioral model not only encourages interdisciplinary treatment, but also provides a framework in which it can occur. What follows is a description of the roles and types of assessment that various professionals may perform.

Child Psychiatrist

The child psychiatrist combines an expertise in diagnosing psychiatric illness with medical knowledge of associated physical disorders that, if present, may cause or exacerbate existing behavior problems. This professional serves as a facilitator and conduit for obtaining the requisite medical, ecobehavioral, and psychological information on the child.

The cornerstone in the psychiatric assessment of children with hyperactivity is the clinical interview. A detailed history, including developmental, medical, social, educational, and both psychosocial and genetic family history, is obtained from the parents at the initial diagnostic interview. In addition, the parents are asked specific questions about any accompanying psychiatric disorder their child may have (e.g., oppositional-defiant disorder, specific learning problems, anxiety and affective disorders, conduct disorder).

Psychologist

The psychologist is responsible for obtaining information about the child from a number of sources. In addition to direct observations and psychological testing, the psychologist obtains relevant information from the child's teachers and parents through a behavioral interview. Information obtained from this interview may or may not contribute directly to treatment, but it still can serve a number of useful functions. For example, it can increase the team's understanding of how certain behavior problems (e.g., aggressiveness) began and the psychosocial variables (e.g., modeling influences) that help to maintain them. It also can help to identify conditions under which problem behaviors may reappear after successful intervention; this information, in turn, can be used to prevent a relapse from occurring. Since treatment effects may be mediated by the resiliency and intelligence of the child, as well as the expectations and compliance of the parents, these issues also should be addressed by the psychologist (Henker & Whalen, 1989; Rapport, 1983).

Direct observations of behavior provide a useful means of assessing the child's behavior at school. Results can be interpreted by comparison with non-hyperactive peers, using the so-called social comparison method, which provides a valid means of gauging problem severity and determining whether treatment is having its intended effect (Kazdin, 1982). The Code for Instructional Structure and Student Academic Response (Hall, Delquadri, Greenwood, & Thurston, 1982) can be used for in-class observations on five major categories of ecological variables: activity, task, teaching structure, teacher position, and teacher activity. This does not preclude the use of other ecologically valid variables, such as peer-based codes (see Singh & Aman, 1990).

Alternative observation systems include the Classroom Observation Code, which is a reliable tool for differentiating hyperactive from normal children (Abikoff, Gittelman, & Klein, 1980), and computer-based observational systems that can be used to collect ecobehavioral data on as many as 40 variables at a time (see Repp, Karsh, Van Acker, Felce, & Harman, 1989).

The psychologist is also responsible for undertaking a functional analysis of the child's problem behaviors to ascertain whether they are environmentally determined (and thus in need of behavioral programming), or intrinsically motivated (and thus in need of pharmacotherapy) (see Singh & Repp, 1988). There are three strategies for performing a functional analysis: (a) behavioral interviews with the child and his caretakers; (b) direct observations of behavior in the natural environment; and (c) systematically manipulating the child's environment to see whether it produces predictable effects on behavior (O'Neill, Horner, Albin, Storey, & Sprague, 1990).

Standardized psychological tests and rating scales provide another means of assessing the hyperactive child's behavior, intelligence, and academic achievement in comparison to normative peers. Hyperactive children usually are rated at least two standard deviations from the mean for their age on the various screening scales used by psychologists. Rating scales assist the psychologist in diagnosing hyperactivity and in ruling out overlapping conditions, such as intellectual deficits, specific learning problems, and conduct disorder.

The psychologist also conducts a number of tests to assess the core features of hyperactivity. These tests include the Continuous Performance Task (Rosvold, Mirsky, Sarason, Bransome, & Beck, 1956), a vigilance-type test usually employed as an index of sustained attention in hyperactive children, and the Matching Familiar Figures Test (Kagan, 1965), which deals with aspects of visual perception and measures impulsivity. Other tests for cognitive functioning may be used depending on the characteristics of the child (Swanson, 1985).

Parents

For obvious reasons, parents are one of the most important sources of information on the child. Both the child psychiatrist and the psychologist will probably have direct contact with one or both parents. As noted above, one of the child psychiatrist's tasks is to conduct a detailed interview with the parents. In addition, parents may be asked to complete any of several rating scales, including (a) the SNAP Rating Scale (Atkins, Pelham, & Licht, 1985) or the Parent Symptom Questionnaire (Conners, 1973) to assist in the diagnosis of hyperactivity; (b) the Home Situations Questionnaire (Barkley, 1981a), which assesses the child's behavior at home; (c) the Child Behavior Checklist (Achenbach & Edelbrock, 1986a), which provides a more general profile of psychopathology and social competence; (d) the Treatment Evaluation Inventory (Kazdin, 1980), which is used to provide a measure of the parents' views of the acceptability of alternative treatments; and (e) perhaps the Parenting Stress Index (Abdin, 1986) to provide an indication of the coping ability of the parent.

Educators

Because a child's hyperactivity may be situation specific (Sleator, 1982; Sleator & Ullmann, 1981), it is important to consult with the teacher to assess the extent of the problem in school. Rating scales have been developed for this purpose and include (a) A Comprehensive Teacher Rating Scale (ACTeRS) used for the diagnosis of hyperactivity (Ullmann, Sleator, & Sprague, 1984); (b) the Abbreviated Conners Teacher Rating Scale (ACTRS) used for assessing the presence and severity of hyperactivity (Werry, Sprague, & Cohen, 1975); (c) the Teacher Report form of the Child Behavior Checklist (Achenbach & Edelbrock, 1986b); and (d) the teachers' version of the Treatment Evaluation Inventory (Kazdin, 1980). In addition, the teacher can provide useful information about auditory, language and other secondary problems from the child's files at school.

Summary

Many hyperactive children have multiple problems for which comprehensive assessment is required. In the ecobehavioral model, a multimethod approach is used to identify areas in need of treatment, to gauge problem severity, and to assess controlling variables. Among the assessment methods commonly used are standardized psychological tests, rating scales, and direct behavioral observations. These can be used to measure different aspects of the child's attention, cognition, self-control, and behavior in different situations. Because the role of setting events or contextual factors is pivotal in an ecobehavioral model, some measure of social context at home is included in the assessment battery. Measures of parental stress and family cohesiveness also may be appropriate.

DIFFERENTIAL DIAGNOSIS

A diagnosis of hyperactivity can be made from the assessment data provided by the various disciplines and collated by the child's primary clinician. One of several diagnostic schemes, such as the DSM-III-R or the ICD-9, can be used as the basis for arriving at a decision. The DSM-III-R provides two subtypes of attention deficit disorder: those with attention difficulties only (attention deficit disorder [ADD]), and those with concomitant hyperactivity (attention deficit hyperactivity disorder [ADHD]). In addition, it has provision for multiple diagnoses if a child with ADHD has a comorbid conduct disorder, oppositional disorder, or one of the specific developmental disorders. Furthermore, if the child has a complicating medical condition such as epilepsy, this can be included as an Axis III diagnosis in the multiaxial system.

The DSM-III-R criteria for diagnosing a child with ADHD are not very specific, and only moderate correlations between raters have been obtained (Rapoport & Ismond, 1984). However, clinicians and researchers may wish to use the more stringent criteria advanced by Barkley (1981b), which can provide for greater reliability between raters. In addition, Rapport (1983) has added two further criteria to Barkley's six to make this a comprehensive diagnostic system.

There is provision in the ecobehavioral model for the diagnosis of children with ADHD alone and for those with comorbid disorders. It is recognized that ADHD children with comorbid disorders well may be different with respect to the course of their disorder, response to various treatments, and long-term outcome (Biederman, Munir, & Knee, 1987a; Gittelman, Mannuzza, Shenker, & Bonagura, 1985; Hechtman, 1989). Thus, differential diagnosis of the more common subtypes of ADHD children is required before informed treatment decisions can be made. This may require further assessment by a number of professionals to differentially diagnose overlapping disorders.

A number of childhood disorders are either similar to or co-occur with ADHD (Rapport, 1987), including anxiety disorder, adjustment disorders (adjustment disorder with anxious mood, adjustment disorder with academic inhibition), disorder of behavior (e.g., conduct disorder, oppositional disorder, childhood antisocial behavior), and supplementary conditions (e.g., parent-child problem, family circumstances). In the following sections we consider a few of these as examples of the methods that can be used in the differential diagnosis of hyperactivity.

ADHD without Associated Disorders

In a sample of 108 children aged 5 to 12 years, Reeves, Werry, Elkind, and Zametkin (1987) found that 36% of them had a diagnosis of ADHD without associated disorder, or "pure" ADHD (Milich, Loney, & Landau, 1982). The diagnosis of pure ADHD children is by exclusion; it is dependent on the absence of any comorbid psychiatric disorder in children who meet the DSM-III-R criteria for ADHD. Usually, the background of such children lacks the family disharmony frequently seen in the families of ADHD children with comorbid disorders (Reeves et al., 1987; Taylor, 1985). As noted elsewhere, the majority of ADHD children have co-occurring psychiatric disorders that must be ruled out before a child can be classified as having a diagnosis of "pure" ADHD.

ADHD with Learning Disabilities

The research literature indicates that learning disabilities co-occur with much greater frequency in children with ADHD than in the general population (Ackerman, Dykman, & Oglesby, 1983; Carparulo et al., 1981). Some researchers have estimated that between 50% and 80% (Lambert & Sandoval, 1980; Safer & Allen, 1976) of hyperactive children experience some type of learning disability. While these estimates may be somewhat high, it is clear that there are distinct subgroups of ADHD children—those who exhibit learning disabilities and those who do not (August & Holmes, 1984).

The intelligence and achievement test scores of the ADHD child should indicate whether there is a severe ability-achievement discrepancy indicative of learning disabilities as defined in Public Law 94-142 (Kavale & Forness, 1992; U.S. Office of Education, 1977). If this indication exists, further tests may be needed, depending on the child's intelligence and patterns of cognitive efficiency rather than on any pattern of scores on specific tests. Researchers and clinicians should be wary of the commonly used ACID pattern on the WISC-R (low scores on arithmetic, coding, information, and digit span) as indicative of learning disabilities because no unique WISC-R patterns have been found that differentiate between learning disabled and normal populations (Kavale & Forness, 1984).

Barkley (1981c) has presented a system for assessing learning disabilities that appears to be practical and effective. His system requires four levels of assessment: *developmental-cognitive processes* (e.g., verbal-linguistic, visual-spatial-constructional, sequential-analytic, planning processes; reading written expression, mathematics, and spelling); *community task demands* (e.g., demands being placed on the child by his or her school teacher, family, and the community at large); *social context and interactions* (e.g., the effects of the child's cognitive deficits and academic failure on significant others in his or her social settings); and *transactional effects over time* (e.g., how the above variables have interacted over time to affect the child's current array of cognitive, behavioral, emotional, and social difficulties). Specific assessment instruments that can be used for this purpose are presented by Sattler (1988). A collaboration of the teachers and school psychologist of psychometrician would be required to provide the data on which to base a diagnosis of learning disability in children with ADHD.

ADHD with Conduct Disorder

Current estimates of the co-occurrence of ADHD and conduct disorder among clinic-referred samples range from 41% to 75% (Loney & Milich, 1982; Sandberg, Wiesel, & Shaffer, 1980; Stewart, Cummings, Singer, & DeBlois, 1981). When compared to children with "pure" ADHD, those with ADHD and conduct disorder appear to be more antisocial and more egocentric. A recent study (Reeves et al., 1987) reported that ADHD children with and without comorbid conduct/oppositional disorder are more alike than different on a number of variables, including age of onset and presentation, frequency of perinatal insults, psychosocial stress, and impairment in cognition and achievement. However, the latter group of children had a higher occurrence of severe adverse family backgrounds and showed greater deficits in social functioning.

Much of the data needed for a diagnosis of coexisting conduct disorder will be available from the initial psychiatric interview and the data obtained by the psychologist. At times, older children with comorbid conduct disorder are referred through the juvenile courts because of legal violations or out-of-control behavior. A functional analysis of the child's behavior, through interviews or direct behavioral observations (O'Neill et al., 1990), and information from the teacher and parent version of the Child Behavior Checklist, provide a substantial data base for this purpose. If needed, supplementary data can be obtained from rating scales that have factors corresponding to conduct disorder; examples include the Behavior Problem Checklist (Quay & Peterson, 1983), the Parent Attitude Test (Cowen, Huser, Beach, & Rapoport, 1970), and the Walker Problem Behavior Identification Checklist (Walker, 1970). Other rating scales that include dimensions of behavior encompassing conduct disorder are also available (see Hammil, Brown, & Bryant, 1989; Sattler, 1988) and can be used for this purpose. A collaboration of the school psychologist, teachers, and parents is usually needed to collect all the pertinent data relating to a comorbid conduct disorder in a child with ADHD.

ADHD with CNS Disorders

Between 3% and 5% of school-age children (Rapport, 1983), or approximately one child in every classroom (Barkley, 1981a), has ADHD. Statistics on how many of these children have a comorbid neurological disorder or how many children with a neurological disorder are also hyperactive are unavailable. Furthermore, the results of longitudinal outcome studies do not partial out of the group the hyperactives who also have a neurological disorder.

Assessment of the child with ADHD and a suspected or diagnosed central nervous system disorder must begin with a full pediatric and/or child neurological examination, as well as a number of laboratory and neuroradiological tests, to clarify the diagnosis. Comorbid disorders, such as epilepsy, require anticonvulsant medication and careful monitoring. Neurobehavioral disorders following head injury require extensive rehabilitative services and often need to be supplemented by neuropsychopharmacological agents (Parmelee & O'Shanick, 1987). The clinician evaluating the child for ADHD must work closely with the physician designated to

assess the child medically, and enlist his or her active collaboration in treatment planning.

ADHD with Mood Disorders

There are two groups of mood disorders that are sometimes seen in children: bipolar disorder and depressive disorders. Although the psychiatric literature is replete with studies of adults with bipolar disorder, there have been only a handful of studies of children with this condition. So far, it appears that many features of the childhood presentation are similar (Carlson, 1983; Dwyer & DeLong, 1987). The essential feature of bipolar disorder is the presence of one or more manic or hypomanic episodes, usually with a history of depressive episodes. In children, the "cycling" appears to be much briefer than in adults (Carlson, 1983). The essential feature of depressive disorders is one or more periods of depression without a manic or hypomanic period. In children with depression, there are more somatic complaints, psychomotor agitation, and mood-congruent hallucinations than in adults with depression. Adolescents who are depressed may display negative or frank antisocial behavior, abuse drugs and alcohol, and do poorly at school. Frequently, there is a family history of significant depression. This finding of mood disorders in first- and second-degree relatives of depressed children also has been found in relatives of children with ADHD (Biederman, Munir, & Knee, 1987b).

Assessment of the child or adolescent with ADHD and a suspected mood disorder includes detailed family, developmental, and primary complaint history. The clinical interview can be supplemented by the use of rating scales such as the Child Depression Inventory or the Beck Depression Inventory (Kazdin & Petti, 1982). Unlike other comorbid disorders, this one may require the clinician to evaluate posthaste the presence of suicide risk.

ADHD with Mental Retardation

The WISC-R scores from the initial assessment will indicate whether the ADHD child falls within the normal range of intelligence. If a score of 70 or lower is obtained, the possibility that the child is mentally retarded must be considered, along with the implications of the diagnosis for school placement and long-range planning. Mental retardation is defined as "significantly subaverage general intellectual functioning resulting in or associated with concurrent impairments in adaptive behavior and manifested during the developmental period" (Grossman, 1983).

Other tests may be needed to assess the child's adaptive behaviors, and the American Association on Mental Deficiency (AAMD) Adaptive Behavior Scale (Nihira, Foster, Shellhaas, & Leland, 1974) or the Vineland Adaptive Behavior Scale (Sparrow, Balla, & Cicchetti, 1984) can be used for this purpose. Information on the child's adaptive behavior is obtained from the teacher, direct-care staff, and family members. In addition, to meet the diagnostic criteria for mental retardation in both the AAMD (Grossman, 1983) and DSM-III-R (APA, 1987) classification systems, it must be established that the onset of the intellectual deficiency occurred before the age of 18. If it was later than that, the syndrome is called dementia instead (APA, 1987). The level of retardation (mild, moderate, severe, profound) is determined on the basis of intelligence test scores and adaptive behavior. For assessment and evaluation of treatment, the Aberrant Behavior Checklist (Aman & Singh, 1986) can be used to provide a measure of the child's problem behaviors across five factors. Unless the child is severely retarded, the combined efforts of parents, psychologist of psychometrician, teachers and/or direct-care staff may be needed to collect all the data on which a diagnosis of mental retardation is made.

Summary

The differential diagnosis of ADHD children with and without comorbid disorders can be difficult in the absence of a comprehensive assessment. Differential diagnosis is made more difficult when ADHD children present several overlapping disorders, such as learning disabilities, conduct disorder, and affective disorders. However, it is essential that the various subgroups of ADHD children be identified because of the differing effects of their comorbidity on subsequent adjustment and response to treatment. The need for comprehensive assessment and treatment of these children underscores the importance of close collaboration between disciplines.

TREATMENT

The treatment of choice in this model is eco-behavioral. It follows logically from a functional analysis in which problem behaviors are identified and hypotheses advanced about their controlling variables. Treatment often is implemented in the child's natural environment by parents and/or teachers who are under the direction of the primary therapist. The primary goal of treatment is to bring the hyperactive child's behavior in line with that of nondeviant peers so that the two are indistinguishable. A social comparison method (Kazdin, 1982; Wolf, 1978) is the main criterion on which the efficacy of treatment is judged. This approach is advocated for hyperactive children whether or not comorbidity is present.

Behavior modification procedures can be used to reduce behavioral excesses (e.g., aggressiveness, temper tantrums) and to remedy deficits in both academic and social behavior. One method is called the keystone behavior approach (Wahler, 1975) because the behavior(s) selected for modification is designed to have beneficial effects that are generalized rather than response-specific. For example, if compliance with parental requests is selected as the keystone behavior, one would expect to see a reduction in noncompliance and argumentativeness, as well as a general improvement in parent-child relationships.

Reductions in hyperactive behavior at school can be brought about by manipulation of both antecedent and consequent events. At the antecedent end, changes in curricula, seating arrangements, and the way in which the teacher gives directives or reprimands can have dramatic effects on how hyperactive children behave (Greenwood, Delquadri, Stanley, Terry, & Hall, 1985). Researchers also have investigated the effects of other variables, including easy versus difficult learning materials, self-paced versus other-paced activities, as well as the amount of ambient (Whalen, Collins, Henker, Alkus, Adams, & Stapp, 1978; Whalen, Henker, Collins, Fink, & Dotemoto, 1979) and within-task stimulation (Radosh & Gittelman, 1981; Zentall, Zentall & Booth, 1978).

On a more molar level, the amount of structure in the classroom has been shown to be a relevant variable. Generally speaking, and in some way contrary to expectation, hyperactive children may do better in a classroom that is relatively open and unstructured (Flynn & Rapoport, 1976; Jacob, O'Leary & Rosenbald, 1978).

Some of the problem behaviors of hyperactive children also can be reduced by training parents and teachers to manipulate consequent events (e.g., rewards, loss of privileges, time-out, token economy systems). This method is particularly helpful in undercontrolled behaviors such as impulsiveness, tantrums, and aggressiveness. The large body of literature on parent training and contingency management approaches has been summarized by other investigators (see Barkley, 1985; Rapport, 1983; Schaughency, Walker, & Lahey, 1988). Dulcan (1986) recommends that caretakers use precise instructions and frequent reminders to avoid misunderstandings on the part of the child. Intervention programs generally work best when positive reinforcers are used in combination with mild negative feedback, such as "soft" reprimands or brief time-out.

The majority of hyperactive children, and indirectly their caretakers and peers, will probably benefit from the aforementioned approaches. Nonetheless, the behavior of some hyperactive children will be refractory to change, or the benefits derived may not be sufficient for the child to function adequately in most situations. In this case, alternative therapies need to be explored, especially pharmacotherapy.

ADHD without Associated Disorders

This group of children usually respond to stimulant medications (Taylor, 1983). However, it is generally recommended that drug therapy be used as an adjunct to psychological and educational interventions (Gadow, 1988).

ADHD with Learning Disabilities

Many of the undercontrolled distractibility and social skill problems of children with concurrent ADHD and learning disabilities can be controlled through the ecobehavioral approach. However, supplemental interventions may be required for specific adademic weaknesses (Singh & Beale, 1992). In some cases, academic problems are the result of poor teaching or motivational deficits rather than underlying disorders, a situation that should be evident if a careful assessment was performed. Under those circumstances, the use of a behavioral treatment model is indicated (Singh & Beale, 1988; Singh, Beale, & Snell, 1988). Learning disabled children seldom require drug treatment in the absence of other psychiatric disorders or specific symptoms (Aman & Rojahn, 1992). Collaboration of behavioral specialists, teachers, and parents is a crucial ingredient for success with these children because much depends on the consistency and continuity of the treatment they receive. A physician should be involved if a determination is made that pharmacological intervention is needed to augment other approaches.

ADHD with Conduct Disorder

At present there are no clear guidelines for the pharmacological treatment of children with a combined ADHD and conduct disorder (Biederman & Steingard, 1989). A trial of stimulant medication may be useful in reducing the impulsiveness and motor restlessness of these children while increasing their responsiveness to verbal instructions. Although lithium carbonate and thioridazine are reported to be effective in controlling the aggressiveness of some children with conduct disorder (Campbell & Spencer, 1988), there are few data to support their use with hyperactive children who have an overlay of conduct problems (DeLong & Aldershof, 1987). Whenever medications are used, it is important that the treating child psychiatrist and the child's teachers and parents work closely together to ensure that the medications are properly administered and the desired effects are achieved. More often than not, these children do best when their parents and teachers have been carefully trained in behavior management techniques. Provision of positive role models through social reprogramming, as well as training in social skills, self-control, and problem-solving strategies also can produce beneficial results with this population (Dumas, 1989).

ADHD with CNS Disorders

Treatment planning for children with ADHD and comorbid central nervous system disorders involves considerable coordination with and between physicians. Probably the most frequently occurring comorbid disorder is epilepsy and, when it is present, great care must be taken to ensure that the most appropriate anticonvulsant is used and its effects are carefully monitored. Before the widespread use of carbamazepine, phenytoin and phenobarbital were the most commonly used anticonvulsants for children, with phenobarbital often causing a number of behavioral changes, including greater impulsivity, distractibility, and hyperkinesis. Since it is suspected that intellectual deterioration may occur with long-term use of phenytoin and phenobarbital (Stores, 1988), many child neurologists have switched to carbamazepine instead. When monitored properly, the negative side effects of this drug are few (Pellock, 1986; Thompson & Trimble, 1982). If a stimulant is recommended for the symptoms of ADHD, there are few, if any, contraindications to the child's being on an anticonvulsant. However, if a tricyclic is recommended, caution is advised as there may be a lowering of seizure threshold when higher doses are used. Other neurological disorders, such as post-traumatic head injury or postencephalitic conditions, do not pose a problem when stimulants are used to reduce the hyperactive features that may occur as sequelae to these insults. Often, however, the symptoms associated with these conditions require extensive behavioral rehabilitation, multiple medication trials, and sometimes the concomitant use of one or more psychotropic drugs (O'Shanick & Parmelee, 1989; Parmelee & O'Shanick, 1987). As before, this treatment requires close collaboration between the prescribing physicians (child psychiatrists and child neurologists) and those who can monitor the child's behavior on a regular basis.

ADHD with Mood Disorders

Effective treatment for children with ADHD and a comorbid mood disorder entails one or more of the psychotherapies (individual, group, family) and pharmacological intervention, although the literature on effective treatment of mood disorders in children is controversial. In general, a child psychiatrist should evaluate the child and monitor the use of whichever antidepressant medication is chosen. In some children with ADHD, a tricyclic antidepressant helps to reduce hyperactive symptoms and may be effective for the comorbid mood disorder as well (Biederman, Baldessarini, & Wright, 1989). A child with an accompanying bipolar illness is best treated with a combination of lithium carbonate and stimulant medication. Close monitoring by the treating physician is essential under these circumstances.

ADHD with Mental Retardation

Mental retardation is first and foremost characterized by generalized behavioral deficits in the social, cognitive, and behavioral domains. The majority of children with co-occurring mental retardation and ADHD can be treated successfully with the ecobehavioral model. However, a small percentage of them may require other treatments, chiefly pharmacological. Children with a dual diagnosis of mental retardation and mental illness may require medication for specific disorders such as schizophrenia or depression (Menolascino & Stark, 1984; Singh, Sood, & Soneklar, 1991). In addition, children with intractable behavior problems that fail to respond to behavioral approaches may require adjunctive medications (Aman & Singh, 1988; Singh & Winton, 1989). Under these conditons, efforts should always be made to facilitate collaboration among the treating child psychiatrist, clinical pharmacist, psychologist, parents, direct-care staff, and teachers.

Summary

The ecobehavioral approach is a system for providing comprehensive care. It is highly appropriate for treating hyperactive children because so many of these children have multiple problems which require broad-based interventions that go beyond the expertise of any single clinician or discipline. The ecobehavioral model is atheoretical and makes no assumptions about etiology or preferred methods of treatment. Psychological and pharmacological interventions fit equally well within the system when used independently or in combination. Its main advantage is that it provides a framework for integrating care around the identified needs of the patient and ensures better accountability. When the ecobehavioral model is used, the child's parents and teachers become an integral part of the treatment team. This enables therapy to be given on a continuous basis and allows its effects to be carefully monitored in the child's natural environment. Generalization and maintenance of treatment effects are enhanced because therapy is not limited to any particular environment or individual. Although the ecobehavioral model is appropriate for treating hyperactive children with or without comorbid psychiatric disorders, its value increases with the complexity of the case and the need for multiple interventions.

REFERENCES

Abidin, R. (1986). *Parenting stress index*. Charlottesville, VA: Pediatric Psychology Press, University of Virginia.

Abikoff, H. (1985). Efficacy of cognitive training interventions in hyperactive children: A critical review. *Clinical Psychology Review, 5*, 479–512.

Abikoff, H., & Gittelman, R. (1985). The normalizing effects of methylphenidate on classroom behavior of ADDH children. *Journal of Abnormal Child Psychology, 13*, 33–44.

Abikoff, H., Gittelman, R., & Klein, D. F. (1980). Classroom observation code for hyperactive children: A replication study. *Journal of Consulting and Clinical Psychology, 48*, 555–565.

Achenbach, T. M., & Edelbrock, C. S. (1986a). *Child behavior checklist and youth self-report*. Burlington, VT: Author.

Achenbach, T. M., & Edelbrock, C. S. (1986b). *Teacher's report form*. Burlington, VT: Author.

Ackerman, D. T., Dykman, R. A., & Oglesby, D. M. (1983). Sex and group differences in reading and attention deficit disordered children with and without hyperkinesis. *Journal of Learning Disabilities, 16*, 407–415.

Aman, M. G., & Rojahn, J. (1992). Pharmacological intervention. In N. N. Singh, & I. L. Beale (Eds.), *Learning disabilities: Nature, theory, and treatment* (pp. 478–525). New York: Springer-Verlag.

Aman, M. G., & Singh, N. N. (1983). Specific reading disorders: Concepts of etiology reconsidered. In K. D. Gadow & I. Bialer (Eds.), *Advances in learning and behavioral disabilities* (Vol. 2, pp. 1–47). Greenwich, CT: JAI Press.

Aman, M. G., & Singh, N. N. (1986). *Aberrant behavior checklist*. New York: Slosson Educational Publications.

Aman, M. G., & Singh, N. N. (1988). *Psychopharmacology of the developmental disabilities*. New York: Springer-Verlag.

American Psychiatric Associaton (1987). *Diagnostic and statistical manual of mental disorders* (3rd ed. rev.). Washington, DC: Author.

Anastopoulos, A. D., & Barkley, R. A. (1988). Biological factors in attention deficit hyperactivity disorder. *The Behavior Therapist, 11*, 47–53.

Atkins, M. S., Pelham, W. E., & Licht, M. H. (1985). A comparison of objective classroom measures and teacher ratings of attention deficit disorder. *Journal of Abnormal Child Psychology, 13*, 155–167.

August, G. J., & Garfinkel, B. D. (1989). Behavioral and cognitive subtypes of ADHD. *Journal of the American Academy of Child and Adolescent Psychiatry, 28*, 739–748.

August, G. J., & Holmes, C. S. (1984). Behavior and academic achievement in hyperactive subgroups and learning-disabled boys: A six-year followup. *American Journal of Disease in Children, 138*, 1025–1029.

Barker, R. G. (1968). *Ecological psychology*. Stanford, CA: Stanford University Press.

Barkley, R. A. (1981a). *Hyperactive children: A handbook for diagnosis and treatment*. New York: Guilford Press.

Barkley, R. A. (1981b). Hyperactivity. In E. J. Mash & L. G. Terdal (Eds.), *Behavioral assessment of childhood disorders* (pp. 441–482). New York: John Wiley & Sons.

Barkley, R. A. (1981c). Learning disabilities. In E. J. Mash & L. G. Terdal (Eds.), *Behavioral assessment of childhood disorders* (pp. 441–482). New York: John Wiley & Sons.

Barkley, R. A. (1985). Attention deficit disorders. In P. H. Bornstein & A. E. Kazdin (Eds.) *Handbook of clinical behavior therpay with children* (pp. 158–217). Homewood, IL: Dorsey Press.

Bennett, F. C., & Sherman, R. (1983). Management of childhood "hyperactivity" by primary care physicians. *Journal of Developmental and Behavioral Pediatrics, 4*, 88–93.

Biederman, J., Baldessarini, R. J., & Wright, V. (1989). A double-blind placebo controlled study of desipramine in the treatment of ADD: I. Efficacy. *Journal of the American Academy of Child and Adolescent Psychiatry, 28*, 777–784.

Biederman, J., Munir, K., & Knee, D. (1987a). Conduct and oppositional disorder in clinically referred children with attention deficit disorder: A controlled family study. *Journal of the American Academy of Child and Adolescent Psychiatry, 26,* 724–727.

Biederman, J., Munir, K., & Knee, D. (1987b). High rate of affective disorders in probands with attention deficit disorder: A controlled family study. *American Journal of Psychiatry, 144,* 330–333.

Biederman, J., & Steingard, R. D. (1989). Attention deficit hyperactivity disorder in adolescents. *Psychiatric Annals, 19,* 587–596.

Bijou, S. W., & Baer, D. M. (1961). *Child development: A systematic and empirical theory.* Englewood Cliffs, NJ: Prentice-Hall.

Bijou, S. W., & Baer, D. M. (1978). *Behavior analysis of child development.* Englewood Cliffs, NJ: Prentice-Hall.

Campbell, M., & Spencer, K. (1988). Psychopharmacology in child and adolescent psychiatry: A review of the past five years. *Journal of the American Academy of Child and Adolescent Psychiatry, 27,* 269–279.

Cantwell, D. P., & Baker, L. (1989). Stability and natural history of DSM-III childhood diagnoses. *Journal of the American Academy of Child and Adolescent Psychiatry, 28,* 691–700.

Carlson, G. (1983). Bipolar affective disorders in childhood and adolescence. In D. P. Cantwell & G. A. Carlson (Eds.), *Affective disorders in childhood and adolescence: An update* (pp. 61–83). Jamaica, NY: Spectrum Publications.

Carlson, G., & Rapport, M. (1989). Diagnostic classification issues in attention deficit hyperactivity disorder. *Psychiatric Annals, 19,* 576–583.

Carparulo, B. K., Cohen, D. J., Rothman, S. L., Young, J. G., Katz, J. D., Shaywitz, S. E., & Shaywitz, B. A. (1981). Computed tomographic brain scanning in children with neuropsychiatric disorders. *Journal of the American Academy of Child and Adolescent Psychiatry, 20,* 338–357.

Conners, C. K. (1973). Rating scales for use in drug studies in children. *Psychopharmacology Bulletin* [Special issue: Pharmacotherapy with children] 24–29.

Cowen, E. L., Huser, J., Beach, D. R., & Rapoport, J. (1970). Parental perceptions of young children and their relations to indexes of adjustment. *Journal of Consulting and Clinical Psychology, 34,* 97–103.

DeLong, G. R., & Aldershof, A. L. (1987). Long term experience with lithium treatment in childhood: Correlation with diagnosis. *Journal of the American Academy of Child and Adolescent Psychiatry, 26,* 389–395.

Drager, S., Prior, M., & Sanson, A. (1986). Visual and auditory attention performance in hyperactive children: Competence or compliance. *Journal of Abnormal Child Psychology, 14,* 411–424.

Dulcan, M. (1986). Comprehensive treatment of children and adolescents with attention deficit disorders: The state of the art. *Clinical Psychology Review, 6,* 539–569.

Dumas, J. (1989). Treating antisocial behavior in children: Child and family approaches. *Clinical Psychology Review, 9,* 197–222.

Dwyer, J. T., & DeLong, G. R. (1987). A family history study of twenty probands with childhood manic-depressive illness. *Journal of the American Academy of Child and Adolescent Psychiatry, 26,* 176–180.

Flynn, N. M., & Rapoport, J. L. (1976). Hyperactivity in open and traditional classroom environments. *Journal of Special Education, 10,* 286–290.

Gadow, K. D. (1988). Attention deficit disorder and hyperactivity: Pharmacotherapies. In J. L. Matson (Ed.), *Handbook of treatment approaches in childhood psychopathology* (pp. 215–247). New York: Plenum Publishing.

Gittelman, R., Mannuzza, S., Shenker, R., & Bonagura, N. (1985). Hyperactive boys almost grown up. *Archives of General Psychiatry, 42,* 937–947.

Greenhill, L. (1989). Treatment issues in children with attention deficit hyperactivity disorder. *Psychiatric Annals, 19,* 604–613.

Greenwood, C. R., Delquadri, J. C., Stanley, S. O., Terry, B., & Hall, R. V. (1985). Assessment of ecobehavioral interaction in school settings. *Behavioral Assessment, 7,* 331–347.

Grossman, H. J. (1983). *Classification in mental retardation.* Washington, DC: American Association on Mental Deficiency.

Hall, R. V., Delquadri, J., Greenwood, C. R., & Thurston, L. (1982). The importance of opportunity to respond in children's academic success. In D. Edgar, N. Haring, J. Jenkins, & C. Pious (Eds.), *Serving young handicapped children: Issues and research.* Baltimore, MD: University Park Press.

Hammil, D. O., Brown, L., & Bryant, B. R. (1989). *A consumer's guide to test in print.* Austin, TX: Pro-Ed.

Heavilon, J. C. (1980). A critical evaluation of treatment modalities for hyperkinesis in children. *Doctoral Abstracts International, 41,* 1915–1916B.

Hechtman, L. (1989). Attention deficit hyperactivity disorder in adolescence and adulthood: An updated follow-up. *Psychiatric Annals, 19,* 597–603.

Hechtman, L., & Weiss, G. (1983). Long-term outcome of hyperactive children. *American Journal of Orthopsychiatry, 53,* 378–389.

Hechtman, L., Weiss, G., Finklestein, J., Werner, A., & Benn, R. (1976). Hyperactives as young adults: Preliminary report. *Canadian Medical Journal, 115,* 625–630.

Hechtman, L., Weiss, G., & Perlman, T. (1984). Young adult outcome of hyperactive children who received long-term stimulant treatment. *Journal of the American Academy of Child Psychiatry, 23,* 261–269.

Henker, B., & Whalen, C. (1989). Hyperactivity and attention deficits. *American Psychologist, 44,* 216–223.

Jacob, R. G., O'Leary, K. D., & Rosenbald, C. (1978). Formal and informal classroom settngs: Effects on hyperactivity. *Journal of Abnormal Child Psychology, 6,* 47–59.

Johnson, C., & Katz, R. C. (1972). Using parents as change agents for their children: A review. *Journal of Child Psychology and Psychiatry, 14,* 181–200.

Jones, M. L., Lattimore, J., Ulicny, G. R., & Risley, T. R. (1986). Ecobehavioral design: Programming for engagement. In R. P. Barrett (Ed.), *Severe behavior disorders in the mentally retarded: Nondrug approaches to treatment* (pp. 123–155). New York: Plenum Publishing.

Kagan, J. (1965). Reflection-impulsivity and reading ability in primary grade children. *Child Development, 36,* 609–628.

Katz, R. C., & Woolley, R. (1975). Improving patient records through problem orientation. *Behavior Therapy, 6,* 119–124.

Kavale, K. A., & Forness, S. R. (1984). A meta-analysis of the validity of Wechsler Scale profiles and recategorizations: Patterns or parodies? *Learning Disability Quarterly, 7,* 136–156.

Kavale, K. A., & Forness, S. R. (1992). History, definition, and diagnosis. In N. N. Singh, & I. L. Beale (Eds.), *Learning disabilities: Nature, theory and treatment* (pp. 3–43). New York: Springer-Verlag.

Kazdin, A. E. (1980). Acceptibility of alternative treatments for deviant child behavior. *Journal of Applied Behavior Analysis, 13,* 259–273.

Kazdin, A. (1982). *Single case research designs: Methods for clinical and applied settings.* New York: Oxford University Press.

Kazdin, A. E., & Petti, T. A. (1982). Self-report and interview measures of childhood and adolescent depression. *Journal of Child Psychology and Psychiatry, 23,* 437–457.

Kinsbourne, M. (1973). Minimal brain dysfunction as a neurodevelopmental lag. *Annals of the New York Academy of Sciences, 205,* 268–273.

Kinsbourne, M. (1975). Models of learning disability: Their relevance to remediation. *Canadian Medical Association Journal, 113,* 1066–1068.

Kinsbourne, M., & Swanson, J. M. (1979). Models of hyperactivity: Implications for diagnosis and treatment.

In R. L. Trites (Ed.), *Hyperactivity in children: Etiology, measurement, and treatment implications.* Baltimore, MD: University Park Press.

Lambert, N. M., & Sandoval, J. H. (1980). The prevalence of learning disabilities in a sample of children considered hyperactive. *Journal of Abnormal Child Psychology, 8,* 33–50.

Loney, J., & Milich, R. (1982). Hyperactivity, inattention, and aggression in clinical practice. *Advances in Developmental and Behavioral Pediatrics, 3,* 113–147.

Mannuzza, S., Gittelman, R., Bonagura, N., Konig, P., Shenker, R. (1988). Hyperactive boys almost grown up. *Archives of General Psychiatry, 45,* 13–18.

Martens, B. K., & Witt, J. C. (1988). Ecological behavior analysis. *Progress in Behavior Modification, 22,* 115–140.

Menolascino, F. J., & Stark, J. (1984). *Handbook of mental retardation and mental illness.* New York: Plenum Publishing.

Milich, R., Loney, J., & Landau, S. (1982). Independent dimensions of hyperactivity and aggression: A validation with playroom observation data. *Journal of Abnormal Psychology, 91,* 183–198.

Nihira, K., Foster, R., Shellhaas, M., & Leland, H. (1974). *AAMD adaptive behavior scale* (rev. ed.), Washington, DC: American Association on Mental Deficiency.

O'Neill, R. E., Horner, R. H., Albin, R. W., Storey, K., & Sprague, J. R. (1990). *Functional analysis: A practical assessment guide.* Sycamore, IL: Sycamore Press.

O'Shanick, G. J., & Parmelee, D. X. (1989). Psychopharmacological agents in the treatment of brain injury. In D. W. Ellis & A. L. Christensen (Eds.), *Neuropsychological treatment after brain injury* (pp. 91–104). Norwell, MA: Kluwer Academic.

Parmelee, D. X., & O'Shanick, G. J. (1987). Neuropsychiatric interventions with head-injured children and adolescents. *Brain Injury, 1,* 41–47.

Pellock, J. M. (1986). The role of antiseizure medications on cognitive function. In *Abstracts of the Proceedings, 10th Annual Medical College of Virginia Conference on the Rehabilitation of the Head-injured Child and Adult.* Richmond, VA: Medical College of Virginia.

Piacentini, J. C., Lahey, B. B., & Hynd, G. (1986). *Personality characteristics of the mothers of conduct disordered and hyperactive children.* Paper presented at the 32nd Annual Meeting of the Southeastern Psychological Association, Kissimmee, FL.

Quay, H. C., & Peterson, D. R. (1983). *Interim manual for the revised behavior problem checklist.* Coral Gables, FL: University of Miami.

Radosh, A., & Gittelman, R. (1981). The effect of

appealing distractors on the performance or hyperactive children. *Journal of Abnormal Psychology, 9,* 179–189.

Rapoport, J. L., & Ismond, D. R. (1984). *DSM-III training guide for diagnosis of childhood disorders.* New York: Brunner/Mazel.

Rapport, M. D. (1983). Hyperactivity: Treatment parameters and applications. *Progress in Behavior Modification, 14,* 219–298.

Rapport, M. D. (1987). Attention deficit disorder with hyperactivity. In M. Hersen, & V. B. Van Hasselt (Eds.), *Behavior therapy with children and adolescents* (pp. 325–361). New York: John Wiley & Sons.

Reeves, J. C., Werry, J. S., Elkind, G. S., & Zametkin, A. (1987). Attention deficit, conduct, oppositional, and anxiety disorders in children: II. Clinical Characteristics. *Journal of the American Academy of Child and Adolescent Psychiatry, 26,* 144–155.

Reimers, T. M., Wacker, D. P., & Koeppl, G. (1987). Acceptability of behavioral interventions: A review of the literature. *School Psychology Review, 16,* 215–227.

Repp, A. C., Karsh, K. G., Van Acker, R., Felce, D., & Harman, M. (1989). A computer-based system for collecting and analyzing observational data. *Journal of Special Education Technology, 9,* 217.

Roberts, M. A., Milich, R., Loney, J., & Capute, J. (1981). A multitrait-multimethod analysis of variance of teachers' ratings of aggression, hyperactivity, and inattention. *Journal of Abnormal Child Psychology, 9,* 371–380.

Rogers-Warren, A., & Warren, S. F. (1977). *Ecological perspectives in behavior analysis.* Baltimore, MD: University Park Press.

Rosvold, R. E., Mirsky, A. F., Sarason, I., Bransome, E. D., & Beck, L. H. (1956). A continuous performance test of brain damage. *Journal of Consulting Psychiatry, 20,* 343–350.

Safer, D. J., & Allen, R. P. (1976). *Hyperactive children: Diagnosis and management.* Baltimore, MD. University Park Press.

Sandberg, S. T., Wiesel, M., & Shaffer, D. (1980). Hyperkinetic and conduct problem children in a primary school population: Some epidemiological considerations. *Journal of Child Psychology and Psychiatry, 21,* 293–311.

Sandoval, J., Lambert, N. M., & Sassone, D. M. (1981). The comprehenisve treatment of hyperactive children: A continuing problem. *Journal of Learning Disabilities, 14,* 117–118.

Satterfield, J. H., Satterfield, B. T., & Cantwell, D., (1981). Three-year multimodality treatment study of 100 hyperactive boys. *Journal of Pediatrics, 98,* 650–655.

Sattler, J. M. (1988). *Assessment of children* (3rd, ed.). San Diego: Jerome M. Sattler.

Schaughency, E. A., Walker, J., & Lahey, B. B. (1988). Attention deficit disorder and hyperactivity: Psychological therapies. In J. L. Matson (Ed.), *Handbook of treatment approaches in childhood psychopathology* (pp. 193–213). New York: Plenum Publishing.

Schroeder, S. R. (1990). *Ecobehavioral analysis and developmental disabilities: The twenty-first century.* New York: Springer-Verlag.

Shaywitz, S. E., & Shaywitz, B. A. (1984). Devising propr drug therapy for attention deficit disorders. *Contemporary Pediatrics, 1,* 12–24.

Singh, N. N., & Aman, M. G. (1990). Ecobehavioral analysis in pharmacotherapy. In S. R. Schroeder (Ed.), *Ecobehavioral analysis and developmental disabilities: The twenty-first century* (pp. 182–200). New York: Springer-Verlag.

Singh, N. N., & Beale, I. L. (1988). Learning disabilities: Psychological therapies. In J. L. Matson (Ed.), *Handbook of treatment approaches in childhood psychopathology* (pp. 525–553). New York: Plenum Publishing.

Singh, N. N. & Beale, I. L. (1992). *Learning disabilities: Nature, theory, and treatment.* New York: Springer-Verlag.

Singh, N. N., Beale, I. L., & Snell, D. (1988). Learning disability. In M. Hersen & C. G. Last (Eds.), *Child behavior therapy casebook,* (pp. 193–206). New York: Plenum Publishing.

Singh, N. N., Epstein, M. H., Luebke, J., & Singh, Y. N. (1990). Psychopharmacological intervention. I: Teacher perceptions of psychotropic medication for seriously emotionally disturbed students. *Journal of Special Education, 24,* 283–295.

Singh, N. N., & Katz, R. C. (1985). On the modification of acceptability ratings for alternative child treatments. *Behavior Modification, 9,* 375–386.

Singh, N. N., & Repp, A. C. (1988). Current trends in the behavioral and psychopharmacological management of behavior problems of mentally retarded persons [Special issue on evaluating services]. *Irish Journal of Psychology, 9,* 362–384.

Singh, N. N., Sood, B., & Soneklar, N. (1991). Mental illness in persons with mental retardation [Special issue on assessment-based interventions for childhood disorders]. *Behavior Modification, 15,* 418–442.

Singh, N. N., & Winton, A. S. W. (1989). Behavioral pharmacology. In J. K. Luiselli (Ed.), *Behavioral medicine and developmental disabilities* (pp. 152–179). New York: Springer-Verlag.

Sleator, E. K. (1982). Office diagnosis of hyperactivity by the physician. *Advances in Learning and Behavioral Disabilities, 1,* 341–364.

Sleator, E. K., & Ullmann, R. K. (1981). Can the physician diagnose hyperactivity in the office? *Pediatrics, 67,* 13–17.

Sparrow, S. S., Balla, D., & Cicchetti, D. V. (1984). *Vineland adaptive behavior scales.* Circle Pines, MN: American Guidance Service.

Stewart, M. A., Cummings, C., Singer, S., & DeBlois, C. S. (1981). The overlap between hyperactive and unsocialized aggressive children. *Journal of Child Psychology and Psychiatry, 22,* 35–45.

Stores, R. (1988). Antiepileptic drugs. In M. G. Aman & N. N. Singh (Eds.), *Psychopharmacology of the developmental disabilities* (pp. 101–118). New York: Springer-Verlag.

Swanson, J. M. (1985). Measures of cognitive functioning appropriate for use in pediatric psychopharmacological research studies. *Psychopharmacology Bulletin, 21,* 887–890.

Taylor, E. (1983). Drug response and diagnostic validation. In M. Rutter (Ed.), *Developmental neuropsychiatry* (pp. 348–368). New York: Guilford Press.

Taylor, E. (1985). Drug treatment. In M. Rutter & L. Hersov (Eds.), *Child and adolescent psychiatry: Modern approaches* (pp. 780–793). Philadelphia: Blackwell.

Thompson, P. J., & Trimble, M. R. (1982). Anticonvulsant drugs and cognitive functions. *Epilepsia, 2,* 531–544.

Ullman, R. K., Sleator, E. K., & Sprague, R. L. (1984). A new rating scale for diagnosis and monitoring of ADD children. *Psychopharmacology Bulletin, 21,* 169–177.

U.S. Office of Education. (1977). *Education of handicapped children.* (Federal Register, August 23, 1977, Vol. 42, No. 163, p. 42478). Washington, DC.: Department of Health, Education, and Welfare.

Wahler, R. G. (1975). Some structural aspects of deviant child behavior. *Journal of Applied Behavior Analysis, 8,* 27–42.

Wahler, R. G., & Fox, J. J. (1981). Setting events in applied behavior analysis: Toward a conceptual and methodological expansion. *Journal of Applied Behavior Analysis, 14,* 327–338.

Walker, H. M. (1970). *Walker problem behavior identification checklist.* Los Angeles: Western Psychological Services.

Weiss, G. (1983). Long-term outcome: Findings, concepts, and practical implications. In M. Rutter (Ed.), *Developmental neuropsychiatry* (pp. 422–436). New York: Guilford Press.

Weiss, G., & Hechtman, L. T. (1986). *Hyperactive children grown up: Empirical finding and theoretical considerations.* New York: Guilford Press.

Werry, J., Sprague, R., & Cohen, M. (1975). Conners teacher rating scale for use in drug studies with children: An empirical study. *Journal of Abnormal Child Psychology, 3,* 217–229.

Whalen, C. K., Collins, B. E., Henker, B., Alkus, S. R., Adams, D., & Stapp, J. (1978). Behavior observations of hyperactive children and methylphenidate (Ritalin) effects in systematically structured environments: Now you see them, now you don't. *Journal of Pediatric Psychology, 3,* 177–187.

Whalen, C. K., & Henker, B. (1980). *Hyperactive children: The social ecology of identification and treatment.* New York: Academic Press.

Whalen, C. K., Henker, B., Collins, B. E., Finck, D., & Dotemoto, S. (1979). A social ecology of hyperactive boys: Medication effects in structured classroom environments. *Journal of Applied Behavior Analysis, 12,* 65–81.

Whalen, C. K., Henker, B., & Dotemoto, S. (1980). Methylphenidate and hyperactivity: Effects on teacher behavior. *Science, 208,* 1280–1282.

World Health Organization. (1977). *Manual of the international classification of diseases, injuries, and causes of death* (9th ed., rev.) Geneva: Author.

Wolf, M. (1978). Social validity: The case for subjective measurement or how applied behavior analysis is finding its heart. *Journal of Applied Behavior Analysis, 11,* 203–214.

Zentall, S. S., Zentall, T. R., & Booth, M. E. (1978). Within-task stimulation: Effects on activity and spelling performance in hyperactive and normal children. *Journal of Educational Research, 74,* 223–230.

CHAPTER 16

PAST DEVELOPMENT AND FUTURE TRENDS

Virginia E. Fee
Johnny L. Matson

In the last 25 years, disorders of childhood have become a focus for researchers and clinicians alike. Countless areas have been explored, and numerous problems can now be successfully treated (Matson, 1988). As many scientists and practitioners have devoted considerable time to childhood disorders, this area of psychopathology has rapidly become a separate field of study. Corresponding to this trend, several volumes are now available summarizing literature on the etiology, assessment, and treatment of childhood problems (e.g., Frame & Matson, 1987; Kazdin, 1988; Matson, 1988; Ollendick & Hersen, 1989).

Among childhood disorders, attention deficit hyperactivity disorder (ADHD) may be the most thoroughly studied. Unfortunately, the disorder is not the best understood. Indeed, ADHD has been one of the most controversial areas in the child psychopathology literature with respect to diagnosis and etiology. This state of affairs may exist for several reasons. First, formulations of ADHD were based on clinical lore for many years. For instance, at one time, the diagnosis was determined via response to stimulant medication. Those who responded to medication were labeled hyperactive; those who did not respond were not given the diagnosis (Gadow, 1988)

Moreover, popular treatments often consisted of restricting the child's intake of sugar and chemical additives (e.g., Feingold, 1976). Our current conclusion is that nutritional therapies are of little benefit (see chapter 13 in this volume).

At the same time, our conceptualization of the problem has changed dramatically over the years. At first an emphasis was placed exclusively on brain damage as the cause of hyperactivity (Still, 1902). However, brain damage could not be demonstrated in most hyperactive children (Fine, 1977; Safer & Allen, 1976) and no consistent pattern occurred among those who did evince unusual findings (Werry, 1988). Next, authors focused on more behavioral definitions of the problem, emphasizing neurological soft signs, and the term *minimal brain dysfunction* was coined (Kessler, 1980). Objections were soon raised concerning the inference of brain damage based on behavioral symptoms alone, and studies showed that many hyperactive children did not display soft signs (Bax & MacKeith, 1963; Casey, 1977). The question then became one of overactivity, inattention, or both as the primary problem (Chess, 1960; Childers, 1935; Douglas, 1972; Levin, 1938; Werry & Sprague, 1970). Thus, the diagnosis is still at issue (Whalen, 1986). Currently, we view ADHD as a multifaceted problem, with varied etiologic and maintaining factors (see chapter 4).

In addition, methodological problems have obscured much of the research literature on ADHD. For instance, subject characteristics have been poorly described, and a variety of diagnostic criteria have been employed (Whalen, 1983). Many of the very early studies on hyperactivity included children with primary brain damage, learning disabilities, and conduct disorders (Ross & Ross, 1982). More recently, changes in the DSM criteria for diagnosing ADHD have contributed to difficulties in generalizing from previous research. First the disorder was called hyperkinetic reaction of childhood, emphasizing excessive motor activity (American Psychiatric Association [APA], 1968). Next, the *Diagnostic and Statistical Manual of Mental Disorders,* 3rd ed. (DSM-III; APA, 1980) focused on the attentional component and provided the diagnoses of attention deficit disorder with hyperactivity and attention deficit disorder without hyperactivity (APA, 1980). Attention and overactivity have been recombined in DSM-III-R (the revised third edition) under the label attention deficit hyperactivity disorder (APA, 1987).

Further contributing to problems in research is the possibility that the literature has not been recently summarized. The purpose of this book was to present current findings against a background of historical developments. In light of the large body of literature reviewed here, a volume devoted entirely to the topic of ADHD in children was considered warranted. Our primary aim has been to acquaint the reader with current data from a variety of research domains. For this purpose, the most notable authorities on ADHD were sought to contribute chapters. The contributors for this book are all accomplished scientists, and their empirical background has markedly influenced ADHD research. It is hoped that this book may provide a basis for those interested in performing further investigations.

The problem of ADHD was shown to be pervasive in that 2% to 5% of all children are afflicted (Barkley, 1982). With ADHD occurring in such proportions, this disorder cannot be ignored. ADHD is problematic to the child, his or her family, and educators. Accordingly, this book was developed for a broad target audience, including child psychiatrists,

pediatricians, clinical child psychologists, school psychologists, and educators. Thus, it provides a detailed scholarly review of the empirical literature of the etiology, assessment, and treatment of ADHD.

The organization of this book followed the basic issues confronted by practitioners. First, a historical and methodological background was presented, followed by sections on assessment and treatment. Within each major section, several perspectives were presented, providing information relevant to various settings and treatment professionals. Thus, discipline-specific information is interwoven within a more general framework.

In the first section, the most basic issues were discussed. Included were chapters on historical developments, analysis, theoretical perspectives, and theories on the etiology of ADHD. Two additional chapters were added because of their significance. First, a chapter on methodology was included, emphasizing the importance of empirical sophistication. Of continued necessity will be consistency and technical precision in research. The second additional chapter discussed the relationship between intellectual functioning and pharmacologic treatment. The second and third sections of the book summarized current assessment and treatment findings.

What can be concluded from the body of research summarized here? First, the area of ADHD has been plagued by controversy. Debate has ensued over etiologic, diagnostic, and treatment issues. In this book, Walters and Barrett suggested that ADHD stems from both physical and environmental causes. We now have reason to believe that ADHD may result from varied and interactive sources, including both biology and environmental factors. These possibilities were reviewed here by several authors.

The diagnosis of ADHD has also been controversial. First, there is a question of the syndrome's very existence. Whether ADHD is a cluster of behaviors separate from conduct disorder has been subject to extensive validation. Many feel further investigation is necessary before this issue can be resolved (Caperaa, Cote, & Thivierge, 1985; Holborow & Berry, 1985; Luk, 1985; Quay, Routh, & Shapiro, 1987). For instance, when the effects of age, sex, and IQ were controlled, Werry, Elkind, and Reeves (1987) found few differences between children with DSM-III diagnoses of ADD-H, anxiety problems, and

ADD-H plus conduct disorder. Others contend that ADHD and conduct disorder are independent syndromes but that a third category exists where ADHD and conduct disorder co-occur (Hinshaw, 1987; McGee, Williams, & Silva, 1985; Reeves, Werry, Elkind, & Zametkin, 1987; Shapiro & Garfinkel, 1986; Stein & O'Donnell, 1985; Walker, Lahey, Hynd, & Frame, 1987; Weiss, 1985; Werry, Reeves, & Elkind, 1987). In a few investigations, the comorbid group displayed greater social dysfunction (Reeves, et al., 1987) and family problems (August & Stewart, 1984; Lahey, Piacentini, McBurnett, & Stone, 1988; Reeves et al., 1987). These findings deserve confirmation. Of interest is the conclusion of Walker et al. (1987) that the children with ADHD and conduct disorder in their study exhibited more aggression and severe antisocial behavior than did children with conduct disorder alone.

Another area of diagnostic confusion concerns the independence of ADHD and learning disabilities. Much less work has been done in this area. In one recent investigation, Dalby (1985) showed that children with developmental reading disorders exhibited greater academic problems than did children with ADD. The ADD group was rated significantly higher than controls on a measure of hyperactivity whereas the reading disordered children were not. Dalby (1985) therefore concluded that ADD and developmental reading disorder constitute separate entities. However, there has been a longstanding suggestion that these disorders constitute separate but ovelapping categories similar to that observed with ADHD and conduct disorder (Conners, 1976; Satz & Fletcher, 1980; Wender, 1976).

There is also the question of the most important symptoms for diagnosing ADHD. Whether motoric or attention components are essential for the diagnosis is still unresolved. Currently, DSM-III-R (APA, 1987) uses inattention, impulsivity, and hyperactivity as core symptoms, but allows emphasis on any of the three. However, there may be diagnostic validity in the categories of ADD and ADD-H previously specified in DSM-III. Brown (1985) found that teacher ratings could discriminate these two categories and that those children with hyperactivity in addition to attentional problems were viewed as more difficult to manage.

A final area of controversy concerns the nature of the disorder, whether it is situation specific or cross-situational. A common finding among ADHD children is that the severity of the problem fluctuates from environment to environment (Barkley, 1989). It has been repeatedly noted that these children have less difficulty in unstructured free-play settings compared to more restrictive environments, such as the learning situation (Barkley, 1985; Jacob, O'Leary, & Rosenblad, 1978; Luk, 1985; Routh & Schroeder, 1976; Whalen, Collins, Henker, Alkus, Adams, & Stapp, 1978). Barkley (1989) reviewed these findings and suggested that the apparent attentional deficit in ADHD may actually be a motivational one, as the child's behavior worsens with increased familiarity with the environment, improves when immediate consequences are provided, and improves when instructions are given frequently. Establishing the core problem in ADHD may be the most important problem facing researchers in the near future.

TRENDS

In recent years, several emerging trends have become apparent in the ADHD literature. These trends reflect an ever-expanding body of accumulated knowledge and the synthesis of many ideas. First, assessment has become more fine grained and observer based. For the purposes of diagnosis and treatment planning, it is popular to supplement interview and checklist data with observation (Morris & Collier, 1987). With this in mind, several observation systems have been evaluated (Abikoff, Gittleman-Klein, & Klein, 1977, 1980; Atkins, Pelham, & Licht, 1985; Blunden, Spring, & Greenberg, 1974; Mayes, 1987; Milich, Loney, & Roberts, 1986; Roberts, 1986; Vincent, Williams, Harris, & Duval, 1981). These observational systems were designed for both playroom (Mayes, 1987; Milich et al., 1986; Roberts, 1986) and classroom environments (Atkins et al., 1985; Blunden et al., 1974; Vincent et al., 1981) and allow the coding of several important behaviors. The classroom codes help to objectify observation in the school, and the playroom codes are so constructed that they may be recreated in a clinic setting. In addition to providing information for diagnosis and treatment planning, these observation systems are valuable research tools, pointing to symptoms most predictive of the disorder (Abikoff et al., 1977, 1980) and those that tend to persist over time (Milich et al., 1986).

A second recent trend concerns the ongoing assessment of behavioral and stimulant interventions using single-subject methodology. These procedures have recently been described in such a way that they may be carried out by clinicians and teachers with the cooperation of medical personnel (Gadow, 1988; Schell, Pelham, Bender, Andree, Law, & Roberts, 1986). Throughout the years, medication has been shown to be effective. Psychologists advocate its use when combined with other treatments (Rosenberg & Beck, 1986). However, its indiscriminate prescription without careful follow-up has been a concern of professionals in the field (Gadow, 1988). Moreover, in the general public many espouse the idea that ADHD is not severe enough to justify the use of medication. For instance, Summers and Caplan (1987) found that lay people viewed pharmacological treatment of ADHD as less acceptable than medication for children with seizure disorders. It may be that in our current era many believe that medical treatment of children is justifiable, but only when conditions are undisputably biological in nature and/or life threatening. With children, behavior control via medication may be unpalatable to many. The advent of a methodology whereby behavioral and medical interventions are assessed alone and together in an ongoing fashion makes the use of medication potentially more acceptable. This approach was supported by Rosenberg and Beck (1986) who surveyed clinical and school psychologists.

Another contemporary theme in the ADHD literature has involved the possibility of various subgroups of hyperactive children (e.g., with and without aggression). The issue of comorbidity and ADHD is extremely important for clarifying current diagnostic problems. The finding that factor analytic studies have sometimes failed to identify the dimension of hyperactivity (Langhorne, Loney, Paternite, & Bechtoldt, 1976; Sandberg, Rutter, & Taylor, 1978; Werry, 1968) has been one of the most puzzling problems in the ADHD literature. In addition to conduct disorder and learning disabilities described previously, other problems have been associated with ADHD. Most recently, childhood depression has been linked with ADHD (Biederman, Munir, Knee, & Armentano, 1987; Bohline, 1985; Borden, Brown, Jenkins, & Clingerman, 1987). Some have suggested that depression results as a sequalae to school failure (Bohline, 1985; Borden et al., 1987) whereas others have implied an inherited predisposition (Biederman et al., 1987). Alternatively, depression in ADHD children could be attributed to untoward side effects of medication (e.g., listlessness, lack of appetite, sleeplessness). In any case, the treatment of coexisting depression would be warranted when present, and these preliminary findings and hypotheses deserve further elaboration and study. They emphasize the view that the problems of ADHD span well beyond overactivity and attention deficits.

In the past several years, researchers have also begun to look carefully at the social skills of ADHD children. Whalen and Henker (1985) suggested these children display high rates of irritating, unsuccessful, and intense or aggressive social behaviors, possibly stemming from dysfunctional attention, modeling influences, and/or an abnormal response to reinforcement. Sociometric studies have repeatedly confirmed poor social skills in ADHD children. For instance, Carlson, Lahey, Frame, and Walker (1987) showed that ADD-H and ADD-WO children received significantly fewer "liked most" nominations and more "liked least" nominations. These children were also frequently nominated as the child who "fights most." Johnston, Pelham, and Murphy (1985) found ADHD boys received more nominations on an Aggression factor and fewer nominations on a Likeability factor using the Pupil Evaluation Inventory. These researchers found no difference by age, but did note that female subjects could not be discriminated using peer ratings. However, DeHaas (1986) found that ADHD girls and boys could be discriminated from normal children using a sociometric measure. Both sexes of ADHD children displayed higher rates of conduct problem behavior relative to controls, with ADHD boys showing the highest rates. Moreover, peer ratings have been shown to be sensitive to medication effects (Whalen, Henker, Castro, & Granger, 1987).

Observational studies have also revealed social skills problems in ADHD children. Researchers have found less verbal reciprocity, more withdrawal and aggression (Clark, Cheyne, Cunningham, & Siegel, 1988), and greater difficulty in managing interpersonal conflict in ADHD children compared to normal controls (Grenell, Glass, & Katz, 1987). Although this discussion has focused on the conduct-related behaviors of ADHD children, there is the suggestion that those with additional depressive features experience significant social problems as well (Asarnow, 1988). Results of studies on social skills in ADHD children lend support to the multifaceted nature of the disorder.

Another recent focus involves the course of ADHD. At this time, data on the outcome of ADHD children in later life has accumulated from follow-up, prospective, and retrospective studies (Cantwell, 1985). After reviewing the literature, some concluded that widely different outcomes have been reported depending on the sample (Shaffer & Greenhill, 1980). However, others claim support for continued problems in the areas of academic achievement, restlessness, immaturity, and self-esteem (Hechtman & Weiss, 1984). Hechtman and Weiss (1986) studied adolescents previously diagnosed with hyperactivity, and they reported drug and alcohol abuse and antisocial behavior for a large percentage, although these problems were not significantly greater than for controls (Hechtman & Weiss, 1986). In addition, although many children with ADHD lose their symptoms with age, the presence of conduct symptoms has been a predictor of antisocial behavior in adolescence (Cantwell, 1985). Family disruption, negative mother-child interactions (Campbell, Breaux, Ewing, & Szumowski, 1986), and initial symptom severity have been associated with children identified in preschool who continue to have problems at school age (Campbell, Ewing, Breaux, & Szumowski, 1986). Moreover, stimulant treatment during childhood does not appear to change adolescent outcome (Milich & Loney, 1980). Finally, recent results from a large study of college men using self-report data indicated that attention problems in adulthood were not necessarily associated with overactivity in childhood (Buchsbaum, 1985).

This trend of mapping the course of ADHD brings to light several points. First, overactivity and/or attentional problems in childhood are sometimes associated with significant difficulty in later life (Hechtman, 1989; Minde, Weiss, & Mendelson, 1972; Weiss, Minde, Werry, Douglas, & Nemeth, 1971). Second, additional research is necessary to identify more clearly the prognostic features of poor outcome. Third, the need for comprehensive treatment is highlighted, especially from the results of Milich and Loney (1980), who found that medical treatment did little to improve adult outcome. What is needed would appear to be long-term multicenter outcome studies with specific dependent measures assessing several problem variables in childhood and their relation to more global measures of overall functioning in adulthood. Longitudinal data of this sort would point to the most important areas for intervention.

With respect to treatment, in recent years investigations have gone from simply testing individual therapies (e.g., Abikoff & Gittelman, 1984; Sherman & Anderson, 1980) to testing treatments against each other (e.g., Rapport, Murphy, & Bailey, 1982). And now, a few studies have tested the additive effects of various interventions. For instance, in a group study, Horn, Ialongo, Popovich, and Peradotto (1987) evaluated cognitive self-control therapy and behavioral parent training alone and combined. Results showed the largest decrease in hyperactivity scores for the self-control group. However, these results did not generalize to the school environment.

As mentioned previously, current opinion holds that medication alone is not sufficient to treat children with ADHD (Wiener, 1984). Supporting this perspective, a study performed by Ullmann and Sleator (1985) showed that methylphenidate improved attention and decreased activity but had only a minor effect on social skills and oppositional behavior. Others have found overall ratings of improved behavior with methylphenidate, but educational gains only with cognitive or behavioral training designed specifically for academic behavior (Hogg, Callias, & Pellegrini, 1986).

Conversely, various authors have suggested that cognitive and behavioral procedures do not fully address the problems when used in isolation (Abikoff, 1985; Pelham, Schnedler, Bologna, & Contreras, 1980; Schaughency, Walker, & Lahey, 1988). In 1986, Wells reviewed behavioral techniques for ADHD children. These approaches included parent training, classroom management procedures, and social skills training. She concluded that these procedures are effective but not maximally so. Only when behavior therapy and medication are combined do ADHD children achieve maximum improvement.

Cognitive and behavioral therapies have therefore been paired with medication and studied. For example, Abikoff and Gittelman (1985) studied a cognitive intervention with medication and failed to find results superior to medication alone for either behavior problems or academics. In this investigation, the cognitive treatment included social skills training.

Behavioral treatments have also been combined with medication. Gadow (1985) reviewed 16 studies that compared medical and behavioral interventions on academics. He concluded that behavioral interventions specifically designed to improve academics were clearly superior to medication. Only limited support was found for the addition of medication to improve academics.

In another investigation, Chase and Clemont (1985) studied the effects of behavioral and medical treatment on reading comprehension questions. In this single case experiment with seven subjects, methylphenidate alone did not result in improvements. However, self-reinforcement led to substantial gains. The combination of self-reinforcement and medication resulted in gains slightly better than self-reinforcement alone.

On the other hand, Speltz, Varley, Peterson, and Beilke (1988) tested dextroamphetamine and contingency management. Previously, the behavioral intervention had not been sufficient to mitigate the problems of the 4-year-old subject with ADHD and oppositional disorder. Improvements on both work behavior and aggressiveness were noted with the combined intervention.

More specifically, the effects of continuous and partial reinforcement when combined with methylphenidate have been examined (Pelham, Milich, & Walker, 1986). Conditions representing no reinforcement, partial reinforcement, and continuous reinforcement with and without medication were studied. Effects were found with both reinforcement conditions and with methylphenidate alone. Maximal effects were achieved when medication and any of the three schedules of reinforcement were combined. However, no differences were found among the reinforcement conditions.

A behavioral parent training program and medication were also combined and studied. Firestone,

Crowe, Goodman, and McGrath (1986) followed children who had been treated 2 years previously to examine long-term gains. At posttest, the medication-alone group had been superior on academic measures, but this effect disappeared at follow-up, suggesting medication is effective only on a short-term basis.

To summarize, in the last several years, researchers have begun to examine the effects of combined interventions. Global measures of functioning and more specific target behaviors have been studied. Moreover, we have seen the hint of microanalytic studies in which specific schedules of reinforcement are compared with and without medication. These issues are not resolved, and while much more needs to be done, there is the strong suggestion that multimodal treatment will be necessary to benefit the child with ADHD. This matter is addressed in the following section, which discusses future directions in ADHD research.

FUTURE DIRECTIONS

ADHD has been studied more extensively than most other disorders of childhood. Researchers have been interested in basic issues related to diagnostic and etiologic factors in addition to more practical problems of assessment and treatment. Large-scale studies have been performed in each area (e.g., Abikoff et al., 1977; Brown, 1985; Satterfield & Schell, 1984; Ullmann & Sleator, 1985). Reatig (1984) noted that between 1976 and 1984, over 300 articles reported studies that had been conducted to examine the etiology and diagnosis of ADHD. Systematic efforts are currently underway to extend what is already known. However, much awaits further confirmation. For instance, concerning etiology, the contribution of both biology and environment need further quantification. More information is needed on the causes of ADHD and their relationship to treatment and prognosis.

Greater attention is needed particularly on environmental causes of ADHD. Thus, the use of functional analysis is recommended as it has been employed successfully with autistic and other developmentally disabled children in the case of self-injurious and stereotyped behavior. With these problems, an assessment approach that suggests treatment strategies has been developed (Carr, 1977; Durand & Crimmins, 1988). With our current understanding that ADHD is probably the result of varied factors, it may be that there are strictly biological cases, strictly environmental cases, and for the bulk of cases, a mixed etiology. With further information, greater emphasis may be placed on prevention.

Moreover, primary questions are unanswered in regard to the diagnosis of ADHD and the existence of comorbidity or narrow-band subgroups. As described earlier, children with concomitant conduct disorder have been shown to differ from cases of pure ADHD in terms of prognosis and response to treatment. Therefore, intruments are needed that differentiate children with ADHD, learning disabilities, and conduct problems. From this review of the literature, an additional problem, anxiety disorders with ADHD, has yet to be extensively examined. However, a few researchers have used relaxation training with ADHD children (Denkowski & Denkowski, 1984; Raymer & Poppen, 1985; Wood & Frith, 1984). Intuitively, this suggests that anxiety may play a role in the development, maintenance, or course of the disorder in at least some cases.

Another future focus should include handicapped groups, such as mentally retarded children. Recently, a few investigators have examined ADHD in developmentally disabled children. The literature describes cases reports and investigations of children with mental retardation, Tourette's syndrome, and hearing impairments who also display the characteristics of ADHD (Alverez & Londono, 1982; Chess & Fernandez, 1981; Epstein, Cullinan, & Gadow, 1986; Fejes & Prieto, 1987; Fisher, Burd, Kuna, & Berg, 1985; Hoge & Biederman, 1986; Litrownik, White, McInnis, & Licht, 1984). The DSM system currently excludes these children from the secondary diagnosis of ADHD. Additional research may be helpful for revising this taxonomy, and further information is needed for the assessment and treatment of these special populations.

With respect to treatment, research has most often incorporated a few specific interventions for a few specific behaviors during a discrete period of time. These behavioral techniques such as positive attention, time-out and response cost have been recommended in a global fashion to be utilized in a variety of situations. Now, they should be investigated in a more situation-specific manner. It is possible that some techniques are more appropriate for certain environments. Additionally, new interventions should be developed and evaluated for leisure time and for particular academic tasks. Information from a variety of sources will be helpful for designing these situation-specific treatments.

With additional research more clearly defining diagnostic categories, it is anticipated that several subtypes of hyperactivity will emerge and specialized treatment packages will be developed for each type. Milich, Widiger, and Landau (1987) described an approach to differentiating diagnostic categories using conditional probabilities. The approach uses a statistical method employing positive predictive power (PPP), or the conditional probability of a disorder given the presence of a symptom, and negative predictive power (NPP), or the conditional probability of the absence of a disorder given the absence of the symptom. Milich et al. (1987) found that "can't sit still," "restless sleeper," and "runs around" were the best symptoms for identifying ADD. However, these symptoms did not identify a large percentage of ADD children. The symptom "easily distracted" when *absent* strongly suggested the *absence* of ADD. Also, for the diagnosis of conduct disorder, the absence of the symptoms "doesn't listen," "acting without thinking," and "easily distracted" were as useful as the presence of any conduct disorder symptom. Although the results of this research will require replication, the approach is promising and warrants further development.

In regard to treatment for ADHD coexisting with conduct disorder, intervention might emphasize family structure, role models, and social skills training in addition to basic interventions for attention and overactivity problems. In the case of learning disabilities overlapping ADHD, comprehensive treatment might include special academic training and the development of nonacademic skills. A few investigators have already begun work on this approach to treatment. For example, Van Hasselt (1984) performed a single case study with a 7.5-year-old boy having both ADHD and conduct disorder. Two components were emphasized in the intervention: social skills training and contingency management. These procedures increased appropriate interactions with peers and decreased withdrawal. However, the long-term effects of such a program should be evaluated.

Further results are anticipated in the area of drug research with ADHD children. We need to know more about the behaviors affected by ADHD and their relation to social and academic behavior. More information on the fine-grained and general effects of behavioral interventions when combined with medication would also be helpful. Medication for children with coexisting problems should be studied to determine the symptoms that improve and the behaviors, if any, that actually worsen the medication. Additionally, a method for assessing the side effects of methylphenidate should be standardized so that these problems can be minimized. Finally, the research community should continue to measure actively the way methylphenidate is being used in the "real world." We have an obligation to ensure that our methodology and recommendations amount to more then just rhetoric.

Some general research directions should also be pursued. For instance, new and innovative behavioral treatment techniques are welcomed. Although stimulant medication as a treatment strategy is well documented, many children are unable to participate in medical therapy because of physical or social factors. These children and nonresponders require an alternative approach. Much more information is needed about nonresponder subgroups and their response to behavioral and medical intervention.

A new research direction should examine behavioral programs that cater to various age groups. As has been demonstrated, the symptom pattern is subject to change as the child matures. A clear picture of the developmental pattern is sorely needed. With this, researchers can determine whether younger and older children respond differently to various treatments. For instance, the type of reinforcers used with young children would not be expected to improve the behavior of adolescents. Of further necessity are treatment packages designed for specific age groups that could be readily carried out by teachers and parents.

Additional information is necessary concerning the diagnosis of ADHD at very early ages. It is important that many children outgrow the problem

(Goyette, Conners, & Ulrich, 1978). However, the search should continue for markers differentiating the chronic from transient case. In this way, effective and economical early intervention strategies may be developed. Barkley (1987) is on the forefront of this movement and included in his parent training program are procedures to help parents accept and cope with the poor self-control of their preschoolers with ADHD.

We can also expect a greater emphasis on adolescents and adults with ADHD. Since the course of the disorder suggests a need for extended intervention, the assessment and treatment of ADHD in later stages of life should be fruitful for researchers in the area.

The social validation of treatment programs implemented by teachers and parents is another crucial research endeavor at this time. How can programs be improved to make them more "user friendly" in order that parents and teachers will be more likely to use them? For the aim of socially valid treatments, the collaboration of disciplines becomes extremely important. In terms of research planning, input should be sought from those in direct contact with ADHD children for long periods of time.

As implied throughout this chapter, it is likely that treatment of ADHD children will become more comprehensive and preventive. As such, the need for multimodal assessment is highlighted. In recent years, authors have presented guidelines for assessment that suggest this comprehensive flavor. For instance, Barkley (1989) recommended the use of several informants in a variety of settings and multiple methods for assessing ADHD. These methods include interviews, rating scales, laboratory measures, and direct observation. Table 16.1 presents a comprehensive assessment strategy recommended by Rapport (1987). Notice that Rapport's (1987) assessment plan includes the evaluation of classroom and clinic behavior. He also provided a table of disorders that should be ruled out when assessing the ADHD child.

Achenbach (1985) described a multiaxial system for the assessment of children. The domains to be sampled included I: Parent Reports, II: Teacher Reports, III: Cognitive Assessment, IV: Physical Assessment, and V: Direct Assessment of the Child. In Table 16.2, we present Achenbach's (1985)

Table 16.1.

Social/Classroom Behavior

Instruments Administered to Parents	Instruments Administered to Teachers
1. Home Situations Questionnaire. Assesses the occurrence and severity of the child's behavior at home (Barkley, 1981).	1. ADD-H: Comprehensive Teacher Rating Scale (ACTeRS). A recently developed rating scale for diagnosis and treatment monitoring (Ullmann, Sleator, & Sprague, 1984).
2. Werry-Weiss-Peters Activity Scale (WWPAS). Assesses the child's behavior in the familial and surrounding environment (Routh, Schroeder, & O'Tuama, 1974).	2. Abbreviated Conners Teacher Rating Scale (ACTRS). Useful in screening and assessing treatment outcome (Werry, Spraque, & Cohen, 1975).
3. SNAP Rating Scale. Incorporates the DSM-III diagnostic criteria in a rating scale format.	3. SNAP Rating Scale. Also for classroom use (Swanson, Nolan, & Pelham, 1981).
4. Personality Inventory for Children (PIC). Provides a comprehensive personality profile. Four scales distinguish ADD-H children from other clinical groups: adjustment, social skills, hyperactivity, delinquency (Lachar, 1982).	4. Teacher's Self-Control Rating Scale (TSCRS). Useful in assessing children's self-control and perceived competency (Humphrey, 1982).

Academic Behavior

Direct Classroom Observations	Classroom Assessment
1. Observational coding of percentage of time on-task, percentage of assignments completed, and percentage correct (Rapport et al., 1982).	1. Assess child's present curricula for appropriateness of content.
2. Classroom Observation Code. A recently developed coding system for differentiating ADD-H from normal children in classroom settings (Abikoff, Gittelman, & Klein, 1980).	2. Assess differences in child's performance in group vs. small-group instructional settings, appropriateness of classroom placement, and seating arrangement.

Clinical Assessment

1. Continuous Performance Test (CPT): Measures the child's ability to sustain attention (indicated by errors of omission) and inhibit impulsive responding (indicated by errors of commission). Clinicians may need to create their own test materials using slides of numeric or

Continued

Table 16.1. *Continued*

alphabetic sequences (see Rapport, DuPaul, Stoner, & Jones, in press), or use the Gordon Diagnostic Test (GDS: Gordon, McClure, & Post, 1983).

2. Matching Familiar Figures Test (MFFT): A standardized test of children's cognitive tempo developed by Kagan, Rosman, Day, Albert, and Phillips (1964). ADD-H children tend to exhibit a "fast-inaccurate" tempo, characterized by a higher number of errors and shorter response latencies. Information regarding standardization, scoring, and developmental norms are available (Salkind, 1978).

3. Delay Test (GDS): A recently developed test of a child's ability to delay responding under appropriate circumstances. Complete information regarding standardization, scoring, and developmental norms as well as computerized administration are available (Gordon, McClure, & Post, 1983).

Rule-Outs

Childhood Disorders Similar to ADD-H[a]

1. *Anxiety Disorders:*
   a. Overanxious Disorder: generalized, persistent anxiety or worry (not related to separation).
   b. Separation Anxiety Disorder: excessive anxiety regarding separation from those to whom the child is attached.
2. *Adjustment Disorders:*
   a. Adjustment Disorder with Anxious Mood: A maladaptive reaction to an identifiable psychosocial stressor that occurs within 3 months of the onset of the stressor (predominant features include nervousness, worry, and jitteriness).
   b. Adjustment Disorder with Academic Inhibition: Predominant manisfestation is an inhibition in academic functioning in a child whose previous performance was adequate.
3. *Supplementary Conditions:*
   a. Parent-Child Problem: Problems not due to a mental disorder, such as child abuse.
   b. Family Circumstances: Problems not due to a mental disorder, such as sibling rivalry, recent change in residence and/or school placement.
4. *Disorders of Behavior:*
   a. Conduct Disorder: A repetitive, persistent pattern of conduct in which the basic rights of others or societal norms are violated. Four types: undersocialized, aggressive; undersocialized, nonaggressive; socialized, aggressive, socialized, nonaggressive.
   b. Oppositional Disorder: A pattern of disobedient, negativistic, and provocative opposition to authority figures without violating the basic rights of others or societal norms (e.g., violation of minor rules, temper tantrums, stubbornness).
   c. Childhood Antisocial Behavior: Involves isolated acts in contrast to repetitive pattern of antisocial behavior.
5. Tourette's Disorder: The essential features are recurrent, involuntary, repetitive, rapid, purposeless motor movements (tics), including vocal tics. The movements can be voluntarily suppressed and may vary in intensity, frequency, and location. First symptom may appear as a single tic (often an eye blink). Other initial symptoms often include tongue protrusion, squatting, sniffing, hopping, skipping, and throat clearing.

Source: From Rapport, M. D. (1987). Attention deficit disorder with hyperactivity. In M. Hersen & V. B. Van Hasselt (Eds.), *Behavior therapy with children and adolescents: A clinical approach.* Reprinted by permission.

[a]Consult DSM-III (American Psychiatric Association, 1980) for specific diagnostic features of these disorders.

Table 16.2. Multiaxial Assessment of ADHD

Axis I: Parent Reports	Axis II: Teacher Reports	Axis III: Intellectual/ Achievement Tests	Axis IV: Physical Assessment	Axis V: Direct Assessment	Axis VI: Comorbidity/ Rule outs
-Child Behavior Checklist (1)	-Child Behavior Checklist (1)	-WISC-R (2)	-Neurologic Exam	-Porteus Mazes (3)	-Child Behavior Checklist (1)
-Conners Parent Rating Scale (5)	-Conners Teacher Rating Scale (6)	-Stanford-Binet (4)	-Monitoring of medication	-Matching Familiar Figures Test (8)	-Children's Depression Inventory (9)
-Werry-Weiss-Peters Activity Rating Scale Peters Activity Rating Scale (14)	-SNAP Checklist (10)	-Woodstock Johnson (7)	-Direct Observation	-Behavior Problem Checklist (11)	
-Monitoring data	-MESSY (12)				-Louisville Fear Survey Schedule (13)
	-Monitoring data				Autism Behavior Checklist (15)

References: (1) Achenbach (1978), (2) Wechsler (1974), (3) Porteus (1959) (4) Thorndike, Hagen, & Sattler (1986), (5) Conners (1970), (6) Conners (1968), (7) Woodcock (1977), (8) Kagan (1965), (9) Kovacs & Beck (1985), (10) Swanson, Nolan, & Pelham, (1981) (11) Quay (1983), (12) Helsel & Matson (1984), (13) Miller et al. (1972), (14) Werry (1968), (15) Krug et al. (1980).

strategy adapted specifically to the assessment of the ADHD child.

Under Parent and Teacher Reports are interviews, behavior rating scales, and monitoring data. Standard intelligence and achievement tests fall under Axis III. On Axis IV, the results of neurological exams and the monitoring of medication are included. Axis V, Direct Assessment of the Child, includes observation in the school, home, and clinic as well as various laboratory measures. In Table 16.2, we added a sixth axis for assessing the presence of comorbid conditions or alternatively for ruling them out. The assessment of these areas would be especially important if information from Axes 1 and 2 suggested other difficulties.

THEORETICAL CONSIDERATIONS

In 1988, Kazdin provided an elaborate discussion of the theoretical shortcomings characterizing the study of childhood psychopathology. He argued for theoretical models in order to avoid unecessary research. Broad theoretical models and minitheories provide a systematic framework for choosing the most fruitful directions in research. Patterson's (1980) model of conduct disorder was used to illustrate the formulation of conduct dirorders in children and adolescents (Kazdin, 1988). Patterson's (1988) work is an example of what Kazdin (1988) called a minitheory. Specifically, Patterson's model addresses the influence of coercive interaction patterns on the development and continuation of antisocial behavior (see Figure 16.1).

The model is exemplary in its ability to guide clinicians and researchers. For clinicians, the model prescribes areas for assessment and intervention. For researchers, the model suggests areas requiring further study or replication and also suggests assessment and treatment questions for investigation.

The work of Gardner and Cole (1988) is another recent example of a theroetical model for conduct disorder. As is evident in Figure 16.2 this model is more comprehensive than that developed by Patterson in that it targets both the person and several categories of environmental events (1986). Of note is the way the models overlap somewhat and differ slightly in focus. Patterson's (1986) model emphasizes communication patterns whereas Gardner and Cole's (1988) is broader and focuses on characteristics of the individual. Both models, however, provide

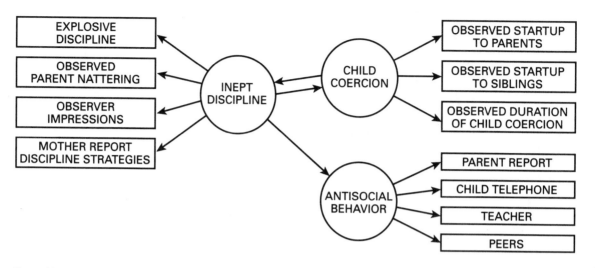

Figure 16.1. Patterson's (1986) model for the development of conduct disorder. Reprinted with permission.

Note: Upper number refers to Cohort I and lower to Cohort II. From *Antisocial Boys* by G. R. Patterson, J. B. Reid, and T. J. Dishion, in press, Eugene, OR: Castalia Publishing Co. Copyright by Castalia Publishing Co. Used by permission.

testable hypotheses and variables to be assessed and treated.

In Figure 16.3, a model for the development and maintenance of ADHD is presented. Our model is a modification of the work pioneered by Gardner and Cole (1988). Considering the overlap between conduct disorder and ADHD, their work is an obvious starting point. Notice, however, the importance of the school environment and comorbid conditions with the present model for ADHD. Within this volume, a great deal of attention has been given to these facets of the disorder. Therefore, they were thought important enough to include in the present model.

Like the models described by Patterson (1986) and Gardner and Cole (1988), the model for ADHD presented here lends itself to the comprehensive assessment and treatment of the child. The first set of variables under the heading "Events that Instigate and/or Increase the Probability of Occurrence" include both environmental events and individual characteristics. Assessment of these factors would include evaluation of the physical and psychosocial environment in addition to such individual characteristics as prenatal history, intellectual ability, and the assessment of social and self-management skills. Academic assessment of the ADHD child falls under

this heading and was reviewed in chapter 9. Behavioral checklists for ADHD would be relevant here as would the diagnostic issues summarized by Werry. Concerning treatment, chapter 11 on medication would fit most appropriately here.

In addition to the general model for the development and maintainence of ADHD presented in Figure 16.3, we also offer two models for the development of conduct disorder and depression in ADHD children. These models are presented in Figures 16.4 and 16.5. Both models include the findings that ADHD children are often subject to negative paternal interactions (Battle & Lacey, 1972; Campbell, 1972), school failure (Cantwell & Satterfield, 1978; Riddle & Rapport, 1976; Trites, Blouin, Ferguson, & Lynch, 1980), and social skills problems (Carlson et al., 1987; DeHaas, 1986; Johnston, Pelham, Murphy, 1985). Notice how the simple addition of antisocial role models contributes to the development of conduct disorder. Should these models be supported by future research, the importance of paternal and peer modeling influences will be highlighted.

Our models also emphasize the prudent use of punishment and reinforcement. They suggest that simply teaching behavioral procedures may not be sufficient to give maximal help to the ADHD child. Experience has taught us that parents and teachers

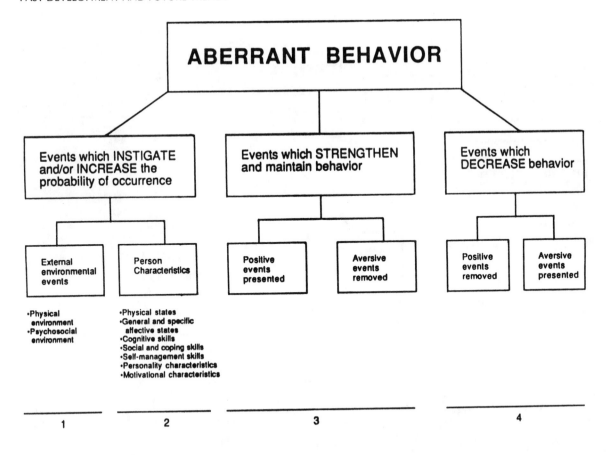

Assessment and Treatment Focus

Figure 16.2. Gardner and Cole's (1988) model for the development and maintenance of conduct disorder. Reprinted with permission.

Source: Gardner, W. I., & Cole, C. (1988). Conduct disorders: Psychological therapies. In J. L. Matson (Ed.), *Handbook of treatment approaches in psychopathology.* New York: Plenum. Reprinted by permission.

often rely on aversive control and forget the second part of the equation, namely, positive reinforcement. Clincians have a responsibility to educate parents and teachers on the long-term consequences of behavior management delivered as such. If our hypothesis are confirmed, Figures 16.4 and 16.5 could be used as valuable teaching tools. In our clinical work, we take care to ensure that the child receives more positive reinforcement than punishment. If not, target behaviors are scaled down and a shaping approach is used. The rationale for this approach is summarized by the models presented in Figures 16.4 and 16.5.

Further, the model for depression in ADHD emphasizes the need for caution in using medication to treat ADHD. The side effects of methylphenidate include appetite loss, problems in sleeping, and increased irritability. The child may have a decreased frustration tolerance and cry easily when medication is excessive (Barkley, 1989). Although these side effects are problems for only some children, their presence especially in combination with other difficulties deserves careful monitoring. Such side effects as "irritability" may be difficult to assess and may present only subclinically, setting the child at an unrecognized risk for the development of depression.

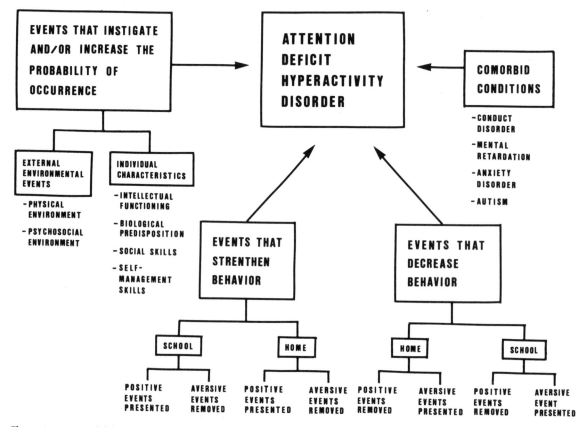

Figure 16.3. Model for the development and maintenance of ADHD.

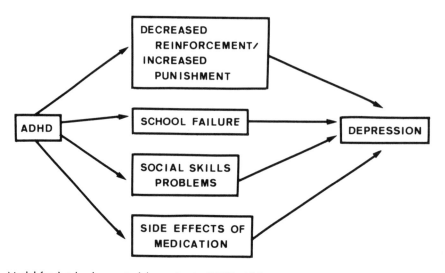

Figure 16.4. Model for the development of depression in ADHD children.

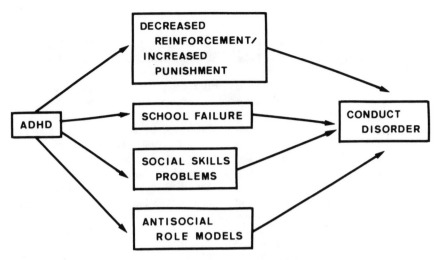

Figure 16.5. Model for the development of conduct disorder in ADHD children.

A final point is that growth retardation has been regarded as an essentially unimportant side effect, since growth is reinstated when medication is discontinued (Barkley, 1989). However, when looking at the total picture of ADHD, where the chid may be at risk for numerous difficulties, the addition of growth retardation could significantly affect the child's developing self-confidence. This matter is important and should be acknowledged when medication is considered.

CONCLUSION

This chapter provided a review of this volume and an overview of the trends in recent ADHD research as well as future directions for the field. Many advances have been made in ADHD research. We have a clearer picture of the course, diagnostic problems, and treatment of the disorder. The section on future directions included more information on the assessment and treatment of comorbid conditions, the use of a developmental approach to assessment and treatment, and further development of behavioral and pharmalogical research. A model for the genesis and maintenance of ADHD was presented as was a comprehensive multiaxial strategy for assessment. Finally, models for the development of conduct

disorder and depression in ADHD children emphasized the importance of multimodal assessment and treatment, long-term intervention, and the cooperation of disciplines working to help the child with ADHD. We are hopeful that these three directions will be among the trends of the next decade of ADHD research.

REFERENCES

Abikoff, H. (1985). Efficacy of cognitive training interventions in hyperactive children: A critical review. *Clinical Psychology Review, 5,* 479–512.

Abikoff, H., & Gittelman, R. (1984). Does behavior therapy normalize the classroom behavior of hyperactive children? *Archives of General Psychiatry, 41,* 449–454.

Abikoff, H., & Gittelman, R. (1985). Hyperactive children treated with stimulants: Is cognitive training a useful adjunct? *Archives of General Psychiatry, 42,* 953–961.

Abikoff, H., Gittelman-Klein, R., & Klein, D. F. (1977). Validation of a classroom observation code for hyperactive children. *Journal of Consulting and Clinical Psychology, 5,* 772–783.

Abikoff, H., Gittelman, R., & Klein, D. (1980). Classroom observation code for hyperactive children: A replication of validity. *Journal of Consulting and Clinical Psychology, 48,* 555–565.

Achenbach, T. M. (1978). The child behavior profile: I.

Boys 6–11. *Journal of Consulting and Clinical Psychology, 46,* 478–488.

Achenbach, T. M. (1985). *Assessment and taxonomy of child and adolescent psychopathology.* Beverly Hills, CA: Sage.

Alvarez, U. L., & Londono, J. P. C. (1982). Application of a DRO program with feedback for the modification of attention, distractibility and passivity in a retarded female adolescent. *Perspectives en Psicologia, 1,* 169–200.

American Psychiatric Association. (1968). *Diagnostic and Statistical Manual of Mental Disorders-II.* Washington, DC: Author.

American Psychiatric Association (1980). *Diagnostic and Statistical Manual of Mental Disorders-III.* Washington, D.C.: Author.

American Psychiatric Association. (1987). *Diagnostic and Statistical Manual of Mental Disorders-III-R.* Washington, DC: Author.

Asarnow, J. R. (1988). Peer status and social competence in child psychiatric inpatients: A comparison of children with depressive, externalizing and concurrent depressive and externalizing disorders. *Journal of Abnormal Child Psychology, 16,* 151–162.

Atkins, M. S., Pelham, W. E., & Licht, M. H. (1985). A comparison of objective classroom measures and teacher ratings of attention deficit disorder. *Journal of Abnormal Child Psychology, 13,* 155–167.

August, G. J., & Stewart, M. A. (1984). Familial subtypes of childhood hyperactivity. *Annual progress in child psychiatry and child development* (pp. 364–377). New York: Bruner/Mazel.

Barkley, R. A. (1982). Hyperactivity. In E. J. Mash & L. G. Terdal (Eds.), *Behavioral assessment of childhood disorders* (pp. 127–184). New York: Guilford Press.

Barkley, R. A. (1985). The social interactions of hyperactive children: Developmental changes, drug effects, and situational variation. In R. McMahon & R. Peters (Eds.), *Childhood disorders: Behavioral-developmental approaches* (pp. 218–243). New York: Brunner/Mazel.

Barkley, R. A. (1987). Poor self-control in preschool hyperactive children. *Medical Aspects of Human Sexuality, 21,* 176–180.

Barkley, R. A. (1989). Attention deficit-hyperactivity disorder. In E. J. Mash & R. A. Barkley (Eds.), *Treatment of childhood disorders* (pp. 39–72). New York: Guilford Press.

Battle, E. S., & Lacey, B. (1972). A context for hyperactivity in children, over time. *Child Development, 43,* 757–773.

Biederman, J., Munir, K., Knee, D., Armentano, M. (1987). High rate of affective disorders in probands with attention deficit disorder and in their relatives: A controlled family study. *American Journal of Psychiatry, 144,* 330–333.

Blunden, D., Spring, C., & Greenberg, L. M. (1974). Validation of the Classroom Behavior Inventory. *Journal of Consulting and Clinical Psychology, 42,* 84–88.

Bohline, D. S. (1985). Intellectual and affective characteristics of attention disordered children. *Journal of Learning Disabilities, 18,* 604–608.

Borden, K. B., Brown, R. T., Jenkins, P., & Clingerman, S. R. (1987). Achievement attribution and depressive symptoms in attention deficit-disordered and normal children. *Journal of School Psychology, 25,* 399–404.

Brown, R. T. (1985). The validity of teacher ratings in differentiating between two subgroups of attention deficit disordered children with or without hyperactivity. *Educational and Psychological Measurement, 45,* 661–669.

Buchsbaum, M. S. (1985). Attention dysfunction and psychopathology in college men. *Archives of General Psychiatry, 42,* 354–360.

Campbell, S. B. (1972). Mother-child interaction in reflective, impulsive and hyperactive children. *Developmental Psychology, 8,* 341–349.

Campbell, S. B., Breaux, A. M., Ewing, L. J., & Szumowski, E. K. (1986). Correlates and predictors of hyperactivity and aggression: A longitudinal study of parent-referred problem preschoolers. *Journal of Abnormal Child Psychology, 14,* 217–234.

Campbell, S. B., Ewing, L. J., Breaux, A. M., & Szumowski, E. K. (1986). Parent-referred problem three-year-olds: Follow-up at school entry. *Journal of Child Psychology and Psychiatry and Allied Disciplines, 27,* 473–488.

Cantwell, D. P. (1985). Hyperactive children have grown up: What have we learned about what happens to them? *Archives of General Psychiatry, 42,* 1026–1028.

Cantwell, D. P., & Satterfield, J. H. (1978). The prevalence of academic underachievement in hyperactive children. *Journal of Pediatric Psychology, 3,* 168–171.

Caperaa, P., Cote, R., & Thivierge, J. (1985). Hyperactivity: Comment Trite's article. *Journal of Child Psychology and Psychiatry and Allied Disciplines, 26,* 485–486.

Carlson, C. L., Lahey, B. B., Frame, C. L., Walker, J. (1987). Sociometric status of clinic-referred children with attention deficit disorders with and without hyperactivity. *Journal of Abnormal Child Psychology, 15,* 537–547.

Carr, E. G. (1977). The motivation of self-injurious behavior: A review of some hypotheses. *Psychological Bulletin, 84,* 800–816.

Chase, S. N., & Clement, P. W. (1985). Effects of self-reinforcement and stimulants on academic performance in children with Attention Deficit Disorder. *Journal of Clinical Child Psychology, 14*, 323–333.

Chess, S. (1960). Diagnosis and treatment of the hyperactive child. *New York State Journal of Medicine, 60*, 2379–2385.

Chess, S., & Fernandez, P. (1981). Do deaf children have a typical personality? *Annual Progress in Child Psychiatry and Child Development*, 295–305.

Childers, A. T. (1935). Hyper-activity in children having behavior disorders. *American Journal of Orthopsychiatry, 5*, 227–243.

Clark, M. L., Cheyne, J. A., Cunningham, C. E., & Siegel, L. S. (1988). Dyadic peer interaction and task orientation in attention-deficit disordered children. *Journal of Abnormal Child Psychology, 16*, 1–15.

Conners, C. K. (1969). A teacher rating scale for use in drug studies. *American Journal of Psychiatry, 126*, 884–888.

Conners, C. K. (1970). Symptom patterns in hyperkinetic, neurotic, and normal children. *Child Development, 41*, 667–682.

Conners, C. K. (1976). Learning disabilities and stimulant drugs in children: Theoretical considerations. In R. Knights & D. J. Bakker (Eds.), *The neuropsychology of learning disorders* (pp. 389–404). Baltimore: University Park Press.

Dalby, J. T. (1985). Taxonomic separation of attention deficit disorders and developmental reading disorders. *Contemporary Educational Psychology, 10*, 228–234.

DeHaas, P. A. (1986). Attention styles and peer relationships of hyperactive and normal boys and girls. *Journal of Abnormal Child Psychology, 14*, 457–467.

Denkowski, K. M., & Denkowski, G. C. (1984). Is group relaxation training as effective with hyperactive children as individual EMG biofeedback treatment? *Biofeedback and Self Regulation, 9*, 353–364.

Douglas, V. I. (1972). Stop, look, and listen: The problem of sustained attention and impulse control in hyperactive and normal children. *Canadian Journal of Behavioral Science, 4*, 259–282.

Durand, V. M., & Crimmins, D. B. (1988). Identifying the variables maintaining self-injurious behavior. *Journal of Autism and Developmental Disorders, 11*, 303–315.

Epstein, M. H., Cullinan, D., & Gadow, K. D. (1986). Teacher ratings of hyperactivity in learning-disabled, emotionally disturbed, and mentally retarded children. *Journal of Special Education, 20*, 219–220.

Feingold, B. F. (1976). Hyperkinesis and learning disabilities linked to the ingestion of artificial colors and flavors. *Journal of Learning Disabilities, 9*, 551–559.

Fejes, K. D., & Prieto, A. G. (1987). The potential of relaxation training for the hyperkinetic trainable mentally retarded child. *Child and Family Behavior Therapy, 9*, 55–66.

Fine, M. J. (1977). Hyperactivity: Where are we? In M. J. Fine (Ed.), *Principles and techniques of intervention with hyperactive children* (pp. 3–46). Springfield, IL: Charles C. Thomas.

Firestone, P., Crowe, D., Goodman, J. T., & McGrath, P. (1986). Vicissitudes of follow-up studies: Differential effects of parent training and stimulant medication with hyperactives. *American Journal of Orthopsychiatry, 56*, 184–194.

Fisher, W., Burd, L., Kuna, D. P., & Berg, D. J. (1985). Attention deficit disorders and the hyperactivities in multiply disabled children. *Rehabilitation Literature, 46*, 250–254.

Frame, C. L., & Matson, J. L. (1987). *Handbook of assessment in childhood psychopathology: Applied issues in differential diagnosis and treatment evaluation*. New York: Plenum Publishing.

Gadow, K. D. (1985). Relative efficacy of pharmacological, behavioral, and combination treatments for enhancing academic performance. *Clinical Psychology Review, 5*, 513–533.

Gadow, K. D. (1988). Attention deficit disorder and hyperactivity. In J. L. Matson (Ed.), *Handbook of treatment approaches in child psychology* (pp. 215–247). New York: Plenum Publishing.

Gardner, W. I., & Cole, C. (1988). Conduct disorders: Psychological therapies. In J. L. Matson (Ed.), *Handbook of treatment approaches in childhood psychopathology* (pp. 163–194). New York: Plenum Publishing.

Gordon, M., McClure, F. D., & Post, E. M. (1983). *Gordon Diagnostic System*. Golden, CO: Clinical Diagnostic.

Goyette, C. H., Conners, C. K., & Ulrich, R. F. (1978). Normative data on revised Conners Parent and Teacher Rating Scales. *Journal of Abnormal Child Psychology, 6*, 221–236.

Grenell, M. M., Glass, C. R., & Katz, K. S. (1987). Hyperactive children and peer interaction: Knowledge and performance of social skills. *Journal of Abnormal Child Psychology, 15*, 1–13.

Hechtman, L. (1989). Attention deficit hyperactivity disorder in adolescence and adulthood: An updated follow-up. *Psychiatric Annals, 19*, 597–603.

Hechtman, L., & Weiss, G. (1984). Long-term outcome of hyperactive children. *Annual Progress in Child Psychiatry and Child Development*, 378–389.

Hechtman, L., & Weiss, G. (1986). Controlled porspective fifteen year follow-up of hyperactives as adults: Non-medical drug and alcohol use and anti-social behaviour. *Canadian Journal of Psychiatry, 31*, 557–567.

Helsel, W. J., & Matson, J. L. (1984). The assessment of depression in children: The internal structure of the child depression inventory (CDI). *Behavior Research and Therapy, 22,* 289–298.

Hinshaw, S. P. (1987). On the distinction between attentional deficits/hyperactivity and conduct problems/aggression in child psychopathology. *Psychological Bulletin, 101,* 443–463.

Hoge, S. K., & Biederman, J. (1986). A case of Tourette's syndrome with symptoms of attention deficit disorder treated with desipramine. *Journal of Clinical Psychiatry, 47,* 478–479.

Hogg, C., Callias, M., & Pellegrini, D. (1986). Treatment of a 7-year-old hyperactive boy with educational problems. *Behavioural Psychotherapy, 14,* 145–161.

Holborow, P., & Berry, P. (1985). Is there an independent syndrome of hyperactivity? A comment on Trites and Laprade. *Journal of Child Psychology and Psychiatry and Allied Disciplines, 26,* 487–489.

Horn, W. F., Ialongo, N., Popovich, S., & Peradotto, D. (1987). Behavioral parent training and cognitive-behavioral self-control therapy with ADD-H children: Comparative and combined effects. *Journal of Clinical Child Psychology, 16,* 57–68.

Humphrey, L. L. (1982). Children's and teachers' perspectives on childrens' self-control: The development of two rating scales. *Journal of Consulting and Clinical Psychology, 50,* 624–633.

Jacob, R. G., O'Leary, K. D., & Rosenblad, C. (1978). Formal and informal classroom settings: Effects on hyperactivity. *Journal of Abnormal Child Psychology, 6,* 47–59.

Johnston, C., Pelham, W. E., & Murphy, B. A. (1985). Peer relationships in ADDH and normal children: A developmental analysis of peer and teacher ratings. *Journal of Abnormal Child Psychology, 13,* 89–100.

Kagan, J., Rosman, B. L., Day, D., Albert, J., & Phillips, W. (1964). Information processing in the child: Significance of analytic and reflective attitudes. *Psychological Monographs, 78* (1, Whole No. 578), 4.

Kazdin, A. E. (1988). *Child psychotherapy.* Elmsford, NY: Pergamon Press.

Kessler, J. W. (1980). History of minimal brain dysfunctions. In H. E. Rie & E. D. Rie (Eds.), *Handbook of minimal brain dysfunction: A critical review* (pp. 18–51). New York: John Wiley & Sons.

Krug, D. A., Arick, J., & Almond, P. (1980). Behavior checklist for identifying severely handicapped individuals with high levels of autistic behavior. *Journal of Child Psychology and Psychiatry, 21,* 221–229.

Lahey, B. B., Piacentini, J. C., McBurnett, K., & Stone, P. (1988). Psychopathology in the parents of children with conduct disorder and hyperactivity. *Journal of the American Academy of Child and Adolescent Psychiatry, 27,* 163–170.

Langehorne, J. E., Loney, J., Paternite, C. E., & Bechtold, H. P. (1976). Childhood hyperkinesis: A return to the source. *Journal of Abnormal Psychology, 85,* 201–209.

Levin, P. M. (1938). Restlessness in children. *Archives of Neurology and Psychiatry, 39,* 764–770.

Litrownik, A. J., White, K., McInnis, E. T., & Licht, B. G. (1984). A process for designing self-management programs for the developmentally disabled. *Analysis and Intervention in Developmental Disabilities, 4,* 189–197.

Luk, S. (1985). Direct observation studies of hyperactive behaviors. *Journal of the American Academy of Child Psychiatry, 24,* 338–344.

Matson, J. L. (1988). *Handbook of treatment approaches in childhood psychopathology.* New York: Plenum Publishing.

Mayes, S. D. (1987). Assessment of preschool hyperactivity: Combining rating scale and objective observation measures. *Topics in Early Childhood Special Education, 6,* 49–61.

McGee, R., Williams, S. M., & Silva, P. A. (1985). Factor structure and correlates of ratings of inattention, hyperactivity, and antisocial behavior in a large sample of 9-year-old children from the general population. *Journal of Consulting and Clinical Psychology, 53,* 480–490.

Milich, R., & Loney, J. (1980). The role of hyperactive and aggressive symptomatology in predicting adolescent outcome among hyperactive children. *Annual Progress in Child Psychiatry and Child Development,* 336–356.

Milich, R., Loney, J., & Roberts, M. A. (1986). Playroom observations of activity level and sustained attention: Two-year stability. *Journal of Consulting and Clinical Psychology, 54,* 272–274.

Milich, R., Widiger, T. A., & Landau, S. (1987). Differential diagnosis of attention deficit and conduct disorders using conditional probabilities. *Journal of Consulting and Clinical Psychology, 55,* 762–767.

Miller, L. C., Barrett, C. L., Hampe, E., & Noble, H. (1972). Revised anxiety scales for the Louisville Behavior Checklist. *Psychological Reports, 29,* 503–511.

Minde, K., Weiss, G., & Mendelson, N. (1972). A 5-year follow-up study of 91 hyperactive school children. *Journal of the American Academy of Child Psychiatry, 11,* 595–610.

Morris, R. J., & Collier, S. J. (1987). Assessment of Attention Deficit Disorder and Hyperactivity. In C. L. Frame & J. L. Matson (Eds.), *Handbook of assessment in childhood psychopathology: Applied issues in diagnosis and treatment evaluation* (pp. 271–312). New York: Plenum Publishing.

Ollendick, T. H., & Hersen, M. (1989). *Handbook of childhood psychopathology*. New York: Plenum Publishing.

Patterson, G. E. (1986). Performance models for antisocial behavior. *American Psychologist, 41*, 432–444.

Pelham, W. E., Milich, R., & Walker, J. L. (1986). Effects of continuous and partial reinforcement and methylphenidate on learning in children with attention deficit disorder. *Journal of Abnormal Psychology, 95*, 319–325.

Pelham, W. E., Schnedler, R. W., Bologna, N. C., & Contreras, J. A. (1980). Behavioral and stimulant treatment of hyperactive children: A therapy study with methylphenidate probes in a within-subject design. *Journal of Applied Behavior Analysis, 13*, 221–236.

Porteus, S. D. (1959). *The Maze Test and clinical psychology*. Palo Alto, CA: Pacific Books.

Quay, H. C. (1983). A dimensional approach to behavior disorder: The Revised Behavior Problem Checklist, *School Psychology Review, 12*, 244–249.

Quay, H. C., Routh, D. K., & Shapiro, S. K. (1987). Psychopathology of childhood: From description to validation. *Annual Review of Psychology, 38*, 491–532.

Rapport, M. D. (1987). Attention deficit disorder with hyperactivity. In M. Hersen & V. B. Van Hasselt (Eds.), *Behavior therapy with children and adolescents: A clinical approach* (pp. 325–361). New York: John Wiley and Sons.

Rapport, M. D., DuPaul, G. J., Stoner, G., & Jones, A. T. (in press). Comparing classroom and clinic measures of attention deficit disorder: Differential, idiosyncratic, and dose-response effects of methylphendate. *Journal of Consulting and Clinical Psychology*.

Rapport, M. D., Murphy, H. A., & Baily, J. S. (1982). Ritalin vs. response cost in the control of hyperactive children: A within-subjects comparison. *Journal of Applied Behavior Analysis, 15*, 205–216.

Raymer, R., & Poppen, R. (1985). Behavioral relaxation training with hyperactive children. *Journal of Behavior Therapy and Experimental Psychiatry, 16*, 309–316.

Reeves, J. C., Werry, J. S., Elkind, G. S., & Zametkin, A. (1987). Attention deficit, conduct, oppositional, and anxiety disorders in children II: Clinical characteristics. *Journal of the American Academy of Child and Adolescent Psychiatry, 26*, 144–155.

Riddle, K. D., & Rapport, J. L. (1976). A 2-year follow-up of 72 hyperkinetic boys. Classroom behavior and peer acceptance. *Journal of Nervous and Mental Disease, 162*, 126–134.

Roberts, M. A. (1986). How is playroom behavior observation used in the diagnosis of attention deficit disorder? *Journal of Children in Contemporary Society, 19*, 65–74.

Rosenberg, R. P., & Beck, S. (1986). Preferred assessment methods and treatment modalities for hyperactive children among clinical child and school psychologists. *Journal of Clinical Child Psychology, 15*, 142–147.

Ross, D. M., & Ross, S. A. (1982). *Hyperactivity: Current issues, research, and theory*. New York: John Wiley and Sons.

Routh, D. K., & Schroeder, C. S. (1976). Standardized playroom measures as indices of hyperactivity. *Journal of Abnormal Child Psychology, 4*, 199–207.

Safer, D. J., & Allen, R. P. (1976). *Hyperactive children*. Baltimore: University Park Press.

Sandberg, S. T., Rutter, M., & Taylor, E. (1978). Hyperkinetic disorder in psychiatric clinic attenders. *Developmental Medicine and Child Neurology, 20*, 279–299.

Satterfield, J. H., & Schell, A. M. (1984). Childhood brain function differences in deliquent and non-delinquent hyperactive boys. *Electroencephalography and Clinical Neurophysiology, 57*, 199–207.

Satz, P., & Fletcher, J. M. (1980). Minimal brain dysfunctions: An appraisal of research concepts and methods. In H. E. Rie & E. D. Rie (Eds.), Handbook of minimal brain dysfunction: A critical review (pp. 669–714). New York: John Wiley & Sons.

Schaughency, E. A., Walker, J., & Lahey, B. B. (1988). In J. L. Matson (Ed.), *Handbook of treatment approaches in childhood psychopathology* (pp. 195–214). New York: Plenum Publishing.

Schell, R. M., Pelham, W. E., Bender, M. E., Andree, J. A., Law, T., & Robbins, F. R. (1986). The concurrent assessment of behavioral and psychostimulant interventions: A controlled case study. *Behavioral Assessment, 8*, 373–384.

Shaffer, D., & Greenhill, L. (1980). A critical note on the predictive validity of "the hyperkinetic syndrome." *Annual Progress in Child Psychiatry and Child Development*, 357–380.

Shapiro, S. K., & Garfinkel, B. D. (1986). The occurrence of behavior disorders in children: The interdependence of attention deficit disorder and conduct disorder. *Journal of the American Academy of Child Psychiatry, 25*, 809–819.

Sherman, C. F., & Anderson, R. B. (1980). Modification of attending behavior in hyperactive children. *Psychology in the Schools, 17*, 372–379.

Speltz, M. L., Varley, C. K., Peterson, K., & Bielke, R. L. (1988). *Journal of the American Academy of Child and Adolescent Psychiatry, 27*, 175–178.

Stein, M. A., & O'Donnell, J. P. (1985). Classification of children's behavior problems: Clinical and quantitative approaches. *Journal of Abnormal Child Psychology, 13*, 269–279.

Still, G. F. (1902). Some abnormal psychical conditions in children. *Lancet, i,* 1008–1012, 1077–1082, 1163–1168.

Summers, J. A., & Caplan, P. J. (1987). Laypeople's attitudes toward drug treatment for behavioral control depend on which behavior and which drug. *Clinical Pediatrics, 26,* 258–262.

Swanson, J., Nolan, W., & Pelham, W. (1981). *The SNAP rating scale for the diagnosis of attention deficit disorder.* Paper presented at the meeting of the American Psychological Association, Los Angeles.

Thorndike, R. L., Hagen, E. P., & Sattler, J. M. (1986). *Technical manual, Stanford-Binet Intelligence Scale: Fourth Edition.* Chicago: Riverside Publishing.

Trites, R. L., Blouin, A. G., Ferguson, H. B., & Lynch, G. (1980). The Conners Teacher Rating Scale: An epidemiologic, inter-rater reliability and followup investigation. In K. D. Gadow & J. Loney (Eds.), *Psychosocial aspects of drug treatment for hyperactivity.* Boulder, CO: Westview Press.

Ullmann, R, Sleator, E., & Sprague, R. (1984). A new rating scale for diagnosis and monitoring of ADD children. *Psychopharmacology Bulletin, 20,* 160–164.

Ullman, R. K., & Sleator, E. K. (1985). Attention deficit disorder children with or without hyperactivity: Which behaviors are helped by stimulants? *Clinical Pediatrics, 24,* 547–551.

Van Hasselt, V. B. (1984). Poor peer interactions and social skills training on a child psychiatric inpatient unit. *Journal of Behavior Therapy and Experimental Psychiatry, 15,* 271–276.

Vincent, J. P., Williams, B. J., Harris, G. E., Jr., & Duval, G. C. (1981). Classroom observation of hyperactive children: A multiple validation study. In K. D. Gadow & J. Loney (Eds.), *Psychosocial aspects of drug treatment for hyperactivity* (pp. 207–248). Boulder, CO: Westview Press.

Walker, J. L., Lahey, B. B., Hynd, G. W., & Frame, C. L. (1987). Comparison of specific patterns of antisocial behavior in children with conduct disorder with or without coexisting hyperactivity. *Journal of Consulting and Clinical Psychology, 55,* 910–913.

Wechsler, D. (1974). *Manual for the Wechsler Intelligence Scale for Children-Revised.* San Antonio: Psychological Corporation.

Weiss, G. (1985). Hyperactivity: Overview and new directions. *Psychiatric Clinics of North America, 8,* 737–753.

Weiss, G., Minde, K., Werry, J. S., Douglas, V. I., & Nemeth, E. (1971). Studies on the hyperactive child, VIII. Five-year follow-up. *Archives of General Psychiatry, 24,* 409–414.

Wells, K. C. (1986). What do we know about the use and effects of behavior therapies in the treatment of ADD? *Journal of Children in Contemporary Society, 19,* 111–122.

Wender, P. H. (1976). Hypothesis for a possible biochemical basis of minimal brain dysfunction. In R. M. Knights and D. J. Bakker (Eds.), *Neuropsychology of learning disorders: Theoretical approaches.* Baltimore: University Park Press.

Werry, J. S. (1968). Studies of the hyperactive child IV: An empirical analysis of the minimal brain dysfunction syndrome. *Archives of General Psychiatry, 19,* 9–16.

Werry, J. S., Sprague, R. L., & Cohen, M. N. (1968). Conners Teacher Rating Scale for use in drug studies with children—An empirical study. *Journal of Abnormal Child Psychology, 3,* 217–229.

Werry, J. S., Reeves, J. C., & Elkind, G. S. (1987). Attention deficit, conduct, oppositional, and anxiety disorders in children: I. A review of research on differentiating characteristics. *Journal of the American Academy of Child and Adolescent Psychiatry, 26,* 133–143.

Werry, J. S., & Sprague, R. L. (1970). Hyperactivity. In C. G. Costello (Ed.), *Symptoms of psychopathology* (pp. 397–417). New York: John Wiley.

Werry, J., Sprague, R., & Cohen, M. (1975). Conners Teacher Rating Scale for use in drug studies with children—An empirical study. *Journal of Abnormal Child Psychology, 3,* 217–229.

Whalen, C. K. (1983). Hyperactivity, learning problems, and the attention deficit disorders. In T. H. Ollendick & M. Hersen, *Handbook of child psychopathology,* (pp. 151–199). New York: Plenum Publishing.

Whalen, C. K., Collins, B. E., Henker, B., Alkus, S. R., Adams, D., & Stapp, J. (1978). Behavior observations of hyperactive children and methylphenidate (Ritalin) effects in systematically structured classroom environments: Now you see them, now you don't. *Journal of Pediatric Psychology, 3,* 177–187.

Whalen, C. K., & Henker, B. (1985). The social worlds of hyperactive (ADDH) children. *Clinical Psychology Review, 5,* 447–448.

Whalen, C. K., Henker, B., Castro, J., & Granger, D. (1987). Peer perceptions of hyperactivity and medication effects. *Child Development, 58,* 816–828.

Wiener, J. M. (1984). Psychopharmacology in childhood disorders. *Psychiatric Clinics of North America, 7,* 831–843.

Wood, J. W., & Frith, G. H. (1984). Drug therapy? Let's take a closer look. *Academic Therapy, 20,* 149–157.

Woodcock, R. W. (1977). *Woodcock-Johnson Psycho-Educational Battery: Technical Report.* Allen, TX: DLM Teaching Resources.

AUTHOR INDEX

SUBJECT INDEX